W9-DJN-724

THE PRESIDENCY
AND THE POLITICAL SYSTEM

353.031
P92

134686

DATE DUE			

WITHDRAWN

THE PRESIDENCY
AND THE POLITICAL SYSTEM

Michael Nelson, editor
Vanderbilt University

CARL A. RUDISILL LIBRARY
LENOIR RHYNE COLLEGE

CQ Press, a division of
Congressional Quarterly Inc.
1414 22nd Street N.W., Washington, D.C. 20037

353.031
P92
134686
apr. 1986

Cover illustration: Ray Driver

Copyright © 1984, Congressional Quarterly Inc.

All rights reserved. No part of this publication may be reproduced or transmitted in any form or by any means, electronic or mechanical, including a photocopy, recording, or any information storage and retrieval system, without permission in writing from the publisher.

Printed in the United States of America

Second Printing

Library of Congress Cataloging in Publication Data

Main entry under title:

The Presidency and the political system.

    1. Presidents—United States—Addresses, essays, lectures. I. Nelson, Michael.
JK516.P639   1983   353.031   83-15006
ISBN 0-87187-276-5

To my beloved wife, Linda.

*She opens her mouth with wisdom
and the teaching of kindness is on
her tongue.*

Proverbs 31:26

TABLE OF CONTENTS

The presidency stands aloof and apart in American political culture. Columnists and commentators often portray the office as the "loneliest job in the world" and its occupants as "alone at the top." Historians commonly organize American political history into a succession of presidential administrations. Periods of great policy change are described by political scientists as eras of "presidential government." Only about half the citizenry—college students not excepted—knows who their representatives or senators are, but almost everyone knows the president's name.

In truth, of course, the presidency is woven into the fabric of the larger political system. The power of the modern presidency is shaped by decisions that were made at the Constitutional Convention in 1787 and by two centuries of change in the system since that event. It is shaped as well by the skills and personalities of individual presidents, who are elected products of the political system.

Politically, presidents can do little without the support of interest groups, the press, the political parties, and the people. Constitutionally, they require the cooperation or acquiescence of the rest of the government—Congress, the judiciary, and the bureaucracy. Both sets of dependencies are apparent in presidential policy making, whether foreign, domestic, or economic.

Each of the 19 essays in this book treats some important aspect of the relationship between the presidency and the political system. The essays are organized into six parts—Approaches to the Presidency, Elements of Presidential Power, Presidential Selection, Presidents and Politics: Nongovernmental Constituencies, Presidents and Politics: Governmental Constituencies, and Presidents and Policy. Each part begins by introducing the authors and their topics.

Some of the contributors to this book are established authorities on the presidency, others are young scholars who are well on their way to becoming established authorities. Several report the results of important new research about the presidency. All have written their essays expressly for this collection.

I do not agree with everything these authors have to say, nor will any reader. But together they have written a collection of essays whose readability is fully matched by its intellectual substance. Students may be assured of gaining the widest possible understanding of the presidency. Scholars will find these essays of real value in their research. Journalists, government officials, and other citizens can read them with interest and profit.

A number of people—the 19 contributors first among them—have helped to bring this book to fruition. Susan Sullivan and Jean Woy, formerly of Congressional Quarterly, offered useful advice and encouragement when I first raised the idea for a book of this kind. Professor Erwin C. Hargrove of Vanderbilt University helped me to think through the organization and line up authors. The staff of the Vanderbilt Department of Political Science—Elizabeth R. McKee and Mildred W. Tyler—were as patient and pleasant as they were helpful in preparing parts of the manuscript. As for Congressional Quarterly's Barbara de Boinville and Joanne Daniels, if I were to thank them in all the ways they deserve, they no doubt would edit me for length and extravagance.

Michael Nelson
Nashville, Tennessee
August 1983

Part I

APPROACHES TO THE PRESIDENCY

First impressions are important in politics as in almost everything else. Americans' first impression of their political system is of the president, and it generally is favorable. Long before children have any real knowledge of what the government actually does, they already think of the president in terms of almost limitless power and benevolence. The president, as described by grade school children, "gives us freedom, . . . worries about all the problems of all the states, . . . makes peace with every country but bad, . . . is in charge of the United States and has many wise men to tell him what is best." [1]

The first chapter in Part I, "Evaluating the Presidency," uncovers powerful traces of these childhood first impressions in the formed impressions of adults. Four groups in particular—journalists, bureaucrats, members of Congress, and members of the voting public—make up constituencies whose support presidents need if they are to function successfully during their terms of office. In all cases, the attitudes of each group seem at first glance to be detrimental to presidential leadership. Reporters are cynical about the presidency, career civil servants are preoccupied with their own careers, representatives and senators are obsessed with pleasing the voters, and the voters themselves are wed to contradictory expectations of the presidency that no individual president can possibly satisfy. Closer inspection, however, reveals that these surface attitudes overlie more fundamental orientations that exalt strong presidential leadership.

As active participants in the political process, journalists, legislators, bureaucrats, and voters cannot be judged severely for a lack of detachment. Detachment and objective analysis of politics and government are the main province of historians and political scientists. Yet what is true for these four groups turns out to be true for presidential scholars as well: visible confusion, but underlying awe with regard to the presidency. "Presidential scholarship in recent years has been marked by a bewildering succession of new models of the presidency, each the product of an admixture of empirical and normative assessments, each constructed in hasty overreaction to the most recent president," Chapter 1 concludes. But "underlying the scholars' confusion is an implicit appreciation that significant policy change, whatever its ideological direction, requires a strong president."

George Edwards, in his chapter on "Studying the Presidency," sheds light on the sources of scholarly confusion. All of the approaches that historians and political scientists traditionally have taken to the presidency are valuable, he argues, but each contains pitfalls that must be avoided if accurate understanding is to be attained. What Edwards calls the legal approach, for example, is particularly subject to an uncomfortable mix of empirical and normative concerns. The psychological approach tends to "stress the pathological aspects of the presidency"; conversely, the political power approach often "carries an implicit assumption that the president should be the principal decision maker in American politics."

Edwards's main purpose, however, is to guide researchers in the selection of an appropriate approach to studying whatever aspect of the presidency interests them and to point them toward research methods that are suitable to their approach. His chapter concludes with a discussion of the available sources of information about the presidency.

NOTES

1. Fred Greenstein, "The Benevolent Leader: Children's Images of Political Authority," *American Political Science Review* (December 1960): 934-944. See also Fred Greenstein, "The Benevolent Leader Revisited: Children's Images of Political Leaders in Three Democracies," *American Political Science Review* (December 1975).

1. EVALUATING THE PRESIDENCY

Michael Nelson

The November 1, 1948, issue of *Life* magazine is a collector's item because of a picture on page 37 that is captioned: "The next president travels by ferry over the broad waters of San Francisco bay." (The picture is of Thomas E. Dewey.) Of greater significance, however, is an article that begins on page 65 called "Historians Rate U.S. Presidents." It was written by Professor Arthur M. Schlesinger, Sr., who had called upon 55 fellow historians to grade each president as either "great," "near great," "average," "below average," or "failure," then tallied up the results. Abraham Lincoln, George Washington, Franklin D. Roosevelt, Woodrow Wilson, and Andrew Jackson scored as great presidents, U. S. Grant and Warren Harding as failures, and the rest fell in between.

As interesting as the Schlesinger evaluations and their many imitators are, the important lessons may be more about the judges than their judgments, more about the office of the presidency than about individual presidents. What standards do scholars use to evaluate presidents? What image of the presidency do they measure the Lincolns and Hardings, or Carters and Reagans, against? What standards for evaluation do other important judges of the presidency use: journalists, citizens, members of Congress, bureaucrats?

Answering these questions can tell us a lot, not only about the presidency's evaluators, but also about the presidency itself.[1] Presidents, after all, want the "verdict of history" that scholars eventually render to be favorable. In the short run, they need the support of journalists, the mass public, and congressional and bureaucratic officeholders if they are to succeed. To do so, presidents must understand the standards of evaluation such groups apply to them.

Scholars: Strength Amid Confusion

Schlesinger followed his 1948 survey of historians with another in 1962. The results were strikingly similar: the same pair of "failures" and, with the narrow exception of Jackson, the same set of "greats." More important, so were the standards that historians in the late 1940s and early 1960s appeared to measure presidents against: strength and the desire to be strong. "Washington apart," Schlesinger wrote," none of [the great presidents] waited for the office to seek the man; they pursued it with all their might and main." Once in office, their greatness was established by the fact that "every one of [them] left the Executive branch stronger and more influential than he found it." When dealing with Congress, they knew "when to reason and to browbeat, to bargain and stand firm, . . . and when all else failed, they appealed over the heads of the lawmakers to the people." Nor did they shy away from confrontations with the Supreme Court. They were, to be sure, inattentive to administration of the bureaucracy, but this freed them, according to Schlesinger, for the more important tasks of "moral leadership." [2] A 1968 survey of historians by sociologist Gary Maranell not only confirmed Schlesinger's conclusion that "strength" and "activeness" were important criteria in the historians' model of the presidency, but also found that "idealism" and "flexibility" were not.[3]

The historians' model was very much like that of the other group of scholars who write and talk about the presidency, political scientists.[4] Their view in the 1950s and 1960s was summed up nicely in the title of an article by Thomas Cronin: "Superman: Our Textbook President." [5] After reviewing dozens of political science textbooks written in those two decades, Cronin found that political scientists characterized the presidency as both "omnipotent" and "benevolent." This idea that strength and goodness go hand in hand shined through, for example, in James MacGregor Burns's assessment that "the stronger we make the Presidency, the more we strengthen democratic procedures." [6] It also animated the most influential book on the presidency of this period, *Presidential Power*. "A president's success" in maximizing power, wrote its author, Richard Neustadt, "serves objectives far beyond his own and his party's. . . . [P]residential influence contributes to the energy of the government and to the viability of public policy. . . . [W]hat is good for the country is good for the president, and *vice versa*." [7]

Underlying the political scientists' model was a quasi-religious awe of the presidency. Clinton Rossiter began his book on *The American Presidency* by confessing his "feeling of veneration, if not exactly reverence, for the authority and dignity of the presidency." He described Lincoln as "the martyred Christ of democracy's passion play" and quoted favorably the "splendid judgment" of Englishman John Bright in 1861 that there is nothing more worthy of reverence and obedience, and nothing more sacred, than the authority of the freely chosen magistrate of a great and free people; and if there be on earth and amongst men any right divine to govern, surely it rests with a ruler so chosen and so appointed.[8]

Herman Finer was equally reverent, although in a polytheistic way. Finer not only characterized the presidency as "the incarnation of the American people in a sacrament resembling that in which the wafer and the wine are seen to be the body and blood of Christ," but also as "belong[ing] rightfully to the offspring of a titan and Minerva husbanded by Mars."[9]

Thus, strength and the desire to be strong, power and virtue, omnipotence and benevolence, all were tied in with each other in what only half-facetiously might be called the "Savior" model of the presidency. The model's underlying rationale was that the president is the chief guardian of the national interest, not only in foreign policy because no one else can speak and act for the nation, but also in domestic affairs because of the pluralistic structure of government and society. Members of Congress cater to wealthy and influential interests within their constituencies, it was argued, but the president can mobilize the unorganized and inarticulate and speak for national majorities against special interest groups.

Clearly, scholars' normative preference for presidential strength in the 1950s and 1960s had more to it than their value judgments about the proper distribution of power among the branches of government. It was rooted in their liberal policy preferences as well. Democratic historians outnumbered Republicans by two-to-one in the Schlesinger samples, for example. One of the reasons they found the strength of the presidents they chose as "great" so appealing was that, as Schlesinger put it, each of these presidents "took the side of liberalism and the general welfare against the status quo."[10] William Andrews observed a similar partisan and ideological bias among his fellow political scientists, many of whom had worked in liberal Democratic administrations. When it comes to the presidency, he concluded, "the constitutional theory follows the party flag."[11]

Presidential strength and ambition would benefit the nation, argued scholars of the "Savior" school in this period. How, then, to explain the nation's experience with Lyndon B. Johnson and Richard Nixon? In foreign affairs the power of these presidents sustained a large-scale war in Vietnam long after public opinion had turned against it. The power of the president as "Chief Legislator," in

Rossiter's phrase, prompted such hasty passage of a host of Great Society social welfare programs that their flaws, which might have been discovered in bargaining between the president and Congress, were not found until later. Many of these flaws were in administrative design and implementation, the very area of activity the Savior model had encouraged presidents to avoid. Finally, in 1972 and 1973, abuses of presidential power, which have been grouped under the umbrella term "Watergate," occurred that forced Nixon's resignation in August 1974.

The flawed presidencies of Johnson and Nixon convinced scholars that presidential strength and the general welfare, far from being synonymous, were more likely to appear as opposites: "Satan" to the earlier model's "Savior." Arthur M. Schlesinger, Jr., had helped to create the Savior model with his glowing biographies of Jackson, Roosevelt, and Kennedy and in eulogistic passages such as this one from *A Thousand Days:* "Thinking of the young Roosevelts, lost suddenly in middle age, and of the young Kennedys, so sure and purposeful, one perceived an historic contrast, a dynastic change, like the Plantagenets giving way to the Yorks." In 1973, he came back with a book berating the "imperial presidency." [12] Marcus Cunliffe called the office a "Frankenstein monster." [13] Nelson Polsby noted that the careers of most of the "great" presidents were tied up with total war.[14]

The new task for scholars, of course, was to explain why strength in the presidency was likely to be harmful to the nation rather than helpful, as previously had been thought. Their search carried them into two primary areas: the person and the office.

The expedition into personality as a source of presidential pathology was led by James David Barber. Barber identified a presidential personality type, the "active-negative," whose efforts to maximize power are born of a deep-seated and psychologically unhealthy need to dominate others.[15] When active-negatives encounter serious challenges to their power while in office, as all presidents eventually do, they react rigidly and aggressively. Such was the case with Johnson and Nixon. The nation survived their presidencies, but given the nature of modern weaponry, Barber argued, even one more active-negative could be too many.

Other scholars looked to the institution to explain why presidential strength was likely to be destructive. Cronin claimed that the "swelling of the presidency"—the sheer growth in the size of the White House staff—had turned it into "a powerful inner sanctum of government isolated from the traditional constitutional checks and balances." [16] George Reedy suggested that "the life of the White House is the life of a [royal] court" in which the president "is treated with all the reverence due a monarch." He added:

> There is built into the presidency a series of devices that tend to remove the occupant of the Oval Office from all of the forces which require most men to rub up against the hard facts of life on a daily basis. . . . No one interrupts presidential contemplation for anything less than a major catastrophe somewhere on the globe. No one speaks to him unless spoken to first. No one ever invites him to "go soak your head" when his demands become petulant and unreasonable. [17]

Ironically, no sooner had the Satan model of a powerful but dangerous presidency taken hold among political scientists and historians than events again intruded: the unusually weak presidencies of Gerald Ford and Jimmy Carter. The response of presidential scholars was not unlike that of the people of ancient Israel to Samson when he transgressed and had his strength cut away: they beheld the new weakness and were distressed by it. The Samson model of the presidency—others have called it the "imperiled" or "tethered" presidency—came in startling contrast to those that had preceded it. [18] It ruefully portrayed a large and growing gap between what presidents can do and what they are expected to do.

The model traced to two sources the presidency's incapacity to deliver: its constitutional dependence on other political institutions for support and the recent decline in the ability or willingness of those institutions to provide it. According to Samson theorists, parties had grown too weak to help, Congress too decentralized to bargain with, the bureaucracy too fragmented and powerful to lead, and the media too adversarial to make its spotlight an asset for the president. Among the public, single-issue groups harshly critical of government were proliferating, while those parts of the population most inclined to support the president—the less educated, religiously fundamentalist, and strongly partisan—were dwindling in number. Thus, presidents "have to work harder to keep the same popularity." [19]

Yet even as the president's ability to meet demands for action supposedly was declining, the volume, intensity, and complexity of those demands were said to be increasing. Godfrey Hodgson argued that the American people expect too much of their president:

> He must simultaneously conduct the diplomacy of a superpower, put together separate coalitions to enact every piece of legislation

required by a vast and complex society, manage the economy, command the armed forces, serve as a spiritual example and inspiration, respond to every emergency.[20]

With demands on the presidency so high, Samson theorists argued, no individual president could be expected to meet them. They cited the recent high turnover in the presidency as a sign of the weakness of the institution. Ronald Reagan's inauguration on January 20, 1981, made him the sixth president to be sworn into office in only 20 years.

But once in office, Reagan quickly refuted the Samson model just as the Johnson and Nixon administrations had the Savior model and Ford and Carter had the Satan model. A political cartoon from the summer of 1981 depicts an angry professor storming out of a door marked "Political Science Department." Papers fly around the office in his wake, one a title page marked "The Limits of Power," another a newspaper with the headline "Stunning Tax, Budget Wins for Reagan." In the foreground a secretary explains to a startled student: "He just completed the definitive, 600-page work on why special-interest groups, weak parties, and a fragmented Congress make presidential leadership impossible."

Savior, Satan, Samson—the sheer velocity of the turnover in these models since the 1960s would seem to indicate that the best single-word description of how scholars evaluate the presidency is "confusion." The sources of this confusion are not hard to trace. Although the models purport to describe the enduring institution of the presidency, they were created in response to specific presidents. Like a newspaper, a topical model becomes obsolete quickly. In addition, each of the three models combined, albeit unwittingly, an empirical question (Is the presidency strong or weak?) and a normative one (Is this condition of presidential strength or weakness good or bad for the American political system?). Both types of questions are worth asking but not in the same breath. Thus in the Savior model, which prevailed from the Roosevelt through the Kennedy administrations, the answers were: the presidency is a strong office, and this is good for the system. The Satan model displaced it when scholars, overreacting to the lessons of Johnson and Nixon, decided that the strength of the presidency, although great, was pathological. Then, startled once again by the weak administrations of Ford and Carter, they went back to the drawing board and constructed the Samson model of the presidency (the office is weak, which is bad).[21]

Yet underlying this confusion has been a recurring, if sometimes implicit, celebration of presidential strength. The Savior model exulted in its presence; the Samson model mourned its apparent demise. As for the Satan school, it may be understood best as the scholarly equivalent of a lovers' quarrel with the presidency. Even while warning of active-negative personality types, for example, Barber placed his hopes for the country in the election of "active-positives," presidents who would seek to dominate the system out of zest rather than zeal. Although Schlesinger, Jr., sharply attacked the excessive power of the "imperial presidency," he stopped short of endorsing any serious effort to limit the office constitutionally.[22]

In the 1980s, strength as the standard for scholarly evaluation of presidents actually may be more solidly grounded than it was in the heyday of the Savior model in the 1950s and 1960s. As always, those who want action from the government—and liberal scholars like those who made up the Schlesinger surveys certainly do—will urge the president to lead. What is new is that conservatives have learned from the Reagan experience that a strong presidency can work to serve their interests too.

Journalists: Strength Amid Cynicism

If confusion is the key word for understanding changing scholarly views of the presidency, the comparable shorthand description of journalistic standards of evaluation in recent years is cynicism. Underlying this surface attitude, however, is an implicit exaltation of presidential strength. Like presidential scholars, the White House press corps encourages a powerful presidency.

Historically, journalistic cynicism toward the presidency can be traced to Vietnam and Watergate.[23] White House reporters felt that a breach of trust occurred in the late 1960s and early 1970s: they had been lied to repeatedly by presidents and their aides and, by reporting those lies in their newspapers and news broadcasts on good faith, had been used. Stephen Hess describes "the residue of that era" among the Washington journalists he interviewed as "distrust of public institutions and politicians in general." [24] That distrust has carried over into such routine events as the presidential press secretary's daily briefing where, according to *Newsweek* editor Mel Elfin, "reporters vie with each other to see who can ask the toughest questions and never let Watergate happen to us again." [25]

A more deeply rooted and important source of cynicism among journalists, however, may be the "status frustration" of the White House press corps. This frustration has developed out of the growing imbalance between their social and professional status, which is exalted, and the nature of the job itself, which is degrading.

Of the high status of the White House press corps, little needs to be said. The White House correspondent, says Martin Tolchin of the *New York Times*, is "part of the whole social circle" of Supreme Court justices, cabinet secretaries, and prominent members of Congress.[26] Professionally, the presidency is among a handful of what Hess calls "high-prestige beats" in Washington; journalist Stewart Alsop listed it as first in the pecking order.[27] White House reporters usually are guaranteed prominent placement for their daily dispatches and tend to be high on the list of journalists who are invited to give paid lectures or write magazine articles or books. The presidential beat also is a gateway to better things in the profession. David Halberstam describes it as "an institutional ticket. The guy who gets to the White House goes on to some bigger job" such as editor, columnist, or television anchor.[28]

In stark contrast to these external indicators of success and prestige is the job itself, which has been well described as "the body watch." The body, of course, is the president's; the purpose of the watch is to find out all that he does in his waking hours, both officially and privately. That means staying near; as Elfin puts it, "the worst thing in the world that could happen to you is for the president of the United States to choke on a piece of meat, and for you not to be there." [29]

Staying near, however, is a goal that usually can be achieved only in the most technical sense. The White House press room is only yards away from the Oval Office, but the distance rarely is spanned. Reporters not only are forbidden to "roam the halls" of the White House and Executive Office Building in the time-honored *modus operandi* of their profession, but their free access even to the office of the press secretary is limited to his assistants' outer sanctums. Charged by their editors to "body-watch" the president, they usually are forced to rely on the secondhand reports of his press secretary, who comes out once a day to brief them, or on other presidential aides or visitors to the Oval Office, who may choose to speak to them or not. When reporters are allowed to see the president, it almost always is in a setting that is defined both physically and procedurally by the White House. Members of the White House press corps enjoy high status in part because they are so visible, but the irony is that "they are visible because of the large amount of time they spend waiting for something to happen—for the briefing to start, for the president to appear for a White House ceremony in the Rose Garden, for a visitor to arrive, for a statement or a transcript to be released." [30]

The frustration that journalists feel in a job whose main activities are stenographic is great. A briefing room full of White House reporters when the press secretary appears is not unlike a classroom full of junior high school students who have just been informed that a substitute teacher is on the way. In their daily dispatches to the public, where professional and editorial standards forbid overtly hostile displays, status frustration, joined to the hangover from Vietnam and Watergate, shows up in subtler form. As one study of the subject records,

> reporters now present news about the White House along with an item that casts doubt on the credibility of what has been said or on the reliability of the person who has said it. They indicate to their viewers that a cynical approach is a realistic approach when analyzing the motives of the president and his advisers.[31]

Yet, on balance, presidents still receive highly favorable press coverage. In their study of how *Time* and the *New York Times* covered the presidency from 1953 to 1978, Michael Grossman and Martha Kumar found that about twice as many stories were favorable to the presidency as were unfavorable. This was true not only for the total period, but for its last five years. Their study of a decade of CBS Evening News coverage showed a similar balance in favor of the presidency from 1974 to 1978, up markedly from the Vietnam and Watergate years of 1968 to 1973. If anything, this two-to-one ratio in favor of the presidency understates the true situation. Flattering pictures of presidents in *Time,* the *Times,* and CBS outnumbered unflattering ones by margins of 33, 34, and six-to-one, respectively.[32] And local and regional media, which the authors did not study, tend to be even more supportive than national organs.

Even more pertinent to our concern with journalists' standards for evaluating the presidency are the kinds of actions by presidents that generate the most favorable coverage. According to Grossman and Kumar, reporters respond enthusiastically to presidential actions that convey strength. They list five categories of such stories:

1) appearing decisive—military leadership;
2) appearing decisive—firing contrary subordinates;
3) being in command—the president as expert;
4) being in command—the president as effective intellectual; and
5) being recognized as a leader—foreign travel.[33]

In sum, when strong action—or the appearance of strong action—comes from the White House, journalists tend to applaud it.

Why do reporters who are cynical about the presidency continue to cover it favorably? One reason is occupational necessity. Most White House correspondents must file at least one story every day. Because of the severe limitations placed on reporters' ability to gather information independently, the president or the press secretary is in a good position to define the agenda they cover. "They have this huge built-in element of control over you," explains Austin Scott of the *Washington Post*. "You're locked into this little press room with only a telephone connecting you to the rest of the White House, and they have the option of taking your calls or not. All you get is staged events—press conferences, briefings, photo opportunities." [34] Dom Bonafede of the *National Journal* observed during the Ford years that "every day when [Press Secretary Ron] Nessen gets out there he determines, with his opening statement, what the news is going to be for that day." [35] Thus, even when reporters tag on a cynical twist, it usually is to a story that the White House has concocted.

Editors demand more than a daily story from their White House correspondents, of course; they also expect an occasional "exclusive" to put them a leg up on the competition. These usually come about through leaks of information from members of the White House staff. Such leaks almost always are intended to make the president look good: the personal success of presidential assistants, after all, is tied very closely to the political success of the president. But according to Peter Lisagor of the *Chicago Daily News,* reporters really have little choice but to use what they get:

> The competition and competitive pressure is such that guys have to get a story. If they get something that someone else might not have—no matter how self-serving [for the White House] it may seem and no matter how hardnosed they may feel themselves to be—they may often go with the story.[36]

Considerations other than occupational necessity contribute to reporters' favorable portrayal of a powerful presidency. Their "world view," or implicit conception of how the political system works, greatly affects how they perform their job. "Journalists define the center of government action as the executive," note David Paletz and Robert Entman, and "personalize the institution as one man." [37] A study by Elmer Cornwell of front-page newspaper headlines from 1885 to 1957 found "a long-term upward trend [in presidency-centered coverage] in absolute terms and relative to news about Congress"; Alan Balutis's extension of Cornwell's data through 1974 found both trends growing stronger.[38] The favorable or unfavorable nature of presidential coverage may be less important than the coverage itself. Simply by dwelling on the presidency, the media reinforces images of its strength and importance.[39] Finally, reporters tend to look at government through the lenses of electoral politics. They often describe relationships between the presidency and other policy-making institutions, especially Congress, in terms of victories and defeats for the president. This, too, reinforces the notion that strong presidents who dominate the system are good presidents.

Citizens: Strength Amid Contradiction

The American presidency combines the roles of chief of government and chief of state. As chief of government, the president is called upon to act in the manner of the British prime minister, as a political leader of the partisan causes and coalition that elected him the office. As chief of state, he is the equivalent of the British monarch: the ceremonial leader of the nation and the living symbol of its unity.

Because the presidency embodies both roles, the general public tends to evaluate it by standards that seem contradictory. According to Cronin, Americans want the president to be "gentle and decent but forceful and decisive," "inspirational but 'don't promise more than you can deliver,'" "open and caring but courageous and independent," a "common man who gives an uncommon performance," and a "national unifier-national divider." [40] George Edwards suggests several similar sets of contradictory public expectations about presidential style, including "leadership vs. responsiveness," "statesman vs. politician," and "empathy vs. uniqueness."[41]

The public's expectations of presidential policy making also seem to be contradictory. On the one hand, they expect the president to reduce unemployment, cut the cost of government, increase government efficiency, deal effectively with foreign policy, and strengthen national defense. In a survey taken shortly after Carter's election in 1976, 59 to 81 percent of the respondents, depending on the policy in question, said that they expected these accomplishments. The comparable figures following Reagan's election ranged from 69 to 89 percent.[42]

Yet the conventional wisdom among scholars is that the public also would prefer that Congress—the other, constitutionally coequal branch they elect—dominate the presidency in the policy-making process. After reviewing a wide variety of poll data from 1936 to 1973, Hazel Erskine concluded: "whenever given a choice between congressional vs. presidential decision-making, the people tend to trust Congress over the chief executive. Whether the issue pertains to specific domestic or military matters, or to authority in general, seems immaterial." [43] Donald Devine agreed: "the American people believe ... that the Congress should be supreme." He cited as evidence the 61 to 17 percent margin by which they chose Congress in response to this 1958 Survey Research Center question: "Some people say that the president is in the best position to see what the country needs. Other people think the president may have some good ideas about what the country needs but it is up to Congress to decide what ought to be done. How do you feel about it?" [44] A 1979 Gallup poll question that asked whether Congress or the president "ought to have major responsibility" in three policy areas found Congress preferred for energy and the economy and the president only for foreign policy. [45]

In apparent contradiction of their high expectations of presidential performance, then, Americans are "philosophical congressionalists." But in truth, all this means is that when pollsters ask abstract questions of a theoretical nature, the public tends to side with Congress against the president. (It is hard to imagine that such questions come up very often in ordinary discussions.)[46] When one looks at evidence about attitudes and feelings that bear more directly on political behavior, the balance shifts. The American public, like American scholars and journalists, wants and admires strength in the presidency.

One finds first that Americans are "operational presidentialists." Whatever they may say about proper institutional roles in theory, the presidents they like are the ones who take the lead and the Congresses they like are the ones that follow. Stephen Wayne provides evidence for the first half of this proposition in his report on a 1979 survey that asked people what qualities they admired most in their favorite president. "Strong" led the list by far; "forceful," "ability to get things done," and "decisive" ranked third, fifth, and seventh, respectively. "Concern for the average citizen," "honest," and "had confidence of people" were the only oft-mentioned qualities that were not clear synonyms for strength. [47] As for Congress, the only times that a majority of the respondents have rated its performance as either "excellent" or "pretty good" in two decades of Harris surveys were in 1964 and 1965, the two years in which Congress was most responsive to strong presidential leadership. [48]

Americans also can be described as "emotional presidentialists." Almost all of their politial heroes from the past are presidents;[49] when candidates run for president, they promise to be like the best of their predecessors. (In contrast, members of Congress—the "only distinctly native American criminal class," in Mark Twain's jest—serve in political folklore as the butt of jokes. Congressional aspirants tend to "run *for* Congress by running *against* Congress.") [50] Heroic feelings about the presidency show up most dramatically when a president dies. Surveys taken shortly after President John F. Kennedy's assassination found Americans to be displaying symptoms of grief that otherwise appear only at the death of a close friend or relative. They "didn't feel like eating" (43 percent), were "nervous and tense" (68 percent), and "dazed and numb" (57 percent). [51] They also feared, for a short time at least, that the Republic was in danger. [52] Similar emotional outpourings seem to have accompanied the deaths in office of all presidents, whether by assassination or natural causes and whether they were popular or not. In Great Britain, it is the monarch's death that occasions such deep emotions, not the death of the prime minister, the chief of government. [53]

The public's emotional attachment to the presidency has implications of its own for strong leadership. The "honeymoon" that each new president enjoys with the people at the start of his term is, in a sense, an affirmation of faith in the office. New and reelected presidents invariably receive the early approval of millions of citizens who had voted against them, and most presidents are able to keep their public approval ratings at near-honeymoon levels for a year or more. As we will see, nothing is more helpful to presidential leadership of Congress than popularity with the voters.

Presidents also can trade on the public's emotional support for the office in foreign affairs. Citizens will "rally 'round the flag" in the form of their chief of state in all sorts of international circumstances. [54] According to a study by Jong Lee, wars and military crises head the list of support-inspiring events, followed by new foreign policy initiatives, peace efforts, and summit conferences. [55] Nixon's approval rating in the Gallup poll went up 12 percentage points after his October 1969 "Vietnamization" speech, Ford's jumped 11 points after he "rescued" the *Mayaguez,* and Carter added 12 points to his rating as a result of the Camp David summit that brought Israel and Egypt together.

Rossiter sums up the symbolic and political importance of the presidency:

> No president can fail to realize that all his powers are invigorated, indeed are given a new dimension of authority, because he is the symbol of our sovereignty, continuity, and grandeur. When he asks a senator to lunch in order to enlist support for a pet project, ... when he orders a general to cease caviling or else be removed from his command, the senator and ... the general are well aware—

especially if the scene is laid in the White House—that they are dealing with no ordinary head of government.[56]

The presidency-evaluators to whom Rossiter refers, of course, are not outside of government but are fellow officeholders. Like scholars, journalists, and the general public, members of Congress and bureaucrats evaluate the presidency in ways that are superficially detrimental to presidential leadership, yet their underlying attitudes offer support for strong presidents.

Members of Congress: Strength Amid Constituency-Centeredness

Whether animated by a selfish urge to do well or a generous desire to do good, the modern member of Congress wants to be reelected.[57] As Richard Fenno explains, "for most members of Congress most of the time, [the] electoral goal is primary. It is the prerequisite for a congressional career and, hence, for the pursuit of other member goals." [58] From 1946 to 1982, an average 91.6 percent of all representatives sought reelection, as did 83.7 percent of all senators.[59]

To be reelected, of course, members must please their constituents, a task best accomplished by working in Congress to advance local interests as defined by local people. A 1977 Harris survey conducted for the House Commission on Administrative Review asked respondents whether they thought their representative should be primarily concerned with looking after the needs and interests of "his own district" or "the nation as a whole." They chose "own district" by a margin of 57 to 34 percent. About twice as many voters in a 1978 survey said that when a legislator sees a conflict between "what the voters think best" and "what he thinks best," he should obey the voters.[60]

Personal ambition and constituents' demands powerfully influence how members of Congress behave in office. Most channel their energy and resources into activities that translate readily into votes. This creates an anomaly: although Congress's main constitutional task is to legislate in the national interest, most of the activities that produce votes for members are nonlegislative, primarily "pork-barreling" and casework.[61] (Pork-barreling involves getting federal grant and project money for their home states and districts; casework is handling constituents' complaints about their personal experiences with the federal bureaucracy.) David Mayhew adds "advertising" to the list of leading congressional activities: newsletters or questionnaires mailed home, personal visits, and similar efforts "to create a favorable image but in messages having little or no issue content." [62]

What time is left for legislative activity generally is spent in two reelection-oriented ways. First, members propose laws pleasing to their voters. This takes little effort but enables them to gain publicity in local media and to answer almost any constituent's inquiry about policy or legislation with: "I introduced (or cosponsored) a bill on that very subject." At the same time, it commits them to none of the difficult, time-consuming, and largely invisible activities needed to get legislation over the hurdles of subcommittee, committee, and floor passage in each house.

Second, legislators work very hard on those few areas of lawmaking that are of particular interest to the local constituency. For example, a representative from a farm district can be certain that his effectiveness, not just his rhetoric, on agricultural issues will be monitored closely by opinion leaders back home. This explains why the Agriculture committees in both houses are dominated by farm-state members, the House Interior and Senate Environmental and Public Works committees by westerners, and the House Merchant Marine and Fisheries committee by coastal-state representatives.[63] Once on these committees, members often enter into mutually beneficial relationships with the interest groups and executive agencies in their policy "subgovernment." By supporting programs that interest groups favor, legislators may obtain campaign contributions and other electoral benefits. From agencies they may receive special consideration for their constituents and influence over the distribution of patronage and contracts in return for generous appropriations and loose statutory reins.

Not surprisingly, representatives and senators also evaluate the presidency by constituency-based criteria. For presidents who have an extensive legislative agenda, this can seem very discouraging. Their difficulty in moving bills through a constitutionally bicameral legislature is compounded by Congress's culture of constituency service, which distracts members away from serious legislative activity into the more electorally rewarding business of pork barreling, casework, and advertising. Successful presidential leadership also requires that members direct their attention to national concerns. But congressional ambition is such that local issues, or the local effects of national issues, come first. Finally, most presidential initiatives call for legislative alteration of the status quo. Such proposals often conflict with the general satisfaction that each component of the various subgovernments, including the congressional committees and subcommittees, has in existing arrangements.

Nevertheless, in other, perhaps more important ways, Congress's constituency-centered culture enhances rather than inhibits presidential strength. These are the power to initiate, the power of popularity, and power in foreign policy.

Power to Initiate

During the past century, the public has placed ever greater demands for action on the federal government, most of which have required the passage of new legislation. To satisfy each of these demands, Congress as an institution has had to move through the long, tortuous, and largely subterranean process of developing programs and steering them past its own internal obstacles to action. Representatives and senators naturally have wanted to see this happen, but as noted earlier, the pursuit of reelection takes them mainly into nonlegislative areas of activity.

Again and again since 1932, members of Congress have found their way out of this dilemma by turning to the presidency. Not only did Congress give Franklin D. Roosevelt a virtual blank check to deal with the Great Depression as he saw fit—in the fabled first hundred days, it passed more than a dozen pieces of Roosevelt-spawned legislation—it also authorized actions that allowed the president to institutionalize his role as policy initiator. The Bureau of the Budget was transferred from the Treasury Department to a newly created Executive Office of the President and empowered to screen all departmental proposals for legislation before Congress could see them. In addition, the president was authorized to hire a personal political staff, largely for the purpose of developing and selling legislation to Congress.

In succeeding administrations, these trends continued. The Employment Act of 1946 called upon the president (with the aid of a new Council of Economic Advisers) to monitor the economy and recommend corrective legislation in times of economic distress. Similar congressional requests for presidential initiative were included in the Manpower Development and Training Act of 1962, the Housing and Urban Development Act of 1968, the National Environmental Policy Act of 1969, and several others. Remarkably, when Congress wanted to express its deep dissatisfaction with President Nixon's economic policies in 1971, it passed a law that forced on him the power to impose wage and price controls on the entire economy. Congress sometimes demands strength from the president even when the president does not want to give it.

Power of Popularity

The power to initiate legislation that members of Congress have ceded to the presidency in the interests of their own reelection is formidable in itself, but what of the power to secure legislative passage? Again, the constituency-centered culture of Congress can work to the advantage of presidential strength. The same congressional preoccupation with reelection that has led members to try to insulate their relationship with the voters from national political forces also has made them extremely sensitive to any national forces that might cost them votes. In particular, when legislators think that the president's support among voters is high, they are likely to follow his legislative leadership.

Perceptions of presidential popularity may grow out of a landslide election victory accompanied by unusually large gains for the president's party in Congress. (Gains of 30 to 40 seats are large enough to seem unusual nowadays; until recently, they were quite ordinary.) Such gains invariably are attributed, accurately or not, to the president's "coattails" or to a mandate that he and Congress share. Either way, the election creates a heightened disposition among legislators of both congressional parties to support the president's legislative agenda: copartisans because they want to ride his bandwagon, electorally vulnerable members of the opposition party because they want to avoid being flattened by it. Such was the case following the landslide elections of Johnson in 1964, whose party gained 37 seats in the House, and Reagan in 1980, when Republicans won 33 new seats in the House and took control of the Senate.

The obsession with reelection that governs legislators' reactions to election results causes them to respond in a similar manner to indices of presidential popularity during a president's term. Because reelection-oriented members of Congress "are hypersensitive to anticipated constituent reaction" to their actions, it is not surprising that the amount of support Congress gives to a president's legislative agenda is strongly related to his Gallup approval rating.[64] Each president, of course, enjoys a honeymoon period of high voter approval at the start of his term. Among recent reelected presidents, Eisenhower and Kennedy maintained their initial popularity throughout their terms, Johnson and Nixon kept theirs for the first two years, and Carter and Reagan held their ground in the polls for at least the first year. Even after their approval ratings declined, all but Johnson were able to revive their initial popularity, at least for short periods.[65] And Johnson and Reagan held on long enough to get their particularly dramatic legislative programs through Congress virtually intact.

As many scholars have pointed out, approval ratings are down in general; both the peaks and the valleys in presidential "fever charts" are lower than they used to be. But as with new-style election "landslides" of 30 to 40 seats, hills now are as impressive to members of Congress as mountains once were. Reagan's highest approval rating barely exceeded Kennedy's lowest, but members were more impressed by Reagan's popularity, which contrasted so favorably with his predecessors', than by Kennedy's, which seemed typical after Eisenhower.

Power in Foreign Policy

Congress's constituency-centered culture also encourages presidential strength in foreign policy. Historically, Congress has been assertive only on the minority of foreign policy issues that concern voters the most, especially unpopular wars. For a member of Congress to pursue an interest in foreign policy much further than that is to tempt electoral fate. Both Senate Foreign Relations Committee Chairman J. William Fulbright and his successor as chairman, Frank Church, were defeated in reelection bids by opponents who charged that they cared more about world politics than about local politics.

Bureaucrats: Strength Amid Careerism

Career civil servants might appear to be the group whose favorable evaluations presidents need the least. In civics book theory, they are part of the president's executive chain of command and perform purely administrative, not policy-making functions. In practice, however, Congress and the courts, as well as the chief executive, have a rightful say over what bureaucrats do. And the nature of administration in modern society increasingly involves those who implement policy in the making of it.

Like members of Congress, career civil servants, who represent some 99.9 percent of the federal civilian workforce, often are motivated by self-interest. "The prime commitments of civil servants," writes Erwin Hargrove, "are to their career, agency, and program. The markers of success are autonomy for their bureaus and expansion of budgets." [66] Such self-interested commitments make life difficult for the remaining one-tenth of 1 percent: the departmental secretaries, undersecretaries, assistant secretaries, bureau chiefs, regional directors, and other "political executives" whom the president appoints to manage the bureaucracy in pursuit of his policies.

The stance of both presidents and their political executives toward the career bureaucrats, observes James Fesler, includes "an assumption that the bureaucracy is swollen, a doubt of careerists' competence, and an expectation of their unresponsiveness to the administration." [67] This view of the unresponsive bureaucrat seemed to be validated by Joel Aberbach's and Bert Rockman's 1970 study of the political beliefs of high-ranking civil servants in several social service agencies.[68] Large majorities of the supergrade bureaucrats they interviewed disapproved of President Nixon's policies to reduce the social agencies' power and budgets. This was especially true for the 47 percent who were Democrats, but the bulk of the 36 percent who were Independents also opposed the president. These data seemed so supportive of the stereotype of the self-centered bureaucrat resisting the policies of the elected president that Nixon actually quoted the authors' conclusion in his memoirs: "Our findings ... pointedly portray a social service bureaucracy dominated by administrators hostile to many of the directions pursued by the Nixon administration in the realm of social policy." [69]

But far from proving Nixon's point, Aberbach and Rockman actually laid the groundwork for a later study that appears to have refuted it. In 1976, Richard Cole and David Caputo conducted a similar survey and discovered that most supergrade bureaucrats, including Democrats and especially Independents, by then supported Nixon's policies. "We find the 'pull' of the presidency to be very strong," they concluded.[70]

What accounts for the apparent willingness of career bureaucrats to respond to strong presidential leadership? In part, it seems the stereotype of bureaucratic self-interest has been overdrawn. As Fesler notes, most careerists feel obliged "to serve loyally the people's choice as president. Because senior careerists have served through several changes in administration, this is a well-internalized commitment." [71] Presumably, the stronger a president's leadership, the easier it is for loyal bureaucrats to follow.

A more important explanation may be the apparent harmony of self-interest between careerist bureaucrats and strong presidents. Cole and Caputo report that the Nixon administration played an unusually purposeful and active role in the job promotion process within the upper reaches of the civil service. Civil servants sympathetic to the administration's policies were favored. This group included Republicans, of course, but also many Independents and some Democrats who recognized that the administration meant business and therefore adapted their views to further their own careers.

In sum, the civics books are not entirely wrong. Some bureaucrats follow the ethic of loyal service to the president because they believe in it. Others will follow when promotions are based on faithful obedience to the president. In either event the result is the same: "senior bureaucrats, like Supreme Court justices, 'follow the election returns.' " [72]

Summary and Conclusion

Presidential scholarship in recent years has been marked by a bewildering succession of new models of the presidency, each the product of an admixture of empirical and normative assessments, each constructed in hasty overreaction to the most recent president. Journalists' coverage of the presidency has been tinged by a Vietnam- and Watergate-induced cynicism whose real source may be the status frustration of the modern White House press corps. Citizens pin all their hopes for chief of state-like symbolic leadership and chief of government-like political leadership on one office, the presidency. Members of Congress view the White House through constituency-colored lenses, judging it by the narrow standard of personal reelection ambitions. Tenured civil servants, whose working life is committed to the bureaucracy, also evaluate the presidency in terms of their own careers.

But in all cases, these evaluations turn out to be superficial. Underlying the scholars' confusion is an implicit appreciation that significant policy change, whatever its ideological direction, requires a strong president. The career needs and world view of journalists lead them to exalt presidential strength as well. Citizens apparently want to have the contradictions in their expectations resolved through presidential actions that are strong but appear unifying. Legislators and bureaucrats realize, albeit reluctantly at times, that their career interests can be served by strong presidential initiatives.

On the whole, the underlying admiration for and celebration of presidential strength by scholars, journalists, citizens, members of Congress, and career bureaucrats should be a source of comfort to presidents and to all who have fretted in recent years about a decline in the authority of the presidency. But two cautionary notes need to be sounded.

First, strength means different things to different people. Scholarly celebrants of a strong presidency traditionally have dismissed the president's administrative duties as distractions from the real tasks of moral and political leadership. Yet many bureaucrats will respond to strong presidential initiatives only when they seem likely to influence their own careers. Similarly, while the public tends to respond enthusiatically to strong presidential action of a unifying kind, journalists write most approvingly when a president defeats his political opponents.

Second, the urge that presidents may feel to impress audiences both present and future as a strong—and hence a "great"—president may lead them to behave in ways that disserve themselves, the government, and the nation. "For fear of being found out and downgraded," writes Nelson Polsby, "there is the temptation to hoard credit rather than share it . . . [and] to export responsibility away from the White House for the honest shortfalls of programs, thus transmitting to the government at large an expectation that loyalty upward will be rewarded with disloyalty down." The final, and most dangerous temptation is "to offer false hopes and to proclaim spurious accomplishments to the public at large." [73]

The complete lesson for presidents who wish to exert strong leadership, then, is that they need not worry about threats from the rest of the political system. Their problems really begin only when the concern for appearing strong distracts them from the business of the presidency.

NOTES

1. Some of the themes in this chapter are discussed in more detail in Erwin Hargrove and Michael Nelson, *Presidents, Politics, and Policy* (New York: Alfred A. Knopf, 1984).
2. Arthur Schlesinger, "Our Presidents: A Rating by 75 Historians," *The New York Times Magazine,* July 29, 1962, 12ff.
3. Gary Maranell, "The Evaluation of Presidents: An Extension of the Schlesinger Polls," *Journal of American History* (June 1970): 104-113.
4. A study of how social scientists rated presidents from Franklin D. Roosevelt through Richard Nixon found economists' rankings to be similar to those of political scientists and historians. Malcolm B. Parsons, "The Presidential Rating Game," in *The Future of the American Presidency,* ed., Charles Dunn (Morristown, N.J.: General Learning Press, 1975), 66-91.
5. Thomas Cronin, "Superman: Our Textbook President," *The Washington Monthly* (October 1970): 47-54.
6. James MacGregor Burns, *Presidential Government: The Crucible of Leadership* (Boston: Houghton Mifflin Co., 1965), 330.

7. Richard Neustadt, *Presidential Power: The Politics of Leadership* (New York: John Wiley & Sons, 1960). The theme of Neustadt's book is that although presidents can do little by direct command, they can and should wield great power through skillful bargaining and persuasion.

8. Clinton Rossiter, *The American Presidency* (New York: Harcourt, Brace & World, 1960), 15-16, 108.

9. Herman Finer, *The Presidency* (Chicago: University of Chicago Press, 1960), 111, 119.

10. Schlesinger, "Our Presidents," 40.

11. William Andrews, "The Presidency, Congress and Constitutional Theory," in *Perspectives on the Presidency,* ed. Aaron Wildavsky (Boston: Little, Brown & Co., 1975), 38. For further evidence of partisan and ideological bias in scholarly assessments of the presidency, see Parsons, "Presidential Rating Game."

12. Arthur M. Schlesinger, Jr., *A Thousand Days* (Boston: Houghton Mifflin Co., 1965), 677; and idem, *The Imperial Presidency* (Boston: Houghton Mifflin Co., 1973).

13. Marcus Cunliffe, "A Defective Institution?" *Commentary* (February 1968): 28.

14. Nelson Polsby, "Against Presidential Greatness," *Commentary* (January 1977): 63.

15. James David Barber, *The Presidential Character* (Englewood Cliffs, N.J.: Prentice-Hall, 1972).

16. Thomas Cronin, *The State of the Presidency* (Boston: Little, Brown & Co., 1975), 138.

17. George Reedy, *The Twilight of the Presidency* (New York: New American Library, 1970), chap. 1. See also Bruce Buchanan, *The Presidential Experience* (Englewood Cliffs, N.J.: Prentice-Hall, 1978); and Irving Janis, *Victims of GroupThink* (Boston: Houghton Mifflin Co., 1972).

18. Gerald Ford, "Imperiled, Not Imperial," *Time,* November 10, 1980, 30-31; and Thomas Franck, ed., *The Tethered Presidency* (New York: New York University Press, 1981).

19. Aaron Wildavsky, "The Past and Future Presidency," *The Public Interest* (Fall 1975): 56-76.

20. Godfrey Hodgson, *All Things to All Men* (New York: Simon & Schuster, 1980), 239.

21. A fourth, "Seraph" model of the presidency, as an institution that is and should be weak, never has dominated presidential scholarship. But it has its adherents. See, for example, Fred Greenstein, "Change and Continuity in the Modern Presidency," in *The New American Political System,* ed. Anthony King (Washington, D.C.: American Enterprise Institute for Public Policy Research, 1978); and Peter Woll and Rochelle Jones, "The Bureaucracy as a Check upon the President," *The Bureaucrat* (April 1974): 8-20.

22. Barber, *Presidential Character,* chap. 13; and Schlesinger, Jr., *Imperial Presidency,* chap. 11.

23. Pre-Vietnam and Watergate press attitudes are described in Tom Wicker, "News Management from the Small Town to the White House," *The Washington Monthly* (January 1978): 19-26.

24. Stephen Hess, *The Washington Reporters* (Washington, D.C.: The Brookings Institution, 1981), 78.

25. Michael Grossman and Martha Kumar, *Portraying the President: The White House and the News Media* (Baltimore: Johns Hopkins University Press, 1981), 131.
26. Ibid., 206-207.
27. Hess, *Washington Reporters,* 49; Stewart Alsop, *The Center* (New York: Popular Library, 1968), 161.
28. Grossman and Kumar, *Portraying the President,* 183.
29. Ibid., 43.
30. Ibid., 36.
31. Ibid., 301.
32. Ibid., chap. 10.
33. Ibid., 232-238.
34. David Paletz and Robert Entman, *Media Power Politics* (New York: Free Press, 1981), 57.
35. Grossman and Kumar, *Portraying the President,* 33.
36. Ibid., 182.
37. Paletz and Entman, *Media Power Politics,* 55.
38. Elmer Cornwell, "Presidential News: The Expanding Public Image," *Journalism Quarterly* (Summer 1959): 282; and Alan Balutis, "The Presidency and the Press: The Expanding Public Image," *Presidential Studies Quarterly* (Fall 1977).
39. Bruce Miroff, "Monopolizing the Public Space: The President as a Problem for Democratic Politics," in *Rethinking the Presidency,* ed. Thomas Cronin (Boston: Little, Brown & Co., 1982), 218-232.
40. Thomas Cronin, "The Presidency and Its Paradoxes," in *The Presidency Reappraised,* 2d ed., edited by Thomas Cronin and Rexford Tugwell (New York: Praeger Publishers, 1977), 69-85.
41. George Edwards, *The Public Presidency* (New York: St. Martin's Press, 1983), 196-198.
42. "Early Expectations: Comparing Chief Executives," *Public Opinion* (February-March 1981): 39.
43. Hazel Erskine, "The Polls: Presidential Power," *Public Opinion Quarterly* (Fall 1973): 488.
44. Donald Devine, *The Political Culture of the United States* (Boston: Little, Brown & Co., 1972), 158.
45. Thomas Cronin, "A Resurgent Congress and the Imperial Presidency," *Political Science Quarterly* (Summer 1980): 211.
46. Richard Fenno, *Home Style: House Members in Their Districts* (Boston: Little, Brown & Co., 1978), 245. According to Fenno, "most citizens find it hard or impossible to think about Congress as an institution. They answer questions about it; but they cannot conceptualize it as a collectivity."
47. Stephen Wayne, "Great Expectations: What People Want from Presidents," in *Rethinking the Presidency,* ed. Cronin, 192-195.
48. Roger Davidson and Walter Oleszek, *Congress and Its Members* (Washington, D.C.: CQ Press, 1981), 152.
49. Devine, *Political Culture,* 128.
50. Fenno, *Home Style,* 168.
51. Paul Sheatsley and Jacob Feldman, "The Assassination of President Kennedy: Public Reactions," *Public Opinion Quarterly* (Summer 1964): 197-202.
52. Ibid., 197.

53. Sebastian de Grazia, *The Political Community* (Chicago: University of Chicago Press, 1948), 112-115.
54. John Mueller, *War, Presidents, and Public Opinion* (New York: John Wiley & Sons, 1973), 69-74, 122-140.
55. Jong R. Lee, "Rally Round the Flag: Foreign Policy Events and Presidential Popularity," *Presidential Studies Quarterly* (Fall 1977): 255.
56. Rossiter, *American Presidency*, 16-17.
57. See Morris Fiorina, *Congress: Keystone of the Washington Establishment* (New Haven: Yale University Press, 1977), 41-49; and David Mayhew, *Congress: The Electoral Connection* (New Haven: Yale University Press, 1974).
58. Fenno, *Home Style*, 31.
59. Calculated from data presented in Norman J. Ornstein et al., *Vital Statistics on Congress, 1982* (Washington: American Enterprise Institute for Public Policy Research, 1982), 46-48. In that same period, 90.6 percent of the representatives and 78.8 percent of the senators who ran were reelected. Ibid., 50-51.
60. Morris Fiorina, "Congressmen and their Constituents: 1958 and 1978," in *The United States Congress*, ed. Dennis Hale (Chestnut Hill, Mass.: Boston College, 1982), 39.
61. Fiorina, *Congress: Keystone of the Washington Establishment*, 41-49.
62. Mayhew, *Congress: The Electoral Connection*, 49.
63. Kenneth A. Shepsle, *The Giant Jigsaw Puzzle: Democratic Committee Assignments in the Modern House* (Chicago: University of Chicago Press, 1978).
64. Roger Davidson, *The Role of the Congressman* (New York: Pegasus, 1968), 121. For evidence about the link between popularity and legislative leadership, see George Edwards, *Presidential Influence in Congress* (San Francisco: W. H. Freeman & Co., 1978), chap. 4; and Harvey G. Zeidenstein, "Presidential Popularity and Presidential Support in Congress: Eisenhower to Carter," *Presidential Studies Quarterly* (Spring 1980): 224-233.
65. Edwards, *Public Presidency*, 219-220.
66. Erwin Hargrove, *The Missing Link* (Washington: Urban Institute, 1975), 114.
67. James Fesler, "Politics, Policy and Bureaucracy at the Top," *Annals* (March 1983): 32.
68. Joel Aberbach and Bert Rockman, "Clashing Beliefs within the Executive Branch: The Nixon Administration Bureaucracy," *American Political Science Review* (June 1976): 456-468.
69. Richard Nixon, *RN* (New York: Grossett & Dunlap, 1978), 768.
70. Richard Cole and David Caputo, "Presidential Control of the Senior Civil Service," *American Political Science Review* (June 1979): 399-412.
71. Fesler, "Politics, Policy and Bureaucracy," 34.
72. Francis Rourke, "Grappling with the Bureaucracy," in *Politics and the Oval Office*, ed. Arnold Meltsner (San Francisco: Institute for Contemporary Studies, 1981), 137.
73. Polsby, "Against Presidential Greatness."

2. STUDYING THE PRESIDENCY

George C. Edwards III

Although many people consider the presidency the most fascinating aspect of American politics, unfortunately it is not easy to research. This chapter is not a "how to study the presidency" essay, nor is it a bibliographic review of the vast literature on the chief executive. Rather it is an attempt to alert students to the implications, both positive and negative, of adopting particular research approaches and methodologies. Armed with this awareness, students of the presidency should be able to construct research designs that better suit their needs. The last portion of the chapter tries to ease the task of research by presenting some of the more accessible and useful sources of data on the presidency.

Approaches

There are many approaches to studying the presidency, ranging from those that are concerned with the constitutional authority of the office to those dealing with the personality dynamics of a particular president. By "approaches" we mean orientations that guide researchers to ask certain questions and employ certain concepts rather than others. In this section four of the principal approaches used by political scientists who study the presidency are examined. The legal, institutional, political, and psychological perspectives are neither mutually exclusive nor comprehensive. The goal here is not to create an ideal typology of scholarship on the presidency. Instead, it is to increase our sensitivity to the implications of different approaches for what is studied, how a subject is investigated, and what types of conclusions may be reached. Similarly, our focus is on approaches per se rather than the works of individual authors or a comprehensive review of the literature.[1]

Legal

The oldest approach to studying the presidency, what we shall term the "legal" perspective, concerns the president's formal powers.

Legal researchers analyze the Constitution, laws, treaties, and legal precedents in order to understand the sources, scope, and use of the president's formal powers, including their legal limitations.[2] Because these have changed over time, the legal approach has an historical orientation. With its emphasis on the historical development of the office and the checks and balances in the Constitution, it also lends itself to discussion of the president's place in our system of government, both as it is and as scholars think it ought to be. Thus, there is often a clear prescriptive or normative element in these studies.

The range of issues involving presidential authority is great. Illustrations from the past decade include the right of the president to impound funds appropriated by Congress, the scope of the president's power to issue executive orders and proclamations, the president's authority to "freeze" federal hiring, the president's use of the pocket veto during brief congressional recesses, the constitutionality of the legislative veto, and claims of executive privilege. Foreign policy issues also have reached the courts. These include Lyndon Johnson's and Richard Nixon's conduct of the Vietnam War without explicit congressional authorization, Jimmy Carter's termination of a defense treaty with Taiwan and his settlement of the Iranian assets and hostage issues, and, more generally, the president's use of executive agreements as substitutes for treaties.

Although the legal perspective has a deservedly honored place both in political science and in a nation that prides itself on the rule of law, it has its limitations. Most of what the president does cannot be explained through legal analysis. The Constitution, treaties, laws, and court decisions describe only a small portion of the president's behavior. Most of the president's relationships with the public, the Congress, the White House staff, and the bureaucracy do not fall easily within the purview of the legal perspective. Instead, this behavior can be described only in terms of informal or extraconstitutional powers. Similarly, since the legal perspective is heavily government-centered, topics such as the press's coverage of the presidency, the public's evaluation of the president, and other relationships that involve nongovernmental actors are largely ignored.

Equally significant, the legal perspective does not lend itself to explanation. Studies of the boundaries of appropriate behavior do not explain why actions occur within those boundaries or what their consequences are. Moreover, the heavy reliance on case studies by scholars employing this approach inevitably makes the basis of their generalizations somewhat tenuous. Thus, although studies that adopt the legal perspective make important contributions to our understanding of American politics, they do not answer most of the questions that entice researchers to study the presidency. For this we must turn to alternative approaches.

Institutional

A second basic approach regards the presidency as an institution in which the president has certain roles and responsibilities and is involved in numerous structures and processes. Thus, the structure, functions, and operation of the presidency become the center of attention. These concerns are broad enough to include agencies such as the Office of Management and Budget (OMB) and units in the White House such as the legislative liaison operation. Scholars who follow this approach can move beyond formal authority and investigate such topics as the formulation, coordination, promotion, and implementation of the president's legislative program or the president's relationship with the media.[3] Like the legal perspective, the institutional approach often traces the persistence and adaptation of organizations and processes over time. This gives much of the literature a historical perspective and also lends itself to evaluations of the success of institutional arrangements.

Although at one time many institutional studies emphasized formal organizational structure and rules, such as organization charts of the White House or budgetary process procedures, in recent years the behavior of those involved in the operation of the presidency has drawn more attention. This has increased the value of institutional research. It is, after all, necessary to collect empirical data about what political actors are doing before we can discuss the significance of their behavior, much less examine analytical questions such as those pertaining to influence. By seeking to identify patterns of behavior and study interactions between the White House and Congress, OMB, or the media, institutional research not only tells us what happens but, more significantly, helps us understand why it happens. When scholars examine presidential efforts to influence the media, for example, they are looking at typical and potentially significant behavior that may explain patterns of media coverage of the White House.

The institutional approach has two principal limitations. First, description often is emphasized at the expense of explanation. We know a great deal more about how presidents have organized their White House staffs, for example, than about how these arrangements have affected the kinds of advice they received. In other words, more is known about the process than about its consequences. This in turn provides a tenuous basis for the prescriptive aspect of some institutional research. We cannot have confidence in recommendations about presidential advisory systems, for example, until we understand their effects.

The second limitation of some institutional studies is that they downplay or even ignore the significance of political skills, ideology, and personality in their emphasis on organizations and processes. Indeed, the implicit assumption that underlies the often extensive attention scholars devote to structures and processes is that they are very significant. Yet this assumption may not always be justified. It may be that the world view a president brings to the White House influences his decisions more than the way he organizes his advisers. Similarly, ideology, party, and constituency views may be more important than the White House legislative liaison operation in influencing congressional votes on the president's program.

Political Power

In the political power approach to the study of the presidency, researchers examine not institutions, but the people within them and their relationships with each other.[4] These researchers view power as a function of personal politics rather than formal authority or position. They find the president operating in a pluralistic environment in which there are numerous actors with independent power bases and perspectives different from his. Thus, the president must marshal his resources to persuade others to do as he wishes.

The president's need to exercise influence in several arenas leads those who follow the power perspective to adopt an expansive view of presidential politics that includes both governmental actors, such as the Congress, bureaucracy, and White House staff, and those outside of government, such as the public, the press, and interest groups. The dependent variables in studying presidential interactions (what authors are trying to explain) are many and may include congressional or public support for the president, presidential decisions, press coverage of the White House, or bureaucratic policy implementation. Because this approach does not assume presidential success or the smooth functioning of the presidency, the influence of bureaucratic politics and other organizational factors in the executive branch are as important to investigate as behavior in more openly adversarial institutions such as Congress.

Although the power approach examines a number of questions left unexplored in other approaches, it also slights certain topics. The emphasis on relationships does not lead naturally to the investigation of the president's accountability, the limitations of his legal powers, or the day-to-day operation of the institution of the presidency.

Some commentators are bothered by the "top-down" orientation of the power approach, that is, its view of the presidency from the perspective of the president.[5] They feel that this carries an implicit assumption that the president should be the principal decision maker in American politics. These critics argue that such a premise is too Machiavellian and that an evaluation of the goals and methods of presidents must be added to analyses of power. Others find exaggerated the depiction of the president's environment as basically confrontational, with political actors' conflicting interests creating centrifugal forces the president must try to overcome. Moreover, they claim that the heavy emphasis on power relationships may lead analysts to underestimate the importance of ideology or other influences on behavior.[6]

Psychological

Perhaps the most fascinating and popular studies of the presidency are those that approach the topic through psychological analysis. Some take the form of psychobiographies of presidents[7]; others are attempts to categorize presidents on the basis of selected personality dimensions.[8] They all are based on the premise that continuing personality needs may be displaced onto political objects and become unconscious motivations for presidential behavior. A psychological perspective forces us to ask why presidents behave as they do and leads us to look beyond external influences for answers. If individual presidents were not strongly affected by their personalities, they would neither be very important nor merit such attention.

Psychological analysis also has a broader application to the study of the presidency. Presidents and their staffs view the world through cognitive processes that affect their perceptions of why people and nations behave as they do, how power is distributed, how the economy functions, and what the appropriate roles of government, presidents, and advisers are. Cognitive processes also screen and organize an enormous volume of information about the complex and uncertain environment in which presidents function. Objective reality, intellectual abilities, and personal interests and experiences merge with psychological needs (such as those to manage inconsistency and maintain self-esteem) to influence the decisions and policies that emerge from the White House. Cognitive processes simplify decision making and lessen stress, especially on complex and controversial policies such as the war in Vietnam. Group dynamics also may influence decision making, limiting the serious appraisal of alternatives by group members. Efforts to sort out the effects of these psychological influences are still in their early stages, but there is little question that we cannot claim to understand presidential decision making until those efforts succeed.[9]

Although psychological studies can make us sensitive to important personality traits that influence presidential behavior, they are probably the most widely criticized writings on the presidency. A fundamental problem is that they often display a strong tendency toward being reductionist, that is, they concentrate on personality to the exclusion of most other behavioral influences. As a result, they convey little information about the institution of the presidency or the relationships between psychological and institutional variables. Alternative explanations for behavior rarely are considered in psychological studies.

A related drawback is that psychological studies tend to stress the pathological aspects of a presidency. Scholars, like others, are drawn quite naturally to investigate problems. Their principal interest often becomes the relationship between the personality flaws of the president and what the author feels to be some of his most unfortunate actions in office. This reinforces the reductionist tendency because it usually is not difficult to find plausible parallels between psychological and decisional deficiencies.

Data are also a problem for psychological studies. It is difficult both to discern unconscious motivations or cognitive processes and to differentiate their effects from those of external influences. Often authors must rely upon biographical information of questionable validity about the behavior and environment of presidents, stretching back to their childhoods.

Summary

The legal, institutional, political power, and psychological approaches all have advantages and disadvantages for the researcher. Each concerns a different aspect of the presidency and concentrates on certain variables at the expense of others. Thus, those thinking of doing research on the presidency should carefully determine what it is they want to investigate before selecting an approach. While the power and psychological perspectives are stronger in their concern for explanation, the legal and institutional orientations are better at providing broad perspectives on the presidency. Selecting an approach is not the only decision one must make in deciding on a research strategy, however. Appropriate methods also must be chosen.

Methods

Although political scientists have always been keenly interested in the American presidency, their progress in understanding it has been very slow. One reason for this is their reliance upon methods of analysis that are either irrelevant or inappropriate to the task of examining the basic relationships in which the presidency is involved. This section examines some of the advantages and limitations of methods used by scholars to study the presidency. Throughout, we should remember that methods are not ends in themselves but techniques for examining research questions generated by the approaches discussed earlier.

Traditional

Studies of the presidency usually describe events, behavior, and personalities. Many are written by journalists or former executive branch officials, who rely upon their personal experiences. Unfortunately, such anecdotal evidence is generally subjective, fragmentary, and impressionistic. The commentary and reflections of insiders, whether participants or participant observers, is limited by their own, often rather narrow, perspectives. For example, the memoirs of aides to Presidents Johnson and Nixon reveal very different perceptions of the president and his presidency. As Henry Kissinger writes about the Nixon White House staff,

> It is a truism that none of us really knew the inner man. More significant, each member of his entourage was acquainted with a slightly different Nixon subtly adjusted to the President's judgment of the aide or to his assessment of his interlocutor's background.[10]

Proximity to power actually may hinder rather than enhance an observer's perspective and breadth of view. The reflections of those who have served in government may be colored by the strong positions they advocated while in office or by a need to justify their decisions and behavior. Faulty memories further cloud such perceptions. Moreover, few insiders are trained to think in terms of analytical generalizations based on representative data and controls for alternative explanations. This is especially true of journalists.

Several examples illustrate the problem. One of the crucial moments in America's involvement in Vietnam came in July 1965 when President Johnson committed the United States to large-scale combat operations. In his memoirs Johnson goes to considerable lengths to show that he considered very carefully all the alternatives available at the time.[11] One of his aide's detailed account of the dialogue between Johnson and some of his advisers shows the president probing deeply for answers, challenging the premises and factual bases of options, and playing the devil's advocate.[12] Yet a presidency scholar has argued persuasively that this "debate" was really a charade, staged by the president to lend legitimacy to the decision he already had made.[13]

Even tapes of conversations in the Oval Office may be misleading. As Henry Kissinger explains regarding the Watergate tapes:

> Anyone familiar with Nixon's way of talking could have no doubt he was sitting on a time bomb. His random, elliptical, occasionally emotional manner of conversation was bound to shock, and mislead, the historian. . . . One of Nixon's favorite maneuvers . . . was to call a meeting for which everybody's view except one recalcitrant's was either known to him or prearranged by him. He would then initially seem to accept the position with which he disagreed and permit himself to be persuaded to his real views by associates, some of whom had been rehearsed in their positions, leaving the potential holdout totally isolated.[14]

Although insiders' accounts have limitations, they often contain useful insights that may guide more rigorous research. They also provide invaluable records of the perceptions of participants in the events of the presidency. As long as the researcher understands the limitations of these works and does not accept them at face value, they can be of considerable use.

Not all studies of the presidency that use traditional methods are written by insiders. Many are written by scholars, based primarily on the observations of others.[15] As one might expect, a common criticism of the traditional literature on the presidency is that it appears to be the same presentation, repeated in slightly different versions. Although such studies may be useful syntheses of the conventional wisdom or present provocative insights about the presidency, they are more likely to suffer from the limitations of their data.

Quantitative

Research on the presidency, then, often has failed to meet all the standards of contemporary political science, including the careful definition of concepts, the rigorous specification and testing of propositions, and the use of empirical theory to develop hypotheses and explain findings. We generally have not concentrated on explanation of why things happen as they do. To explain we must examine relationships, and to generalize we must look at these relationships under many circumstances. Quantitative analysis can be an extremely useful tool in these endeavors.[16]

There have been three principal constraints on the use of quantitative analysis to study the presidency. The frequent failure to pose analytical questions already has been discussed. The second constraint has been the small number of presidents. Viewing the presidency as a set of relationships, however, helps to overcome this problem. Although the number of presidents may be small, many people are involved in relationships with them, including the entire public, members of Congress, federal bureaucracy, and world leaders. Because there are so many people interacting with the president, we are no longer inhibited by the small universe of presidents.

The third constraint on the quantitative study of the presidency is lack of data. When we pose analytical questions, we naturally are led to search for information about the causes and consequences of presidential behavior. For example, we may ask what the president wants people to do. Among other things, the president wants support from the public, positive coverage from the media, votes for his programs from Congress, sound analysis from his advisers, and faithful policy implementation from the bureaucracy. Thus, we can look for data on these political actors, whose behavior is usually the dependent variable in our hypotheses, that is, what we are trying to explain.

The advantage of quantitative analysis of the presidency can be seen in the quantitative studies that already have been done. For example, one of the most important relationships of the presidency is that between the president and the public. Why are presidents as popular or unpopular as they are? We are just beginning to make some headway in the investigation of this question.[17] Related to these studies are those of the attitudes and beliefs of children toward the presidency and the president.[18] This research has come out of the subfield of political socialization. Substantial progress in understanding public support for the president would be impossible without the use of quantitative analysis and the techniques of survey research.

The other side of this relationship is the president's leadership of public opinion. We know that presidents devote considerable efforts to this task, but without quantitative analyses our understanding of the effects of presidential attempts to lead or manipulate public opinion will remain almost completely conjectural. Fortunately, a few scholars have begun to explore this area with quantitative techniques, including experimentation. Some have examined the public's response to presidential leadership,[19] while others have looked at the content of what the president presents to the public.[20] The nature of media coverage[21] and its effect on public approval and expectations of the president[22] are other topics of research.

The study of presidential-congressional relations also has been advanced through the use of quantitative analysis. We have been able to test propositions about the extent of presidential coattails, the pull of the president's party affiliation, the influence of the president's public approval and electoral support, and the significance of presidential skills.[23] Many findings have been counterintuitive, and none would have been possible without the use of quantitative analysis.

Quantitative analysis may be applied to less developed areas of presidency research, such as presidential decision making. Who influences the president? How do external constraints and pressures, such as public opinion, the state of the economy, and international events, affect presidential decisions? What are the effects of a crisis on decision-making processes? How does the public's approval of the president affect the scheduling and conduct of press conferences? What are staff attitudes, communications, and influence patterns in domestic policy making? Quantitative analyses of presidential decision making explore these and other questions.[24]

Policy implementation is another area that invites quantitative analysis. Scholars generally have given the president's role as "executor" of the law limited attention, and most of what attention it has received has been of an anecdotal or case-study nature. Identifying the variables that are critical to successful implementation, such as communications, resources, implementors' dispositions, bureaucratic structure, and follow-up mechanisms, is an important first step.[25] Measures of these variables as well as of implementation itself then can be developed. To understand presidential policy implementation, we should use quantitative methods to relate, systematically and empirically, possible causes with possible effects.

Although quantitative analysis can help to answer many fundamental questions about the presidency, it is important to remember that methods and models must be appropriate to the questions under investigation. If researchers ignore this seemingly obvious rule, their conclusions are likely to be inaccurate. Impressive, and therefore authoritative-looking, statistics only make matters worse. Time-series analyses of "presidential popularity" are a good example of the use of inappropriate methods.[26] The conclusions many of these studies reach are unreliable and often uninterpretable.

The proper use of quantitative analysis, like any other type of analysis, is predicated upon a close affinity between the methods selected and the theoretical arguments that underly the hypotheses being tested. A statement that something causes something else to happen is an assertion, not a theoretical argument. A theoretical argument requires an emphasis on explanation of why two variables are related.

Even at its best, quantitative analysis is not equally useful for studying all areas of the presidency. It is least useful when there is little change in the variables under study. If the subject of research is just one president, and the researcher is concerned, not with the president's interactions with others, but with how his personality, ideas, values, attitudes, and ideology influenced his decisions, then quantitative analysis will be of little help. These independent variables are unlikely to change much during a president's term. Similarly, important elements in the president's environment, such as the federal system or the basic capitalist structure of our economy, vary little over time. It is therefore difficult to employ quantitative analysis to gauge their influence on the presidency.

Quantitative methods also are unlikely to be useful for the legal approach to studying the presidency. There are well-established techniques for interpreting the law, and scholars with this interest will continue to apply them.[27]

Normative questions and arguments have always occupied a substantial percentage of the presidency literature, and rightly so. Can quantitative analyses aid scholars in addressing these concerns? The answer is "partially." For example, to reach conclusions about whether the presidency is too powerful or not powerful enough (the central normative concern regarding the presidency) requires a three-part analysis. The first is an estimation of just how powerful the presidency is. The second step requires an analysis of the consequences of the power of the presidency. In other words, given the power of the presidency, what difference does it make? Is the power of the presidency relevant? Or is it important only when it interacts with other crucial variables such as crisis conditions or public support? To answer these and similar questions requires that we correlate levels of power with policy consequences.

Quantitative research will be much less useful in the third part of the analysis: Do we judge the consequences of presidential power to be good or bad? Our evaluation of these consequences will be determined, of course, by our values. Nevertheless, it is important to remember that quantitative analysis can be very useful in helping us to arrive at the point where our values dominate our conclusions.

Quantitative analysis can help us to test and refine theoretical relationships. The question remains, however, whether quantitative analysis is useful for developing theories themselves, basic conceptions of the relationships between variables.

Although quantitative studies cannot replace the sparks of creativity that lie behind conceptualizations, they may produce findings upon which syntheses may be built. Conversely, they may produce findings contrary to the conventional wisdom and thus prod scholars into challenging dominant viewpoints. To the extent they make these contributions, they will be useful in theory building.

Case Studies

One of the most widely used methods for studying the presidency is the case study of an individual president, a presidential decision, or presidential involvement in a specific area of policy. The case study method offers the researcher several advantages. It is a manageable way to present a wide range of complex information about individual and collective behavior. Since scholars typically have found it difficult to generate quantitative data regarding the presidency, the narrative form often seems to be the only available choice.

Conversely, case studies are widely criticized on several grounds. First, they have been used more for descriptive than for analytical purposes, a failing not inherent in the nature of the case study. A more intractable problem is the idiosyncratic nature of case studies and the failure of authors to reapply the same analytical frameworks. This makes the accumulation of knowledge difficult because scholars often, in effect, talk past each other. In the words of one case-studies scholar:

> The unique features of every case—personalities, external events and conditions and organizational arrangements—virtually ensure that studies conducted without the use of an explicit analytical framework will not produce findings that can easily be related to existing knowledge or provide a basis for future studies.[28]

Naturally, reaching generalizations about the presidency on the basis of unrelated case studies is a hazardous task. But case studies can be very useful in increasing our understanding of the presidency. For example, analyzing several case studies can serve as the basis for identifying chronic problems in decision making or in policy implementation.[29] These in turn may serve as the basis for recommendations to improve policy making. Case studies also may be used to test hypotheses or refute theories such as propositions about group dynamics drawn from social psychology.[30]

Some authors use case studies to illustrate the importance of certain aspects of the presidency that have received little scholarly attention, such as presidential influence over interest groups.[31] On a broader scale, Richard Neustadt used several case studies to help develop his influential model of presidential power.[32] Graham Allison used a case study of the Cuban missile crisis to illustrate three models of policy making.[33]

Writing a case study that has strong analytical content is difficult. It requires considerable skill, creativity, and rigor because it is very easy to slip into a descriptive rather than an analytical gear. Those who embark on preparing case studies are wise to remind themselves of their pitfalls.

Sources of Information

Research requires facts, and the difficulty of obtaining them has been one of the greatest frustrations of presidency scholars. Although information on the presidency usually is not as neatly packaged or easily generated as, say, data on Congress, many sources are readily accessible to researchers. This section reviews the most helpful of these sources and also alerts researchers to some of their limitations.

Locating the Law

A student wishing to research questions about the president's legal authority or the substance of presidential policy making may need to locate the text of a statute, treaty, regulation, or court decision. In addition, the researcher may need to know whether these are still in force and how others have interpreted them. Fortunately, the task is not as difficult as it may first appear.[34]

The *U.S. Statutes at Large* contain public laws, private laws (legislation intended for the relief of private parties, especially claims against the national government and exceptions to immigration and naturalization requirements), reorganization plans, joint resolutions, concurrent resolutions, and proclamations issued by the president. Since 1938 (Volume 52), each volume has contained the laws enacted during a calendar year. Citations are to volume first and then page, as in 94 STAT. 2957.

After 1950 (Volume 64), treaties and other international agreements no longer were printed in the *Statutes at Large*. Instead, they were printed in a series entitled *United States Treaties and Other International Agreements*. Citations are given to the volume and then page number, as in 31 UST 405. Each volume has a country and subject index. All the treaties and other international agreements prior to 1950 have been collected in a single work: *Treaties and Other International Agreements of America, 1776-1949*.

Laws that are enacted may be modified or repealed by Congress later on. The permanent body of U.S. law is in the *United States Code*. During the last 50 years new editions of the code have been published in 1934, 1940, 1946, 1952, 1958, 1964, 1970, and 1976. Supplements to the code are issued after each session of Congress. The code consists of 50 titles organized by subject matter, such as The Congress, The President, and Armed Forces. Index references are to title, section, and year, as in 3 U.S.C. 246 (1976) and 3 U.S.C. 53 (Supp. II 1978).

The *Federal Register* includes all presidential proclamations and executive orders that have general applicability and legal effect as well as other presidential directives, including memoranda, presidential determinations, letters, directives, reorganization plans, designations, and lists of messages transmitting budget rescissions and deferrals. The *Federal Register* is published each weekday, except for official holidays. A typical citation would be 48 Fed. Reg. 2311 (1983), designating the volume, page, and year, respectively. An index of the previous year is published monthly. The earliest forms of executive orders were not numbered. Clifford Lord compiled these in the *List and Index of Executive Orders: Unnumbered Series*. The first volume is a chronological listing of titles (up to January 11, 1941), and the second volume is a subject index.

The subject matter of the *Federal Register* is codified into 50 titles that generally parallel those of the *United States Code*. Each of the 50 titles is published annually in pamphlet form, containing all rules, regulations, and orders in force at the time, and is entitled the *Code of Federal Regulations* (CFR). Citations are by title and section, as in 19 CFR 123 (1980). The *CFR* is indexed annually.

The full decisions of the Supreme Court are published in bound volumes of the *United States Reports*. Citations are in the form of Baker v. Carr, 369 U.S. 186 (1962), which indicates that the decision may be found in Volume 369, beginning on page 186. The first 90 volumes of the *Reports* were named after court reporters Dallas, Cranch, Wheaton, Peters, Howard, Black, and Wallace. Thus, references take the form of McCulloch v. Maryland, 4 Wheaton 316 (1819). An invaluable aid is the "citator" or citation book, which tells whether a decision is still valid and authoritative. A decision by a lower court may be affirmed, reversed, or modified.

The *Index to Legal Periodicals* and, since 1980, the *Current Law Index* cite articles from several hundred legal journals and newspapers. The coverage of the *Current Law Index* is more comprehensive, and its indexing is more refined and specific than the *Index to Legal Periodicals.*

General Sources

There are two general collections of presidential documents and several general indexes that students of the presidency may find helpful for a wide variety of research projects.[35] The *Weekly Compilation of Presidential Documents (Weekly Comp.)* is a selective compilation of press releases. It generally contains presidential proclamations, executive orders, addresses, remarks, letters, messages and telegrams, memorandums to federal agencies, communications to Congress, bill-signing statements, presidential press conferences, communiqués with foreign heads of state, appointments, and nominations. The *Weekly Comp.* began August 2, 1965, and is published every Monday for the week ending the previous Saturday. Each issue contains a cumulative index to issues in the current quarter, and separate indexes are published semiannually and annually.

Unfortunately, the *Weekly Comp.* does not use a standard, controlled vocabulary. Thus, it is necesary to examine all possible synonyms for the topic of research. Another difficulty is that all index terms are grouped under broad generic headings such as Addresses and Remarks; Communications to Congress; and Letters, Messages, Telegrams, and Statements by the President. If in doubt concerning the index term under which a research topic falls, consult the listings under each type of heading.

The National Archives has published official compilations of the presidential papers of Presidents Hoover, Truman, Eisenhower, Kennedy, Johnson, Nixon, Ford, and Carter. Each annual volume contains an index but not a cumulative index. KTO Press, however, has published single-volume indexes for each administration from Truman through Nixon. Private presses have published the papers of Presidents Washington, Adams, Jefferson, Madison, Wilson, and Eisenhower.

Another useful index to valuable primary documents is *The Federal Index,* published monthly. It indexes a diversity of publicly and privately published sources, including the *Congressional Record, Federal Register, Weekly Comp., Washington Post,* the *Code of Federal Regulations,* the *U.S. Code,* House and Senate bills, and other documents of the federal government.

The Monthly Catalog of United States Government Publications is the basic bibliography of U.S. government publications. Each issue lists government publications for that month, organized according to the agency or congressional committee that issued them. There is an index at the end of each issue, and indexes are cumulated semiannually, annually, and every five years. Before 1976 the *Monthly Catalog* was indexed only by subject; since then it has been indexed by author, title, subject, series, key words, and other criteria.

The American Statistics Index is a comprehensive source of information regarding all executive branch publications. It employs a standard vocabulary and provides lengthy annotations of each monograph. This valuable source lessens considerably the burden of conducting a thorough review of a subject.

Congressional Quarterly published an annual review of the Nixon, Ford, and Carter presidencies and an assessment of the beginning of Reagan's presidency entitled *President Reagan's First Year.* These books include transcripts of press conferences and major speeches, and coverage of nominations, congressional-executive relations, and general policy developments. The *Congressional Quarterly Almanac* covers presidents' legislative initiatives each year. The *National Journal* provides regular coverage of the White House and the executive branch; it publishes the White House phone list semiannually.

Congress

The Congressional Information Service's *Index to Congressional Publications and Public Laws* is the best source for locating congressional documents, which often are excellent sources of information about the presidency.[36] The *Index* has two parts. One is an annual volume that includes a subject and name index, a title index, and indexes by bill, document, and report numbers for all significant congressional documents published that year. Cumulative indexes are published every four or five years. The second annual volume contains detailed abstracts that describe the contents of the publications of all congressional committees, including quotations from the testimony of witnesses at hearings, statements from committee reports, and lists of those testifying at hearings. The abstracts are an efficient means of obtaining a sense of the substance of congressional hearings and the principal arguments in committee reports. Also useful are the detailed legislative histories that list all of the documents relevant to each bill enacted into law during the year. These are found at the end of each abstract volume.

The Congressional Information Service's *U.S. Serial Set Index, 1789-1969* is the only complete index to the materials published in the Serial Set of congressional documents. It is composed of 12 chronological units of several volumes each. Each unit includes one volume with a finding list arranged by report and document numbers and several additional volumes arranged by subject.

The *Congressional Quarterly Weekly Report* is an indispensable aid to following the daily activities of Congress, the president's interactions with it, and the substance of public policy. Both in the *Weekly Report* and its yearly *Almanac,* Congressional Quarterly provides an extraordinary amount of quantitative data on congressional roll-call voting and election results. The *Weekly Report* also carries the president's veto messages and transcripts of his press conferences. It has a cumulative, quarterly index.

The *Almanac* provides an extensive review of the year organized by policy area in addition to the data mentioned above. Another authoritative reference work on Congress that is published by Congressional Quarterly is *Congress and the Nation.* Volume 1 covers major legislation between 1945 and 1964; Volumes 2-5 cover four-year periods coterminous with presidential terms. The *Guide to Congress* provides useful background on the president and Congress, and the *Guide to U.S. Elections* and its biennial paperback supplements are the best single source of presidential election statistics. They are even broken down to the congressional district level.

Finally, the Inter-University Consortium for Political Research (ICPSR) at the University of Michigan provides data in the form of machine readable tapes to its member universities. These include congressional roll-call voting records since 1789 and, for more recent years, indexes of voting records calculated by Congressional Quarterly and various interest groups.

Public Opinion

There is an enormous amount of data on public evaluations of the president, voting behavior, and other relevant public attitudes waiting to be analyzed.

The ICPSR makes its extensive biennial election studies, covering the years 1948 to 1982, available to members. These studies contain questions on a variety of matters, including evaluations of the president, in addition to those of purely electoral concern. The ICPSR also compiles opinion surveys of elites, bureaucrats, children (useful for socialization studies), and the general public.

Since 1965 the results of Gallup polls have been published monthly in *The Gallup Report* (formerly the *Gallup Political Index* and the *Gallup Opinion Index*). Gallup polls since 1935 have been compiled in a set of volumes entitled *The Gallup Poll*. Gallup polls, as well as those from many other polling organizations, are available from the Roper Center, which is affiliated with the University of Connecticut, Williams College, and Yale University.

A number of surveys that are relevant to studying the presidency are kept at the Louis Harris Data Center at the University of North Carolina at Chapel Hill, and many libraries now receive press releases containing new Harris poll results. Similarly, the National Opinion Research Center (NORC), affiliated with the University of Chicago, contains relevant surveys of public opinon taken over the past four decades.

The Press

Although the press plays a vital role in the operation of the presidency, it often has been overlooked by researchers. As noted earlier, many of the materials that the White House formally prepares for the press are available in the *Weekly Comp.*, and transcripts of press conferences are available from several sources.

News coverage of the president is a much discussed and rarely studied phenomenon, particularly in nonelection periods. The Television Archive at Vanderbilt University contains videotapes of television news programs, and researchers can use the elaborate indexes it publishes monthly to order tapes of specific time periods or subjects. The ICPSR's holdings include a data collection of media content. In addition, most libraries contain indexes of daily newspapers, including the *New York Times, Washington Post, Chicago Tribune, Los Angeles Times,* and *Wall Street Journal* and the *Reader's Guide to Periodical Literature,* which indexes magazine coverage. These can be used to help the student follow media coverage of the president as well as the president's activities. Magazines such as the *Columbia Journalism Review* and the *Washington Journalism Review* regularly carry commentary on press coverage of Washington.

Presidential Libraries

A resource of enormous potential importance is the presidential libraries, although they have not been widely used by students of the presidency.[37] A presidential library contains millions of pages of memos, reports, and letters from a president's White House years; a collection of relevant books, articles, and audiovisual materials; and oral histories. Libraries exist for all past presidents since Herbert Hoover with the exceptions of Richard Nixon and Jimmy Carter. They are widely dispersed in West Branch, Iowa (Hoover); Hyde Park, New York (Roosevelt); Independence, Missouri (Truman); Abilene, Kansas (Eisenhower); Dorchester, Massachusetts (Kennedy); Austin, Texas (Johnson); and Ann Arbor, Michigan (Ford). The Nixon and Carter libraries will be in San Clemente, California, and Atlanta, Georgia, respectively.

Although most people use the libraries as ends in themselves, they can equip researchers with the background information needed to interview persons involved in the subject being studied. Specifically, library material can help researchers grasp the general context of events, trace the development of a policy, or understand the operation of the White House. Each library provides extensive finding guides and well-trained archivists to aid researchers.

Unfortunately, the widespread location and complex filing system of presidential libraries limit their usefulness for students of the presidency. White House files are kept for ease in operating the presidency and not for the future convenience of political scientists. If one wants to discover how cognitive processes affected decision making in the war in Vietnam, for example, one cannot simply go to a set of files with this specific heading. The task will be an extremely lengthy one, requiring the reading of material in thousands of files. In addition, not all top presidential aides leave extensive files, and there are not always records of oral advice or small meetings. Many records may be classified.

The researcher also must be sensitive to possible distortions in records. Some advisers write self-serving memos to make themselves look good in the light of history and exaggerate their own role in the policy-making process. Moreover, some memos from the president or documents prepared at his request were never officially issued or meant to be taken seriously but rather were a means of letting off steam.

The oral histories in the libraries vary greatly in length and quality. Although some provide real insight into a president and his presidency, others are rambling accounts of an anecdotal nature. Nevertheless, they may prove very useful in a project, and since many important officials have died, there is no other way to "interview" them. Many oral histories, unlike other materials in the presidential libraries, are available through interlibrary loan.

Interviews

Much of what occurs in the operation of the presidency is not open to public observation. The executive branch, especially at its peak, is not as accessible as Congress. Moreover, many potentially important topics of research, such as those involving interpersonal interactions, may not be well represented by a trail of paper. Thus, researchers seeking to understand the presidency may find it necessary to interview the participants themselves. The researcher should also keep in mind that it is not only the most promiment members of an administration that have worthwhile things to say. Lower-level officials may be knowledgeable and have more time for interviews. With fewer political axes to grind, they may be fertile sources of accurate information.

Despite their obvious usefulness, interviews are a mixed blessing. Some participants may refuse to be interviewed, especially while they are in office, because they fear political repercussions or simply are too busy. Those who consent to interviews may forget or repress information, or they may be unable to communicate in terms of the concepts the investigator is employing. There is also the ever-present problem of lack of candor and embellishment on behalf of themselves or their administration.

Successful interviews require considerable skill and hard work.[38] Both careful preparation and personal interaction skills are essential. A sophisticated understanding of the context in which interviewees operate and of the issues with which they deal are necessary to elicit useful comments. So is a sensitivity to the interviewees' needs, because it is necessary to win their confidence before they will speak candidly.

Conclusion

Few topics in American politics are more interesting or more important to understand than the presidency. Studying the presidency is not a simple task, however. There are many reasons for this, including the relative sparsity of previous research that applies the approaches and methods of modern political science and the small number of models to follow. But the obstacles to studying the presidency also present researchers with an opportunity. Few questions about the presidency are settled; there is plenty of room for committed and creative researchers to make significant contributions to our understanding. The prospects for success will be enhanced if researchers realize the implications of the approaches and methods they employ and choose those that are best suited to shed light on the questions they wish to investigate.

NOTES

* Portions of this essay are reprinted by permission of The University of Tennessee Press. From Edwards, George, C., III and Wayne, Stephen J.: *Studying the Presidency*. Copyright © 1983 by The University of Tennessee Press.

1. For a more extensive discussion of approaches to studying the presidency, see Stephen J. Wayne, "Approaches," in *Studying the Presidency*, ed. George C. Edwards III and Stephen J. Wayne (Knoxville, Tenn.: University of Tennessee Press, 1983), 17-49.
2. The classic work from the legal perspective is Edward S. Corwin, *The President: Office and Powers,* 4th rev. ed. (New York: New York University Press, 1957). An excellent recent example is Louis Fisher, *Presidential Spending Power* (Princeton, N.J.: Princeton University Press, 1975).
3. See, for example, Stephen J. Wayne, *The Legislative Presidency* (New York: Harper & Row, 1978); and Michael Baruch Grossman and Martha Joynt Kumar, *Portraying the President: The White House and the News Media* (Baltimore: John Hopkins University Press, 1981).
4. The political power approach is best represented in Richard E. Neustadt, *Presidential Power: The Politics of Leadership from FDR to Carter* (New York: John Wiley & Sons, 1980).
5. Bruce Miroff, "Beyond Washington," *Society* 17 (July/August 1980): 66-72.
6. Peter W. Sperlich, "Bargaining and Overload: An Essay on Presidential Power," in *The Presidency,* ed. Aaron Wildavsky (Boston: Little, Brown & Co., 1969), 168-192.
7. See, for example, Alexander L. George and Juliette L. George, *Woodrow Wilson and Colonel House: A Personality Study* (New York: Dover Publications, 1964).
8. The most notable example is James David Barber, *The Presidential Character: Predicting Performance in the White House,* 2d ed. (Englewood Cliffs, N.J.: Prentice-Hall, 1977).
9. Some relevant studies include, Alexander L. George, *Presidential Decisionmaking in Foreign Policy: The Effective Use of Information and Advice* (Boulder, Colo.: Westview Press, 1980); Bruce Buchanan, *The Presidential Experience: What the Office Does to the Man* (Englewood Cliffs, N.J.: Prentice-Hall, 1978); John D. Steinbruner, *The Cybernetic Theory of Decision* (Princeton, N.J.: Princeton University Press, 1974); and Irving L. Janis, *Groupthink,* 2d ed. (Boston: Houghton Mifflin Co., 1982).
10. Henry Kissinger, *Years of Upheaval* (Boston: Little, Brown & Co., 1982), 1182.

11. Lyndon Baines Johnson, *The Vantage Point: Perspectives of the Presidency, 1963-1969* (New York: Popular Library, 1971), 144-153.
12. Jack Valenti, *A Very Human President* (New York: W. W. Norton & Co., 1975), 317-319.
13. Larry Berman, *Planning a Tragedy: The Americanization of the War in Vietnam* (New York: W. W. Norton & Co., 1982), 105-121.
14. Kissinger, *Years of Upheaval,* 111-112.
15. See, for example, Richard Tanner Johnson, *Managing the White House* (New York: Harper & Row, 1974).
16. For a more extensive discussion of quantitative analysis of the presidency, see George C. Edwards III, "Quantitative Analysis," in *Studying the Presidency,* ed. Edwards and Wayne, 99-124.
17. Samuel Kernell, "Explaining Presidential Popularity," *American Political Science Review* 72 (June 1978): 506-522; Stephen J. Wayne, "Great Expectations: Contemporary Views of the President," in *Rethinking the Presidency,* ed. Thomas Cronin (Boston: Little, Brown & Co., 1982); and George C. Edwards III, *The Public Presidency* (New York: St. Martin's Press, 1983), chap. 6.
18. Fred I. Greenstein, "The Benevolent Leader Revisited: Children's Images of Political Leaders in Three Democracies," *American Political Science Review* 69 (December 1975): 1371-1398; and Jack Dennis and Carol Webster, "Children's Images of the President and of Government in 1962 and 1974," *American Politics Quarterly* 3 (October 1975): 386-405.
19. Lee Sigelman, "Gauging the Public Response to Presidential Leadership," *Presidential Studies Quarterly* 10 (Summer 1980): 427-433; Carey Rosen, "A Test of Presidential Leadership of Public Opinion: The Split-Ballot Technique," *Polity* 6 (Winter 1973): 282-290; and Lee Sigelman and Carol K. Sigelman, "Presidential Leadership of Public Opinion: From 'Benevolent Leader' to Kiss of Death?" *Experimental Study of Politics* 7, no. 3 (1981): 1-22.
20. Lawrence C. Miller and Lee Sigelman, "Is the Audience the Message? A Note on LBJ's Vietnam Statements," *Public Opinion Quarterly* 42 (Spring 1978): 71-80; John H. Kessel, "The Parameters of Presidential Politics," *Social Science Quarterly* 55 (June 1974): 8-24, and "The Seasons of Presidential Politics," *Social Science Quarterly* 58 (December 1977): 418-435.
21. Grossman and Kumar, *Portraying the President,* chap. 10.
22. David L. Paletz and Richard I. Vinegar, "Presidents on Television: The Effects of Instant Analysis," *Public Opinion Quarterly* 41 (Winter 1977-78): 488-497; Dwight F. Davis, Lynda L. Kaid, and Donald L. Singleton, "Information Effects of Political Commentary," *Experimental Study of Politics* 6 (June 1978): 45-68, and "Instant Analysis of Televised Political Addresses: The Speaker Versus the Commentary," in *Communication Yearbook I,* ed. Brent D. Ruben (New Brunswick, N.J.: Transaction Books, 1977), 453-464; and Thomas A. Kazee, "Television Exposure and Attitude Change: The Impact of Political Interest," *Public Opinion Quarterly* 45 (Winter 1981): 507-518.
23. George C. Edwards III, *Presidential Influence in Congress* (San Francisco: W. H. Freeman & Co., 1980) chaps. 3-7; and idem, *The Public Presidency,* 83-93.
24. Richard L. Cole and Stephen J. Wayne, "Predicting Presidential Decisions on Enrolled Bills: A Computer Simulation," *Simulation and Games* 11 (September 1980): 313-325; Lee Sigelman and Dixie Mercer McNeil, "White House Decision-Making Under Stress: A Case Analysis," *American Journal of Political*

Science 24 (November 1980): 652-673; Jarol B. Manheim and William W. Lammers, "The News Conference and Presidential Leadership of Public Opinion: Does the Tail Wag the Dog?" *Presidential Studies Quarterly* 11 (Spring 1981): 177-188; and John H. Kessel, *The Domestic Presidency: Decision-Making in the White House* (North Scituate, Mass.: Duxbury Press, 1975).

25. Some very interesting survey work has been done on bureaucratic dispositions. See Joel D. Aberbach and Bert A. Rockman, "Clashing Beliefs Within the Executive Branch: The Nixon Administration Bureaucracy," *American Political Science Review* 70 (June 1976): 456-468; and Richard L. Cole and David A. Caputo, "Presidential Control of the Senior Civil Service: Assessing the Strategies of the Nixon Years," *American Political Science Review* 73 (June 1979): 399-413.

26. For a discussion of these studies, see Edwards, *The Public Presidency,* 257-260.

27. For more on legal analysis of the presidency, see Louis Fisher, "Making Use of Legal Sources," in *Studying the Presidency,* ed. Edwards and Wayne, 182-198.

28. Norman C. Thomas, "Case Studies," in *Studying the Presidency,* ed. Edwards and Wayne, 50-78.

29. Alexander L. George, "The Case for Multiple Advocacy in Making Foreign Policy," *American Political Science Review* 66 (September 1972): 765-781; and George C. Edwards III, *Implementing Public Policy* (Washington, D.C.: CQ Press, 1980).

30. Janis, *Groupthink.*

31. Bruce Miroff, "Presidential Leverage Over Social Movements: The Johnson White House and Civil Rights," *Journal of Politics* 43 (February 1981): 2-23.

32. Neustadt, *Presidential Power.*

33. Graham T. Allison, *Essence of Decision: Explaining the Cuban Missile Crisis* (Boston: Little, Brown & Co., 1971).

34. For more on locating the law, see Fisher, "Making Use of Legal Sources," in *Studying the Presidency,* ed. Edwards and Wayne, 188-198.

35. For more on general sources of data on the presidency, see Jennifer DeToro, "A Guide to Information Sources," in *Studying the Presidency,* ed. Edwards and Wayne, 127-155.

36. For more on congressional sources of data, see G. Calvin Mackenzie, "Research in Executive-Legislative Relations," in *Studying the Presidency,* ed. Edwards and Wayne, 156-181.

37. For discussions of researching in presidential libraries, see Martha Joynt Kumar, "Presidential Libraries: Gold Mine, Booby Trap, or Both?" and Larry Berman, "Presidential Libraries: How *Not* to be a Stranger in a Strange Land," in *Studying the Presidency,* ed. Edwards and Wayne, 199-256.

38. For discussions of the proper techniques for interviewing presidential aides, see Dom Bonafede, "Interviewing Presidential Aides: A Journalist's Perspective" and Joseph A. Pika, "Interviewing Presidential Aides: A Political Scientist's Perspective," in *Studying the Presidency,* ed. Edwards and Wayne, 257-302.

Part II

ELEMENTS OF PRESIDENTIAL POWER

A longstanding issue in the life sciences is the "nature-nurture" or heredity vs. environment controversy. Do people turn out as they do because of their genetic makeup at birth or because of external forces that influence their lives afterward? Theologians argue a third position, free will: we are masters not prisoners of our fate. In truth, of course, the answer is some blend of "all of the above": our lives are determined by what we bring into the world, what happens to us later, and what choices we make. So it is with the power of the presidency, which is shaped first by the Constitution— the presidency's "genetic code"; second, by the political environment in which the presidency functions; and third, by a "free will" element: the political skills and personality that each president brings to the office.

To many students of government and politics, the most impressive thing about the American political system has been the capacity of the Constitution to endure by adapting to changing conditions. In Chapter 3, Jeffrey Tulis traces the development of "The Two Constitutional Presidencies"—the enduring one that the framers defined in 1787 and whose formal provisions remain substantially unaltered, and the adapted one that Woodrow Wilson prescribed and that most twentieth-century presidents have practiced.

Tulis is less than sanguine about the harmony of the blend between the two constitutions. Both the framers and Wilson, he shows, defined the presidency in terms of "energy"—a "vigorous executive," in Alexander Hamilton's phrase.[1] But in the framers' view, presidential energy was to derive from the Constitution itself, particularly its provisions for a unitary executive with ample enumerated powers and the prospect for reelection. Popular leadership by the president, which to the framers was a synonym for demagoguery, was to be avoided at all costs. In the second constitutional presidency, however, popular leadership is regarded as the very essence of energy in the presidency: "Woodrow Wilson prescribes" what "*The Federalist* and the Constitution proscribe." In Tulis's view, "Many of the dilemmas and frustrations of the modern presidency may be traced to the president's ambiguous constitutional station, a vantage place composed of elements in conflict with each other."

Because the constitutional, environmental, and skill elements of presidential power are parts of a unified institution, it is not surprising that Tulis's discussion of the presidency and the Constitution leads him to consider the relationship between the presidency and the people. Stephen Skowronek's concern in "Presidential Leadership in Political Time" is with the political environment more broadly defined: not just the people, but also legislators, interest groups, and other political "elites."

Skowronek argues in Chapter 4 that "a broad view of American development reveals patterned sequences of political change with corresponding patterns of presidential performance." A sequence begins when voters hand the old ruling coalition a stunning electoral defeat. The challenge for the newly elected president is to "undermine the institutional support for existing interests, restructure institutional relationships between state and society, and secure the dominant position of a new political coalition"—in short, to build a "regime" that will survive his administration. Some presidents who came to office after such an election failed to meet this challenge, and even for those who succeeded, their accomplishment contained the ingredients of its own eventual demise. Each "success created a new establishment," concludes Skowronek, which eventually became old and politically vulnerable.

In what Skowronek calls "political time," the Jacksonian regime of the nineteenth century corresponds to the New Deal regime of the twentieth. The election of 1828 comes at a "parallel juncture" with the election of 1932, Andrew Jackson with Franklin D. Roosevelt, James K. Polk with John F. Kennedy, and Franklin Pierce with Jimmy Carter. President and system—accent on the system—are the basic ingredients of Skowronek's understanding of the American presidency.

President and system—accent on the president—is the concern of those who write about the third element of presidential power: the political skills and personalities of individual presidents. Most students of presidential skill have dwelled on technique: bargaining, persuasion, rhetoric, management, and the like. In Chapter 5, Paul J. Quirk looks instead at "Presidential Competence" to exercise such skills, asking "how much must a president know?" Quirk rejects the widely advocated "self-reliant" model of presidential competence as impossibly demanding and the "minimalist" or "chairman of the board" model as not demanding enough. His own model calls for "strategic competence": presidents need not know everything if they know how to find what they need to know. Specifically, Quirk argues, presidents must pay enough attention to the substantive debates about important national issues so that they can evaluate policy recommendations and must keep the policy process sufficiently fluid that they hear a wide range of such recommendations. They also must have—or obtain the services of others who have—Washington experience, the better to promote their policy decisions once they make them.

Quirk's final point in his essay—that voters and commentators should study presidential candidates for signs of strategic competence—is not unlike James David Barber's first point in *The Presidential Character,* which urges them to examine candidates for evidence of psychological health. In Barber's view, presidential success depends above all on the president's having an "active-positive" personality.[2] But according to Chapter 6, "The Psychological Presidency," history belies his claim: only a modest share of the "great" presidents have been active-positives. This essay, which applauds Barber for drawing attention to the psychological aspects of the presidency, concludes by assessing his theory of presidential elections, the subject of Part III.

NOTES

1. Alexander Hamilton, James Madison, and John Jay, *The Federalist Papers,* with an introduction by Clinton Rossiter (New York: New American Library, 1961), no. 70, 423.
2. James David Barber, *The Presidential Character: Predicting Performance in the White House,* 2d ed. (Englewood Cliffs, N.J.: Prentice Hall, 1977).

3. THE TWO CONSTITUTIONAL PRESIDENCIES

Jeffrey Tulis

The modern presidency is buffeted by two "constitutions." Presidential action continues to be constrained and presidential behavior shaped by the institutions created by the original Constitution. The core structures established in 1789 and debated during the founding era remain essentially unchanged. For the most part, later amendments to the Constitution have left intact the basic features of the executive, legislative, and judicial branches of government. Great questions, such as the merits of unity or plurality in the executive, have not been seriously reopened. Because most of the structure persists, it seems plausible that the theory upon which the presidency was constructed remains relevant to its current functioning.[1]

Presidential and public understanding of the character of the constitutional system and of the president's place in it have changed, however. This new understanding is the "second constitution" under whose auspices presidents attempt to govern. Central to this second constitution is a view of statecraft that is in tension with the original Constitution—indeed is opposed to the founders' understanding of the presidency's place in the political system. The second constitution, which puts a premium on active and continuous presidential leadership of popular opinion, is buttressed by several institutional, although extra-Constitutional, developments. These include the proliferation of presidential primaries as a mode of selection and the emergence of the mass media as a pervasive force.[2]

Many of the dilemmas and frustrations of the modern presidency may be traced to the president's ambiguous constitutional station, a vantage place composed of conflicting elements. The purpose of this chapter is to lay bare the theoretical core of each of the two constitutions in order to highlight those elements that are in tension between them.

To uncover the principles that underly the original Constitution, this chapter relies heavily upon *The Federalist,* a set of papers justifying the Constitution that was written by three of its most articulate proponents, Alexander Hamilton, James Madison, and John

Jay. The purpose of this journey back to the founders is not to point to their authority nor to lament change. Neither is it meant to imply that all the supporters of the Constitution agreed with each of their arguments. *The Federalist* does represent, however, the most coherent articulation of the implications of, and interconnections among, the principles and practices that were generally agreed upon when the Constitution was ratified.[3]

The political thought of Woodrow Wilson is explored to outline the principles of the second constitution. Wilson self-consciously attacked *The Federalist* in his writings; as president he tried to act according to the dictates of his reinterpretation of the American political system. Presidents have continued to follow his example, and presidential scholars tend to repeat his arguments. Of course, most presidents have not thought through the issues Wilson discussed—they are too busy for that. But if pushed and questioned, modern presidents probably would (and occasionally do) justify their behavior with arguments that echo Wilson's. Just as *The Federalist* represents the deepest and most coherent articulation of generally held nineteenth-century understandings of the presidency, Wilson offers the most comprehensive theory in support of contemporary impulses and practices.

The Founding Perspective

Perhaps the most striking feature of the founding perspective, particularly in comparison with contemporary political analyses, is its synoptic character. The founders' task was to create a whole government, one in which the executive would play an important part, but only a part. By contrast, contemporary scholars of American politics often study institutions individually and thus tend to be partisans of "their institution" in its contests with other actors in American politics.[4] Presidency scholars often restrict their inquiries to the strategic concerns of presidents as they quest for power. Recovering the founding perspective gives one a way to think about the systemic legitimacy and utility of presidential power as well. To uncover such a synoptic vision, one must range widely in search of the principles that guided or justified the founders' view of the executive. Some of these principles are discussed most thoroughly in *The Federalist* in the context of other institutions, such as Congress or the judiciary.

The founders' general and far-reaching institutional analysis was preceded by a more fundamental decision of enormous import. Federalists and Anti-Federalists alike sought a government devoted to limited ends. In contrast to polities that attempt to shape the souls of its citizenry and foster certain excellences or moral qualities by penetrating deeply into the "private" sphere, the founders wanted their government to be limited to establishing and securing a private sphere. Politics would extend only to the tasks of protecting individual rights and fostering liberty for the exercise of those rights.

Proponents and critics of the Constitution agreed about the proper ends of government, but they disagreed over the best institutional means to secure them.[5] Some critics of the Constitution worried that its institutions actually would undermine or subvert its limited "liberal" ends. While these kinds of arguments were settled *politically* by the federalist victory, *The Federalist* concedes that they were not resolved *fundamentally*, since they continued as problems built into the structure of American politics.

"[Is] a vigorous executive ... inconsistent with the genius of republican government[?]" The founders hoped that executive energy and republican freedom were compatible, but they were not certain.[6]

Demagoguery

The founders worried especially about the danger a powerful executive might pose to the system if his power derived from a role as popular leader. Nearly all references to popular leadership in their writings are pejorative. In fact, for them, popular leadership was a synonym for demagoguery, which, combined with the possibility of majority tyranny, was regarded as the peculiar vice to which democracies were susceptible. While much historical evidence supported this insight, the founders were made more acutely aware of the problem by the presence in their own midst of popular leaders such as Daniel Shay, who led an insurrection in Massachusetts. The founders' preoccupation with demagoguery may appear to us as quaint, unscientific, or both. Yet it may be that we do not fear demagoguery today because the founders were successful in institutionally proscribing it.

The original Greek meaning of demagogue was simply "leader of the people." As James Ceaser points out, the term has been more characteristically applied to a certain quality of leadership—that which attempts to sway popular passions.[7] Since most speech contains a mix of "rational" and "passionate" appeals, it is difficult to define demagoguery with precision. But as Ceaser argues, one should not ignore a phenomenon merely because it is difficult to define; the term has enough intuitive clarity that few would consider, say, President Dwight Eisenhower a demagogue, while most would not hesitate to so label

Sen. Joseph McCarthy. The defining characteristic of demagoguery seems to be an excess of passionate appeals.

Ceaser categorizes demagogues according to the means that they employ, dividing them into "soft" and "hard" types. The soft demagogue flatters his constituents "by claiming that they know what is best, and makes a point of claiming his closeness [to them] by manner or gesture." [8] The hard demagogue attempts to create or encourage divisions among the people in order to build and maintain a constituency. Typically, this sort of approach employs extremist rhetoric that appeals to fear. James Madison worried about the possibility of class appeals that would pit the poor against the wealthy. But the hard demagogue might appeal to a very different passion. "Excessive encouragement of morality and hope" might be employed to create a division between those who claim to be compassionate, moral, or progressive, and those thought insensitive, selfish, or backward. Hard demagogues are not restricted to the "right" or to the "left." [9]

Demagogues also can be classified by their object. Here the issue becomes more complicated. Demagoguery might be good if it were a means to a good end, such as preservation of a decent nation or successful prosecution of a just war. The difficulty is to ensure by institutional means that demagoguery would be employed only for good ends and not simply to satisfy the overweening ambition of an immoral leader or potential tyrant. How are political structures created that permit demagoguery when appeals to passion are needed, but proscribe it for normal politics?

The founders did not have a straightforward answer to this problem, perhaps because there was no unproblematic institutional solution. Yet they did address it indirectly in two ways: they attempted both to narrow the range of acceptable demagogic appeals through the founding itself and to mitigate the effects of such appeals in the day-to-day conduct of governance through the particular institutions they created. Certainly they did not choose to make provision for the institutional encouragement of demagoguery, refusing to adopt, for example, the Roman procedure of planned dictatorship for emergencies.[10] Behind their indirect approach may have been the thought that excessive ambition needs no institutional support and the faith that in extraordinary circumstances popular rhetoric, even forceful demagoguery, would gain legitimacy through the pressure of necessity.

Many references in *The Federalist* and in the ratification debates over the Constitution warn of demagogues of the hard variety who through divisive appeals would aim at tyranny. *The Federalist* literally begins and ends with that issue. In the final paper Hamilton offers "a lesson of moderation to all sincere lovers of the Union [that] ought to put them on their guard against hazarding anarchy, civil war, a perpetual alienation of the states from each other, and perhaps the military despotism of a victorious demagogue." [11] The founders' concern with "hard" demagoguery was not merely a rhetorical device designed to facilitate passage of the Constitution. It also reflected the thought that, by the deliberate act of founding, the nation could "settle" the large issue of whether the one, few, or many ruled in favor of the many acting "through" a constitution, and could reconfirm the limited purposes of government. To the extent that these divisive issues were settled and were replaced by a politics of "administration," as Hamilton referred to it, demagogues would be deprived of part of their once powerful arsenal of rhetorical weapons. [12]

If the overriding concern about demagoguery in the extraordinary period before the ratification of the Constitution was to prevent social disruption, division, and possibly tyranny, the concerns expressed through the Constitution for normal times were broader: to create institutions that would be most likely to generate and execute "good" policy or be most likely to resist "bad" policy. Underlying the institutional structures and powers created by the Constitution are three principles designed to address this broad concern: representation, independence of the executive, and separation of powers.

Representation

As the founders realized, the problem with any simple distinction between good and bad law is that it is difficult to provide clear criteria to distinguish the two in any particular instance. It will not do to suggest that in a democracy good legislation reflects the majority will. A majority may tyrannize a minority, violating its rights; even a nontyrannical majority may be a foolish one, preferring policies that do not further its interests. These considerations lay behind the founders' distrust of "direct" or "pure" democracy. [13] Yet an alternative definition—that legislation is good if it objectively furthers the limited ends of the polity—is also problematic. It is perhaps impossible to assess the "interests" of a nation without giving some attention to what the citizenry considers its interests to be. This consideration underlay the founders' animus toward monarchy and aristocracy. [14] They wrestled with the problem of how to give due weight to popular opinion but not rely upon it in the day-to-day conduct of government. Their understanding of republicanism as representative government contains this dilemma and its attempted resolution.

Practically, the founders attempted to accommodate the requisites of good government by four devices. First, they established popular election as the fundamental basis of the Constitution and of the government's legitimacy. They modified that requirement by allowing "indirect" selection for some institutions (e.g., the Senate, Court, presidency); that is, selection by others who were themselves chosen by the people. With respect to the president, the founders wanted to elicit the "sense of the people," but they feared an inability to do so if the people acted in a "collective capacity." They worried that the dynamics of mass politics would at best produce poorly qualified presidents and at worst open the door to demagoguery and regime instability. At the same time, the founders wanted to give popular opinion a greater role in presidential selection than it would have if Congress chose the executive. The institutional solution to these concerns was the Electoral College, originally designed as a semi-autonomous locus of decision for presidential selection, and chosen by state legislatures at each election.[15]

Second, the founders established differing lengths of tenure for officeholders in the major national institutions, which corresponded to the institutions' varying "proximity" to the people. House members were to face reelection every two years, thus making them more responsive to constituent pressure than members of the other national institutions. The president was given a four-year term, sufficient time, it was thought, to "contribute to the firmness of the executive" without justifying "any alarm for the public liberty."[16]

Third, the founders derived the authority and formal power of all of the institutions and their officers ultimately from the people but immediately from the Constitution. This would serve to insulate officials from rapidly changing currents of public opinion, while leaving them open to the assertion of deeply felt and widely shared public opinion through constitutional amendment.

Finally, the founders envisioned that the extent of the nation itself would insulate governing officials from sudden shifts of public opinion. In his well-known arguments for an extended republic, Madison reasoned that large size would improve democracy by making the formation of majority factions difficult. But again, argued Madison, extent of the territory and diversity of factions would not prevent the formation of a majority if the issue was an important one.[17]

It is the brakes upon public opinion rather than the provision for its influence that causes skepticism today.[18] Because of the centrality of popular leadership to modern theories of the presidency, the rationale behind the founders' distrust of "direct democracy" should be noted specifically. This issue is joined dramatically in *The Federalist* No. 49, in which Madison addresses Jefferson's suggestion that "whenever two of the three branches of government shall concur in [the] opinion . . . that a convention is necessary for altering the Constitution, *or correcting breaches of it,* a convention shall be called for the purpose." Madison recounts Jefferson's reasoning: because the Constitution was formed by the people it rightfully ought to be modified by them. Madison admits "that a constitutional road to the decision of the people ought to be marked out and kept open for great and extraordinary occasions." But he objects to bringing directly to the people disputes among the branches about the extent of their authority. In the normal course of governance, such disputes could be expected to arise fairly often. In our day they would include, for example, the war powers controversy, the impoundment controversy, and the issue of executive privilege.

Madison objects to recourse to "the people" on three basic grounds. First, popular appeals would imply "some defect" in the government: "Frequent appeals would, in great measure, deprive the government of that veneration which time bestows on everything, and without which perhaps the wisest and freest governments would not possess the requisite stability." *The Federalist* points to the institutional benefits of popular veneration—stability of government and the enhanced authority of its constitutional officers. Second, the tranquility of the society as a whole might be disturbed. Madison expresses the fear that an enterprising demagogue might reopen disputes over "great national questions" in a political context less favorable to their resolution than the Constitutional Convention.

Finally, Madison voices "the greatest objection of all" to frequent appeals to the people: "the decisions which would probably result from such appeals would not answer the purpose of maintaining the constitutional equilibrium of government." The executive might face political difficulties if frequent appeals to the people were permitted because other features of his office (his singularity, independence, and executive powers) would leave him at a rhetorical disadvantage in contests with the legislature. Presidents will be "generally the objects of jealousy and their administrations . . . liable to be discolored and rendered unpopular," Madison argued. "[T]he Members of the legislatures on the other hand are numerous. . . . Their connections of blood, of friendship, and of acquaintance embrace a great proportion of the most influential part of society. The nature of their public trust implies a personal influence among the people. . . .[19]

Madison realizes that there may be circumstances "less adverse to the executive and judiciary departments." If the executive power were "in the hands of a peculiar favorite of the people . . . the public decision might be less swayed in favor of the [legislature]. But still it could never be expected to turn on the true merits of the question." The ultimate reason for the rejection of "frequent popular appeals" is that they would undermine *deliberation,* and result in bad public policy:

> The *passions,* not the *reason,* of the public would sit in judgment. But it is the reason alone, of the public, that ought to control and regulate the government. The passions ought to be controlled and regulated by the government.[20]

There are two frequent misunderstandings of the founders' opinion on the "deliberative" function of representation. The first is that they naively believed that deliberation constituted the whole of legislative politics—that there would be no bargaining, logrolling, or nondeliberative rhetorical appeals. The discussion of Congress in *The Federalist* Nos. 52 to 68 and in the Constitutional Convention debates reveals quite clearly that the founders understood that the legislative process would involve a mixture of these elements. The founding task was to create an institutional context that made deliberation most likely, not to assume that it would occur "naturally" or, even in the best of legislatures, predominantly.[21]

The second common error, prevalent in leading historical accounts of the period, is to interpret the deliberative elements of the founders' design as an attempt to rid the legislative councils of "common men" and replace them with "better sorts"—more educated and above all, more propertied individuals.[22] Deliberation, in this view, is the byproduct of the kind of person elected to office. The public's opinions are "refined and enlarged" because refined individuals do the governing. While this view finds some support in *The Federalist* and was a worry of several Anti-Federalists, the founders placed much greater emphasis upon the formal structures of the national institutions than upon the backgrounds of officeholders.[23] Indeed, good character and high intelligence, they reasoned, would be of little help to the government if it resembled a direct democracy: "In all very numerous assemblies, of whatever characters composed, passion never fails to wrest the sceptre from reason. Had every Athenian citizen been a Socrates, every Athenian assembly would still have been a mob."[24]

The presidency thus was intended to be representative of the people, but not merely responsive to popular will. Drawn from the people through an election (albeit an indirect one), the president was to be free enough from the daily shifts in public opinion so that he could refine it and, paradoxically, better serve popular interests. Hamilton expresses well this element of the theory in a passage in which he links the problem of representation to that of demagoguery:

> There are those who would be inclined to regard the servile pliancy of the executive to a prevailing current in the community of the legislature as its best recommendation. But such men entertain very crude notions, as well of the purposes for which government was instituted, as of the true means by which public happiness may be promoted. The republican principle demands that the deliberative sense of the community should govern the conduct of those to whom they intrust the management of the affairs; but it does not require an unqualified complaisance to every transient impulse which the people may receive from the arts of men, who flatter their prejudices to betray their interests ... when occasions present themselves in which the interests of the people are at variance with their inclinations, it is the duty of the persons whom they have appointed to be the guardians of those interests to withstand the temporary delusion in order to give them time and opportunity for more cool and sedate reflections.[25]

Independence of the Executive

To "withstand the temporary delusions" of popular opinion, the executive was made independent. The office would draw its authority from the Constitution rather than from another governmental branch. The framers were led to this decision from their knowledge of the states, where according to John Marshall, the governments (with the exception of New York) lacked any structure "which could resist the wild projects of the moment, give the people an opportunity to reflect and allow the good sense of the nation time for exertion." As Madison stated at the Convention, "experience had proved a tendency in our governments to throw all power into the legislative vortex. The executives of the states are in general little more than Cyphers."

While independence from Congress was the immediate practical need, it was a need based upon the close connection between legislatures and popular opinion. Because independence from public opinion was the source of the concern about the legislatures, the founders rejected James Wilson's arguments on behalf of popular election as a means of making the president independent of Congress.[26]

Independence of the executive created the conditions under which presidents would be most likely to adopt a different perspective from Congress on matters of public policy. Congress would be dominated by local factions that, according to plan, would give great weight to constituent opinion. The president, as Thomas Jefferson was to argue, was the only national officer "who commanded a view of the whole ground." Independence thus was not only necessary for executive discretion incident to carrying out the will of Congress or executing the law, it was useful for the construction of good laws in the first place, laws that would be responsive to the long-term needs of the nation at large.[27]

Separation of Powers

The constitutional role of the president in lawmaking raises the question of the meaning and purpose of separation of powers. What is the sense of separation of power if power is shared among the branches of government? Clearly, legalists are wrong who have assumed that the founders wished to distinguish so carefully among executive, legislative, and judicial power as to make each the exclusive preserve of a particular branch. However, their error has given rise to another.

Political scientists, following Richard Neustadt, have assumed that since powers were not divided according to the principle of "one branch, one function," the founders made no principled distinction among kinds of power. Instead, according to Neustadt, they created "separate institutions sharing power.'"[28] The premise of that claim is that power is an entity that can be divided up to prevent any one branch from having enough to rule another. In this view, the sole purpose of separation of powers is to preserve liberty by preventing the arbitrary rule of any one center of power.

The Neustadt perspective finds some support in the founders' deliberations. Much attention was given to making each branch "weighty" enough to resist encroachment by the others. Yet this "checks and balances" view of separation of powers can be understood better in tandem with an alternative understanding of the concept: Powers were to be separated and structures of each branch differentiated because each branch would be best equipped to perform different tasks. Each branch would be superior (although not the sole power) in its own sphere and in its own way. The purpose of separation of powers was to make effective governance more likely.[29]

Ensuring the protection of liberty and individual rights was one element of effective governance as conceived by the founders, but not the only one. Government also needed to ensure the security of the nation and to craft policies that reflected popular will. These three governmental objectives may conflict; for example, popular opinion might favor policies that violated rights. Separation of powers was thought to be an institutional way of accommodating the tensions between governmental objectives.

Table 3-1 presents a simplified view of the purposes behind the separation of powers. Note that the three objectives of government—popular will, popular rights, and self-preservation—are mixed twice in the Constitution; they are mixed among the branches and within each branch so that each objective is given priority in one branch. Congress and the president were to concern themselves with all three, but the priority of their concern differs, with "self preservation" or national security of utmost concern to the president.

The term "separation of powers" perhaps has obstructed understanding of the extent to which different structures were designed to give each branch the special quality needed to secure its governmental objectives. Thus, while the founders were not so naive as to expect that Congress would be simply "deliberative," they hoped that its plural

Table 3-1 Separation of Powers

Objectives (in order of priority)	Special Qualities and Functions (to be aimed at)	Structures and Means
Congress 1. popular will 2. popular rights 3. self-preservation	deliberation	a. plurality b. proximity (frequent House elections) c. bicameralism d. competent powers
President 1. self-preservation 2. popular rights 3. popular will	energy and "steady administration of law"	a. unity b. four-year term and eligibility c. competent powers
Court 1. popular rights	"judgment, not will"	a. small collegial body b. life tenure c. power linked to argument

membership and bicameral structure would provide necessary, if not sufficient, conditions for deliberation to emerge. Similarly, the president's "energy," it was hoped, would be enhanced by unity, the prospect of reelection, and substantial discretion. As we all know, the Court does not simply "judge" dispassionately; it also makes policies and exercises will. But the founders believed that it made no sense to have a Court if it were intended to be just like a Congress. The judiciary was structured to make the dispassionate protection of rights more likely, if by no means certain.

The founders differentiated powers as well as structures in the original design. These powers ("the executive power" vested in a president in Article II and "all legislative power herein granted," given to Congress in Article I) overlap and sometimes conflict. Yet both the legalists' view of power as "parchment distinction" and the political scientists' view of "separate institutions sharing power" provide inadequate guides to what happens and what was thought ought to happen when power collided. The founders urged that "line drawing" among spheres of authority be the product of political conflict among the branches, not the result of dispassionate legal analysis. Contrary to more contemporary views, they did not believe that such conflict would lead to deadlock or stalemate.[30]

Consider the disputes that sometimes arise from claims of "executive privilege."[31] Presidents occasionally refuse to provide information to Congress that its members deem necessary to carry out their special functions. They usually justify assertions of executive privilege on the grounds of either national security or the need to maintain the conditions necessary to sound execution, including the unfettered canvassing of opinions.

Both Congress and the president have legitimate constitutional prerogatives at stake: Congress has a right to know and the president a need for secrecy. How does one discover whether in any particular instance the president's claim is more or less weighty than Congress's? The answer will depend upon the circumstances—for example, the importance of the particular piece of legislation in the congressional agenda versus the importance of the particular secret to the executive. There is no formula independent of political circumstance with which to weigh such competing institutional claims. The most knowledgeable observers of those political conflicts are the parties themselves: Congress and the president.

Each branch has "weapons" at its disposal to use against the other. Congress can threaten to hold up legislation or appointments important to the president. Ultimately, it could impeach and convict him. For his part, a president may continue to "stonewall"; he may veto bills or fail to support legislation of interest to his legislative opponents; he may delay political appointments; and he may put the issue to public test, even submitting to an impeachment inquiry for his own advantage. The lengths to which presidents and Congresses are willing to go was thought to be a rough measure of the importance of their respective constitutional claims. Nearly always, executive-legislative disputes are resolved at a relatively low stage of potential conflict. In 1981, for example, President Ronald Reagan ordered Interior Secretary James Watt to release information to a Senate committee after the committee had agreed to maintain confidentiality. The compromise was reached after public debate and "contempt of Congress" hearings were held.

It is important to note that this political process is dynamic. Viewed at particular moments, the system may appear deadlocked; considered over time, considerable movement becomes apparent. Similar scenarios could be constructed for the other issues over which congressional and presidential claims to authority conflict, such as the use of executive agreements in place of treaties, the deployment of military force, or the executive impoundment of appropriated monies.[32]

While conflict may continue to be institutionally fostered or constrained in ways that were intended by the founders, one still may wonder whether their broad objectives have been secured and whether their priorities should be ours. At the outset of the present century, Woodrow Wilson mounted an attack on the founders' design, convinced that it had not secured its objectives. More importantly, his attack resulted in a reordering of these objectives in the understandings that presidents have of their roles. His theory underlies the second constitution that buffets the presidency.

The Modern Perspective

Woodrow Wilson's influential critique of *The Federalist* contains another synoptic vision. Yet his comprehensive reinterpretation of the constitutional order appears, at first glance, to be internally inconsistent. Between writing his classic dissertation, *Congressional Government*, in 1885, and the publication of his well-known series of lectures, *Constitutional Government in the United States*, in 1908, Wilson shifted his position on important structural features of the constitutional system.

Early in his career Wilson depicted the House of Representatives as the potential motive force in American politics and urged reforms to make it more unified and energetic. He paid little attention to the presidency or judiciary. In later years the presidency became the focus of his attention. In his early writings Wilson urged a plethora of constitutional amendments that were designed to emulate the British parliamentary system, including proposals to synchronize the terms of representatives and senators with that of the president and to require presidents to choose leaders of the majority party as cabinet secretaries. Later Wilson abandoned formal amendment as a strategy, urging instead that the existing Constitution be reinterpreted to encompass his parliamentary views.

Wilson also altered his views at a deeper theoretical level. Christopher Wolfe has shown that while the "early" Wilson held a "traditional" view of the Constitution as a document whose meaning persists over time, the "later" Wilson adopted a historicist understanding, claiming that the meaning of the Constitution changed as a reflection of the prevailing thought of successive generations.[33]

As interesting as these shifts in Wilson's thought are, they all rest upon an underlying critique of the American polity that he maintained consistently throughout his career. Wilson's altered constitutional proposals, indeed his altered understanding of constitutionalism itself, ought to be viewed as a series of strategic moves designed to remedy the same alleged systemic defects. This section outlines the theory Wilson developed to contend with those defects—a theory whose centerpiece ultimately would be popular leadership.

Wilson's doctrine can be nicely counterpoised to the founders' understanding of demagoguery, representation, independence of the executive, and separation of powers. For clarity, these principles will be examined here in a slightly different order than before: separation of powers, representation, independence of the executive, and demagoguery.

Separation of Powers

For Wilson, separation of powers was the central defect of American politics. He was the first and most sophisticated proponent of the now conventional argument that separation of powers is a synonym for "checks and balances," the negation of power by one branch over another. Yet Wilson's view was more sophisticated than its progeny because his ultimate indictment of the founders' conception was a functionalist one. Wilson claimed that under the auspices of the founders' view, formal and informal political institutions failed to promote true deliberation in the legislature and impeded energy in the executive.

Wilson characterized the founders' understanding as "Newtonian," a yearning for equipoise and balance in a machine-like system:

> The admirable positions of the *Federalist* read like thoughtful applications of Montesquieu to the political needs and circumstances of America. They are full of the theory of checks and balances. The President is balanced off against Congress, Congress against the President, and each against the Court ... politics is turned into mechanics under [Montesquieu's] touch. The theory of gravitation is supreme.[34]

The accuracy of Wilson's portrayal of the founders may be questioned. He reasoned backward from the malfunctioning system as he found it to how they must have intended it. Wilson's depiction of the system rather than his interpretation of the founders' intentions is of present concern.

Rather than equipoise and balance, Wilson found a system dominated by Congress, with several attendant functional infirmities: major legislation frustrated by narrow-minded committees, lack of coordination and direction of policies, a general breakdown of deliberation, and an absence of leadership. Extra-Constitutional institutions— "boss"-led political parties chief among them—had sprung up to assume the functions not performed by Congress or the president, but they had not performed them well. Wilson also acknowledged that the formal institutions had not always performed badly, that some prior Congresses (those of Webster and Clay) and some presidencies (those of Washington, Adams, Jefferson, Jackson, Lincoln, Roosevelt, and, surprisingly, Madison) had been examples of forceful leadership.[35]

These two strands of thought—the growth of extra-Constitutional institutions and the periodic excellence of the constitutional structures—led Wilson to conclude that the founders had mischaracterized their own system. The founders' rhetoric was "Newtonian," but their constitutional structure, like all government, was actually 'Darwinian." Wilson explains:

> The trouble with the Newtonian theory is that government is not a machine but a living thing. It falls, not under the theory of the universe, but under the theory or organic life. It is accountable to Darwin, not to Newton. It is modified by its environment, necessitated by its tasks, shaped to its functions by the sheer pressure of life.[36]

The founders' doctrine had affected the working of the structure to the extent that the power of the political branches was interpreted mechanically and that many of the structural features reflected the Newtonian yearning. A tension arose between the "organic" core of the system and the "mechanical" understanding of it by politicians and citizens. Thus, "the constitutional structure of the government has hampered and limited [the president's] actions but it has not prevented [them.]" Wilson tried to resolve the tension between the understanding of American politics as Newtonian and its actual Darwinian character to make the evolution self-conscious and thereby more rational and effective.[37]

Wilson attacked the founders for relying on mere "parchment barriers" to effectuate a separation of powers. This claim is an obvious distortion of founding views. In *Federalist* Nos. 47 and 48, the argument is precisely that the federal constitution, unlike earlier state constitutions, would *not* rely primarily upon parchment distinctions of power but upon differentiation of institutional structures.[38] However, through Wilson's discussion of parchment barriers an important difference between his and the founders' view of the same problem becomes visible. Both worried over the tendency of legislatures to dominate in republican systems.

To mitigate the danger posed by legislatures, the founders had relied primarily upon an independent president with an office structured to give its occupant the personal incentive and means to stand up to Congress when it exceeded its authority. These structural features included a nonlegislative mode of election, constitutionally fixed salary, qualified veto, four-year term, and indefinite reeligibility. Although the parchment powers of the Congress and president overlapped (contrary to Wilson's depiction of them), the demarcation of powers proper to each branch would result primarily from political interplay and conflict between the political branches rather than from a theoretical drawing of lines by the judiciary.[39]

Wilson offered a quite different view. First, he claimed that because of the inadequacy of mere parchment barriers, Congress, in the latter half of the nineteenth century, had encroached uncontested upon the executive sphere. Second, he urged that when the president's institutional check was employed it took the form of a "negative"— prevention of a bad outcome rather than provision for a good one. In this view separation of powers hindered efficient, coordinated, well-led policy.[40]

Wilson did not wish to bolster structures to thwart the legislature. He preferred that the president and Congress should be fully integrated into, and implicated in, each others' activities. Rather than merely assail Congress, Wilson would tame or, as it were, domesticate it. Separation would be replaced by institutionally structured cooperation. Cooperation was especially necessary because the president lacked the energy he needed, energy that could be provided only by policy backed by Congress and its majority. Although Congress had failed as a deliberative body, it could now be restored to its true function by presidential leadership that raised and defended key policies.

These latter two claims actually represent the major purposes of the Wilsonian theory: leadership and deliberation. Unlike the founders, who saw these two functions in conflict, Wilson regarded them as dependent upon each other. In "Leaderless Government" he stated:

> I take it for granted that when one is speaking of a representative legislature he means by an "efficient organization" an organization which provides for deliberate, and deliberative, action and which enables the nation to affix responsibility for what is done and what is not done. The Senate is deliberate enough; but it is hardly deliberative after its ancient and better manner.... The House of Representatives is neither deliberate nor deliberative.... For debate and leadership of that sort the House must have a party organization and discipline such that it has never had.[41]

At this point, it appears that the founders and Wilson differed on the means to common ends. Both wanted "deliberation" and an "energetic" executive, but each proposed different constitutional arrangements to secure those objectives. In fact, their differences went much deeper, for each theory defined deliberation and energy to mean different things. These differences, hinted at in the above quotation, will become clearer as we examine Wilson's reinterpretation of representation and independence of the executive.

Representation

In the discussion of the founding perspective, the competing requirements of popular consent and insulation from public opinion as a requisite of impartial judgment were canvassed. Woodrow Wilson gave much greater weight to the role of public opinion in the ordinary conduct of representative government than did the founders. Some scholars have suggested that Wilson's rhetoric and the institutional practices he established (especially regarding the nomination of presidential candidates) are the major sources of contemporary efforts toward a more "participatory" democracy. However, Wilson's understanding of representation, like his views on separation of powers, is more sophisticated than his followers'.[42]

Wilson categorically rejected the Burkean view of the legislator who is elected for his quality of judgment and position on a few issues and then left free to exercise that judgment:

> It used to be thought that legislation was an affair to be conducted by the few who were instructed for the benefit of the many who were uninstructed: that statesmanship was a function of origination for which only trained and instructed men were fit. Those who actually conducted legislation and conducted affairs were rather whimsically chosen by Fortune to illustrate this theory, but such was the ruling thought in politics. The Sovereignty of the People, however . . . has created a very different practice. . . . [I]t is a dignified proposition with us—is it not?—that as is the majority, so ought the government to be.[43]

Wilson did not think that his view was equivalent to "direct democracy" or to subservience to public opinion (understood, as it often is today, as response to public opinion polls). He favored an interplay between representative and constituent that would, in fact, educate the constituent. This process differed, at least in theory, from the older attempts to "form" public opinion: it did not begin in the minds of the elite but in the hearts of the mass. Wilson called the process of fathoming the people's desires (often only vaguely known to the people until instructed) "interpretation." Interpretation was the core of leadership for him.[44] Before exploring its meaning further, it will be useful to dwell upon Wilson's notion of the desired interplay between the "leader interpreter" and the people so that we may see how his understanding of deliberation differed from the founders'.

For the founders, deliberation simply meant reasoning on the merits of policy. The character and content of deliberation thus would vary with the character of the policy at issue. In "normal" times, there would be extensive squabbles by competing interests. To the extent that such interests and factions were compelled to offer and respond to arguments made by the others, there would be deliberation. Such arguments might be relatively crude, specialized, or technical, or they might involve matters of legal or constitutional propriety. But in none of these instances would they resemble the great debate over fundamental principles.

Wilson effaced the distinction between "crisis" and "normal" political argument. "Crises give birth and a new growth to statesmanship because they are peculiarly periods of action ... [and] also of unusual opportunity for gaining leadership and a controlling and guiding influence.... And we thus come upon the principle ... that governmental forms will call to the work of the administration able minds and strong hearts constantly or infrequently, according as they do or do not afford *at all times* an opportunity of gaining and retaining a commanding authority and an undisputed leadership in the nation's councils." [45]

Woodrow Wilson's lament about the lack of deliberation that took place in Congress was not that the merits of policies were left unexplored, but rather that because the discussions were not elevated to the level of major contests of principle the public generally did not interest itself. Wilson rested this view on three observations. First, the congressional workload was parceled among specialized standing committees, whose decisions usually were ratified by the respective houses without any general debate. Second, the arguments that did take place in committee were technical and structured by the "special pleadings" of interest groups, whose advocates adopted the model of legal litigation as their mode of discussion. As Wilson characterized committee debates:

> They have about them none of the searching, critical, illuminating character of the higher order of parliamentary debate, in which men are pitted against each other as equals, and urged to sharp contest and masterful strife by the inspiration of political principle and personal ambition, through the rivalry of parties and the competition of policies. They represent a joust between antagonistic interests, not a contest of principles.

Finally, because debates were hidden away in committee, technical, and interest-based, the public cared little about them. "The ordinary citizen cannot be induced to pay much heed to the details, or even the main principles of lawmaking," Wilson wrote, "unless something more interesting than the law itself be involved in the pending decision of the lawmaker." [46] For the founders this would not have been disturbing, but for Wilson the very heart of representative government was the principle of publicity: "the informing function of Congress should be preferred even to its legislative function." [47] The informing function was to be preferred both as an end in itself and because the accountability of public officials required policies that were connected with one another and explained to the people. Argument from "principle" would connect policy and present constellations of policies as coherent wholes to be approved or disapproved by the people. "Principles, as statesmen conceive them, are threads to the labyrinth of circumstances." [48]

Wilson attacked separation of powers in an effort to improve leadership for the purpose of fostering deliberation. "Congress cannot, under our present system . . . be effective for the instruction of public opinion, or the cleansing of political action." As mentioned at the outset of this chapter, Wilson first looked to Congress itself, specifically to its Speaker, for such leadership. Several years after the publication of *Congressional Government,* Wilson turned his attention to the president. "There is no trouble now about getting the president's speeches printed and read, every word," he wrote at the turn of the century. [49]

Independence of the Executive

The attempt to bring the president into more intimate contact with Congress and the people raises the question of the president's "independence." Wilson altered the meaning of this notion, which originally had been that the president's special authority came independently from a Constitution, not from Congress or the people. The president's station thus afforded him the possibility and responsibility of taking a perspective on policy different from either Congress or the people. Wilson urged us to consider the president as receiving his authority independently through a mandate from the people. For Wilson, the president remained "special," but now because he was the only governmental officer with a national mandate. [50]

Political scientists today have difficulty in finding mandates in election years, let alone between them, because of the great number of issues and the lack of public consensus on them. Wilson understood this problem and urged the leader to sift through the multifarious currents of opinion to find a core of issues that he believed reflected majority will even if the majority was not yet fully aware of it. The leader's rhetoric could translate the people's felt desires into public policy. Wilson cited Daniel Webster as an example of such an interpreter of the public will:

> The nation lay as it were unconscious of its unity and purpose, and he called it into full consciousness. It could never again be anything less than what he said it was. It is at such moments and in the mouths of such interpreters that nations spring from age to age in their development. [51]

"Interpretation" involves two skills. First, the leader must understand the true majority sentiment underneath the contradictory positions of factions and the discordant views of the mass. Second, the leader must explain the people's true desires to them in a way that is easily comprehended and convincing.

Wilson's desire to raise politics to the level of rational disputation and his professed aim to have leaders educate the mass are contradictory. Candidly, he acknowledges that the power to command would require simplification of the arguments to accommodate the mass: "The arguments which induce popular action must always be broad and obvious arguments; only a very gross substance of concrete conception can make any impression on the minds of the masses."[52] Not only is argument simplified but disseminating "information," a common concern of contemporary democratic theory, is not the function of a deliberative leader in Wilson's view:

> Men are not led by being told what they don't know. Persuasion is a force, but not information; and persuasion is accomplished by creeping into the confidence of those you would lead.... Mark the simplicity and directness of the arguments and ideas of true leaders. The motives which they urge are elemental; the morality which they seek to enforce is large and obvious; the policy they emphasize, purged of all subtlety.[53]

Demagoguery

Wilson's understanding of leadership raises again the problem of demagoguery. What distinguishes a leader-interpreter from a demagogue? Who is to make this distinction? The founders feared that there was no institutionally effective way to exclude the demagogue if popular oratory during "normal" times was encouraged.

Wilson was sensitive to this problem. "The most despotic of governments under the control of wise statemen is preferable to the freest ruled by demagogues," he wrote. Wilson relied upon two criteria to distinguish the demagogue from the leader, one based upon the nature of the appeal, the other upon the character of the leader. The demagogue appeals to "the momentary and whimsical popular mood, the transitory or popular passion," while the leader appeals to "true" and durable majority sentiment. The demagogue is motivated by the desire to augment personal power, while the leader is more interested in fostering the permanent interests of the community. "The one [trims] to the inclinations of the moment, the other [is] obedient to the permanent purposes of the public mind."[54]

Theoretically, there are a number of difficulties with these distinctions. If popular opinion is the source of the leader's rhetoric, what basis apart from popular opinion itself is there to distinguish the "permanent" from the "transient"? If popular opinion is constantly evolving, what sense is there to the notion of "the permanent purposes of the public mind"? Yet the most serious difficulties are practical ones. Assuming it theoretically possible to distinguish the leader from the demagogue, how is that distinction to be incorporated into the daily operation of political institutions? Wilson offered a threefold response to this query.

First, he claimed that his doctrine contained an ethic that could be passed on to future leaders. Wilson hoped that politicians' altered understanding of what constituted success and fame could provide some security. He constantly pointed to British parliamentary practice, urging that long training in debate had produced generations of leaders and few demagogues. Wilson had taught at Johns Hopkins, Bryn Mawr, Wesleyan, and Princeton, and at each of those institutions he established debating societies modeled on the Oxford Union.[55]

Second, Wilson placed some reliance upon the public's ability to judge character:

> [M]en can scarcely be orators without that force of character, that readiness of resource, that cleverness of vision, that grasp of intellect, that courage of conviction, that correctness of purpose, and that instinct and capacity for leadership which are the eight horses that draw the triumphal chariot of every leader and ruler of freemen. We could not object to being ruled by such men. [56]

According to Wilson, the public easily could recognize "courage," "intelligence," and "correctness of purpose"—signs that the leader was not a demagogue. The major difficulty with this second source of restraint is that public understanding of the leader's character would come from his oratory rather than from a history of his political activity or from direct contact with him.

Finally, Wilson suggests that the natural conservatism of public opinion, its resistance to innovation that is not consonant with the speed and direction of its own movement, will afford still more safety:

> Practical leadership may not beckon to the slow masses of men from beyond some dim, unexplored space or some intervening chasm: it must daily feel the road to the goal proposed, knowing that it is a slow, very slow, evolution to the wings, and that for the present, and for a very long future also, Society must walk....[57]

Woodrow Wilson's assurances of security against demagogues may seem unsatisfactory because they do not adequately distinguish the polity in which he worked from others in which demagogues have prevailed, including some southern states in this country. However, his arguments should be considered as much for the theoretical direction and emphases that they imply as for the particular weaknesses they reveal. Wilson's doctrine stands on the premise that the need for more energy in the political system is greater than the risk incurred through the possibility of demagoguery.[58] This represents a major shift, indeed a reversal, of the founding perspective. If Wilson's argument regarding demagoguery is strained or inadequate, it was a price he was willing to pay to remedy what he regarded as the founders' inadequate provision for an energetic executive.

Conclusion

Both constitutions were designed to secure an energetic president, but they differ over the legitimate sources and alleged virtues of popular leadership. For the founders, the president draws his energy from his authority. His authority rests upon his independent constitutional position. For Woodrow Wilson and for presidents ever since, power and authority are conferred directly by the people. *The Federalist* and the Constitution proscribe popular leadership. Woodrow Wilson prescribes it. Indeed, Wilson urges the president to minister continually to the moods of the people as a preparation for action. The founders' president was to look to the people, but less frequently, and to be judged by them, but usually after acting.

The second constitution gained legitimacy because presidents were thought to lack the resources necessary for the energy that was promised but not delivered by the first constitution. The second constitution did not replace the first, however. Because many of the founding structures persist, while our understanding of the president's legitimate role has changed, the new view should be thought of as superimposed upon the old, altering without obliterating the original structure.[59]

For example, the inconsistency of popular appeals common to recent presidents may be traced to competing constitutional imperatives. Urged by the Wilsonian perspective (and a selection system that embodies its prescriptions) to appeal continually to the people, all recent presidents have begun their terms as popular leaders. Jimmy Carter promised to be "as good as the people"; Ronald Reagan has sounded the same theme. But the vantage point structured by the original design also has offered presidents the opportunity to "hide" in the White House and to act "presidential," that is, more as a constitutional officer than a popular leader. President Carter found it in his interest to do so during the Iranian hostage crisis. Such retreats from public view, however justifiable, are rendered hypocritical by the legitimacy of the second constitution. Presidential hypocrisy might not be as much a reflection of defects of character as it is the unintended by-product of the constitutional hybrid.

Many commentators have noted the tendency of recent presidents to raise public expectations about what they can achieve. Public disenchantment with government altogether might stem largely from disappointment in presidential performance, since the presidency is the most salient American political institution. Again personality or character may not be the most important cause of how presidents behave. Rather, all presidents face the same institutional dilemma. Under the auspices of the second constitution, presidents continually must craft rhetoric that pleases their popular audience. But while presidents are always in a position to promise more, the only additional resource they have to secure their promises is public opinion itself. Because Congress retains the independent status conferred upon it by the first constitution, it can resist the president.

The second constitution seemed particularly necessary and suitable for presidents who faced crises as profound as World War II and the Great Depression. The continuous use of the "crisis tool" of popular leadership, however, was meant to make the president more effective in normal times as well. The unintended consequence may have been to make presidents less capable of leadership at any time. If crisis politics are now routine, we may have lost the ability as a people to distinguish genuine from spurious crises. Moreover, the continuous attempts to mobilize the populace through "charismatic" power delegitimizes constitutional or "normal" authority, making the tasks of governance still more difficult. Garry Wills recently has described how presidents, since Kennedy, attempt to pit public opinion against the rest of the government, indeed sometimes against the president's own executive establishment. Successors to a charismatic leader then inherit "a delegitimated set of procedures" and are themselves compelled "to go outside of procedures—further delegitimating the very office they [hold.]" The routinization of crisis is accompanied by attempted repetitions of charisma.[60] These feed the cynicism endemic to contemporary American politics.

Yet the founders' presidency may have seemed to Woodrow Wilson, and still may seem, inadequately "energetic" because the tasks of modern governance appear inordinately greater than those that faced George Washington. While government still attempts to secure rights, it does so much differently. Wilson's Progressivism marks the beginning of the welfare state as well as of the emergence of the United States as a world power. It can be argued that the expanded politics of the twentieth century was facilitated by the very Constitution Wilson opposed and is presaged in the theory behind it. However that may be, changed conditions may have heightened the need for popular leadership while making the dilemmas inherent in the constitutional hybrid even more acute.

NOTES

1. Notable structural changes in the Constitution are the Twelfth, Seventeenth, Twentieth, and Twenty-second Amendments dealing respectively with change in the Electoral College system, the election of senators, presidential succession, and presidential reeligibility. While all are interesting, only the last seems manifestly inconsistent with the founders' plan. There also have been interesting nonconstitutional developments in internal arrangements of the major organs of government. See, for example, Roger H. Davidson, "Two Avenues of Change: House and Senate Reorganization," in *Congress Reconsidered*, 2d ed., edited by Lawrence C. Dodd and Bruce I. Oppenheimer (Washington, D.C.: CQ Press, 1981), 107-136. For a detailed discussion of the relation of constitutional forms to political behavior, see Joseph M. Bessette and Jeffrey Tulis, "The Constitution, Politics, and the Presidency," in *The Presidency in the Constitutional Order*, ed. Joseph M. Bessette and Jeffrey Tulis (Baton Rouge, La.: Louisiana State University Press, 1981), 3-30.
2. James Ceaser, *Presidential Selection: Theory and Development* (Princeton, N.J.: Princeton University Press, 1979); Doris Graber, *Mass Media and American Politics* (Washington, D.C.: CQ Press, 1980); and Harvey C. Mansfield, Jr., "The Media World and Democratic Representation," *Government and Opposition*, 14 (Summer 1979): 35-45.
3. This essay does not reveal the founders' personal and political motives except as they were self-consciously incorporated into the reasons offered for their constitution. For a good discussion of the literature on the politics of the founding fathers, see Erwin Hargrove and Michael Nelson, *Presidents, Politics, and Policy* (New York: Random House, 1984), chap. 2. In this chapter, the founders' views are treated on their own terms, as a constitutional theory; Hamilton's statement in the first number of *The Federalist* is taken seriously: "My motives must remain in the depository of my own breast. My arguments will be open to all and may be judged by all." James Madison, Alexander Hamilton, and John Jay, *The Federalist Papers*, introduction by Clinton Rossiter (New York: New American Library, 1961), no. 1, 36.
4. The most influential study of the presidency is by Richard Neustadt. See *Presidential Power: The Politics of Leadership from FDR to Carter* (New York: John Wiley & Sons, 1979, originally published 1960), vi: "... one must try to view the Presidency from over the President's shoulder, looking out and down with the perspective of *his* place."
5. Herbert J. Storing, *What the Anti-Federalists Were For* (Chicago: University of Chicago Press, 1981), 83 (note 7).

6. *Federalist,* no. 70, 423.
7. Ceaser, *Presidential Selection,* 166-167, 318-327.
8. *Federalist,* no. 71, 432.
9. *Federalist,* no. 10, 82; Ceaser, *Presidential Selection,* 324.
10. Clinton Rossiter, *Constitutional Dictatorship: Crisis Government in the Modern Democracies* (Princeton, N.J.: Princeton University Press, 1948), chap. 3.
11. *The Federalist,* no. 85, 537.
12. Harvey Flaumenhaft, "Hamilton's Administrative Republic and the American Presidency," in *The Presidency in the Constitutional Order,* ed. Bessette and Tulis, 65-114.
13. *The Federalist,* no. 10, 77; no. 43, 276; no. 51, 323-325; no. 63, 384; no. 73, 443. Contemporary political scientists note that it is often theoretically and practically impossible to discover a majority will—that is, to count it up—because of the manifold differences of intensity of preferences and the plethora of hierarchies of preferences. See, for example, Kenneth Arrow, *Social Choice and Individual Values* (New York: John Wiley & Sons, 1963); and Benjamin I. Page, *Choices and Echoes in Presidential Elections* (Chicago: University of Chicago Press, 1978), chap. 2.
14. *The Federalist,* no. 39, 241; see also Martin Diamond, "Democracy and *The Federalist:* A Reconsideration of the Framers' Intent," *American Political Science Review* 53 (March 1959): 52-68.
15. *The Federalist,* no. 39, 241; no. 68, 412-423. See also James Ceaser, "Presidential Selection," in *The Presidency in the Constitutional Order,* ed. Bessette and Tulis, 234-282. Ironically, the founders were proudest of this institutional creation; the Electoral College was their most original contrivance. Moreover, it escaped the censure and even won a good deal of praise from anti-federal opponents of the Constitution. Because electors were chosen by state legislatures for the sole purpose of selecting a president, the process was thought *more* democratic than potential alternatives, such as selection by Congress.
16. *Federalist,* no. 72, 435.
17. *Federalist,* no. 9; no. 10.
18. Gordon Wood, *The Creation of the American Republic: 1776-1787* (New York: W. W. Norton & Co., 1969); Michael Parenti, "The Constitution as an Elitist Document," in *How Democratic is the Constitution?,* ed. Robert Goldwin (Washington, D.C.: American Enterprise Institute for Public Policy Research, 1980), 39-58; and Charles Lindblom, *Politics and Markets* (New York: Basic Books, 1979), conclusion.
19. *Federalist,* no. 49, 313-317.
20. Ibid., 317.
21. See *Federalist,* no. 57; Joseph M. Bessette, "Deliberative Democracy," in *How Democratic?,* ed. Goldwin, 102-116; and Michael Malbin, "What Did the Founders Want Congress To Be—and Who Cares?" (Paper presented to the American Political Science Association, Denver, Colo., September 2, 1982).
22. Wood, *Creation of the American Republic,* chap. 5; and Ceaser, *Presidential Selection,* 48.
23. *Federalist,* no. 62, no. 63, 376-390; "Agrippa," in *The Antifederalists,* ed. Cecilia M. Kenyon (New York: Bobbs Merrill Co., 1966), 134-160.
24. *Federalist,* no. 55, 342; Max Farrand, ed., *The Records of the Federal Convention of 1787,* 4 vols. (New Haven, Conn.: Yale University Press, 1966), I:53.

25. *Federalist,* no. 71, 432; no. 63, 384.

26. John Marshall, quoted in Charles Thatch, *The Creation of the Presidency,* reprinted ed. (Baltimore: Johns Hopkins University Press, 1969), 51; Farrand, *Records* 2:35, 2:22, 32.

27. *Federalist,* no. 68, 413; no. 71, 433; no. 73, 442; see also Herbert Storing, "Introduction," in Thatch, *Creation of the Presidency,* vi-viii.

28. Neustadt, *Presidential Power,* 26, 28-30, 170, 176, 204. See also James Sterling Young, *The Washington Community* (New York: Columbia University Press, 1964), 53.

29. Farrand, *Records,* 1:66-67; *Federalist,* no. 47, 360-380; see also U.S. Congress, *Annals,* 1:384-412, 476-608. See generally, Louis Fisher, *The Politics of Shared Power: Congress and the Executive* (Washington: CQ Press, 1981).

30. See, for example, Lloyd Cutler, "To Form a Government," *Foreign Affairs* (Fall 1980): 126-143.

31. Gary J. Schmitt, "Executive Privilege: Presidential Power to Withhold Information from Congress," in *Presidency in the Constitutional Order,* ed. Bessette and Tulis, 154-194.

32. Gary J. Schmitt, "Executive Agreements and Separation of Powers," (Ph.D. diss., University of Chicago, 1980); Gary J. Schmitt, "Separation of Powers: Introduction to the Study of Executive Agreements," *American Journal of Jurisprudence,* vol. 27, 114-138; Richard Pious, *The American Presidency* (New York: Basic Books, 1979), 372-415; and Louis Fisher, *Presidential Spending Power* (Princeton, N.J.: Princeton University Press, 1975), 147-201.

33. Woodrow Wilson, *Congressional Government: A Study in American Politics* (1884; reprint ed., Gloucester, Mass.: Peter Smith, 1973), preface to 15th printing, introduction; idem, *Constitutional Government in the United States* (New York: Columbia University Press, 1908); Christopher Wolfe, "Woodrow Wilson: Interpreting the Constitution," *Review of Politics* 41, no. 1 (January 1979): 131. See also Woodrow Wilson, "Cabinet Government in the United States," in *College and State,* ed. Ray Stannard Baker and William E. Dodd, 2 vols. (New York: Harper & Brothers, 1925), I:19-42; Paul Eidelberg, *A Discourse on Statesmanship* (Urbana: University of Illinois Press, 1974), chaps. 8 and 9; Harry Clor, "Woodrow Wilson," in *American Political Thought,* ed. Morton J. Frisch and Richard G. Stevens (New York: Charles Scribner's Sons, 1971); and Ceaser, *Presidential Selection,* 171.

34. Wilson, *Constitutional Government,* 56, 22; idem, "Leaderless Government," in *College and State,* ed. Baker and Dodd, 337.

35. Wilson, *Congressional Government,* 141, 149, 164, 195.

36. Wilson, *Constitutional Government,* 56.

37. Ibid., 60; see also Wilson, *Congressional Government,* 28, 30, 31, 187.

38. *Federalist,* nos. 47 and 48, 300-313. Consider Madison's statement in *Federalist,* no. 48, 308-309: "Will it be sufficient to mark with precision, the boundaries of these departments in the Constitution of the government, and to trust to these parchment barriers against the encroaching spirit of power? This is the security which appears to have been principally relied upon by the compilers of most of the American Constitutions. But experience assures us that the efficacy of the provision has been greatly overrated; and that some more adequate defense is indispensably necessary for the more feeble against the more powerful members of the

government. The legislative department is everywhere extending the sphere of its activity and drawing all power into its impetuous vortex."

39. Schmitt, "Executive Privilege."
40. Woodrow Wilson, "Leaderless Government," in *College and State,* ed. Baker and Dodd, 340, 357; idem., *Congressional Government,* 158, 201; idem, "Cabinet Government," 24-25.
41. Wilson, "Leaderless Government," 346; at the time he wrote this, Wilson was thinking of leadership internal to the House, but he later came to see the president performing this same role. Wilson, *Constitutional Government,* 69-77; see also idem, *Congressional Government,* 76, 97-98.
42. Eidelberg, *Discourse,* chaps. 8 and 9; Ceaser, *Presidential Selection,* chap. 4, conclusion.
43. Woodrow Wilson, *Leaders of Men,* ed. T. H. Vail Motter (Princeton: Princeton University Press, 1952), 39. This is the manuscript of an oft-repeated lecture that Wilson delivered in the 1890s. See also idem, *Congressional Government,* 195, 214.
44. Wilson, *Leaders of Men,* 39; idem, *Constitutional Government,* 49. See also, *Congressional Government,* 78, 136-137.
45. Wilson, "Cabinet Government," 34-35. See also idem, "Leaderless Government," 354; idem, *Congressional Government,* 72, 136-137.
46. Wilson, *Congressional Government,* 69.
47. Ibid., 72.
48. Ibid., 82.
49. Ibid., 197-198, 72; Wilson, "Cabinet Government," 20, 28-32.
50. Wilson, *Leaders of Men,* 46.
51. Wilson, *Congressional Government,* 76; ibid., Preface to 15th printing, 22-23.
52. Wilson, *Constitutional Government,* 49.
53. Wilson, *Leaders of Men,* 22-23.
54. Ibid., 20, 26.
55. Ibid., 29.
56. Wilson, "Cabinet Government," 37; idem, *Leaders of Men,* 45-46.
57. Wilson, *Congressional Government,* 143-147.
58. Ibid., 144.
59. For a more detailed discussion of some of the consequences of the second constitution for the conduct of the presidency today, see James W. Ceaser, Glen E. Thurow, Jeffrey Tulis, and Joseph M. Bessette, "The Rise of the Rhetorical Presidency," *Presidential Studies Quarterly,* 1:11 (Spring 1981): 158-171; and Jeffrey Tulis, "The Decay of Presidential Rhetoric," in *Rhetoric and Statesmanship,* ed. Glen E. Thurow and Jeffrey Wallin (Durham, N.C.: Carolina Academic Press, 1983).
60. Garry Wills, "The Kennedy Imprisonment: The Prisoner of Charisma," *The Atlantic* (January 1982): 34; and H. H. Gerth and C. Wright Mills, eds., *From Max Weber* (New York: Oxford University Press, 1958), 247-248.

4. PRESIDENTIAL LEADERSHIP IN POLITICAL TIME

Stephen Skowronek

Three general dynamics are evident in presidential history. The locus of the first is the Constitution. It links presidents past and present in a timeless and constant struggle over the definition of institutional prerogatives and suggests that although much has changed in two hundred years, the basic structure of presidential action has remained essentially the same. The locus of the second dynamic is national development. It links presidents past and present in an evolutionary sequence culminating in the expanded powers and governing responsibilities of the "modern presidency," and it suggests that the modern presidents stand apart—their shared leadership situation distinguished from that of the early presidents by the scope of governmental concerns, the complexity of national and international issues, and the sheer size of the institutional apparatus. The third dynamic is less well attended by students of the American presidency. Its locus is in political change, and it links presidents past and present at parallel junctures in "political time." [1] This third dynamic is the point of departure for our investigation.

To read American history with an eye toward the dynamics of political change is to see that within the linear sequence of national development there have been many beginnings and many endings. Periods are marked by the rise to power of new political coalitions, with one, in particular, exerting a dominant influence over the federal government. The dominant coalition operates the federal government and perpetuates its position through the development of a distinctive set of institutional arrangements and approaches to public policy questions. Once established, however, coalition interests have an enervating effect on the governing capacities of these political-institutional regimes. From the outset, conflicts among interests within the dominant coalition threaten to cause political disaffection and may weaken regime support. Then, beyond the problems posed by conflicts among established interests, more basic questions arise concerning the nature of the interests themselves. Not only does the nation change in ways that the old ruling coalition finds increasingly difficult to address, but as disaffection within the coalition makes the mobilization of political support more difficult, the regime becomes increasingly dependent on sectarian interests with myopic demands and momentary loyalties. Generally speaking, the longer a regime survives, the more its approach to national affairs becomes encumbered and distorted. Its political energies dissipate, and it becomes less competent in addressing the manifest governing demands of the day.

Thinking in terms of regime sequences rather than linear national development, one can distinguish many different political contexts for presidential leadership *within* a given historical period. Leadership situations might be distinguished by whether or not the president is affiliated with the dominant political coalition. Looking at the modern Democratic period, regime outsiders like Republicans Dwight D. Eisenhower and Richard Nixon might be said to have faced a different political problem in leading the nation than regime insiders like John F. Kennedy and Lyndon B. Johnson. Leadership situations also might be distinguished in political time, that is, by when in a regime sequence the president engages the political-institutional order. Thus, Presidents Franklin D. Roosevelt, John F. Kennedy, and Jimmy Carter—all Democrats who enjoyed Democratic majorities in Congress—may be said to have faced different problems in leading the nation as they were arrayed along a sequence of political change that encompassed the generation and degeneration of the New Deal order.

It is not difficult to relate this view of the changing relationship between the presidency and the political system to certain outstanding patterns in presidential leadership across American history. First, the presidents who traditionally make the historians' roster of America's greatest—George Washington, Thomas Jefferson, Andrew Jackson, Abraham Lincoln, Woodrow Wilson, and Franklin D. Roosevelt—all came to power in an abrupt break from a long-established political order, and each led an infusion of new political interests into control of the federal government.[2] Second, after the initial break with the past and the consolidation of a new system of governmental control, a general decline in the political effectiveness of regime insiders is notable. Take, for example, the sequence of Jeffersonians. After the galvanizing performance of Jefferson's first term, we observe increasing political division and a managerial-style presidency under James Madison. Asserting the sanctity of an indivisible Republican majority, James Monroe opened his administration to unbridled sectarianism and oversaw a debilitating fragmentation of the federal establishment. A complete political and institutional breakdown marked the shortened tenure of John Quincy Adams.

But is it possible to go beyond these general observations and elaborate a structural and temporal dimension in presidential leadership? What are the characteristic political challenges that face a leader at any given stage in a regime sequence? How is the quality of presidential performance related to the changing shape of the political-institutional order? These questions call for an investigation that breaks presidential history into regime segments and then compares leadership problems and presidential performances at similar stages in regime development across historical periods. Taking different regimes into account simultaneously, this essay will group presidents together on the basis of the parallel positions they hold in political time.

The analysis focuses on three pairs of presidents drawn from the New Deal and Jacksonian regimes: Franklin D. Roosevelt and Andrew Jackson; John F. Kennedy and James K. Polk; and Jimmy Carter and Franklin Pierce. All are Democrats and thus affiliated with the dominant coalition of their respective periods. None took a passive, caretaker view of his office. Indeed, each aspired to great national leadership. Paired comparisons have been formed by slicing into these two regime sequences at corresponding junctures and exposing a shared relationship between the presidency and the political system.

We begin with two beginnings—the presidency of Franklin D. Roosevelt and its counterpart in political time, the presidency of Andrew Jackson. Coming to power upon the displacement of an old ruling coalition, these presidents became mired in remarkably similar political struggles. Although separated by more than a century of history, they both faced the distinctive challenge of regime construction. Leadership became a matter of securing the political and institutional infrastructure of a new governmental order.

Beyond the challenges of regime construction lie the ever more perplexing problems of managing an established regime in changing times. The regime manager is constrained on one side by the political imperatives of coalition maintenance and on the other by deepening factional divisions within the ranks. Leadership does not penetrate to the basics of politics and government. It is caught up in the difficulties of satisfying regime commitments while stemming the tide of internal disaffection. Consequently, the president is tested at the level of interest control and conflict manipulation. Our examination of the manager's dilemma focuses on John F. Kennedy and his counterpart in political time, James K. Polk.

Finally, we come to the paradoxes of establishing a credible leadership posture in an enervated regime. Jimmy Carter and Franklin Pierce came to power at a time when the dominant coalition had degenerated into myopic sects that appeared impervious to the most basic problems facing the nation. Neither of these presidents penetrated to the level of managing coalition interests. Each found himself caught in the widening disjunction between established power and political legitimacy. Their affiliation with the old order in a new age turned their respective bids for leadership into awkward and superficial struggles to escape the stigma of their own irrelevance.

All six of these presidents had to grapple with the erosion of political support that inevitably comes with executive action. But, while this problem plagued them all, the initial relationship between the leader and his supporters was not the same, and the terms of presidential interaction with the political system changed sequentially from stage to stage. Looking within these pairs, we can identify performance challenges that are shared by leaders who addressed the political system at a similar juncture. Looking across the pairs, we observe an ever more awkward leadership situation, an ever more constricted universe of political action, and an ever more superficial penetration of the political system.

Jackson and Roosevelt: Political Upheaval and the Challenge of Regime Construction

The presidencies of Andrew Jackson and Franklin D. Roosevelt were both launched on the heels of a major political upheaval. Preceding the election of each, a party long established as the dominant and controlling power within the federal government had begun to flounder and fragment in an atmosphere of national crisis. Finally, the old ruling party suffered a stunning defeat at the polls, losing its dominant position in Congress as well as its control of the presidency. Jackson and Roosevelt assumed the office of chief executive with the old ruling coalition thoroughly discredited by the electorate and, at least temporarily, displaced from political power. They each led a movement of general discontent with the previously established order of things into control of the federal establishment.

Of the two, Jackson's election in 1828 presents this crisis of the old order in a more purely political form. New economic and social conflicts had been festering in America since the financial panic of

1819, but Jackson's campaign gained its special meaning from the confusion and outrage unleashed by the election of 1824. In that election, the Congressional Caucus collapsed as the engine of national political unity. The once monolithic Republican party disintegrated into warring factions during the campaign, and after an extended period of political maneuvering, an alliance between John Quincy Adams and Henry Clay secured Adams a presidential victory in the House of Representatives despite Jackson's pluralities in both popular and electoral votes. The Adams administration was immediately and permanently engulfed in charges of conspiracy, intrigue, and profligacy in high places. Jackson, the hero of 1815, became the hero wronged of 1824. The Jackson campaign of 1828 launched a broadside assault on the degrading "corruption of manners" that had consumed Washington and on the conspiracy of interests that had captured the federal government from the people.[3]

In the election of 1932, the collapse of the old ruling party dovetailed with and was overshadowed by the Depression. The Democratic party of 1932 offered nothing if not hope for economic recovery, and in this Roosevelt's candidacy found its special meaning almost in spite of the candidate's own rather conservative campaign rhetoric. The Depression had made a mockery of President Herbert Hoover's early identification of his party with prosperity, and the challenge of formulating a response to the crisis broke the Republican ranks and threw the party into disarray. The Roosevelt appeal was not grounded in substantive proposals or even partisan ideology, but in a widespread perception of Republican incompetence, if not intransigence, in the face of national economic calamity. As future Secretary of State Cordell Hull outlined Roosevelt's leadership situation in January 1933: "No political party at Washington [is] in control of Congress or even itself . . . there [is] no cohesive nationwide sentiment behind any fundamental policy or idea today. The election was an overwhelmingly negative affair. . . ."[4]

Thus, Jackson and Roosevelt each engaged a political system cut from its moorings by a wave of popular discontent. Old commitments of ideology and interest suddenly had been thrown into question. New commitments were as yet only vague appeals to some essential American value (republican virtue, economic opportunity) that had been lost in the indulgences of the old order. With old political alliances in disarray and new political energies infused into Congress, these presidents had an extraordinary opportunity to set a new course in public policy and to redefine the terms of national political debate. They recaptured the experience of being first.

But this situation is not without its characteristic leadership challenge. The leader who is propelled into office by a political upheaval in governmental control ultimately must confront the imperatives of establishing a new order in government and politics. Naturally enough, this challenge is presented by the favored interests and residual institutional supports of the old order, and, once posed, the unencumbered leadership environment that was created by the initial break with the past quickly fades. As the nation and the government begin to redivide themselves politically, the president is faced with the choice of either abandoning his revolution or consolidating it with structural reforms. Situated just beyond the old order, presidential leadership crystallizes as a problem of regime construction.

The leader as regime builder grapples with the fundamentals of political regeneration—institutional reconstruction and party building. He must undermine the institutional support for opposition interests, restructure institutional relations between state and society, and secure the dominant position of a new political coalition. Success in these tasks is hardly guaranteed. Wilson had to abandon this course when the Republicans reunited and preempted his efforts to broaden the Democratic base. Lincoln was assassinated just as the most critical questions of party building and institutional reconstruction were to be addressed. This disaster ushered in a devastating confrontation between president and Congress and left the emergent Republican regime hanging in a politically precarious position for the next three decades. Even Jackson and Roosevelt—America's quintessential regime builders—were not uniformly successful. Neither could keep the dual offensives of party building and institutional reconstruction moving in tandem long enough to complete them both.

Andrew Jackson

Republican renewal was the keynote of Jackson's first term. The president was determined to ferret out the political and institutional corruption that he believed had befallen the Jeffersonian regime. This meant purging incompetence and profligacy from the civil service, initiating fiscal retrenchment in national projects, and reviving federalism as a system of vigorous state-based government.[5] Jackson's appeal for a return to Jefferson's original ideas about government certainly posed a potent indictment of the recent state of national affairs and a clear challenge to long-established interests. But there was a studied political restraint in his initial program that defied the attempts of his opponents to characterize it as revolutionary.[6] Indeed, while holding out an attractive standard with which to rally supporters, Jackson was careful to yield his opposition precious little ground upon which to mount an effective counterattack. He used the initial upheaval in governmental control to cultivate an unreproachable political position as the nation's crusader in reform.

Significantly, the transformation of Jackson's presidency from a moral crusade into a radical program of political reconstruction was instigated, not by the president himself, but by the premier institution of the old regime, the Bank of the United States.[7] At the time of Jackson's election, the Bank was long established as both the most powerful institution in America and the most important link between state and society. It dominated the nation's credit system, maintained extensive ties of material interest with political elites, and actively involved itself in electoral campaigns to sustain its own political support. It embodied all the problems of institutional corruption and political degradation toward which Jackson addressed his administration. The Bank was a concentration of political and economic power able to tyrannize over people's lives and to control the will of their elected representatives.

During his first years in office, Jackson spoke vaguely of the need for some modification of the Bank's charter. But since the charter did not expire until 1836, there appeared to be plenty of time to consider appropriate changes. Indeed, although Jackson was personally inclined toward radical hard-money views, he recognized the dangers of impromptu tinkering with an institution so firmly entrenched in the economic life of the nation and hesitated at embracing untested alternatives. Moreover, Jackson foresaw an overwhelming reelection endorsement for his early achievements and knew that to press the Bank issue before the election of 1832 could only hurt him politically. After a rout of Henry Clay, the architect of the Bank and the obvious challenger in the upcoming campaign, Jackson would have a free hand to deal with the institution as he saw fit.

But Jackson's apparent commitment to some kind of Bank reform and the obvious political calculations surrounding the issue led the Bank president, Nicholas Biddle, to join Henry Clay in a preelection push to recharter the institution without any reforms a full four years before its charter expired. Biddle feared for the Bank's future in Jackson's second term. Clay needed to break Jackson's unreproachable image as a national leader and to expose his political weaknesses. An early recharter bill promised to splinter Jackson's support in Congress. If the president signed the bill, his integrity as a reformer would be destroyed; if he vetoed it, he would provide a sorely needed coherence to anti-Jackson sentiment.

As expected, the recharter bill threw Jackson enthusiasts into a quandary and passed through Congress. The president saw the bill not only as a blatant attempt by those attached to the old order to destroy him politically, but also as proof certain that the Bank's political power threatened the very survival of republican government. He accepted the challenge and set out to destroy the Bank. Pushed beyond the possibility of controlling the modification of extant institutions without significant opposition, Jackson had to press for an irrevocable break with established governmental arrangements. The 1828 crusade for republican renewal became in 1832 an all-fronts offensive for the establishment of an entirely new political and institutional order.

The president's veto of the recharter bill clearly marked this transition. The political themes of 1828 were turned against the Bank with a vengeance. Jackson defined his stand as one that would extricate the federal government from the interests of the privileged and protect the states from encroaching federal domination. He appealed directly to the interests of the nation's farmers, mechanics, and laborers, claiming that this great political majority stood to lose control over the government to the influential few. This call to the "common man" for a defense of the republic had long been a Jacksonian theme, but now it carried the portent of sweeping governmental changes. Jackson not only was declaring open war on the premier institution of the old order, he was challenging long-settled questions of governance. The Supreme Court, for example, had upheld the constitutionality of the Bank decades before. Jackson's veto challenged the assumption of executive deference to the Court and asserted presidential authority to make an independent and contrary judgment about judicial decisions. Jackson also challenged executive deference to Congress, perhaps the central operating principle of the Jeffersonian regime. His veto message went beyond constitutional objections to the recharter bill and asserted the president's authority to make an independent evaluation of the social, economic, and political implications of congressional action. In all, the message was a regime builder's manifesto that looked toward the fusing of a broad-based political coalition, the shattering of established institutional power relationships between state and society, and the transformation of power relationships within the government itself.

Of course, regime construction requires more than a declaration of presidential intent. Jackson had his work cut out for him at the beginning of his second term. His victory over Clay in 1832 was certainly sweeping enough to reaffirm his leadership position, and having used the veto as a campaign document, Jackson could claim a strong mandate to complete the work it outlined. But the veto also had been used as an issue by Clay, and the threat to the Bank was fueling organized political opposition in all sections of the country.[8] More important still, the Senate, which had been shaky enough in Jackson's first term, moved completely beyond his control in 1833, and his party's majority in the House returned in a highly volatile condition. Finally, the Bank's charter still had three years to run, and Bank President Biddle had every intention of exploiting Jackson's political vulnerabilities in hope of securing his own future.

Jackson clearly needed to neutralize the significance of the Bank for the remainder of its charter and to prevent any new recharter movement from emerging in Congress. His plan was to have the deposits of the federal government removed from the Bank on his own authority and transferred to a select group of politically friendly state banks. The president would thus circumvent his opponents and, at the same time, offer the nation an alternative banking system. The new banking structure had several potential advantages. It promised to work under the direct supervision of the executive branch, to forge direct institutional connections between the presidency and local centers of political power, and to secure broad political support against a revival of the national bank.

Jackson's plan faced formidable opposition from the Treasury Department, the Senate, and most of all from the Bank of the United States. Biddle responded to the removal of federal deposits with an abrupt and severe curtailment of loans. By squeezing the nation into a financial panic, Biddle hoped to turn public opinion against Jackson. The Senate followed suit with a formal censure of the president, denouncing his pretentions to independent action on the presumption of a direct mandate from the people.

The so-called "Panic Session" of Congress (1833-1834) posed the ultimate test of Jackson's resolve to forge a new regime. Success hinged on consolidating the Democratic party in Congress and reaffirming its control over the national government. The president moved quickly to deflect blame for the panic onto the Bank. Destroying Biddle's credibility, he was able by the spring of 1834 to solidify Democratic support in the House and gain an endorsement of his actions (and implicitly, his authority to act) from that chamber. Then, undertaking a major grass-roots, party-building effort in the midterm elections of 1834, Jackson and his political lieutenants were able to secure a loyal Democratic majority in the Senate. The struggle was over, and in a final acknowledgment of the legitimacy of the new order, the Democratic Senate expunged its censure of the president from the record.

But even as Congress was falling into line, the limitations of the president's achievement were manifesting themselves throughout the nation at large. Jackson had shattered the old governmental order, consolidated a new political party behind his policies, secured that party's control over the entire federal establishment, and redefined the position of the presidency in its relations with Congress, the courts, the states, and the electorate. But his institutional alternative for reconstructing financial relations between state and society—the state deposit system—was proving a dismal failure.

In truth, Jackson had latched onto the deposit banking scheme out of political necessity as much as principle. The president had been caught between his opponents' determination to save the Bank and his supporters' needs for a clear and attractive alternative to it. Opposition to Biddle and Clay merged with opposition to any national banking structure, and the interim experiment with state banking quickly became a political commitment. Unfortunately, the infusion of federal deposits into the pet state banks fueled a speculative boom and threatened a major financial collapse.

Hoping to stem the tide of this disaster, the Treasury Department began to choose banks of deposit less for their political soundness than for their financial soundness, and Jackson threw his support behind a gradual conversion to hard money. In the end, however, the president was forced to accept the grim irony of his success as a regime builder. Congress had moved solidly behind him, but in so doing members had begun to see for themselves the special political attractions of the state deposit system. With the passage of the Deposit Act of 1836, Congress expanded the number of state depositories and explicitly limited executive discretion in controlling them.[9]

Thus, although Jackson had reconstructed American government and politics, he merely substituted one irresponsible and uncontrollable financial system for another. Institutional ties between state and society emerged as the weak link in the new order. Jackson's chosen successor, Martin Van Buren, understood this all too well as he struggled to extricate the federal government from the state banks in the midst of the nation's first great depression.

Franklin D. Roosevelt

As a political personality, the moralistic, vindictive, and tortured Jackson stands in marked contrast to the pragmatic, engaging, and buoyant Franklin D. Roosevelt. Yet, their initial triumphs over long-established ruling parties and the sustained popular enthusiasm that accompanied their triumphs propelled each into grappling with a similar set of leadership challenges. By late 1934, Roosevelt himself seemed to sense the parallels. To Vice President John Nance Garner he wrote: "The more I learn about Andy Jackson, the more I love him." [10]

The interesting thing about this remark is its timing. In 1934 and 1935, Roosevelt faced mounting discontent with the emergency program he had implemented from the favored interests of the old order. Moreover, he saw that the residual bulwark of institutional support for that order was capable of simply sweeping his programs aside. Like Jackson in 1832, Roosevelt was being challenged either to reconstruct the political and institutional foundations of the national government or to abandon the leadership initiatives he had sustained virtually without opposition in his early years in power.

The revival of the economy was the keynote of Roosevelt's early program.[11] Although collectivist in approach and bold in their assertion of a positive role for the federal government, the policies of the early New Deal did not present a broadside challenge to long-established political and economic interests. Roosevelt adopted the role of a bipartisan national leader reaching out to all interests in a time of crisis. He carefully courted the southern Bourbons, who controlled the old Democratic party, and directly incorporated big business into the government's recovery program. The problem was not that Roosevelt's program ignored the interests attached to and supported by the governmental arrangements of the past, but that it implicated those interests in a broader coalition. The New Deal bestowed legitimacy on the interests of organized labor, the poor, and the unemployed, leaving southern Bourbons and northern industrialists feeling threatened and increasingly insecure.

This sense of unease manifested itself politically in the organization of the American Liberty League in the summer of 1934. The league mounted an aggressive assault on Roosevelt and the New Deal, but Roosevelt's party received a resounding endorsement in the midterm elections, actually broadening the base of enthusiastic New Dealers in Congress. The congressional elections vividly demonstrated the futility of political opposition, but in the spring of 1935, a more potent adversary arose within the government itself. The Supreme Court, keeper of the rules for the old regime, handed down a series of anti-New Deal decisions. The most important of these nullified the centerpiece of Roosevelt's recovery program, the National Industrial Recovery Act. With the American Liberty League sorting out friend from foe and the Court pulling the rug out from under the cooperative approach to economic recovery, Roosevelt turned his administration toward structural reform. If he could no longer lead all interests toward economic recovery, he could still secure the interests of a great political majority within a new governmental order.

Roosevelt began the transition from national leader to regime builder with a considerable advantage over Jackson. He could restructure institutional relations between state and society simply by reaching out to the radical and irrepressibly zealous 74th Congress (1935-1937) and offering it sorely needed coherence and direction. The result was a "second" New Deal. The federal government extended new services and permanent institutional supports to organized labor, the small businessman, the aged, the unemployed, and later, the rural poor. At the same time, the president revealed a new approach to big business and the affluent by pressing for tighter regulation and graduated taxation.[12]

In their scope and vision, these achievements far surpassed the makeshift and flawed arrangements that Jackson had improvised to restructure institutional relations between state and society in the Bank war. But Roosevelt's comparatively early and more thoroughgoing success on this score proved a dubious advantage in subsequent efforts to consolidate the new order. After his overwhelming reelection victory in 1936, Roosevelt pressed a series of consolidation initiatives. Like Jackson in his second term, he began with an effort to neutralize the remaining threat within the government.

Roosevelt's target, of course, was the Supreme Court. He was wise not to follow Jackson's example in the Bank war by launching a direct ideological attack on the Court. After all, Roosevelt was challenging a constitutional branch of government and hardly could succeed in labeling that branch a threat to the survival of the republic. The president decided instead to kill his institutional opponent with kindness. He called for an increase in the size of the Court, ostensibly to ease the burden on the elder justices and increase overall efficiency. Unfortunately, the real stakes of the contest never were made explicit, and the chief justice deflected the attack by simply denying the need for help. More importantly, the Court, unlike the Bank, did not further exacerbate the situation. Instead it reversed course in the middle of the battle and displayed a willingness to accept the policies of the second New Deal.

The Court's turnabout was a great victory for the new regime, but it eliminated even the implicit justification for Roosevelt's proposed judicial reforms. With the constituent services of the New Deal secure, Congress had little reason to challenge the integrity of the Court. Bound by his own efficiency arguments, Roosevelt did not withdraw his proposal. Although stalwart liberals stood by the president to the end, traditional Democratic conservatives deserted him. A bipartisan opposition took open ground against Roosevelt, defeated the "court packing" scheme, and divided the ranks of the New Deal coalition. It was a rebuke every bit as portentous as the formal censure of Jackson by the Senate.

With Roosevelt, as with Jackson, the third congressional election of his tenure called forth a major party-building initiative. Stung by the Court defeat, the president moved to reaffirm his hold over the Democratic party and to strengthen its liberal commitments. Ironically, this effort was handicapped by the sweeping character of Roosevelt's early successes. Unlike Jackson in 1834, Roosevelt in 1938 could not point to any immediate threat to his governing coalition. The liberal program was already in place. The Court had capitulated, and despite deep fissures manifested during the Court battle, the overwhelming Democratic majorities in Congress gave no indication of abandoning the New Deal. Even the southern delegations in Congress maintained majority support for Roosevelt's domestic reform initiatives.[13] Under these conditions, party building took on an aura of presidential self-indulgence. Although enormously important from the standpoint of future regime coherence, at the time it looked like heavy-handed and selective punishment for the ungrateful defectors. In this guise, it evoked little popular support, let alone enthusiasm.

The party-building initiative failed. Virtually all of the conservative Democrats targeted for defeat were reelected, and the Republicans showed a resurgence of strength. As two-party politics returned to the national scene, the division within the majority party between the old southern conservatism and the new liberal orthodoxy became more ominous than ever.

Despite these setbacks, Roosevelt's effectiveness as a regime builder still was not completely exhausted. A final effort at strengthening the new order met with considerable success. In 1939, Roosevelt received congressional approval for a package of administrative reforms that promised to bolster the position of the president in his relations with the other branches of government. Following the precepts of his Commission on Administrative Management, the president asked for new authority to control the vastly expanded federal bureaucracy and for new executive offices to provide planning and direction for governmental operations. Congress responded with a modest endorsement. While deflating Roosevelt's grand design, it clearly acknowledged the new governing demands of the large federal bureaucracy he had forged. The establishment of the Executive Office of the President closed the New Deal with a fitting symbol of the new state of affairs.[14]

Polk and Kennedy:
The Dilemmas of Interest Management in an Established Regime

The administrations of Jackson and Roosevelt shared much in both the political conditions of leadership and the challenges undertaken. The initial upheaval, the ensuing political confusion, and the enduring popular enthusiasm for reform set the stage for America's quintessential regime-building presidencies. Opposition from the favored interests of the old order and their residual institutional supports eventually pushed these presidents from an original program to meet the immediate crisis at hand into structural reforms that promised to place institutional relations between state and society on an entirely new footing. After a second landslide election, Jackson and Roosevelt each moved to consolidate their new order by eliminating the institutional opposition and forging a more coherent base of party support. As the nation redivided politically, they secured a new ruling coalition and institutionalized a new position of power for the presidency itself.

It is evident from a comparison of these performances that where Rooseveltian regime building was triumphant, Jacksonian regime building faltered and vice versa: Roosevelt left institutional relations between state and society thoroughly reconstructed but his performance as a party builder was weak and his achievement flawed; Jackson left institutional relations between state and society in a dangerous disarray but his performance and achievement as a party builder remain unparalleled. The more important point, however, lies beyond these comparisons. It is that few presidents have either the incentive or the opportunity to address the political system at the level of institutional reconstruction and party building. Most presidents must use their skills and resources—however extensive these may be—to work within an already established governmental order.

The successful regime builder leaves in his wake a more constricted universe for presidential action. To his partisan successors, in
particular, he leaves the difficult task of keeping faith with a ruling coalition. In an established regime, the majority-party president comes to
power as a representative of the dominant political alliance and is
expected to offer a representative's service in delegate style. Commitments of ideology and interest are all too clear, and the fusion of
national political legitimacy with established power relationships argues against any attempt to tinker with the basics of government and
politics. The leader is challenged not to break down the old order and
forge a new one, but to complete the agenda, adapt the vision, and de-
fuse the potentially explosive choices among competing obligations. He
is partner to a highly structured regime politics, and to make the
partnership work, he must assert preemptive control over impending
disruptions.

The presidencies of James K. Polk and John F. Kennedy clearly
illustrate the problems and prospects of leadership circumscribed by the
challenge of managing an established coalition. Both of these men came
to the presidency after an interval of opposition-party control and
divided government. The intervening years had seen some significant
changes in the tenor of public policy, but there had been no systemic
transformations of government and politics. Ushering in a second era of
majority-party government, Polk and Kennedy promised to revive the
commitments and revitalize the vision of the regime founder.

Neither Polk nor Kennedy could claim the leadership of any
major party faction. Indeed, their credibility as regime managers rested
largely on their second rank status in regular party circles. Each
schooled himself in the task of allaying mutual suspicions among the
great centers of party strength. Their nominations to the presidency
were the result of careful posturing around the conflicts that divided
contending party factions. What they lacked in deep political loyalties,
they made up for with their freedom to cultivate the support of all interests.

Once the office was attained, the challenge of interest management
was magnified. Each of these presidents had accepted one especially
virulent bit of orthodoxy that claimed majority support within the party
as a necessary part of the new regime agenda. Their ability to endorse
their party's most divisive enthusiasm (Texas annexation, civil rights)
without losing their broad base of credibility within it was fitting
testimony to their early education in the art of aggressive maintenance.
But their mediating skills did not alter the fact that each came into of-

CARL A. RUDISILL LIBRARY
LENOIR RHYNE COLLEGE

fice with a clear commitment to act on an issue which had long threatened to split the party apart. In addition, Polk and Kennedy each won astonishingly close elections. There was no clear mandate for action, no discernible tide of national discontent, no mass repudiation of what had gone before. The hairbreadth Democratic victories of 1844 and 1960 suggested that the opposition could continue to make a serious claim to the presidency and reinforced an already highly developed sense of executive dependence on all parts of the party coalition. With maintenance at a premium and an ideological rupture within the ranks at hand, Polk and Kennedy carried the full weight of the leadership dilemma that confronts the majority-party president of an established regime.

James K. Polk

For the Democratic party of 1844, the long-festering issue was the annexation of Texas with its implicit threat of prompting a war of aggression for the expansion of slave territory.[15] Even Andrew Jackson, an ardent nationalist, had eyed Texas as forbidden fruit. Despite his passion for annexation, Old Hickory steered clear of the issue during the last years of his presidency in the certain knowledge that it would divide along sectional lines the national party he had just consolidated.[16] Democratic loyalists followed Jackson's lead until 1843 when the party-less "mongrel president" John Tyler, desperate to build an independent political base of support for himself, latched onto the annexation issue and presented a formal proposal on the subject to Congress. With Texas finally pushed to the forefront, expansionist fever heated up in the South and the West and antislavery agitation accelerated in the North.

Jackson's political nightmare became reality on the eve of his party's nominating convention in 1844. Martin Van Buren, Jackson's successor to the presidency in 1837 and still the nominal head of the Democracy, risked an all but certain nomination by coming out against the immediate annexation of Texas. The New Yorker's pronouncement fused a formidable opposition in the southern and western wings of the party and left the convention deadlocked through eight ballots. With Van Buren holding a large bloc of delegates but unable to get the leaders of the South and West to relinquish the necessary two-thirds majority, it became clear that only a "new man" could save the party from disaster. That man had to be sound on Texas without being openly opposed to Van Buren. On the ninth ballot, James Knox Polk became the Democratic nominee.

Polk was a second-choice candidate, and he knew it. As leader of the Democratic party in Tennessee, he had the unimpeachable credentials of a stalwart friend of Andrew Jackson. He had served loyally as floor leader of the House during the critical days of the Bank war, and he had gone on to win his state's governorship. But after Polk tried and failed to gain his party's vice-presidential nomination in 1840, his political career fell on hard times. Calculating his strategy for a political comeback in 1844, Polk made full use of his second-rank standing in high party circles. Again he posed as the perfect vice-presidential candidate and cultivated his ties to Van Buren. Knowing that this time Van Buren's nomination would be difficult, Polk also understood the special advantages of being a Texas enthusiast with Van Buren connections. As soon as that calculation paid off, Polk ventured another. In accepting the presidential nomination, he pledged that, if elected, he would not seek a second term. Although he thus declared himself a lame duck even before he was elected, Polk reckoned that he would not serve any time in office at all unless the frustrated party giants in all sections of the nation expended every last ounce of energy for the campaign, which they might not do if it meant foreclosing their own prospects for eight years.[17]

The one-term declaration was a bid for party unity and a pledge of party maintenance. But the deepening divisions that were exposed at the convention of 1844 and their uncertain resolution in a Texas platform and a dark-horse nomination suggested that the party was likely to chew itself up under a passive caretaker presidency. If Polk was to avoid a disastrous schism in the party of Jackson, he would have to order, balance, and service the major contending interests in turn. He would have to enlist each contingent within the party in support of the policy interests of all the others. Polk submerged himself in a high-risk strategy of aggressive maintenance in which the goal was to satisfy each faction of his party enough to keep the whole from falling apart. The scheme was at once pragmatic and holistic, hard-headed and fantastic. The most startling thing of all is how well it worked.

The president opened his administration (appropriately enough) with a declaration that he would "know no divisions of the Democratic party." He promised "equal and exact justice to every portion."[18] His first action, however, indicated that the going would be rough. Scrutinizing the cabinet selection process, Van Buren judged that New York (whose electoral votes had put Polk over the top) had not had its interests sufficiently recognized. The frustrated ex-president thought he saw a determination on the new president's part to turn the party toward the slave South. Polk tried to appease Van Buren with other patronage offers, but relations between them did not improve. From the outset Van Buren's loyalty was tinged with a heavy dose of suspicion.

The outcry over patronage distribution indicated that any action the president took would evoke charges of favoritism. Van Buren's was but the first in an incessant barrage of such charges.[19] But Polk was not powerless in the face of disaffection. He had an irresistible agenda for party government to bolster his precarious political position.

Polk's program elaborated the theme of equal justice for all coalition interests. On the domestic side, he reached out to the South with support for a lower tariff, to the Northwest with support for land price reform, to the Northeast by endorsing a warehouse storage system advantageous to import merchants, and to the old Jackson radicals with a commitment to a return to hard money and a reinstatement of the independent Treasury. (Van Buren had dedicated his entire administration to establishing the independent Treasury as a solution to Jackson's banking dilemma, but his work had been undermined in the intervening four years.) It was in foreign affairs, however, that the president placed the highest hopes for his administration. Superimposed on his carefully balanced program of party service in the domestic arena was a missionary embrace of "Manifest Destiny." Reaching out to the South, Polk promised to annex Texas; to the Northwest, he promised Oregon; and to bind the whole nation together, he made a secret promise to himself to acquire California. In all, the president would complete the Jacksonian program of party services and fuse popular passions in an irresistible jingoistic campaign to extend the Jacksonian Republic across the continent.

Driven by a keen sense of the dual imperatives of maintenance and leadership, Polk embarked on a course of action designed to transform the nation without changing its politics. Party loyalty was the key to success, but it would take more than just a series of favorable party votes to make this strategy of aggressive maintenance work. The sequence, pace, and symbolism of Polk's initiatives had to be assiduously controlled and coordinated with difficult foreign negotiations so that the explosive moral issues inherent in the program would not enter the debate. Sectional paranoia and ideological heresies had to be held in constant check. Mutual self-interest had to remain at the forefront so that reciprocal party obligations could be reinforced. Polk's program was much more than a laundry list of party commitments. If he did not get everything he promised in the order he promised it, he risked a major party rupture. Here, at the level of executive management and interest control, the president faltered.

After the patronage tiff with Van Buren demonstrated Polk's problems with the eastern radicals, disaffection over the Oregon boundary settlement exposed his difficulties in striking an agreeable balance between western and southern expansionists. The president moved forward immediately and simultaneously on his promises to acquire Oregon and Texas. In each case he pressed an aggressive, indeed belligerent, border claim. He demanded "all of Oregon" (extending north to the 54° 40′ parallel) from Great Britain and "Greater Texas" (extending south below the Nueces River to the Rio Grande) from Mexico.

The pledge to get "all of Oregon" unleashed a tidal wave of popular enthusiasm in the Northwest. But Great Britain refused to play according to the presidential plan, and a potent peace movement spread across the South and the East out of fear of impending war over the Oregon boundary. Polk used the belligerence of the "54° 40′ or fight" faction to counter the peace movement and to prod the British into coming to terms, but he knew he could not risk war on that front. An impending war with Mexico over the Texas boundary promised to yield California in short order, but a war with both Mexico and Great Britain promised disaster.

When the British finally agreed to settle the Oregon boundary at the 49th parallel, Polk accepted the compromise. Then, after an appropriate display of Mexican aggression on the Texas border, he asked Congress for a declaration of war against that nation. Abandoned, the 54° 40′ men turned on the president, mercilessly accusing him of selling out to the South and picking on defenseless Mexico instead of standing honorably against the British. A huge part of the Oregon territory had been added to the Union, but a vociferous bloc of westerners now joined the Van Burenites in judging the president to be willfully deceptive and dangerously prosouthern. Polk had miscalculated both British determination and western pride. His accomplishment deviated from the pace and scope of his grand design and in so doing undermined the delicate party balance.

Polk's designs were further complicated by the effects of wartime sensibilities on his carefully balanced legislative program. The independent Treasury and warehouse storage bills were enacted easily, but old matters of principle and simple matters of interest were not enough to calm agitated eastern Democrats. They demanded the president's assurance that he was not involved in a war of conquest in the

Southwest. Polk responded with a vague and evasive definition of war aims. There was little else he could do to ease suspicions.

More portentous still was the influence of the tariff initiative on wartime politics. Polk had to court northwestern Democrats to make up for expected eastern defections on a vote for a major downward revision of rates. To do so, he not only held out his promised land price reform as an incentive to bring debate to a close, he also withheld his objections to a legislative initiative brewing among representatives of the South and West to develop the Mississippi River system. The northwestern- ers swallowed their pride over Oregon in hopeful expectation and threw their support behind the tariff bill.

After the tariff bill was enacted, Polk vetoed the internal improve- ment bill. It had never been a part of his program, and it was an offense to all orthodox Jacksonians. Needless to say, the deviousness of the president's maneuverings was an offense to the West that all but eclipsed the veto's stalwart affirmation of Jacksonian principles. To make matters worse, the land bill failed. The president made good his pledge to press the measure, but he could not secure enactment. Burned three times after offering loyal support to southern interests, the northwesterners no longer were willing to heed the counsels of mutual restraint. The president's effort to bring the war to a quick and triumphant conclusion provided them with their opportunity to strike back.

The war with Mexico was in fact only a few months old, but that already was too long for the president and his party. To speed the peace, Polk decided to ask Congress for a $2 million appropriation to settle the Texas boundary dispute and to pay "for any concessions which may be made by Mexico." This open offer of money for land was the first clear indication that the United States was engaged in— perhaps had consciously provoked—a war of conquest in the South- west. With it, the latent issue of 1844 manifested itself with a vengeance. Northern Democrats, faced with the growing threat of antislavery agitation at home, saw unequal treatment in the adminis- tration's handling of matters of interest, intolerable duplicity in presidential action, and an insufferable southern bias in national policy. They were ready to take their stand on matters of principle.

It is ironic that Polk's implicit acknowledgment of the drive for California, with its promise of fulfilling the nationalist continental vision, would fan the fires of sectional conflict. Surely he had intended just the opposite. The president was, in fact, correct in calculating that no section of the party would oppose the great national passion for expansion to the Pacific. But he simply could not stem the tide of party disaffection in the East, and unfulfilled expectations fueled disaffection in the West. He was thus left to watch in dismay as the disaffected joined forces to take their revenge on the South.

Northern Democrats loyally offered to support the president's effort to buy peace and land, but added a demand that slavery be prohibited from entering any of the territory that might thus be acquired. This condition, known as the "Wilmot Proviso" after Pennsylvania Democrat David Wilmot, splintered the party along the dreaded sectional cleavage. An appropriation bill with the proviso was passed in the House, but it failed in the Senate when an effort to remove the proviso was filibustered successfully. Now it was Polk's turn to be bitter. In a grim confession of the failure of his grand design, he claimed that he could not comprehend "what connection slavery had with making peace with Mexico." [20]

Ultimately, Polk got his peace with Mexico, and with it he added California and the greater Southwest to the Union. He also delivered on tariff revision, the independent Treasury, the warehouse storage system, Oregon, and Texas. Interest management by Polk had extorted a monumental program of party service from established sources of power in remarkably short order. Indeed, except for the conclusion of peace with Mexico, everything had been put in place between the spring of 1845 and the summer of 1846. But the Jacksonian party was ruptured in the very course of enacting this most orthodox of party programs. Polk's monument to Jacksonian nationalism proved a breeding ground for sectional heresy.

The failure of interest management manifested itself in political disaster for the Democratic party. By the fall of 1846, the New York party had divided into two irreconcilable camps, with Van Buren leading the radicals who were sympathetic to the Wilmot Proviso and opposed to the administration. While Polk maintained an official stance of neutrality toward the schism, party regulars rallied behind Lewis Cass, a westerner opposed to the proviso. Cass's alternative—"popular" or "squatter sovereignty" in the territories—promised to hold together the larger portion of the majority party by absolving the federal government of any role in resolving the questions of slavery extension and regional balance that were raised by Polk's transformation of the nation. When the Democrats nominated Cass in 1848, the Van Buren delegation bolted the convention. Joining "Conscience Whigs" and "Liberty Party" men, they formed the Free Soil Party, dedicated it to the principles of the Wilmot Proviso, and nominated Van Buren as their presidential candidate.[21]

After the convention, Polk abandoned his studied neutrality. In the waning months of his administration, he withdrew administration favors from Free-Soil sympathizers and threw his support behind the party regulars.[22] But it was Van Buren who had the last word. Four years after putting aside personal defeat, loyally supporting the party, and electing Polk, he emerged as the leader of the "heretics" and defeated Cass.

John F. Kennedy

John F. Kennedy had every intention of spending eight years in the White House, but this ambition only compounded the leadership dilemma inherent in his initial political situation. Kennedy's presidential campaign harkened back to Rooseveltian images of direction and energy in government. It stigmatized Republican rule as a lethargic, aimless muddle, and roused the people with a promise to "get the country moving again." At the same time, however, the party of Roosevelt maintained its awkward division between northern liberals and southern conservatives. The candidate assiduously courted both wings, and the narrowness of his victory reinforced his debts to each. The president's prospects for eight years in the White House seemed to hinge on whether or not he could, in his first four, vindicate the promise of vigorous national leadership without shattering an already fractured political base.

Kennedy's "New Frontier" was eminently suited to the demands of aggressive maintenance. It looked outward toward placing a man on the moon and protecting the free world from communist aggression. It looked inward toward pragmatic adaptations and selective adjustments of the New Deal consensus. Leadership in the international arena would fuse the entire nation together behind bold demonstrations of American power and determination. Leadership in the domestic arena would contain party conflict through presidential management and executive-controlled initiatives.

This leadership design shared more in common with Polk's pursuits than a frontier imagery. Both presidents gave primacy to foreign enthusiasms and hoped that the nation would do the same. Facing a politically divided people and an internally factionalized party, they set out to tap the unifying potential of America's missionary stance in the world and to rivet national attention on aggressive (even provocative) international adventures. By so doing, they claimed the high ground as men of truly national vision. At the same time, each countered deepening conflicts of principle within the ruling coalition with an attempt to balance interests. They were engaged in a constant struggle to mute the passions that divided their supporters and stem the tide of coalition disaffection. Resisting the notion of irreconcilable differences within the ranks, Polk and Kennedy held out their support to all interests and demanded in return the acquiescence of each in executive determination of the range, substance, and timing of policy initiatives.

Of course, there were notable differences in the way these presidents approached regime management. Kennedy, who was not unaware of Polk's failings, avoided Polk's tactics.[23] Polk had gone after as much as possible as quickly as possible for as many as possible in the hope that conflicts among interests could be submerged through the ordered satisfaction of each. Kennedy seemed to feel that conflicts could be avoided best by refraining from unnecessarily divisive action. He was more circumspect in his choice of initiatives and more cautious in their pursuit. Interest balance was translated into legislative restraint and aggressive maintenance into contained advocacy. Kennedy's "politics of expectation" kept fulfillment of the liberal agenda at the level of anticipation.[24]

At the heart of Kennedy's political dilemma was the long-festering issue of civil rights for black Americans. Roosevelt had seen the fight for civil rights coming, but he refused to make it his own, fearing the devastating effect it would have on the precarious sectional balance in his newly established party coalition.[25] Harry S. Truman had seen the fight break out and temporarily rupture the party in 1948.[26] His response was a balance of executive amelioration and legislative caution. When the Republicans made gains in southern cities during the 1950s, the prudent course Truman had outlined appeared more persuasive than ever. But by 1961, black migration into northern cities, Supreme Court support for civil rights demands, and an ever more aggressive civil rights movement in the South had made it increasingly difficult for a Democratic president to resist a more definitive commitment.

In his early campaign for the presidential nomination, Kennedy developed a posture of inoffensive support on civil rights.[27] While keeping himself abreast of the liberal orthodoxy, he held back from leadership and avoided pressing the cause upon southern conservatives. Such maneuvering became considerably more difficult at the party' convention of 1960. The liberal-controlled platform committee presented a civil rights plank that all but committed the nominee to take the offensive. It pledged presidential leadership on behalf of new legislation, vigorous enforcement of existing laws, and reforms in congressional procedures to remove impediments to such action. Adding insult to injury, the plank lent party sanction to the civil rights demonstrations that had been accelerating throughout the South.

Although the Democratic platform tied Kennedy to the cause that had ruptured the party in 1948, it did not dampen his determination to hold onto the South. Once nominated, he reached out to the offended region and identified himself with more traditional Democratic strategies. Indeed, by offering the vice-presidential nomination to Lyndon Johnson, he risked a serious offense to the left. Johnson was not only the South's first choice and Kennedy's chief rival for the presidential nomination, but his national reputation was punctuated by conspicuous efforts on behalf of ameliorative civil rights action in the Senate. Kennedy himself seems to have been a bit surprised by Johnson's acceptance of second place. The liberals were disheartened.[28] Together, however, Kennedy and Johnson were to make a formidable team of regime managers. Riding the horns of their party's dilemma, they balanced the boldest Democratic commitment ever on civil rights with a determination not to lose the support of its most passionate opponents. Their narrow victory owed as much to those who were promised a new level of action as to those promised continued moderation.

The president's inaugural and State of the Union addresses directed national attention to imminent international dangers and America's world responsibilities. Civil rights received only passing mention. Stressing the need for containment in the international arena, these speeches also reflected the president's commitment to containment in the domestic arena. In the months before the inauguration, Kennedy had decided to keep civil rights off the legislative agenda. Instead, he would prod Congress along on other liberal issues such as minimum wage, housing, aid to education, mass transit, and health care. The plan was not difficult to rationalize. If the president pressed for civil rights legislation and failed, his entire legislative program would be placed in jeopardy, and executive efforts on behalf of blacks would be subject to even closer scrutiny. If he withheld the civil rights issue from Congress, southerners might show their appreciation for the president's circumspection. His other measures thus would have a better chance for enactment, and blacks would reap the benefits of these programs as well as Kennedy's executive-centered civil rights initiatives.

Accordingly, Kennedy avoided a preinaugural fight in the Senate over the liberalization of the rules of debate. The effort failed. He did lend his support to a liberal attempt to expand the House Rules Committee, but this was a prerequisite to House action on Kennedy's chosen legislative program. The Rules effort succeeded, but the new committee members gave no indication of an impending civil rights offensive.[29]

Feelings of resentment and betrayal among civil rights leaders inevitably followed the decision to forego the bold legislative actions suggested in the party platform. But by giving substance to the promise of aggressive executive action, the president hoped to lay aside resentment and persuasively demonstrate a new level of commitment to civil rights. The administration moved forward on several fronts. The centerpiece of its strategy was to use the Justice Department to promote and protect black voter registration drives in the South. This promised to give blacks the power to secure their rights and also to minimize the electoral costs of any further Democratic defections among southern whites. On other fronts, the president liberalized the old Civil Rights Commission and created a Committee on Equal Employment Opportunity to investigate job discrimination. When Congress moved to eliminate the poll tax, the president lent his support. When demonstrations threatened to disrupt southern transportation terminals, Attorney General Robert Kennedy enlisted the cooperation of the Interstate Commerce Commission in desegregating the facilities. When black applicant James Meredith asserted his right to enroll at the University of Mississippi, the administration responded with protection and crisis mediation. Even more visibly, the president appointed a record number of blacks to high civil service positions.

Kennedy pressed executive action on behalf of civil rights with more vigor and greater effect than any of his predecessors. Still, civil rights enthusiasts were left with unfulfilled expectations and mounting suspicions. Ever mindful of the political imperatives of containing advocacy, the president was trying not only to serve the interests of blacks, but also to manage those interests and serve the interests of civil rights opponents as well. Indeed there seemed to be a deceptive qualification in each display of principle. For example, the president's patronage policies brought blacks into positions of influence in government, but they also brought new segregationist federal judges to the South. The FBI that provided support for the voter registration drive also tapped civil rights activist Martin Luther King's phone. The poll tax was eliminated with administration support, but the administration backed away from a contest over literacy tests. Kennedy liberalized the Civil Rights Commission, but he refused to endorse its controversial report recommending the withholding of federal funds from states that violated the Constitution. While he encouraged the desegregation of interstate transportation terminals, the president put off action on a key campaign pledge to promote the desegregation of housing by executive order. (When the housing order was finally issued, it adopted the narrowest possible application and was not made retroactive.) And although the administration ultimately saw to the integration of the University of Mississippi, the attorney general first tried to find some way to allow the racist governor of the state to save face.

Executive management allowed Kennedy to juggle contradictory expectations for two years. But as an exercise in forestalling a schism within the ranks, the administration's efforts to control advocacy and balance interests ultimately satisfied no one and offered no real hope of resolving the issue at hand. The weaknesses in the president's position became more and more apparent early in 1963 as civil rights leaders pressed ahead with their own timetable for action.

While civil rights leaders clearly needed the president's support, they steadfastly refused to compromise their demands and relinquish de facto control over their movement to presidential management. The president and his brother became extremely agitated when movement leaders contended that the administration was not doing all that it could for blacks. Civil rights groups, in turn, were outraged at the implication that the movement represented an interest like any other and that claims of moral right could be pragmatically "balanced" against the power of racism and bigotry in a purely political calculus. Independent action already had blurred the line between contained advocacy and reactive accommodation in the administration's response to the movement. Continued independence and intensified action promised to limit the president's room to maneuver still further and to force him to shift his course from interest balancing to moral choice.

The first sign of a shift came on February 28, 1963. After a season of rising criticism of presidential tokenism, embarrassing civil rights advocacy by liberal Republicans in Congress, and portentous planning for spring demonstrations in the most racially sensitive parts of the South, the president recommended some mild civil rights measures to Congress. His message acknowledged that civil rights was indeed a moral issue and indicated that it no longer could be treated simply as another interest. But this shift was one of words more than action.

Kennedy did not follow up his legislative request in any significant way.

Although civil rights agitation clearly was spilling over the channels of presidential containment, the prospect for passing civil rights legislation in Congress had improved little since the president had taken office. Kennedy's circumspect attitude on civil rights matters during the first two years of his administration had been only moderately successful in winning support from southern Democrats for his other social and economic measures. Several of the administration's most important successes—minimum wage, housing, and area redevelopment legislation—clearly indicated the significance of southern support. On the other hand, the president already had seen southern Democrats defect in droves to defeat his proposed Department of Urban Affairs, presumably because the first department head was to be black.[30] If Kennedy no longer could hope to contain the civil rights issue, he still faced the problem of containing the political damage that inevitably would come from spearheading legislative action.

Kennedy's approach to this problem was to press legislation as an irresistible counsel of moderation. This meant holding back still longer, waiting for the extreme positions to manifest themselves fully, then offering real change as the only prudent course available. He did not have to wait long. A wave of spring civil rights demonstrations that began in Birmingham, Alabama, and extended throughout the South brought mass arrests and ugly displays of police brutality to the center of public attention. Capitalizing on the spectre of social disintegration, the administration argued that a new legislative initiative was essential to the restoration of order and sought bipartisan support for it on this basis. Congressional Republicans were enlisted with the argument that the only way to get the protesters off the streets was by providing them with new legal remedies in the courts. Kennedy then seized an opportunity to isolate the radical right. On the evening of the day that Gov. George Wallace made his symbolic gesture in defiance of federal authority at the University of Alabama (physically barring the entrance of a prospective black student), the president gave a hastily prepared but impassioned television address on the need for new civil rights legislation.

In late June the administration sent its new legislative proposal to Congress. The bill went far beyond the mild measures offered in February. It contained significantly expanded voting rights protections and for the first time called for federal protection to enforce school desegregation and to guarantee equal access to public facilities. But even with this full bow to liberal commitments, the struggle for containment continued. The administration tried to counter the zeal of urban Democrats by searching for compromise in order to hold a bipartisan coalition of civil rights support. When civil rights leaders planned a march on Washington in the midst of the legislative battle, the president tried without success to dissuade them.

Containing the zeal of the left was the least of the president's problems. Kennedy had struggled continually to moderate his party's liberal commitments and thus avoid a rupture on the right. Now as a landmark piece of civil rights legislation inched its way through Congress, the president turned to face the dreaded party schism. His popularity had plummeted in the South. George Wallace was contemplating a national campaign to challenge liberal control of the Democratic party, and an ugly white backlash in the North made the prospects for such a campaign brighter than ever. Conservative reaction, party schism, and the need to hold a base in the South were foremost in the president's thinking as he embarked on his fateful trip to Texas in November 1963.

Pierce and Carter:
Establishing Credibility in an Enervated Regime

For Polk and Kennedy, leadership was circumscribed by the dilemmas of interest management and the test of aggressive maintenance. With a preemptive assertion of executive control, each attempted to orchestrate a course and pace for regime development that would maintain an established coalition in changing times. Their governing strategies involved them in convoluted conflict manipulations calculated to accommodate all coalition interests, uphold regime commitments, and stave off party rupture. Grounded in established power, leadership cast a dark cloud of duplicity over its greatest achievements.

Indeed, it would be difficult to choose the greater of these two performances. Polk was able to deliver on an impressive array of policy promises, but his success was premised on the exclusion of the basic moral issue inherent in these policies from the arena of political debate. Kennedy delivered little in the way of outstanding policy, but he eventually acknowledged the great moral choice he confronted and made a moral decision of enormous national significance. Despite these manifest differences, Polk's and Kennedy's limited claims to greatness actually rest on a similar response to the dilemmas of interest management. These presidents began with a credible claim to executive control and a promise of respectful service to all the interests of the majority party. Within two years, however, the delicate interest balance they had been at pains to maintain began to unravel, and the effort to stave off coalition disaffection became a matter of limiting the effects of an open rupture. When interest management no longer could hold the old majority coalition together, these presidents took their stand with the party orthodoxy and helped to secure the greater part.

The irony in these performances is that while upholding their respective regime commitments and vindicating their party orthodoxies, Polk and Kennedy raised serious questions about the future terms of regime survival and left orthodoxy politically insecure. Because Polk's nationalism and Kennedy's liberalism ultimately came at the expense of the old majority coalition, a new appeal to the political interests of the nation seemed imperative. In vindicating orthodoxy, Polk and Kennedy set in motion a pivotal turn toward sectarianism in regime development.

For the Jacksonian Democrats, the turn toward sectarianism grew out of a political defeat. The election of 1848 exposed the weaknesses of stalwart Jacksonian nationalism and spurred party managers to overcome the political damage wrought by sectional divisiveness. In 1850, Democratic votes secured passage of a bipartisan legislative package designed to smooth the disruptions that had rumbled out of the Polk administration.[31] This incongruous series of measures, collectively labeled the "Compromise of 1850," repackaged moderation in a way that many hoped would isolate the extremes and lead to the creation of a new Union party. But the dream of a Union party failed to spark widespread interest, and Democratic managers grasped the sectarian alternative. Using the compromise as a point of departure, they set out to reassemble the disparate parts of their broken coalition. While supporting governmental policies that were designed to silence ideological conflict, they renewed a partnership in power with interests at the ideological extremes.[32]

For the New Deal regime, the turn came on the heels of a great electoral victory. Running against a Republican extremist, Lyndon Johnson swept the nation. But the disaffection stemming from the Kennedy administration was clearly visible: southern Democrat Johnson lost five states in his own region to the Republican outlier. In 1965 and 1966, Johnson tried to fuse a new consensus with policies that ranged across the extremes of ideology and interest. He dreamed of superseding the New Deal with a Great Society, but his vast expansion of services to interests added more to governmental fragmentation than to regime coherence. He also hoped to supersede the old Democratic party with a "party for all Americans," but his extension of regime commitments did more to scatter political loyalties than to unify them.[33]

By the time of the next incarnation of majority-party government (1852 and 1976, respectively), the challenge of presidential leadership had shifted categorically once again. By 1852, the nationalism of Jackson had degenerated into a patchwork of suspect compromises sitting atop a seething sectional division. By 1976, the liberalism of Roosevelt had become a grab bag of special interest services all too vulnerable to political charges of burdening a troubled economy with bureaucratic overhead. Expedience completely eclipsed enthusiasm in the bond between the regime and the nation. Supporters of orthodoxy were on the defensive. The energies that once came from advancing great national purposes had dissipated. A rule of myopic sects defied the very notion of governmental authority.

Expedience also eclipsed enthusiasm in the bond between the majority party and its president. Franklin Pierce and Jimmy Carter each took the term "dark horse" to new depths of obscurity. Each was a minor local figure, far removed from the centers of party strength and interest. Indeed, each hailed from the region of greatest erosion in majority-party support. Pierce, a former governor of New Hampshire, was called to head the Democratic ticket in 1852 after 48 convention ballots failed to yield a consensus on anyone who might have been expected to actually lead the party. His appeal within regular party circles (if it may be so called) lay first in his uniquely inoffensive availability, and second, in his potential to bring northeastern Free Soil Democrats back to the standard they so recently had branded as proslavery. Carter, a former governor of Georgia, was chosen to head the Democratic ticket in 1976 after mounting a broadside assault on the national political establishment. To say that he appealed to regular party circles would be to mistake the nature of his campaign and to exaggerate the coherence of the Democratic organization at that time. Still, Carter offered the Democrats a candidate untainted by two decades of divisive national politics and capable of bringing the South back to the party of liberalism.

The successful reassembling of broken coalitions left Pierce and Carter to ponder the peculiar challenge of leading an enervated regime. These presidents engaged the political system at a step removed from either an assertion of executive control or a submersion of energies in interest management. Tenuously attached to a governmental establishment that itself appeared barren of any interest in addressing the most pressing problems of the day, their leadership turned on a question so narrow that it really is prerequisite to leadership—that of their own credibility. Despite determined efforts to establish credibility, neither Pierce nor Carter could reconcile his own awkward position in the old order with the awkward position of the old order in the nation at large. Caught between the incessant demands of regime interests and the bankruptcy of the assumptions about the government and the nation that had supported those interests in the past, neither could find secure ground on which to make a stand and limit the inevitable political unraveling that comes with executive action. What began in expedience simply dissolved into irrelevance.

Franklin Pierce

In 1852, Franklin Pierce carried 27 of the 31 states for a hefty 250 out of 296 electoral votes.[34] In the process, the Democratic party strengthened its hold over both houses of Congress. But the Pierce landslide was more apparent than real, and the election was anything but a mandate for action. As a presidential candidate, Pierce had simply endorsed the past work of a bipartisan group of Senate moderates. His campaign was confined to a declaration of support for the Compromise of 1850 and a pledge to resist any further agitation on slavery, the issue that underlay all other national concerns. The Pierce campaign was nothing if not a dutiful bow to senatorial authority and moderate political opinion.

It is possible that the new president might have enhanced his position at the start of his term by taking a second bow to the center and placing the full largesse of his office at the disposal of the Senate moderates. But there were other aspects of the election that argued against this approach. Pierce actually had received less than 51 percent of the popular vote. He had not won the presidency because the moderate center of national opinion had rallied to his standard, but because the party managers working in the field had reassembled support at the political extremes. To these extremes, the Compromise of 1850 was a source of suspicion rather than satisfaction; it was a matter of reluctant acquiescence rather than loyal support.

Pierce was sensitive to the precariousness of his victory but thought the logic of his situation was fairly clear. He believed that the election of 1848 had demonstrated that it was not enough for the Democratic party to stand with the moderates and let the extremes go their own way and that the narrow victory of 1852 amply demonstrated the electoral imperative of consolidating party loyalties at the extremes. Pierce refused to ignore this renewed display of Democratic support—

however reluctantly given—in the vague hope that the centrists of both parties might join him in a national coalition government. He therefore decided to reach out to the old party coalition and to try to heal the wounds of 1848 once and for all.

In a bold bid for leadership, Pierce held himself aloof from the moderate Democratic senators and set out to rebuild the political machinery of Jacksonian government under presidential auspices. As the mastermind of a party restoration, he hoped to gain a position of respectability in his dealings with Congress, to take charge of national affairs, and ultimately—in 1856—to claim the mantle of Andrew Jackson. The basic problem with this plan for establishing a credible leadership posture was that no interest of any significance depended on the president's success. Pierce had exhausted his party's national strength and legitimacy simply by letting the various party leaders elect him. These leaders had no stake in following their own creation and no intention of withholding their mutual suspicions in order to enhance the president's position. Pierce quickly discovered that his claims to the office of Andrew Jackson had no political foundation, and that by asserting his independence at the outset, he had robbed the alternative strategy—a bow to senatorial power—of any possible advantage.

As a political vision, Pierce's goal of resuscitating the old party machinery was ideologically and programmatically vacuous. It was conceived as a purely mechanical exercise in repairing and perfecting the core institutional apparatus of the regime and thereby restoring the regime's operational vitality. There was no reference to any of the substantive concerns that had caused the vitality of the party apparatus to dissipate in the first place. Those concerns were simply to be forgotten. Pierce recalled Polk's dictum of "equal and exact justice" for every portion of the party, but not the wide-ranging appeal to unfinished party business that had driven Polk's administration. He held up to the nation the vision of a perfect political machine purged of all political content.[35]

The rapid unraveling of the Pierce administration began with the president's initial offer to forget the Free Soil heresy of 1848 and provide all party factions in the North their due measure of presidential favor for support given in 1852. Much to the president's dismay, many of the New York Democrats who had remained loyal in 1848 refused to forgive the heretics and share the bounty. The New York party disintegrated at a touch, and the Whigs swept the state's elections in 1853.

Within months of Pierce's inauguration, his strategy for establishing leadership credibility was in a shambles. The president's key appointment to the Collectorship of the Port of New York had yet to be confirmed by the Senate, and if the party leaders withheld their endorsement—a prospect that Pierce's early standoffishness and the New York electoral debacle made all too possible—the rebuke to the fledgling administration would be disastrous. But Pierce not only had placed himself at the mercy of the Senate, he had also placed the Senate at the mercy of the radical states' rights advocates of the South. This small but potent faction of southern senators felt shortchanged by the distribution of patronage in their own region and resolved to use the president's appeal for the restoration of Free Soilers as a basis to seek their revenge. They characterized the distribution of rewards in the North as representing a heightened level of commitment to the Free Soil element, and they challenged their more moderate southern cohorts to extract an equal measure of new commitment for their region as well.

The radical southerners found their opportunity in Illinois Senator Stephen Douglas's bill to organize the Nebraska territory. Douglas pushed the Nebraska bill because it would open a transcontinental railroad route through the center of his own political base. His bill followed the orthodox party posture, a posture confirmed in the Compromise of 1850, by stipulating that the new territory would be organized without reference to slavery and that the people of the territory would decide the issue. Southerners who ostensibly had accepted this formula for settling new lands by electing Pierce in 1852 were offended by his northern political strategy in 1853 and felt compelled to raise the price of their support in 1854. They demanded that the Douglas bill include a repeal of the Missouri Compromise of 1820 and thus explicitly acknowledge that slavery could become permanently established anywhere in the national domain. Douglas evidently convinced himself that the expected benefits of his Nebraska bill were worth the price extracted by the South. After all, it could be argued that the repeal would only articulate something already implicit in the squatter sovereignty doctrine. The change in the formal terms of sectional peace would be more symbolic than real. In any case, Douglas accepted the repeal, and by dividing the Nebraska territory in two (Nebraska and Kansas) hinted that both sections might peacefully lay claim to part of the new land.

In January 1854, less than a year into Pierce's administration, Douglas led his southern collaborators to the White House to gain a presidential endorsement for the Kansas-Nebraska bill. With Douglas's railroad and the confirmation of Pierce's New York Collector nominee hanging in the balance, the cornerstone of the Pierce presidency was placed on the line. Confronted with his very first legislative decision, the president was being told to disregard his electoral pledge not to reopen the issue of slavery. If he chose to stand by his pledge, he stood to lose all credibility within his party. If he endorsed the handiwork of the party leaders, he stood to lose all credibility in the nation at large. Pierce chose to stand with the party leaders. He convinced himself that the Kansas-Nebraska bill was faithful to the spirit of the Compromise of 1850 and offered to help Douglas convince the northern wing of the party. The Collector of the Port of New York was confirmed.

Between March 1853 and January 1854, Pierce had tried and failed to prove himself to his party on his own terms; between January and May of 1854, he struggled to prove himself to his party on the Senate's terms. The president threw all the resources of the administration behind passage of the Kansas-Nebraska bill in the House. Despite a Democratic majority of 159 to 76, he fought a no-win battle to discipline a party vote. Midway into the proceedings, 66 of the 90 northern Democrats stood in open revolt against this northern Democratic president. Even a no-holds-barred use of presidential patronage persuaded only 44 members to give a final assent. Instead of perfecting a political machine, Pierce found himself defying a political revolution. Passage of the bill was secured through the support of southern Whigs. Forty-two northern Democrats openly voted no. Not one northern Whig voted yes.[36]

In the winter of 1854, Pierce lost his claim to credibility in the nation at large. Exhausted after the passage of Douglas's bill, the administration turned to reap northern revenge for the broken pledge of 1852. The Democrats lost every northern state except New Hampshire and California in the elections of 1854. The once huge Democratic majority in the House disappeared, and a curious new amalgamation of political forces prepared to take over. Adding to the rebuke was the threat of civil war in the territories. Free Soil and slave factions rushed into Kansas and squared off in a contest for control. The president called for order, but the call was ignored.

Pierce never gave up hope that his party would turn to him. But once the North rejected his administration, the South had no more use for him, and the party Pierce so desperately had wanted to lead became increasingly anxious to get rid of him. Ironically, when faced with the unmitigated failure of his leadership and his political impotence at midterm, Pierce seemed to gain his first sense of a higher purpose. He threw his hat into the ring for a second term with a spirited defense of the Kansas-Nebraska Act and a biting indictment of the critics of the Missouri Compromise repeal. He appealed to the nation to reject treason in Kansas. He wrapped his party in the Constitution and cast its enemies in the role of uncompromising disunionists bent on civil war.[37]

This was the president's shining hour. Rejecting the spectre of party illegitimacy and the stigma of his own irrelevance, standing firm with the establishment against the forces that would destroy it, Pierce pressed the case for his party in the nation and with it, his own case for party leadership. Still, there was no rally of political support. The party took up the "friends of the Constitution" sentiment, but it hastened to bury the memory of the man who had articulated it. Pierce's unceasing effort to prove his significance to those who had called him to power never bore fruit. The Democratic convention was an "anybody but Pierce" affair.

Jimmy Carter

There is no better rationale for Jimmy Carter's mugwumpish approach to political leadership than Franklin Pierce's unmitigated failure. No sooner had Pierce identified his prospects for gaining credibility as a national leader with the revitalization of the old party machinery under presidential auspices than he fell victim to party interests so factious that the desperate state of national affairs was all but ignored. Gripped by myopic sects, the party of Jackson proved itself bankrupt as a governing instrument. Its operators no longer were capable of even recognizing that they were toying with moral issues of explosive significance for the nation as a whole. Pierce's plan for claiming party leadership first and then taking charge of the nation dissolved with its initial action, pushing the president down a path as demoralizing for the nation as it was degrading to the office. The quest for credibility degenerated into saving face with the Senate over patronage appointments, towing the line on explosive territorial legislation for the sake of Douglas's railroad, and forswearing a solemn pledge to the nation.

It was Jimmy Carter's peculiar genius to treat his remoteness from his party and its institutional power centers as a distinctive asset rather than his chief liablity in his quest for a credible leadership posture. He called attention to moral degeneration in government and politics, made it his issue, then compelled the political coalition that had built that government to indulge his crusade against it. In a style reminiscent of Andrew Jackson, Carter identified himself with popular disillusionment with political insiders, entrenched special interests, and the corruption of manners that consumed Washington. He let the liberals of the Democratic party flounder in their own internal disarray until it became clear that liberalism no longer could take the political offensive on its own terms. Then, in the 1976 Florida primary, Carter pressed his southern advantage. The party either had to fall in line behind his campaign against the establishment or risk another confrontation with the still greater heresies of George Wallace.

The obvious problem in Carter's approach to the presidency was that while it claimed a high moral stance of detachment from the establishment, it also positioned itself within the established coalition. This curiosity afforded neither the regime outsider's freedom to oppose established interests nor the regime insider's freedom to support them. The tension in Carter's campaign between an effort to reassemble the core constituencies of the traditional Democratic coalition and his promise to reform the governmental order that served it suggested the difficulties he would face establishing a credible leadership posture in office. Carter's narrow victory in the election magnified those difficulties by showing the regime's supporters in Congress to be a good deal more secure politically than their strange new affiliate in the executive mansion.

On what terms, then, did Carter propose to reconcile his outsider's appeal with his position within the old order? The answer of the campaign lay in Carter's preoccupation with problems of form, procedure, and discipline rather than in the substantive content of the old order. It was not bureaucratic *programs*, Carter argued, but bureaucratic *inefficiency* that left the people estranged from their government. It was not the system *per se* that was at fault but the way it was being run. In the eyes of this late-regime Democrat, the stifling weight and moral decay of the federal government presented problems of technique and personnel rather than problems of substance.

Like Jackson's early efforts, Carter's reform program called for governmental reorganization, civil service reform, and fiscal retrenchment. But coming from an outsider affiliated with the old order, the political force and ideological energy of this program for revitalization were largely nullified. What Jackson presented as an ideological indictment of the old order and a buttress for supporters newly arrived in power, Carter presented as institutional engineering plain and simple. Carter's Jackson-like appeal to the nation translated into an ideologically passionless vision of reorganizing the old order without challenging any of its core concerns.[38]

It is in this respect that the shaky ground on which Carter staked his credibility as a leader begins to appear a good deal more like that claimed by Franklin Pierce than their different party postures would at first lead us to suppose. Both pinned their hopes on the perfectability of machinery. Carter would do for the bureaucratic apparatus of the liberal regime what Pierce had intended to do for the party apparatus of the Jacksonian regime—repair the mechanical defects and realize a new level of operational proficiency. With their perfection of the apparatus, they hoped to save the old regime from its own self-destructive impulses and, at the same time, eliminate the need to make any substantive choices among interests. Political vitality was to be restored simply by making the engines of power run more efficiently.

Sharing this vision, Pierce and Carter also shared a problem of action. Neither could point to any interest of political significance that depended on his success in reorganization. Carter's plan for instilling a new level of bureaucratic discipline was not the stuff to stir the enthusiasm of established Democrats, and once the plan became concrete action, there was plenty for party interests to vehemently oppose. Carter's vision of institutional efficiency dissolved in a matter of weeks into institutional confrontation.

The Carter administration immediately engaged the nation in an elaborate display of symbolism that was designed to build a reservoir of popular faith in the president's intentions and confidence in his ability to change the tenor of government.[39] The economic difficulties the old regime faced in simply maintaining its programmatic commitments at current levels dampened whatever enthusiasm there was for reaching out to the interests with bold new programs in traditional Democratic style. The impulse to lead thus focused on an early redemption of the pledge to be different. With his "strategy of symbols," the president bypassed Congress and claimed authority in government as an extension of his personal credibility in the nation at large.

The first material test of this strategy came in February 1977 when Carter decided to cut 19 local water projects from the 1978 budget. As mundane as this bid for leadership was, it placed the disjunction between the president's appeal to the nation and his political support in government in the starkest possible light. For the president, the water projects were a prime example of the wasteful and unnecessary expenditures inherent in the old ways government did business. The cuts offered Carter a well-founded and much needed opportunity to demonstrate to the nation how an outsider with no attachments to established routines could bring a thrifty discipline to government without really threatening any of its programmatic concerns. Congress—and, in particular, the Democratic leadership in the Senate—saw the matter quite differently. The president's gesture was received as an irresponsible and politically pretentious assault on the bread and butter of congressional careers. Its only real purpose was to enhance the president's public standing, yet its victims were those upon whom presidential success in government must ultimately depend. The Democratic leaders of the Senate pressed the confrontation. They reinstated the threatened water projects on a presidentially sponsored public works jobs bill. Carter threatened to stand his ground, and majority-party government floundered at the impasse.

As relations with Congress grew tense, the president's bid for national leadership became even more dependent on public faith and confidence in his administration's integrity. By standing aloof from "politics as usual," the administration saddled itself with a standard of conduct that any would find difficult to sustain. A hint of shady dealing surfaced in the summer of 1977, and by the fall, the symbolic supports of Carter's leadership were a shambles.

Like the water projects debacle, the Bert Lance affair is remarkable for its substantive insignificance. The administration's "scandal" amounted to an investigation of financial indiscretions by one official before he took office. But the Carter administration was nothing if not the embodiment of a higher morality, and the budget director was the president's most important and trusted political appointee. The exposé of shady dealings on the part of the man whose hand was on the tiller of the bureaucratic machine not only indicted the administration on the very ground that it had asserted a distinctive purpose, but also made a sham of the Democratic Senate's nomination review process. Shorn of its pretentions to a higher standard of conduct, the outsider status of the administration became a dubious asset. Attention now was directed to the apparent inability of the outsiders to make the government work and address the nation's manifest problems.

Despite these first-year difficulties in establishing a credible leadership posture on his own terms, Carter still refused to abdicate to the party leaders. Indeed, as time went on the intransigence of the nation's economic difficulties seemed to stiffen the president's resistance to social policy enthusiasms he felt the nation could no longer afford to support. There was to be no alliance between Carter and Sen. Edward M. Kennedy to recapitulate the Douglas-Pierce disaster. But what of the prospects for continued resistance? The core constituencies of the Democratic party—blacks and organized labor in particular—found the president's program of governmental reorganization and fiscal retrenchment tangential to their concerns at best. They had little use for a Democratic president who seemed to govern like a Republican, and their disillusionment added to the dismay of the congressional leadership. Stalwart liberals admonished the president not to forsake the traditional interests but to rally them and, in Kennedy's words, "sail against the wind." [40] If the shaky state of the economy made this message perilous for the president to embrace, his awkward political position made it equally perilous to ignore.

Following the Lance affair, Carter did attempt to dispel disillusionment with an appeal to the neoliberal theme of consumerism. He had identified himself with consumer issues during his campaign and opened the second year of his administration with a drive to establish a consumer protection agency. The proposal hardly could be said to address the demands of the old Democratic constituencies, but it had enthusiastic backing from consumer groups, a general appeal in the nation at large, and support from the Democratic leadership in Congress, as well as the additional attraction of posing little direct cost to the government. In consumer protection, Carter found all the makings of a great victory, one that not only would wash away the memory of the first year but also define his own brand of political leadership. But the legislation failed, and with it his prospects for leadership all but collapsed.

Indeed, this defeat underscored the paradox that plagued Carter's never-ending struggle for credibility. Opposition fueled by business interests turned the consumer protection issue against the administration with devastating effect. Identifying governmental regulation of industry with the grim state of the national economy, business made Carter's neoliberalism appear symptomatic of the problem and counterproductive to any real solution. [41] Carter's own critique of undisciplined governmental expansion actually became the property of his critics, and the distinctions he had drawn between himself and the old liberal establishment became hopelessly blurred. While this most distant of Democratic presidents was alienating the liberal establishment by his neglect of its priorities, he was being inextricably linked to it in a conservative assault on the manifest failings of the New Deal liberal regime as a whole. Carter's liberalism-with-a-difference simply could not stand its ground in the sectarian controversies that racked the liberal order in the 1970s. It was as vulnerable to the conservatives for being more of the same as it was vulnerable to the liberals for being different.

As tensions between the old regime politics and new economic realities intensified, all sense of political definition was eclipsed. Notable administration victories—the Senate's ratification of a bitterly contested treaty with Panama, the endorsement of a version of the much heralded administrative reorganization, the negotiation of an accord between Israel and Egypt—offered precious little upon which to vindicate the promise of revitalization. Moreover, the president's mugwumpish resolve to find his own way through deepening crises increasingly came to be perceived as rootless floundering. His attempt to assert forceful leadership through a major cabinet shake-up in the summer of 1979 only added credence to the image of an administration out of control. His determination to support a policy of inducing recession to fight inflation shattered the political symbolism of decades past by saddling a Democratic administration with a counsel of austerity and sacrifice and passing to the Republicans the traditional Democratic promise of economic recovery and sustained prosperity.

The administration was aware of its failure to engage the political system in a meaningful way well before these momentous decisions. By early 1979, the president had turned introspective. It was readily apparent that his credibility had to be established anew and that an identification of the administration with some clear and compelling purpose was imperative. Carter's response to the eclipse of political definition was not, of course, a Pierce-like defense of the old order and its principles. It was, if anything, a sharpened attack on the old order and a renewed declaration of presidential political independence.

In what was to be his most dramatic public moment, Carter appeared in a nationally televised appeal to the people in July 1979 with a revised assessment of the crisis facing the nation.[42] This new bid for leadership credibility began with an acknowledgment of widespread disillusionment with the administration and its "mixed success" with Congress. But the president detached himself from the "paralysis, stagnation, and drift" that had marked his tenure. He issued a strong denunciation of the legislative process and reasserted his campaign image as an outsider continuing the people's fight against a degenerate politics. Attempting to restore the people's faith in themselves and to rally them to his cause, Carter all but declared the bankruptcy of the federal government as he found it. Thirty months in office only seemed to reveal to him how deeply rooted the government's incapacities were.

It was the system itself, not simply its inefficiencies, that the president now placed in question.

Trying once again to identify his leadership with the alienation of the people from the government, Carter again exposed himself as the one with the most paralyzing case of estrangement. The awkward truth in this presidential homily lent credence to the regime's most vehement opponents by indicting the establishment controlled by the president's ostensible allies. On the face of it, Carter had come to embrace a leadership challenge of the greatest moment, but beneath the challenge lay the hopeless paradox of his political position. The Democratic party tore itself apart in a revolt against him and the sentiments he articulated. It rejected his message, discredited his efforts, and then, in its most pathetic display of impotence, revealed to the nation that it had nothing more to offer. Carter finally may have seen the gravity of the problems he confronted, but as the people saw it, he was not part of the solution.

Studying the Presidency in Political Time

Presidential leadership often is pictured as a contest between the man and the system. Timeless forces of political fragmentation and institutional intransigence threaten to frustrate the would-be leader at every turn. Success is reserved for the exceptional individual. It takes a person of rare political skill to penetrate the system and manipulate the government in politically effective ways. It takes a person of rare character to give those manipulations national meaning and constructive purpose.

Although the significance of the particular person in office cannot be doubted, this perspective on leadership presents a rather one-sided view of the interaction between the presidency and the political system. It is highly sensitive to differences among individual incumbents, but it tends to obscure differences in the political situations in which they act. If presidential leadership is indeed something of a struggle between the individual and the system, it must be recognized that the system changes as well as the incumbent. The changing universe of political action is an oft-noted but seldom explored dimension of the leadership problem.

While changes in the political conditions and challenges of presidential leadership have been incessant, they have not been entirely erratic. A broad view of American political development reveals patterned sequences of political change with corresponding patterns in presidential performance. Presidential history in this reading has been episodic rather than evolutionary, with leadership opportunities gradually dissipating after an initial upheaval in political control over government. Presidents intervene in—and their leadership is mediated by—the generation and degeneration of political orders. The clock at work in presidential leadership keeps political rather than historical time.

The leaders who stand out at a glance—Washington, Jefferson, Jackson, Lincoln, Wilson, and Roosevelt—are closer to each other in the political conditions of leadership than they are to any of their respective neighbors in historical time. In *political* time all were first. As the analysis of the Jacksonian and New Deal regimes has shown, successive incarnations of majority-party government produced progressively more tenuous leadership situations. Presidents approached ever more perplexing problems of regime governance with ever more superficial governing solutions; regime supporters approached ever more perplexing leadership choices with ever less forbearance.

The regime builders rode into power on an upheaval in governmental control and tested their leadership in efforts to secure a political and institutional infrastructure for a new governing coalition. Their success created a new establishment, thrust their partisan successors into the position of regime managers, and posed the test of aggressive maintenance. Ultimately, visions of regime management dissolved into politically vacuous mechanical contrivances, and leadership was preempted in the political contradictions of simply establishing presidential credibility.

Comparing the leadership performances of Jackson and Roosevelt, Polk and Kennedy, and Pierce and Carter is a suggestive but hardly exhaustive exercise. No attention has been given to the minority-party presidents, let alone to other regime sequences and fragments. These sketches are but the outlines of the study of the presidency in political time, a study in which the past is something more than an extended prelude to "modernity," and the modern presidents are something more than a group apart.

It is appropriate, then, to conclude with a few thoughts about how this notion of the presidency-in-time might be elaborated and how our understanding of the institution in its relationship to the changing political system might thereby be enhanced. For example, our pairing of Pierce and Carter in the analysis of presidential leadership may prompt consideration of other presidents similarly situated. The other late-regime presidents—John Quincy Adams, James Buchanan, and Herbert Hoover immediately come to mind—are a uniformly uninspiring lot, but when they are taken out from the shadows of the luminaries who succeeded them and studied as a group, it becomes difficult to simply dismiss them for personal failings. The apparent preemption of leadership in the advanced stages of regime development and the peculiar predicament of the president caught in the crisis of the old order makes the study of such administrations something more than the study of individual failures and something indicative of the capacities of the institution itself.

Similarly, our pairing of Polk and Kennedy may prompt consideration of other majority-party leaders of established regimes. This is an especially enigmatic group including such extraordinarily successful mediocrities as James Monroe and Ulysses S. Grant and such frustrated giants as Theodore Roosevelt and Lyndon Johnson. Curiously, while Monroe and Grant abdicated all but the pretense of leadership to fellow partisans in Congress and the bureaucracy, each managed in the process to maintain a virtually uncontested position as the balance wheel among his party's factions through two landslide elections. Roosevelt and Johnson, accidental presidents who went on to win one landslide election of their own, each dreamed of fashioning something new out of established political power. They managed to extort significant policy achievements, but their leadership quickly became mired in opposition from within their own ranks, and their careers ended in political rejection. These connections between political success and presidential mediocrity and between the impulse to lead and political failure delimit this peculiar universe of presidential action and seem to suggest the range of the institution in an already established regime.

Finally, our pairing of Jackson and Roosevelt may prompt consideration of the other presidents whose rise to power displaced long-established political orders. It is not only the full flowering of leadership in the interregnum of political order that deserves close attention here but also the compulsion to reestablish order. The significance of the presidency in regime construction has often been noted, but since the study of regime sequences has concentrated largely on the dynamics of party alignments and mass behavior, this subject has not received the systematic attention it demands.[43] Party building and institutional reconstruction need to be examined as leadership challenges at the elite level; then, the relationship between these challenges and the peculiar conjunction of institutional and mass politics in which they have been undertaken most successfully needs to be more fully elaborated. It hardly needs be said that the study of the presidency in the interregnum is especially timely at the present juncture. The question of political regeneration is likely to figure prominently in future evaluations of Ronald Reagan's leadership.

NOTES

1. Other recent works investigating distinctly political patterns in presidential history include Erwin C. Hargrove and Michael Nelson, "Presidents, Ideas, and the Search for a Stable Majority," in *A Tide of Discontent: The 1980 Elections and Their Meaning*, ed. Ellis Sandoz and Cecil V. Crabb, Jr. (Washington, D.C.: CQ Press, 1981); and James David Barber, *The Pulse of Politics: Electing Presidents in the Media Age* (New York: W. W. Norton & Co., 1980).

2. Thomas A. Bailey, *Presidential Greatness: The Image and the Man from George Washington to the Present* (New York: Appleton-Century-Crofts, 1966), 23-34. Bailey critically discusses the ratings by professional historians. The important point here, however, is that the presidents who rated highest in the Schlesinger surveys of 1948 and 1962 all shared this peculiarly structured leadership situation at the outset of their terms.

3. Robert Remini, *Andrew Jackson and the Course of American Freedom, 1822-1832*, vol. 2 (New York: Harper & Row Publishers, 1981), 12-38, 74-142.

4. Quoted in Frank Freidel, *FDR and the South* (Baton Rouge: Louisiana State University Press, 1965), 42.

5. Remini, *Andrew Jackson*, 152-202, 248-256.

6. The famous veto of the Maysville Road, for example, was notable for its limited implications. It challenged federal support for *intrastate* projects and was specifically selected as an example for its location in Henry Clay's Kentucky. On Jackson's objectives in civil service reform, see Albert Somit, "Andrew Jackson as an Administrative Reformer," *Tennessee Historical Quarterly*, 13 (September 1954): 204-223; and Eric McKinley Erikson, "The Federal Civil Service Under President Jackson," *Mississippi Valley Historical Review*, 13 (March 1927): 517-540. Also significant in this regard is Richard G. Miller, "The Tariff of 1832: The Issue that Failed," *The Filson Club History Quarterly*, 49, 3 (July 1975): 221-230.

7. The analysis in this and the following paragraphs draws on the following works: Remini, *Andrew Jackson*; Robert Remini, *Andrew Jackson and the Bank War: A Study in the Growth of Presidential Power* (New York: W. W. Norton & Co., 1967); Marquis James, *Andrew Jackson: Portrait of a President* (New York: Grosset & Dunlap, 1937), 283-303, 350-385; and Arthur Schlesinger, Jr., *The Age of Jackson* (Boston: Little, Brown & Co., 1945), 74-131.

8. Charles Sellers, Jr., "Who Were the Southern Whigs?" *American Historical Review*, 49 (January 1954): 335-346.

9. Harry Scheiber, "The Pet Banks in Jacksonian Politics and Finance, 1833-1841," *Journal of Economic History*, 23 (June 1963): 196-214; Frank Otto Gatell, "Spoils of the Bank War: Political Bias in the Selection of Pet Banks," *American Historical Review*, 70 (October 1964): 35-58; and Frank Otto Gatell, "Secretary Taney and the Baltimore Pets: A Study in Banking and Politics," *Business History Review*, 39 (Summer 1965): 205-227.

10. Quoted in James MacGregor Burns, *Roosevelt: The Lion and the Fox* (New York: Harcourt, Brace & World, 1956), 208.

11. The analysis in this and the following paragraphs draws on Burns, *Roosevelt*; and Freidel, *FDR and the South.*

12. Burns, *Roosevelt*, 223-241.

13. Freidel, *FDR and the South*, 99.

14. Richard Polenberg, *Reorganizing Roosevelt's Government: The Controversy Over Executive Reorganization, 1936-1939* (Cambridge, Mass.: Harvard University Press, 1966).

15. The analysis in this and the following paragraphs draws on the following works: Charles Sellers, *James K. Polk: Continentalist, 1843-1846* (Princeton, N.J.: Princeton University Press, 1966); John Schroeder, *Mr. Polk's War: American Opposition and Dissent, 1846-1848* (Madison, Wis.: University of Wisconsin Press, 1973); Norman A. Graebner, "James Polk," in *America's Ten Greatest Presidents*, ed. Morton Borden (Chicago: Rand McNally & Co., 1961), 113-138; and Charles McCoy, *Polk and the Presidency* (Austin, Texas: University of Texas Press, 1960).

16. Sellers, *James K. Polk*, 50.

17. Ibid., 113-114, 123.

18. Ibid., 282-283.

19. Ibid., 162-164; Joseph G. Raybeck, "Martin Van Buren's Break with James K. Polk: The Record," *New York History*, 36 (January 1955): 51-62; and Norman A. Graebner, "James K. Polk: A Study in Federal Patronage," *Mississippi Valley Historical Review*, 38 (March 1952): 613-632.

20. Sellers, *James K. Polk*, 483.

21. Frederick J. Blue, *The Free Soilers: Third Party Politics, 1848-54* (Urbana, Ill.: University of Illinois Press, 1973), 16-80; and John Mayfield, *Rehearsal for Republicanism: Free Soil and the Politics of Antislavery* (Port Washington, N.Y.: Kennikat Press, 1980), 80-125.

22. McCoy, *Polk and the Presidency*, 197-198, 203-204.

23. Arthur M. Schlesinger, Jr., *A Thousand Days: John F. Kennedy in the White House* (Boston: Houghton Mifflin Co., 1965), 675-676.

24. Caroll Kilpatrick, "The Kennedy Style and Congress," *The Virginia Quarterly Review*, 39 (Winter 1963): 1-11; and Henry Farlie, *The Kennedy Promise: The Politics of Expectation* (New York: Doubleday & Co., 1973), especially 235-263.

25. Freidel, *FDR and the South*, 71-102.

26. Herbert S. Parmet, *The Democrats: The Years After FDR* (New York: Oxford University Press, 1976), 80-82.

27. The analysis in this and the following paragraphs draws on material presented in the following works: Carl M. Bauer, *John F. Kennedy and the Second Reconstruction* (New York: Columbia University Press, 1977); Schlesinger, *A Thousand Days*; Parmet, *The Democrats*, 193-247; Bruce Miroff, *Pragmatic Illusions: The Presidential Politics of John F. Kennedy* (New York: David McKay Co., 1976), 223-270; and Farlie, *The Kennedy Promise*, 235-263.

28. Bauer, *John F. Kennedy*, 30-38; and Schlesinger, *A Thousand Days*, 47-52.

29. Bauer, *John F. Kennedy*, 61-88; and Schlesinger, *A Thousand Days*, 30-31.

30. Parmet, *The Democrats*, 211; and Bauer, *John F. Kennedy*, 128-130.

31. Holman Hamilton, *Prologue to Conflict: The Crisis and Compromise of 1850* (Lexington, Ky.: University of Kentucky Press, 1964), especially 156-164.

32. Roy F. Nichols, *The Democratic Machine, 1850-1854* (New York: AMS Press, 1967).

33. Parmet, *The Democrats*, 220-228.
34. The analysis in this and the following paragraphs draws on Roy F. Nichols, *Franklin Pierce: Young Hickory of Granite Hills* (Philadelphia: University of Pennsylvania Press, 1969); and Nichols, *The Democratic Machine*, 147-226.
35. Nichols, *Franklin Pierce*, 292-293, 308-310; and Nichols, *The Democratic Machine*, 224.
36. Roy F. Nichols, "The Kansas-Nebraska Act: A Century of Historiography," *Mississippi Valley Historical Review*, 43 (September 1956): 187-212; and Nichols, *Franklin Pierce*, 292-324, 333-338.
37. Nichols, *Franklin Pierce*, 360-365, 425-434.
38. Jack Knott and Aaron Wildavsky, "Skepticism and Dogma in the White House: Jimmy Carter's Theory of Governing," *The Wilson Quarterly* 1 (Winter 1977): 49-68; and James Fallows, "The Passionless Presidency: The Trouble With Jimmy Carter's Administration," *The Atlantic Monthly*, May 1979, 33-58, and June 1979, 75-81.
39. The analysis in this and the following paragraphs draws on the following works: Robert Shogun, *Promises to Keep: Carter's First Hundred Days* (New York: Thomas Y. Crowell Co., 1977); Haynes Johnson, *In the Absence of Power: Governing America* (New York: Viking Press, 1980); Robert Shogun, *None of the Above: Why Presidents Fail and What Can Be Done About It* (New York: New American Library, 1982), 177-250; Thomas Ferguson and Joel Rogers, eds., *The Hidden Election: Politics and Economics in the 1980 Presidential Campaign* (New York: Pantheon Books, 1981), 200-230; and Alan Wolfe, *America's Impasse: The Rise and Fall of the Politics of Growth* (New York: Pantheon Books, 1981), 200-230.
40. Shogun, *None of the Above*, 220.
41. Johnson, *In the Absence of Power*, 233-245.
42. *New York Times*, July 16, 1979, 1, 10.
43. Recent studies that point in this direction include: Jerome M. Clubb, William H. Flanigan, and Nancy Zingale, *Partisan Realignment: Voters, Parties, and Government in American History* (Beverly Hills: Sage Publications, 1980); and Kristi Andersen, *The Creation of a Democratic Majority, 1928-1936* (Chicago: Chicago University Press, 1979).

5. PRESIDENTIAL COMPETENCE

Paul J. Quirk

The presidency is the most difficult job in the world. So, at least, Americans have long said, seeming more proud than concerned. But a recent string of failed presidencies has turned this pride to apprehension. Perhaps, some now are saying, the president's job has become not just difficult but impossible.

Whether the contemporary presidency can be executed successfully is a complicated matter. But it depends in large part on the answer to one question that has not been carefully examined: In order to preserve his chances to succeed politically and serve the country well, how much must a president know? To what extent must the president be his own expert in governing, whatever that may entail, and to what extent can he rely on other officials to supply knowledge and understanding that he may lack? Only if the demands for presidential competence are feasible—that is, consistent with the capacities of ordinary men and women—is it at all likely that presidents can succeed.

Although the requirements for a competent presidency cannot be reduced to a formula, their general outlines should be susceptible to analysis. This chapter examines three distinct conceptions of the president's personal tasks and expertise—three models of presidential competence. Two of them—an orthodox approach of long standing and a more novel one associated with the presidency of Ronald Reagan—are criticized as seriously defective. I then propose a third model, based on the notion of "strategic competence," and discuss its application in three major areas of presidential activity.

The Self-reliant Presidency

Most commentary on the presidency assumes a conception of the president's personal tasks that borders on the heroic. Stated simply, the

* This chapter is an extensively revised and elaborated version of "What Must a President Know?" by Paul J. Quirk in Transaction/SOCIETY, no. 23 (January/February 1983) © 1983 by Transaction Publishers.

president must strive to be self-reliant and bear personally a large share of the burden of governing. And he therefore must meet intellectual requirements that are correspondingly rigorous.

The classic argument for the self-reliant presidency is presented in Richard Neustadt's *Presidential Power*.[1] In arguing for an enlarged conception of the presidential role, Neustadt stressed that the president's political interests, and therefore his perspective on decisions, are unique. Only the president has political stakes that correspond with the national interest somehow construed. For no other government official is individual achievement so closely identified with the well-being of the entire nation. Thus the president's chances for success depend on what he can do for himself: his direct involvement in decisions, his personal reputation and skill, his control over subordinates.[2]

It is in this spirit that students of the presidency often hold up Franklin D. Roosevelt as the exemplary modern president—if not for his specific policies or administrative practices, at least for his personal orientation to the job. A perfect "active-positive" in James David Barber's typology of presidential personalities,[3] Roosevelt made strenuous efforts to increase his control and to improve his grasp of issues and situations. For example, he would set up duplicate channels within the government to provide him information and advice, and when this did not seem enough, he looked outside the government for persons who could offer additional perspectives.[4] The ideal president, in short, is one with a consuming passion for control, and thus for information.

This image of the president—as one who makes the major decisions himself, depends on others only in lesser matters, and firmly controls his subordinates—also appeals to the general public, which seems to evaluate presidents partly by how well they live up to it. But is the self-reliant presidency sensible, even as an ideal? Both experience and the elementary facts of contemporary government indicate strongly that it is not.

Even for Roosevelt, self-reliance carried certain costs. In an admiring description of Roosevelt's administrative practices, Arthur Schlesinger, Jr., concedes that his methods hampered performance in some respects. Roosevelt's creation of unstructured, competitive relationships among subordinates, a method he used for control, caused "confusion and exasperation on the operating level"; it was "nerve-wracking and often positively demoralizing." Because Roosevelt reserved so many decisions to himself, he could not make all of them promptly, and aides often had to contend with troublesome delays.[5] The overall effect of Roosevelt's self-reliant decision making on the design, operation, and success of New Deal programs is open to question. Indeed, the New Deal is revered (by those who do) mainly for its broad assertion of governmental responsibility for the nation's well-being, not for the effectiveness of its specific programs. Roosevelt took pride in an observer's estimate that for each decision made by Calvin Coolidge, he was making at least 35. Perhaps some smaller ratio would have been better.

In later administrations the weaknesses of the self-reliant presidency have emerged more clearly. Presidents who have aspired to self-reliance have ended up leaving serious responsibilities badly neglected. Lyndon Johnson, another president with prodigious energy and a need for control, gravitated naturally to the self-reliant approach.[6] Eventually, however, he directed his efforts narrowly and obsessively to the Vietnam War. Meeting daily with the officers in charge, Johnson directed the American military strategy from the Oval Office, going into such detail, at times, as to select specific targets for bombing. Every other area of presidential concern he virtually set aside. Although such detailed involvement would have been unobjectionable had there been any cause to believe it would help to resolve the conflict, the reverse seems more likely. Guided by the president's civilian subordinates, the military officers themselves should have been able to decide matters of strategy at least as well as the president, probably better. Moreover, Johnson's direct operational control of military strategy may have impaired his ability to take a broader, "presidential" perspective. After all, doing a general's job, to some inevitable degree, means thinking like a general. Johnson illustrated a dangerous tendency for self-reliance to become an end in itself.

Jimmy Carter, although less a driven personality than Johnson, preferred self-reliance as a matter of conviction. It led him toward a narrowness of a different kind. From the first month in office, Carter signaled his intention to be thoroughly involved, completely informed, and prompt. "Unless there's a holocaust," he told the staff, "I'll take care of everything the same day it comes in." Thus he spent long hours daily poring over stacks of memoranda and took thick briefing books with him for weekends at Camp David. Initially, he even checked arithmetic in budget documents. Later he complained mildly about the number of memoranda and their length, but he still made no genuine effort to curb the flow.[7] Carter's extreme attention to detail cannot have contributed more than very marginally to the quality of his administration's decisions. Yet it took his attention from other, more essential tasks. Carter was criticized as having failed to articulate the broad themes or ideals that would give his presidency a sense of purpose—a natural oversight, if true, for a president who was wallowing in detail. He certainly neglected the crucial task of nurturing constructive relationships with other leaders in Washington.[8]

The main defect of the self-reliant presidency, however, is none of these particular risks, but rather the blunt, physical impossibility of carrying it out. Perhaps Roosevelt, an extraordinary man who served when government was still relatively manageable, could achieve some sort of approximation of the ideal. But the larger and more complex government has become, the more presidents have been forced to depend on the judgments of others. Today, any single important policy question produces enough pertinent studies, positions, and proposals to keep a conscientious policy maker fully occupied. In any remotely literal sense, therefore, presidential self-reliance is not so much inadvisable as inconceivable.

Even as an inspirational ideal (like perfect virtue), the self-reliant presidency is more misleading than helpful. It can lead to an obsessive narrowness, and it is too far removed from reality to offer any concrete guidance. Rather than such an ideal, presidents need a conception of what a competent, successful performance would really consist of—one that takes the nature of government and the limits of human ability as they exist.

The Minimalist Presidency

A second approach to presidential competence rejects the heroic demands of self-reliance altogether. In this approach, the president requires little or no understanding of specific issues and problems and instead can rely almost entirely on subordinates to resolve them. Although rarely if ever advocated by commentators, the "minimalist" approach commands close attention if only because of the Reagan administration's attempt to use it.

Minimalism does not imply a passive conception of the presidency as an institution, the view of some nineteenth-century American presidents. Accepting the "Whig theory of government," they believed that Congress, as the most representative branch, should lead the country, and thus they left it to Congress to shape and pass legislation without much presidential advice.[9] The Whig theory has been abandoned in the twentieth century, and minimalism, as here defined, is not an attempt to restore it. With the help of a large personal staff, the Office of Management and Budget, and other presidential agencies in the

Executive Office of the President, a minimalist president can exercise his powers as expansively as any.

Nor does minimalism describe the "hidden-hand" leadership ascribed to Dwight D. Eisenhower in the notable reinterpretation of his presidency by Fred Greenstein.[10] Long viewed as a passive president, who reigned rather than ruled, Eisenhower has been thoroughly misinterpreted, according to Greenstein's provocative thesis. In truth, Eisenhower, seeing a political advantage, merely cultivated this image. He worked longer hours, gave closer attention to issues, and exercised more influence than the public was allowed to notice. His methods of influence were indirect. In the long dispute between the administration and Joseph McCarthy over the senator's charges of Communist infiltration of the government, Eisenhower resolutely withheld any public criticism of McCarthy by name. Privately, however, the president and his aides arranged the format of the Senate's Army-McCarthy hearings and plotted strategy for the executive branch, which ultimately led to the senator's downfall.[11]

The hidden-hand style, Greenstein argues, generally permitted Eisenhower to get what he wanted, yet insulated him from politically harmful controversy. By remaining "above politics," Eisenhower could achieve a political feat as yet unmatched by any of his successors—serving two complete four-year terms, popular to the end. Eisenhower was no minimalist, if Greenstein is correct: he was merely a closet activist.

The only recent minimalist president has been Ronald Reagan, whose administration often flatly rejected the self-reliant approach. President Reagan's role in decision making, his spokesmen said during the first year, would be that of a chairman of the board. He would personally establish the general policies and goals of his administration, select cabinet and other key personnel who shared his commitments, then delegate broad authority to them so that they could work out the particulars.[12]

In part, the very limited role for the president was clearly designed to accommodate Reagan's particular limitations—especially his disinclination to do much intellectual work—and to answer critics who questioned his fitness for office. By expounding a minimalist theory, the Reagan administration was able to defend the president's frequent lapses and inaccuracies in news conferences as harmless and irrelevant. It is a "fantasy of the press," said communications director David Gergen, that an occasional "blooper" in a news conference has any real importance.[13]

Nevertheless, the administration presented this minimalist model not merely as an ad hoc accommodation, but as a sensible way in general for a president to operate. The model has at least one claim to be taken seriously: unlike self-reliance, it has the merit of being attainable. For several reasons, however, it can neither be defended in general nor judged satisfactory even in Reagan's case.

First, chairman-of-the-board notions notwithstanding, a minimalist president and his administration will have serious difficulties reaching intelligent decisions. This is so if only because a minimalist president—or rather, the sort of president to whom minimalism might be suited—will not fully appreciate his own limitations. By never paying attention to the complexities of careful policy arguments, one never comes to understand the importance of thorough analysis. In politics and government, at least, people generally do not place a high value on discourse that is much more sophisticated than their own habitual mode of thought.

That President Reagan lacked a sense of his limits emerged in late 1981 as the administration drew up a proposal for the 1983 budget. After weeks of internal debate over whether to propose a tax increase to hold deficits down to reasonable levels, a united front in favor of doing so formed among the administration's key economic policy makers— Office of Management and Budget Director David A. Stockman, Treasury Secretary Donald Regan, and White House Chief of Staff James Baker. When the last hold-out, Regan, came on board, the press began to treat the president's concurrence as a foregone conclusion. But this assumed that Reagan felt compelled to heed the unanimous advice of his principal advisers—which, to their public humiliation, he did not. Instead Reagan went along with the recommendations of Rep. Jack Kemp and the U.S. Chamber of Commerce and followed his own instinct not to retreat. The resulting proposal was a total failure: Congress, including the Republican Senate, dismissed the president's budget out-of-hand.

Even if a minimalist president is willing to delegate authority and dutifully accept advice, his aides and cabinet members cannot be counted on to make up for his limitations. As they compete to please him, they will tend to assume his likeness. At high levels of the executive branch, policies are advanced competitively through vigorous internal debate. But the arguments that tend to weigh most heavily are those that would impress the president himself if he were to become involved. Arguments, therefore, are stated in the president's idiom, and when deciding what policies to advocate, officials lean toward those that can easily be defended by arguments he would like. Such imitation apparently produced the Environmental Protection Agency (EPA) scandals that embarrassed the Reagan administration and led to the removal of numerous high-level officials, including Administrator Anne Gorsuch Burford. Rather than being corrupt, it seems, Reagan's EPA appointees merely took their cue from the president, whose sweeping antiregulatory rhetoric they interpreted to mean that they should do hardly any regulating at all.

Because the president's appointees consider it an achievement—a sign of power—to influence a presidential action, they are likely to propose almost anything that the president might like and defend it somehow as plausible. Because Reagan had made a campaign promise to restore tax exemptions for racially segregated private schools, Treasury and Justice Department officials, who should have known it was legally and politically unsound, offered such a proposal. The result was charges that the administration was anti-civil rights, months of harmful publicity, and, in the end, resounding disapproval of the administration's position by an eight-to-one vote in the Supreme Court.[14] In short, the president's intellectual approach is not just his own; it shapes the tone and the actions of his entire administration.

Second, a minimalist president's lack of attention to the substance of issues will reduce his effectiveness in promoting his policies. A president's influence with congressional leaders, public figures, and heads of state depends partly on his being persuasive in private, face-to-face communications with them. But a minimalist president, lacking any firm understanding of the issues, perhaps lacking even a compatible style of argument and thought, will be at his greatest disadvantage in just those situations.

Of course, the effectiveness of direct, personal lobbying by the president does not depend on his being able to make the best substantive arguments for the administration's policies. There are always subordinates more thoroughly versed in the subject. Clearly, presidential lobbying works by political pressure and exploiting respect for the office more than by rational persuasion. Nevertheless, politicians and officials who are given the personal treatment expect the president to be reasonably informed and able to talk sensibly about the issues on which he seeks their support. It demonstrates the seriousness of his interest; it gives them confidence in the soundness of the administration's decision making; and, perhaps above all, it enables them to rationalize "conversion," at least in part, as persuasion on the merits. The more one is influenced by a show of power, psychologists have argued, the more one wants to believe there are also other good reasons to go along.[15]

Even senior Republican senators have been distressed, therefore, by Reagan's inability to engage in orderly, responsive argument. Sen. Bob Packwood, an outspoken moderate Republican, complained to a reporter that in private meetings the president seemed to respond "on a different wavelength." In the rather extreme example he gave, Packwood was present when Sen. Pete V. Domenici, the chairman of the Budget Committee, tried to warn the president about huge impending deficits in the administration's budget. Reagan answered, irrelevantly, by launching into a story of how someone had used food stamps to buy liquor, despite the rules against it. "That's the problem," Reagan concluded, finding a connection the senators did not see.

Persuasion in Washington usually involves explicit arguments about the public interest, reinforced by obvious allusions to political self-interest that, for the sake of politeness, are not spelled out. By failing to address issues credibly, a president not only foregoes the public-interest argument, but weakens his political appeal by leaving it too naked.

Finally, if a president is known in Washington to delegate most of his major decisions, the press will draw attention to it and make it a source of embarrassment. From this one learns something about the operational priorities of the press. National political reporters, whose politics are generally liberal, have not appeared impressed with Reagan's personal capabilities.[16] One might assume, then, that they would prefer not to see Reagan take firm, personal control of the affairs of state. But because the public expects self-reliant leadership from the president, the press, to stir up controversy, would rather emphasize his failure to meet those expectations than encourage what is perhaps a sensible adaptation to personal limits. Thus reporters continually have challenged Reagan to prove what they secretly may hope is not the case: that he is deeply involved in all the administration's major decisions and ultimately makes them himself. Exposed to such criticism, Reagan probably has made more decisions than he would have otherwise.

Neither self-reliance nor minimalism offers a reliable, or even a plausible, route to presidential competence. The question is whether there is another possible model that corrects the defects of both— making feasible demands on the president yet allowing for competent performance.

Strategic Competence

The third conception of presidential competence, proposed and defended in the rest of the chapter, lies between the two extremes of minimalism and self-reliance. But it does not represent merely a vague compromise between them. It is based on a notion of *strategic competence,* from which it derives some needed definition.

Strategic competence does not refer to the correct but not very helpful observation that presidents need to be competent in the choice of strategies. It refers primarily to the idea that, in order to achieve competence, presidents must have a well-designed (even if mostly implicit) strategy *for* competence. This strategy, it seems, must recognize and take appropriately into account three basic elements of the president's situation:

(1) The president's time, energy, and talent, and thus his capacity for direct, personal competence, must be regarded as a scarce resource. *Choices must be made concerning what things a president will attempt to know.*

(2) Depending on the task (for example, deciding issues, promoting policies), the president's ability to substitute the judgment and expertise of others for his own and still get satisfactory results varies considerably. *Delegation works better for some tasks than for others.*

(3) The success of such substitutions will depend on a relatively small number of presidential actions and decisions concerning the selection of subordinates, the general instructions they are given, and the president's limited interactions with them. *How well delegation works depends on how it is done.*

Achieving competent performance, then, can be viewed as a problem of allocating resources. The president's personal abilities and time to use them are the scarce resources. For each task, the possibilities and requirements for effective delegation determine how much of these resources should be used, and how they should be employed.

The rest of this chapter will work out the implications of strategic competence in three major areas of presidential activity: policy decisions, policy processes, and policy promotion.[17] The test of the model is twofold. For each area of presidential activity, does it provide adequately for competent performance? Taken as a whole, does it call for a level of expertise and attentiveness that an average president can be expected to meet?

Policy Decisions

When it comes to substantive issues, vast presidential ignorance is simply inevitable. No one understands more than a few significant issues very well. Fortunately, presidents can get by—controlling subordinates reasonably well and minimizing the risk of policy disasters—on far less than a thorough mastery. Some prior preparation, however, is required.

As a matter of course, each president has a general outlook or philosophy of government. The principal requirement beyond this is for the president to be familiar enough with the substantive policy debates in each major area to recognize clearly the signs of serious, responsible argument. This especially includes having enough exposure to the work of policy analysts and experts in each area to know, if only in general terms, how they reach conclusions and the contribution they make. The point is not that the president will then be able to work through all the pertinent materials on an issue, evaluate them properly, and reach a sound, independent conclusion—that is ruled out if only for lack of time. However, as he evaluates policy advice, the president will at least be able to tell which of his subordinates are making sense. Whatever the subject at hand, the president will be able to judge: Is an advocate bringing to bear the right kinds of evidence, considerations, and arguments, and citing appropriate authorities?

One can observe the importance of this ability by comparing two, in some respects, similar episodes. Both John F. Kennedy in 1963 and Ronald Reagan in 1981 proposed large, controversial reductions of the individual income tax, each in some sense unorthodox. But in the role played by respectable economic opinion, the two cases could not be more different.

Kennedy brought to bear on federal fiscal policy the prescriptions of Keynesian economics, by then the dominant school of professional economic thought for nearly three decades. The Kennedy administration had taken office when the economy was in a deep recession. From the beginning, therefore, Walter Heller, a leading academic economist and Kennedy's chairman of the Council of Economic Advisors (CEA), sought tax reductions to promote economic growth, which was the appropriate Keynesian response even though it might increase the federal deficit. Long familiar with the Keynesian argument for fiscal stimulation, Kennedy did not require persuasion on the economic merits, but he did have political reservations. "I understand the case for a tax cut," he told Heller, "but it doesn't fit my call for sacrifice." Nor did it fit the economic views of Congress or the general public—both of which remained faithful on the whole to the traditional belief in an annually balanced budget. But the CEA continued its internal lobbying and Kennedy—first partially, later completely—went along. Finally, in 1963 Kennedy proposed to reduce income taxes substantially.

The novelty of this proposal, with the economy already recovering and the budget in deficit, alarmed traditionalists. "What can those people in Washington be thinking about?" asked former president Eisenhower in a magazine article. "Why would they deliberately do this to our country?" Congress, which also had doubts, moved slowly but eventually passed the tax cut in 1964. The Keynesian deficits proved right for the time: the tax cut stimulated enough economic activity that revenues, instead of declining, actually increased.[18]

Aside from being a tax cut and being radical, Reagan's proposal bore little resemblance to Kennedy's. Pushed through Congress in the summer of 1981, the Kemp-Roth bill (named for its congressional sponsors Rep. Jack F. Kemp and Sen. William V. Roth, Jr.) represented an explicit break with mainstream economic thinking, both liberal and conservative. The bill embodied the ideas of a small fringe group of economists whose views conservative Republican economist Herbert Stein dismissed in the *Wall Street Journal* as "punk supply side economics." In selling the bill to Congress, which was submissive in the aftermath of the Reagan election landslide, the administration made bold, unsupported claims. Despite tax rate reductions of 25 percent in a three-year period, it promised, the bill would so stimulate investment that revenues would increase and deficits decline. This resembled the claims for the Kennedy bill except that, under the prevailing conditions, nothing in conventional economic models or empirical estimates remotely justified the optimistic predictions. Senate Republican leader Howard Baker, a reluctant supporter, termed the bill "a riverboat gamble." The gamble did not pay off. Within a year, policy makers were contemplating deficits in the $200 billion range—twice what they had considered intolerable a short time earlier and enough, nearly all agreed, to damage the economy severely.[19]

A president with some measure of sophistication about economic policy would have dismissed the extraordinary claims made for the Kemp-Roth bill as economic demagoguery.[20] He would have become aware of several things at least: that mainstream economists have methods with which they attempt to predict the effects of tax policies; that these methods are very imperfect; but that, however much one might prefer some other result, they still give the best estimates anybody has. President Reagan probably knew that most economists did not endorse Kemp-Roth. Yet he had never paid enough attention to how they argued, it seems, to recognize as important the distinction between ideological faith and empirical measurement.

None of this means that presidents should set ideology aside or simply defer to experts, somehow conceived as neutral. Next to Ronald Reagan, the most conservative recent president was Gerald Ford, who believed strongly in the free market and assembled a cabinet and staff almost exclusively from persons sharing this belief. But the Ford administration also insisted on sound professional analysis for its decisions and took pains to consider a variety of views. Ford's CEA chairman and most influential economic adviser was Alan Greenspan, whose pronounced conservatism was evidenced and partly shaped by his earlier association with Ayn Rand, the literary exponent of an uncompromising laissez-faire capitalism. Even so, to broaden the president's perspective, Greenspan encouraged Ford (and Ford agreed) to meet occasionally with panels of outside economists. Selected for diversity, the panels even included former advisers in Democratic administrations. Greenspan did not regard his main advisory function—producing the administration's economic forecasts—as an appropriate vehicle for ideological expression. Unlike successors in the Reagan administration, he relied on variants of standard economic models and sponsored no major forecasting innovations.[21]

This did not prevent Ford's conservative ideology from shaping his administration's economic policies. The Ford administration held down government spending, stressed controlling inflation more than reducing unemployment, and initiated efforts (markedly successful in the long run) to reduce anticompetitive regulation of business. Part of the knowledge about policy experts needed by a president, and exhibited by Ford, is to understand where "the facts" leave off in making a decision, and thus where moral judgment, guesswork, and ideology have their place.

An adequate level of policy expertise cannot be acquired in a hurry—for example, during the presidential transition. A president needs to have been over the years the kind of politician who participates responsibly in decision making and debate and who does his homework. This means occasionally taking the time to read some of the advocacy documents (such as hearing testimony and committee reports) that are prepared especially for politicians and their staff. Such documents tend to be pitched toward the high end of the politician's scale of sophistication, attention span, and tolerance for technical detail. For one who takes the opportunity, they provide a fairly rigorous education.

If properly prepared, a president need not spend long hours immersed in policy memoranda, the way Jimmy Carter did. If, after a thorough briefing on a decision of ordinary importance, the president still does not see which course he prefers, he is probably just as well off delegating the decision or taking a vote of his advisers. Other tasks will make more of a contribution to his success than further reading or discussion on a decision that is a close call anyway.

Policy Processes

In addition to policy issues, presidents must be competent in the processes of policy making.[22] Most presidential policy decisions are based on advice from several agencies or advisory groups in the executive branch, each with different responsibilities and points of view. To be useful to the president, all the advice must be brought together in a timely, intelligible way, with proper attention to all the significant viewpoints and considerations. Unfortunately, complex organizational and group decision processes like these have a notorious capacity to produce self-defeating and morally unacceptable results. The specific ways in which they go awry are numerous, but in general terms there are three major threats: intelligence failures, in which critical information is filtered out at lower organizational levels (sometimes because subordinates think the president would be upset by or disagree with it);[23] group-think, in which a decision-making group commits itself to a course of action prematurely and adheres to it because of social pressures to conform;[24] and noncoordination, which may occur in formulating advice, in handling interdependent issues, or in carrying out decisions.[25]

Many of the frustrations of the Carter administration resulted from its failure to organize decision processes with sufficient care and skill. Carter's original energy proposals, which affected numerous federal programs, were nonetheless formulated by a single drafting group under the direction of Energy Secretary James Schlesinger. The group worked in secrecy and isolation, as well as under severe time pressure, which the president had imposed. The resulting proposals had serious flaws that, combined with resentment of the secrecy, led to a fiasco in Congress. Such problems were typical. The Carter administration's system of interagency task forces for domestic policy making generally was chaotic and not well controlled by the White House.[26] Moreover, the White House itself was weakly coordinated, a problem widely recognized and also substantiated very concretely in quantitative evidence provided by John Kessel. Compared with the Reagan White House, which he also studied, not only did Carter's have fewer high-level coordinators; but even those that it had were less often in communication with the rest of the staff.[27]

In foreign policy, the major criticisms of the Carter administration concerned its propensity for vacillation and incoherence. Those tendencies resulted largely from its failure to manage the conflict between national security assistant Zbigniew Brzezinski and Secretary of State Cyrus Vance. Despite their different approaches to foreign policy, neither their respective roles and relative authority nor the administration's operative doctrines were ever adequately clear. One crucial issue was whether the American stance toward negotiating with the Soviets on strategic arms would be linked with Soviet activities in the Horn of Africa (as Brzezinski wanted), or decided solely for its direct effects on American strategic interests (the preference of Vance). Instead of being reconciled, both policies were stated in public, each by the official who favored it, which cast doubt on America's ability to act consistently on either of them.[28]

In part, the failure to coordinate foreign policy represented sheer thoughtlessness and naiveté about the management of decision making. To avoid the stereotyped discussion and bureaucratic posturing that plague fully staffed, interdepartmental meetings (an ironic attempt at organizational sophistication), Carter, Brzezinski, and Vance met alone for a weekly principals' lunch. For orderly decision making, the lunches were disastrous. No stenographer was present, so the three would tell their respective aides, often very casually, what had been decided. When the aides checked with their counterparts to confirm the understandings reached, they regularly discovered sharp discrepancies in what each had heard and reported—an outcome no better, perhaps, than no meeting at all.[29] In part, too, the problems resulted from Carter's personal unwillingness to discipline subordinates—to insist, for example, that Brzezinski abide by the more modest role that in theory had been assigned to him.

In short, serious presidential failures often will result not from individual ignorance—his own or that of his advisers—but from their collective failure to maintain reliable processes for decision. But what must a president know to avoid this danger, and how can he learn it?

The effort to design the best possible organization for presidential coordination of the executive branch is exceedingly complex and uncertain—fundamentally a matter of hard trade-offs and guesses, not elegant solutions. Rather than adopt any one organizational plan or carefully study the debates about them, a president needs to possess a high degree of generalized *process sensibility.* He should be generally conversant with the risks and impediments to effective decision making and strongly committed to avoiding them; he should recognize the potentially decisive effects of structure, procedures, and leadership methods; and he should be prepared to assign these matters a high priority. In short, the president should see organization and procedure as matters both difficult and vital.

The main operational requirements are straightforward. One or more of the president's top-level staff should be a process specialist— someone with experience managing large organizations, ideally the White House, and whose role is defined primarily as a manager and guardian of the decision process, not as an adviser on politics and policy.[30] Certainly one such person is needed in the position of White House chief of staff; others, perhaps much lower in rank, are needed to manage each major area of policy. A suitable person would be sophisticated about the problems of organizational design and the subtleties of human relationships—in addition to just being orderly. The president would have to invest the process specialist with the support and authority needed to impose a decision-making structure and help him insist on adherence to it. Since any organizational arrangement will have weaknesses, some of them unexpected, the president and other senior officials must give the decision-making process continual attention—monitoring its performance, and making needed adjustments.

Finally, if any of this is to work, the president also must be willing to discipline his own manner of participation. A well-managed, reliable decision-making process sometimes requires the president to perform, so to speak, unnatural acts. For example, in the heat of debate about a major decision, the inclination to enforce general plans about structures and roles does not come naturally. A procedural "point-of-order" appears to distract from urgent matters at hand. In any case, the president's temptation is to react according to the substantive outcome he thinks he prefers: if an official who is supposed to be a neutral coordinator has a viewpoint the president likes, let him be heard; if an agency will make trouble over a decision that seems inevitable, let them stay out of it. Whatever the established procedures, senior officials sometimes will try to bypass them—asking for more control of a certain issue or ignoring channels to give the president more direct advice.

On important decisions that require intensive discussion—decisions in major foreign policy crises, for example—the requirements are even more unnatural. In order to make such decisions well (or just avoid terrible mistakes), it is crucial not to suppress disagreement or close off debate prematurely. Thus, it is desirable, perhaps essential, for the president to assume a scrupulously neutral stance until the time comes to decide. According to psychologist Irving Janis's study of the Kennedy administration's disastrous decision to invade the Bay of Pigs, the president unwittingly inhibited debate just by his tone and manner of asking questions, which made it obvious that he believed, or wanted to believe, the invasion would work.[31] Thus the president must restrain tendencies that are perfectly normal: to form opinions, perhaps optimistic ones, before all the evidence is in, and then want others to relieve his anxiety by agreeing. He must have a strong process sensibility if only because without it he would lack the motivation to do his own part.

On the whole, the Reagan administration performed well in organization and policy management. But it was not without its failings, some of which demonstrate the need for sophistication and awareness by the president himself. The administration's principal device for making policy decisions, a system of "cabinet councils," was designed by Chief of Staff Baker and Counselor Edwin Meese, both of whom showed a strong interest in organizational issues. Each cabinet council was designed to be, in effect, a subcommittee of the full cabinet, staffed by the White House and chaired by a cabinet officer or the president. The system generally has worked well in blending departmental and White House perspectives and reaching decisions in a timely manner, and it seems to have helped to keep cabinet officers oriented toward broad administration goals.[32]

In some respects Reagan played his part. Unlike Carter, he got rid of people who interfered with effective organization or did not fit in. Richard Allen, who had not been effective as coordinator of the foreign policy machinery, was eased out. At one point Secretary of State Alexander Haig and Defense Secretary Caspar Weinberger were both on notice to curtail their infighting or face possible dismissal; ultimately, Reagan was persuaded that Haig should be replaced by someone more cooperative. In other respects, though, Reagan has been the main threat to rational, orderly processes. Instead of being restrained and conscious of procedures, Reagan was natural and spontaneous. No one could ever predict, it seems, what decisions he would make, when he would intervene, or on whose advice he would act. In the development of the 1983 budget, Reagan showed a willingness to go it alone within his administration. Quite unexpectedly, he chose to "cast the one vote that counts," insisting on a budget that not even congressional Republicans would consider seriously. Despite the attentiveness of Reagan's top advisers, in other words, decisions have sometimes been made by haphazard, unreliable methods because of a lack of procedural sensibility and discipline by the president himself.

Policy Promotion

Good policy decisions, carefully made, are not enough. Presidents also need competence in policy promotion—the ability to get things done in Washington and especially in Congress. For no other major presidential task, it seems, is the necessary knowledge any more complicated or esoteric. Nevertheless, it is also a task in which delegation can largely substitute for the president's own judgment and thus one in which strategic competence places a modest burden on the president.[33]

To promote his policies effectively, a president must act upon good judgment on complex, highly uncertain problems of strategy and tactics. Which presidential policy goals are politically feasible and which must be deferred? With which groups or congressional leaders should coalitions be formed? When resistance is met, should the president stand firm, perhaps taking the issue to the public, or should he compromise? In all these matters what is the proper timing? Such decisions call for a form of political expertise that has several related elements (all of them different from winning elections): a solid knowledge of the main coalitions, influence relations, and rivalries among groups and individuals in Washington; personal acquaintance with a considerable number of important or well-informed individuals; and a fine-grained, practical understanding of how the political institutions work. This distinctive expertise can be acquired, clearly enough, only through substantial and recent experience in Washington. For a president who happens to lack this experience, however, this need not pose much difficulty. Like any technical skill, which in a sense it is, it can easily be hired; the president needs merely to see his need for it.

Because the government has many jobs that require political skill, people with the requisite experience abound. Many of them (to state the matter politely) would be willing to serve in the White House, and by asking around it is not hard to get good readings on their effectiveness. Most importantly, having hired experienced Washington operatives, a president can delegate to them the critical judgments about feasibility, strategy, and political technique. It is not that such judgments are clear-cut, of course. But unlike questions of policy, in these matters there is no difficult boundary to discern between the realm of expertise and that of values and ideology. Political strategy, in the narrow sense of how to achieve given policy objectives to the greatest possible extent, is ideologically neutral. It is even nonpartisan: Republican and Democratic presidents attempt to influence Congress in much the same way.[34] In any case, a political expert's performance in the White House can be measured primarily by short-term results, that is, by how much the administration's policy goals are actually being achieved.

Both the value and the necessity of delegating policy promotion emerge from a comparison of Carter and Reagan—the two recent presidents who had no prior Washington experience. If there was a single, root cause of the failure of the Carter administration (underlying even its mismanagement of decision making), it was its refusal to recruit people with successful experience in Washington politics for top advisory and political jobs in the White House.

One of the more unfortunate choices was that of Frank Moore to direct legislative liaison. Although he had held the same job in Georgia when Carter was governor, Moore had no experience in Washington and came to be regarded in Congress as out of his depth. Among Moore's initial staff, which consisted mostly of Georgians, two of the five professionals had worked neither in Congress nor as a lobbyist. In organizing them, Moore chose a plan that had been opposed by the former Democratic liaison officials asked for advice. Instead of using the conventional division by chambers and major congressional groups, Moore assigned each lobbyist to specialize in an area of policy. This kept them from developing the stable relationships with individual members of Congress that would enhance understanding and elicit trust, and it ignored the straightforward consideration that not all the issues in which the lobbyists specialized would be actively considered at the same time.[35] The Carter administration's reputed incompetence in dealing with Congress might have been predicted: the best of the many Georgians on the Carter staff were able and effective, but others were not, and collectively they lacked the orientation to operate well in Washington.[36]

After this widely condemned failure of his immediate predecessor, it is not surprising that President Reagan did not make the same mistake. But it is still impressive how thoroughly he applied the lesson, even setting aside sectarian considerations for some of the top White House positions. Chief of Staff Baker, who assumed responsibility for political operations, not only had been a Ford administration appointee and campaign manager for George Bush, but was considered too moderate for a high-level position by many of Reagan's conservative supporters. Max Friedersdorf, the first congressional liaison director, was a mainstream Republican with excellent standing among members of both parties and had worked on congressional relations for Nixon and Ford. Friedersdorf put together a lobbying staff with extensive Capitol Hill experience and prior connections with all elements of the Republican party.[37] In short, the political strategy by which the "Reagan revolution" was pushed through Congress in 1981 was devised and executed by highly experienced hired hands who were late-comers, at best, to Reaganism.

Later, when Reagan suffered some major, apparently unnecessary political defeats, it was because in his occasional assertiveness he did not choose to rely on the political experts' advice. In 1983, after he had re-fused repeatedly to compromise with a clear, determined majority of the Senate Budget Committee, the committee cut Reagan's defense spend-ing figures drastically and embarrassingly. His political advisers had pointed out the necessity for compromise, but Reagan had not believed them.

Although the task of formulating strategy for policy promotion can be delegated, much of the hard work cannot. Nothing can draw attention to a proposal and build public support like a well-presented speech by the president. Further, there are always certain votes available in Congress if the president makes the necessary phone calls or meets with the right members. The latter task is often tedious, however, if not somewhat degrading—pleading for support, repeating the same pitch over and over, and promising favors to some while evading requests from others. Presidents therefore often neglect this duty, a source of frustration for their staffs. Carter "went all over the country for two years asking everybody he saw to vote for him," his press secretary complained, "but he doesn't like to call up a Congress-man and ask for his support on a bill." [38] In making speeches and lobbying, of course, the president's effectiveness depends very much on his basic skills in persuasive communication. Here, therefore, we confront a limitation on *any* strategy for competence. Persuasive skills cannot be supplied by presidential aides; moreover, because they are not in any simple way matters of knowledge, they mainly cannot be learned.

The Possibility of Competence

The presidency is not an impossible job. The requirements for personal knowledge, attention, and expertise on the president's part seem wholly manageable—but only if the president has a *strategy* for competence that puts his own, inherently limited capacities to use where and how they are most needed.

With regard to the substance of *policy decisions*, it is enough if the president over the years has given reasonably serious attention to the major national issues and thus is able to recognize the elements of responsible debate. Waking before sunrise to read stacks of policy memoranda is neither necessary nor especially productive. To maintain an effective *policy process*, the president needs mainly to have a strong process sensibility, that is, a clear sense of the need for careful and self-conscious management of decision making and a willingness to discipline himself as he participates in it. He need not claim any facility in drawing the boxes and arrows of organization charts himself. Although this substantive and procedural competence will not ensure that the president will always make the "right" decision—the one he would make with perfect understanding of the issues—it will minimize the likelihood of decisions that are intolerably far off the mark. Finally, and easiest of all, the president must know enough to avail himself of the assistance of persons experienced in *policy promotion* in the political environment of Washington, and especially in dealing with Congress—whether they have been long-time supporters or not. Then he must respect their advice and do the work they ask of him.

Also suggested by the analysis, it seems, is a lesson for the electorate and for commentators on future presidential campaigns. In scrutinizing candidates for president, it is not sufficient to be concerned with partisan, ideological, and moral criteria. For a candidate to be considered credible, he or she should manifest this modest, and very feasible, form of competence. Rank amateurism and lack of sophistication should be denied the benefit of the doubt.

NOTES

* This chapter has been improved greatly as the result of advice from several people: Stella Herriges Quirk, Irving Louis Horowitz, A. James Reichley, Robert A. Katzmann, Martha Derthick, and especially Michael Nelson, who led me to bring out some implicit analytic features of the earlier version.

1. Richard E. Neustadt, *Presidential Power: The Politics of Leadership* (New York: John Wiley & Sons, 1960). Later editions, most recently in 1980, have updated the analysis and in some ways modified the argument.
2. Ibid., chap. 7.
3. James David Barber, *The Presidential Character: Predicting Performance in the White House*, 2d ed. (Englewood Cliffs, N.J.: Prentice-Hall, 1977).
4. Arthur M. Schlesinger, Jr., "Roosevelt as Administrator," in *Bureaucratic Power in National Politics*, 2d ed., edited by Francis E. Rourke (Boston: Little, Brown & Co., 1972), 126-138.
5. Ibid., 132-133, 137.
6. On Johnson's personality and his presidency, see Doris Kearns, *Lyndon Johnson and the American Dream* (New York: Harper & Row, 1976).
7. James Fallows, "The Passionless Presidency," *The Atlantic* (May 1979): 33-48.
8. See Nelson W. Polsby, *Consequences of Party Reform* (New York: Oxford University Press, 1983), 108-109.
9. On the Whig theory and the changing conceptions of the presidency as an institution, see James L. Sundquist, *The Decline and Resurgence of Congress* (Washington, D.C.: The Brookings Institution, 1981), chap. 2.
10. Fred I. Greenstein, *The Hidden-Hand Presidency: Eisenhower as Leader* (New York: Basic Books, 1982).
11. Ibid., 61, 155-227.
12. Dick Kirtschen, "White House Strategy," *National Journal*, February 21, 1981, 300-303.
13. John Herbers, "The Presidency and the Press Corps," *New York Times Magazine*, May 9, 1982, 45ff.
14. The case was *Bob Jones University* v. *United States* (1983).
15. Leon Festinger, *Conflict, Decision, and Dissonance* (Stanford, Calif.: Stanford University Press, 1964).
16. For a discussion of the political and other attitudes of national political reporters, see Stephen Hess, *The Washington Reporters* (Washington, D.C.: The Brookings Institution, 1981), chap. 4.
17. For the sake of brevity, I omit the president's problems and potential strategies for managing policy implementation by the bureaucracy. See Richard P. Nathan, *The Administrative Presidency* (New York: John Wiley & Sons, 1983). This function depends heavily on the appropriate selection of political executives. See G. Calvin Mackenzie, *The Politics of Presidential Appointments* (New York: Free Press, 1980).
18. Arthur M. Schlesinger, Jr., *A Thousand Days: John F. Kennedy in the White House* (Boston: Houghton Mifflin Co., 1965), 628-630, 1002-1008.
19. At least one Reagan administration leader has been candid about the role of faith in its 1981 economic proposals. See William Greider, "The Education of David Stockman," *The Atlantic* (December 1981): 27ff.
20. The same cannot be said of members of Congress, whom one expects to be more prone to demagoguery, and who came under intense political pressure, stimulated in large part by the president.
21. See A. James Reichley, *Conservatives in an Age of Change: The Nixon and Ford Administrations* (Washington, D.C.: The Brookings Institution, 1981), chap. 18; and Roger Porter, *Presidential Decision Making: The Economic Policy Board* (New York: Cambridge University Press, 1980), chap. 3.

22. The president's task in managing decision making is more difficult than that of chief executives in some of the parliamentary democracies because they have more elaborate and better institutionalized coordinating machinery. See Colin Campbell and George J. Szablowski, *The Super-Bureaucrats: Structure and Behavior in Central Agencies* (New York: New York University Press, 1979).

23. Harold Wilensky, *Organizational Intelligence: Knowledge and Policy in Government and Industry* (New York: Basic Books, 1967).

24. Irving Janis, *Victims of GroupThink: A Psychological Study of Foreign-Policy Decisions and Fiascoes* (Boston: Houghton Mifflin Co., 1972).

25. Fundamentally, all organization theory concerns the problem of coordination. See Anthony Downs, *Inside Bureaucracy* (Boston: Little, Brown & Co., 1967), chap. 11; Jay R. Galbraith, *Organization Design* (Reading, Mass.: Addison Wesley, 1977). Problems of coordination in the executive branch are emphasized in I. M. Destler, *Making Foreign Economic Policy* (Washington, D.C.: The Brookings Institution, 1980).

26. Lester M. Salamon, "The Presidency and Domestic Policy Formulation," in *The Illusion of Presidential Government,* ed. Hugh Heclo and Lester Salamon (Boulder, Colo.: Westview Press, 1982), 177-212.

27. For this and other Reagan-Carter comparisons, see John H. Kessel, "The Structures of the Reagan White House," (Paper delivered at the annual meeting of the American Political Science Association, Chicago, Ill., September 1-4, 1983). More generally on Carter, however, see Kessel, "The Structures of the Carter White House," *American Journal of Political Science* 22 (August 1983).

28. The resulting mutual recriminations constitute leading themes in the recently published memoirs of the two officials. See Cyrus Vance, *Hard Choices: Critical Years in America's Foreign Policy* (New York: Simon & Schuster, 1983); and Zbigniew Brzezinski, *Power and Principle: Memoirs of the National Security Advisor, 1977-1981* (New York: Farrar, Straus & Giroux, 1983).

29. Personal conversations with two Carter administration national security aides who were involved in this process.

30. An influential argument for separating the roles of process manager and policy adviser is in Alexander George, "The Case for Multiple Advocacy in Making Foreign Policy," *American Political Science Review,* 66 (September 1972): 751-785; see also idem, *Presidential Decision Making: The Effective Use of Information and Advice* (Boulder, Colo.: Westview Press, 1980).

31. Janis, *Victims,* chap. 2.

32. Dick Kirtschen, "Reagan's Cabinet Councils May Have Less Influence Than Meets the Eye," *National Journal,* July 11, 1981, 1242-1247. The title of this article is misleading. Kirtschen argues that the councils play the main role in developing issues for the president's decision, but points out that decisions have been modified through negotiations with Congress, a process in which James Baker and his political staff are most influential.

33. On the president's relations with Congress, see Anthony King, ed., *Both Ends of the Avenue: The Presidency, the Executive Branch, and Congress in the 1980s* (Washington, D.C.: American Enterprise Institute for Public Policy Research, 1983).

34. For a historical treatment and analysis of organization for White House liaison, see Stephen J. Wayne, *The Legislative Presidency* (New York: Harper & Row, 1978).

35. Eric L. Davis, "Legislative Liaison in the Carter Administration," *Political Science Quarterly,* 95 (Summer 1979): 287-302. Eventually, organization of the taff by issues was dropped.

36. In *Consequences of Party Reform*, 105-114, Polsby details the Carter administration's major mistakes in dealing with Congress and argues persuasively that its difficulties were not importantly the result of internal changes in Congress.

37. Dick Kirtschen, "The Pennsylvania Ave. Connection—Making Peace on Capitol Hill," *National Journal,* March 7, 1981, 384-387.

38. Quoted in Polsby, *Consequences of Party Reform*, 109.

6. THE PSYCHOLOGICAL PRESIDENCY

Michael Nelson

The United States elects its president every four years, which makes it unique among democratic nations. Since 1972, *Time* magazine has run a story about James David Barber every presidential election year, which makes him equally singular among political scientists. The two quadrennial oddities are not unrelated.

The first *Time* article was about Barber's just-published book *The Presidential Character: Predicting Performance in the White House,* in which he argued that presidents could be divided into four psychological types: "active-positive," "active-negative," "passive-positive," and "passive-negative." What's more, according to Barber via *Time,* with "a hard look at men before they reach the White House," voters could tell in advance what candidates would be like if elected: healthily "ambitious out of exuberance" like the active-positives; or pathologically "ambitious out of anxiety," "compliant and other-directed," or "dutiful and self-denying" like the three other, lesser types, respectively. In the 1972 election, Barber told *Time,* the choice was between an active-positive, George McGovern, and a psychologically defective active-negative, Richard Nixon.[1]

Nixon won the election, but Barber's early insights into Nixon's personality won notoriety for both him and his theory, especially in the wake of Watergate. So prominent had Barber become by 1976 that Hugh Sidey used his entire "Presidency" column in the October 4 *Time* just to tell readers that Barber was refusing to "type" candidates Gerald Ford and Jimmy Carter this time around. "Barber is deep into an academic study of this election and its participants, and he is pledged to restraint until it is over," Sidey reported solemnly.[2] (Actually, more than a year before, Barber had told interviewers from *U.S. News & World Report* that he considered Ford an active-positive.)[3] Carter, who read Barber's book twice when it came out, was left to tell the *Washington Post* that active-positive is "what I would like to be. That's what I hope I prove to be."[4] And so Carter would, wrote Barber in a special postelection column for *Time.*[5]

The 1980 election campaign witnessed the appearance of another Barber book, *The Pulse of Politics: Electing Presidents in the Media Age,* and in honor of the occasion, two *Time* articles. This was all to the good, because the first, a Sidey column in March, offered more gush than information: "The first words encountered in the new book by Duke's Professor James David Barber are stunning: 'A revolution in presidential politics is underway.'. . . Barber has made political history before." [6] A more substantive piece in the May 19 "Nation" section described the new book's cycle theory of twentieth-century presidential elections: since 1900, steady four-year "beats" in the public's psychological mood, or "pulse," have caused a recurring alternation among elections of "conflict," "conscience," and "conciliation." *Time* went on to stress, although not explain, Barber's view of the importance of the mass media, both as a reinforcer of this cycle and as a potential mechanism for helping to break the nation out of it.[7]

Time's infatuation with Barber brought him fame that comes rarely to scholars, more rarely still to political scientists. For Barber, it has come at some cost. Although widely known, his ideas are little understood. The media's cursory treatment of them has made them appear superficial or even foolish—instantly appealing to the naive, instantly odious to the thoughtful. Partly as a result, Barber's reputation in the intellectual community as an *homme sérieux* has suffered. In the backrooms and corridors of scholarly gatherings, one hears "journalistic" and "popularizer," the ultimate academic epithets, muttered along with his name.

This situation is in need of remedy. Barber's theories may be seriously flawed, but they are serious theories. For all their limitations—some of them self-confessed—they offer one of the more significant contributions a scholar can make: an unfamiliar but useful way of looking at a familiar thing that we no longer see very clearly. In Barber's case, the familiar thing is the American presidency, and the unfamiliar way of looking at it is through the lenses of psychology.

Psychological Perspectives on the Presidency

Constitutional Perspectives

Looking at politics in general, or the American presidency in particular, from a psychological perspective is not new. Although deprived of the insights (and spared the nonsense) of twentieth-century psychology, the framers of the Constitution constructed their plan of government on a foundation of Hobbesian assumptions about what motivates political man. James Madison and most of his colleagues at the Constitutional Convention assumed that "men are instruments of their desires"; that "one such desire is the desire for power"; and that "if unrestrained by external checks, any individual or group of individuals will tyrannize over others." [8] Because the framers believed this, a basic tenet of their political philosophy was that the government they were designing should be a "government of laws and not of men." Not just psychology, but recent history had taught them to associate liberty with law and tyranny with rulers who departed from law, as had George III and his colonial governors.

In the end the convention yielded to those who urged, on grounds of "energy in the executive," that the Constitution lodge the powers of the executive branch in a single person, the president.[9] There are several explanations for why the framers were willing to put aside their doubts and inject such a powerful dose of individual "character," both in the moral and psychological senses of the word, into their new plan of government. The first is the framers' certain knowledge that George Washington would be the nation's first president. They knew that Washington aroused powerful and, from the standpoint of winning the nation's support for the new government, vital psychological reactions from the people. As Seymour Martin Lipset has shown, Washington was a classic example of Max Weber's charismatic leader, a man "treated [by the people] as endowed with supernatural, superhuman, or at least specifically exceptional powers or qualities." [10] Marcus Cunliffe notes that

> Babies were being christened after him as early as 1775, and while he was still President, his countrymen paid to see him in waxwork effigy. To his admirers he was "godlike Washington," and his detractors complained to one another that he was looked upon as a "demigod" who it was treasonous to criticize. "Oh Washington!" declared Ezra Stiles of Yale (in a sermon of 1783). "How I do love thy name! How have I often adored and blessed thy God, for creating and forming thee the great ornament of human kind!" [11]

Just as Washington's charismatic "gift of grace" would legitimize the new government, the framers believed, so would his personal character ensure its republican nature. The powers of the president in the Constitution "are full great," wrote South Carolina convention delegate Pierce Butler to a British kinsman,

> and greater than I was disposed to make them. Nor, entre nous, do I believe they would have been so great had not many of the delegates cast their eyes towards General Washington as President; and

shaped their Ideas of the Powers to be given to a President, by their opinions of his Virtue.[12]

The framers were not so naive or short-sighted as to invest everything in Washington. To protect the nation from power-mad tyrants after he left office, they provided that the election of presidents, whether by electors or members of the House of Representatives, would involve selection by peers—personal acquaintances of the candidates who could screen out those of defective character. And even if someone of low character slipped through the net and became president, the framers felt that they had structured the office to keep the nation from harm. "The founders' deliberation over the provision for indefinite reeligibility," writes Jeffrey Tulis, "illustrates how they believed self-interest could sometimes be elevated." [13] Whether motivated by "avarice," "ambition," or "the love of fame," argues Alexander Hamilton in the *Federalist,* a president will behave responsibly in order to secure reelection to the office that allows him to fulfill his desire.[14] Underlying this confidence was the assurance that in a relatively slow-paced world, a mad or wicked president could do only so much damage before corrective action could remove him. As John Jay explains, "So far as the fear of punishment and disgrace can operate, that motive to good behavior is amply afforded by the article on the subject of impeachment." [15]

Scholarly Perspectives

The framers' decision to inject personality into the presidency was a conscious one. But it was made for reasons that eventually ceased to pertain, the last of them crumbling on August 6, 1945, when on orders of an American president, an atomic bomb was dropped on Hiroshima. The destructive powers at a modern president's disposal are ultimate and swift; the impeachment process now seems uncertain and slow. "Peer review" never took hold in the Electoral College. The rise of the national broadcast media makes the president's personality all the more pervasive. In sum, the framers' carefully conceived defenses against a president of defective character are gone.

Clearly, then, a sophisticated psychological perspective on the presidency was overdue in the late 1960s when Barber began offering one in a series of articles and papers that culminated in *The Presidential Character.*[16] Presidential scholars long had taken as axiomatic that the American presidency is an institution shaped in some measure by the personalities of individual presidents. But rarely had the literature of personality *theory* been brought to bear, in large part because scholars of the post-Franklin D. Roosevelt period no longer seemed to share the framers' assumptions about human nature, at least as far as the presidency was concerned. As we saw in Chapter 1, historians and political scientists exalted not only presidential power, but presidents who were ambitious for power. Richard Neustadt's influential book *Presidential Power,* published in 1960, was typical in this regard:

> The contributions that a president can make to government are indispensable. Assuming that he knows what power is and wants it, those contributions cannot help but be forthcoming in some measure as by-products of his search for personal influence.[17]

As Erwin Hargrove reflected in post-Vietnam, post-Watergate 1974, this line of reasoning was the source of startling deficiencies in scholarly understandings of the office: "We had assumed that ideological purpose was sufficient to purify the drive for power, but we forgot the importance of character."[18]

Scholars also had recognized for some time that Americans' attitudes about the presidency, like presidents' actions, are psychologically as well as politically rooted. Studies of school children indicated that they first come into political awareness by learning of, and feeling fondly toward, the president. As adults, they "rally" to the president's support, both when they inaugurate a new one and in times of crisis.[19] Popular nationalistic emotions, which in constitutional monarchies are directed toward the king or queen, are deflected in American society onto the presidency. Again, however, scholars' awareness of these psychological forces manifested itself more in casual observation (Dwight Eisenhower was a "father figure"; the "public mood" is fickle) than in systematic thought.

The presidencies of John F. Kennedy, Lyndon B. Johnson, and Richard Nixon altered this state of scholarly quiescence. Surveys taken shortly after the Kennedy assassination recorded the startling depth of the feelings that citizens have about the presidency. A large share of the population experienced symptoms classically associated with grief over the death of a loved one. Historical evidence suggests that the public has responded similarly to the deaths of all sitting presidents, popular or not, by murder or natural causes.[20]

If Kennedy's death illustrated the deep psychological ties of the public to the presidency, the experiences of his successors showed even more clearly the importance of psychology in understanding the connection between president and presidency. Johnson, the peace candidate who rigidly pursued a self-defeating policy of war, and Nixon, who promised "lower voices" only to angrily turn political disagreements into personal crises, projected their personalities onto policy in ways that were both obvious and destructive. The events of this period brought students of the presidency up short. As they paused to consider the nature of the "psychological presidency," they found Barber standing at the ready with the foundation and first floor of a full-blown theory.

James David Barber and the Psychological Presidency

Barber's theory offers a model of the presidency as an institution shaped largely by the psychological mix between the personalities of individual presidents and the public's deep feelings about the office. It also proposes methods of predicting what those personalities and feelings are likely to be in given instances. These considerations govern *The Presidential Character* and *The Pulse of Politics,* books that we shall examine in turn. The question of how we can become masters of our own and of the presidency's psychological fate also is treated in these books but it receives fuller exposition in other works by Barber.

Presidential Psychology

> The primary danger of the Nixon administration will be that the President will grasp some line of policy or method of operation and pursue it in spite of its failure. . . . How will Nixon respond to challenges to the morality of his regime, to charges of scandal and/or corruption? First such charges strike a raw nerve, not only from the Checkers business, but also from deep within the personality in which the demands of the superego are so harsh and hard. . . . The first impulse will be to hush it up, to conceal it, bring down the blinds. If it breaks open and Nixon cannot avoid commenting on it, there is a real setup here for another crisis. . . .

James David Barber is more than a little proud of that prediction, primarily because he made it in a talk he gave at Stanford University on January 19, 1969, the eve of Richard Nixon's first inauguration. It was among the first in a series of speeches, papers, and articles whose purpose was to explain his theory of presidential personality and how to predict it, always with his forecast for Nixon's future prominently, and thus riskily, displayed. The theory received its fullest statement in *The Presidential Character.*

"Character," in Barber's usage, is not quite a synonym for personality.[21] A politician's psychological constitution also includes two other components: his adolescence-born "world view," which Barber defines as his "primary, politically relevant beliefs, particularly his conceptions of social causality, human nature, and the central moral conflicts of the time"; and his "style," or "habitual way of performing three political roles: rhetoric, personal relations, and homework," which develops in early adulthood. But clearly Barber regards character, which forms in childhood and shapes the later development of style and world view, to be "the most important thing to know about a president or candidate." As he defines the term, "character is the way the President orients himself toward life—not for the moment, but enduringly." It "grows out of the child's experiments in relating to parents, brothers and sisters, and peers at play and in school, as well as to his own body and the objects around it." Through these experiences, the child—and thus the man to be—arrives subconsciously at a deep and private understanding of his fundamental worth.

For some, this process results in high self-esteem, the vital ingredient for psychological health and political productiveness. Others must search outside themselves for evidence of worth that at best will be a partial substitute. Depending on the source and nature of their limited self-esteem, Barber suggests, they will concentrate their search in one of three areas: the affection from others that compliant and agreeable behavior brings, the sense of usefulness that comes from performing a widely respected duty, or the deference attendant with dominance and control over other people. Because politics is a vocation rich in opportunities to find all three of these things—affection from cheering crowds and backslapping colleagues, usefulness from public service in a civic cause, dominance through official power—it is not surprising that some insecure people are attracted to a political career.

This makes for a problem, Barber argues: if public officials, especially presidents, use their office to compensate for private doubts and demons, it follows that they will not always use it for public purposes. Affection-seekers will be so concerned with preserving the good will of those around them that they rarely will challenge the status quo or otherwise rock the boat. The duty-doers will be similarly inert, although in their case inertia will result from their feeling that to be "useful" they must be diligent guardians of time-honored practices and procedures. Passive presidents of both kinds may provide the nation with "breathing spells, times of recovery in our frantic political life," or even "a refreshing hopefulness and at least some sense of sharing and caring." Still, in Barber's view, their main effect is to "divert popular attention from the hard realities of politics," thus leaving the country to "drift." And "what passive presidents ignore, active presidents inherit." [22]

Power-driven presidents pose the greatest danger. They will seek their psychological compensation not in inaction but in intense efforts to maintain or extend their personal sense of domination and control through public channels. When things are going well for the power-driven president and he feels that he has the upper hand on his political opponents, there may be no problem. But when things cease to go his way, as eventually they must in a democratic system, such a president's response almost certainly will take destructive forms, such as rigid defensiveness or aggression against opponents. Only those with high self-esteem will be secure enough to lead as democratic political leaders must lead, with persuasion and flexibility as well as action and initiative.

Perhaps more important than the theoretical underpinnings of Barber's character analysis is the practical purpose that animates *The Presidential Character*: to help citizens choose their presidents wisely. The book's first words herald this purpose:

> When a citizen votes for a presidential candidate he makes, in effect, a prediction. He chooses from among the contenders the one he thinks (or feels, or guesses) would be the best president.... This book is meant to help citizens and those who advise them cut through the confusion and get at some clear criteria for choosing presidents.

How, though, in the heat and haste of a presidential election, with candidates notably unwilling to bare their souls publicly for psychoanalytical inspection, are we to find out what they are really like? Easy enough, argues Barber: to answer the difficult question of what motivates a political man, just answer two simpler ones in its stead: Is he active or passive? ("How much energy does the man invest in his presidency?"); and is he positive or negative? ("Relatively speaking, does he seem to experience his political life as happy or sad, enjoyable or discouraging, positive or negative in its main effect?") According to Barber, the four possible combinations of answers to these questions turn out to be almost synonymous with the four psychological strategies people use to enhance self-esteem. The "active-positive" is the healthy one in the group. His high sense of self-worth enables him to work hard at politics, have fun at what he does, and thus be fairly good at it. Of the four eighteenth- and nineteenth-century presidents and 14 twentieth-century presidents whom Barber has "typed," he places Thomas Jefferson, Franklin D. Roosevelt, Harry S. Truman, Kennedy, Ford, and Carter in this category. The "passive-positive" (James Madison, William Howard Taft, Warren Harding, Ronald Reagan) is the affection-seeker; although not especially hard-working in office, he enjoys it. The "passive-negative" (Washington, Calvin Coolidge, Eisenhower) neither works nor plays; it is duty, not pleasure or zest, that gets him into politics. Finally, there is the power-seeking "active-negative," who compulsively throws himself into his presidential chores with little satisfaction. In Barber's view, active-negative Presidents John Adams, Woodrow Wilson, Herbert Hoover, Johnson, and Nixon all shared one important personality-rooted quality: they persisted in disastrous courses of action (Adams's repressive Alien and Sedition Acts, Wilson's League of Nations battle, Hoover's depression policy, Johnson's Vietnam, Nixon's Watergate) because to have conceded that they were wrong would have been to cede their sense of control, something their psychological constitutions could not allow.[23] Table 6-1 summarizes Barber's four types and his categorizations of individual presidents.

Not surprisingly, *The Presidential Character* was extremely controversial when it came out in 1972. Many argued that Barber's theory was too simple, that his four types did not begin to cover the range of human complexity. At one level, this criticism is as trivial as it is true. In spelling out his theory, Barber states very clearly that "we are talking about tendencies, broad directions; no individual man exactly fits a category." His typology is offered as a method for sizing up potential presidents, not for diagnosing and treating them. Given the nature of election campaigning, a reasonably accurate shorthand device is about all we can hope for. The real question, then, is whether Barber's shorthand device is reasonably accurate.

Barber's intellectual defense of his typology's soundness, quoted here in full, is not altogether comforting:

> Why might we expect these two simple dimensions [active-passive, positive-negative] to outline the main character types? Because they stand for two central features of anyone's orientation toward life. In nearly every study of personality, some form of the active-passive contrast is critical; the general tendency to act or be acted upon is evident in such concepts as dominance-submission, extraversion-introversion, aggression-timidity, attack-defense, fight-flight, engagement-withdrawal, approach-avoidance. In every life we sense quickly the general energy output of the people we deal with. Similarly we catch on fairly quickly to the affect dimension—whether the person seems to be optimistic or pessimistic, hopeful or

Table 6-1 Barber's Character Typology, with Presidents Categorized According to Type

Affect Toward the Presidency

	POSITIVE	NEGATIVE
ACTIVE	Thomas Jefferson Franklin Roosevelt Harry Truman John Kennedy Gerald Ford Jimmy Carter "consistency between much activity and the enjoyment of it, indicating relatively high self-esteem and relative success in relating to the environment ... shows an orientation to productiveness as a value and an ability to use his styles flexibly, adaptively"	John Adams Woodrow Wilson Herbert Hoover Lyndon Johnson Richard Nixon "activity has a compulsive quality, as if the man were trying to make up for something or escape from anxiety into hard work ... seems ambitious, striving upward, power-seeking ... stance toward the environment is aggressive and has a problem in managing his aggressive feelings."
PASSIVE	James Madison William Taft Warren Harding Ronald Reagan "receptive, compliant, other-directed character whose life is a search for affection as a reward for being agreeable and co-operative ... low self-esteem (on grounds of being unlovable)"	George Washington Calvin Coolidge Dwight Eisenhower "low self-esteem based on a sense of uselessness ... in politics because they think they ought to be ... tendency is to withdraw, to escape from the conflict and uncertainty of politics by emphasizing vague principles (especially prohibitions) and procedural arrangements."

Energy Directed Toward the Presidency

SOURCE: Barber's discussions of all presidents but Ford, Carter, and Reagan are in *The Presidential Character: Predicting Performance in the White House* (Englewood Cliffs, N.J.: Prentice-Hall, 1972). For Ford and Carter, see "After Eight Months in Office—How Ford Rates Now," *U.S. News & World Report*, April 28, 1975, and James David Barber, "An Active-Positive Character," *Time*, January 3, 1977, 17. For Reagan, see James David Barber, "Worrying About Reagan," *The New York Times*, September 8, 1980, 19.

skeptical, happy or sad. The two baselines are clear and they are also independent of one another: all of us know people who are very active but seem discouraged, others who are quite passive but seem happy, and so forth. The activity baseline refers to what one does, the affect baseline to how one feels about what he does.

Both are crude clues to character. They are leads into four basic character patterns long familiar in psychological research.[24]

In the library copy of *The Presidential Character* from which I copied this passage, there is a handwritten note in the margin: "Footnote, man!" But there is no footnote to the psychological literature, here or anywhere else in the book. Casual readers might take this to mean that none is necessary, and they would be right if Barber's types really were "long familiar in psychological research" and "appeared in nearly every study of personality." [25] But they aren't and they don't; as Alexander George has pointed out, personality theory itself is a "quagmire" in which "the term 'character' in practice is applied loosely and means many different things." [26] Barber's real defense of his theory—that it works; witness Nixon—is not to be dismissed, but one wishes he had explained better why he thinks it works.[27]

Interestingly, Barber's typology also has been criticized for not being simple enough, at least not for purposes of accurate preelection application. Where, exactly, is one to look to decide if Candidate Jones is, deep down, the energetic, buoyant fellow his image-makers say he is. Barber is quite right in warning analysts away from their usual hunting ground—the candidate's recent performances in other high offices. These offices "are all much more restrictive than the Presidency is, much more set by institutional requirements," [28] and thus much less fertile cultures for psychopathologies to grow in. (This is Barber's only real mention of what might be considered a third, coequal component of the psychological presidency: the rarefied, court-like atmosphere—so well described in George Reedy's *The Twilight of the Presidency*[29]— that surrounds presidents and allows those whose psychological constitutions so move them to seal themselves off from harsh political realities.)

Barber's alternative—a study of the candidate's "first independent political success," or "fips," in which he found his personal formula for success in politics—is not very helpful either. How, for example, is one to tell which "ips" was first? According to Barber's appropriately broad definition of "political," Johnson's first success was not his election to Congress, but his work as a student assistant to his college president.

Hoover's was his incumbency as student body treasurer at Stanford. Sorting through someone's life with the thoroughness necessary to arrive at such a determination may or not be an essential task. But clearly it is not a straightforward one.

Some scholars question not only the technical basis or practical applicability of Barber's psychological theory of presidential behavior, but also the importance of psychological explanation itself. Psychology appears to be almost everything to Barber, as this statement from his research design reveals:

> What is de-emphasized in this scheme? Everything which does not lend itself to the production of potentially testable generalizations about presidential behavior. Thus we shall be less concerned with the substance or content of particular issues . . . less concern[ed] for distant phenomena, such as relationships among other political actors affecting events without much reference to the president, public opinion, broad economic or historical trends, etc.—except insofar as these enter into the president's own approach to decision-making.[30]

But is personality all that matters? Provocative though it may be, Barber's theory seems to unravel even as he applies it. A "healthy" political personality turns out not to be a guarantor of presidential success: Barber classed Ford and Carter early in their presidencies as active-positives, for example. Carter, in fact, seemed to take flexibility—a virtue characteristic of active-positives—to such an extreme that it approached vacillation and inconsistency, almost as if in reading *The Presidential Character* he had learned its lessons too well.

Nor, as Table 6-2 shows, does Barber's notion of psychological unsuitability seem to correspond to failure in office. The ranks of the most successful presidents in three recent surveys by historians include some whom Barber classified as active-positives (Jefferson, Truman, and Franklin Roosevelt), but an equal number of active-negatives (Wilson, Lyndon Johnson, and John Adams), and others whom Barber labeled passive-negatives (Washington and Eisenhower).[31] The most perverse result of classifying presidents by this standard involves Abraham Lincoln, whom Jeffrey Tulis, correctly applying Barber's theory, found to be an active-negative.[32]

Clearly, personality is not all that matters in the modern presidency. As Tulis notes, Lincoln's behavior as president can be explained much better by his political philosophy and skills than by his personality. Similarly, one need not resort to psychology to explain the failures of "active-negatives" Hoover and, in the latter years of his

Table 6-2   "Great" Presidents and Barber's Character Typology

	POSITIVE	NEGATIVE
ACTIVE	Thomas Jefferson Franklin Roosevelt Harry Truman	John Adams Woodrow Wilson Lyndon Johnson (Abraham Lincoln)
PASSIVE		George Washington Dwight Eisenhower

NOTE: For the purposes of this table, a "great" president is defined as one who ranked among the first ten in at least one of these three polls of historians: Steve Neal, "Our Best and Worst Presidents," *Chicago Tribune Magazine,* January 10, 1982, 9-18; Lloyd Shearer, "U.S. Presidents: How They Rate," (report on a 1982 survey by Robert Murray), *Parade,* December 12, 1982, 10; and David L. Porter, letter to author, January 15, 1982. Four others who achieved this ranking (Jackson, Polk, T. Roosevelt, and McKinley) are not included because Barber did not classify them according to his typology.

presidency, Lyndon Johnson. Hoover's unbending resistance to federal relief in the face of the depression may have stemmed more from ideological beliefs than psychological rigidity. Johnson's refusal to change the administration's policy in Vietnam could be interpreted as the action of a self-styled consensus leader trying to steer a moderate course between "hawks" who wanted full-scale military involvement and "doves" who wanted unilateral withdrawal.[33] These presidents' actions were ineffective, but not necessarily irrational.

The theoretical and practical criticisms that have been mentioned are important ones, and they do not exhaust the list. (Observer bias, for example. Since Barber's published writings provide no clear checklist of criteria by which to type candidates, subjectivity is absolutely inherent.) But they should not blind us to his major contributions in *The Presidential Character:* a concentration (albeit an overconcentration) on the importance of presidential personality in explaining presidential behavior, a sensitivity to its nature as a variable (power does not always corrupt; nor does the office always make the man), and a boldness in approaching the problems voters face in predicting what candidates will be like if elected.

Public Psychology

The other side of the psychological presidency—the public's side—is Barber's concern in *The Pulse of Politics: Electing Presidents in the Media Age.* The book focuses on elections, those occasions when, because citizens are filling the presidential office, they presumably feel (presidential deaths aside) their emotional attachments to it most deeply. Again Barber presents us with a typology. The public's election moods come in three variations: *conflict* ("we itch for adventure, . . . [a] blood-and-guts political contest"), *conscience* ("the call goes out for a revival of social conscience, the restoration of the constitutional covenant"), and *conciliation* ("the public yearns for solace, for domestic tranquility").[34] This time the types appear in recurring order as well, over 12-year cycles.

Barber's question—What is the nature of "the swirl of emotions" with which Americans surround the presidency?—is as important and original as the questions he posed in *The Presidential Character.* But again, his answer is as puzzling as it is provocative. Although Barber's theory applies only to American presidential elections in this century, he seems to feel that the psychological "pulse" has beaten deeply, if softly, in all humankind for all time. Barber finds conflict, conscience, and conciliation in the "old sagas" of early man and in "the psychological paradigm that dominates the modern age: the *ego,* instrument for coping with the struggles of the external world [conflict]; the *superego,* warning against harmful violations [conscience]; the *id,* longing after the thrill and ease of sexual satisfaction [conciliation]." He finds it firmly reinforced in American history. Conflict is reflected in our emphasis on the war story ("In isolated America, the warmakers repeatedly confronted the special problem of arousing the martial spirit against distant enemies. . . . Thus our history vibrates with *talk* about war"); conscience is displayed in America's sense of itself as an instrument of divine providence ("our conscience has never been satisfied by government as a mere practical arrangement"); and conciliation shows up in our efforts to live with each other in a heterogeneous "nation of nationalities." In the twentieth century, Barber argues, these themes became the controlling force in the political psychology of the American electorate, so controlling that every presidential election since the conflict of 1900 has fit its place within the cycle (conscience in 1904, conciliation in 1908, conflict again in 1912, and so on). What caused the pulse to start beating this strongly, he feels, was the rise of national mass media.

The modern newspaper came first, just before the turn of the century. "In a remarkable historical conjunction," writes Barber, "the sudden surge into mass popularity of the American daily newspaper coincided with the Spanish-American War." Since war stories sold papers, daily journalists also wrote about "politics as war" or conflict. In the early 1900s, national mass circulation magazines arrived on the scene, taking their cues from the Progressive reformers who dominated that period. "The 'muckrakers'—actually positive thinkers out to build America, not destroy reputations"—wrote of "politics as a moral enterprise," an enterprise of conscience. Then came the broadcast media, radio in the 1920s and television in the 1950s. What set them apart was their commercial need to reach not just a wide audience, but the widest possible audience. "Broadcasting aimed to please, wrapping politics in fun and games . . . conveying with unmatched reach and power its core message of conciliation."

As for the cyclic pulse, the recurring appearance of these public moods in the same precise order, Barber suggests that the dynamic is internal: each type of public mood generates the next. After a conflict election ("a battle for power . . . a rousing call to arms"), a reaction sets in. Conscience calls for "the cleansing of the temple of democracy." But "the troubles do not go away," and four years later "the public yearns for solace," conciliation. After another four years, Barber claims, "the time for a fight will come around again," and so on.

In *The Pulse of Politics*, difficulties arise not in applying the theory (a calendar will do: if it's 1980, this must be a conciliating election), but from the theory itself. Barber needs an even more secure intellectual foundation here than in his character theory, for this time he not only classifies all presidential elections into three types, but also asserts that they will recur in a fixed order. Once again, however, there are no footnotes; if Barber is grounding his theory in external sources, it is impossible to tell—and hard to imagine—what they are. Nor does the theory stand up sturdily under its own weight. If, for example, radio and television are agents of conciliation, why did we not have fewer conciliating elections before they became our dominant political media and more since? Perhaps that is why some of the "postdictions" Barber's theory leads to are as questionable as they are easy to make: Did conflict typify the 1924 Coolidge-Davis election, conscience the Eisenhower-Stevenson election in 1952, and conciliation the 1968 contest between Nixon, Humphrey, and Wallace?

The most interesting criticism pertinent to Barber's pulse theory, however, was made in 1972 by a political scientist concerned with the public's presidential psychology, which he described in terms of a "climate of expectations" that "shifts and changes." This scholar wrote: "Wars, depressions, and other national events contribute to that change, but there is also a rough cycle, from an emphasis on action (which begins to look too 'political') to an emphasis on legitimacy (the moral uplift of which creates its own strains) to an emphasis on reassurance and rest (which comes to seem like drift) and back to action again. One need not be astrological about it." (A year earlier this scholar had written that although "the mystic could see the series ... marching in fateful repetition beginning in 1900 ... the pattern is too astrological to be convincing.") Careful readers will recognize the identity between the cycles of action-legitimacy-reassurance and conflict-conscience-conciliation. Clever ones will realize that the passages above were written by James David Barber.[35]

Man, Mood, and the Psychological Presidency

There is, in fact, a good deal about the public's political psychology sprinkled through *The Presidential Character,* and the more of it one discovers, the more curious things get. Most significant is the brief concluding chapter on "Presidential Character and the Moods of the Eighth Decade" (reprinted unchanged in the 1977 second edition), which contains Barber's bold suggestion of a close fit between the two sides of his model. For each type of public psychological climate, Barber posits a "resonant" type of presidential personality. This seems to be a central point in his theory of the presidency: "Much of what [a president] is remembered for," he argues, "will depend on the fit between the dominant forces in his character and the dominant feelings in his constituency." Further, "the dangers of discord in that resonance are great." [36]

What is the precise nature of this fit? When the public cry is for action (conflict), Barber argues, "[i]t comes through loudest to the active-negative type, whose inner struggle between aggression and control resonates with the popular plea for toughness. . . . [The active-negative's] temptation to stand and fight receives wide support from the culture." In the public's reassurance (conciliation) mood, he writes, "they want a friend," a passive-positive. As for the "appeal for a moral cleansing of the Presidency," or legitimacy (conscience), Barber suggests that it "resonates with the passive-negative character in its emphasis on *not doing* certain things." This leaves the active-positive, Barber's president for all seasons.[37] Blessed with a "character firmly rooted in self-recognition and self-love, Barber's "active-positive can not only *perform* lovingly or aggressively or with detachment, he can *feel* those ways." [38]

What Barber first offered in *The Presidential Character,* then, was the foundation of a model of the psychological presidency that was not only two-sided, but integrated as well, one in which the "tuning, the resonance—or lack of it" between the public's "climate of expectations" and the president's personality "sets in motion the dynamic of his Presidency." He concentrated on the personality half of his model in *The Presidential Character,* then firmed it up (after de-"astrologizing" it) and filled in the other half—the public's—in *The Pulse of Politics.* And here is where things get so curious. Most authors, when they complete a multivolume opus, trumpet their accomplishment. Barber does not. In fact, one finds in *The Pulse of Politics* no mention at all of presidential character, of public climates of expectations, or of "the resonance—or lack of it" between them. [39]

At first blush, this seems doubly strange, because there is a strong surface fit between the separate halves of Barber's model. As Table 6-3 indicates, in the 19 elections since Taft's in 1908 (Barber did not type twentieth-century presidents farther back than Taft), presidential character and public mood resonated 13 times. The six exceptions— active-negative Wilson's election in the conscience year of 1916, passive-negative Coolidge's in conflictual 1924, active-negative Hoover's and passive-negative Eisenhower's in the conciliating elections of 1928 and 1956, active-negative Johnson's in conscience-oriented 1964, and active-negative Nixon's in conciliating 1968—perhaps could be explained in terms of successful campaign image-management by the winners, an argument that also would support Barber's view of the media's power in presidential politics. In that case, a test of Barber's model would be: did these six "inappropriate" presidents lose the public's support when it found out what they really were like after the election? In every presidency but Eisenhower's and Coolidge's, the answer would have been yes.

On closer inspection it also turns out that in every case but these two, the presidents whose administrations were unsuccessful were active-negatives, whom Barber tells us will fail for reasons that have nothing to do with the public mood. As for the overall 13 for 19 success rate for Barber's model, it includes seven elections that were won by active-positives, whom he says resonate with every public mood. A good hand in a wild-card game is not necessarily a good hand in straight poker; Barber's success rate in the elections not won by active-positives is only six of 12. In the case of conscience elections, only once did a rep-

Table 6-3 Resonance of Character Type and Public Mood in Presidential Elections, 1908-1980

	ELECTION		WINNING PRESIDENTIAL CANDIDATE	
Year	Public Mood	*"Resonant"* Character Types	Name	Character Type
1908	Conciliation	Passive-positive (Active-positive)	Taft	Passive-positive
1912	Conflict	Active-negative (Active-positive)	Wilson	Active-negative
1916	Conscience	Passive-negative (Active-positive)	Wilson	Active-negative
1920	Conciliation	Passive-positive (Active-positive)	Harding	Passive-positive
1924	Conflict	Active-negative (Active-positive)	Coolidge	Passive-negative
1928	Conscience	Passive-negative (Active-positive)	Hoover	Active-negative
1932	Conciliation	Passive-positive (Active-positive)	Roosevelt	Active-positive
1936	Conflict	Active-negative (Active-positive)	Roosevelt	Active-positive
1940	Conscience	Passive-negative (Active-positive)	Roosevelt	Active-positive
1944	Conciliation	Passive-positive (Active-positive)	Roosevelt	Active-positive
1948	Conflict	Active-negative (Active-positive)	Truman	Active-positive
1952	Conscience	Passive-negative (Active-positive)	Eisenhower	Passive-negative
1956	Conciliation	Passive-positive (Active-positive)	Eisenhower	Passive-negative
1960	Conflict	Active-negative (Active-positive)	Kennedy	Active-positive
1964	Conscience	Passive-negative (Active-positive)	Johnson	Active-negative
1968	Conciliation	Passive-positive (Active-positive)	Nixon	Active-negative
1972	Conflict	Active-negative (Active-positive)	Nixon	Active-negative
1976	Conscience	Passive-negative (Active-positive)	Carter	Active-positive
1980	Conciliation	Passive-positive (Active-positive)	Reagan	Passive-positive

resentative of the resonant type (passive-negative) win, while purportedly less suitable active-negatives won three times.

Barber's Prescriptions

In *The Presidential Character* and *The Pulse of Politics* Barber developed a suggestive and relatively complete model of the psychological presidency. Why he has failed even to acknowledge the connection between the theories in each book much less present them as a unified whole remains unclear. Perhaps he feared that the lack of fit between his mood and personality types—the public and presidential components—would have distracted critics from his larger points.

In any event, the theoretical and predictive elements of Barber's theory of the presidency are sufficiently provocative as to warrant him a hearing for his prescriptions for change. Barber's primary goal for the psychological presidency is that it be "de-psychopathologized." He wants to keep active-negatives out and put healthy active-positives in. He wants the public to become the master of its own political fate, breaking out of its electoral mood cycle, which is essentially a cycle of psychological dependency. Freed of their inner chains, the presidency and the public, Barber claims, will be able to forge a "creative politics" or "politics of persuasion," as he has variously dubbed it. Just what this kind of politics would be like is not clear, but apparently it would involve greater sensitivity on the part of both presidents and citizens to the ideas of the other.[40]

It will not surprise readers to learn that Barber, by and large, dismisses constitutional reform as a method for achieving his goals: if the presidency is as shaped by psychological forces as he says it is, then institutional tinkering will be, almost by definition, beside the point.[41] Change, to be effective, will have to come in the thoughts and feelings of people: in the information they get about politics, the way they think about it, and the way they feel about what they think. Because of this, Barber believes, the central agent of change will have to be the most pervasive—media journalism— and its central channel, the coverage of presidential elections.[42]

It is here, in his prescriptive writings, that Barber is on most solid ground, here that his answers are as good as his questions. Unlike many media critics, he does not assume imperiously that the sole purpose of newspapers, magazines, and television is to elevate the masses. Barber recognizes that the media is made up of commercial enterprises that must sell papers and attract viewers. He recognizes, too, that the basic format of news coverage is the story, not the scholarly treatise. His singular contribution is his argument that the media can improve the way it does all of these things at the same time, that better election stories will attract bigger audiences in more enlightening ways.

The first key to better stories, Barber argues, is greater attention to the candidates. Election coverage that ignores the motivations, developmental histories, and basic beliefs of its protagonists is as lifeless as dramas or novels that did so would be. It also is uninformative; elections are, after all, choices among people, and as Barber has shown, the kinds of people candidates are influences the kinds of presidents they would be. Good journalism, according to Barber, would "focus on the person as embodying his historical development, playing out a character born and bred in another place, connecting an old identity with a new persona—the stuff of intriguing drama from Joseph in Egypt on down. That can be done explicitly in biographical stories." [43]

Barber is commendably diffident here; he does not expect reporters to master and apply his own character typology. But he does want them to search the candidates' lives for recurring patterns of behavior, particularly the rigidity that is characteristic of his active-negatives. (Of all behavior patterns, rigidity, he feels, "is probably the easiest one to spot and the most dangerous one to elect.")[44] With public interest ever high in "people" stories and psychology, Barber probably is right in thinking that this kind of reporting not only would inform readers, but engage their interest as well.

This goal—engaging readers' interest—is Barber's second key to better journalism. He finds reporters and editors notably, sometimes belligerently, ignorant of their audiences. "I really don't know and I'm not interested. . . ," he quotes Richard Salant of CBS News. "Our job is to give people not what they want, but what we decide they ought to have." Barber suggests that what often is lost in such a stance is an awareness of what voters need to make voting decisions, namely, information about who the candidates are and what they believe. According to a study of network evening news coverage of the 1972 election campaign, which he cites, almost as much time was devoted to the polls, strategies, rallies, and other "horse-race" elements of the election as to the candidates' personal qualifications and issue stands combined. As Barber notes, "The viewer tuning in for facts to guide his choice would, therefore, have to pick his political nuggets from a great gravel pile of political irrelevancy." [45] Critics who doubt the public's interest in long, fleshed-out stories about what candidates think, what they are like, and what great problems they would face as president would do well to check the ratings of CBS's "60 Minutes."

An electorate whose latent but powerful interest in politics is engaged by the media will become an informed electorate because it wants to, not because it is supposed to. This is Barber's strong belief. So sensible a statement of the problem is this, and so attractive a vision of its solution, that one can forgive him for cluttering it up with types and terminologies.

NOTES

* An early version of this essay appeared in *The Virginia Quarterly Review* (Autumn 1980).

1. "Candidate on the Couch," *Time,* June 19, 1972, 15-17; James David Barber, *The Presidential Character: Predicting Performance in the White House* (Englewood Cliffs, N.J.: Prentice-Hall, 1972).
2. Hugh Sidey, "The Active-Positive Searching," *Time,* October 4, 1976, 23.
3. "After Eight Months in Office—How Ford Rates Now," *U.S. News & World Report,* April 28, 1975, 28.
4. David S. Broder, "Carter Would Like to Be an 'Active Positive,'" *The Washington Post,* July 16, 1976, A12.
5. James David Barber, "An Active-Positive Character," *Time,* January 3, 1977, 17.
6. Hugh Sidey, "'A Revolution Is Under Way,'" *Time,* March 31, 1980, 20.
7. "Cycle Races," *Time,* May 19, 1980, 29.
8. Robert A. Dahl, *A Preface to Democratic Theory* (Chicago: University of Chicago Press, 1956), 6-8.
9. The phrase is Alexander Hamilton's. See Alexander Hamilton, James Madison, John Jay, *The Federalist Papers,* with an introduction by Clinton Rossiter (New York: New American Library, 1961), no. 70, 423.
10. Seymour Martin Lipset, *The First New Nation* (New York: Basic Books, 1963), chap. 1; and Max Weber, *The Theory of Social and Economic Organization* (New York: Oxford University Press, 1947), 358.
11. Marcus Cunliffe, *George Washington: Man and Monument* (New York: New American Library, 1958), 15.
12. Max Farrand, *The Records of the Federal Conventions of 1787,* 4 vols. (New Haven: Yale University Press, 1966), I: 65.
13. Jeffrey Tulis, "On Presidential Character," in *The Presidency in the Constitutional Order,* ed. Jeffrey Tulis and Joseph M. Bessette (Baton Rouge: Louisiana State University Press, 1981), 287.
14. *Federalist,* nos. 71 and 72, 431-440.
15. *Federalist,* no. 64, 396.
16. See, for example, James David Barber, "Adult Identity and Presidential Style: The Rhetorical Emphasis," *Daedalus* (Summer 1968): 938-968; idem, "Classifying and Predicting Presidential Styles: Two 'Weak' Presidents," *Journal of Social Issues* (July 1968): 51-80; idem, "The President and His Friends" (Paper presented at the annual meeting of the American Political Science Association, New York, September 1969) and idem, "The Interplay of Presidential Character and Style: A Paradigm and Five Illustrations," in *A Source Book for the Study of Personality and Politics,* ed. Fred I. Greenstein and Michael Lerner (Chicago: Markham, 1971), 383-408.

17. Richard E. Neustadt, *Presidential Power: The Politics of Leadership* (New York: John Wiley & Sons, 1960), 185.
18. Erwin C. Hargrove, *The Power of the Modern Presidency* (New York: Alfred A. Knopf, 1974), 33.
19. See, for example, Fred I. Greenstein, *Children and Politics* (New Haven: Yale University Press, 1965); and John E. Mueller, *War, Presidents, and Public Opinion* (New York: John Wiley & Sons, 1973).
20. Paul B. Sheatsley and Jacob J. Feldman, "The Assassination of President Kennedy: Public Reactions," *Public Opinion Quarterly* (Summer 1964): 189-215.
21. Unless otherwise indicated, all quotes from Barber in this section are from *The Presidential Character*, chap. 1.
22. Ibid., 145, 206.
23. Barber's discussions of all presidents but Ford, Carter, and Reagan are in *The Presidential Character*. For Ford and Carter, see notes 3 and 5, respectively. For Reagan, see James David Barber, "Worrying about Reagan," *The New York Times*, September 8, 1980, 19.
24. Barber, *Presidential Character,* 12.
25. Barber told me that he plans to discuss the sources of his typology in psychological theory in the third edition of *The Presidential Character*.
26. Alexander George, "Assessing Presidential Character," *World Politics* (January 1974): 234-282.
27. Ibid. George argues that Nixon's behavior was not of a kind that Barber's theory would lead one to predict.
28. Barber, *Presidential Character,* 99.
29. George Reedy, *The Twilight of the Presidency* (New York: New American Library, 1970). See also Bruce Buchanan, *The Presidential Experience: What the Office Does to the Man* (Englewood Cliffs: Prentice-Hall, 1978).
30. James David Barber, "Coding Scheme for Presidential Biographies," January 1968, mimeographed, 3.
31. The surveys are reported in Steve Neal, "Our Best and Worst Presidents," *Chicago Tribune Magazine,* January 10, 1982, 9-18; Lloyd Shearer, "U.S. Presidents—How They Rate" (report on a 1982 survey by Robert Murray), *Parade,* December 12, 1982, 10; and David L. Porter, letter to author, January 15, 1982.
32. Tulis, "On Presidential Character."
33. Erwin C. Hargrove, "Presidential Personality and Revisionist Views of the Presidency," *Midwest Journal of Political Science* (November 1973): 819-836.
34. James David Barber, *The Pulse of Politics: Electing Presidents in the Media Age* (New York: W. W. Norton & Co., 1980). Unless otherwise indicated, all quotes from Barber in this section are from chapters 1 and 2.
35. The first quote appears in *The Presidential Character*, 9; the second in "Interplay of Presidential Character and Style," footnote 2.
36. Barber, *Presidential Character,* 446.
37. Ibid., 446, 448, 451.
38. Ibid., 243.
39. Barber did draw a connection between the public's desire for conciliation and its choice of a passive-positive in the 1980 election: "Sometimes people want a fighter in the White House and sometimes a saint. But the time comes when all we want is a friend, a pal, a guy to reassure us that the story is going to come out all right. In

1980, that need found just the right promise in Ronald Reagan, the smiling American." James David Barber, "Reagan's Sheer Personal Likability Faces Its Sternest Test," *The Washington Post*, January 20, 1981, 8.

40. James David Barber, "Tone-Deaf in the Oval Office," *Saturday Review/World*, January 12, 1974, 10-14.
41. James David Barber, "The Presidency After Watergate," *World*, July 31, 1973, 16-19.
42. Barber, *Pulse of Politics*, chap. 15. For other statements of his views on how the press should cover politics and the presidency, see James David Barber, ed. *Race for the Presidency: The Media and the Nominating Process* (Englewood Cliffs: Prentice-Hall, 1978), chaps. 5-7; and idem, "Not Quite the New York Times: What Network News Should Be," *The Washington Monthly*, September 1979, 14-21.
43. Barber, *Race for the Presidency*, 145.
44. Ibid., 171, 162-164.
45. Ibid., 174, 182-183.

Part III

PRESIDENTIAL SELECTION

F ew contrasts in American politics seem sharper than that between the presidential selection process that existed through the election of 1968 and the process since then. In 1968, only 17 states held presidential primaries; by 1980, 36 states did. In 1968, two-thirds of the national convention delegates were not chosen in primaries; most of them were appointed by each state's party chair or governor. In 1980, only one-fourth were chosen outside the primary system, and their selection was made at open party caucuses. At the 1968 Democratic convention, 5 percent of the delegates were black and 13 percent were women, compared with 14 percent and 49 percent, respectively, in 1980. The party's 1968 nominee was Hubert Humphrey, who had not entered a single primary. In 1980, as in 1972 and 1976, the presidential candidates of both major parties received their nominations because they had won most of the primaries, especially the early ones. During the fall campaign of 1968, each candidate was free to raise and spend as much money as he could; in 1980, each received—and was limited to— a check from the federal treasury. In 1968, debates between the Republican and Democratic candidates remained the exception; by 1980, they were the rule.

Dramatic historical changes like these cry out for explanations that are rooted in equally dramatic causes. Scholars and journalists commonly have offered the Democratic party's 1969 McGovern-Fraser commission on party reform, which "opened up" the nominating process to wider public participation, as the only event that possibly could account for the recent changes in presidential politics. The two chapters in this section suggest that H. L. Mencken's aphorism is applicable to that line of analysis: "There is a simple explanation for everything, and it is wrong."

In Chapter 7, "The Presidency and the Nominating System," Jack L. Walker describes the McGovern-Fraser reforms and those that were instituted by subsequent party commissions, both Democratic and

Republican. But according to Walker, the effects of these changes in the rules are less important than their causes, which can only be understood by placing them in an appropriately broad context. "American society is in the midst of an extraordinary period of social change and economic transformation that has been under way since World War II," he writes. These changes have triggered new styles of political mobilization among the citizenry—demonstrations, ideological interest groups, referendums, and other forms of participatory politics. Alterations in the presidential nominating system have reflected these deeper tides of change. "There will be no returning to the 'good old days' of the 1950s, which were marked by relative calm and political predictability," Walker concludes.

To Walker, the important dates to keep in mind when trying to understand modern presidential selection would include not just 1969, but 1955, when the Montgomery, Alabama, bus boycott occurred; 1962, the year of the first Supreme Court decision on reapportionment; 1965, when the Voting Rights Act became law; and many others. In Chapter 8, "The Presidency and the Contemporary Electoral System," Morris P. Fiorina traces the roots of recent changes in the effects of elections on presidential leadership back even further—to 1787, the year of the Constitutional Convention.

The Constitution, Fiorina notes, not only created an executive that was formally independent of the legislature, but also separated the two branches electorally. Members of Congress represent small parts of the nation, the president the whole; congressional elections sometimes coincide with presidential elections, sometimes they do not. Historically, political parties have helped to bridge this separation by giving reelection-minded members of Congress "a compelling personal incentive," as Fiorina describes it, "to do what they could to see that a national administration of their party was perceived as effective." This incentive can exist, however, only as long as voters link their choices for Congress with their choices for president. In the post-World War II polity that Walker describes in the first chapter of this section, it is not surprising that fewer and fewer voters have been making that link, or that presidents seem to have a harder and harder time bridging the constitutional gap between the White House and Capitol Hill.

7. THE PRESIDENCY AND THE NOMINATING SYSTEM

Jack L. Walker

The 1980 presidential campaign, an exhausting affair that stretched over almost two years and involved more than a dozen candidates, led many observers to conclude that the much-reformed nominating process urgently needed even more reform. As David S. Broder observed in a June 1980 *Washington Post* column:

> The 1980 presidential primary season has ended—at last— with a prize political paradox. On the face of it, the system worked perfectly. The two men, Jimmy Carter and Ronald Reagan, who were the favorites of their party's rank-and-file, have emerged as the victors. And yet there is more widespread dissatisfaction being expressed with the choices for the general election than I have heard in 25 years on the political beat. There is a sense that something has gone terribly wrong.[1]

Once the election was over, the target of criticism shifted from the choices facing the voters to the electoral process that produced those choices. A proliferation of primaries, some said, had prolonged the 1980 campaign needlessly, given undue importance to television, and put a premium on candidates' personalities rather than on their performance in past offices or their positions on the central policy questions facing the country. Changes in party rules, others asserted, had destroyed the deliberative functions of the nominating conventions and gravely diminished the mediating role of political parties in America. Critics argued that the increasingly complex task of winning a major party's nomination for president no longer has much to do with the task of governing as president, that the qualities now required for success in one endeavor are largely irrelevant to success in the other.[2]

Pressure for Reform

Criticism of the procedures used to nominate presidential candidates is hardly confined to the 1980s. The elaborate procedure based upon the Electoral College that was provided for in the Constitution was one of the first aspects of the constitutional system to be changed with the Twelfth Amendment in 1804. The Electoral College was short-circuited during the early nineteenth century by members of Congress who decided to choose presidential candidates for their parties at meetings of their own. These choices were routinely endorsed by the electors, but the system, labeled "King Caucus" by its critics, was itself supplanted a few decades later by national nominating conventions. Staged by the political parties, the conventions brought together state and local party leaders and elected officials from across the country. The Progressive reformers of the early twentieth century, complaining of the nondemocratic and sometimes corrupt methods used to select delegates to the nominating conventions, managed to have them chosen in direct primaries in a few states, a system they felt would be more responsive to the public will. In recent years the conventions have lost their deliberative character almost entirely—nominations have been made on the first ballot of every convention since 1952.

Since 1968 the Democratic party has been debating further changes in its nominating procedures. The result has been the spread of direct primaries, the selection of more women and minorities as delegates, the elimination of winner-take-all selection systems, and the adoption of requirements that delegates be legally bound to carry out their pledges to vote for candidates at the convention. Republicans have been much slower to change their nominating procedures. But pulled along by the Democrats, they often have been affected against their wishes when Democratic-controlled state legislatures have passed legislation requiring the use of direct primaries to select convention delegates or have mandated other changes in party rules.

The process of change is still under way, partly in reaction to the unanticipated consequences of earlier reforms. In 1982 a Democratic party-sponsored commission, headed by Gov. James Hunt of North Carolina, made far-reaching changes in the rules that will affect the nominating process in 1984. Numerous privately financed study groups and conferences on procedural reform still are busily debating further alterations in the rules, and the newspapers are always full of commentary and reports of proposals for new nominating procedures. Even after almost two decades of reform, scholars such as James Ceaser still argue that "the situation today presents a new opportunity for genuine party revitalization through structural changes." [3] The pressure for reform continues, and it seems unlikely that the new rules governing presidential nominations in 1984 will satisfy the critics.

Jack L. Walker

Social Changes in the Electorate

Why is there such widespread dissatisfaction among both liberals and conservatives with the procedures used to nominate presidential candidates? Can we identify any social or political trends that have led to the enactment of so many procedural reforms? Have these new procedures produced the results expected by the reformers? If even more changes are to be attempted, can we establish any guidelines for evaluating proposals? Whose interests should be served by change, and more importantly, what should be the overriding goal of reform?

The first thing any aspiring reformer must recognize is that there will be no returning to the "good old days" of the 1950s, which were marked by relative calm and political predictability. American society is in the midst of an extraordinary period of social change and economic transformation that has been under way since World War II. Massive population shifts to the South and West have created a new regional balance of political power. As many as 10 million Hispanics have moved into the United States from Mexico, Cuba, and elsewhere in Latin America, touching off political changes and creating social tensions in many southern and southwestern states. The fast pace of urbanization and suburbanization has reduced the percentage of the population living in rural areas from 34 percent in 1950 to 26 percent in 1980. All of these rapid changes have unsettled state and local political systems and have altered the relative power of states and regions in Congress. For those concerned with the performance of the political system, however, the most significant long-term change in the American electorate during the past three decades has been the truly revolutionary increase in average educational attainments, a development that has greatly expanded the pool of potential civic activists.

Only 15 percent of the electorate that chose Dwight D. Eisenhower for president in 1952 had ever attended college, and more than 40 percent had received only an elementary school education. In 1976, 34 percent of the electorate had attended college—more than double the number less than a quarter-century earlier—and those with only an elementary education had shrunk to 17 percent. Evidence that these trends will continue can be seen among young voters born since World War II, only 2 percent of whom have only elementary schooling and 46 percent of whom have attended college.[4]

Social researchers have found that one of the most powerful influences on political attitudes and behavior in any population is its level of education. The more education people have, the more tolerant they are likely to be of new ideas, the more willing to associate with members of other social or ethnic groups, and the more likely to engage in political activity of all kinds.[5] As education has increased in America, so has public awareness of abstract questions of public policy, and with it the amount of pressure members of Congress feel from their constituents. The percentage of adults in the United States who reported that they had written letters to public officials about policy questions grew from 17 percent in 1964 to 28 percent in 1976, an increase of 65 percent. As members of this active political stratum have become more involved in the governmental process, they also have become more willing to reinforce their opinions with financial contributions. Surveys reveal that more than 16 percent of the electorate—some 21 million people—reported making campaign contributions in 1976, compared with only 4 percent in 1952.[6]

The entry of greater numbers of well-educated citizens into the potential electorate has unsettled the political system and created many surprises for unsuspecting candidates. As voters gather more information on their own about the candidates and issues in elections, they are more likely to ignore party loyalties and split their ballots. A large, shifting, independent political force is emerging that all candidates seek to influence through the mass media. Much publicity has been given to declines in voter turnout throughout the 1960s and 1970s—only 53.9 percent of the eligible voters turned out to vote in 1980—but this is partly a result of the large proportion of young people in the potential electorate and also the restrictive systems of voter registration employed in many states. Not nearly enough attention has been paid to the steady expansion during this same period in the American electorate's active core. These new, better educated voters can be reached by appeals to broad ideological principles and are willing to consider new, unconventional solutions to social problems. This volatile electorate, increasingly dominated by the post-World War II "baby-boom" generation, already has reshaped the American political landscape and promises even more change in the future.

Political Mobilization in the 1960s and 1970s

The American public's extraordinary propensity to write letters to members of Congress is not entirely an outgrowth of rising educational levels, nor is the increase in financial contributions explained only by growing affluence. Citizens are being encouraged to engage in these activities through their memberships in organized groups. Since 1950 a nationwide process of political mobilization has generated new groups and civic organizations at an unprecedented rate, bringing many formerly quiescent elements of the population into closer contact with the nation's political leaders.

Social Protests

This burst of organizational activity began in 1955 with the Montgomery, Alabama, bus boycott to protest segregation and continued with sit-ins, freedom rides, and civil rights marches, events that eventually led to the transformation of the American political system. Armed with the symbolic authority of affirmative decisions from the Supreme Court, and backed by a broad coalition of liberal religious groups, labor unions, and white civic leaders, the civil rights movement called into question the moral foundations upon which political leadership had been based in the postwar years. Its demand for the immediate implementation of the promises of political equality that were fundamental parts of the American democratic creed led many other groups who also believed they were victims of discrimination to make similar appeals. Their campaigns included class-action law suits, acts of civil disobedience, and initiatives and referenda, as well as conventional electoral politics. The same mixture of tactics that had been pioneered by the civil rights movement thus spurred on the process of mobilization.

White college students who were veterans of the early years of protest came home from one concentrated civil rights campaign, the Mississippi Freedom Summer in 1964, and immediately made efforts to convince their fellow students that they were somehow members of an oppressed class in need of liberation.[7] Plans to give students an equal voice in curriculum development, academic tenure decisions, campus planning, and budget making were advanced—first at Berkeley in 1964 and later at other schools across the country. Many of these universities were soon wracked by civil disorder. Confrontations with college administrators and local police had all the rhetorical and tactical earmarks of the civil rights protests in Atlanta and Birmingham. Some student leaders had been initiated into civic life through participation in these protests; others, who had not been directly involved, patterned their actions after the heroic style of the southern black students.

The 1960s were marked by the birth of movements involving women, Hispanics, the elderly, the handicapped, homosexuals, and many other formerly unmobilized and often despised segments of society. Hundreds of groups were formed in attempts to make the same kind of gains for their constituents that they believed blacks were achieving through the civil rights movement. The National Organization for Women (NOW) has been described as the "NAACP of the women's movement";[8] the Mexican-American Legal Defense and Education Fund (MALDEF), one of the most active of the new Hispanic groups, was incorporated by a former staff member of the NAACP.[9] Established institutions were placed under great pressure as one group after another engaged in angry egalitarian polemics against customary procedures for hiring employees or measuring achievement. Most of the society's fundamental assumptions about human relations and the basis for authority were subjected to searching criticism.

Once this process of political mobilization of the disadvantaged sectors of the society was well under way, other kinds of social movements, mainly from the educated middle class, began to arise. Many of these groups were founded early in this century and slowly developed broad public support. They were dedicated to forwarding the rights of consumers against the power of large businesses, placing restraints on the ability of businesses and individuals to exploit the environment, or granting the government extensive powers to ensure higher standards of industrial health and safety. Ideological feuds, lack of money, or personality clashes destroyed some of the groups, but politicians began to pay heed, and so did the voters.

Technological Advances

In the 1970s several technological advances made the task of organizing large groups with nationwide memberships easier. Computerized systems that could store and classify millions of names and addresses enabled associations to target mailings to the individuals who would be most likely to contribute money or communicate with their elected representatives. The country's long distance telephone network, which expanded rapidly after World War II, allowed associations to reach members almost instantly at little cost. The art of public opinion polling also was perfected and put into widespread use.

Nevertheless, it was not only technological breakthroughs but the atmosphere of protest and the weakened authority of established institutions that provided the impetus for the explosive growth of environmental and consumer groups in the 1960s. The tactics and symbolic appeals of the civil rights movement were not directly applicable to these largely white, middle-class groups, which competed with the movement for the limited space on the society's agenda of controversy. But by joining forces in Washington and arguing their cases for change in public policy, consumer advocates and environmentalists added to the conflicting pressures upon members of Congress and the president.

Public Pressures

Through elaborate networks of associations and advocacy groups, public preferences and opinions can be both molded and transmitted to the political leadership. The degree to which they have transformed the political system is graphically illustrated by the striking differences in the reactions of the American public to the wars in Korea and Vietnam. If public opinion polls that measured support for the war in Korea in the 1950s are compared with the results of similar polls about the war in Vietnam, the patterns look very similar. As casualties mounted and frustration grew over the limited goals of American forces in both conflicts, the number of citizens who expressed disapproval of the war effort began to rise at about the same rate.[10] President Harry S. Truman's public approval rating dropped rapidly to less than 25 percent as the war dragged on, just as President Lyndon B. Johnson's declined to its lowest point toward the end of his term in 1968.[11] Voters in both the national elections of 1952 and 1968 shifted toward those candidates who promised to end the fighting.

In the 1960s, however, the more highly mobilized public, accustomed to unconventional forms of political expression, voiced its dissatisfaction with the war more forcefully than in the previous decade. Once public support for the war in Vietnam began to evaporate during 1968 and 1969, political leaders began to feel pressure almost immediately in the form of letters from constituents, visits from delegations of concerned citizens, negative testimony in Congress, and protest demonstrations in cities and towns across the country. Political leaders found that they no longer were as well insulated as they had been from the shifting tides of public opinion.

Conservative Countermovements

Most of the groups formed in the 1950s and 1960s were dedicated to liberal causes. But they soon were matched by conservative countermovements that grew in the 1970s. Planned Parenthood, Inc., was confronted by the National Right to Life Committee; the Fellowship of Reconciliation encountered the Committee on the Present Danger; the National Council of Churches was matched by the Moral Majority. These new conservative groups—often adopting techniques perfected by the liberals, such as computer-assisted direct-mail solicitation for funds—began campaigns against the central policies of the Kennedy-

Johnson years. Several new policy initiatives were launched by this rapidly growing network, and some, such as the tax limitation movement, exerted a major influence on the course of political debate in the country.

These movements, like the liberal ones that preceded them, drew many elements of the population—housewives opposed to abortion, new groups of business executives, and Protestant evangelicals—into active participation in political life for the first time. With the help of sympathetic business firms and foundations, an imposing network was created consisting of think tanks, public interest law firms, and political magazines dedicated to conservative causes. This conservative movement, although rising in opposition to the existing liberal movements, extended the process of political mobilization that began with the Montgomery bus boycott in 1955. The civil rights movement had a profound effect on the American political system that has reverberated through American society, steadily expanding the boundaries of the active political community.

Political Cynicism and Distrust of Government

Americans are better mobilized for political action than ever before, but, paradoxically, they view their country's leaders and governmental institutions with much more cynicism and distrust. After violent civil disorders, two highly unpopular Asian wars, a string of spectacular political scandals that culminated with Watergate, the assassination of several of the country's most admired public figures, a steady increase in unemployment and inflation, and a prolonged period of economic recession, it should come as no surprise that the extraordinary confidence expressed by Americans in their government during the fifties plummeted in the sixties and seventies.

When a sample of voting age adults was asked in 1958 whether they could "trust the government in Washington to do what is right," 76 percent said that they could "most of the time" or "always." Answers to this same question, asked periodically over the next two decades, revealed a steady decline in public confidence. By 1976 only 34 percent of the respondents answered positively.[12] Distrustfulness and cynicism about politicians and government has become part of the civic culture of America, affecting even those who work actively for political groups, make financial contributions, or express their opinions to political leaders. Public cynicism greatly complicates the task of political leadership. In a world in which mistakes are inevitable, American political leaders are allowed very little margin for error.

The Reformers' Response to Political Mobilization

Faced with the pressures that were generated by the political mobilization and rising ideological conflict of the 1960s and 1970s, political leaders responded with an extraordinary series of legal and constitutional changes in society's central institutions. Such far-reaching reforms had not been implemented since the turn of the century and the introduction of the secret ballot, the direct primary, the referendum and recall, nonpartisan elections and the city manager form of government.

Like the Progressives in the early 1900s, the reformers in the 1960s and 1970s wanted to increase participation in the deliberative processes of government. Their first impulse was to bring to the bargaining table those who were pursuing their interests through protests and threats of violence. The reformers hoped that procedural changes eventually leading to changes in public policy would follow. They also wished to reestablish order and accommodate pressures for change so that the legitimacy of the American political system might be restored. These were not entirely compatible goals, as events in the late 1960s were to reveal, but they were the principal motives behind the extensive changes in the rules of the political game during this period. The system for nominating presidential candidates was only one of many different areas that the reformers of the 1960s and 1970s marked for change.

Reapportionment

Three landmark reforms laid the groundwork for efforts to change the system of presidential nomination. First, the Supreme Court decided in *Baker v. Carr* (1962), *Reynolds v. Sims* (1964), *Wesberry v. Sanders* (1964), and subsequent rulings that state legislatures, local city councils, and U.S. congressional districts must be apportioned according to equal population size. In the words of the Court, "one man's vote is to be worth as much as another's." [13]

The immediate result of reapportionment was rapid turnover in all representative bodies. Prior to reapportionment, 20 percent of those elected to the state Senate in the 1959 general election in New Jersey were new members, while in 1967, soon after reapportionment, 75 percent of those returned were serving for the first time. Many southern states hotly disputed reapportionment decisions. No sooner was the issue settled than the 1970 census figures became available, requiring yet another round of district drawing. The Tennessee state legislature, for example, was redistricted six times in the nine years between 1963 and 1972.

The constant shifting of district lines allowed newly organized political forces centered in the suburbs and central cities to exert a much greater voice in state politics and led to the unsettling of state political systems for more than a decade.[14] Reapportionment decisions had their greatest effects on southern states, such as Georgia and Mississippi, which had long been controlled by a single dominant party, the Democrats, and in states such as New Jersey and Michigan, where carefully constructed political coalitions based in rural areas and small towns had blocked proportional representation of urban areas. In all these states the continual turmoil lasting over an entire decade fractured local political organizations.

Voting Rights

The second landmark reform was a double-barreled assault on voting restrictions, the effect of which was felt mainly in the South. Ratification of the Twenty-fourth Amendment in 1964 eliminated the poll tax in Alabama, Arkansas, Mississippi, Texas, and Virginia, and passage of the Voting Rights Act in 1965 barred the use of literacy tests and sent federal examiners to register blacks in southern counties where their voting participation was below specified levels. These were the final strokes that ended a century of discrimination against black voters. Within a decade the black vote in most southern states doubled. In 1964 only 28,500 blacks were registered to vote in Mississippi compared with 525,000 whites; in 1974 there were 286,000 registered blacks and 690,000 registered whites. Complete political equality was still far off, but this tenfold increase in registered black voters transformed Mississippi politics, leading in 1974 to the election of 191 blacks to public office—an unthinkable event prior to 1965—and to open courting of black voters by all candidates for state-wide office.[15]

Beginning in the late 1960s, the new political role of blacks and the new legislative influence of cities and suburbs as a result of reapportionment led to vigorous two-party competition for state-wide offices in the South for the first time in the twentieth century. Republicans were elected to the U.S. Senate in North Carolina, Florida, and Alabama—also unthinkable events—and liberal governors such as Reubin Askew of Florida, Jimmy Carter of Georgia, and later even George Wallace of Alabama, once a militant segregationist, ran successfully on platforms that made straightforward appeals to blacks and to the interests of cities and suburbs. The procedural reforms of the

1960s finally caused a true reconstruction of southern politics, a century after the end of the Civil War.

The 18-Year-Old Vote

The third landmark reform affected the entire country, although its effects were not as great as many reformers had expected. Eighteen-year-olds were granted the right to vote in 1971 with the Twenty-sixth Amendment to the Constitution, thus bringing about the largest expansion of the electorate since 1920 when the vote was extended to women. Democrats made special efforts to cultivate these new voters in 1972 but were disappointed to find that they were hard to register and get to the polls. Only 48 percent of all 18- to 20-year-olds voted in the 1972 election, compared with 71 percent of those age 45 to 54. Even more than their parents, they tended to avoid firm ties to the Democratic or Republican parties; nor did they vote as a cohesive bloc.[16]

Conclusion

All of these unsettling reforms contributed to the collapse of local party machines and opened the political system to participation by elements of the population that had been excluded in the past. It was inevitable that having successfully transformed state and local party organizations, reformers would begin to press for similar changes in the processes through which the parties' nominees for president were chosen.

Presidential Nomination Reforms

The process of reform in presidential nominations began in earnest in the wake of the Democratic party's stormy 1968 nominating convention in Chicago. The campaign for the nomination, set against the background of urban riots and Vietnam protests, had already been upset by President Johnson's surprise announcement that he would not run for reelection and the tragic assassinations of Martin Luther King, Jr., and Robert Kennedy. The convention itself was marked by a steady stream of angry complaints about the rules governing the meeting, near-violent disputes by delegates on the convention floor, and by what an investigating commission later described as a "police riot" in the streets of Chicago.[17]

As the convention drew to a close, a resolution was passed that called for a commission to establish new rules to govern the 1972 convention. This body, chaired in the beginning by Sen. George

McGovern and later by Rep. Donald Fraser, was followed a few years later by a commission chaired by Rep. Barbara Mikulski to establish the rules for 1976. Morley Winograd, state chairman of the Michigan Democratic party, chaired the commission to set the 1980 rules. Most of the reform efforts of the 1970s have been centered in these party commissions, with the Republicans adopting many of the proposed reforms after the Democrats took the initiative. The work of the Democratic commissions have transformed the nominating process.

The most dramatic change in nomination procedures after 1968 was the rapid increase in the number of states holding direct primaries to choose their delegates to the national nominating conventions. There were 17 state primaries in 1968, 23 in 1972, 30 in 1976, and 36 in 1980. Members of the Fraser-McGovern Commission had not intended to encourage this swift departure from the traditional system of caucuses and conventions, but the complicated rules they created to govern the conduct of caucuses had this effect. Many state party leaders, afraid that they would lose all control over their party apparatus to volunteers representing various candidates if they continued to use the caucus system, adopted the primary system as the lesser evil.[18]

The Democrats also transformed the makeup of state delegations by requiring that at least one-half of the delegates be women, no matter what system was used to choose them, and that all states develop plans for increasing the number of delegates chosen from among racial minorities. As a result of these reforms, women increased as a proportion of total delegates at Democratic conventions from 13 percent in 1968 to 49 percent in 1980, and blacks from 5 percent in 1968 to 14 percent in 1980. Republicans did not enact similar rules concerning delegate representativeness, and the proportion of black delegates at Republican conventions has remained steady at about 3 percent of the total. Even without explicit quotas, however, the proportion of female delegates at Republican conventions increased steadily from 16 percent in 1968 to 29 percent in 1980.[19]

Despite all this attention to the racial and sexual makeup of state convention delegations, the real effect of the reforms was to reduce the autonomy of convention delegates. Biological traits aside, delegates now were chosen in most states, not because of their personal qualifications, but because of their support for certain presidential candidates. After the 1972 election, the Democrats prohibited any state from using a "winner-take-all" system in allocating delegates after a primary. The Republicans did not require states to follow this practice, but soon both parties in most states apportioned delegates in rough accordance with the number of votes each candidate received in the primary. Delegates also were legally bound to vote for their candidate on at least the first ballot of the convention, regardless of the circumstances.

Campaign Finance Reforms

The rules changes that emanated from the 1972, 1976, and 1980 Democratic party reform commissions led to the rapid spread of presidential primaries, proportional allocation of delegates, a dramatic change in the racial and sexual composition of state delegations, and the transformation of the legal status and political role of convention delegates. But the movement for reform was not confined to the parties themselves. Another extremely important part of the reform package was the passage by Congress during the 1970s of a series of laws governing campaign finance, the most important of which was the Campaign Finance Act of 1974.

This reform, which went into effect with the 1976 election, made far-reaching changes in the political process. It established limits on the permissible size of individual and organizational contributions to candidates—$1,000 for individuals, $5,000 for political action committees (PACs)—and required candidates to report the source of all contributions of more than $200 to a newly created regulatory agency, the Federal Elections Commission.

Reporting laws had been enacted before, but this one included several other, more significant provisions. Most important, it provided for an equal match from public funds, dollar for dollar, of all individual contributions under $250 up to a limit to be established in each election ($7.3 million in 1980). Political action committees were excluded from the matching provisions. Candidates were not required to accept public funding, but if they decided to do so—as all 1980 presidential candidates except John Connally did—they also were required to accept limitations both upon the total amount of money they could spend and upon the amount they could spend in each state.

Although the overall limitations on campaign expenditure were generous ($14.7 million in 1980, plus 20 percent for fund-raising costs), reformers saw this law as a significant step toward limiting the control of large vested interests over party nominations. Critics of the reform feared that it would encourage a rash of candidates running highly divisive campaigns centered on narrow controversial issues, all at public expense. To guard against that possibility, candidates were not eligible for federal matching funds until they had raised $100,000 in individual contributions, including at least $5,000 from 20 different states in individual contributions of no more than $250. Any candidate who failed to receive as much as 10 percent of the vote in two consecutive primary elections would stop receiving public funds. Vast amounts of money were needed to conduct national presidential campaigns through the mass media. With public financing, the creation of the PACs, strict reporting provisions, and limits on expenditures, the reformers were trying to provide the necessary funds and at the same time maintain an important measure of competitive equity.

Campaigning in 1972, 1976, and 1980

The rapid increase in the number of primaries, the first of them more than six months before the party conventions, along with the proportional rule in allocating delegates, conceivably could have led to a stalemate among several candidates, with none of them able to build a majority. This result would have revived the convention as the key instrument of choice. But as both the McGovern nomination in 1972 and the Carter nomination in 1976 demonstrated, the reformed system produced forces that not only prevented stalemate, but also led to overwhelming victories for the early front-runner. Candidates who won or did better than the press expected them to in the early primaries were able to drain away from their competitors financial contributions, volunteer workers, and exposure on the national television networks. The popularity of those "thrusting candidates" sometimes began to sag toward the end of the long primary season, as Carter's did in both 1976 and 1980, but by then they already had gained enough pledged delegates to win the nomination easily on the first ballot at the convention.

Public financing for primary campaigns in 1976 and 1980 also had surprising effects. It increased the importance of private contributions rather than decreasing them as the reformers intended. The federal matching dollars greatly benefited candidates whose popularity accelerated after early successes by doubling the surge of contributions that they received in the wake of primary victories.[20]

Once it became evident that early successes were the key to victory in the reformed system, the marathon campaign was born. To win, candidates needed to devote two years or more to the exhausting, full-time pursuit of public exposure and support. Candidates with heavy responsibilities in government, such as members of the leadership in the House or Senate or state governors—positions that provide experience a successful president might need—were virtually precluded from consideration because their duties did not allow them enough time to mount a successful campaign.

Ronald Reagan's success in the 1980 race for the Republican nomination reminds us that there are limits to the effectiveness of marathon campaigning by a little-known candidate in a single election. Reagan was defeated in his first confrontation with George Bush in the highly publicized Iowa caucuses, but he was able to recover quickly and win the nomination once he increased his efforts in later primaries. Despite this early defeat, Reagan was a near consensus choice within his party by the time the primaries began in 1980; he had built a dedicated following over 15 years of Republican advocacy and two major bids for his party's nomination in 1968 and 1976—a kind of "supermarathon" campaign.

Incumbent presidents evidently have some of these same advantages in the race for the nomination, as shown by the successful campaigns of Gerald Ford in 1976 and Jimmy Carter in 1980 against powerful challengers. The new system, however, provided encouragement for those who wanted to challenge incumbent presidents within their own party. The challenger enjoyed public exposure and notoriety that might lead to victory in later elections, while the incumbent president was presented with a serious distraction that threatened to transform every official announcement or policy decision during the final two years of the term into a partisan campaign gesture.[21]

The Hunt Commission Reforms and the 1984 Presidential Nomination Campaign

Contemporary reformers can learn a valuable lesson from the ironic history of recent changes in the presidential nominating process. Most of the reforms of the 1970s produced surprising and wholly unintended results, especially as soon as ambitious candidates and their managers were able to devise new ways to manipulate the reformed procedures for their own benefit. The resulting system was not really designed; it developed haphazardly as state party leaders, national candidates, campaign consultants, and financial backers struggled to gain an advantage. The result is a set of rules that is widely criticized but for which nobody feels responsible.

The weaknesses in presidential nominating procedures that were uncovered during the 1972, 1976, and 1980 elections led the Democrats to create yet another reform commission. Chaired by Gov. James Hunt of North Carolina, the new commission met during 1981 and recommended several modifications in the rules governing presidential nominations for 1984, most of which were adopted by the Democratic National Committee in March 1982.

Like its three predecessors, the Hunt Commission spent most of its time refighting the last war, that is, seeking to make procedural changes that would rectify shortcomings in the rules that governed the most recent campaign for the nomination. For example, it concluded that the reformed system's greatest weakness was its vulnerability to media-based campaigns by little-known outsiders who generated overwhelming momentum from a few early primary victories. As the 1972 and 1976 elections had demonstrated, the reformed system could produce candidates who lacked longstanding political alliances, or even prior assurances of support, from powerful members of their own party in Congress.

The Hunt Commission reforms were designed mainly to limit the possibility of another such insurgency. Three major rules changes were devised. First, the commission shortened by almost two months the period during which delegate selection occurs. The Iowa caucuses now begin in late February rather than in early January as they did in 1980. The New Hampshire primary still retains its traditional leadoff spot, but it takes place only a week after the Iowa caucuses rather than five weeks later as in 1980. The New Hampshire primary is followed in one week by simultaneous primaries in several large states. This rule was intended to reduce the effects of early victories or surprisingly strong showings by obscure candidates: less time would remain for them to capitalize upon their good fortune. In practice, however, it may enhance the importance of a surprise early victory. Not enough time may be left for better-known candidates to reassert themselves after a defeat, as Reagan did in the 1980 New Hampshire primary. Such a result might arise despite the Hunt Commission's hope that by shortening the total length of the campaign, increasing the number of states being contested at once, and putting less time between each round of primaries, an advantage would be provided for candidates with established reputations based upon records of public service.

Second, the Hunt Commission relaxed the rule requiring strict adherence to proportional representation in allocating delegates, thus allowing "loophole" primaries. Although state-wide winner-take-all primaries still are prohibited, states will now be allowed to conduct primaries within subjurisdictions, such as congressional districts, on a winner-take-all basis. They also may use what is sometimes referred to as a "winner-take-more" system in which candidates would be awarded "bonus" delegates for each victory in a congressional district.

Candidates with narrow ideological followings or with support that is heavily concentrated in a few constituencies will lose delegates under this system to candidates with broad support who can muster pluralities in most of a state's subjurisdictions.

The third major rule change affecting the 1984 presidential nomination represents the most dramatic departure from the reforms of the sixties and seventies. In 1984 one-seventh of the delegates to the Democratic convention will be selected outside the caucus or primary system. All of them will remain formally uncommitted to any candidate. Approximately 200 of these uncommitted delegates will be Democratic members of the House and Senate; the remainder will be officials in state and local party organizations. The commission recommended this rule to reverse the pronounced decline in participation in the national conventions by elected party leaders. In 1976, for example, only 18 percent of Democratic senators, 15 percent of Democratic representatives, and about one-half of Democratic governors served as delegates to the party's national convention. This rule also is intended to create a bloc of uncommitted party loyalists who might wield the balance of power in a deadlocked convention that otherwise would be dominated by strongly committed candidate loyalists.

The Hunt Commission reforms were designed to improve the competitive position of presidential candidates who have strong ties to the party organization and whose campaigns are likely to appeal to a diverse majority during the general election in November.[22] Yet, like previous rules changes, they are certain to have many unintended consequences. It may not be possible, for example, for the national news media to wait until the formal beginning date for caucuses and primaries to find out how popular the candidates are likely to be. In the autumn of 1979, months before the primary season began, a straw vote held by the Florida Democratic party during county caucuses of party workers was covered intensively by national television networks and wire services even though the outcome had no effect on the selection of Florida's convention delegation. Once the media appeared, however, all the national candidates were forced to open campaigns in Florida, like rival armies suddenly meeting on a battlefield that neither had chosen.

Similarly, although it is possible to allocate seats to uncommitted delegates, it is impossible, once the national campaign begins, to prevent them from announcing their support for a candidate long before the convention, especially if straw votes and public opinion polls point toward a clear front-runner or if a political logjam seems about to be broken by an unexpected primary result. In a primary system of nomination early victories usually create irresistible momentum. Thus, several large states that once wanted to hold decisive contests in the final few days before the convention recently have decided to move their primaries to the beginning of the season. After the first three weeks of primaries in 1972, only 17 percent of the Democratic convention delegates were committed; after three weeks in 1980, 44 percent were.[23] A single, national primary might even emerge without any central body designing or consciously choosing such a system.

Reform and the Conduct of the Presidency

What have been the effects of a decade of reforms in the presidential nomination process? Critics have charged that by changing the rules and bringing new, sometimes volatile constituencies into the process the reformers seriously eroded the ability of the parties to build durable coalitions, mediate among contending factions, and decide what the issues would be in an election campaign. Reformers have responded that no set of rules could offset the enormous effects on presidential fortunes of the civil rights movement, the war in Vietnam, or disputes over environmental pollution, abortion, inflation, and the declining competitiveness of American industry. With so many pressures pulling in different directions at once, it is doubtful that any president could have exercised strong, consistent leadership during the 1970s, no matter what procedures were employed by the political parties to nominate their candidates. The response of reformers to these intense pressures was to open the system to larger and larger numbers of people so that the country could make a safe passage through one of the most conflictual periods in American history with its democratic traditions intact.

The reforms not only brought new groups into the political process, they also made possible, in the case of Jimmy Carter, the selection of a party outsider as president who sometimes was unable to gain the cooperation of other powerful leaders in Washington. Reformers argued, in defense of the new rules, that the choice of an outsider in the immediate aftermath of Watergate—the most serious constitutional crisis ever faced by the American presidency—was a stroke of collective political genius. In their view, President Carter's problems in office were the result of the international energy crisis and the Iranian revolution, not the nominating procedures of the Democratic party.

The rules governing presidential nominations cannot be used to explain every fault that might be found in the performance of recent presidents. Neither should they be regarded as insignificant. The reforms require that candidates campaign for months or even years before the nominating conventions. As aspiring candidates begin their campaigns, incumbent presidents must either defend their records or run for reelection themselves, thus causing many of their decisions about appointments or policies to appear as campaign gestures that are unworthy of support. The heavy investments of time, energy, and money that are needed to mount a successful presidential campaign virtually exclude from serious contention congressional leaders or active state governors—unless they are willing to ignore most of their duties for almost two years prior to the national election. The changes made by the Hunt Commission in the rules of the Democratic party for the 1984 election, which were meant to address some of the problems of the reformed system of presidential nominations, do little to remedy this situation.

The Dilemmas of Reform

Controversy over the rules that govern presidential nominations reveals a central paradox that exists at the heart of all democratic systems of government, a paradox that often frustrates the best efforts of reformers and party leaders. The principal force that diffuses authority and fragments power in a democracy—active citizen participation—is also the fundamental justification for authority and leadership. The same process that provides the system its reason for being can render it so unmanageable that no collective goals can be reached. The process of participation itself can sometimes deteriorate into a selfish, aimless, scramble for private gain.

The principal aim of reformers in the 1960s and 1970s was to recognize newly mobilized elements of American society and peacefully resolve social conflicts that easily could have led to widespread violence or bloodshed. Had the events of these tumultuous years been mismanaged, the governmental system could have been engulfed in an uncontrollable political rampage that might have undermined the country's democratic traditions. Reformers were willing to trade away some of the political leaders' capacity to ascertain preferences, establish agendas, and determine presidential nominees in order to increase the participation of women, blacks, and other minorities that had not been adequately consulted in the past. They also intended to force onto the political agenda controversial new questions of public policy that they believed had been ignored or suppressed by the established party leadership.

The stability of American democracy ultimately will depend upon the willingness of elected officials and interest group leaders to exercise self-restraint and engage in compromise. Although this willingness can never be entirely a product of formal procedures, rules are extremely important. Whatever rules future reformers may enact, they must be evaluated by a dual standard that grows out of democracy's central paradox. First, the public must be convinced that the procedures governing election campaigns are not unfairly tilted toward some predetermined outcome; second, leaders must be given enough political and administrative resources so that after the election the government can actually reach the goals they have set for it. Reformers have vacillated between these seemingly conflicting demands of legitimacy and governability, but in the end the two goals are linked and neither can safely be ignored. In short, the overriding purpose of procedural reform in a democracy is to encourage enough citizen participation in government to create a legitimate moral basis for the effective exercise of political authority.

NOTES

*This chapter is an expanded and revised version of the author's presentation before the Duke University-Woodrow Wilson Center Forum on Presidential Nominations at the Smithsonian Institution in Washington, D.C., May 11, 1981.

1. David S. Broder, *The Washington Post,* June 5, 1980, 5.
2. Terry Sanford presents a good summary of contemporary critics of reform in *A Danger of Democracy: The Presidential Nominating Process* (Boulder, Colo.: Westview Press, 1981).
3. James W. Ceaser, *Reforming the Reforms: A Critical Analysis of the Presidential Selection Process* (Cambridge, Mass.: Ballinger Publishing Co., 1982), 157.
4. These figures came from random samples of the adult population surveyed by the Center for Political Studies at the University of Michigan. Results are reported in *American National Election Data Sourcebook: 1952-1978,* ed. Warren E. Miller, Arthur H. Miller, and Edward J. Schneider (Cambridge, Mass.: Harvard University Press, 1980).
5. For an insightful discussion of the importance of education in determining political behavior, see Philip E. Converse, "Change in the American Electors," in *The Human Meaning of Social Change,* ed. Angus Campbell and Philip E. Converse (New York: Russell Sage Foundation, 1972), 263-338.
6. Miller, Miller, and Schneider, eds., *American National Election Data Sourcebook.*
7. Thousands of college students from across the country worked in southern communities during this summer to register black voters. The project was organized by the Student Nonviolent Coordinating Committee (SNCC), and the work was often dangerous. On June 21, 1964, three civil rights workers, one a

New York college student, were brutally killed in Philadelphia, Mississippi. On July 14, the bodies of two 19-year-old black students were found in the Mississippi River. The FBI was called in to investigate.

8. Maren Lockwood Carden, *The New Feminist Movement* (New York: Russell Sage Foundation, 1974), 103-118.

9. David S. Broder, *Changing of the Guard: Power and Leadership in America* (New York: Simon & Schuster, 1980), 283.

10. For an analysis of these data, see John E. Mueller, *Wars, Presidents and Public Opinion* (New York: John Wiley & Sons, 1973).

11. *The Gallup Opinion Index,* Report No. 182 (October-November 1980).

12. Miller, Miller, and Schneider, eds., *American National Election Data Sourcebook.*

13. *Wesberry v. Sanders* (1964).

14. Timothy G. O'Rourke, *The Impact of Reapportionment* (New Brunswick, N.J.: Transaction Books, 1980).

15. Richard E. Cohen, "Changing Racial Conditions May Shape 1975 Voting Rights Act," *National Journal,* October 26, 1974, 1606-1613.

16. "Whatever Happened to the Youth Vote?" *Congressional Quarterly Weekly Report,* July 15, 1978, 1792-1795.

17. Daniel Walker, *Rights in Conflict* (Report of the National Commission on the Causes and Prevention of Violence, 1968).

18. Patricia Bonom, James MacGregor Burns, and Austin Ranney, eds., *The American Constitutional System Under Strong and Weak Parties* (New York: Praeger Publishers, 1981), 97-114.

19. Ceaser, *Reforming the Reforms,* 52.

20. William R. Keech and Donald R. Matthews, *The Party's Choice* (Washington, D.C.: The Brookings Institution, 1976); and John H. Aldrich, *Before the Convention: Strategies and Choices in Presidential Nomination Campaigns* (Chicago: University of Chicago Press, 1980).

21. During his final year in the White House, Gerald R. Ford spent more than 20 percent of his working time engaged directly in campaigning for renomination. See Mr. Ford's testimony at the Duke University-Woodrow Wilson Center Forum on Presidential Nominations, May 11, 1981.

22. For a critique of the Hunt Commission's work, see Michael J. Malbin, "The Democratic Party's Rules Changes: Will They Help or Hurt It?" *National Journal,* January 23, 1982, 139, 165.

23. Ibid.

8. THE PRESIDENCY AND THE CONTEMPORARY ELECTORAL SYSTEM

Morris P. Fiorina

This essay takes seriously the key words in its title: "presidency," rather than simply presidential candidates, and "electoral system," rather than simply elections. The discussion naturally revolves around elections, but it focuses on the implications of the structure and operation of the contemporary electoral system for the contemporary presidency. In particular, it emphasizes how the evolution of the electoral system has exacerbated the political difficulties faced by recent presidents and how those heightened difficulties have in turn contributed to the decline of responsible government in the United States.[1] For responsible government to exist, citizens must be able to determine whom to credit or blame for the state of the nation, and must vote on the basis of such determinations. By doing so they provide public officials with a compelling personal incentive to concern themselves about national conditions. The decline of responsible government lies at the core of the aforementioned difficulties confronting the contemporary presidency. These difficulties are systemic and not the transient echoes of a singularly inept Jimmy Carter which can be dispelled by an especially skilled Ronald Reagan or some future president. For in fact, and despite much popular commentary to the contrary, the politics of the early 1980s fits comfortably with themes developed in writings of the 1970s.

A Question of Incentives

To a greater degree than behavioral political scientists have acknowledged, institutional arrangements shape individual incentives, which in turn affect behavior. Both formal institutions and informal ones, such as custom or practice, are important, and while in most stable democracies the former are more fundamental, their constancy means that their specific effects are more likely to be overlooked. In the United States two aspects of our formal institutions warrant discussion:

the independent executive and the electoral law laid down by the Constitution.

Americans take for granted the opportunity to indicate a preference among presidential candidates who are explicitly listed on the ballot. In the 1983 British general election, however, electors had the opportunity to cast a vote specifically for Margaret Thatcher in only one of 650 constituencies. Similarly, in only one constituency (not the same one) did voters have an opportunity to vote for Michael Foot. In the 1977 elections in the Netherlands *no* voter had an opportunity to cast a vote for the current prime minister, Ruud Lubbers; the Dutch ballot lists only parties, not personal names. The same is true in Israel. German voters in one constituency had the opportunity to vote for Helmut Kohl for chancellor in 1980. As a result of the election and subsequent maneuvering, however, Helmut Schmidt of the Social Democratic party assumed the office; but in the fall of 1982, with no new elections having taken place, Kohl replaced Schmidt.

Most of the advanced democracies do not elect their chief executives independently from the members of their legislature. Rather, the executives are the leaders of parties that control blocs of legislative seats (not necessarily a majority). And once selected, these chief executives have no *legal* hold on the office; their tenure depends on maintaining the support of the parties that selected them. As Anthony King observes, the American system is unusual in permitting the accession to office of presidents who have little national political experience and little acquaintance with, let alone preexisting support among, members of the legislature.[2] Although the typical European parliamentarian has some direct responsibility for choosing an executive whom he or she knows firsthand, the typical American representative or senator has neither direct responsibility for, nor firsthand knowledge of, the elected president.

The formal separation of executive and legislative offices in the United States is reinforced further by the differences in the electoral systems that determine the officeholders. Representatives are elected from geographically distinct single-member districts in which the high vote getter, majority or not, wins the seat. Only half of all House elections and two-thirds of all senatorial elections coincide with presidential elections. Formally, the electoral coalitions of legislative and executive officeholders are completely independent. All voters in a district or state conceivably could cast a vote for a legislative candidate of one party and a presidential candidate of the other. A substantial and increasing segment of the citizenry does choose to avail itself of this opportunity.

Again, contrast the American situation with that in the majority of other democracies. In Great Britain, for example, electors who wished to see Margaret Thatcher win office in 1983 had only one means of registering their choice—by casting a vote for the Conservative candidate for member of Parliament (MP) in the constituency regardless of the personal characteristics, achievements, and beliefs of that individual. In some of the continental democracies such considerations cannot even arise; the choice is that of voting for a particular party, not for any particular candidate.

In sum, in the United States no two representatives have a common constituency (only pairs of senators), and while the president's geographic constituency necessarily overlaps those of representatives and senators, his electoral support within any particular constituency might have little overlap with that of the relevant representative or senator. Besides, all these officeholders never stand for election simultaneously.

Informal institutional arrangements also play a critical role in any political system. After all, British MPs also represent constituencies different from that of the prime minister, but if anything, the unity and cohesion of British government traditionally has been viewed as even higher than in the more formally centralized governments of most continental democracies. Evidently, informal practices can unify what formal institutions put asunder, and perhaps vice versa. The informal institutions of major importance here are practices that are associated with political parties, especially the nomination of candidates for office.

Throughout U.S. history, political parties have helped to overcome the formal separation of offices that was established by the Constitution. Whenever voters and elites can be induced to think and act in partisan terms, a degree of cohesion is overlaid on the political system. If a party's officeholders do not differ on the policies they can be expected to support, voters have little reason to differentiate among individual candidates and greater reason to support or oppose the entire party. And if voters think more in terms of parties than individuals, candidates will have greater reason to concern themselves with the performance and prospects of the party as a whole. These behavior patterns are mutually reinforcing.[3]

In the contemporary period, however, various factors have brought the capacity of parties to stimulate such unifying forces to a low ebb. For one thing, today's parties do not have as much control of tangible resources, such as jobs and contracts, as the parties did in the pre-Progressive era. Thus, their ability to motivate activists now must rest largely on other grounds, and one tool for fostering cohesion among officeholders is no longer available. Probably of much greater importance is the decline in the parties' ability to control nominations. The spread of the direct primary has expanded the arena in which nominations are won, and in this expanded arena, party endorsement—if it is permitted—may count for little or nothing. The increased importance of money and the new campaign technologies it can purchase, which also can be provided outside the party, have further contributed to the decline in party influence over nominations. What is the result of such changes? Parties that do not nominate candidates and elect their nominees hardly can be expected to enforce cohesion on those who are elected. And voters react in natural fashion: when candidates differentiate themselves, sensible voters take account of the differences and do not vote blindly for party labels.

Again, such behavior is mutually reinforcing. And again, we might contrast this situation with that in the other Western democracies. Only in the United States are candidates chosen directly through mass participation. Only in the United States do elected legislators have so little influence in the choice of candidates for chief executive. Only in the United States do the formal party organizations have so little control over the campaigns for legislative or executive office.

In sum, the formal institutional structure and informal institutions that are associated with political parties in most Western democracies provide relatively stronger incentives for cohesive behavior in the political realm than do American institutions. This is certainly true in the abstract, but what about the reality? Are the incentive patterns implicit in institutional structure discernible in the actual behavior of politicians and voters?

Voting Behavior in Contemporary American Elections

Presidential Elections

So much is known about voting behavior in presidential elections that any attempt to provide a concise summary inevitably oversimplifies a rich and constantly growing body of knowledge. Nevertheless, most analysts would accept the following general portrait.[4]

Americans cast their presidential votes on the basis of four general factors: longstanding party affiliations, attitudes toward individual candidates, general conditions in the country which are taken as a

Table 8-1 Decline of Party-Line Voting in U.S. National Elections, 1956-1980

Year	Presidential		House		Senate	
	Party-line*	Defector*	Party-line*	Defector*	Party-line*	Defector*
1956	76%	15%	82%	9%	79%	12%
1958	—	—	84	11	85	9
1960	79	13	80	12	77	15
1962	—	—	83	12	**	**
1964	79	15	79	15	78	16
1966	—	—	76	16	**	**
1968	69	23	74	19	74	19
1970	—	—	76	16	78	12
1972	67	25	75	17	69	22
1974	—	—	74	18	73	19
1976	74	15	72	19	70	19
1978	—	—	69	22	71	20
1980			69	23	71	21

* Party-line + Defector + Independent = 100%
** Data not available.

SOURCE: Gary Jacobson, *The Politics of Congressional Elections* (Boston: Little, Brown & Co., 1983), 85; and Thomas Mann and Raymond Wolfinger, "Candidates and Parties in Congressional Elections," *American Political Science Review* 74 (September 1980): 617-632.

reflection on the performance of the incumbent administration, and the policies advocated by the candidates. The relationship of party affiliation to voting has declined somewhat in the past 15 years, although it remains a major correlate of the vote, as Table 8-1 indicates. The other three factors have waxed and waned somewhat more. In 1956, 1964, and 1972, the characteristics of one or both of the candidates appear to have made an especially large difference. In 1968 and 1980, reactions to the performance of the incumbent administration were particularly important. In 1964 and 1972, the ideologies of certain candidates and the policies associated with those ideologies were especially significant.

Of course, the four factors are not so distinct either logically or in reality as casual commentary sometimes presumes. For example, reactions to the performance of past administrations underpin the party affiliations that exist among the citizenry—hardly a revolutionary idea.[5] Moreover, voter attitudes toward candidates surely are related to the policies they advocate and, at least for incumbents, their performance in office. Certainly, the perceived policy positions of the candidates depend somewhat on the party affiliations they carry, and on the record of their past actions. The close connections among these influences on presidential voting make it imprudent to rank them in terms of relative importance. Each must be considered if an analysis of any presidential election is to be complete.

Congressional Elections

While the study of presidential elections flourished during the 1950s and 1960s, the study of congressional elections languished. Several early analyses suggested that congressional elections were low information party-line affairs and by implication less interesting than the more complex presidential elections.[6] Of late, however, congressional elections have attracted a major share of academic attention, and we now know quite a bit about the more recent ones—1978 and 1980 especially.[7]

Party affiliation remains the single most influential correlate of the vote in congressional elections, although as Table 8-1 indicates, party-line voting has declined steadily since 1956.[8] Nevertheless, in both American executive and legislative elections party affiliation continues to be important and provides the major point of commonality in these election returns.[9] We cannot say the same for other factors, however. The issue basis of congressional elections remains very thin; congressional voters are more informed and aware than scholars previously believed, but—especially in House elections—only a small minority has any knowledge of the incumbent's voting record and issue stands, let alone the stands of the much less well-known challenger.[10]

During the period in which scant attention was paid to congressional elections, prevailing scholarly opinion held that deviations from the basic partisan vote division stemmed largely from the influence of national conditions and presidential level forces, such as presidential coattails and referenda voting on the president's handling of the economy. Surprisingly, recent congressional elections research has found little support for this traditional conception of congressional elections. There is virtually no evidence that evaluations of Jimmy Carter's performance played any direct role in the 1978 congressional elections; one relevant analysis is entitled "The Fiction of Congressional Elections as Presidential Events."[11] The elections of 1974 and 1980 were similar, although effects of presidential performance evaluations were discernible in 1976.[12] Some effects of economic conditions (as opposed to the president's perceived success in dealing with them) are evident in recent elections, but again, these effects are smaller than anticipated, inconsistent across studies, and the issue of how they affect individual voting is very controversial.[13]

If the importance of party affiliations is declining, and issues, national conditions, and national performance have only weak effects on congressional elections, what then underlies voter choice? In particular, what accounts for the election to election changes that are overlaid on the basic partisan division?

Clearly, the answer lies in the fourth general factor—the candidates. But if, as mentioned, the issue stands of the candidates are not so important, what then is? The principal reason for the reawakening of interest in congressional elections in the late 1970s was the discovery that a significant incumbency effect had developed. Scholars such as Robert Erikson and David Mayhew called attention to important changes in the patterns of election outcomes, changes that seemed most pronounced in the mid- to late-1960s.[14] At the same time that the relationship between party affiliation and the vote showed signs of loosening, the relationship between incumbency and the vote increased from a marginal one to a significant one. Erikson estimated that the electoral advantage stemming from incumbency status increased from less than 2 percent in the 1950s to approximately 5 percent in the 1960s.[15]

Figure 8-1 illustrates the increased importance of incumbency in the congressional vote. In the early postwar period the outcomes in most congressional districts were clustered around the point representing a 50-50 split between the parties. As one looked at more lopsided margins, one found fewer and fewer districts, except at the extremes where uncontested southern Democratic districts and a few rock-ribbed Republican districts fell. As the years went by, however, the distribution gradually became more bimodal. The marginal, or closely contested districts became fewer, and the safe, lopsided outcome districts became more numerous. This shift in the shape of the distribution was complete by 1972 and has persisted to the present. The 5 to 10 percent increase in the vote going to incumbents accounts for the shift in the distribution, but what accounts for that increase?

Recent studies suggest that various factors underlie the increased advantage of congressional incumbency. Incumbents have voted themselves ever more "perks"—staff, offices, trips home, access to mass communications—which can be used to form a taxpayer-financed political organization. Observers have estimated that the campaign resources that are provided free to incumbents would cost as much as a

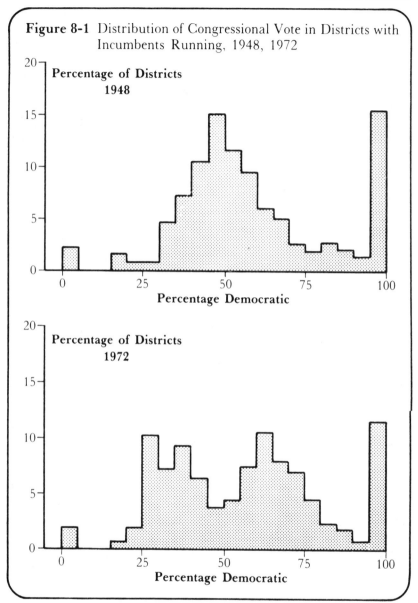

Figure 8-1 Distribution of Congressional Vote in Districts with Incumbents Running, 1948, 1972

million dollars per term on the open market. To a great extent, the information constituents receive *about* their incumbent is provided *by* their incumbent, and one would certainly expect such information to be highly favorable.[16]

Among other things, today's incumbents emphasize their efforts to aid constituents in dealing with the federal bureaucracies. As government has grown, both the number of individuals and groups receiving (or trying to receive) government benefits and the number encountering regulatory constraints has increased accordingly. Traditionally, members of Congress have played the role of ombudsman for their constituents and have tried to broker federal dollars into their districts. Thus, as the supply of government services, money, and regulation has grown, the demand for congressional assistance has increased. And, like most entrepreneurs, members probably have done what they could to stimulate demand.[17] Some appreciative constituents appear to support attentive incumbents regardless of their party ties or ideological considerations. Constituency service is nonpartisan and nonideological; it is highly individualistic; and it is not an important source of votes for presidents. In short, increased voting for congressional incumbents that is based on constituency service inevitably weakens the electoral links between presidents and members of their party in Congress.

The preceding characterizations describe House elections more accurately than Senate elections, which have received much less academic scrutiny, in part because of technical problems in using national surveys to study them, and in part because their smaller number and highly variable nature makes them more difficult to generalize about. In one important respect, contemporary Senate elections clearly differ from House elections: constituency service—and thus the advantage of incumbency—plays a smaller role. On the other hand, Senate and House elections are similar in several ways. Party affiliation is very important, although less so than in earlier times (see Table 8-1). The same studies that were cited in connection with House elections show that national conditions and presidential performance also have little effect on Senate voting in recent elections. These studies indicate that the particular candidates running make a major difference in the voting, although the qualities that voters care about in candidates appear to differ across the two arenas—issue stands and ideology are more important in Senate elections. Specific differences notwithstanding, contemporary Senate elections are as idiosyncratic as House elections; thus, the gap between Senate and presidential voting also has widened in recent years.

Finally, the decline in the importance of party affiliations among voters enhances or even creates the situation in which individual candidate behavior matters. Candidates emphasize the personal and particularistic because they believe they can win votes that way, and they can win votes that way only if citizens ignore such impersonal factors as party and ideology and vote on personal and particularistic grounds. Once the dynamic starts, it is self-reinforcing: increased emphasis on the particular further weakens the relevance of the general, which further enhances the importance of the particular.

Have Congressional Elections Always Been That Way?

Although recent congressional election studies provide a convincing portrait of the past few congressional elections, it would be a mistake to presume that the portrait would accurately describe the congressional elections of two decades ago. As mentioned, the influence of party has declined, and the importance of incumbency has increased. What little historical data we have suggests that constituency attentiveness was not so important 20 years ago as it is today.[18] Moreover, there is good reason to believe that the anemic relationships between national conditions, including presidential performance and congressional voting, were far stronger in past times. For example, in the late 1950s one could predict the presidential and the House vote about equally well on the basis of party identification and measures of national performance. By the late 1960s, however, the relationship between such measures and the House vote declined considerably relative to their relationships with the presidential vote.[19] Apparently the constituency oriented behavior of new incumbents led to a weakening of some voters' tendencies to hold legislators of the president's party responsible for national conditions.

This helps to explain why some highly sophisticated and well-publicized statistical models of expected seat losses have missed their mark so widely in recent elections. Edward Tufte's well-known model, for example, predicted that the Democrats would lose more than 30 House seats in the 1978 midterm elections.[20] The actual loss was 15 seats. Even by political science standards, 100 percent overestimates are unsatisfactory. Douglas Hibbs's model predicted a Republican loss of 40 House seats in 1982; using highly conservative assumptions, Tufte's prediction was about 5 seats less.[21] Given the actual loss of 26 seats, the predictions are somewhat better, but 50 percent overestimates are still disappointing. The basic problem with such models is that they are based on longitudinal data—typically all midterms in the post-World War II period—and implicitly presume that the essential features of congressional elections have not changed over time, including the importance to voters of their opinions about the president. But the cross-sectional evidence strongly suggests that presidential performance was not as closely related to House voting decisions in 1978 as in 1950, and that national economic conditions were not as closely related to House voting decisions in 1982 as they were in 1958. Pre-1966 congressional midterms differ from those that have followed precisely in their stronger association with national events and conditions. As more elections take place, this temporal shift can be built into the models.

Implications for the Presidency

If the American Constitution formally separates presidents and Congress, if the capacity of informal institutions to overcome the formal separation has declined, and if citizens increasingly vote for presidents and members of Congress for somewhat different reasons, what results follow? Walter Dean Burnham and others have argued that the presidential and congressional electoral arenas are becoming increasingly separate as individual career incentives reinforce the formal separation of offices.[22] The increased importance of incumbency and decreased importance of national effects in congressional elections are central components of this argument.

Since the post-Civil War era when careerist ambitions became widespread among senators and representatives, a president could count on a degree of self-interested support from members of his congressional party. When voters supported parties rather than individual candidates, and national conditions and presidential performance became major factors in determining party support, the party in government faced Ben Franklin's classic choice of hanging together lest they all hang separately. Individual members of Congress had a compelling personal incentive to do what they could to see that a national administration of their party was perceived as effective.

Consider that the Democrats lost 116 seats in the midterm elections of 1894, the Republicans 75 seats in the midterm of 1922, the Democrats 56 seats in 1946, and the Republicans 49 seats in 1958. In contrast to 1946, a Democratic president who was widely believed to be in over his head lost a mere 15 seats in 1978; in contrast to 1958, a Republican president presiding over the most serious recession since the Depression lost only 26 seats in 1982. If, as in earlier elections, a quarter to a half of the congressional party faced a real threat of defeat from an unsatisfactory presidential performance, one can be rather confident that members of that party would be more concerned about their president's standing and performance than Jimmy Carter's congressional compatriots were in 1978.[23]

Similarly, when presidential coattails were longer than they are today, members of the congressional party did not wish to run on the same ticket with an unattractive presidential candidate. In 1920 James Cox helped make his party's House delegation 59 seats poorer, and in 1932 Herbert Hoover presided over a Republican loss of 101 seats. By comparison, the Democrats lost only 12 seats in the George McGovern debacle in 1972, and in 1980 Carter helped drag down only 33. If members of the president's party in Congress do not believe that his coattails helped them win office, they naturally will be less inclined to bear any burdens for the sake of his success in office. As Gary Jacobson observes:

> ... [M]embers of Congress who believe that they got elected with the help of the president are more likely to cooperate with him, if not from simple gratitude than from a sense of shared fate; they will prosper politically as the administration prospers. Those convinced that they were elected on their own, or despite the top of the ticket, have much less incentive to cooperate.[24]

Presidential coattails and performance have declined as factors in congressional elections. For any given swing in the national vote for a party's House candidates, fewer seats will change hands than in the 1940s, when more seats were near the tipping point (see Figure 8-1). Tufte precisely characterized this effect of the increased incumbency advantage in a 1973 article on "swing ratios," which measure the responsiveness of the legislative seat division to the national vote division in legislative elections. A ratio of approximately 3 percent of the seats to each 1 percent gain for a party in the national vote in the early postwar period declined to one of approximately 2 percent of the seats to each 1 percent vote gain by the 1970s.[25] Thus, members of the president's party in Congress today need to be less fearful of any given swing against their president than a generation ago simply because fewer of their districts fall in the range where the swing will exceed their normal vote margin.

Recent research also suggests that any given swing in presidential voting is less likely to carry over into the congressional vote today than was the case a generation ago. Studies by Randall Calvert and John Ferejohn show that effects of presidential level factors in general have declined as an influence in congressional elections.[26]

As Table 8-2 indicates, the connection between aggregate presidential and House voting has dropped 75 percent since the New Deal period. The table also shows the 33 percent decline in the swing ratio.

Table 8-2 Responsiveness of House Party Division to Presidential Voting, 1868-1976

Historical Period	Responsiveness of Congressional Vote to Presidential Vote*	Swing Ratio*	Overall Responsiveness**
1868-1896	.95	4.40	4.18
1900-1928	.57	1.95	1.11
1932-1944	.81	3.20	2.51
1948-1964	.37	2.40	.89
1968-1976	.19	2.02	.38

* Numerical entries are regression coefficients.
** Numerical entries are the product of the two preceding columns. The interpretation is the percentage gain in House seats associated with a 1 percent gain in the *presidential* vote.

SOURCE: Randall Calvert and John Ferejohn, "Presidential Coattails in Historical Perspective," *American Journal of Political Science*, forthcoming.

Calvert and Ferejohn observe that "the remaining responsiveness of the composition of the House to the presidential vote is a pale reflection of its previous levels." [27]

The decline in party voting and coattails voting and the lessened influence of national conditions on the congressional vote lead each individual officeholder to see a different mandate in the election returns. Perhaps the most graphic single demonstration of that assertion appears in Table 8-3. At the turn of the century, fewer than 15 congressional districts gave majorities of their votes to a congressional candidate of one party and a presidential candidate of the other. The number of such districts remained relatively small until after 1940, when ticket splitting began to increase dramatically. In 1980, 34 percent of congressional districts were carried by congressional and presidential candidates of different parties. One can hardly blame members today for seeing mixed signals in the returns. They run on their personal records and attribute their reelections to their personal records. Republican or Democrat, members of Congress belong to the "Reelect Me" party.[28]

The implications of this electoral disintegration for the contemporary presidency are clear and disturbing. Generations of American political commentators have argued that the president is the only elected official with a *direct* political interest in the state of the entire nation. Members of Congress may agree with the president that a

Table 8-3   Districts Carried by Congressional and Presidential Candidates of Different Parties, 1900-1980

Year	Percentage
1900	3%
1908	7
1916	11
1924	12
1932	14
1940	15
1948	21
1952	19
1956	30
1960	26
1964	33
1968	32
1972	44
1976	29
1980	34

SOURCE: John Bibby, Thomas Mann, and Norman Ornstein, *Vital Statistics on Congress, 1980* (Washington, D.C.: American Enterprise Institute for Public Policy Research, 1980).

problem, say inflation, has become a pressing national concern. They also may agree that no easy solution exists, that any effective action to address the problem will impose significant costs on some elements of the nation. But here the agreement ends. The president's national constituency bears the burdens of public policies but also enjoys the benefits. Therefore, the president will bite the bullet and push policies that impose costs, as long as the corresponding benefits are significantly greater.

Congressional districts and states, however, are not microcosms of the country. The United States has never seen a national inflation so severe that a representative would accept 25 percent unemployment in his district in order to halt it. Even in the 1890s, one of the heydays of party government in the United States, such extreme local effects split presidents and their fellow partisans in Congress. Today's members refuse to accept even modest costs in their districts in order to provide significant national benefits. In Sen. Howard H. Baker, Jr.'s, colorful words, they walk up to the bullet and gum it a little bit. Carter's embarrassing struggles with the inflation and energy problems in the late 1970s provide a good illustration. Each proposal his administration put forth was taken apart by members who were disturbed by differential effects, especially geographical ones. Their refusal to back the president is perfectly comprehensible in an era of weak party ties, weaker coattails, weak effects of national conditions, and "every man for himself" politics.

Thus, the situation of the contemporary presidency is not a happy one. The occupant of that office must expect to be judged on his success in maintaining peace, high employment, low inflation, adequate and inexpensive energy, harmonious racial relations, an acceptable moral climate, and a generally contented nation. Meanwhile, his copartisans on the Hill are relatively insulated from such concerns. No longer expecting to gain much from the president's successes or suffer much from his failures, they have little incentive to bear any risk on his behalf. In a recent interview Speaker Thomas P. O'Neill, Jr., lamented that the Democratic congressional party had become little more than an organizational convenience: "Members are more home-oriented. They no longer have to follow the national philosophy of the party. They can get reelected on their newsletter, or on how they serve their constituents." [29] By holding only the president responsible for national conditions, the electorate has removed the critical incentives that have brought some cohesion to an institutionally fragmented national government. By holding only the presidency responsible, the citizenry allows the Congress to profit electorally from irresponsibility.

The 1980s: A New Era?

The themes that are developed in the preceding sections emerge from research conducted during the 1970s, based primarily on data gathered in the 1960s and 1970s. How well do those themes apply to the elections of the 1980s and the presidency that will be shaped by them? On the surface, the 1980 and 1982 elections appear to constitute a break with those of the past decade and a half, but a closer view reveals a picture more impressive for its familiarity than for its freshness.

In 1980 the Republicans won an impressive victory. Added to Ronald Reagan's personal triumph was evidence of a seemingly strong coattail effect—33 seats gained in the House and 12 seats in the Senate, which gave the Republicans control of a chamber for the first time since the 83rd Congress (1953-1955). Such gains also gave surface credence to the argument that the nation had "turned to the right," and numerous commentators of a conservative stripe lost little time in advancing such interpretations. Many Democratic politicians accepted that view or at least considered it plausible enough to justify lying low for a decent interval. The legislative successes of the first year of Reagan's presidency certainly were aided by the seeming clarity of the election returns.

Yet the Republican victory was not so sweeping as it first appeared. In the House, when all was tallied up, 90 percent of the unindicted Democratic incumbents who ran, won—a slightly smaller percentage than in 1976. In 1964, however, only 75 percent of the Republican House incumbents managed to reach safe harbor against the Democratic tide. Even if the value of incumbency relative to national forces dropped marginally between 1976 and 1980, it still appears quite impressive in comparison with the pre-1966 period. Calvert and Ferejohn thus assess coattail effects for recent elections:

> Although the 1972 and 1980 elections exhibited a partial return to the higher levels of efficiency [responsiveness of congressional vote to presidential vote] characteristic of the 1956-1964 period, the efficiency levels after 1968 are on the order of two-thirds of their earlier levels.[30]

What of the Senate? Here, there surely was a political sea change. Or was there? After the initial shouts of jubilation and lamentation had subsided, more sober analysts noticed an interesting feature of the voting. Nationally, Democratic senatorial candidates actually received more votes than did Republicans: the latter simply did extremely well in close races in the small states. An examination of the 12 seats that the Democrats lost reveals some additional information. In three of the 12 cases, the Democrats' loss followed the primary defeat of the Democratic incumbent (Mike Gravel of Alaska, Donald Stewart of Alabama, and Richard Stone of Florida), something that seldom helps a party in the general election.

Table 8-4 presents the percentage of the 1974 and 1980 vote received by the nine Democratic Senate incumbents who were defeated in 1980 general elections. Of the nine, Herman Talmadge and Warren Magnuson had showed no sign of difficulty in previous elections. Talmadge, however, was mired in personal and financial scandals. Whether he should be counted as a casualty of the Reagan landslide is dubious, especially since Carter carried Georgia. Magnuson was attacked by his opponent as old and tired, a tactic that also nearly defeated his comparably aged colleague on the conservative Republican side of the political spectrum—Barry Goldwater.

The remaining seven incumbents, particularly the six liberals, are more often viewed as central to the interpretation of the 1980 returns.

Table 8-4   Democratic Senate Incumbents Defeated in 1980

| | Percentage of the Total Vote | |
	1974	1980
Birch Bayh (Ind.)	50.7%	46.2%
Frank Church (Idaho)	56.1	46.8
John C. Culver (Iowa)	52.0	45.5
John A. Durkin (N.H.)	53.6*	47.8
George McGovern (S.D.)	53.0	39.4
Warren G. Magnuson (Wash.)	60.7	45.8
Robert B. Morgan (N.C.)	62.1	49.4
Gaylord Nelson (Wis.)	61.8	48.3
Herman E. Talmadge (Ga.)	71.7	49.1

* Special 1975 election called after 1974 general election resulted in a virtual tie.

SOURCE: *America Votes 14: A Handbook of Contemporary American Election Statistics, 1980,* compiled and edited by Richard M. Scammon and Alice V. McGillivray (Washington, D.C.: Congressional Quarterly, 1981).

When one looks closely, however, one sees a group of extremely weak candidates. With the exception of Gaylord Nelson, these liberal senators were living on borrowed time. In all probability, only the Watergate-induced Democratic tide of 1974 gave them the opportunity to run in 1980. Ronald Reagan's coattails might have done them in, the National Conservative Political Action Committee (NCPAC) might have done them in, almost anything might have done them in. It did not take much. If this group had lost in a more normal 1974 election, the Republicans still might have taken control of the Senate in 1980. But they would have done so with about half the number of Democratic defeats, not including the most widely publicized liberal ones, and there would have been less talk of a "shift to the right" or a new era in American politics.

What about the widely discussed "shift to the right?" All but the most ideological Republican hard-core rejected this interpretation after examining the plentiful poll data from November 1980. Such data indicate that the presidential voting hinged on Jimmy Carter's perceived poor performance in handling the economy and maintaining a secure American presence in the world; issues dear to the New Right motivated only small proportions of the electorate. Moreover, the ideological self-assessment of Americans changed scarcely a whit. The principal lesson of the 1980 election is that voters hold contemporary

Table 8-5 Presidential Support Among In-Party Members of the House and Senate, 1953-1981

Year	President	House	Senate
1953	Eisenhower	74%	68%
1961	Kennedy	73	65
1965	Johnson	74	64
1969	Nixon	57	66
1977	Carter	63	70
1981	Reagan	68	80

NOTE: These presidential support scores are a rough measure of the comity between the president and members of his own party in the House and Senate. The scores represent the percentage of votes on which the House and Senate voted "yea" or "nay" *in agreement* with the president's recorded position.

SOURCE: *Congressional Quarterly Almanacs* for the years 1953, 1961, 1965, 1969, 1977, 1981; pages 78, 620, 1099, 1040, 23-B, 20-C, respectively.

presidents, if not contemporary members of Congress, responsible for permitting a perceived deterioration in the state of the nation.[31]

Of course, perceptions of reality can be as important as reality itself. After the 1980 election, Democrats appeared to lie low, and some actually may have feared continued Republican electoral gains. For their part, the Republicans maintained near-perfect party cohesion on the principal elements of Reagan's economic program.[32] Thus, even if one can discount the inherent significance of the 1980 returns, what about their perceived significance? Did not Reagan's leadership performance in 1981 and 1982 recall the glory days of Lyndon B. Johnson and Franklin D. Roosevelt? Did it not mark a return to an earlier era when presidents and their congressional parties were more apt to govern together and then electioneer together?

To be sure, Reagan won some impressive early legislative victories, but even Jimmy Carter won a few. What about the overall pattern of executive-legislative relations in the early years of the Reagan administration? Richard Fleisher and Jon Bond report a fascinating analysis of congressional support for Presidents Carter and Reagan.[33] Using data from 1959 to 1974, they developed a model of presidential support in Congress based on party membership, popular support in the Gallup poll, and ideological similarity, as measured by conservative coalition support scores. The model predicts legislative support for presidents in their first year, given the characteristics of the

Congresses they faced. Fleisher and Bond conclude that, overall, Reagan's support was not strikingly high; rather, Carter's was abnormally low. Reagan's support was actually 1 percent *lower* than their model predicted, while Carter's was 7 percent lower. Only 26 representatives (including 21 southern Democrats) supported Reagan at a level 10 percent or more higher than predicted, while 167 representatives (including 166 Democrats) supported Carter at a level 10 percent or more lower than expected.

Table 8-5 contains additional data on presidential leadership. Evidently Reagan did enjoy unprecedented first-year support among senators of his own party. In the House, however, he fared less well. Although Reagan's first-year support among his House copartisans was higher than Carter's, and noticeably higher than Richard Nixon's, it was lower than that of Dwight Eisenhower and other presidents elected prior to the mid-1960s growth in the congressional incumbency advantage. In the short term, Reagan's political record is impressive. When viewed from a more historical perspective, however, it appears less remarkable.

To discount the purported significance of the 1980 and 1982 elections and the political success of the Reagan presidency is not to disparage the recent achievements of Republicans. To be sure, the defeat of 40 to 50 Republican representatives and a few senators in 1982 would have furthered the cause of responsible government, as would have the defeat of 30 or 35 Democratic representatives under the less severe conditions of 1978. Collectively, members of Congress are every bit as responsible for the state of the nation as the president, but the electorate does not treat them that way.

To their credit, the Republicans of late have behaved more like a serious political party than has anyone for at least two decades. In 1980, for example, Reagan appealed not just for personal support, but also for the election of Republicans in the House and Senate. In 1982 Reagan explicitly appealed for continued support of his policies rather than distance himself from his party's candidates. Even more importantly, because it transcends the commitment of a single party leader, the Republican National Committee (RNC) is leading the way to a resurgence of party interest in candidate recruitment and the conduct of campaigns. Given the importance of good candidates in American elections, the RNC has begun to build a solid base by actively recruiting and helping train candidates for local offices and state legislatures. These candidates also have received financial support for their campaigns. At the federal level the RNC has targeted Democratic

House and Senate seats where Republican prospects look favorable and has intervened actively to recruit and help nominate strong challengers. These challengers have been sent to RNC "campaign schools" and have received financial assistance through the party's congressional campaign committees. In these and other ways the Republicans are reviving a collective party spirit not often seen in recent years.[34] Their performance is particularly refreshing because it comes on the heels of the Democratic party's disheartening performance between 1976 and 1980. Current DNC efforts and accomplishments still pale by comparison to the Republicans', but they too are on the upswing.

Such indications of party resurgence, especially on the Republican side, offer one of the few possibilities for containing and reversing the fissiparous tendencies discussed in this chapter. If members of Congress can be made more dependent on their party, and if the party apparatus is under firm presidential control, greater cohesion can be enforced. The first "if" obviously is the bigger of the two. Simple gratitude for their selection and training does not suffice; candidates must *need* their party. One possibility is continued change in the pattern of campaign financing so that congressional candidates increasingly would rely on party rather than individual and PAC contributions. This would entail statutory change, of course, and we should not expect members to submit happily to presidential and party control. But campaign financing reforms are probably the best means of strengthening party cohesion and national party leadership. "Follow the money" applies quite generally to human activity, not just to Watergate coverups.

Summary

The contemporary presidency constitutes one electoral system and the Congress 535 others. Although these systems overlap, their intersection now has less in common than in much of our earlier history. As a result of the increased separation of the electoral systems, the contemporary presidency occupies a lonely position. The citizenry attaches high expectations to the occupant of the office and expresses its disappointment at the polls when those expectations are not met. But no president can accomplish much without the help of Congress, and the contemporary Congress is not the focus of the same expectations as the presidency. Each individual member emphasizes his or her personal qualities and record, each is expected to work for the interests of the district or state, and electoral success is largely dependent on meeting these expectations. Unfortunately, members often profit by protecting short-term particular interests, which hinders efforts to advance longer-term national interests. As modern social science theory has demonstrated convincingly, adding up the preferences of the parts need not result in a good thing for the whole.[35] Thus, until members of Congress believe that their personal fates coincide with that of the president, and that both depend on doing well by the country, the political failure that has become so familiar in recent years will continue.

NOTES

*This essay was prepared while the author was a Fellow at the Center for Advanced Study in the Behavioral Sciences. He gratefully acknowledges the financial support provided by the Guggenheim Foundation and the National Science Foundation (BNS8206304).

1. The argument that follows is synthetic. Among the scholars who have most stimulated my thinking are Walter Dean Burnham, Robert Erikson, John Ferejohn, David Mayhew, and Edward Tufte. Numerous useful studies by these and other scholars are cited below. Parts of the argument are developed more fully in my article "The Decline of Collective Responsibility in American Politics," *Daedalus* (1980): 25-45.
2. Anthony King, "How Not to Select Presidential Candidates: A View from Europe," *The American Elections of 1980,* ed. Austin Ranney (Washington, D.C.: American Enterprise Institute for Public Policy Research, 1981), 303-328.
3. Fiorina, "Decline of Collective Responsibility."
4. For excellent scholarly treatments of recent elections, see John Kessel, *Presidential Campaign Politics* (Homewood, Ill.: The Dorsey Press, 1980); and Herbert Asher, *Presidential Elections and American Politics,* rev. ed. (Homewood, Ill.: The Dorsey Press, 1980). For an analysis of the 1980 voting, see Paul Abramson, John Aldrich, and David Rohde, *Change and Continuity in the 1980 Elections,* rev. ed. (Washington, D.C.: CQ Press, 1983).
5. Morris Fiorina, *Retrospective Voting in American National Elections* (New Haven: Yale University Press, 1981).
6. The *locus classicus* is Donald Stokes and Warren Miller, "Party Government and the Saliency of Congress," *Public Opinion Quarterly* 26 (1962): 531-546.
7. Two books that synthesize this expanding body of knowledge are Barbara Hinckley, *Congressional Elections* (Washington, D.C.: CQ Press, 1981); and Gary Jacobson, *The Politics of Congressional Elections* (Boston: Little, Brown & Co., 1983).
8. Bruce Cain, John Ferejohn, and Morris Fiorina, "The Constituency Service Basis of the Personal Vote for U.S. Representatives and British MPs," *American Political Science Review* 78 (1984).
9. John Ferejohn, "On the Decline of Competition in Congressional Elections," *American Political Science Review* 71 (1977): 166-176.
10. Jacobson, *The Politics of Congressional Elections,* 121. He writes, "Alert readers will have noticed that issues were hardly a prominent item in the discussion of voting behavior. The reason is that they show up so infrequently as having any

measurable impact on individual voting in these election studies once other variables have been taken into account."

11. Lyn Ragsdale, "The Fiction of Congressional Elections as Presidential Events," *American Politics Quarterly* 8 (1980): 375-379.

12. On the effects of presidential performance on the 1974 and 1976 congressional elections, see Fiorina, *Retrospective Voting,* chap. 8. On 1980 see Abramson, Aldrich, and Rohde, *Change and Continuity,* 220-221.

13. The failure to find a direct effect of economic conditions or presidential performance on the congressional vote does not preclude those factors influencing the voting in other less direct ways. Jacobson and Kernell, for example, argue that national conditions and presidential performance affect the voting indirectly by influencing the calculations of potential candidates and contributors. The latter lie low in bad years for their party and ante up in good years (bad and good being defined in terms of national conditions). This behavior leads to self-fulfilling expectations as poorly funded bad candidates go down to defeat in bad years and adequately funded good candidates drive to victory in good ones. The argument undoubtedly has considerable merit (not to mention empirical support), but it is doubtful that candidates and contributors would continue to delude themselves were there not some basis for their expectations in reality. See Gary Jacobson and Samuel Kernell, *Strategy and Choice in Congressional Elections* (New Haven: Yale University Press, 1981).

14. Robert Erikson, "Malapportionment, Gerrymandering and Party Fortunes in Congressional Elections" *American Political Science Review* 66 (1972): 1234-1245; and David Mayhew, "Congressional Elections: The Case of the Vanishing Marginals" *Polity* 6 (1974): 195-317.

15. Erikson, "Party Fortunes."

16. Glenn Parker, "The Advantage of Incumbency in House Elections," *American Politics Quarterly* 4 (1980): 449-464.

17. Morris P. Fiorina, *Congress: Keystone of the Washington Establishment* (New Haven: Yale University Press, 1977).

18. Morris P. Fiorina, "Congressmen and their Constituents: 1958 and 1978," in *Proceedings of the Thomas P. O'Neill, Jr., Symposium on the U.S. Congress,* ed. Dennis Hale (Boston: Eusey Press, 1982), 33-64.

19. Fiorina, *Retrospective Voting,* 42-43. This decline is consistent with Richard Born's pinpointing of the mid-1960s as the period in which the value of incumbency grew fastest. See Richard Born, "Generational Replacement and the Growth of Incumbent Reflection Margins in the U.S. House," *American Political Science Review* 73 (1979): 811-817.

20. Edward Tufte, "Determinants of the Outcomes of Midterm Congressional Elections," *American Political Science Review,* 69 (1975): 812-826. The model incorporates three variables: the "benchmark," or standing division of party support, presidential performance ratings, and election-year variation in real per capita income.

21. Douglas A. Hibbs, "President Reagan's Mandate from the 1980 Election: A Shift to the Right?" *American Politics Quarterly* (1982): 387-420.

22. Walter Dean Burnham, "Insulation and Responsiveness in Congressional Elections," *Political Science Quarterly,* 90 (1975): 411-435.

23. The objection might be raised that as recently as 1974 an incumbent congressional party paid dearly for the sins of the national administration: the Republicans lost

49 seats in the House. As Burnham points out, however, 1974 was noteworthy in that Republican losses were relatively small by historical standards: "In all probability, considerably more than a dozen Republican incumbents survived the 1974 tide who would have lost under pre-1960 conditions." Burnham, "Insulation and Responsiveness," 426.

24. Jacobson, *The Politics of Congressional Elections,* 132.
25. Edward Tufte, "The Relationship between Seats and Votes in Two-Party Systems," *American Political Science Review* 67 (1973): 540-554.
26. Randall Calvert and John Ferejohn, "Coattail Voting in Recent Presidential Elections" *American Political Science Review* 77 (June 1983) and "Presidential Coattails in Historical Perspective," *American Journal of Political Science,* forthcoming.
27. Calvert and Ferejohn, "Coattail Voting."
28. "The Thoughts of Chairman Scammon," *Regulation* (August/September 1982), 9.
29. *Congressional Quarterly Weekly Report,* September 13, 1980, 2696.
30. Calvert and Ferejohn, "Coattail Voting," 27-28.
31. Such conclusions are common. For an excellent compilation and analysis of the evidence, see Hibbs, "President Reagan's Mandate."
32. Similarly, even after a modest 26-seat gain in the 1982 elections, the Democrats appeared confident that the electorate had demanded a tempering of Reaganomics. Many Republicans appeared to share that view.
33. Richard Fleisher and Jon Bond, "Assessing Presidential Support in the House: Lessons from Reagan and Carter," *Journal of Politics,* forthcoming.
34. Gary Jacobson, "Congressional Campaign Finance and the Revival of the Republican Party," in *The United States Congress,* ed. Hale.
35. Several theoretical propositions underlie this claim. See Kenneth Arrow, *Social Choice and Individual Values,* 2d ed. (New Haven: Yale University Press, 1970). Arrow has shown that any method of aggregation that is responsive to unrestricted individual preferences (e.g., majority rule) will fail in certain specified ways. In addition, game theory has studied the now well-known idea of the "Prisoner's Dilemma": rational individual behavior may lead inexorably to poor collective outcomes. For a comprehensive discussion see Russell Hardin, *Collective Action* (Washington, D.C.: Resources for the Future, 1982).

Part IV

PRESIDENTS AND POLITICS:
NONGOVERNMENTAL CONSTITUENCIES

After two or more years of relentless campaigning, a newly elected president may earnestly desire that "politics" is over and "government" can begin. The endless search for popular votes, the ceaseless wooing of interest group support, the constant cultivation of the press, the steady accumulation of debts to the political party—all this is behind, he may hope, with only the most serious matters of state ahead. In practice, of course, the presidency does not work that way. To deal effectively with the great issues, presidents need the cooperation of others in government, cooperation that is most likely to be forthcoming when presidential popularity is high, interest groups are mobilized, the press accepts the president's policy agenda, and the party is faithful.

The need for political support from the presidency's nongovernmental constituencies is not new. But according to Samuel Kernell (Chapter 9: "The Presidency and the People") and Martha Joynt Kumar and Michael Baruch Grossman (Chapter 11: "The Presidency and Interest Groups"), the challenges of rousing such support are different from what they were a quarter century ago. "Once Washington was a city filled with hierarchies," Kernell observes. "To these hierarchies were attached leaders or at least authoritative representatives"—congressional committee chairmen, party leaders, press barons, and the like—who were empowered to bargain with presidents on behalf of their colleagues. Similarly, note Kumar and Grossman, presidents generally could negotiate for the support of interest groups through " 'go-betweens,' political leaders who dealt with representatives of specific organizations and with whom the president could deal." But recent decades have witnessed a breakdown in the authority of leaders and intermediaries such as these. As Kernell puts it, "From the president's vantage, Washington has become a big city in which the number of exchanges necessary to secure others' support has increased dramatically."

To some extent, recent presidents have tried to reduce their need to make all those exchanges by "going public" on the issues that concern them most, the idea being that a tidal wave of popular support will wash all opposition in the Washington community before it. Kernell documents a steady rise in the number of presidential speeches and appearances, both on television and before live audiences, in Washington and around the country. He notes some spectacular policy victories for what he calls the "public president." But inevitably, Kernell argues, the public president strategy runs up against a wall of indifference from the public and declining popularity for the president.

Denied the possibility of moving Washington either through bargains with power brokers or a steady stream of appeals to the general public, presidents have increased their efforts to assemble support coalitions fragment by fragment, issue by issue. Kumar and Grossman describe the development within the White House of a variety of new roles that presidential assistants play as they try to manage relations with interest groups. " 'Markers' deal with the accumulated credits held by groups that supported the president's nomination and selection," they write. " 'Communicants' establish a basis of shared interest with groups that the president needs in his ongoing governmental and political efforts. 'Constructors' seek group support for policy campaigns, particularly those that involve congressional lobbying. 'Brokers' make agreements with groups for the president and intercede with him on behalf of interest groups."

The pressures that interest groups can bring to bear on presidents are well known. What is intriguing about Kumar's and Grossman's analysis is their conclusion that if all four staff roles are performed skillfully and with presidential support, then "ultimately, the relationship with interest groups, for all its potential pitfalls, provides a president with some advantages."

The press is another White House constituency whose constraining influences on recent presidents, although real, may be exaggerated. In Chapter 10, "The Presidency and the Press," James Fallows identifies four subjects on which the White House press corps feels sufficiently confident to offer an independent, and thus sometimes critical, assessment of a president: suspected scandal, dissension within the administration, tactical blunders, and "politics in the narrow sense: the business of winning elections and gaining points in the opinion polls." Such stories often vex the White House and prompt charges that the press is a presidential adversary. But according to Fallows, when it comes to substantive issues—"the *what* of government"—presidents generally are able to secure the press's acquiescence to their policy agenda. "If you listen to the press secretary make his morning announcement," he writes, "you know—barring scandal or gaffe— what the lead will be on the evening news that night."

If interest groups and the press are not as hostile to presidents as is commonly thought, neither are political parties as useless. To be sure, "presidents have shown little desire to have party organizations strengthen their influence," notes Roger G. Brown in Chapter 12, "The Presidency and the Political Parties." And the recent decline of parties, both in their hold on the loyalties of voters and their power relative to other political institutions, has allowed presidents to free themselves to some extent from their traditional obligations as party leader. But, Brown argues, the parties may be in the midst of an organizational comeback that not only will increase their attractiveness to presidents, but remind them that historically, when the general public has turned fickle, the interest groups have grown uncooperative, and the press has become adversarial, the president's political party has been his last, best friend.

9. THE PRESIDENCY AND THE PEOPLE: THE MODERN PARADOX

Samuel Kernell

In February 1982, as President Reagan and his budget director, David Stockman, were preparing a second round of budget cuts, White House reporters asked White House Director of Communications David Gergen what the president would do if this session's Congress proved less compliant. "Well," replied Gergen, "the president has a reservoir of public support to draw upon." The word "compromise" never came up, and the president's actions subsequently confirmed Gergen's prognosis. Shunning a deal with the leaders of the House Democrats and Senate Republicans until a crisis arose in late summer, Reagan chose to reaffirm his electoral mandate with a strategy of public statements and travel to such remote but predictably sympathetic gatherings as Republican rallies in Wyoming and southern state legislatures.

Reagan's tactics seem to epitomize the way presidents increasingly approach Washington problems. Impatient with Washington politics, they are inclined more than ever to "go public." No president espoused this view more frequently than Jimmy Carter. For example, consider the exchange that took place at a White House press conference in 1979 when Carter was pressed by a reporter to say how he planned to improve his notably poor performance with the heavily Democratic Congress.

> Q. Mr. President, even though it might not be your favorite way of doing things with Congress, why don't you get tough to the extent of saying to Members of Congress individually that, "If you won't help me on these major programs that I feel are important to the entire country, I won't go along with my administration providing the individual, district-by-district services that you are interested in as a Member of Congress"?
>
> The President. I represent those districts also. Every one of the people who lives in any congressional district is my constituent. And I don't think it's right to punish the people of our Nation who live in a particular farming community or city or congressional district

because a particular Member of Congress does not comply with the proposals that I make that I believe to be in the best interest of our Nation.

The best approach that I have been able to make—and we've had a very good success in having the Congress approve my proposals in previous years—has been to deal, first of all, with the Congress directly, both as a body and also individual Members of the Congress.

When I do face a serious problem, like with the windfall profits tax when the prediction was we had no chance to get it passed, I take my case to the public as strongly and effectively as I can. I think that's the best way to induce the Congress Members to vote in the best interests of their constituents and mine, not to punish the constituents in a district.[1]

This development toward a more "public president" is important because as public strategies are substituted for subtler forms of persuasion, they yield a qualitatively different form of leadership. The degree to which the president draws upon public opinion determines the kind of leader he will be. Will the president bargain with other elites as a way of building winning coalitions, or will he blithely construct bandwagons that others will mount out of their own self-interest? Conventionally, students of the presidency have applauded the former;[2] the latter increasingly appears more likely.

The reasons for this are numerous and complex. The proximate causes reflect both who the modern presidents are and what Washington has become. When Jimmy Carter states in his memoirs that "We came as outsiders ... and we left as outsiders," he may well be speaking for the next generation of presidents.[3] The multitude of presidential selection reforms—among them, the proliferation of primaries, proportional representation in delegate selection, campaign spending limitations and federal financing—has largely removed traditional party leaders from the process of selecting nominees. More frequently than not, the nominee will be decided in the primary elections, well before the party convention.

These reforms have allowed candidates with little Washington experience (much less talent in the art of bargaining) and with political views beyond the mainstream of the party to contest and win their party's nomination. Once elected, these presidents—unfamiliar with and unknown by the Washington community—will be disinclined to practice the detailed day-to-day rituals of exchange necessary to cultivate support among fellow Washingtonians. Instead, they are likely to continue to pursue those strategies that placed them in the

White House. For outsiders, governing may be little more than an extension of the campaign.

There is also good reason to suspect that public strategies of leadership are coming into vogue because they succeed. Once Washington was a city filled with hierarchies. To these hierarchies were attached leaders or at least authoritative representatives. Such leaders sometimes extracted a dear price for cooperation with the president, and at times they defeated him outright. But as difficult as a Lyndon Johnson, a Wilbur Mills, an Otto Passman, a Robert Kerr, or even a J. Edgar Hoover could be when he got his back up, they each were indispensable trading partners. Consider what such men had to offer: a Senate majority leader (Johnson) who could strike a deal with the president on legislation, then return to the chamber floor and deliver the critical votes for its passage; a committee chairman (Mills, Passman, or Kerr) who spoke so authoritatively for his commitee that its mark-up session was spent detailing the language of the general bargain he had struck earlier; or an agency head (Hoover) who, once persuaded, effectively redirected his agency's activities.

Today, Washington is substantially different.[4] These changes consistently point to a community governed less by leaders and more by the requirements of independent, egocentric actors. Subpresidential coalitions founded largely upon institutional proximity have given way to more casual and voluntary associations, such as congressional caucuses and work groups, founded upon an affinity of interest. For the president who attempts to assemble a coalition across a broad institutional landscape, these changes are unattractive. From his vantage, Washington has become a big city in which the number of exchanges necessary to secure others' support has increased dramatically. At the same time, a city of free agents unencumbered by commitments to party leaders may well be more susceptible to the political winds that a public president can stir up.

The new leadership style of the modern president as a "public president" is demonstrated in this chapter by a systematic record of the public behavior of recent incumbents. Although some tactics of the public president are private and escape close scrutiny, they generally involve an implied or expressed threat to "go public" to mobilize support. This increasingly popular strategy, however, introduces a profound paradox for modern presidential leadership. Consider the inference that follows from these three empirical propositions:

(1) Presidents increasingly go public.
(2) The effectiveness of a president's public appeal depends upon his popular support.
(3) But presidents are becoming less popular, more quickly.

Therefore, presidents are going public precisely at the time when they can least afford to do so.

If these propositions are accurate and the inference sound, the modern president faces an inescapable dilemma. Disposed to a public strategy by who he is and by what Washington has become, the president finds himself perched on a rostrum before an audience that quickly becomes bored with, if not hostile to, his appeals. The implications of this paradox for presidential leadership are discussed at the close of the chapter. First, however, the accuracy of the three empirical claims upon which the paradox is based must be tested.

Proposition 1:
Presidents increasingly go public.

Going public can take a variety of forms. The most obvious is a formal occasion, such as an inaugural address or State of the Union message, when official duty places the president prominently before the nation. Going public, however, may involve no more than a pregnant aside to a news reporter at a strategic moment. Given this variety, we shall, for the sake of analysis, divide the president's public behavior into three broad, nonexclusive classes: direct public appeals for support, presidential appearances, and political travel. Each has been further dichotomized according to the locale or prominence of the activity.[5]

Public Addresses

Appeals for support from non-Washington constituencies is at the heart of the public president. Even within this core of activities, great variety is evident. Form, audience, and content make each appeal unique. President John F. Kennedy's October 1962 address to the nation, in which he announced a quarantine of Soviet ships laden with surface-to-surface missiles enroute to Cuba, is different in each respect from President Carter's trip to Iowa in 1977 to sell his agricultural policies before a gathering of farmers. With such diversity one reasonably may wonder what any trends discerned in the volume of public addresses could mean.

Without delving too deeply into the form, audience, and content, we shall distinguish between major and minor presidential addresses.

The former are those in which the president speaks directly to a national audience via radio or television, while the latter are targeted to some special audience. By these definitions, Kennedy's Cuban missile crisis statement qualifies as a major address while Carter's farm speech is classified as minor.[6]

Of the major addresses, the most numerous and potentially the most dramatic kind involves the president's use of prime-time television for special reports to the nation. The subjects of these television talks, listed in Table 9-1, provide a calendar of the crises and national exigencies that have preoccupied post-World War II presidents. But President Carter's repeated use of this forum to campaign for energy conservation and his legislative program and President Reagan's regular appeals for public support for his economic policies suggest that "normal" politics are replacing international crises as the main occasions of these prime-time appeals.[7]

Televised talks, along with other major appeals, such as addresses to joint sessions of Congress, may be the most dramatic and effective devices available to the public president, but they also can be the most taxing. One might suspect that public attentiveness would drop off sharply with successive appeals. If every presidential tribulation were taken to the country on prime-time television, people soon would lose interest.[8] Each appeal of this type, therefore, entails opportunity costs for the president because it potentially reduces the size and responsiveness of the audience for his next appeal.

Minor presidential addresses—those directed toward special constituencies—are different. Whatever institutional change has occurred in Washington during the past two decades, presidential governance remains largely the process of assembling temporary coalitions from among diverse, sometimes antagonistic, constituencies. For the public president, the value of directly mobilizing special constituencies is great. Appeals to targeted audiences may succeed where "major" addresses to the undifferentiated citizenry would not.

President Reagan demonstrated this approach when he addressed a Chicago conference of Catholic lay organizations in 1982 on behalf of his proposal to provide federal assistance for private school tuition.[9] For the Catholic church, financially strapped by rising costs and declining enrollments in many communities, and for parents who send their children to these schools (or who would like to), enactment of the president's proposal would be a godsend. Considering President Reagan's penurious domestic budget and his generous cutbacks for education, the trip to Chicago may have been inspired more by an immediate

Table 9-1 Calendar of Presidential "Reports to the Nation" on National Television, 1953-1982

Year	Jan.	Feb.	Mar.	Apr.	May	June	July	Aug.	Sept.	Oct.	Nov.	Dec.
Eisenhower												
1953												
1954	Review			World affairs		Review		Congress				
1955							Geneva Conference					
1956		Reelection announcement; Middle East		Veto-Agriculture						Middle East		
1957					Mutual aid			Labor reform	Little Rock		Science, security	
1958												
1959			Berlin						Europe			International peace
1960		National defense	Latin America		Paris summit							
Kennedy												
1961						Far East Europe meetings	Berlin					
1962			Nuclear tests							Cuba	Cuba	
1963						Civil rights		Taxes; Test ban	Tax cut			
Johnson												
1964								Tonkin Gulf		International Affairs		
1965				Railroad Labor dispute (2); Dominican Rep.	Dominican Rep.			Steel strike	Steel strike			
1966	Bombing North Vietnam											
1967						Violence	Riots					
1968	Pueblo		Vietnam; non-candidacy	Martin Luther King						Halt of bombing		

President	Year								
Nixon	1969	Veto-H.E.W.	Welfare	S.E. Asia					
	1970	Postal strike	Cambodia (2) Economy	Peace initiative Economy					
	1971	Vietnam (2)	S.E. Asia SALT						
	1972 1973	S.E. Asia Vietnam	Busing Economy	Vietnam Watergate	Vietnam	Economy	China trip	Economy Watergate	Energy crisis (2)
Ford	1974	Egypt-Israel	Watergate	Middle East Crisis	USSR trip (2); economy	Pardon of Nixon			
	1975	National issues	Tax cut	Mayaguez (2); energy	Tax cut				
	1976								
Carter	1977	Fireside chat Panama Canal Treaty							
	1978	Energy	Inflation	Energy	China				
	1979	Economy	Energy	SALT II	Crisis of Confidence	Soviet troops in Cuba			
	1980	Economy							
Reagan	1981	Farewell (Carter)	Tax bill	Economy	Economy; budget Middle East (2)	Poland			
	1982	Economy	Budget	Arms control					

SOURCE: The entries from 1953 through November 1963 were compiled from "Presidents on TV: Their Live Records," *Broadcasting*, November 8, 1965, 55–58; those from December 1963 through December 1975 were taken from a Congressional Research Service report by Denis S. Rutkus entitled, "A Report on Simultaneous Television Network Coverage of Presidential Addresses to the Nation," unpublished manuscript, 1976, appendix; entries since 1976 were drawn from the *Public Papers of the Presidents* series and a tentative compilation by Denis Rutkus.

political need to shore up support with this constituency than by a
desire to give his stalled legislation a push in Congress.[10] The trip also
promised an enthusiastic reception before a traditionally Democratic
audience that would receive prominent coverage on the evening news.

Aside from being more focused and publicly less obtrusive than
major addresses (and therefore less taxing on future public appeals),

Table 9-2 President Carter's "Minor" Addresses During October
1977

Date	Location	Audience	Subject
October 4	United Nations	General Assembly	Controlling nuclear proliferation
October 4	United Nations	U.S. Delegation	Thanks for fine job, importance of the U.N.
October 5	United Nations	Not Stated	Remarks on signing international covenants on human rights
October 5	United Nations	Foreign Ministers, Heads of Delegations	Changing international relationships
October 7	Washington Hilton Hotel	Democratic National Committee	Political support for Panama Canal treaties
October 19	State Department	Conference for International Nuclear Fuel Cycle Evaluation	Provisions for adequate power sources
October 21	Des Moines, Iowa	Not Stated	Importance of Iowa farm bill
October 21	Des Moines, Iowa	Democratic Party Dinner	New farm legislation, energy issues
October 22	Denver, Colorado	Western States Governors	Western water policy
October 22	Denver, Colorado	Citizens from Rocky Mountain West	Panama Canal
October 22	Los Angeles, California	Democratic National Committee Dinner	Human rights, peace in the Middle East, energy issues

SOURCE: *Public Papers of the Presidents of the United States: Jimmy Carter, 1977,* in two books,
January 20-June 24, 1977; June 25-December 31, 1977 (Washington, D.C.: U.S. Government
Printing Office, 1978), book two, 1715-1898.

minor addresses are attractive to presidents because the opportunities to give them are plentiful. The president is importuned daily to appear before graduation exercises, union conferences, and trade and professional association conventions. Not surprisingly, the advantages of minor addresses make this form of going public a common device of presidential leadership today. Just how common and varied can be seen by looking at President Carter's October 1977 calendar of speaking engagements, which is presented in Table 9-2. On eleven occasions in that month, he personally addressed nine different constituencies in five cities on both coasts. And this tally does not include the similar itineraries of other members of his administration.

The average yearly numbers of major and minor addresses for each president since Herbert Hoover are displayed in Figure 9-1. Both forms of presidential oratory have been on the rise in recent years, although to far different degrees. Given the opportunity costs (as well as network resistance) to commandeering prime-time television, it is not surprising that recent presidents have increased their use of this approach only marginally. Nonetheless, the eight major addresses by President Reagan in 1981 (a month of which was spent convalescing) is a first-year record for any president.[11]

The real explosion in presidential talk has occurred in the class of minor addresses. Presidents Nixon, Carter, and Reagan have surpassed their predecessors' use of such rhetoric by nearly fivefold. If asked to name a president who could speak skillfully, one probably would think first of Franklin Roosevelt or perhaps John Kennedy, two men whose speeches have weathered time and relistening well. President Nixon's pronouncements—such as his Watergate denials and prepresidential "Checkers" speech—will be remembered mostly as objects of ridicule and, ultimately, of historical curiosity. Addresses by Presidents Johnson and Carter will be recalled, if at all, as instructive examples of poor elocution. Yet, Nixon, Carter, and Reagan stand apart from their more polished predecessors as chronic practitioners of the ancient art of public speaking. President Reagan, nicknamed the Great Communicator by underlings and the press, is clearly an able speaker who presently is matching recent records in frequency and topping them in success. Overall, however, it is not success that breeds presidential rhetoric but the evolving requirements of the job.

Public Appearances and Travel

Visual images at times can convey messages more effectively than talk. The audience to whom the president speaks, where, and under

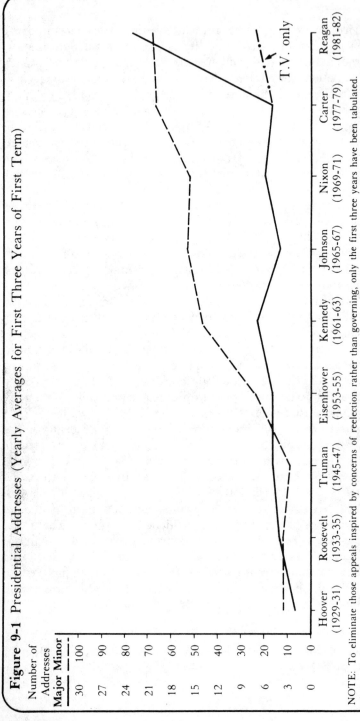

Figure 9-1 Presidential Addresses (Yearly Averages for First Three Years of First Term)

NOTE: To eliminate those appeals inspired by concerns of reelection rather than governing, only the first three years have been tabulated.

SOURCE: Figures for Hoover, Roosevelt, Truman, Eisenhower, Nixon, and Carter have been recompiled from William W. Lammers, "Presidential Attention-Focusing Activities," in *The President and the American Public*, ed. Doris A. Graber (Philadelphia: Institute for the Study of Human Issues, 1982), Table 6-1, 152. Figures for Kennedy, Johnson, and Reagan have been compiled from *Public Papers of the President* series. See Appendix.

what circumstances may contribute as much to his message's effectiveness as what he has to say. The image of President Nixon donning a hard hat and waving to cheering construction workers on the scaffolding above him was a stronger pitch for support among his "silent majority" than mere words or political appointments could have accomplished.

Sometimes presidents travel in search of opportunities to appear "presidential." Foreign travel especially can remind the electorate of the weighty responsibilities of the presidency. Could the salutary effects of Kennedy's confrontation with Nikita Khrushchev in Vienna and Nixon's trip to China on these presidents' popularity long escape a future incumbent? In the age of television, every president may be suspected of, and perhaps forgiven for, engaging in strategic travel and posing for the continuous "photo opportunities."

The indices for both types of public activities—appearances and travel—are broken down in Figures 9-2 and 9-3 according to locale. Figure 9-2 shows days of both domestic and foreign travel because the public traditionally has given greater support to the president in the conduct of foreign affairs than in his handling of domestic problems. Appearances, on the other hand, are distinguished in Figure 9-3 according to whether they occurred within or beyond Washington. Public appearances outside of the city generally are more symbolic of the president's non-Washington origins and sympathies.[12] They also afford the president a brief escape from what invariably comes to be viewed by the White House as an unappreciative and overly critical Washington press. In the spring of 1983, President Reagan blamed his falling prestige on press carping and exaggerated stories of disarray among his staff that were all the more irritating because they were based on anonymous leaks from within the White House. According to one unnamed White House source, the president planned to remedy this unsatisfactory situation with shorter press conferences and more frequent out-of-town travel.[13]

As Figures 9-2 and 9-3 show, recent presidents have logged far more time in public view, whether measured by travel days or public appearances. Compared with their early predecessors' average of 15 appearances a year outside of Washington, Presidents Nixon and Carter averaged about 70 such appearances, and for Carter this figure excludes his numerous and lengthy "town meetings." Add to this an average of 25 Washington appearances and 11 days of foreign travel annually, and one has accounted for nearly a third of these presidents' time in office during the first three years.[14] By comparison, Franklin

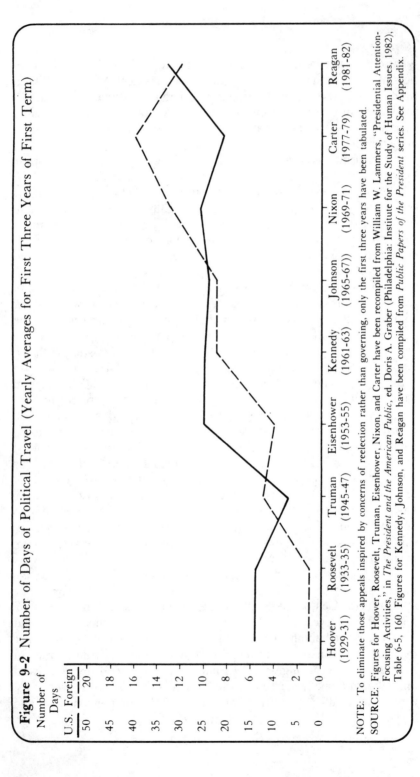

Figure 9-2 Number of Days of Political Travel (Yearly Averages for First Three Years of First Term)

NOTE: To eliminate those appeals inspired by concerns of reelection rather than governing, only the first three years have been tabulated.

SOURCE: Figures for Hoover, Roosevelt, Truman, Eisenhower, Nixon, and Carter have been recompiled from William W. Lammers, "Presidential Attention-Focusing Activities," in *The President and the American Public*, ed. Doris A. Graber (Philadelphia: Institute for the Study of Human Issues, 1982), Table 6-5, 160. Figures for Kennedy, Johnson, and Reagan have been compiled from *Public Papers of the President* series. See Appendix.

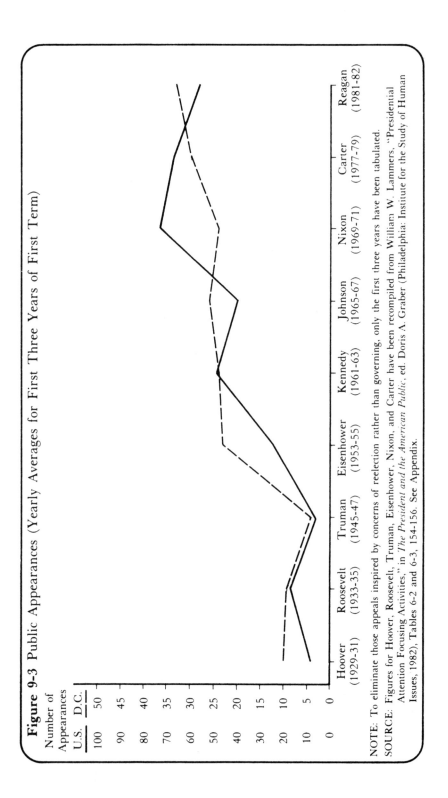

Figure 9-3 Public Appearances (Yearly Averages for First Three Years of First Term)

Number of
Appearances

U.S.	D.C.
100	50
90	45
80	40
70	35
60	30
50	25
40	20
30	15
20	10
10	5
0	0

Hoover (1929-31) Roosevelt (1933-35) Truman (1945-47) Eisenhower (1953-55) Kennedy (1961-63) Johnson (1965-67) Nixon (1969-71) Carter (1977-79) Reagan (1981-82)

NOTE: To eliminate those appeals inspired by concerns of reelection rather than governing, only the first three years have been tabulated.

SOURCE: Figures for Hoover, Roosevelt, Truman, Eisenhower, Nixon, and Carter have been recompiled from William W. Lammers, "Presidential Attention Focusing Activities," in *The President and the American Public*, ed. Doris A. Graber (Philadelphia: Institute for the Study of Human Issues, 1982), Tables 6-2 and 6-3, 154-156. See Appendix.

Roosevelt, whose command of rhetoric and public attention has long been heralded by students of the presidency, appears to have been a recluse.

Of course, the quality and the quantity of public appeals are different matters. But whatever the quality or success of their efforts to go public, outsiders in the White House have no choice but to do so as they engage in a politics that has become increasingly less tractable to "inside" methods of bargaining and persuasion.

Proposition 2:
The effectiveness of a president's appeal depends upon his popular support.

The political cognoscenti probably always have recognized some association between the president's support in the country and his success in Washington. Under present conditions, however, this relation has been elevated to a principle *sine qua non* among Washingtonians. The relation stated in Proposition 2 informs the strategic calculations of presidents and those who advise them, of politicians who must respond to presidential initiatives or who wish to offer their own, and of journalists who must explain and interpret presidential performance as well as report it. Consider the following examples of strategic behavior guided by knowledge of the president's public standing.

Case 1. On March 30, 1981, President Reagan was wounded in an attempted assassination. His public support, which had begun to sag, much to the concern of his advisers, turned upward dramatically. According to a Reagan aide, "It [the shooting] focused uniquely on the President. It did a lot to endear the President with the people. If the endearing thesis is right, his personal attributes might never have come across without the assassination attempt." [15] When White House pollster Richard Wirthlin confirmed the groundswell of support, Michael Deaver, one of the president's chief counselors, convened a strategy meeting to consider how this new "political capital" should be invested. The result came on April 28 when President Reagan, in his first major appearance since the shooting, addressed a wildly jubilant joint session of Congress to lobby for his budget. Shortly thereafter, Democratic opposition to his proposal crumbled.

Case 2. In late 1978 and early 1979, with his approval rating less than 50 percent in the monthly Gallup polls, President Carter complained that it was difficult to gain Congress's attention for his legislative proposals. As one staffer in the congressional liaison office observed, "When you go up to the Hill and the latest polls show Carter isn't doing well, then there isn't much reason for a member to go along with him." [16] A member of Congress concurred, "The relationship between the President and Congress is partly the result of how well the President is doing politically. Congress is better behaved when he does well. . . . Right now, it's almost as if Congress is paying no attention to him." [17]

Case 3. On May 29, 1974, President Nixon summoned the network cameras to announce an Arab-Israeli crisis and an alert of the armed forces for emergency deployment. With the House Judiciary Committee deliberating Nixon's impeachment and barely a quarter of the public endorsing his performance as president, members of the press became suspicious. The next day they bluntly confronted Secretary of State Henry Kissinger at a press conference with the charge that the crisis had been fabricated to deflect public attention away from the president's Watergate troubles.[18]

These examples illustrate just how dramatically elites' responses to presidential messages can vary with the president's standing in the polls. In the first, a popular president rushed through convalescence to take advantage of his newly acquired fame in the most dramatic fashion imaginable. In the second, an unpopular president futilely worked to gain the attention, if not the respect, of a Congress controlled by his own party. Finally, a president disgraced and on the brink of departure tried to fend off the open contempt that greeted his pronouncements. To appreciate the significance of presidential popularity on elite behavior, one need only ask if Reagan would have dared to show his face on Capitol Hill if he had possessed Nixon's popularity. Conversely, would the reporters have been so brazen had Nixon enjoyed Reagan's prestige?

Underlying Opinion Dynamics

The value of Proposition 2 as a principle by which politicians may anticipate the immediate future would seem to rest upon the accuracy of a circuitous path of opinion formation. The proposition implicitly assumes four primary relationships displayed in Figure 9-4 that commonly appear in social-psychological research on opinion change: A) The president's communicated preferences are perceived accurately by the citizenry. This means simply that the public recognizes a positive association between the president and his messages $(P-M=+)$. B) Following the tenet that, "If you like the source, you will like the message," citizens who approve of the president $(P-C=+)$ adopt his preferences as their own $(C-M=+)$. Conversely, those who disapprove $(P-C=-)$ reject his message $(C-M=-)$. C) Politicians

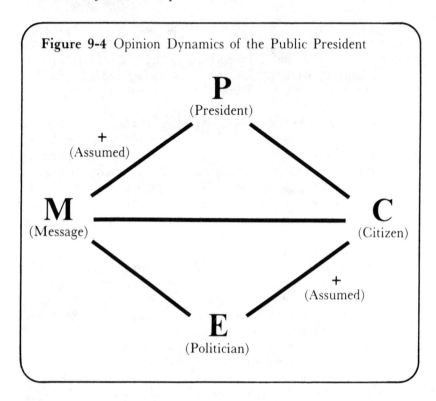

Figure 9-4 Opinion Dynamics of the Public President

whom the president ultimately hopes to persuade accurately perceive the level of popular support for the president's policy. D) To secure their own political welfare (hence, $E - M = +$), politicians reorganize their own publicly stated preferences to agree with the majority preferences of the citizenry ($E - M = C - M$). These are the *formal* preconditions that must be satisfied if the president is to wield influence in Washington through his leadership of public opinion.

With such draconian requirements for influence, one may wonder how public strategies could ever succeed. At each juncture the potential for slippage is great. Inaccurate communication, misperception, and rationalization—the troika of false attitude consistency—threaten conditions A and C, while an unrealistically deterministic psycho-logic of citizens and politicians burdens conditions B and D.[19] How can these conditions, so rife with misconception, hold? More to the point, should public presidents invest heavily in strategies that depend upon these opinion dynamics?

The answer to both questions is that the formal system of opinion dynamics need only be approximated to satisfy the requirements of the public president. There are several reasons why this is true. They concern features peculiar to the presidency, its place in public opinion, and the nature of strategic elite behavior.

Presidents build coalitions at the margin of elite support. On any policy issue that a president is likely to sponsor, a substantial share of the relevant politicians and the American public already will share his position for reasons of their own. In constructing a working majority, a president's public campaign may succeed if it shifts as few as, say, 20 votes on the House floor. The position of the modern presidency in the sequence of policy formation frequently minimizes the degree of influence required for success.

Another reason why imperfect consistency may be sufficient is that the slippage in condition B between evaluations of the president and opinions about his policies does not necessarily weaken the effect of the president's appeal on public opinion. There is good reason to suspect that those citizens who approve of the president's overall performance but disagree with his position will be offset by those who disapprove of but nonetheless defer to his judgment. This is because the president's singular visibility, constitutional legitimacy, and acknowledged institutional expertise preserve for him a special place in public opinion.[20] In judicial parlance, the president enjoys standing. Citizens take note of his appeals whether they like him or not.

An example of this form of compensation was the public response to the Truman Doctrine speech in March 1947, when the president made a dramatic appeal for American assistance to war-torn Europe. Although 34 percent of President Truman's admirers who heard or read about his appeal resisted his argument for emergency aid to Greece, their numbers were more than compensated by the 36 percent of his detractors who supported him on this issue. The net effect was not much different from what would have been yielded by perfect attitude consistency among the mass public.[21]

Another form of compensation, which in this instance operates to soften condition C, can be found in the way representatives receive information about their constituents. Rarely will a politician have instant access to polls that tell him how strongly the citizens he represents agree or disagree with a president's appeal. Generally, politicians must infer the opinions of their constituents from national polls. More often than not, these surveys fail to register the intensity of sentiment on each side of an issue—vital information for assessing its potential political damage. While most Washingtonians probably study the numerous national opinion barometers that are routinely reported in the press, they can ill afford to rely exclusively upon such sources.

Just as presidents operate at the margin of support in Congress, so too do representatives operate at the margin within their constituencies. For them, the opinions of those members of their electorate who are moved to act are far more consequential than mere numbers might indicate. Information about these voters emanates directly from the districts in the form of phone calls, letters, telegrams, editorials and letters in the local papers, and the posturings of local politicians. If the president can motivate even a small fraction of the citizenry to engage in these activities, he will skew the elite's perceptions of public opinion and inspire their compliance.

Finally, politicians frequently short-circuit the process of reading public opinion to the president's advantage. Operating under classic conditions of "limited rationality," many politicians, especially those who are worried about the next election, will infer from the president's overall approval ratings support for his policies and alter their own positions accordingly. Richard Neustadt, in his classic book, *Presidential Power,* acknowledges this when he argues that popularity purchases the president "leeway" in his dealings with others.[22]

In sum, when it comes to telling the country what it needs to hear, no one is in a better position than the president. This is good news for the public president because his influence requires an attentive audience that is sympathetic to his messages. The association described in Figure 9-4 is the foundation of the public president. Without it he is adrift.

A Case Study of Opinion Influence: Reagan's Budget Message

A Gallup poll on the public's responses to President Reagan's nationally televised speech of September 24, 1981, illustrates the dynamics of public presidential leadership. That speech, in which he called for a second round of budget cuts, is an unambiguous example of "going public" as a device for influencing Congress.

During the summer, as unemployment continued its ascent and President Reagan's approval rating its correspondingly steep descent, many members of Congress began to express second thoughts about the administration's supply-side economic policies. As documented in *Newsweek's* lead paragraph on the president's speech, the Republican euphoria of the summer had given way to a growing disillusionment:

Ronald Reagan appealed to the nation again last week in behalf of his economic program—but this time, his avuncular delivery seemed at odds with the pressures that had brought him before his national television audience. Buffeted by disbelieving financial markets and an increasingly combative Congress, the President outlined a second wave of $13 billion in spending cuts aimed at containing an outside budget deficit in the next fiscal year and reassuring the skeptics that Reaganomics could work.[23]

The article went on to describe the "chilly reception" the president's proposal received on the Hill and Wall Street.

On Capitol Hill, GOP leaders publicly applauded the President's resolve to take a second bite out of the budget. But privately, Republicans acknowledged that they would be forced to slice more from the Pentagon budget than the $2 billion Reagan had proposed for fiscal 1982. . . . The Democrats were lying in wait, plainly eager to capitalize on Reagan's new attack on entitlements and quick to underscore their improving fortunes. . . . Wall Street, meanwhile, continued to vote no on the Presidential program. The day after Reagan's speech, bond prices plunged and the Dow Jones industrial average of 30 stocks fell more than 11 points to its lowest level since May 1980.[24]

Within two weeks of the speech, the public's reaction was recorded in unusual detail by a nationwide Gallup survey that devoted eight questions to the president's budget proposals.[25] Sixty-one percent of those queried by Gallup recalled having seen or heard about the speech. Among the president's natural constituency of high-income and well-educated respondents, familiarity was significantly greater. On a follow-up question they also demonstrated a more accurate recall of the details of the president's proposal.

Those who said they were familiar with the speech were asked their opinions of the proposed cuts. Their answers, as well as the full wording of these questions, are provided in Table 9-3. By tabulating these opinions according to the respondent's party identification and evaluation of President Reagan's job performance—both potentially independent sources of an affinity relation $(P-C)$—we can test the degree to which support for (or partisan affinity with) the president influenced support for his message.

Both variables, job performance evaluation and party identification, appear in Table 9-3 to contribute independently to policy support, with the former being the stronger of the two. Comparing overall assessments of the budget cuts (Question 1) by the president's

Table 9-3 Approval of President Reagan's Performance and Support for his Budget (Percentages Read Across)

Respondent's: Party Identification	Job Evaluation[1]	Question 1 "In general, are you in favor of budget cuts in addition to those approved earlier this year or are you opposed to more cuts?"		Question 2 "The additional cuts for social programs came to about $11 billion. Do you feel this amount is too high, too low or about right?"			Question 3 "The additional cuts for defense programs came to about $2 billion. Do you feel this amount is too high, too low or about right?"		
		Favor	Oppose	Too High	About Right	Too Low	Too High	About Right	Too Low
Republican	Approve	76	17	16	60	14	23	52	17
	Disapprove	29	62	57	24	0	24	29	19
Independent	Approve	73	20	13	58	12	22	48	22
	Disapprove	26	68	64	23	1	20	45	24
Democrat	Approve	51	42	33	39	10	24	38	18
	Disapprove	11	85	80	12	4	21	43	28

[1] Question: "Do you approve or disapprove of the way President Reagan has handled his job as president?

NOTE: Table includes only respondents who answered "yes" to the prior question, "Did you happen to see or read about President Reagan's TV speech on September 24 in which he proposed Federal budget cuts in addition to those approved earlier this year?" "No opinion" responses are included in the percentaging.

SOURCE: American Institute of Public Opinion, Survey No. 183-G, October 2-5, 1981.

approvers and disapprovers within each party, we find differences in support ranging from 40 to 47 percentage points. Conversely, controlling for performance evaluations by comparing the opinions of respondents who agree in their job performance evaluation but differ in their party affiliation, we turn up a much smaller range of differences in policy support. Approving Republicans, for example, are more favorable to the overall budget than approving Democrats by 25 percentage points. The party differences are even smaller among the president's detractors. When employed jointly, these variables strongly discriminate among respondents' receptivity to the president's appeal. More than three-quarters of the approving Republicans, but only a tenth of the disapproving Democrats, volunteered general support for further budget reductions. Clearly, the ideal situation for the public president is to be popular and to head the majority party.[26]

The implication of these relationships for the public president's leadership of Congress is equally unambiguous. In the early summer of 1981, White House advisers boasted, "some Democrats are getting the picture that by going with Reagan they are doing the popular thing." At the time, Reagan's approval rating stood near 60 percent. By the fall of 1982 with the president's rating barely 40 percent, his staffers were conceding, "Congress is no longer dictated by a fear that Ronald Reagan can go to the country." [27]

Proposition 3:
Presidents are becoming less popular, more quickly.

Since the mid-1930s, when the Gallup organization began routinely soliciting public evaluations of presidential performance, every president has managed to leave office less popular than when he entered. (See Table 9-4.) For at least one reason, this decline is unavoidable: the levels of support with which presidents begin are artificially high. Whether elected by the narrowest of margins, as Kennedy was in 1960, or serving, as Ford did, as the unelected successor to a president who resigned in disgrace, the president is widely approved when he enters office. But since Johnson, Nixon, Ford, and Carter ended their terms, not only with their popularity down, but also with more citizens disapproving their performance than approving, the argument that the loss of popular support is merely a consequence of their unrealistically high beginnings is not altogether convincing.

For most presidents, public disfavor can be traced to some specific event or condition. Truman was saddled initially with the high

Table 9-4   The Record of Postwar Presidents in Public Opinion

	Beginning of Term	Ending of Term[1]	Percentage Point Decline
Harry Truman	87	32	55
Dwight Eisenhower	68	49	19
John Kennedy	72	58	14
Lyndon Johnson	78	40	38
Richard Nixon	59	24	35
Gerald Ford	71	45	26
Jimmy Carter	66	33	33
Ronald Reagan	51	41[2]	10

[1] For full terms as of July preceding the presidential elections.
[2] As of January 1983.
SOURCE: Various issues of the *Gallup Opinion Index*.

inflation that followed postwar price decontrols and later with Korea. Johnson was immensely popular until the Vietnam War began to take a steady and eventually heavy toll on American lives.[28] Nixon finished his first full term with his standing in public opinion untarnished and proceeded to win reelection over George McGovern by a record share of the vote. His precipitous decline in the polls occurred only as the tangle of misdeeds, summarized under the rubric of Watergate, was revealed. But Ford managed to forfeit his popularity in a few moments when he announced on prime-time television that he had pardoned ex-President Nixon. Seventy-one percent had approved of Ford's performance initially; within a month of the announcement, this figure had plummeted to 40 percent, the largest single-month drop in Gallup's history. His public standing never much improved.[29]

The reasons for Carter's and Reagan's loss of public confidence are less obvious. This is all the more curious because Carter and Reagan each managed to eclipse his predecessors' declines. President Carter easily surpassed Johnson's fall in the polls, for example, even without the assistance of a protracted and controversial war. And Reagan, despite his impressive handling of Congress at the beginning of his term, progressed down the slippery slope of public opinion at a pace that threatened existing speed and distance records. The poor fortunes of these two presidents in the polls, which exceeded any fair reading of their records, have stimulated much speculation about the reasons for public disfavor.

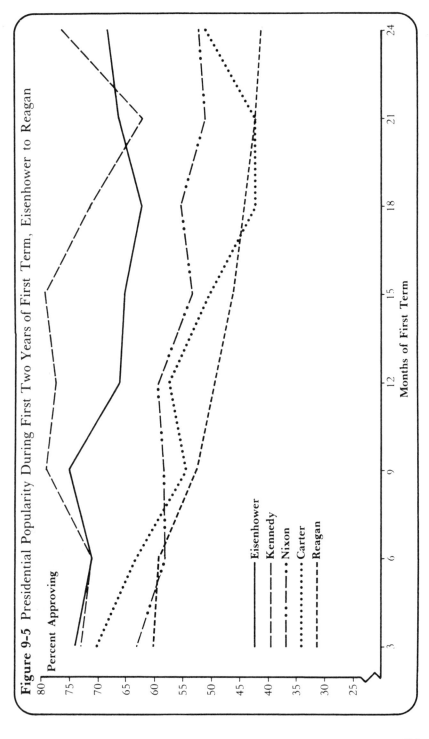

Figure 9-5 Presidential Popularity During First Two Years of First Term, Eisenhower to Reagan

For the most part, recent explanations have shifted the focus from "bad presidents" to "bad times." Independent of the occurrence of dramatic, injurious events late in the term, such as Watergate and Vietnam, the declining popularity of recent presidents appears to reflect both lower beginning levels of approval and an accelerated rate of decline over the first two years in office. Each initially elected president's track record since 1953 is plotted in Figure 9-5.[30]

The differences in initial approval ratings are not great, but each president in the figure clearly began his term less popular than his party's most recent incumbent. Among the Democratic presidents, Carter was slightly less popular than Kennedy, and among the Republicans, Reagan was substantially less popular than either Nixon or Eisenhower. This adds emphasis to the second, more prominent development displayed in the figure: recent presidents also have managed to lose their support more quickly.

The early decline in popular support has become so serious that by the 1978 and 1982 midterm elections both Carter and Reagan had become distinct liabilities to their parties' congressional candidates. Each, as a result, campaigned selectively, as much not to embarrass himself as to avoid hurting his colleagues.[31] No wonder that by the end of his term President Carter was virtually unelectable and by midterm President Reagan found numerous Democrats queuing to offer themselves as his replacement. Although the source of this secular decline in presidential support remains elusive, it does not minimize the degree to which future presidents must plan for their own loss in public confidence.

Conclusion: The President's Rhythm

Edwin Meese, who was among those charged to plan President-elect Reagan's administation, proclaimed that the president would "hit the ground running." During the next few months, as his prophecy was borne out, several White House staffers elaborated on Meese's theme to journalist Elizabeth Drew. She writes, "The President's advisors sensed that if they were to obtain congressional consent for the radical changes they were seeking they would have to do it quickly." As one aide told her, "We had to do it all at once. I don't think the President's going to have a second chance at getting control of spending." And another confided, "We're fighting the clock. We think about that all the time." [32]

Such soundings are familiar from administrations-in-waiting. More than a natural, high-spirited eagerness is involved. Presidents always have been anxious to get started. The more time they have, the better are their prospects of negotiating a coalition that traverses the congressional labyrinth. As one Kennedy aide explained:

> It just makes sense to move as fast as humanly possible. A major program like Medicare takes a good year just to pass through Congress. It will take at least two to implement. By that time, you'll want to make some changes—increase the funding, rewrite some regulations. That may take another two years. If you don't get going early, you'll be out of office before you get the program set.[33]

If the president dallies, he also may find himself confronted with unattractive choices that flow from agendas set by others. In trying to account for his president's feckless legislative performance, one of Carter's officials described the four-year term as a race: "The first months are the starting line. If you don't get off the blocks fast, you'll lose the race. Congress will come in first." Then he averred, "You might say we had a false start." [34]

With the new president or without him, coalitions begin forming, and their goals and priorities can be expected to differ from and often contradict his own. This is the explanation offered by a staffer after President Nixon's highly touted Family Assistance Plan was waylaid in the Senate Finance Committee by an unlikely alliance of liberals (for whom the proposed expenditures were too low) and conservatives (for whom they were too high).

> We gave our opponents a great deal of time to fight the Family Assistance Plan. They had at least six months to prepare for the initial announcement. Then, because we were late, the program bogged down in committee. We gave them too many chances to hit us.[35]

The congressional process can be both time consuming and hazardous for any president, but it is especially so for those who seek to lead by negotiating their way through Congress. Presumably, the public president who leads by summoning popular support can, if the political environment is sufficiently benign, move Congress quickly through a public appeal. So why was Meese, whose mentor adopted a public leadership style, also intent on starting fast?

The answer, of course, is the paradox of the modern or public president. The clock against which the public president races is set not so much by the legislative process as by the public's fickleness. While past presidents began early in order to spend their resources wisely, modern public presidents do so because their resources are being depleted even without their expenditure. The old saw "Don't put off until tomorrow what you can do today"—to which we can append "because you'll never again be so popular"—is an admonition appropriate to the public president. According to the schema in Figure 9-4, the president's declining fortunes across the country will be matched in Washington. As one of President Reagan's "chief strategists" observed, "You can push Congress only so long. Eventually they get tired of the pressure, tired of the complaints back home about some program that's being cut, and they get mad." [36]

However similar the need to begin their journeys quickly, by the third year the public president clearly has proceeded down a different path from past presidents. For the president of earlier times who had succeeded at bargaining, the third year brought the fruits of time well spent cultivating a winning coalition. Neustadt wrote of this in describing a "certain rhythm of the modern [circa 1960] Presidency."[37] The rewards of success are reaped just as the president turns his attention toward winning reelection. But the public president's record will be made early if it is made at all. In the absence of unforeseen events, he will exhaust his resource base more quickly, and hence his success will be short-lived. Rather than a time of harvest, the third year will be one of conservation— preserving whatever popular support remains, identifying targets of opportunity, and fending off efforts to undo his policies. If the public president somehow can survive politically, perhaps his mandate will be renewed at the next election, but the odds are against him. Since Eisenhower, only Nixon has managed to win reelection to a second full term; presidents since Nixon have even had trouble retaining their party's nomination.

Ever since Franklin Roosevelt's astounding early success in 1933, political journalists have felt compelled to assess each new president's first hundred days, even though not much generally happens. Rarely in the past have assessments been appropriate and then only during exceptional moments when normal political relationships were suspended temporarily by lopsided party majorities in Congress. Given the rhythm of the public presidents now entering office, however, the first hundred or two hundred days not only may be appropriate time for assessing the incumbent's record, it may even suffice.

APPENDIX

To make the times-series consistent in Figures 9-1, 9-2, and 9-3, I followed as closely as possible the coding scheme used by William

Lammers. The three classifications below are designed to be neither mutually exclusive nor exhaustive. Press conferences, purely ceremonial functions, and minor activities, such as receptions and brief remarks at the White House, have been excluded from the analysis.

Addresses. *Major* addresses are those given in Washington, broadcast on television or radio, and focused on more than a narrow potential audience. Inaugural, State of the Union, and renomination speeches are included in this category. *Minor* addresses are all other addresses delivered outside of the White House in which the president spoke more than 1,000 words. Question and answer sessions—even outside of a formal press conference setting—are excluded. (See Figure 9-1.)

Political Travel. To distinguish purely vacation travel from work-related travel, the president must engage in public political activities during the day in order to be included in Figure 9-2. For political travel in the United States, the president during the day must do more than briefly talk to reporters. For foreign travel, such comments qualify if they exceed 200 words. Moreover, attendance at international conferences qualifies even if the president does not engage in public activities.

Appearances. *Washington* appearances include all appearances in Washington and surrounding suburbs outside the White House or the Executive Office Building. For *U.S.* appearances, brief comments to reporters are excluded but prepared remarks on arrival are included. Lammers reports that President Carter's town-meeting format created so many coding difficulties that these activities were excluded from those figures presented in Figure 9-3.

NOTES

1. *Public Papers of the Presidents of the United States: Jimmy Carter,* 1979 (Washington, D.C.: U.S. Government Printing Office, 1980): 963-964.
2. Richard Neustadt, *Presidential Power: The Politics of Leadership* (New York: John Wiley & Sons, 1960).
3. Jimmy Carter, *Keeping the Faith* (New York: Bantam Books, 1983).
4. Two prominent chronicles of change in Washington are *The New American Political System,* ed. Anthony King (Washington, D.C.: American Enterprise Institute for Public Policy Research, 1978); and *The New Congress,* ed. Thomas E. Mann and Norman J. Ornstein (Washington, D.C.: American Enterprise Institute for Public Policy Research, 1981).
5. This discussion of classes of public presidential behavior relies heavily upon William W. Lammers, "Presidential Attention-Focusing Activities," in *The*

President and the American Public, ed. Doris A. Graber (Philadelphia: Institute for the Study of Human Issues, 1982): 145-171. The definitions and methodology are described in an appendix to this chapter.

6. Omitted from major addresses are presidential press conferences and purely ceremonial functions (e.g., the annual Christmas tree lighting statements). Press conferences have received more scholarly attention than the other public activities examined in this chapter. The evidence suggests that presidents may adapt press conference schedules to a variety of strategic goals. See William W. Lammers, "Presidential Press-Conference Schedules: Who Hides and When?" *Political Science Quarterly* 96 (Summer 1981): 261-267.

7. As a cautionary note, the sources used to compile this list of television addresses appear to provide a more generous definition in recent years. Those addresses through 1965 are drawn from "Presidents on TV: Their Live Records," *Broadcasting,* November 8, 1965, 55-58. From 1966 to 1975, the entries represent only formally requested air time listed in Denis S. Rutkus, "A Report on Simultaneous Network Coverage of Presidential Addresses to the Nation," Library of Congress, mimeo, January 12, 1976. Addresses since 1976 have been compiled from the *Public Papers of the Presidents* series.

8. Hedrick Smith, "A High-Risk Tactic," *New York Times,* April 28, 1983, 9. He also observes that such appeals are risky because the effects of misstatements and wrong impressions may greatly damage the president's position.

9. According to the *National Journal,* "Reagan fulfilled his campaign promises to propose [tax] credits" in his April 15, 1982, speech to the National Catholic Education Association. See pages 736 to 737 of the April 24, 1982, issue. See also Harrison Donnelly, "Little Hope Seen for Tuition Tax Credit Plan," *Congressional Quarterly Weekly Report,* April 24, 1982, 911-913.

10. Since the preceding fall, Reagan's pollster Richard Wirthlin had been advising the president of his slipping popularity among blue-collar Democrats—many of whom are Catholic—who had supported him against Carter in 1980. See B. Drummond Ayres, Jr., "G.O.P. Keeps Tabs on Nation's Mood," *New York Times,* November 16, 1981, A20; and Howell Raines, "Reagan's Gamble: Bid for Popularity," *New York Times,* March 30, 1982, A27. See also Hedrick Smith, "Blue-Collar Workers' Support for Reagan Declines," *New York Times,* March 8, 1982, 1.

11. Partly as an effort to improve his public support, President Reagan initiated a series of five- to ten-minute Saturday radio broadcasts in the spring of 1982. As shown in Figure 9-1, inclusion of these broadcasts in the "major" address category to which they technically qualify increases the number of major addresses dramatically. Because the radio addresses are so numerous and concern less immediate or dramatic issues, a second entry has been created for Reagan's major addresses that includes only televised speeches.

12. An example of this genre is President Reagan's warm-up routine at a Jaycees convention in San Antonio during the summer of 1981 while pressuring Democrats to accept his budget. To a roaring audience Reagan intoned, "Where on earth has he [Tip O'Neill] been for the last few years?" After a pause he continued, "The answer is, right in Washington, D.C." See "Reagan's Sweet Triumph," *Newsweek,* 48 (July 1981): 18.

13. Raines, "Reagan's Gamble," A27.

14. Although scored separately, public addresses, appearances, and travel are nonexclusive categories. A president, after all, may travel to appear before some

organization and deliver a major, televised policy address. Nor are these categories exhaustive of public activities that take place within the White House. (For example, receptions for foreign dignitaries have not been tallied.)

15. Sidney Blumenthal, "Marketing the President," *New York Times Magazine,* September 13, 1981, 43, 110-113.

16. Gary C. Jacobson, *The Politics of Congressional Elections* (Boston: Little, Brown & Co., 1983): 179-180. Jacobson goes on to note, "Carter did not enjoy broad public support during most of his presidency . . . [and when] he was most popular early in his term . . . he was unable to turn public support into political influence."

17. This statement is by Rep. Richard B. Cheney. See Charles O. Jones, "Congress and the Presidency," in *The New Congress,* ed. Mann and Ornstein, 241.

18. Henry Kissinger, *Years of Upheaval* (Boston: Little, Brown & Co., 1982). See also John Herbers, "Nixon's Motives in Alert Questioned and Defended," *New York Times,* October 26, 1973, 20; and "Was the Alert Scare Necessary?" *Time,* November 5, 1973, 15.

19. For the best discussion of these alternative routes to consistent political attitudes, see Richard A. Brody and Benjamin R. Page, "Comment: The Assessment of Policy Voting," *American Political Science Review* 66 (June 1972): 450-459.

20. In an earlier study on diffuse support for the presidency, Aaron Wildavsky, Peter W. Sperlich, and I found strong endorsement for the president as the nation's leader. Among a sample of 700 Bay Area residents in late 1965, early 1966, we recorded the following levels of support:

	Percent
Question	*Agreeing*
"More nearly than any other person the President stands for our country."	85
"One sleeps better knowing that a President one trusts is watching over the country."	72
"The President should first be given a chance to work out his policies before he is criticized."	70

See Samuel Kernell, Peter W. Sperlich, and Aaron Wildavsky, "Public Support for Presidents," in *Perspectives on the Presidency,* ed. Aaron Wildavsky (Boston: Little, Brown, & Co., 1975), 148-183.

For similar findings and discussion of the president's special status in public opinions, see Fred I. Greenstein, "Popular Images of the President," *American Journal of Psychiatry* 122 (November 1965): 523-529; Roberta S. Sigel, "Image of the American Presidency: Part II of an Exploration into Popular Views of Presidential Power," *Midwest Journal of Political Science* 10 (February 1966): 123-137. For a more recent and richly analytic statement, see Donald R. Kinder, Susan T. Fiske, and Randolph G. Wagner, "Presidents in the Public Mind," Yale University, July 1980, mimeo.

21. The data used in the analysis were taken from the American Institute of Public Opinion, Survey No. 393, March 26-27, 1947. For a detailed analysis of the impact of the Truman Doctrine speech in public opinion, see Samuel Kernell, "The Truman Doctrine Speech: A Case Study of the Dynamics of Opinion Leadership," *Social Science History* 1 (Fall 1976): 20-45.

22. Richard E. Neustadt, *Presidential Power: The Politics of Leadership with Reflections on Johnson and Nixon*, 2d ed. (New York: John Wiley & Sons, 1976). If Washington were sealed off from the rest of the country so that an elected officeholder could only guess how opinion in the district were shifting, such an anticipated response would constitute a self-fullfilling prophesy: to wit, the president would influence elites *only* because he was believed to have such influence with the citizenry. But Washington is not a closed community. Through a complex network of conduits, information continuously trickles into Washington to attentive politicians. Anticipated responses arise only because the assumptions on which they are founded are periodically demonstrated. The following example reveals the acute calculations that drive anticipated responses:

> President [Carter] evidently believes that he can translate his high personal popularity into grassroots support for his policies, thereby forcing Congress and interest groups to bend. Other politicians doubt this, contending that the President's popularity isn't solid because it is built merely on his style rather than any substantive achievements. "His support is gossamer-thin," says a Democratic politician. "It isn't transferable in legislative fights."

In Norman C. Miller, "Carter Not Playing by the Unwritten Rules of the Game," *Wall Street Journal*, April 22, 1977, 16.

On the general importance of "anticipated responses" in elite behavior, see Carl J. Friedrich, "Public Policy and the Nature of Administrative Responsibility," *Public Policy* 1 (1940): 3-24.

23. "Running to Stay in Place," *Newsweek* 48 (October 5, 1981): 24.

24. Ibid. See also, "Rough Waters Ahead," *Time* 118 (October 5, 1981): 8-11.

25. The data used in the following analysis came from American Institute of Public Opinion, Survey No. 183-G. The overall results are described in the Gallup Opinion Index, Report No. 194 (November, 1981): 3-8.

26. Because only 42 percent favored additional budget cuts in October 1981—when the president's popularity was still healthy at 56 percent approving—one may wonder just how unpopular his proposal of further retrenchment had become by the following August, when the next year's budget that incorporated many of these cuts was finally acted on by Congress. By then, Reagan's popularity had plunged to 42 percent approving. If we assume, however, that the relationships displayed in Table 9-3 are stable, we can make an educated guess of the decline of policy support as a function of falling popularity. Extrapolating from the relationships in this table, we can project that by the next August, when the president's popularity hovered around 42 percent approving, his policy support would have declined to 37 percent.

27. Elizabeth Drew, "Reporter at Large," *The New Yorker*, June 8, 1981, 138-142; and Rich Jarosolvsky, "Reagan's 'Revolution' Stalls as Policies Falter Both Here and Abroad," *Wall Street Journal*, December 23, 1982, 1.

28. Samuel Kernell, "Explaining Presidential Popularity" *American Political Science Review* 72 (June 1978): 506-522.

29. For public opinion on the pardon issue, see "Public Would Have Put Nixon On Trial, Not Granted Pardon," *Gallup Opinion Index* (October 1974): 23-25.

30. These particular presidents and time periods have been selected for closer scrutiny for several reasons. By limiting ourselves to elected first-termers we remove contamination from past performance ratings or the special circumstances of their

entry which would make comparisons of initial support levels especially hazardous. Also, these terms were of highly disruptive, "negative" events that depressed a president's level of support. Of the presidents included in Figure 9-5, Kennedy easily had the most eventful presidency; the Bay of Pigs fiasco, the Berlin crisis, his confrontation with Khrushchev in Vienna, and the Cuban missile crisis all appeared to temporarily buoy his public support.

31. Godfrey Sperling Jr., "Memo Sends Carter Campaigning," *Christian Science Monitor,* November 3, 1978, 1; and Dick Kirschten, "Reagan Picks His Spots. . . ," *National Journal,* October 16, 1982, 1744.

32. Drew, "Reporter at Large," 138-142.

33. Paul C. Light, "The President's Agenda," *Presidential Studies Quarterly* 11 (Winter 1981): 74.

34. Ibid.

35. Ibid., 75; and Daniel Patrick Moynihan, *The Politics of Guaranteed Income* (New York: Random House, 1973).

36. Drew, "Reporter at Large," 138-142.

37. Neustadt, *Presidential Power,* 2d ed., 198-199.

10. THE PRESIDENCY AND THE PRESS

James Fallows

In January 1983, halfway through his term, Ronald Reagan paid an impromptu call on a neighborhood tavern while on a tour of Boston. After raising a glass with the other, startled customers, the president made one of the off-the-cuff remarks about national policy that had caused him political difficulty in the previous few months. Some people thought that the "Reagan revolution" was on the wane, that the president could not recapture the mandate for bold innovation he had enjoyed in his first year in office. He didn't agree, the president said; he had lots of new projects he'd like to undertake. He proceeded to give his listeners an example. Although he guessed he'd probably kick himself in the morning for saying so, President Reagan said he thought it might make sense to abolish the corporate income tax.

His premonitions about regretting the remark showed how well Ronald Reagan had come to understand the press. In the week after his statement, newspapers and television news reports were full of stories about his comments, nearly all of them unfavorable. Many of the accounts treated Reagan's remarks as a "gaffe": here was one more piece of evidence that Ronald Reagan could say almost anything, once he slipped the leash usually held by his handlers in the White House. Other accounts dwelt on the political meaning of the incident. The biggest threat to the administration, according to this reasoning, was the "fairness issue," the idea that Reagan's policies took from the poor and gave to the rich. Abolishing the corporate income tax, at a time when more than ten million people were out of work, offered a caricature of a president in anguish over the burdens borne by giant corporations but indifferent to the downtrodden.

Many of these analyses were intelligently presented. From the political point of view, they might even have been correct. But what was missing from nearly all of them was the conception that the president's proposal might possibly have been a good idea.

On this as on so many other questions of public policy, economists disagree. But a strong faction within the profession has argued for many years that the corporate income tax serves no reasonable public purpose. Among other things—this faction argues—the corporate tax drives big companies even farther from the healthy rigors of the competitive market system. In corporate life as in personal life, expenses that are tax-deductible cost less than they seem to. Why should a profitable company really worry about spending a thousand dollars for an executive's country club membership or agreeing to an unrealistic wage agreement with a union? Even if management won a fight to save money on such items, nearly half the savings would be taxed away. But if there were no corporate income tax, a dollar saved would be a dollar earned; market forces would be strengthened, and companies would be more efficient as a result.

There are sound economic arguments on the other side, too; the point is that there *is* a lively debate on the merits of the corporate income tax. In that debate, many who are known as liberals, such as Lester Thurow of MIT, take the same side as the president.

Why was this perspective missing from the coverage of Ronald Reagan's remarks? If it had been included, the event certainly would have looked better for the president. Its absence, therefore, might seem to reflect the press's liberal bias against a conservative administration. If the Reagan administration is anything like its predecessors, that is precisely the explanation that will seem most plausible to members of the White House staff. Similarly, Jimmy Carter's assistants thought that nasty news stories reflected the press's Washington-insider bias against southerners and outsiders. Members of Gerald Ford's entourage thought the press held a biased view of Ford as a dolt. Richard Nixon, of course, thought himself the victim of an unending smear campaign by the press. Lyndon Johnson got bad coverage because of a bias against his Texas-usurper ways.

As this long list of comparable complaints might indicate, the corporate-tax story suggests that there is something more complicated, and more disturbing, at play than the tensions between left-wing reporters and a right-wing president. It illustrates, instead, a kind of bias that rises above merely partisan disputes. It reveals reporters' clear preference to write about *politics,* rather than about the history, the substance, or the day-by-day truths of government's operation. Sometimes this bias works to the president's advantage, sometimes to his disadvantage. But in all cases, the public is disserved.

Press Definitions of News: Government as Politics

In its broadest sense, of course, "politics" embraces everything that matters about a citizen's relationship with his government. It is the web of connections between elected leaders and the diverse national factions whose interests they must meld. It is the long history of previous choices that restrict the choices that are available today. It is the setting of world history and economic change that forces one administration to confront dilemmas that its predecessors had ignored.

But in this chapter politics will be considered as the press defines it: in its narrowest sense, the sense most akin to sports. Newspaper sports pages have improved dramatically in the last generation. On a typical day the reader will find discussions of great sophistication about the why and how of sports. Will the new football or soccer or team-tennis league survive? How did a certain coach win a crucial game? Why was Russell greater than Chamberlain? Why are baseball players paid so much? Who are the future greats now in the high school leagues? If the answers aren't available in the newspapers, there is always *Sports Illustrated.*

Behind the sophistication, however, there is ... nothing. Sports has no ultimate purpose apart from the skill of its execution. And that is its crucial difference from politics. Like sports, politics has a dimension of pure tactics, skill, wins, and losses: the horserace among candidates for the presidency or other offices, the long pennant race, in which campaign organizations gain ground on one another. But in politics, unlike sports, there is something else beyond these details of execution. The game of politics is played not for its own sake but to manage the social, economic, and at times military forces that affect the nation. If the game is played poorly, lives can be lost, societies ruined. Yet the stakes in the game are the missing element in most of what we read about government, and nowhere more so than in coverage of the White House.

Explaining why this is so is not hard. Reporters, like others whose performance is open to public view, are wary of falling on their faces. In the news business, there is usually more to be lost through a big mistake than there is to be gained through a display of unusual insight. Reporters naturally minimize their risks by concentrating on the areas where they are most confident. For members of the White House press corps, that almost always means horse-race politics. When it comes to economics or the workings of the domestic bureaucracy, the White House correspondent probably will feel unsure about discriminating between the trends that matter and those that do not. He will not lack that confidence about politics. Many of the reporters, especially for the television networks, qualify for the White House beat by covering a presidential campaign. As a result, White House reporters typically pour more of themselves into the attempt to explain the politics of a new development than its substance.

During the last year and a half of the Carter administration, for example, one of the biggest political stories was the contest between President Carter and Sen. Edward Kennedy to be the Democratic nominee. By the middle of 1980, it had become clear that Carter would run away with the nomination, but in 1979 it looked like a close, and therefore exciting, race.

In July of 1979, Carter went on television to discuss the latest version of his energy-conservation plans. Shortly afterwards, Kennedy held a press conference to describe an energy program of his own. The major newspapers assigned their crack political reporters to the story and covered it as yet another warmup to the 1980 race. The *Wall Street Journal* headline, typical of the others, was "Kennedy Offers $58 Billion Energy Plan as Prospect for 1980 Election Seems Likelier." Twelve of the 15 paragraphs in the story were devoted to handicapping the next election; only three, to the plan itself.

That kind of coverage may have made perfect sense to the members of the Kennedy and Carter campaign teams. Assessing the effects of each new event on the 1980 election was exactly what they did each day. But from the public point of view, even from the viewpoint of those who are abundantly interested in the horse-race aspect of politics, there was a more important story to be done, or at least started, that day. It was a story that would compare the two energy plans, seriously appraise their consequences, dig out the differences between them and the alternatives that exist. In the end, it might be a more profoundly "political" form of coverage; for, unlike another recap of developments among the campaign teams, it would give the public more information on which to base its choices among the candidates.

An equivalent episode in the Reagan administration was the portrayal of the battle over "Reaganomics" in 1981. In many press accounts the economic decisions were depicted as grudge matches, fought on many fronts. The executive branch locked horns with the legislative; Ronald Reagan faced off against Tip O'Neill. David Stockman fought with Caspar Weinberger; the advocates of pure "supply side economics" fought against those who would betray the faith. Meanwhile, Edward Meese, James Baker, and Michael Deaver struggled for the upper hand. The play-by-play of each of these contests was lavishly and expertly reported.

In fairness, by the end of that same year, many newspapers, news magazines, and networks *had* begun to complement their reports of political jockeying among the supply-siders with an examination of the economic consequences. From the Reagan administration's point of view, much of the resulting coverage must have seemed vexatious. In dwelling on the extreme cases—the ailing pensioners whose disability checks were cut off, the steel- and auto-workers who lost their jobs— the coverage may have appeared, to the administration, to distort the meaning of the long-range changes the new policies were designed to promote. But even if we assume, for the moment, that the complaint was correct, the new direction in economic coverage was still a plus be- cause it directed attention to the results of political struggles, not to the struggles themselves.

This changed emphasis may have been a natural response to the administration's bold claims that it was setting a decisively different course. Perhaps, as many conservatives suspected, it arose from liberal reporters' and editors' hostility to the Reagan administration's goals. But it also could have meant that journalists were broadening their conception of "politics" to embrace more than the play-by-play of Washington infighting. If so, the reading public—Republicans as well as Democrats—has reason to cheer.

The other great public controversy of the early 1980s concerned the control of nuclear weapons. Here, as with economic policy, press re- ports gradually evolved away from the sports-page approach. Eventu- ally, there were informative discussions of the strategic and technical foundations on which the nuclear arsenals had been built, of the risks and consequences of different approaches. Still, these "documentaries" and "special series," admirable and constructive as they were, seemed to represent special, unsustainable exertions. When not pushing themselves to unusual effort, most members of the White House press fell back to viewing nuclear policy as the Sugar Bowl and economic pol- icy as the Rose Bowl. What really mattered to them was how well the teams played the game.

The clearest single illustration of this tendency was the treatment of Kenneth Adelman. In January 1983, Adelman was nominated to direct the Arms Control and Disarmament Agency, succeeding Eugene Rostow, whom President Reagan had dismissed. Over the next three months, Adelman's nomination became the object of a bitter, partisan fight in the Senate.

At one level, the fight reflected fundamental disagreements about the course of arms control policy. On the administration's left, many advocates of the Strategic Arms Limitation Treaties (known as SALT I and SALT II) feared irreparable rupture between the Soviet Union and the United States. The two treaties might not have accomplished miracles, these advocates would concede; but if the two great nuclear powers stopped talking about controlling nuclear weapons, who could say what horrors would follow?

From the administration's right came an argument made with equal passion and intensity. Those who saw the early 1980s as a parallel to the late 1930s thought that Western governments, even the one led by Ronald Reagan, were in danger of appeasing a ruthlessly aggressive power, as the English and French had done with Hitler, to the world's lasting regret. In the shuffling of Rostow and Adelman, they saw a battle for the administration's soul. The question, in their minds, was whether the United States would regain the moral courage necessary to speak the truth about Soviet intentions in general, and their violation of arms-control treaties in particular.

Some press reports on the Adelman nomination depicted this clash of world views. The journalists who took this tack often had a reflexively partisan outlook. Conservatives overlooked the reasonable complaints that could be made about Adelman's credentials for the job; liberals exaggerated how much difference this one nominee could make in the administration's policy. But most accounts portrayed the nomination struggle as just another contest, another test of the administration's power and dexterity. Adelman himself took on a sports-page identity, as the error-prone shortstop who keeps muffing easy grounders. In the first of his three appearances before the Senate Foreign Relations Committee, which was considering his nomination, Adelman discussed the administration's goals in arms control and outlined the philosophical premises that led the Reagan administration to its specific arms-control proposals. But he also responded "I don't know" or "I haven't thought about it" to several questions, and when the television networks covered his testimony, they ran those answers—the bobbled grounders—back to back.

From that point on, the Adelman nomination story had less to do with arms control than with arguments about this particular player, and whether he ever would learn big-league skills. When his nomination was finally confirmed, the White House and Capitol Hill reporters chalked it up as another extra-innings win for the big right-hander, Dutch Reagan. Most reports were as unrevealing about the real stakes in arms control as the controversy over Anne Gorsuch Burford, the director of the Environmental Protection Agency, was about environmental protection.

Presidential Advantages

From the president's point of view, the press's predisposition to cover government as politics has some clear advantages. If he understands the reporters' preference for sports-style political coverage, it becomes far easier for him to control the kind of reports that are written about him. The pioneer in this area was Richard Nixon, who in 1968 laid down the rules for running a presidential campaign in the modern (that is to say, the television-dominated) era.

Nixon understood that in the two or three months between the national convention and the general election, a candidate no longer had to worry about getting *enough* coverage, as he had during the primaries. He was going to get all the news he could handle, the most important of which would be two or three minutes on the network broadcasts each evening. The challenge was to make those few minutes turn out right, to get as much of the candidate's own material across as possible, with the minimum of distraction. Nixon knew that the television reporters would find some way to fill those minutes each day—and that they would leap on misstatements and blunders, like so many fielding errors, if given the chance.

Aware of these hazards, Nixon developed the appropriate plan. To put out his message, he gave one big speech a day, no later than the very early afternoon and in plenty of time for the evening news. Then he did nothing else—nothing, since every extra event increased the danger of tripping over your own news, making a mistake, giving the correspondents too much choice about what to use. He wouldn't give interviews promiscuously, or speak off the cuff, or make any unnecessary noise. The people whose town he was visiting might complain, and the press occasionally grumbled about his attempts to "manage the news." But these criticisms were dwarfed by Nixon's success—even more dramatic in 1972 than in 1968—in getting his point across.

Two of Nixon's successors demonstrated, in opposite ways, the effectiveness of his approach. Jimmy Carter and his entourage in the 1976 presidential campaign were determined to avoid doing anything that smacked of resemblance to Richard Nixon; they were hardly the only Americans with such feelings at the time. After Carter had won the party's nomination, he stuck with the approach that had proven so phenomenally successful during the primary campaigns. This was a campaign style based on making news rather than controlling it—on maximum personal contact with individual voters through endless extemporaneous speeches, countless town meetings, six-a-day rallies.

During the primary elections, this approach had worked well. In Iowa and New Hampshire, a candidate could visit enough towns and give enough speeches to physically *see* a significant share of the voters.

The general election campaign was different: no matter how hard he tried, a candidate could never meet more than a tiny fraction of the national electorate. To communicate with the rest, he would have to rely on newspapers and, especially, television. But Carter stuck with his original approach. He made one big speech, sometimes at nine in the morning and sometimes at nine at night. Whenever it came, it was accompanied by a handful of other pronouncements and performances during the day—brief remarks and impromptu interviews that reinforced the candidate's image as "accessible" and "open."

As human qualities, these may have been more appealing than Nixon's isolation; but as a matter of political tactics, they nearly cost Carter the election. Whenever someone stuck a microphone near Carter's mouth and asked him a question, he would get an answer. Since those answers were so much more juicy than the points Carter wanted to make in his speeches about nuclear proliferation or crime, they dominated the story on the evening news. For days and days, reporters kept asking—and Carter kept answering—questions about an interview with *Playboy* magazine, in which he had discussed, among other subjects, his "lust in my heart" for women other than his wife. This interview was covered to death, but Carter was able to deliver one speech on inflation, in virtually unchanged form, three different times without any detectable news coverage. Partly as a result, Carter sank during the four-month general election campaign from an enormous lead over Gerald Ford to a hair's-breadth victory.

Four years later, Ronald Reagan began walking down the same road Carter had taken earlier, making off-the-cuff remarks about evolution and the Ku Klux Klan. But unlike Carter, he recovered quickly enough to return to the Nixon approach of 1968. His tactics were not the only, or even the major, explanation for his sweeping victory. A change in political ideology, and a widespread revulsion against Carter, were certainly at least as important. But Reagan's approach enabled him to stop hurting himself, a trick that Carter mastered only imperfectly and too late.

The principles of news-management during presidential campaigns apply even more once a candidate has reached the White House. There he has physical control over the main sources of news. His assistants, instead of riding on the campaign airplane with the reporters, work in office buildings, protected by guards and security barriers from reporters who hope to drop by for a chat. The president has at his disposal the machinery of the entire federal government, which means that he can "generate news"—by greeting a foreign leader or forming a presidential commission—at will.

Presidential Disadvantages

If their knowledge of the press's preference for politics gives them all these advantages, why, then, are presidents from both parties united in their belief that the White House press has given them a bad deal? Because their control is always limited: it determines subject matter, not tone.

A president is least able to control the news, and a reader is most likely to enjoy the benefits of an independent, critical assessment, when reporters move onto terrain where they feel comfortable. When given a chance to cover a subject they know well and can handle confidently, reporters will use their powers to observe, inquire, and appraise. Unfortunately, for most of the White House reporters there are only four such subjects.

The first is anything that smacks of indictable criminal scandal. The regulars of the White House press corps, aware that they had been burned by accepting President Richard Nixon's protestations of innocence too quickly, emboldened by the downfalls of Carter's budget director, Bert Lance, and Reagan's national security adviser, Richard Allen, will not let any potential scandal go unexamined. Nor will any ambitious young reporter, aware of how life has changed for the Messrs. Woodward and Bernstein. Little "judgment" or discretion is required in pursuing these stories because of the reporter's confidence that the standard of criminality will be clear. With enough digging, the reporter feels, he may turn up the incriminating photo, the signed document. Such expectations—so necessary in the courtroom, so misleading in understanding real political life—were intensified by the Watergate scandal. There, contrary to the whole human history of high-level political scheming, clear-cut evidence of misbehavior *did* come to light, when the White House tapes revealed that President Nixon had been involved in a conspiracy to thwart justice. This evidence was referred to as the "smoking gun," which linked a suspect to his crime.

The search for the smoking gun is the theme that unites many White House stories since Watergate, whether the immediate subject is the behavior of Carter staffer Hamilton Jordan, who was accused (but later cleared) of snorting cocaine or the Reagan campaign's acquisition of Jimmy Carter's debate briefing book. During the Kenneth Adelman controversy, the senators who opposed the nominee, and the reporters covering the case, really dug in only twice—once to determine whether Adelman had used the word "sham" in a newspaper interview conducted two years before his nomination and once to find out whether he had studied a memorandum recommending personnel changes, contrary to his assertion that he had not made any decisions about hiring or firing. Both of these controversies proved dramatic, at least for a little while; both carried a connotation of lying or other provable misbehavior. But neither had much to do with the supposed purpose of the confirmation hearings, which was to determine the nominee's philosophy on nuclear weaponry.

Politicians sometimes claim that reporters are doing "the easy thing" when they concentrate on scandal. That complaint is imprecise, at least as far as sheer man-hours are concerned. Searching for scandals and smoking guns is exhausting work. It is "easy" only in that it relieves the reporter of the burden of explaining why a certain policy or decision is important. If he can show that it *broke the law*, his work is done.

Understanding this about reporters, shrewd presidents are compelled to deal with potential scandal the way Ronald Reagan dealt with Richard Allen (who was accused of accepting watches from Japanese businessmen), and not the way Jimmy Carter dealt with Bert Lance. As soon as one of his associates is tainted, a president must jettison him promptly—as Reagan did Allen. Otherwise, the story may drag on for months, as it did when Carter stood by Lance, who was accused of financial improprieties. When the briefing-book story broke in the summer of 1983, President Reagan initially compounded his troubles by attempting to pooh-pooh the whole thing, but then tried to recover by turning over great volumes of documents in hopes of deflecting stories of a "cover-up."

The second area where reporters will make the news, rather than follow it, includes stories of dissension, internal rivalry, unhappy passengers rocking the boat. This is why Midge Costanza, a controversial White House assistant, became the most famous member of the Carter administration during its first year, even though she returned to anonymity soon afterwards. Similarly, it is why the reported rivalry between President Reagan's three principal assistants, James Baker, Edwin Meese, and Michael Deaver, became the subplot of much White House reporting in 1981 and 1982. Two assistants on the next lower rung in the White House, David Gergen and Richard Darman, became household words, at least in Washington, largely because reports of the top-level rivalry prominently featured them.

Politicians well understand that reporters love stories about internal feuds. Therefore, the first test of loyalty within any administration is to avoid making comments that could prop up a "dissent from within" article. If anonymous quotes from the State Department suggest that the secretary of state doesn't like the national security adviser, if second-level assistants at the Pentagon are complaining about the White House staff, reporters will eagerly convey details of the controversy to their readers. But if an administration can manage to present a unified face to the world—or at least that portion of the world represented by the White House press—reporters are less likely to draw harsh conclusions for themselves.

The third area is the "gaffe," or tactical blunder. In most cases the substance of the mistake matters very little; what counts is that the fielder dropped the ball. During his debate with Jimmy Carter in the 1976 presidential campaign, Gerald Ford made an inept comment, roughly summarized as "Poland is not dominated by the Soviet Union." No one aware of the history of the Republican party or of Gerald Ford's mainstream anti-communism could have mistaken the remark as anything other than a bit of unfortunate phrasing. What Ford was trying to say, as everyone knew, was that the Poles were proud and independent people whose spirit had not been broken. Indeed, as the Polish labor movement expressed its independence in the next three years, Ford's comments began to appear somewhat prescient. In the harshest interpretation, they might have been taken as further evidence that he was not always quick on his feet—but not that he was soft on communism or ignorant of the shape of the post-1945 world.

But because this presidential debate, like many other events in a president's public career, was interpreted by many reporters as a gaffe-avoidance contest, Ford "lost" the debate in a big way. For nearly two weeks after the episode, the Carter campaign reveled in (and encouraged) lurid coverage of the blunder. From Hamtramck to Buffalo, network correspondents interviewed Polish-Americans-in-the-street and asked, in apparent seriousness, whether they had grown more concerned about the administration's commitment to the Captive Nations of Eastern Europe.

A little more than a year later, Jimmy Carter went to Warsaw and had his own taste of a Polish "gaffe." When he arrived at the Warsaw airport, he made standard welcoming remarks in English—and then stood by as a State Department official translated them into

Polish. Almost immediately, a controversy broke out over the "mistakes" in the translation. On calm, later reflection, it turned out that the mistakes were nowhere near as glaring as initial reports had implied. One crucial sentence, for example, had read in English, "I have come here to understand your desires for the future." For "desire," the translator used a Polish word, *pozadania,* whose carnal connotations are more pronounced than those of "desire." But the translator never said some of the things that were reported, as fact, in the American press. (For example, "I lust after the Poles.") In any case, the whole episode was simply silly, since it made no dent in Polish-American relations or in the business the president had come to transact.

As his comments on the corporate income tax, mentioned at the beginning of this chapter, might indicate, Ronald Reagan also suffered from the press's concentration on gaffes. During his first year in office, he would offer in his press conferences an inventive history of the partition of Vietnam, or an interpretation of federal law for which no legal support could be found. Each time this happened, analyses of the gaffes would overshadow whatever other news the president hoped to produce at the press conference.

Yet by the second half of his administration, the gaffe stories had all but disappeared. The explanation was not so much that Reagan had grown more precise in his language as that his imprecision had become old news. Because his misstatements were so common, the president drained them of news value.

Fourth, there is politics in the narrow sense: the business of winning elections and gaining points in the opinion polls. Reporters will apply their highest powers of analysis and put their reputations on the line to predict whether Walter Mondale or Ronald Reagan or some other candidate is most likely to serve as president in 1985. Washington journalism boasts three dozen men and women who can tell their readers, with authority and with hard-won facts, *how* any politician is doing: in his local campaign organizations, while working the crowd, in staying ahead of the popular trend. Most people in Washington, myself included, will read these stories first when they open the paper. The only thing the stories omit is the *what:* what effect the candidates' promises would have, if implemented, what happened the last time a similar approach was tried. In the prelude to the 1984 election, for example, readers saw expert analyses of whether arms control was a potent enough issue to give Sen. Alan Cranston of California a chance for the Democratic nomination. They had very little opportunity to learn what Cranston's plans for arms control might be, or to read informed analysis of whether his proposals were likely to work.

The *what* of government is usually missing from White House stories because of the same imbalance in the reporters' knowledge mentioned earlier. When it comes to stories about scandal, dissension, gaffes, and horse-race politics, most reporters have both the interest and the confidence necessary to set the agenda by themselves. They will break a story, even if official spokesmen tell them it's not important. They will move beyond presenting a balanced set of pro- and con-quotations, if they are convinced that the quotations fail to give the reader a full appreciation of the truth. If the subject is the prospect for the Iowa caucus vote, a good White House reporter would laugh at any colleague who interviewed each side's campaign manager and thought he'd told all there was to tell. The expert political reporter would want to get out and make his own judgments, by talking to the voters, probing the different levels of the campaign organization, seeing for himself how the candidate came across. These are the tools of appraisal, but the same reporters who use them so adroitly in political stories hesitate to do so on questions of substance.

In this preference, the best White House reporters resemble their counterparts on the president's staff. A Hamilton Jordan in Jimmy Carter's White House or a Lyn Nofziger in Ronald Reagan's might look on a Sam Donaldson or Jack Germond as a creature from another culture, with opposite loyalties, on the other side of the fence. But in the most important ways, they are the same: intelligent pros, gifted handicappers, in love with the skill and detail of politics and faintly interested in anything else.

Conclusion

The result of the reporters' uneven confidence is an important division of labor between president and press. When a story falls into one of the four categories, the reporters determine how much prominence it will have, and how long it will be pursued. But when it falls outside the categories—that is, when it concerns what the government actually does—then the White House controls the topic of the news. Over drinks, during slow moments on the beat, White House reporters will complain bitterly about their status as the press room's trained seals. They describe how confining it all is, how little their editors understand the pointlessness of their beat, how they detest waiting in the press room for Jody Powell or Larry Speakes to show up with the day's press releases.

Nonetheless, if you listen to the press secretary make his morning announcement, you know—barring scandal or gaffe—what the lead will be on the evening news that night. During the Carter years, his appointments staff prepared weekly summaries of the president's schedule. For each day, they listed what the likely "news event" would be. Under normal circumstances, the predictions almost always came true. If the president was making an announcement about the U.S. Forest Service, the Forest Service would get that day's news—and would not be in the news again until another announcement was planned, or until it was the scene of scandal or internal dispute.

But, having accepted the president's chosen topic, reporters treat it in their own chosen way, usually with reflexive cynicism about an administration's intentions. The true lesson of the Watergate scandal was the value of hard digging—not only into scandals, but everywhere else. The *perceived* lesson of Watergate in the White House press room is the Dan Rather lesson: that a surly attitude, such as Rather, then a White House correspondent, displayed toward Richard Nixon, can take the place of facts or analysis. Since the days of Watergate, reporters often have proved their tough-mindedness by asking insulting questions at presidential news conferences. TV correspondents feel they've paid their homage to the shade of Bob Woodward by ending their reports not with intelligent criticism but with a mock-significant twist. "The administration says its plans will work, but the true result is *still to be seen.* Dan Daring, NBC News, the White House."

The Public's Stake

The peculiarities of the White House press corps obviously matter to the few Americans who are presidents, candidates for president, or members of the White House staff. But do they matter to anybody else? They do because they shape the citizen's view of his government and of the public choices to be made in his name. The reporters' most important effect comes through the things their dispatches leave out.

One of those missing ingredients is a sense of history. By history, I do not mean ostentatious references to the Tariff of Abominations or the XYZ Affair. Rather, I mean a prudent awareness that others have walked many of the same paths before and that, by learning from their errors, we may be spared errors of our own.

For example, in the summer of 1979, Jimmy Carter decreed a sudden shake-up in his cabinet. He fired secretaries of several departments and shifted others to new jobs. The press coverage left no doubt in readers' minds that this was more than gaffe, it was disaster.

Such turbulence had only one precedent, the reports implied—one that deepened the stain on Carter. On the day after his reelection in 1972, Richard Nixon had demanded resignation letters from everyone on his staff.

In fact, there were many other precedents, less automatically damning to Carter. In 1830, the second year of Andrew Jackson's first term, tensions between two factions in his administration grew acute. The disputes were personified in the bitter rivalry between Martin Van Buren, then secretary of state, and John C. Calhoun, the vice president. Both men hoped to succeed Jackson as president. As the hostility became intolerable, Van Buren offered his resignation, and Jackson seized the opportunity to dissolve the whole cabinet, replacing it with one in which Calhoun's influence was diminished. Four years later, shortly after beginning his second term, Jackson juggled his cabinet again. To end bickering over economic policy, he fired and transferred half a dozen secretaries. Afterwards, wrote Arthur M. Schlesinger, Jr., in *The Age of Jackson,* "the administration was streamlined for action."

Jackson's case was not an exact parallel to Carter's, but it resembled the Carter changes more than did any of Richard Nixon's acts. Had such a suggestion informed the frantic press commentary in the first days after Carter's firings (or had the administration thought to steer reporters to anecdotes like these), it might have indicated that changing a cabinet was not necessarily a sign of desperation or mental instability.

The nonhistorical approach of White House reporting is, if anything, more important when it comes to the consideration of public issues than to perceptions of a president's performance. By ignoring past attempts to grapple with enduring problems, the press can make presidents look less competent than they are, while misleading the public about the real choices that are available.

The safest bet about any administration's foreign policy is that, sooner or later, it will be the subject of stories about "Split in Middle East Policy." Reagan's administration was plagued by such stories, as was Carter's before it, and Nixon's and Ford's before that. Anything else would be a surprise, since American policy toward the Middle East has been divided at least since Israel became a nation in 1948. The struggles between President Harry S. Truman and James Forrestal, which eventually led to Forrestal's removal as secretary of defense in 1949 and his suicide five days later, can be read in part as a history of disagreement over the Zionist cause. American policy toward the Middle East always has been divided because, by American standards, there is something to be said for the claims of each side. To present this deep-seated dilemma as an indication of chaos in a particular administration is to undermine public comprehension of the problem, and to diminish the chances of solving it.

The same pattern applies to discussions of nuclear policy. Since the early seventies, each president has been accused of ordering a "drastic" or "radical" change in America's retaliatory strategy. In the Ford administration, the change was the "counterforce" strategy announced by James Schlesinger, then the secretary of defense. In the Carter administration, it was "Presidential Directive 59." And in the Reagan administration, it was the proposal to improve "command and control" systems and inaugurate a "nuclear war-fighting" capacity. What these decisions had in common, to judge by the coverage, was a stark departure from past practice. Before the change, according to the stories, the United States had stood by the policy of deterrence, in which its threat to destroy the Soviet population prevented the Soviet Union from destroying ours. After the change, it was said, the United States had seemingly made nuclear warfare more likely, by viewing it less cataclysmically.

In fact, at least since the early sixties, American policy has contained both "counterforce" and "countervalue" elements. ("Counterforce" implies attacking an enemy's military systems; "countervalue," attacking the cities.) The technical and political premises that underly this strategy may be flawed, or they may be sound. But the public debate over nuclear strategy is distorted or retarded each time a news story emphasizes what is new in a particular administration's approach, rather than what has been constant for several decades.

Other illustrations abound. They include the plans to "reform" welfare or the civil service, which each new president announces on arrival, before running into the same obstacles that stopped his predecessors' plans. They also include the commitment to "cabinet government" that the last four presidents have made as they began their terms, only to abandon it two or three years later for reasons that were perfectly predictable to those who had studied the previous administration.

Presidents and their assistants are slow to learn from recent history because of the arrogance that naturally surrounds those who have just won a national election. If the old gang had so much to teach, why did it get beaten? Jimmy Carter was elected largely on the strength of anti-Nixon sentiment, and Ronald Reagan on anti-Carter feelings. It would have been as unnatural for Carter and his advisers to think that Nixon's experience with cabinet government might instruct them as for Reagan's advisers to stop and learn from Carter's record.

This indifference to past experience is often reflected within the White House press, which suggests to its readers that each campaign, each inauguration, wipes the historical slate clean. This leaves the reading public in the same position as a teenaged boy on the verge of puberty, unaware of the powerful hormones that will soon be coursing through his body. As those hormones take hold and work their predictable effect, the young man will not understand the strange things happening to him.

The problems most likely to embroil an administration, from controlling the threat of nuclear war, to containing conflict in the Middle East, to reenergizing the great public and private bureaucracies on which the nation depends for schooling and medical care and economic expansion, did not start on one inauguration day, and they will not be solved by the next. The best an administration can hope for is steady progress. But if there is to be progress, rather than cycles of making the same mistakes every four years, each president must build on the work already done. That, in turn, requires a public that understands why the "Social Security problem" is more than a slogan for Democrats to use against Republicans at campaign time, why reinvigorating the federal bureaucracy involves more than denouncing it in speeches, and why the crucial issue in defense spending is not whether the Republicans are too wasteful and the Democrats too stingy but how the military organization really works. And where will most of the information necessary for citizens to understand these choices come from, if not from the press?

Many political reporters, echoing many politicians, would respond that such an emphasis on the "what" of government would take them too far away from their mission of "objectively" covering the news. There is a place for objectivity, in the sense of giving all sides to a political dispute a fair hearing; but political reporters unhesitatingly step beyond the strictures of objectivity when it comes to analyzing a campaign or pursuing a scandal. They do not see themselves as editorializing; instead, they are trying hard to give the reader a fuller understanding of the truth, as they have been able to discern it. Is it not at least as important for them to do so about the military budget or Medicare? An objective story about Medicare might report that its budget rose faster than that of any other major program during the late 1970s and early 1980s. That story is essential; but the reader also should be exposed to other stories, which explain why the increase occurred, how it might be contained, and whether proposed reforms have worked, when tried elsewhere.

This is not a call for reporters to vent their untutored opinions; on the contrary, reporters ought to apply the hard standards of appraisal and analysis to the substance of government. One illustration of this approach occurred in 1983. After a presidential commission declared that the American education system was failing, some political reporters converted "the education issue" into one more ingredient in the political horse race. But at many newspapers and magazines, reporters took a close look at *education,* not the politics of education. They compared schools where test scores were rising with ones where they were falling; they asked whether teachers' unions were serving students' interests, and whether and where more money would help. No single, simple answer emerged from these stories, but they gave their readers a way to think more constructively about improving schools.

Stories about gaffes and scandals, campaigns and internal dissent, do no harm in themselves. They may distort the meaning of presidential leadership, as the unremitting violence and conspiracy of television dramas distort the nature of day-by-day American life. The damage comes only from the neglect of the stories these reports displace, the ones that would help readers understand the public business that remains to be done.

White House reporters are ever suspicious about a president's efforts to manipulate them, in an attempt to make himself look good. They deserve to be more worried about another form of manipulation: the campaign, in which press and president unintentionally collude, to keep citizens from understanding how their government works.

11. THE PRESIDENCY AND INTEREST GROUPS

Martha Joynt Kumar and Michael Baruch Grossman

Even though interest groups have become of central importance to the modern presidency only recently, a president needs to manage his relations with them effectively just as he needs effective management of other important domestic relationships, such as those with Congress, the media, and the bureaucracy. Direct contacts between the White House and representatives of interest groups, which were relatively infrequent and unplanned 20 years ago and almost a rarity during Franklin D. Roosevelt's administration, are commonplace in the 1980s.

Interest groups, of course, have been an important part of the American political scene for most of our history. Early observers such as Alexis de Tocqueville, writing in 1832, noted the tendency of Americans to form groups and organizations. But until recently, those groups' energies were not directed at the White House. Ordinarily a president dealt with interest groups through his allies in Congress, the political parties, and other elements of a leadership structure that subsequently has lost considerable authority. As that loss occurred, presidents and their assistants had to establish direct contact with interest groups if they were to maintain ties with the groups' leaders and the powerful political forces they represented. At the same time, group leaders also changed their strategies in response to the decline in the traditional structure. They turned directly to the president, recognizing that the White House had become the central political institution of American government.

The transition was not easy for the White House to make. Presidents and their staffs did not immediately perceive that cultivating hostile but important groups was useful, even if no negotiations took place and no bargains were struck. Even as the new pattern of relations emerged in the 1960s, a few White House aides wondered if meetings with some groups were not merely futile public relations tactics. In the summer of 1962, after a meeting that President John F. Kennedy's staff had arranged with business leaders, a senior adviser named Carl Kaysen questioned the value of White House efforts to curry favor with the business community, asking "Is it merely bailing out the ocean with a spoon—and a silver one at that?" [1] Subsequent administrations have recognized that they have no choice. The modern president must woo interest group representatives carefully with a mixture of commitments and demands. The White House, it might be said, has become the "Order of the Silver Spoon."

This chapter begins by examining the contemporary setting of the relationship between the White House and interest groups, what political scientists like to call the "political environment." We then move to our central theme, how the relationship is managed. Finally we offer an assessment of its importance for the contemporary presidency.

The Political Environment

Some fundamental changes in the Washington environment and the climate of national politics have led presidents and their advisers to reevaluate the status of their relations with interest groups. Three developments stand out as particularly important: 1) the decline in the authority of "go-betweens," political leaders who deal with representatives of specific organizations and with whom the president can deal; 2) the resulting need to bring interest groups into both ad hoc and ongoing coalitions; and 3) the need to provide for and respond to the growing financial and organizational power of organized interests.

The Decline in the Authority of Political Leaders

Institutional changes in Congress and the political party system since the Eisenhower era have weakened these institutions' governing capacities. Congress once was ruled by a few important committee chairmen and elected leaders who, by and large, decided what would and would not get done. Political parties, although never highly centralized or coherent in terms of policy goals, produced strong local and regional leaders who could speak for large numbers of people. Similarly, interest groups were not the myriad of small-but-powerful political action committees (PACs) that we see today but a much smaller number of "umbrella organizations" representing broader concerns such as business, labor, and agriculture. A president would try to reach his goals through alliances and negotiations with a few important leaders, especially those who headed his party in Congress.

President and Party. Until recently, presidents and their staffs viewed interest group politics in terms of campaign strategy. The White House dealt mostly with groups that had supported the president's election and could be relied upon to provide general support for the administration. When the president needed to mobilize support for particular policies, he could reach the relevant interest groups through his political allies. But the days of interest groups' loyal support for a political party are over. Except on brief and infrequent occasions, neither political party today can command a coalition with the potential to form an electoral or governing majority.

The White House established direct contact with some important interests before the current era, especially groups whose representation in the party organization was weak but whose assistance the president needed. For example, minority groups were an important part of the New Deal electoral coalition, but because the Democratic party with its strong southern wing did not serve as an intermediary for their interests, Franklin D. Roosevelt had his aide Philleo Nash meet with Jewish and black groups. But neither Roosevelt nor his successor, Harry S Truman, felt comfortable with the notion of making such arrangements a regular part of the White House organization. Roosevelt informed his advisers that he didn't want a formal structure "on the theory that it brought in people with vested interests," according to Richard Neustadt, an aide in the Truman administration. "Truman didn't like it either for the same reason." [2] Both presidents wanted aides to meet with particular interest groups, but assigned them to work at the Democratic National Committee rather than the White House. Molly Dewson, for example, worked with women's groups for many years from her position at the DNC.

Of course presidents did at times go beyond their parties to build support for their policies, especially foreign policy matters that were outside the realm of most party leaders' concern. When President Truman sought legislative approval for his post-World War II reconstruction program for Europe, he worked with a bipartisan committee to build support among business, labor, religious, and charitable groups that party leaders could not (or would not) provide. But when Truman needed group support on domestic policy proposals, the White House provided only informal contacts. "Truman didn't like to use the White House staff to lobby on [Capitol] Hill," Neustadt recalled. "The organizations did a lot of the switchboard work on the Hill. They kept in touch with the White House, but informally." [3]

President and Congress. As parties grew weaker, White House officials became more interested in having direct contacts with interest groups. Party leaders lost their intermediary position except in special cases. Similarly, congressional leaders, some of whom also had been party leaders, lost a great deal of their ability to speak for their institution.

During Dwight D. Eisenhower's administration, the Office of Congressional Liaison was established as part of the White House office. At about the same time, the White House staff began to reach out directly to interest groups that they once had spoken to through congressional power brokers. When President Kennedy sought passage of his Trade Expansion Act, he appointed a trade adviser who gathered a staff that operated as part of the White House. For President Richard M. Nixon to prevail in Congress, especially on controversial "conservative" issues, communications links to organized interests were essential. Nixon's program for an antiballistic missile system required support that party leaders could not provide. He put his assistant Charles Colson in charge of what proved to be a successful effort to develop interest group support that would help him gain a majority in Congress.[4] Colson worked on several similar campaigns, and his efforts convinced Nixon of the value of an operation that generated support for the president and his programs on a routine basis. Nixon later explored the possibility of developing a public liaison operation, but his own political demise occurred before he took any formal steps. Soon after, Gerald R. Ford created the Office of Public Liaison (OPL) as the White House institution responsible for both responding to interest groups and mobilizing their support for the president.[5]

President and Cabinet. Historically, the executive departments served as the normal conduit of group demands on the executive branch. Interest groups often had been instrumental in the birth of a department, bureau, or agency. Political appointees frequently were recruited from the organizations that worked with the department. Through their continued contact with group representatives, civil servants in some cases assimilated their views. Interest group leaders characteristically expected the department to be receptive to their desires or even act as their advocate within the government.

Increasingly, however, departmental constituencies are comprised of competing interest groups whose clashes may be reflected in conflicts between the White House, the cabinet, and the bureaucracy. The numerous conflicts during the Reagan administration involving the Department of the Interior and the Environmental Protection Agency (EPA) provide an example. Organized environmental and conservationist groups regarded Interior and EPA as their representatives in the executive branch. Yet President Ronald Reagan had been elected with strong support from land-owning and manufacturing groups that regarded Interior and EPA as unsympathetic to their interests. He appointed as secretary of the interior and director of the EPA individuals who represented the production groups rather than the environmentalists. Environmentalists in government and in the interest groups then used their alliances in Congress and the media to pressure the White House to break its exclusive relationship with the producers.

In this situation, the president rallied his political supporters to bolster his appointees in their struggle with opposing interest groups. Yet in other cases, the president may find that cabinet officers represent the opinions of interest groups outside his support coalition. It is for this reason that recent presidents have turned to the White House staff rather than the cabinet to build their own relations with interest groups, especially through the Office of Public Liaison.

Forming a Postelection Coalition

When presidents could no longer make their administrations function by dealing with a few dozen leaders in the public and private sectors, the White House staff began to work with the small, cohesive, and often wealthy organizations that represented the new muscle on the political beach. Relations had to be established in order for the president to find a majority to support each of his policy goals, to win reelection, or simply to maintain the foundation of support necessary for managing conflict in the nation. The nature of his relations with interest groups came to depend on how he and his staff saw them aiding the administration's objectives.

During the early years of the modern presidency, when the president and his staff still relied on party and congressional leaders to structure their political contacts, the strength of the president's personal electoral base and his party's coalition shaped the interest group relationship. The patterns established during Roosevelt's administration were followed by his successors through Lyndon B. Johnson. When the electoral coalition was a fragmented alliance, as was the case with Truman and Kennedy, White House assistants sought support beyond their allies in Congress and the party. When the coalition was cohesive enough to stick together after the election, as with Eisenhower, the president was able to use it to convince members of Congress and other policy makers that they should assist him in his efforts to achieve his major policy goals. He did not have to court interest group support on a continuing basis because his goals were not far out of line with what Congress was willing to do. Johnson, like Eisenhower, had a strong base of support among those who elected him president, but this loyalty cracked around the fault line created by the Indochina war.

By the time Gerald R. Ford took office, leaders of the major organizations that had supported presidents' elections no longer could provide the continuing support that Ford would need throughout his term. Vietnam and Watergate hastened the collapse, delegitimating and destabilizing the "natural" coalitions that had provided support for presidents from Roosevelt through Johnson. Presidents needed mechanisms that could continue to build coalitions when their task shifted from winning office to finding the power to make use of their office.

The White House response to a weakened support system was to expand the scope of conflict. By involving supportive lobbies in legislative lobbying, presidents enlarged or found alternatives to the electoral coalitions that had sent them to office. Presidents also found that they needed to translate the support they received from traditional supporters—those who supported them personally and those who supported the general direction of their programs—into something more specific. Involvement by a motivated public was crucial to presidents in tight contests such as the 1969 antiballistic missile vote in the Senate or the Panama Canal Treaty vote that Jimmy Carter won in 1978, each after an arduous struggle to round up the votes.

The problems faced by Ford, Carter, and Reagan indicate that the fragmentation of the political system was not merely a temporary phenomenon created by the tensions of the Johnson-Nixon era. Groups that had supported a party or candidate no longer can be counted on to support either after the election. Thus, while Carter was able to put together major elements of the Roosevelt coalition of the 1930s for the 1976 election, those forces did not provide him with legislative majorities. Labor, for example, was unable to secure passage of administration-backed legislation to revise the National Labor Relations Act; the bill died in a Senate filibuster in 1978. Carter's successful legislative efforts resulted more from the ability of his White House staff to pull together fragmentary alliances on each of the numerous occasions that his lengthy policy agenda required than from a strong, enduring coalition.

While President Carter was unable to secure many legislative advantages from his electoral coalition, President Reagan did better with a narrow but strong coalition based on a core of conservative supporters. His staff's skills in broadening the base of his support, especially in the business community, were largely responsible for his legislative successes in 1981 and 1982. By late 1982 and early 1983, however, Reagan had begun to develop Carter-like problems in holding together a coalition that required constant attention. That both Carter and Reagan received support on so many of their major policy objectives is a tribute to their staffs' ability to build and hold coalitions of interest groups that could serve as fellow lobbyists.

Responding to the Power of Organized Interests

As the authority of political leaders has declined, interest groups and their representatives have proliferated. The number of people lobbying in Washington rose from approximately 4,000 in 1977 to between 10,000 and 20,000 in 1982.[6] Their ranks include lawyers, trade association representatives, foreign representatives, political operatives, and a host of others. From its traditional base of labor and business groups, the interest group structure has expanded to include consumer, environmental, human rights, social, and religious groups among its successful members. In addition to the growth in the number of organizations represented in Washington, there has been an increase in their strength as well.

One of the most important developments in American politics since the 1970s has been the spread of political action committees (PACs), the campaign arm of many interest groups. Their numbers grew from approximately 600 in 1974 to 3,500 at the end of 1982.[7] In 1976, PACs spent $23 million on congressional races. By 1982 that amount had grown to approximately $80 million.

In spite of 1974 legislation that provides for public financing of presidential elections, interest groups also retain an important role in the presidential campaign through their PACs. Inventive fund-raisers have discovered various loopholes in contribution limitations, loopholes "big enough to drive a president through," noted Democratic consultant Robert Keefe.[8] For example, independent political groups that maintain formal independence from a candidate can spend as much money in his behalf as they want without being subject to the restrictions of the campaign laws. Sen. Jesse Helms's Congressional Club spent $4.5 million on the 1980 Reagan cause; Paul Dietrich's Fund for a Conservative Majority spent $2 million.[9] Americans for an Effective Presidency, another independent conservative group, was able to spend $1.3 million by avoiding any direct ties to a candidate.

Interest groups not only are a major source of financing for all levels of elections, but frequently command vast resources for legislative and administrative lobbying as well. The rise to power of these groups is part of the new political reality that the White House has to confront.

With their power and organizational strengths, interest groups have been able to represent themselves and move into the vacuum created by the decline of traditional political authorities.

Organizations welcome White House support when they can get it, but they seldom achieve the same degree of success with the president and his staff that they do with Congress. Lobbying the president is inherently more difficult than attempting to influence Congress. Internal White House procedures are far less visible than those of either branch of Congress. Most elements of the decision-making process on Capitol Hill are discoverable, even though many are not conducted in the open. At the White House, however, the president and his aides take the position that the way in which they operate on specific matters is proprietary information, and its public dissemination is subject to their discretion. Staff members not only try to play policy cards close to the vest, but often succeed for relatively long periods in keeping information about what they are doing within a small circle. By and large they are successful in maintaining this control unless internal staff disputes lead to leaks. Thus, the White House staff has an advantage in responding to interest group lobbying: it is less likely than congressional staffs to be besieged at its most vulnerable points because lobbyists are less likely to know where these points are.

The tremendous prestige of the presidency even makes it possible for the president to use the interest groups to further his own objectives. Furthermore, the White House centralizes power in the person of the president; no equivalent centralization takes place in Congress. If the president and his assistants become familiar with managing the routines of their relations with interest groups, they can translate the presidency's prestige and power into influence.

Still, recent administrations have provided interest groups with channels of access to the president and his staff largely because these groups—particularly their PACs—have become so adept at influencing members of Congress. When organizations recognize that a decision affecting their interests is about to be made, they will direct their efforts to where they believe power lies or where they hope to find a friendly ear. The White House staff, in turn, responds to these groups either because it shares their concern or because it wants to avoid a potential conflict. The contemporary relationship between the presidency and interest groups, although based on mutual advantage, requires considerable management. From the perspective of the presidency, this has meant that the White House staff must take on a variety of roles in order to respond to the groups' expectations.

Managing Relations with Interest Groups

A survey of the functions performed by White House staff members who deal directly with interest groups provides a picture of the demands placed on a president. Since these demands arise both from past commitments and the imperatives of governing, and because they often conflict with each other, their resolution is a high priority for all levels of assistants, from the president's closest advisers to lower level operations personnel.

Presidential assistants who manage White House relations with interest groups play at least four major roles, labeled here as 1) "the marker," 2) "the communicant," 3) "the constructor," and 4) "the broker." Markers deal with the accumulated credits held by groups that supported the president's nomination and election. Communicants establish a basis of shared interest with groups that the president needs in his ongoing governmental and political efforts. Constructors seek group support for policy campaigns, particularly those that involve congressional lobbying. Brokers make agreements with groups for the president and intercede with him on behalf of interest groups.

The Marker

Markers are members of the White House entourage who keep track of the president's political debts to interest groups. The president's political advisers, and those on the staff who are assigned responsibility for working with labor, business, minorities, and other specific constituency groups, assume the marker's role most frequently.

Interest groups want to cash in the chips earned during the nomination and election campaigns in exchange for appointments in the administration, continuing access to the White House, and a role in policy making. In fact the prospect of getting the prestige and influence that comes with appointments and access often is what leads groups to back presidential candidates in the first place. From the groups' perspective, the campaign is the time to give and the White House years are the period to receive. Although the more sophisticated group leaders recognize that their expectations for support on particular policies must be lower than for appointments and access, they press for all three.

Appointments. At the beginning of an administration, groups often want appointments mostly for their symbolic value. In the long run, however, they hope to gain the advantages of having their people on the inside. Not only do they hope that their case will be presented sympathetically within the White House, but that their inside position will enable them to obtain better intelligence about who the important actors are and what they are doing with regard to decisions that affect the group's interests.

There are a variety of inside and outside locations from which groups seek to influence the appointment process. For example, the American Bar Association (ABA) is in an ideal position to influence the selection of federal judges because no president appoints a judge without taking the Bar Association into account. President Ford succeeded in getting former Connecticut Governor Thomas Meskill confirmed as a circuit court judge against the ABA's recommendation, but only after a protracted Senate fight. (The last time the Senate confirmed a circuit court nomination opposed by the ABA was in 1965.)[10]

After the election, groups scramble for prominent positions in the new administration.[11] The level of appointments they are awarded is determined by their support in the nomination and election contests and by the White House staff's perception of their ability to continue to help the president.

President Carter began hearing group demands well before his election. Women's groups had been working for more than five months with the Democratic National Committee to assemble a list of possible female appointees. By election day their list had more than 4,000 names on it.[12] Hispanics, acting through Raul Yzaguirre, the director of the National Council of La Raza, gave the postelection transition team a list of more than 1,000 candidates for appointment. Organized labor was in perhaps the best position to see that its demands for appointments were heard and answered. The AFL-CIO had three representatives with desks in the transition office itself.

During the summer of 1976, interest group leaders made their way to Carter's hometown of Plains, Georgia, to put in their requests for appointments. Candidate Carter, like all Democratic nominees, heard from a wide variety of groups representing environmental and consumer interests, women, blacks, labor, and Hispanics, among others. But as president, Carter found that appointments did not necessarily win him gratitude. Groups that had supported the Democrats talked instead about those on their lists who were not appointed. David Rubenstein, a deputy in Carter's Domestic Policy staff, observed that "groups want 100 percent of what they want."[13] The accuracy of Rubenstein's statement is illustrated by the change in the Hispanic vote between 1976 and 1980: although Carter appointed large numbers of

Hispanics, his support among them dropped from 75 percent in 1976 to 54 percent in 1980.[14]

Republican administrations usually emerge from the appointment phase of interest group relations with fewer losses than the Democrats for at least two reasons: they have fewer groups to contend with, and their staunchest ally—business—tends to assume Republican support for its major goals. Consequently, business groups do not insist on as many appointments as do the groups that support the Democrats. President Reagan, however, faced more discord over appointments than other recent Republican presidents. He had added to the traditional Republican election coalition by wooing conservative religious and social groups. These new segments of the coalition, spearheaded by organizations such as the Moral Majority, reminded the president of what they expected in appointments. At the same time, conservative leaders, such as Paul Weyrich and Richard Viguerie, spoke publicly of their concerns about appointees whom they deemed unacceptable. Their Senate spokesman, Jesse Helms, slowed down the appointment process for State Department designates Lawrence Eagleburger and Helmut Sonnenfeldt, whom many conservatives identified with the policy of détente with the Soviet Union.

Groups that are not part of the winning coalition but that represent a force in the Washington community also must be taken into account, if only in a negative way. Such groups may be able to prevent the president from making appointments they actively oppose. In recent years labor and civil rights groups have shown Republican presidents that they have this kind of informal veto power, even though they do not provide many votes for Republican presidential candidates. President Nixon was unsuccessful in his efforts to get two of his Supreme Court nominees (Judges Clement F. Haynsworth, Jr., and G. Harrold Carswell) confirmed by the Senate because a coalition of labor and civil rights groups led a vigorous opposition.[15] Civil rights groups also showed their ability to veto Reagan appointee Sam Hart, a conservative, black Baptist minister whom the president nominated to be chairman of the Civil Rights Commission. Similarly, Democratic presidents often appoint individuals who are at least minimally acceptable to business to the Federal Reserve Board, many of the regulatory agencies, and the Treasury Department.

The "spoils" of the appointment process include more than 2,000 executive positions, one- or two-hundred judgeships (Carter had a record 297 judicial posts to fill), and several hundred advisory commission slots. There also are more than 600 White House staff jobs, and as executive decision making has moved toward the White House in recent years, the perception that positions there command at least as much prestige as those at the departments and agencies has grown stronger among interest groups. Several former members of consumer advocate Ralph Nader's staff were named to White House jobs in the Carter administration, partly in recognition of the importance of the Nader groups' support. Harrison Wellford, a Nader assistant, served as the deputy to the director of the Office of Management and Budget. The Environmental Defense Fund, another Nader organization, saw one of its staff, Katherine Fletcher, appointed to Stuart Eizenstat's Domestic Policy staff.

Of course, there is no guarantee that the person from the originating group is going to remain loyal to the parent organization when loyalties to president and group come into conflict. Nader had harsh words for his former deputy, Joan Claybrook, who headed the automobile safety division of the Transportation Department in the Carter administration. After Carter's defeat, with no such conflicting loyalites dividing her, she and Nader were able to patch up their quarrel.

Access. Access is particularly important to interest groups because it is very difficult to influence the White House policy process from the outside. "The White House is so involved in so many issues at a time that groups don't know where to focus," Stuart Eizenstat observed.[16] Influence in the policy process can be derived from knowing which decisions are being made at a particular time and by whom. Interest group leaders assume that access to the White House will enhance their ability to find out.

What access means politically is that once the White House staff perceives the policy objective of an interest group to be important to the president, that group will get a hearing. The White House staff members involved in the policy area will arrange to meet with the group and hear its proposals and concerns. If the group and the issue are important enough, the top political adviser or the president himself will provide the sympathetic ear.

Conservative social and religious groups had such access to the Reagan White House, in contrast to what they felt were closed gates when Carter was in office. Their support for President Reagan during the 1980 election campaign gained them a friend in the White House. When the Reverend Morton Hill told White House officials that he wanted to discuss government antipornography actions, a meeting was

Table 11-1 One White House Staff Member's Interest Group Meetings, 1981

| Groups | Meeting With | | | Total |
	President & Vice President	Cabinet & Key White House Staff	Others	
Conservatives and Limited Government	6	16	66	88
Fraternal	0	1	2	3
Veterans/Defense	4	22	39	65
American Indian	0	12	48	60
Religious	1	3	33	37
Total	11	54	188	253

held.[17] Later a conference on the enforcement of obscenity laws was scheduled at the White House. Even if few legislative proposals came out of this meeting, Hill and his antipornography group did get their meeting. In the long run, groups may become more result-oriented, but at the beginning of an administration, access itself is a benefit for both the group and the White House.

A basic measure of interest group access is the number of meetings sponsored by or held at the White House. The portfolio of one staff member from the Office of Public Liaison indicates what access means as measured in meetings. In the first year of the Reagan administration, the aide in charge of dealing with social and religious groups arranged the schedule illustrated in Table 11-1.[18]

Policy. The Reagan White House provides good illustrations of how groups involve themselves in the policy process. Several social and religious groups that were central to Reagan's electoral coalition later became involved in formulating legislation for tuition tax credits designed to aid parents who sent their children to private schools. Representatives of these conservative groups were invited to exchange views with White House officials. They presented their case and subsequently were consulted as the legislation was drafted. Among the 22 people who attended the meeting were religious figures such as Jerry Falwell, John Cardinal Krol, Pat Robertson, and James Robison, as well as secular conservative leaders such as Viguerie and Weyrich.

Following the meeting, Morton C. Blackwell, a staff member in Reagan's OPL, became involved in writing tuition credit legislation. "We spent from two in the afternoon to ten at night hammering legislation that would have the broadest support and meet the president's requirement for the bill," Blackwell recalled. "We were in constant communication with outside groups to make sure it was consistent with what they wanted." [19] The legislation then was sent to Congress.

Other administrations have had the staff assume the marker role, but with variations that depended on the nature of the groups in the president's coalition and his needs at the time. The Maritime Union's pressure on the Carter White House is a clear example of a group that was important to a presidential candidate's election cashing in its chips for favorable legislation. The Maritime Union, a strong backer of Carter, asked for his support on a cargo preference bill that would require a minimum percentage of foreign oil to be carried to the United States aboard U.S. ships. The president was less concerned with the added petroleum costs that would result from such legislation than he was with repaying the political debt he incurred during the 1976 campaign. "It was a straight political call," a White House adviser observed.[20] The same principle applied in Carter's legislative call for the creation of a Department of Education. In 1976, the National Education Association, with its 1.7 million members, supported a presidential candidate for the first time in its history—Jimmy Carter. Presumably, Carter's preelection promise to establish a separate education department—which was realized during his administration—was the price paid for the NEA's support.

The Communicant

Communicants form the first line of the president's offense and defense in dealing with groups. Staff members who are responsible for specific domestic policy areas hear from groups that want their interests embodied in presidential proposals. The political staff responds to group recommendations for appointments, and public relations staffers receive requests for presidential appearances. These communicants control traffic in the White House corridors that lead to "him." Although constant pressure from groups may annoy White House personnel, they recognize that the appearance of open communications channels is important for the president's political and governmental success. In return, the White House staff expects group leaders to generate support for the president among their members. Also, groups often possess political and technical information of a sort that is not routinely available within the White House.

Communicants send out and receive information, ideas, people, and policies for the White House. As might be expected of an activity that is at the core of the presidency, a broad range of the White House staff acts as communicants. They are most concentrated in the Press Office, the Office of Policy Development, the Office of the National Security Adviser, the Office of Public Liaison, the vice president's office, and among the president's political advisers.

The communicant role develops during the campaign when the presidential candidate is eager to find out what groups think and assess their strength. A well-established relationship at this time can be very fruitful for both sides. It provides a basis of personal trust, something that is very difficult to acquire after the inauguration when the walls around the White House limit as well as protect the president and his staff from the consequences of close relations.

Casting the Net. The communicant who is a trusted adviser of the presidential candidate begins the process of establishing group contacts on the road to the nomination. For example, when Carter developed his nomination coalition in 1976, his assistants concentrated on the groups that are traditionally vital for Democratic candidates. After receiving the nomination, Carter cast out his net for the general support he would need to win the election. He sought the support of business, an interest not usually part of the Democratic coalition, but one whose fears of a Democratic president required some attention lest they provoke business groups to disrupt his plans. The week after his nomination, Carter met for lunch with 52 corporate executives in New York City. The meeting, hosted by J. Paul Austin of the Coca-Cola Company, Edgar M. Bronfman of Joseph E. Seagram & Sons, Inc., and Henry Ford II of Ford Motor Company, was characterized by a spokesman for Bronfman as "successful in the sense that there was an exchange of views both ways." [21]

In addition to this New York luncheon meeting, Carter considered a request made by Irving Shapiro that he meet with the Business Roundtable's policy committee.[22] Although he did not meet with that group, Carter invited approximately two dozen business leaders to Atlanta for an afternoon session at which each of the guests spoke for three minutes on a subject of his choosing. Carter then asked the executives to draw up their policy agendas and send them to Bert Lance, whom he designated to be his business liaison. Each group presented Lance with a paper detailing its positions on several subjects. "Carter was simply pleased that industry was offering options instead of making demands," Shapiro observed.[23]

Carrying the Flag. The White House seeks to inform groups about its ideas through both formal meetings with top White House officials and institutional communications. The staff hopes that regular contacts will maintain a flow of positive information that suggests the president is using his office to assist the group, its cause, or the community with which it is associated. Stuart Eizenstat met regularly with important groups in the domestic policy area. "I met on a regular basis with staff members of the AFL-CIO," he recalled. "Those were sessions where we informed them of legislation we were working on, keeping them abreast of what was happening." [24] Eizenstat had the same kind of meetings with representatives of the Business Roundtable, the National Association of Manufacturers, and the Chamber of Commerce.

The vice president is a communicant at the higher levels of the White House. He serves as a stand-in for the president, emphasizing presidential respect for various groups' importance to the administration. For example, Vice President George Bush was assigned to deal with organized labor because although unions had not provided many endorsements for candidate Reagan in 1980, many union members voted for him. In one week during the summer of 1982, Vice President Bush met with Lane Kirkland, the president of the AFL-CIO, and Jesse Calhoon of the Maritime Engineers.[25] He also had lunch with Roy Williams of the Teamsters Union during the hiatus between Williams's indictment and trial (and later conviction) on charges of conspiring to bribe Sen. Howard Cannon.

During the Ford administration, the Office of Public Liaison had an ambitious program of meetings scheduled in Washington and around the country. Beginning in October 1974, the White House held 24 conferences in small cities such as Concord, New Hampshire; Peoria, Illinois; and Hollywood, Florida. Staffers also traveled to larger cities such as San Diego, Knoxville, Seattle, Atlanta, and St. Louis. Interest groups were the major source of information on who should be invited to these conferences; indeed, the Chamber of Commerce frequently was the cosponsor. "The conferences created the concept of an open presidency, an open administration," said John Shlaes, the conference coordinator for the OPL.[26] President Ford attended 12 conferences at which national issues such as energy and the economy were discussed. Local issues also were integrated into the discussions. These meetings gave the president exposure not only to the 40,000 who attended, but to all of the people in the cities where the conferences were held who watched them on television or read about them in local newspapers.[27] In the larger cities the conferences were covered gavel-to-gavel by the local public television stations and were heavily featured in the evening news broadcasts.

Recent administrations also have sent out newsletters to inform groups of administration policies that affect them. The White House uses these newsletters as a billboard for its achievements. In the Carter administration a variety of newsletters were sent to groups whose support the White House courted. Sarah Weddington, an adviser responsible for dealing with women's groups, sent out a monthly letter of around a dozen pages entitled "White House News on Women" to 7,000 people.[28] Louis E. Martin, the adviser who worked with blacks, sent a newsletter to black groups, as did Esteban E. Torres to Hispanics and Stephen A. Aiello to white ethnic groups. Theirs were not the first newsletters to be sent regularly from the White House. Perhaps the most widely distributed newsletter was *Consumer News*, published by the White House Office of Consumer Affairs and distributed to 22,000 subscribers between 1971 and 1979.[29]

Relaying Messages to the White House. One important element of the communicant role is to carry messages from interest groups to the White House. This requires an ability to articulate two points of view. The staff member's value lies in being able to present the president in terms that appeal to the groups, then communicate the groups' responses back to the president.

During the Carter administration, Bert Lance had both the political and business knowledge needed to relay the two kinds of messages. A banker and a close friend of Carter's, Lance was widely sought after by business groups. "He was an effective spokesman for the president," Irving Shapiro commented. He was useful "in summing up viewpoints and carrying them back to the president. He was very effective as a bridge to the outside, and a lot was lost when he had to return to Georgia."[30] Later, when the absence of even the minimal support that Democratic presidents usually receive from business plagued the Carter administration, aides lamented that the loss of Lance had been a severe blow.

There are times when staff members have to deliver unpleasant messages to the White House. One of the last things the Reagan White

House wanted to hear when it was mapping out its economic plans in 1981 was that a group not only refused to go along with proposed budget cuts, but was ready to fight and had the ability to prevail. This was the message delivered to White House staff members who were responsible for veterans' affairs. Morton Blackwell of the White House staff believed that senior advisers needed to understand the strength of those opposing the cuts. He saw it as his job to "facilitate communication between the forces opposed to the cuts and OMB." A meeting was arranged between OMB Director David Stockman on the one side and veterans' groups and G. V. "Sonny" Montgomery, the chairman of the House Veterans' Affairs Committee, on the other. "Montgomery explained to the people at OMB how the cow ate the cabbage," Blackwell observed. The cuts were restored.[31]

The Constructor

Constructors build support for the White House by assembling interest group coalitions. They build functional coalitions for broad policy areas such as economic policy and specific coalitions for individual pieces of legislation such as a tax bill. Since no interest group can support every issue, it is important that the president develop both general alliances and specific coalitions.

All presidents maintain a continuing interest in the outcome of policy, but their willingness to become involved in the processes that lead to enactment and implementation varies according to their individual goals and personalities. The Office of Public Liaison has proved to be the most significant institution for constructing legislative policy coalitions. Public Liaison is concerned with building group support and grass-roots sentiment that eventually will influence members of Congress.

The staff members most involved with the president's electoral base are his political advisers. In the Reagan administration, these advisers were located in the Political Affairs Office, but other administrations have hidden them behind more subtle titles. For example, Carter's political advisers were associated with Hamilton Jordan, who simply carried the title of Assistant to the President. Staff members from the Domestic Policy office and the National Security Council also help to form functional coalitions in response to the president's need to maintain his sources of electoral and governing strength.

Presidential Style. A president's style influences the ways in which White House aides go about forming coalitions. The staff must work around the president's personal strengths and weaknesses. Lyndon B. Johnson not only enjoyed getting into the process of coalition building, he insisted on it. In contrast, Richard Nixon preferred to leave the process to his staff.

During the Carter administration, developing coalitions and stroking individuals whose support was needed were matters for the staff to handle. "You need to build the support and enthusiastic response to programs," observed Eugene Eidenberg, Carter's staff assistant for intergovernmental relations. "As a matter of style, [Carter] didn't relish that part of the job." [32] Carter's personal role was as "explainer" of the administration's position. In meetings set up by the staff, he addressed groups that wanted to hear how particular policies would affect their interests.

In Reagan's case, he and his staff agreed that his presence should be saved for tasks that could not be performed by anyone else with the same effect, especially those involving personal persuasion. "You try to nurse that chit along," commented Wayne Valis, Reagan's business liaison. "We use him only when it will make the difference." During the fight for the 1981 tax cut proposal, the centerpiece of the Reagan administration's "supply-side" economic program, the president was involved at several points in the coalition-building process. Reagan talked with "some of the companies with the biggest tax problems. He tried to get them to mute their opposition, and in some cases, he was successful." He provided the "final inning motivation" as the coalition was put to work, Valis recalled. Reagan talked with about 30 association leaders in the Cabinet Room and gave them a "let's get moving right now, and do nothing else for the next two days" pitch. Then he spoke with members of Congress, meeting in person with about 40 legislators and speaking on the phone to another 150.[33]

Office Work: The OPL. The Carter administration provides an example of what happens when the White House attempts to forge presidential coalitions without an institutional operation. When Carter became president, he used the White House staff position for public liaison to repay a campaign debt to an individual and a group. Midge Costanza, an early supporter, was the highest ranking woman on the White House staff, but her visibility did not correspond to her relatively small influence in decision making. Costanza did not use the Office of Public Liaison to develop policy support for the president. "She saw OPL as a place to bring in disenfranchised groups," Stuart Eizenstat recalled. She was involved in symbolic interactions with groups, some of which, such as gay rights activists, had no previous White House access. By the time Costanza left the White House 18 months after Carter's inauguration, the office had few staff members and less influence. "There was not a recognition of the vital connection between a proposal and the role of interest groups in its passage," Eizenstat concluded about Costanza's office.[34]

The real work of coalition building was done by Carter's political advisers, who kept track of the president's relations with labor and business. But the political operation, which was under the wing of Hamilton Jordan, tended to view group relations in terms of past electoral support rather than present legislative need. It took a full year and a half for the staff to convince the president that interest groups were potentially powerful allies in policy initiatives, not merely winning gamblers whose markers had to be paid.

After staffers recognized the importance of integrating the management of interest group relations into the mainstream of White House activities, they improved their record. Hamilton Jordan used in-house task forces on policy issues to bring together the staff members who developed policy with those who were responsible for selling it. "For the first time we used all of our resources," Jordan said in the aftermath of their success on the Panama Canal issue. "We used that model time and time again." [35] Jordan's task forces often were chaired by Anne Wexler, Costanza's successor as director of the public liaison operation. A task force would attempt to determine the significance of an issue for the administration, discuss alternatives, and estimate the basis of support.

In the summer of 1980, an economic policy task force met to consider how the administration should present its recommendations to the public. Wexler and her associates considered the groups to be consulted and assigned responsibility for meeting with their leaders to Secretary of Labor Ray Marshall, Domestic Policy Chief Stuart Eizenstat, Council of Economic Advisers Chairman Charles Schultze, and Office of Management and Budget Director James McIntyre. Their consultations were scheduled for a three-day period. A congressional leadership breakfast to discuss the policy and inform Congress of the groups' reactions was scheduled early the following week. Then Wexler took on the following responsibilities: she made certain that interest groups were contacted before the announcement of the economic program; that an audience including business, labor, state and local government officials, minorities, and social action groups was assembled for the announcement; and that briefings for interest group leaders would be held soon after the president's statement. In addition, the White House contacted representatives of interest groups at the state and local levels and asked traveling administration officials to sell the president's economic program at meetings with mayors, governors, labor councils, and business organizations.[36]

Wexler brought large numbers of group leaders to the White House where, she later recalled, she would "lobby the lobbyists . . . to get a large constituency on an issue." [37] "She tries to enhance the public's understanding of the real issues involved and develop a climate for legislative acceptance," her aide Michael H. Chanin explained.[38] Because she had to deal with so many constituencies in order to hold together the fragments of Carter's tenuous coalition, Wexler met with a substantial number of groups whenever there was a major legislative initiative. On one policy proposal, Wexler recalled 11 meetings in one week with labor, environmentalists, consumers, small business, the elderly, civil rights groups, trade associations, and the Business Roundtable.[39]

Meetings became the forum the Carter administration used to call groups to action. "All in all the East Room briefing was part selling job, part pep rally, part show biz, and part educational forum," journalist Dom Bonafede wrote about a SALT II presentation.[40] The White House wanted participants to leave a meeting firmly committed and go back to their local areas to mobilize grass-roots support.

A White House meeting provides the public liaison office with an opportunity to put the finishing touches on its efforts to persuade interest group leaders. Group representatives are brought into a setting that exposes them to the charisma of the presidential office as well as whatever talents the incumbent has as a persuader. This setting and the staff's strong lobbying efforts were particularly important to such Reagan administration initiatives as the proposed sale of the Airborne Warning and Control System (AWACS) to Saudi Arabia. At the onset of discussions about the issue, the Senate seemed unlikely to go along. "We came in when we nearly had our hats handed to us," Wayne Valis said. "We went out to every ally and used three or four classes of arguments." If the groups did not have a specific interest in the issue, Valis recalled, "I would say that if the president's leadership is impaired on this issue, his ability to deliver on anything is impaired." [41] Thus, groups that supported the administration's business policies were made to see how the sale of AWACS related to the president's ability to deliver on issues of more direct concern to them. Approximately 200 companies signed up as part of a coalition in support of the sale, and

Clark MacGregor of United Technologies led a steering committee. Business groups contacted their members to relay pro-AWACS arguments. "My very strong recommendation to the White House was that there would be no press gangs, no broken arms on AWACS," Valis declared.[42] The technique seemed to work.

The finishing touches were provided by the president, who made phone calls, held small meetings, and spoke to larger delegations. Business groups provided information that the president could use in his personal contacts with senators. "Congressional Relations and the business community were asked about the concerns of each senator before Reagan met with them," Valis said. "He was prepared to deal with their major concerns."[43]

The key to the success of operations designed to build grass-roots support is the willingness and ability of interest groups to activate their followers. Business groups provided that kind of support on behalf of President Reagan's tax increase proposal in 1982, even though it called for increasing their taxes. In order to discover what the political landscape would be like on the bill, the public liaison operation relied on the information provided by business groups. A steering committee was established that included the leaders of the American Business Conference, National Association of Home Builders, National Association of Realtors, National Council of Life Insurance, and the National Association of Manufacturers. The committee was expanded first to 30 and finally to 70 members. The business groups alerted the administration to prospective opposition from particular organizations, among them the Chamber of Commerce, the National Federation of Independent Businesses, and the American Farm Bureau Federation.

The Office of Public Liaison represented the "muscle" in this case, while the president took the high road in meetings and used his powers of personal persuasion to maintain business groups' support or reduce their objections.[44] After the issue was resolved without Chamber of Commerce support, Chamber leaders were excluded from White House functions. "Guys that fight against me have big welts all over their bodies," Valis mused in the aftermath of the struggle.[45]

Minding the Electoral Coalition. The next election is never far from the minds of most presidents and their aides. The Reagan White House staff, aware of the political mistakes of its predecessors, made sure that the president's electoral coalition was managed by aides in the OPL as well as by the political staff. To a greater extent than in previous administrations, the Reagan operation filled staff positions with representatives of the particular constituencies whose support they sought. Michael Gale, who was responsible for working with Jewish groups, was hired from the staff of the American Israel Public Affairs Committee. Morton Blackwell, who worked with conservatives, had worked for Richard Viguerie and was on the staff of *Conservative Digest*.

White House aides regard building and maintaining the campaign coalition as an ongoing priority. "The majority of the groups I deal with happen to be part of the president's winning coalition," Blackwell noted. "I want to make sure that those people who were with the president get things around here." [46] Blackwell worked closely with Ed Rollins, the president's chief White House political adviser. The Reagan political staff made sure that its supporters on Capitol Hill were taken care of at election time by steering PAC funds to them. [47]

The president's political advisers also play prominent roles in the organization and activities of the White House staff. Carter gave the most important White House posts to those who were closest to him during the campaign. Their location at points of high visibility ensured that politics would be considered in policy making. Although the Reagan administration did not find as many major positions for campaign supporters as some of its predecessors had, legislative strategy meetings included representatives from the political adviser's office as well as from public liaison.

The Broker

Members of the White House staff serve as brokers or intermediaries between interest groups and the president. Interest groups may know the kinds of actions they want government to take or to halt, but rarely do they know where to go in a new administration to present their case. In the executive branch, officials reveal only as much about the roles they play as they want to. The more that is known about individuals in decision-making positions, the greater the likelihood that interest groups will try to influence their actions. Consequently, few policy makers willingly reveal more than they believe they must about their operations. Groups often find themselves scrambling for tidbits of information about what is going on. When they find out, they use their access to determine where, when, and by whom actions are being taken and how to ask the White House to get involved on their behalf. The White House can smooth what may otherwise be a rocky road for groups that deal with executive agencies.

Legislative Brokers. Presidents ordinarily do not press for legislation that will affect supportive interests until they resolve differences among the specific organizations that make up the interest. Although the staff urges settlement, it does not necessarily indicate what the president will accept. There are times, however, when the White House makes it clear that when the groups reach an accord, the president will support it. Such pledges often persuade participants to overcome their reluctance to bargain with antagonists.

For example, during the Carter administration the White House sought to frame legislation to limit the participation of American companies in the Arab boycott of businesses that dealt with Israel. Jewish groups endorsed legislation that would inhibit participation by American companies in the boycott. The White House staff had to find a way to satisfy both the companies, which did not want to lose valuable trading partners, and Jewish groups, which represent an important source of support for a Democratic president. "The White House endorsed in principle a proposal worked out by the two sides," said Irving Shapiro, who was involved in formulating the legislation.

The two main participants in the negotiations were groups with which Shapiro had strong ties, the Business Roundtable and the Anti-Defamation League of B'nai B'rith. A task force was appointed that included three representatives of each organization. "Both sides were in touch with Eizenstat and he played the honest broker role," Shapiro observed. "He was looking for solutions, not rhetoric or theory." [48] After falling apart more than once, the task force finally came to an agreement, which Carter forwarded to Congress.

The broker role in legislative policy making involves White House advocacy of specific proposals from groups in the president's electoral coalition. Almost every administration accepts policies developed by groups and advances them as part of the president's program. The Carter administration introduced legislation that had been developed by the AFL-CIO to reform the National Labor Relations Act. "We had discussions on labor law reform," Stuart Eizenstat said, "actual negotiating sessions with Larry Gold, general counsel for the AFL-CIO.... There were few differences when the bill was submitted." [49] Eizenstat had acted effectively as a broker between an element in the president's electoral coalition and the president himself.

Administrative Brokers. Interest groups frequently seek the White House staff's intercession with the bureaucracy. "A lot of what we do is casework," said Robert Bonitati, who handled labor affairs for

President Reagan. "If the National Maritime Union has a particular problem with something the Department of Commerce is doing, you track it down and set up a session where everybody can talk." [50] Organizations want access to all of government, not just the president. But the bureaucracy is more likely to cooperate after it receives a call from the White House. "It has a great impact when you call from here," Blackwell noted. [51]

In addition to interceding with the bureaucracy, White House officials provide interest group leaders with an insider's knowledge of government. The staff knows or can find out who the group needs to persuade on a particular issue. "The key person might be a deputy assistant; it helps for us to help them get to the right person so that the appropriate action is taken," Blackwell explained. [52] White House staffers also can find out when decisions are being made in the bureaucracy that might affect interest groups. Sometimes they even alert the groups. "When Health and Human Services was developing its contraception regulations," said Wendy Borcherdt, who handled women's issues for OPL during the first year of the Reagan administration, "I sent out notices to the groups about it." Borcherdt knew which groups were interested in particular issues from the results of a questionnaire she had sent to a wide range of women's groups when she first joined the public liaison staff. Borcherdt had asked the women's groups to list three issues on which they could work with the administration. "We have coded them all by area of interest and then we bring the groups in when their issues come up," she said. [53]

White House assistants want the organizations that are part of their portfolios to be taken into account when policies affecting them are being considered. Thus, staff brokers need to be aware of what is brewing elsewhere in the White House and throughout the bureaucracy. Bonitati asserted that a central task in managing the labor portfolio was "to see that all points of view are represented and considered as policy is developed." A staff person learns which groups are interested in which policies. "Sam Church is interested in mine safety and regulatory change, Bob Georgine about Davis-Bacon repeal, Jesse Calhoon in civilian manning of naval ships," Bonitati explained, naming several labor leaders. [54]

Broker for Whom? As constituency representatives have made their way onto the White House staff, the risk for the president is that they will reflect the interests of particular groups rather than those of the president. For example, several constituency representatives in the

Carter and Reagan administrations had close ties to organized ethnic groups. Their loyalties were more than occasionally tested, and in some instances, the president lost. Mark Siegal, the Carter administration aide who served as the liaison to Jewish groups, left the White House in a public break with the president over his Middle East policies. Siegal's successor, Ed Sanders, left the White House in a policy dispute that did not become public. The first constituency representative to leave the Reagan White House, Jack Stein, was also responsible for the Jewish constituency. The drift of recent presidents away from the strong pro-Israel positions they took in their election campaigns has taken its toll on liaison staffers with Jewish group ties.

Some presidents have hoped to avoid potential conflicts by eliminating the position of group specialist from the White House staff. When President Carter took office, he intended to end the practice of assigning aides to particular constituency groups. Shortly after he made a public statement to that effect, however, he reorganized his staff to include assistants responsible for contacting blacks, women, Jews, and Hispanics. The Reagan administration also learned that this kind of assignment was necessary. Wendy Borcherdt explained:

> When the Office of Public Liaison was set up, the staff felt that ethnic, sexual, and racial groups would be brought in the arena not because they were Hispanic or black, but rather because they were interested in particular issues. In reality, they weren't being brought in. They realized that it would have to occur here.[55]

The Reagan White House moved quickly to assign group responsibilities to what have become their "account executives."

Few presidents want to risk the adverse publicity that comes when a White House aide publicly breaks with the chief executive. President Carter even faced a situation in which his adviser on old-age issues went to Capitol Hill to oppose the president's program. Nelson H. Cruikshank, an aide in the Domestic Policy staff, testified that the president's proposed Social Security benefit cuts were "ill advised" and "trumped up."[56] This experience made the president's advisers somewhat suspicious of Cruikshank. "It obviously helps to have ties with groups," remarked David Rubenstein, Stuart Eizenstat's deputy. "Cruikshank was useful politically, but if I wanted to know what I should do, then I would look to someone else."[57] Constituency representatives with close ties to the groups in their portfolios may provide valuable information about how the groups will react to particular policies, but their usefulness as presidential loyalists is likely to be marginal.

The President and Interest Groups

"One of the most important pieces of legislation to be considered by the Congress this year is being held hostage by a small but highly funded and organized special interest group," President Reagan angrily declared when passage of the 1983 Social Security and unemployment benefits bill was jeopardized by a banking interest's attempt to repeal the 10 percent withholding tax on savings.[58] Other recent presidents also have condemned the power that groups exercise in determining the shape of policy. When Presidents Ford and Carter met together at the Ford Library for a discussion on the presidency, both of them singled out interest groups as an obstacle in the governing process.

Yet whether intentionally or not, all recent presidents have structured their relations with groups in such a way as to increase their strength within the system. When Ford established the Office of Public Liaison, he formally brought groups into the White House on a regular basis. There they learned more about the executive decision-making process as well as who the players were on individual policies. Having such information allowed groups to insinuate themselves into the policy process in a way they had not been able to in earlier administrations. President Carter appointed a broad range of constituency representatives to the White House staff and brought groups into policy coalitions such as those put together by Wexler and Jordan. Reagan allowed groups to become deeply enmeshed in the policy process through his staff's use of their political intelligence and operational skills, particularly in contacting organization members. In addition, the Reagan White House used these groups' political resources to reward those in Congress who were loyal to the president.

President Reagan became angry at the efforts of the banking industry to repeal the withholding tax provision because he saw the stakes as so high. Indeed they are. Presidents are affected by their relations with groups in at least three areas: electoral success, policy success, and their image as leaders.

As the loopholes in campaign financing of presidential elections grow wider, each candidate, the president included, is going to be looking for new ways to increase his electoral resources, relative to those of his opponents. Groups provide incumbent presidents with significant opportunities to get ahead of the pack.

In policy terms, groups can provide political intelligence and build the coalitions needed to get legislation enacted. The best relationship from the White House perspective is one in which the staff serves as the liaison for organizations that are working for the president's goals. Groups ordinarily have a more flexible organizational structure than do government institutions, including the White House. When organizations contact their members, the White House reaps two benefits: first, the staff does not have to spend time and resources on the project; second, the information sent to the members comes from a source they trust. "Direct mail is a whole alternate communications system," Wayne Valis noted. "It appeals to people who distrust the general avenue of communications. It is like privileged communications," which has implications for the White House because members "mobilize behind their own." [59] Groups can get to their members—or target categories within the larger membership—quickly. "The Realtors can send out half a million Mailgrams within 24 hours," Valis noted. "If they have a hundred target congressmen, they can get out 100,000 Mailgrams targeted by district." [60] That kind of capacity is the stuff of which White House dreams are made.

Finally, the image that a president projects as a leader can be affected strongly by his relationships with groups. He is going to be judged on his ability to develop support for his programs. A president can use his staff to enhance his strengths and compensate for his weaknesses as a coalition builder, but the president himself must have a sense of how the process works and where groups fit into his policy efforts. The Carter administration provides an example of how staff people can offer important but limited support to a president. President Carter was more concerned with how things worked than with meeting and negotiating with the people involved. The kinds of political machinations that Lyndon B. Johnson thrived on did not appeal to him. Moreover, domestic policy was less interesting to him than foreign policy, where he had more success. The result was that Carter left coalition building to others. "Carter liked the process of governing," Eugene Eidenberg noted. "What he was bad at was the politicking of people." Eidenberg, secretary to the cabinet in the latter part of the administration, suggested that this was an important defect in the president's style:

> He never secured the support, the trust that was so important. He used politics because it led to the place of governing. There was no human connection between Carter and the public; it was catastrophic for his presidency. No one was there when the going got rough.[61]

Most presidents possess at least some of the skills needed for coalition politics. After all, these are the kinds of talents one expects to find among those at the top in politics. They also bring people into the White House who understand that, ultimately, the relationship with interest groups, for all its potential pitfalls, provides a president with some advantages.

Still, by bringing interest groups into the White House, the president and his staff implicitly have made others move over to make room for them on center stage. The political parties and the leadership in Congress have lost much of the authority they once had in fashioning the coalitions a president needs to enact his policies. Yet the objectives of parties and congressional leaders merge with the president's goals more frequently than do those of individual groups. Presidents themselves, therefore, have been a party to narrowing the range of power sources on whom they can rely in realizing their own goals.

NOTES

1. Carl Kaysen to Palmer Hoyt, August 27, 1962, Howard Petersen Files, White House Central Files, John F. Kennedy Library, Boston.
2. Richard E. Neustadt, interview with M. J. Kumar, Boston, September 29, 1982.
3. Ibid.
4. See Michael B. Grossman and Martha J. Kumar, *Portraying the President: The White House and the News Media* (Baltimore: Johns Hopkins University Press, 1981), 105-107.
5. See Joseph A. Pika, "Dealing with the People Divided: The White House Office of Public Liaison." (Paper delivered at the annual meeting of the Midwest Political Science Association, Milwaukee, Wis., April 28-May 1, 1982).
6. Congressional Quarterly, *Guide to Congress*, 3d ed. (Washington, D.C.: Congressional Quarterly, 1982), 792.
7. Elizabeth Drew, "Politics and Money—Part I," *The New Yorker*, December 6, 1982, 60. This article and its companion piece, Part II, detail the growth of PACs and discuss their influence in national politics.
8. Elizabeth Drew, "Politics and Money—Part II," *The New Yorker*, December 13, 1982, 57.
9. Ibid., 87, 91, and 95.
10. On the role of the American Bar Association and other interest groups in federal judicial nominations, see Richard Harris, *Decision* (New York: Ballantine Books, 1971); Harold W. Chase, *Federal Judges: The Appointing Process* (Minneapolis: Minnesota University Press, 1972); Joel B. Grossman, *Lawyers and Judges: The ABA and the Politics of Judicial Selection* (New York: John Wiley & Sons, 1965); and Martin and Susan Tolchin, *To the Victor...* (New York: Random House, 1971).
11. See G. Calvin MacKenzie, *The Politics of Presidential Appointments* (New York: Free Press, 1981), 206-216.
12. Joel Havemann, "The TIP Talent Hunt - Carter's Original Amateur Hour?" *National Journal*, February 19, 1977, 272. (The discussion of the participation of labor and Hispanic groups can be found on pages 269 and 271, respectively.)

13. David Rubenstein, deputy to Stuart Eizenstat, interview with authors, Washington, D.C., January 6, 1981.
14. Gerald Pomper, *The Election of 1980* (Chatham, N.J.: Chatham House Publishers, 1981), 71.
15. See Harris, *Decision*.
16. Stuart Eizenstat, chief of Carter's Domestic Policy Staff, interview with authors, Washington, D.C., August 13, 1982.
17. Morton C. Blackwell, staff member in Reagan's Office of Public Liaison, interview with authors, Washington, D.C., July 7, 1982.
18. Ibid.
19. Ibid.
20. Richard E. Cohen, "Regulatory Rhetoric," *National Journal*, July 23, 1977, 1164.
21. Richard E. Cohen, "Carter's Team Message to Business—'We Hear You,'" *National Journal*, March 5, 1977, 345.
22. James Singer, "Business and Government—A New 'Quasi-Public' Role," *National Journal*, April 15, 1978, 597. For a discussion of the influence of the Business Roundtable in recent presidential politics, see Kim McQuaid, *Big Business and Presidential Power: From FDR to Reagan* (New York: William Morrow & Co., 1982), 284-305.
23. Irving S. Shapiro, former head of the Business Roundtable and president of the DuPont Co., interview with M. J. Kumar, Wilmington, Del., July 13, 1982.
24. Eizenstat interview.
25. Robert F. Bonitati, staff member in Reagan's Office of Public Liaison, interview with authors, Washington, D.C., July 22, 1982.
26. John Shlaes, director of the conferences held by Ford's Office of Public Liaison, interview with M. J. Kumar, Washington, D.C., November 18, 1976.
27. William J. Baroody, Jr., director of Ford's Office of Public Liaison, interview with authors, Washington, D.C., December 3, 1976.
28. Timothy Clark, "Carter Plays Santa Claus for His Reelection Campaign," *National Journal*, April 5, 1980, 553. (The article contains figures on newsletters sent to women, blacks, Hispanics, and white ethnic groups.)
29. "At a Glance," *National Journal*, July 14, 1979, 1178.
30. Shapiro interview.
31. Blackwell interview.
32. Eugene Eidenberg, cabinet secretary in the Carter White House, interview with authors, Washington, D.C., Janary 13, 1981.
33. Wayne Valis, staff member responsible for business relations in Reagan's Office of Public Liaison, interview with M. B. Grossman, Washington, D.C., August 30, 1982.
34. Eizenstat interview.
35. Hamilton Jordan, chief of staff to President Carter, interview with authors, Washington, D.C., January 11, 1979.
36. Information comes from memo entitled, "Program for Economic Renewal—Consultation and Announcement Scenario," August 25, 1980.
37. Anne Wexler, staff assistant responsible for Carter's public liaison, interview with authors, Washington, D.C., July 24, 1979.
38. Dom Bonafede, "To Anne Wexler, All the World is a Potential Lobbyist," *National Journal*, September 8, 1979, 1478.
39. Wexler interview.

40. Bonafede, "To Anne Wexler," 1476.
41. Wayne Valis, interview with authors, Washington, D.C., July 22, 1982.
42. Valis, August interview.
43. Valis, July interview.
44. Valis, August interview.
45. "The Washington Connection: Reagan's Lobbyist to Business," *Fortune*, January 24, 1983, 26. The "guys," most likely the Chamber of Commerce, won the final round with Valis: he was fired at the time of the changing of the leadership at OPL following Elizabeth Dole's appointment as secretary of transportation. Faith Ryan Whittlesey, Reagan's appointee as ambassador to Switzerland, took over as the head of OPL.
46. Blackwell interview.
47. Drew, "Politics and Money—Part I," 67-68.
48. Shapiro interview.
49. Eizenstat interview.
50. Bonitati interview.
51. Blackwell interview.
52. Ibid.
53. Wendy Borcherdt, staff member responsible for dealing with women's groups in Reagan's Office of Public Liaison, interview with authors, Washington, D.C., July 22, 1982.
54. Bonitati interview.
55. Borcherdt interview.
56. Timothy B. Clark, "The Power Vacuum Outside the Oval Office," *National Journal*, February 24, 1979, 296.
57. Rubenstein, interview with authors, Washington, D.C.
58. Statement by the president, "Social Security and Unemployment Benefits Legislation," March 22, 1983, *Presidential Documents*, vol. 19, no. 12, March 28, 1983, 439.
59. Valis, August interview.
60. Ibid.
61. Eidenberg interview.

12. THE PRESIDENCY AND
THE POLITICAL PARTIES

Roger G. Brown

To the casual observer, presidents and political parties seem inextricably joined as institutions in the American governmental process. One of the first clues offered the electorate about a prospective president's political identity is his party affiliation. Many voters will decide whether to give or withhold support for that candidate primarily on the basis of his party label. Candidates and parties join forces to seek the nation's highest electoral prize, and a party can have no more tangible evidence of its strength and its correct interpretation of the popular will than to have its banner carried victoriously into the White House.

In spite of these seemingly natural and inescapable interdependencies, many analysts have portrayed deep estrangement between party organizations and their nominal chief, the president. In 1980, a leading text proclaimed, "No president is an effective party leader." [1] Such appraisals stem in part from long-established peculiarities in the American system such as the constitutional provisions for a separation of powers and a decentralized federal structure. In addition, our political culture has included a deep mistrust of political organizations of any kind. These inherent obstacles to a close president-party relationship have been greatly exacerbated by a number of relatively recent developments. The increased use of presidential primaries, larger White House staffs, instant presidential access to the electronic media, and independent sources of campaign financing have made presidents both less indebted and less accountable to their parties.

Nevertheless, once in office a president must rely on his party for a dependable source of support in an increasingly fragmented and unpredictable political environment. Presidents also look to party label as one indicator of the policy or philosophical biases of executive and judicial appointees. Chief executives hope, of course, that by appointing fellow party members they can expect an additional measure of loyalty to the administration on the part of those who are chosen.

Besides serving as a support group for the president, a political party is one of the primary links between the voters and the White House. It thus offers an opportunity to impose a measure of control and accountability on one of the most powerful forces in our governing system—the presidency. So the public, too, has a stake in a strong relationship between presidents and their parties.

American presidents and their party organizations are not married in a state of blissful harmony; areas of tension are plentiful and significant. But some important ties between the two institutions are inescapable. This chapter examines many of the reasons why recent presidents have depended less on party organizations for both winning and managing the presidency. The ties that continue to bind presidents to their political parties are then described.

Weaknesses of the American Party System

Historical weaknesses in the American party system are in large part a reflection of our institutional underpinnings and political culture. The framers of the Constitution deliberately sought to preclude a centralized and cohesive government, which they feared would serve as a vehicle for the very oppression against which they had so recently revolted. Their devices for preventing such concentrations of governmental power were the creation of separate branches that could check and balance each other and the further dispersion of authority among levels of government in a federal system.

The semi-autonomy of the executive and legislative branches of the federal government has presented the greatest obstacle to effective party leadership by the president. Unlike a British-style parliamentary system in which the prime minister is creature, then master, of the legislative party, the American chief executive has severely limited means for imposing his will on members of his party in Congress. Not only do the president and the legislators answer to entirely different constituencies, but the president also lacks meaningful sanctions or rewards with which to control the behavior of individual members.

Presidential coattails, for instance, have been shown to have little effect on the election of most members of Congress.[2] Thus the president has difficulty in commanding party loyalty on the basis of his vote-getting power at the head of the ticket. The president also has no direct control over the selection of his party's leaders in Congress, and most presidents would be reluctant to become involved in such heated intraparty struggles even if they could. In addition, patronage appointments, which can serve as bargaining chips to entice or reward congressional party members' loyalty to the administration, have become more scarce in an era of expanded civil service protections and increased emphasis on merit hiring and professionalism in government service. Therefore, American presidents cannot look to their parties in Congress for dependable support, even when theirs is the majority party.

Members of the president's party in the executive branch often have different goals, priorities, and agendas from those of the congressional party. This is the central dilemma of one subdivision of the party system, the so-called *party in the government*.[3] Each of the other two segments of the party, the *party organizations* and the *party in the electorate*, presents a different set of problems to the president as he attempts to exercise party leadership.

Federal, state, and local divisions in our formal governing institutions are mirrored in the party organizations. Unlike government, however, organizational strength traditionally has flowed upward in the party system, from relatively strong urban and state party committees to weaker, intermittently active national party committees. Presidential control over such a system is tenuous. The state and local party organizations are outside the president's sphere of direct authority, and the national party committees are not sufficiently powerful to enforce the president's wishes on the lower levels. Besides those handicaps, there are wings, factions, and splinter groups within the party organizations at all levels. The notion of political party organizations as strictly responsible to the president is not, and never has been, a reality in the American system.

These structural difficulties in the party organizations and the party in the government are complicated further by a deep-seated cultural aversion to partisan organizations within the voting public. Role models for such distrust include two of our most revered forebears, George Washington and James Madison. Madison issued his famous caveat against the divisiveness of factions in Number 10 of *The Federalist*, while Washington devoted much of his farewell address to the nation to "an extended and concentrated counterblast against parties." [4]

No sooner had political parties attained their zenith of organizational strength and governmental influence at the end of the nineteenth century than our antiparty heritage flowered again into a sweeping reform movement aimed at wresting political control from entrenched party "machines."[5] In recent years other reforms to increase participation and responsiveness in our electoral and governing processes have made the American party system even less cohesive and more difficult for the president to head. Many of the changes in the party system from 1960 to the present, a period of broad-ranging political and technological transformations, have altered, perhaps permanently, the relationship between presidents and their parties.

An Apartisan Presidency?

Political parties have been less useful to presidents in recent decades because of a host of systemic changes that have affected the three components of the party system: party in the government, party organizations, and party in the electorate. As a consequence, institutional adjustments have occurred as presidents have sought alternative means to perform functions formerly left to the political party.

Changes in the Electoral Party

The mass base of the party, or the party in the electorate, has shrunk in proportion to the total number of eligible voters. In 1960, 73 percent of voters identified themselves as members of one of the two major parties.[6] Another 15 percent described themselves as independents who "leaned" toward one of the major parties. Only 8 percent of eligible voters were pure independents, while the remaining 4 percent considered themselves apolitical. By 1980 the percentages had changed as follows: 63.5 percent were members of a major party, independent leaners made up 21 percent, and pure independents had increased to 13 percent of total voters.

A closer look at these figures shows that those who considered themselves strong Democrats decreased from 21 percent in 1960 to 18 percent in 1980. The percentage of strong Republicans declined even further, from 14 percent in 1960 to 8.5 percent in 1980. Independent voters of all types represented the biggest change, increasing from 23 percent in 1960 to 34 percent in 1980. Clearly, presidential candidates and incumbents no longer can rely as heavily on party label as an attraction for prospective voters or for popular support for their programs. Instead, they must use campaign themes and issues that appear to cut across party lines and thus attract those voters who do not support any party.

Besides the decline in the party in the electorate, the formal party organizations also have lost strength during the last quarter-century. Many of the functions that once defined the very existence of those organizations have been displaced. These functions include candidate recruitment and selection, voter education and mobilization, campaign financing, and liaison between the White House and specialized groups throughout society.

Primary Elections

The recruitment and selection of candidates for office has always been considered an important task of parties. But national nominating conventions, once decisive in the choice of the presidential nominee, have become anticlimactic exercises. In their place are dozens of state primary elections, which have the cumulative effect of removing candidate recruitment and selection from the control of party organizations. Such a nominating system can produce presidential candidates with little incentive to maintain close ties to a party organization, a point best illustrated by the 1976 nomination of Jimmy Carter. According to Walter Dean Burnham, a leading student of political parties, Carter's extraparty campaign may have signaled "the final liberation of the presidency from all organized coalitions or other external constraints," especially political parties.[7]

Vigorous debate continues over the relative merits of presidential primaries and old-style nominating conventions run by party professionals. Reform-minded proponents of primaries argue that presidential nominations have been wrested from the grasp of a powerful, entrenched elite and made more responsive to the popular will.[8] Opponents of the proliferating primary elections counter that the essential institution of party has been drastically weakened, thereby contributing to fragmentation and incoherence in the broader political system.[9] It appears likely, however, that primaries will remain a substantial part of the presidential selection process.

Campaign Finance Reforms

Public financing of presidential campaigns is another election reform that has weakened the ties between the presidency and the parties. In 1971 Congress passed the Federal Election Campaign Act, which together with its subsequent amendments provided federal funds for qualified presidential candidates. The act limits candidates who accept federal funds to specified spending ceilings. For example, Ronald Reagan and Jimmy Carter each were limited in the 1980 campaign to expenditures of $14.7 million in the primaries and $29.4 million in the general election.[10]

Party scholar Austin Ranney has argued that public financing weakens organized parties by giving federal funds directly to candidates rather than to their parties.[11] This allows a candidate to ignore the party as a source of campaign management and adds to the distance between the prospective president and his party's organization.

Electronic Media

The nearly universal reliance on television by presidential candidates and incumbent presidents has further displaced party organizations from their former jobs of soliciting votes, mobilizing public support for programs, and simply attempting to project a particular presidential image. An army of party volunteers sporting buttons and waving campaign pamphlets cannot compete with a 30-second spot on prime-time TV.

Radio and television have been part of presidential politics for more than three decades, but the debates between John F. Kennedy and Richard Nixon in 1960 marked a sea change in the relationship between presidents and television. According to some estimates, nine out of ten adult viewers saw at least one of the Kennedy-Nixon debates. It is not at all surprising in light of such statistics that television campaigning soon became a necessity for every serious presidential candidate. Theodore White summed up the implications for party organizations: "The parties no longer controlled loyalties as they once had; the parties no longer delivered responses as they once had. . . . The stage of politics was changing as television became its most important platform of action." [12]

Once in office, the president has virtually unlimited access to the broadcast media. Skill in using this powerful tool of persuasion has become one of the more important attributes required for presidential success. However, such a visible national forum is a risky place for a president to make overly partisan appeals or to allow his party's symbols to override his image as the representative of all Americans. Therefore, televised presentations by the president are often scrubbed clean of overt attempts to bolster a party's fortunes.

White House Staffs

Party organizations have been weakened not only by primaries, public campaign financing, and the constant use of electronic media, but also by larger White House staffs that oversee many functions formerly performed by party officials. The distribution of patronage jobs, liaison with members of the president's party in Congress, and relations with groups ranging from women and minorities to environmentalists and chambers of commerce are among the tasks party organizations have relinquished to the expanded network of presidential aides. Although party officials continue to exert influence in all of these areas, their presence today is a mere shadow of the central role played by former party chiefs such as James Farley, Democratic National Chairman and long-time adviser to President Franklin D. Roosevelt. During Roosevelt's first two terms, Farley helped to distribute tens of thousands of government jobs to fellow Democrats, shepherded congressional votes for New Deal programs, and kept White House lines of communication open to groups throughout society. In recent administrations, the job of advising the president on personnel appointments in the executive and judicial branches has been done chiefly by White House staff members instead of by the national party chairperson. Many of those White House advisers—Lawrence O'Brien in the Kennedy administration and James Baker and Lyn Nofziger in the Reagan administration, for example—had longtime associations with the regular party organizations. They maintained those ties by consulting party leaders in the organizations and in Congress as they sought top-level appointees to the administration. Others, such as John Ehrlichman in the Nixon White House and Carter adviser Hamilton Jordan, had no strong ties to the party leadership and paid much less attention to the advice of party regulars on personnel selection.

Since 1960 White House officials have taken other important functions from party organizations in addition to appointments. Among them are liaison with the president's party in Congress and the maintenance of relations between the administration and important interest groups.

During the Kennedy and Johnson years, political adviser Larry O'Brien developed a highly effective Office of Congressional Relations in the White House. Since then, this office has performed tasks that once were part of the job description of the national party chairperson. The tasks include monitoring White House relations with individual representatives and senators, handling requests for patronage appointments, and providing information to members of Congress about administration-sponsored bills, construction projects, and presidential trips affecting their state or district.

The enlarged White House establishment also has assumed many of the party organizations' liaison duties with interest groups. National party committees traditionally have included divisions that deal with women's groups, labor, agriculture, and racial and ethnic minorities. Today, however, the White House Office of Public Liaison maintains communications with all those groups, as well as with consumers, environmentalists, the aged, cultural groups, and youth organizations, to name a few. The presidency, once the institution with ostensibly the best vantage point for viewing the broad national interest, has become in part a clearinghouse for the divergent demands of special interests.

Reluctant Presidential Leadership

Among the obstacles to a close relationship between presidents and their parties are presidents themselves. Recent presidents have shown little desire to have party organizations strengthen their influence in politics or governance. The same party network that can provide support and communications channels for the president also can act as a constraining force if party leaders choose to dissent from administration policies. For example, growing criticism from within their respective parties signaled the beginning of the end for both Lyndon B. Johnson and Richard Nixon when they found themselves entangled in the Vietnam War and in the Watergate scandal.

Presidents and Parties: The Ties That Bind

Even in the age of personal campaign organizations, mass media, and nonparty funding, party support remains a prerequisite for electoral success. The president, in Woodrow Wilson's words, "is at once the choice of a party and of the nation." [13] The absence of party backing can thwart the aims even of incumbent candidates. The reelection efforts of Gerald Ford and Jimmy Carter fell victim, not only to an unconvinced electorate, but also to party organizations whose undivided loyalties they could not command. Presidents have been forced to court these organizations simply to win and keep their positions.

Political exigencies and other role demands make vigorous party leadership a precarious venture for presidents once in office. Nevertheless, no president can conveniently ignore the responsibility. His organizational duties begin as soon as he is nominated at the national convention. By naming the national chairperson, the president determines the tone and direction of the national committee and establishes a link between his administration and party organizations nationwide.

National Party Organizations

In recent years the party chair has not been the essential political adviser that earlier party heads had been. Nevertheless, even President Carter, an outsider to party channels, found it necessary to make at least nominal efforts to communicate with national and state party organizations through Democratic National Chairman John White. According to one close observer of national party affairs, White, although not part of the inner circle of Carter assistants, was a regular participant in White House discussions of the domestic political environment.[14]

President Reagan demonstrated his active concern for close relations with the national Republican organization in 1982 when he selected his personal friend Sen. Paul Laxalt as general chairman of the GOP. Reagan's choice represented a break with recent trends in relations between the White House and the national party leadership. Presidents since Harry S. Truman have tended to choose national party chairpersons to mend fences with competing factions of the party or to reward political allies who were instrumental in securing the nomination. Thus, Democratic chairman John Bailey during the Kennedy and Johnson administrations, Republican chiefs George Bush and Robert Dole during the Nixon years, Republican National Committee chair Mary Louise Smith, who was chosen by Gerald Ford, and Kenneth Curtis and John White, Jimmy Carter's choices, all lacked the open access and important advisory roles of earlier national chairpersons. However, Laxalt, a former Nevada governor and longtime adviser to Reagan, brought to his job as head of the national party the advantage of being an administration insider. Furthermore, President Reagan proposed a new role for Laxalt as general chairman of the GOP, which would allow him to coordinate the activities of the Republican National Committee, the Republican campaign committees in Congress, and the reelection attempt by Reagan, if he chose to run in 1984. (The traditional post of Republican National Committee chair was given to Frank Fahrenkopf, former chairman of the Nevada Republican party.) Laxalt's high standing with the Reagan administration could pave the way for closer relations between the White House and the national party organizations than had been possible under many of his predecessors.

The desire to influence party leadership has led some recent presidents to intervene directly in party disputes at the state level. Both Presidents Kennedy and Johnson became involved in the bitter struggle between the vestiges of the Tammany Hall machine and New York's party reformers. Both also were drawn into intraparty battles in Texas. More commonly, presidents have influenced party politics by recruiting or endorsing candidates in state and local elections. Following Chicago Mayor Jane Byrne's unexpected defeat in the 1983 Democratic mayoral primary, the Reagan administration reportedly offered her its support if she would run as a Republican candidate in the city's general election.[15]

The Reagan administration also took the unusual step of privately indicating a preference in the struggle for leadership of the Republican Senatorial Campaign Committee in 1982. White House opposition to the incumbent chairman, Sen. Robert Packwood of Oregon, came after Packwood accused the president of turning the Republican party into "an assemblage of white males over 40." [16] According to the *New York Times,* the president encouraged Sen. Richard Lugar of Indiana to challenge Packwood for the job and let it be known that he would feel more comfortable with Lugar in charge of the campaign committee in 1984, when 19 Republican senators would be up for reelection.[17] Presidential adviser Laxalt nominated Lugar and worked for him within the Senate.

Packwood apparently lost the contest because his Republican colleagues thought that he had used the chairmanship to heighten his own political visibility and that his six years in the job were more than enough.[18] But Reagan's behind-the-scenes support for Lugar underscored emphatically the White House perception that workable ties must be maintained with party organizations inside the government as well as outside it. Furthermore, it was an unusually clear attempt by the president to enforce a unified point of view among Republican leaders in Congress.

Presidential Appointments

Despite the lessened influence of party organizations in the appointments process, all recent presidents have staffed both their administrations and the federal courts overwhelmingly from the ranks of their own parties. Table 12-1 shows the percentages of top-level appointees to the executive branch since 1961 who have shared the party affiliation of the president who hired them. Only 3 to 11 percent of the positions of authority in these administrations were filled by members of the opposition party. Those who were appointed, such as Democrats Jeane Kirkpatrick and Eugene Rostow—Reagan appointees to the United Nations and the Arms Control and Disarmament Agency, respectively—were likely to be "friendly Indians." [19] In other words, their policy views were thought to be in essential agreement with those of the president, in spite of their different party labels.

Unlike traditional patronage appointments to bolster party organizations and reward loyal party workers, most partisan appointments

Table 12-1 Distribution of Party Affiliation Among Presiden-tial Appointees, 1961-1982

Administration	Number of Appointees	Percent from President's Party	Percent from Opposition Party	Percent/Un-affiliated
Kennedy	430	63	10	27
Johnson	524	47	11	42
Nixon	737	65	8	27
Ford	293	56	8	36
Carter (1977-78)	402	58	7	35
Reagan (1981-82)	379	83	3	14

NOTE: Major appointments as listed by the *Congressional Quarterly Almanac* include cabinet, subcabinet, and lower policy-level positions in the executive branch, including ambassadorships and positions on various boards and commissions. In the case of some positions, particularly those on independent regulatory commissions, the ratio of party affiliation among appointees is legislatively prescribed. Therefore, those cases were not included in the annual totals. The *CQ Almanac* indicates the party affiliation for every appointee for whom that information is available. When not listed or listed as "independent," the appointee's affiliation was included here as "unaffiliated." Less than 2 percent of these appointees identified themselves as independent.

   CQ Almanac lists of major presidential appointees confirmed during 1979 and 1980 contained a high proportion of names for whom no information on party affiliation was made available by the Carter administration. In 1979, out of a total of 256 appointees listed, only 48 were assigned a party affiliation. For 1980, only 22 of 148 listings included this information.

SOURCE: Listings of confirmed presidential appointees in the *Congressional Quarterly Almanac* (Washington, D.C.: Congressional Quarterly, 1961-1982), vols. 17-37, and listings in *Congressional Quarterly Weekly Report*, January-December 1982.

by recent presidents reflect more personal political motives. Shared party affiliation continues to serve as a symbolic source of kinship between the president and the appointees, who he hopes will interpret his will to the permanent bureaucracy. Republican presidents, for example, have tended to identify career bureaucrats with the Democratic party and have felt compelled to counterbalance them with Republican political appointees.[20] A related and more substantive reason for appointments from the president's party is that party label provides one indicator of the appointee's policy bias. Presidents and their personnel advisers reasonably expect to find more agreement on broad questions of policy among fellow party members than among other similarly qualified candidates.

   Appointments to the federal judiciary are still among the richest patronage plums available to the president. These prestigious lifetime positions can be used as bargaining chips to secure the support of party

Table 12-2 Distribution of Party Affiliation Among Presidential Appointees to the Federal Judiciary, 1961-1982

Administration	Number of Appointees	Percent from President's Party	Percent from Opposition Party	Percent/Un-affiliated
Kennedy	152	90	7	3
Johnson	175	84	4	12
Nixon	237	86	7	7
Ford	68	92	19	0
Carter (1977-78)	77	79	3	18
Reagan (1981-82)	106	65	1	35

NOTE: Because the *Congressional Quarterly Almanac* listings of confirmed nominees to the federal judiciary include many names for whom no party affiliation was ascertained, the percentages of appointees from the president's party shown here are likely to be lower than the actual percentages. In the case of President Carter, for example, he actually appointed Democrats to 95 percent of the judicial posts filled through August 1978, according to Steven A. Shull, *Presidential Policy Making* (Brunswick, Ohio: King's Court Communications, 1979), 153. If we exclude the Reagan judicial appointees in 1981 and 1982 whose party affiliations were not identified, the percentage of Republican judges would also be more than 95 percent.

SOURCE: Listings of confirmed presidential appointees in the *Congressional Quarterly Almanac* (Washington, D.C.: Congressional Quarterly, 1961-1982), vols. 17-37, and listings in *Congressional Quarterly Weekly Report*, January-December 1982.

organizations or members of Congress. As shown in Table 12-2, presidents during the last two decades have continued to fill the supposedly nonpolitical judiciary with fellow party members.

Campaigning and Fund Raising

As midterm campaigner and fund-raiser for his party's organizations and candidates, the president makes his most visible and tangible contribution to their welfare. Although such duties have been undertaken with a reluctance that sometimes borders on open disgust, all recent presidents have performed them to greater or lesser degree. John F. Kennedy spoke at eight party fund-raising dinners in the first year alone. Lyndon Johnson grudgingly made similar appearances, but he complained that these political obligations were personally distasteful and demeaning to the office.[21] Gerald Ford spoke proudly of his success at raising money for Republican organizations at the national, state, and local levels. Remarking that he had raised more than $2 million at rallies and dinners in 1974 and 1975, Ford explained that he felt an "obligation to try and strengthen and rebuild the Republican Party organization." [22] President Reagan brought high technology to the fund-raising process, using closed circuit and satellite transmission hookups to speak to Republican rallies all over the country simultaneously.

The results of midterm congressional campaigns are influenced by many factors, among them the president's rating in public opinion polls, the state of the nation's economy, and the amount of campaign money spent by each party. These variables, however, rarely alter one very predictable midterm result: the president's party loses seats in the House of Representatives. This has happened in every midterm election this century, except for the one in 1934. The losses have been as high as 70 seats in 1938 and as low as 5 seats in 1962. Recent presidents have become more active on behalf of their party's congressional candidates in an effort to minimize these midterm losses. They also hope that successful candidates will return the favor and side with the administration in future legislative battles.

The actual effects of presidential involvement in individual congressional races are very difficult to gauge. Most congressional campaigns hinge on local issues, whether an incumbent is running, and whether the challenger's face and name are familiar to voters. Some candidates prefer not to have the president and his record become an issue in their campaigns because they fear to be associated with unpopular administration policies. Nevertheless, most party leaders in and out of government continue to expect presidents to lead their congressional party into midterm combat. Many candidates view the prestige of the White House as a highly desirable campaign aid. If elected, these candidates are very likely to remember the president's help when they are asked to consider an administration proposal in Congress.

More significantly, the president's value as a fund-raiser is nothing short of essential to party organizations, which increasingly have lost ground in their efforts to raise money because of competition from a myriad of special interest groups, political action committees, and independent candidate organizations. The aphorism that money greases the wheels of politics has never been more true than at present, and without the president's fund-raising assistance, party organizations would be substantially weaker cogs in the political mechanism.

Presidents as Symbols of Party

The president's importance to political parties is symbolic as well as substantive. The president is the highly visible embodiment of his party. According to Frank Sorauf:

> The successes and failures of executives are party successes and
> failures; their imaginativeness and vigor are the party's. . . . They
> can choose not to lead their party organizations, not to lead their
> party in the legislature, not to intervene in local or congressional
> elections, or not to cater to their special constituency—but they
> cannot avoid their symbolic impact on their parties.[23]

The symbolic connection between presidents and parties operates
two ways: the president serves as a prestigious and powerful titular
figure for his party, and the party enables the president to share the
mythology and symbolism of its traditions. Few, if any, recent
Republican presidents have missed an opportunity to invoke the name
of Abraham Lincoln as their party's founder or of Dwight Eisenhower,
the respected soldier-statesman. Democratic candidates and presidents
can solemnly cloak themselves with the memories of Thomas Jefferson,
Woodrow Wilson, Franklin D. Roosevelt, or the martyred John F.
Kennedy, as if to suggest that their party's name might confer similar
wisdom or greatness on them. In his nomination acceptance speech at
the 1976 Democratic convention, Jimmy Carter intoned the names of
Wilson, Roosevelt, Truman, Kennedy, and Johnson in a manner
befitting a pantheon of political demigods. Thus, while the president
may lend material support to his party, his symbolic embodiment of it
may be the most important—and most inescapable—facet of his
leadership role.

Presidential Attitudes

The differing attitudes of recent presidents toward party organizations can be explained in part by their personal backgrounds and
previous political experiences. Before their accession to the presidency,
some chief executives, notably Kennedy and Ford, came to view parties
as useful and essential governing agents. Once in office, when other
political considerations permitted, they pursued the duties of party
leadership vigorously. On the other hand, presidents whose backgrounds had engendered negative attitudes toward party organizations
were reluctant to assume the responsibilities of active party leadership
as president. Dwight Eisenhower and Jimmy Carter are examples of
this phenomenon.

Both Kennedy and Ford achieved their political successes by
working with their respective party organizations. Kennedy's father,
Joseph Kennedy, Sr., was a strong financial supporter of the Demo-

cratic party and was rewarded by Franklin D. Roosevelt with an ambassadorship. Although he was regarded as something of an outsider by the old pols of the Massachusetts Democratic establishment, John Kennedy still considered himself a "partisan Democrat." [24] During the first year of his presidency he commented on the value of party organizations:

> I believe in strong political organizations in our country.... The party is the means by which programs can be put into action—the means by which people of talent can come to the service of the country. And in this great free society of ours, both of our parties ... serve the interests of the people.[25]

Gerald Ford's commitment to help rebuild the Republican organizations after the debilitating Watergate disclosures already has been mentioned. Ford had been a well-respected workhorse for his party in Congress for many years. In the White House his loyalty to the Republican party and its organizations was never questioned.

In sharp contrast, Eisenhower and Carter, widely regarded as outsiders by party regulars, were openly disdainful of the duties of party leadership. President Eisenhower's sense of himself as a basically apolitical military hero has been contrasted with Kennedy's self-image by political scientist Samuel Eldersveld: "Obviously these two presidents saw their 'party political' and 'politics' role differently. Kennedy saw himself as the party leader; Eisenhower shrank from that image." [26]

Throughout his career in state politics, Jimmy Carter had frequent and bitter skirmishes with the Georgia Democratic party. In his campaign autobiography he was contemptuous of entrenched, special interest elites disguised as political parties.[27] His attitudes accompanied him into the Oval Office, where he was frequently criticized for failing to support and sustain the Democratic party and its traditions. Thus, the attitudes and values of presidents can exert a powerful influence on the vigor with which they pursue the duties of party leadership.

Prospects for Party Renewal

The future of party organizations and presidential leadership of them has become the subject of a vigorous debate among scholars, journalists, and political professionals. For more than a decade, the opinion has prevailed that American parties are in a serious, perhaps irremediable, decline.[28] Many of the reasons adduced for the weakening of an already weak party system have been discussed: fewer party identifiers among voters, greater reliance on television for voter education and campaign announcements, larger White House staffs that have taken over party functions, and legal reforms such as primaries and nonparty financing that have had strong, apartisan influences on elections. Some scholars have argued that lamentations over the weakened state of party affairs are symptomatic of rose-colored nostalgia. According to Michael Nelson, "The good old days of party politics embody the quality of most good old days: they just weren't that good." [29] The old, pre-reform party procedures did not produce better candidates or lead to more effective and responsive government, according to this view.

Other scholars, however, point to nascent signs on the political horizon that party organizations are not declining in influence but broadening their base of support. Proponents of strong political parties have reason to be optimistic, according to Cornelius Cotter and John Bibby in their study of recent developments in the national party committees:

> While the presidential campaign role of the national commit-tees has been receding, the committees have expanded their non-presidential activities. For example, both the DNC and the RNC have become increasingly involved in midterm and special congres-sional elections, and the RNC under former national chairman Bill Brock has become heavily involved in state and even local election campaigns. . . . As the national committees move to regionalize their offices, maintain staff in the field, and provide services to state party organizations, it is likely that they will develop a firmer base of grass-roots support. [30]

New Technologies

Other developments signal a revival of political parties. Party organizations now seem to be profiting from the very sources of their widely reported decline. The new technologies of direct mail, mass media, and custom-designed telecommunications networks, which threatened to turn parties into political dinosaurs, are being used to expand and strengthen their financial bases and communications channels. Improved fund-raising techniques are particularly important.

The Republican National Committee, which traditionally has been better financed than its Democratic counterpart, has become so successful at computerized, direct-mail fund raising that the Demo-cratic organizations are openly emulating it. So marked are trends in this direction for both parties that F. Christopher Arterton has likened the national party committees to "super PACs." He also argues that the 1979 amendments to the Federal Election Campaign Act of 1971 may aid party committees since they limit contributions to, and expenditures by, candidate committees.[31]

New technology has offered party organizations more than increased efficiency in fund raising. Closer ties among party levels and divisions are enhanced by communication links between Washington and every other party office in the country. According to a report by scholars, party officials, journalists, and others attending the 1982 American Assembly at Columbia University, through the use of "comparatively inexpensive satellite link-ups, tele-conferencing, and various forms of television, party organizations can be systematically activated, stimulated, nourished, and sustained."[32] Thus, party organizations may not wither in the face of the technological revolution. The new capabilities are well suited to the modern mass-based parties that have replaced, possibly forever, yesterday's closed, smoke-filled caucus rooms.

Moderation of Reforms

Not only have parties begun to harness the electronic marvels that once seemed destined to render them obsolete, but they have changed many of the legal reforms of the 1970s, considered by some as the true harbingers of doom for party organizations. The intent of these recent reappraisals was to restore to party officials and elected leaders some of the control they lost in the rush to open conventions and other selection processes to the mass electorate. This was the intent of the rules changes by the Democratic party for the 1984 presidential nominating process, which are discussed in Chapter 7.

The nomination of Jimmy Carter in 1976 convinced many proponents of stronger parties that the nominating system no longer favored candidates who were recruited and supported by regular party organizations. After the 1980 election, the Democratic National Committee appointed North Carolina Gov. James B. Hunt to chair another in the succession of commissions dealing with presidential selection. The Hunt Commission recommended, and the party's midterm convention agreed, that a large group of delegates to the 1984 national convention should be made up of party officials and elected Democrats. These delegates will go to the convention formally uncommitted to any candidate, thus increasing the organized party's leverage on the final nominating decision.

Ideological Parties

According to some observers, increased organizational strength is not the only evidence of party renewal. They also have detected a greater sense of ideological definition in party rhetoric and actions. James Sundquist has argued that the internal philosophical diversity that at times has made the major parties difficult to distinguish from one another is decreasing. Regional migrations have made both parties "more homogeneous across the country. . . . The basis for ideological national parties, then, exists." [33] Well-informed, issue-oriented voters who have abandoned party identification as a meaningless label may be attracted by more ideological parties.

The parties' 1982 televised campaign ads reveal a new emphasis on ideological themes. According to political analyst Ben Wattenberg, "These commercials represent something new in American politics: public connection between party and substance." [34] Wattenberg pointed to the emphasis on "institutional advertising," which promoted the Democratic and Republican parties rather than candidate images. He concluded that such advertising "ends up also linking candidates to the themes of their party. As party-based TV grows, it becomes more difficult for a candidate to ignore his party's stance." [35]

In sum, although the preponderance of evidence is on the side of continuing party weakness, the debate over the future of political parties has been joined by academics, political journalists, and party professionals who believe that reports of the death of the American party system were greatly exaggerated. They claim that the parties' vital signs—organizational cohesion, financial health, and ideological stirrings—are becoming stronger. It will be some time before either side of this scholarly exchange can fully substantiate its arguments. Meanwhile, another question must be considered: Are closer ties between parties and the presidency desirable, either for those institutions or for the public?

Presidents, Parties, and the Public: Mutual Benefits

Political parties have much to gain from closer ties with the presidents who carry their banners: prestigious jobs in the administration for their members, help in building party treasuries, White House backing in campaign efforts, and symbolic recognition from the nation's highest office. The national parties have survived the increased distance between them and recent presidents, but they would have fared better with a congenial working relationship. After all, in a loosely federated party system, the presidency serves as the unifying institution.

Although a president may view his party as a source of annoying criticism and tedious demands, it is often the last vestige of solid support in times of political need. Most recent presidents, especially Richard Nixon in 1973 and 1974 and Jimmy Carter in 1979 and 1980, have found themselves in periods of desperate political trouble with only friends, family, and the core of party supporters to defend them from their critics. Gary Orren describes the importance to a president of the party faithful: "A President who must depend overwhelmingly on his personal image to sustain himself, who cannot count on the obligations of party elites to support him, is an isolated and vulnerable leader." [36] In recent decades the presidency has faced uncooperative or hostile audiences: a more aggressive press, a more independent Congress, and a multitude of hard-to-please single interest groups. One source of dependable support, although not always given unconditionally, has been the president's political party.

Parties provide more than moral support to the president. Their organizational networks can be used to mount campaign efforts or mobilize grass-roots and elite support for administration proposals. The fund-raising assistance the president is able to offer his party often is reciprocated: much of the national party machinery is geared for raising money to be spent on the election of the party's presidential nominee. Presidents have always had their difficulties with party organizations, but, as Thomas E. Cronin has pointed out, "Many historians and political scientists hold that the effective presidents have been those who have, like Jackson, strengthened their position by becoming strong party leaders." [37]

The possibilities for mutual campaign aid, mutual fund-raising assistance, and mutual symbolic support mean that both presidents and parties would profit from a closer working relationship. But what is the public's stake in such a partnership? After all, Americans view political organizations and particularly partisan politics with a good deal of skepticism. Few citizens would support a president who appeared interested only in his party's welfare to the exclusion of a consideration of the commonweal.

The fear of an imperial presidency, which surfaced during the Johnson and Nixon administrations, brought to the fore another important public consideration. A party organization with close connections to the White House can serve as a constraint to keep an administration from losing touch with public opinion or with political probity. For example, the excesses of the Nixon administration that led to the break-in of Democratic national headquarters at the Watergate office building in Washington, D.C., may never have occurred if Nixon's 1972 reelection campaign had been in the hands of the Republican National Committee. The Committee to Reelect the President (CREEP) was an ad hoc group assembled for the sole purpose of helping Richard Nixon retain the presidency. By contrast, the RNC presumably would not have gambled its future on the ill-conceived cover-ups that became Nixon's ultimate undoing. From this perspective, the public would profit from a strong party presence in administration circles as a possible check on the abuse of presidential power.

An overarching public concern, of course, is for effective, coherent management of the government's business. Such a goal is considerably enhanced when the president commits time and resources to working closely with his party's establishment. Within this relationship lies the nexus between the presidency, the elective office most ideally situated to represent the national interest, and the political party, the only broad-based institution that can effectively bridge the gulf between the people and their government.

NOTES

1. Richard M. Pious, *The American Presidency* (New York: Basic Books, 1979), 121.
2. George C. Edwards III, *Presidential Influence in Congress* (San Francisco: W. H. Freeman & Co., 1980), 70-78.
3. Frank J. Sorauf, *Party Politics in America,* 4th ed. (Boston: Little, Brown & Co., 1980), 8-10.
4. Richard Hofstadter, *The Idea of a Party System* (Berkeley: University of California Press, 1969), 97.
5. Richard Hofstadter, *The Age of Reform: From Bryan to F.D.R.* (New York: Vintage Books, 1955).
6. Samuel J. Eldersveld, *Political Parties in American Society* (New York: Basic Books, 1982), 76.
7. Walter Dean Burnham, "Jimmy Carter and the Democratic Crisis," *The New Republic,* July 3 and 10, 1976, 17-19.
8. Michael Nelson, "Two Cheers for the National Primary," in *Rethinking the Presidency,* ed. Thomas E. Cronin (Boston: Little, Brown & Co., 1982), 55-64; and William J. Crotty, "Two Cheers for the Presidential Primaries," in *Rethinking the Presidency,* ed. Cronin, 65-71.
9. James W. Ceaser, *Reforming the Reforms: A Critical Analysis of the Presidential Selection Process* (Cambridge, Mass.: Ballinger Publishing Co., 1982).
10. Data provided by the Federal Election Commission.

11. Austin Ranney, "The Political Parties: Reform and Decline," in *The New American Political System*, ed. Anthony King (Washington, D.C.: American Enterprise Institute for Public Policy Research, 1978), 213-247.
12. Theodore H. White, *The Making of the President, 1972* (New York: Atheneum Publishers, 1973), xviii.
13. Woodrow Wilson, *Constitutional Government in the United States* (New York: Columbia University Press, 1908), 67.
14. Vera Murray, confidential assistant to former Democratic National Chairman Robert Strauss, interview with author, February 13, 1981, Washington, D.C.
15. Lou Cannon, "Political Notes," *Washington Post*, March 11, 1983, A-4.
16. Mary McGrory, "More Mixed Signals," *Washington Post,* December 5, 1982, C-1.
17. Steven Roberts, "Packwood Loses Party Job in Senate," *New York Times,* December 3, 1982, A-19.
18. Ibid.
19. John Macy, interview with James Graham and Victor Kramer as part of the U.S. Senate study, *Appointments to the Regulatory Commissions* (Washington, D.C.: U.S. Government Printing Office, 1976).
20. Herbert Kaufman, "The Growth of the Federal Personnel Service," in *The Federal Government Service*, ed. Wallace Sayre (Englewood Cliffs, N.J.: Prentice-Hall, 1965), 49-50; and Richard P. Nathan, *The Plot That Failed: Nixon and the Administrative Presidency* (New York: John Wiley & Sons, 1975), 30-31, 45-54.
21. Joseph A. Califano, Jr., *A Presidential Nation* (New York: W. W. Norton & Co., 1975), 152.
22. *Presidency, 1975* (Washington, D.C.: Congressional Quarterly, 1976), 87-A.
23. Sorauf, *Party Politics in America*, 355.
24. David S. Broder, *The Party's Over: The Failure of Politics in America* (New York: Harper & Row, 1972), 23.
25. *Public Papers of the President: John F. Kennedy, 1961* (Washington, D.C.: U.S. Government Printing Office, 1962), 4.
26. Eldersveld, *Political Parties in American Society*, 373.
27. Jimmy Carter, *Why Not the Best?* (Nashville: Broadman Press, 1975).
28. See, for example, William J. Crotty and Gary C. Jacobson, *American Parties in Decline* (Boston: Little, Brown & Co., 1980); and Ranney, "Political Parties," in *The New American Political System*, ed. King.
29. Michael Nelson, "Sentimental Science: Recent Essays on the Politics of Presidential Selection," *Congress and the Presidency* 9 (Autumn 1982): 103.
30. Cornelius P. Cotter and John F. Bibby, "Institutional Development of Parties and the Thesis of Party Decline," *Political Science Quarterly* 95 (Spring 1980): 8-9.
31. F. Christopher Arterton, "Political Money and Party Strength," in *The Future of American Political Parties: The Challenge of Governance,* ed. Joel L. Fleishman (Englewood Cliffs, N.J.: Prentice-Hall, 1982), 135.
32. Final Report of the 62nd American Assembly, Columbia University, "The Future of American Political Parties" (New York: American Assembly, 1982), 9.
33. James L. Sundquist, "Party Decay and the Capacity to Govern," in *The Future of American Political Parties*, ed. Fleishman, 7-59.
34. Ben Wattenberg, "TV Ads: Reviving the Parties," *Washington Post*, September 29, 1982, A-24.
35. Ibid.

36. Gary R. Orren, "The Changing Styles of American Party Politics, in *The Future of American Politics,* ed. Fleishman, 41.
37. Thomas E. Cronin, "Presidents and Political Parties," in *Rethinking the Presidency,* ed. Cronin, 288.

Part V

PRESIDENTS AND POLITICS:
GOVERNMENTAL CONSTITUENCIES

The essays in Part II described three interrelated elements of presidential power: the constitutional presidency, the political environment in which the presidency functions, and the personal qualities, including political skills, that each president brings to the office. The essays in this part—"The Presidency and the Bureaucracy," by Francis E. Rourke, "The Presidency and Congress," by Roger H. Davidson, and "The Presidency and the Judiciary," by Robert Scigliano—each draw attention to one of these three elements as it affects the ability of presidents to lead the rest of the government.

In Chapter 13, Rourke places the accent on political skill in considering how presidents can lead the bureaucracy. Drawing primarily on his research into the administrations of Lyndon B. Johnson and Richard M. Nixon, Rourke describes three general strategies a president can use to control the bureaucracy, depending on how much he distrusts it: "1) he can fill the top echelon of executive organizations with political appointees that he hopes will share his values and protect his interests in agency decisions; 2) he can assign to the members of his White House staff the continuing task of monitoring the work of executive agencies; and 3) he can create organizational structures in the White House that will take the lead in areas of policy that are particularly important to him."

Although presidential leadership can have a real effect on executive agencies, presidents seldom turn the full force of their attention to the bureaucracy. The reason is that "presidents achieve fame for policy, not administration." [1] Because policy accomplishments are more likely to require the cooperation of Congress, that is where presidents tend to direct most of their efforts at skillful leadership. Yet as Roger H. Davidson indicates in Chapter 14, power elements other than skill seem to make the greatest difference in presidential leadership of Congress.

Davidson draws particular attention to the political environment, notably to three patterns of partisan control of the presidency and

Congress. From the president's standpoint, "party government" usually is the best arrangement because his political party controls both houses of Congress. A "truncated majority," in which the president's party controls only one house, and "divided government" (Congress is controlled by the other party) are the next best and least best patterns, respectively. But, Davidson shows, party government is neither a necessary condition for presidential leadership of Congress—witness President Ronald Reagan's success in leading a divided Congress—nor a sufficient one (witness the failure of Reagan's immediate predecessor, Jimmy Carter, with a Democratic Congress). Other conditions in the political environment—"high turnover on Capitol Hill, a landslide presidential election, a sense of national urgency"—also contribute to presidential leadership.

Even under the least favorable political conditions, of course, there is some sort of relationship between president and Congress—the Constitution's blending of the two branches' powers assures that. And when it comes to the presidency's relationship with the judiciary, Robert Scigliano argues in Chapter 15, the Constitution is perhaps the most important power element of all.

Certainly the framers intended it that way. Delegates to the Constitutional Convention feared legislative power and tried to encourage what Scigliano calls a "limited alliance" between the executive and the judiciary that would restrain it. In the framers' plan, "the hope was that these two 'weaker branches' would support each other against congressional encroachments on themselves and against legislative oppressions originating in the people." Through most of American history, the limited alliance seemed to hold.

The past half century, Scigliano shows, has been marked by greater conflict between the presidency and the judiciary, particularly the Supreme Court. But this may represent a fulfillment of the framers' real concern, which was that no one branch outstrip the others. In recent times, it has been the presidency whose power most often has seemed ascendant, and it should not surprise us that the modern judiciary has been more inclined to restrain presidential power than to buttress it.

NOTES

1. Erwin C. Hargrove, *The Power of the Modern Presidency* (New York: Alfred A. Knopf, 1974), 249.

13. THE PRESIDENCY AND THE BUREAUCRACY: STRATEGIC ALTERNATIVES

Francis E. Rourke

Increasingly prominent in American politics has been the struggle for control over national policy between the White House and the bureaucratic organizations that are nominally under its jurisdiction.[1] In a sense this is only a family squabble, since the participants are both parts of the executive branch of government. But the outcome of their disputes may significantly affect the direction and character of American public life. For it is certainly no less true today than it was in the nineteenth century that, as Henry Jones Ford wrote in 1898, "no vexed question is settled except by executive policy."[2]

The president commonly regards the executive apparatus he inherits when he takes office with nervous suspicion. This distrust is born of the belief that executive agencies see national problems not from the broad perspective that the White House fancies itself as taking but from a narrow outlook shaped by selfish organizational and professional interests. Every modern president has lived with the fear that the bureaucracy will cooperate only reluctantly with his administration's objectives and may even defy or sabotage its programs.

The White House thus sees bureaucracy as having formidable power in its own right. This power comes in large part from the expertise of executive agencies on which presidents frequently must rely for information and advice. Bureaucracies also provide the chief instruments through which most presidential policies and programs must be carried out. While a president may have many grand designs in mind when he is first elected, his success in office ultimately will turn on which of these schemes executive agencies are able to translate into concrete results.

Presidential dependence on bureaucracy goes far to explain why the White House is so often resentful of it. Such dependence helps to breed a sense of "victimization"—a feeling not infrequently expressed that the bureaucracy is as much a nuisance to the White House as it is to the country. Thus, many recent presidents—Ronald Reagan is a notable example—give the odd impression that the bureaucracy is the government, and that they are no less opposed to it than any other "right" thinking American citizen.

But the fact that a branch of government, which should in theory be the president's subordinate, so often seems to be his equal or even his superior is not the only reason why bureaucracy provokes so much "fear and loathing" in the White House. It is equally unsettling that executive agencies often seem joined in hostile conspiracy with interest groups or congressional committees that are bent on making life difficult for the president. From the White House perspective these alliances are chiefly designed to frustrate presidential objectives or to force the president to accept the continuance of programs he would like to see curtailed or abolished.

Thus the president may view the bureaucracy as an adversary with its own set of powers, a group of professionalized principalities that he must treat as equals or actually defer to in some cases. But, along with the apprehension this situation may arouse, the president also must consider that many executive agencies are in league with his opponents in the country at large or in Congress. Consequently, bureaucracies may be either themselves enemies of the president or, no less disturbing, closely allied with his enemies.

Conservative presidents are particularly incensed when executive agencies persist in carrying on activities for which the White House and its supporters no longer see any need. Liberal presidents are more likely to complain that bureaucrats are unwilling to step out in the bold new directions that the Oval Office would like the country to travel. Bureaucracy thus can be a source of trouble from the president's point of view either because of its activity or its inactivity.

Hence, a major task a president faces when he takes over the helm of government is to decide on the strategies he should follow in trying to control, or at least limit, the damage the bureaucracy can do to his administration. A number of alternatives are open to him in structuring his relationship with the bureaucracy, and the character and development of his presidency will be very much affected by the strategies he decides to follow and by the skill with which he implements his chosen course of action.

A president can take three general directions in his efforts to control the bureaucracy: 1) he can fill the top echelon of executive organizations with political appointees that he hopes will share his values and protect his interests in agency decisions; 2) he can assign to the members of his White House staff the continuing task of monitoring the work of executive agencies; and 3) he can create organizational structures in the White House that will take the lead in areas of policy that are particularly important to him.

This list of alternatives reflects an ascending order of distrust between the president and bureaucracy. The first strategy—relying on agency appointees to control bureaucracy—came very naturally to Dwight D. Eisenhower, who was fundamentally at ease with a bureaucratic system in which he had served so long. The second strategy of using White House staff members as presidential surrogates in dealing with bureaucracy reflects a heightened degree of concern about the loyalty of executive organizations to the White House. Although the bureaucracy's responsibility for handling government business is left intact, White House aides are charged to monitor the way in which it discharges this responsibility. Since World War II, the use of this method of controlling bureaucracy by the White House has increased steadily.

When the third strategy is employed, it sends a clear signal that presidential dissatisfaction with bureaucratic performance has increased substantially. White House staff organizations begin to play a leading role in policy development, initiating in some instances major changes in policy. Although this alternative has found its firmest institutional expression in the area of foreign affairs, it recently has become significant in the domestic policy process as well. In no presidency in modern times was greater use made of this strategy than during the Nixon administration.

None of these strategies provides the president with a foolproof course of action. Each can generate very severe problems for him—even a crisis in public confidence in his administration. Within any administration, there may be considerable uncertainty as to which is the appropriate path for the president to follow. The Nixon administration, according to Richard Nathan, became convinced by the end of the president's first term in office that its strategy of controlling the bureaucracy from the White House simply did not work.[3] It thus began an effort during Nixon's second term—aborted by Watergate and the president's resignation—to shift to a strategy of "presidentializing" the bureaucracy by putting Nixon loyalists in important positions in all executive agencies.

The use of each of these alternatives will be examined in this chapter, with particular attention to White House relations with the bureaucracy during the administrations of two presidents, Lyndon B. Johnson and Richard M. Nixon. We will describe these and other presidents' efforts to shape the behavior and decisions of the executive apparatus, looking very closely at the activities of the Federal Communications Commission (FCC). We also will examine the kinds of problems that arose for the White House and for other participants in executive policy making when these various strategies were employed.

Presidentializing the Executive Bureaucracy

The most traditional and in many ways the simplest method by which presidents control bureaucracy is through their power to appoint the principal executives of each of the varied agencies that make up the executive branch of government in the United States. While the president cannot himself take "hands-on" responsibility for the operation of all executive agencies, his appointing power does ensure that their activities will be directed by people who are, at least in some sense, his surrogates.

To be sure, the president's power in this regard is far from an unlimited prerogative. His appointments to executive positions within the bureaucracy ordinarily must be confirmed by the Senate and not altogether odious to the House. They also must be palatable to a variety of groups in the community, which in some cases have the power of veto over presidential appointments to agencies in which they have a particular interest. But in the end, it is the president who makes the final decisions on executive personnel, and it is certainly the president who is most severely damaged when, for whatever reason, an appointment turns out badly.[4]

The way in which presidents can employ their appointment power to alter an agency's policy direction was clearly illustrated by President Lyndon Johnson's success in reshaping communications policy at the FCC after taking office in 1963. When a president ascends to the office as Johnson did, as the result of an assassination, he is not in a strong position to use his appointing power to control the bureaucracy. The voters have neither repudiated his predecessor's policies nor given him a mandate for change through victory at the polls. Indeed he is ordinarily expected to complete the unfinished work of the assassinated president, as was certainly true in Johnson's case.

Yet the record shows that Johnson was able to use his appointing power to put an unmistakable LBJ brand on the FCC. During the Kennedy presidency, the FCC had been moving gradually toward a more activist conception of its role—a more vigorous use of its coercive authority, especially in the area of broadcast regulation. Three of Kennedy's four appointees to the seven-member commission, Newton

Minow, Kenneth Cox, and William Henry, were very strongly in this activist mold. The fourth, Lee Loevinger, was a liberal Democrat who surprised the White House after his appointment by opposing what he regarded as excessive government interference with private business activities.

Thus, when Johnson took over the presidency, the way was open for him to decide on the direction of national communications policy. He could have made an immediate difference by giving a strong public endorsement to the activist role that Kennedy's FCC chairman, William Henry, was playing at the agency. But he did not. While serving as vice president, Johnson had been able to observe at first hand the aggressive stance that Kennedy's first FCC chairman, Newton Minow, had taken toward the broadcast industry, and it was Minow's strong impression that Johnson did not like what he saw. This, at least, is how Minow recalled the situation in a talk he later had with Joe Frantz, who interviewed him in 1978 for the oral history archive at the Johnson library in Texas:

> Frantz: Did the Vice President ever comment to you on your own campaign to give television a little higher level?
>
> Minow: No, except I sort of had the impression—and it was not from anything that was said—that I don't think he approved of it. I think he felt we were stepping too hard on the industry.
>
> Frantz: On private toes?
>
> Minow: Yes. It was never said to me, but I had that impression.[5]

While serving as FCC chairman under Lyndon Johnson, William Henry also had the impression that the president was unsympathetic to the stringent government regulation of business that Kennedy had seemed to encourage. Henry, a southerner from Tennessee, was a quintessential New Frontiersman. An early recruit to John Kennedy's presidential campaign, he was a close friend of Robert F. Kennedy, and he and his family were very much part of the Kennedy circle in Washington. As one observer described it: "The children went to the same school, their wives socialized, and he was part of the inner, beautiful people set." [6]

Moreover, Henry was young (33 when appointed to the commission in 1962), energetic and aggressive—attributes that the Kennedys were always looking for in their legendary and sometimes lamented search for the "best and the brightest." Although a product of Tennessee politics, he certainly was a far cry from an old-style

Tennessee politician such as Gov. Buford Ellington, whom Johnson was later to appoint to high office in his own administration.

As FCC chairman, Henry was very much attached to the activist style of his predecessor, Newton Minow. While he never said anything as disturbing to the broadcast industry as Minow's highly publicized description of television programming as a "vast wasteland," Henry did arouse the industry's anger by spearheading an effort within the FCC to force the broadcast industry to abide by its own self-imposed restrictions on commercials.[7]

For Henry, the change that took place when Johnson succeeded Kennedy in the presidency was a dramatic one:

> Oh, it was night and day! Johnson's first meeting with heads of agencies took place, I think, in December at the White House—I think in the Cabinet room—and the catchword of that little talk that he gave to us was cooperation, not coercion. I remember it, you know, to this day, and it set the tone, the implication being that there had been coercion before. Now, none of that boys![8]

Although there is no indication of any direct White House pressure on Henry to resign as chairman, he felt that he had been greatly weakened because "everyone knows that I was not Johnson's boy." [9] Eventually, he resigned from his FCC position.

With Henry's resignation, Johnson had a chance to reverse the direction in which the Kennedy FCC had been going, and he quickly took advantage of that opportunity. He named as Henry's successor Rosel Hyde, a technocrat who had been with the agency as a member of the staff as well as the commission for nearly 40 years, going back to the days when it was the Federal Radio Commission. Hyde was nominally a Republican, but he had been with the FCC so long as to become in effect a career commissioner—abandoning his attachment to his political party and acquiring instead a strong identification with the communications field itself. He was also very well known in the industry and quite acceptable to it.

When President Johnson called Hyde to his office, he revealed his intention of naming him chairman of the commission and made clear how he expected him to perform in his new role. According to Hyde, Johnson said that "he expected me to chair the agency firmly but that he didn't expect a lot of harassment." Johnson also told Hyde that he hoped he would avoid the "flair and showmanship" that some of his predecessors had exhibited as FCC chairmen.[10]

The designation of Hyde as chairman of the commission was one of seven appointments Johnson made to the FCC. With these appointments Johnson ultimately succeeded in pointing the agency toward the moderate regulatory posture he preferred. As a leading communications journal put it at the time of the Hyde appointment: "President Johnson formally brought to an end the New Frontier era at the FCC—an era that had been marked by controversy and studded with proposals that would affect the foundation of the broadcasting industry." [11]

With one exception to be discussed below, Johnson's appointments to the FCC were men of moderate views whose presence on the commission would not be upsetting to the groups regulated by the agency. The story of Johnson and the FCC is thus a success story as far as the president's relationship with bureaucracy is concerned. He inherited an agency that President Kennedy had oriented toward a very militant conception of its role as promoter and protector of the public interest in communications policy making. Through the skillful use of his appointing power, Johnson was able to moderate the agency's policies and to make the FCC much less threatening to the industry.

Yet aspects of this case reveal that the president's power to appoint agency executives has its limits as a source of presidential influence over agency policy making. Sometimes the goal of influencing an agency's policy decisions may have to take a back seat to some other presumably higher presidential purpose. Johnson's first opportunity to make an FCC appointment came during the election year of 1964, when in view of his own family's deep personal involvement in the communications industry, the last thing Johnson wanted was to be seen exercising power over any aspect of national communications policy.[12] So the president was forced to persuade Franklin Ford, an incumbent Republican whose term had expired, to stay on at the commission in order to keep things quiet.

The appointment of Nicholas Johnson to the FCC in 1966 illustrates the same point. Earlier, as maritime administrator, Johnson had been very unpopular with the maritime interest groups, particularly the trade unions. He was appointed to the FCC, not to put him on the commission, but to get him out of the maritime agency. If the president had any policy goal in making this FCC appointment, it was to influence maritime and not communications policy.

Nicholas Johnson's case parallels that of Lee Loevinger, who was appointed to the FCC in 1963 by President Kennedy as a way of removing him from his position as head of the anti-trust division of the Justice Department, where he had become *persona non grata* to Attorney General Robert F. Kennedy. In each of these cases, Presidents Kennedy and Johnson found themselves locked into the position of using their power of appointment essentially as a power of removal. Since the FCC is a seven-member body, it provided a convenient organizational setting for neutralizing the views of administration mavericks.

What White House officials usually complain about, however, is not that the appointing power often must be used for purposes that have little to do with increasing presidential control over bureaucracy. Rather their chief grievance is with the fabled tendency of agency appointees to be captured by the agencies to which they are appointed. "Marrying the natives" is how presidential aides disparagingly describe the process by which agency appointees come to identify with the needs of their agency and its clients rather than with the concerns and priorities of the president.

But what the case of the FCC under President Johnson strongly suggests is that "marrying the natives" may be precisely what the president has in mind when he makes his appointments. What Johnson most desperately wanted from his FCC appointees was an ability to keep things quiet on the communications policy front. His chief problem when he came to power was that the natives in the communications industry were quite restless because the Kennedy appointees at the FCC were refusing their hand in marriage. Except for Nicholas Johnson, who ultimately proved to be a thorn in the flesh for the communications industry, every Johnson appointee was an eminently suitable marriage prospect. They were not "captured" by the agency's parochial perspective. Happily from the president's point of view, they already had this perspective when they were named to office.

White House Monitoring

As the previous discussion has sought to demonstrate, the president's use of his appointing power to shape the policies of executive agencies is a formidable weapon. But it also has its limitations, and these limitations generate a desire for additional ways of keeping the bureaucracy in line with presidential goals. Chief among these strategies is the assignment of White House staff members to the task of monitoring policy development and agency decision making within the executive establishment.

The way in which such assignments are parcelled out within the White House varies from president to president. Lyndon Johnson's White House was characterized by a high degree of informality. A number of the president's White House aides dealt with communications policy during his administration, if for no other purpose than to answer letters from private citizens with complaints against the FCC. But it was not easy to anticipate beforehand who in the White House might take on a particular task in the communications field, or how long anyone's responsibility for a special set of problems might last.

One new staff member, who came to the Johnson White House from a military background, expected to find a very formal White House staff structure, with a well-defined division of labor and a clear distribution of authority. About three weeks after joining the administration, he asked William Hopkins, a career official who had worked at the White House for 30 years, if there was an organization chart available on the operation of the White House staff under Johnson. Hopkins's amusement at this question was evident in his reply: "We don't have any organization chart at the White House," he told the newcomer, "because we don't have any organization." [13]

In the Johnson administration a White House staff member could have a role in the communications field as a small part of a wide range of quite different responsibilities. When Ernest Goldstein arrived at the White House in late 1967 to begin work as a presidential aide, he met with one of Johnson's chief assistants, Joseph Califano, and they mapped out territory for Goldstein that included exports (stimulating American sales abroad), foreign travel (getting more foreigners to visit the United States), luncheons with ambassadors, anti-trust, and regulatory agencies.[14] It was the last of this clutch of assignments that ultimately got Goldstein involved with the FCC, although his expertise lay largely in other areas.

No role that White House staff members performed in the area of communications policy was more important than that of keeping the president informed about decisions that executive agencies involved in this field were about to make. These "early warning" alerts were an especially important staff function for a president such as Johnson who disliked surprises that were not of his own making.

For example, on February 17, 1968, White House aide DeVier Pierson sent Johnson a memo telling him that the FCC and the State Department finally had reached a tentative agreement on a fifth transatlantic cable that was to be laid between the United States and Spain to facilitate communications with southern Europe.[15] This agreement was an effort to resolve a long-standing dispute among government agencies about whether international communications could best be carried on through the traditional cable or the newly emerging satellite system. The new interagency pact also gave its blessing to an advanced satellite, Intelstat IV, that had been developed to serve southern Europe. From Pierson's point of view, the advantage of the agreement was that it got the Johnson administration out of a troublesome political predicament. In his memo he wrote:

> Although the need for a cable on purely economic ground is open to doubt, this is a pretty good result. It keeps the pressure on for satellite development in accordance with your mandate to provide communications to the developing nations. Denial of the cable would have put the administration in the middle of a hot political fight on a close question.[16]

The intelligence system of the White House staff could penetrate even the inner recesses of the FCC, a supposedly independent regulatory agency. On June 30, 1967, presidential aide Jim Jones sent Johnson a memo reporting on a meeting that Joseph Califano had just had with the FCC chairman, Rosel Hyde. The contents of the memo provide a striking illustration of the way the White House staff served the president as a source of intelligence on what was happening within the bureaucracy:

> 1. Joe met with Rosel Hyde of the FCC today. He reports Robert E. Lee, the Republican member of the FCC, is sending his letter of resignation to Macy today. Lee's term expires June 30 (today). Hyde told Joe he would like us to urge Lee to stay on.
> 2. Hyde said he thought there would be a decision on the ATT rate case next week. He expected it would give about a 7 to 7½ percent rate of return. This is slightly less than what ATT wanted— about 8 percent. Hyde thought he could get a 6-1 decision, but it might turn out to be another 4-3 decision with a bitter dispute among the commissioners. Joe told Hyde that the decision was up to him, and that all we wanted was what is right and just.[17]

This memo shows not only how a White House staff member could meet in an informal way and obtain information from the head of an independent regulatory agency that is not altogether under the president's supervisory authority, but also how the head of such an agency could use the meeting to send a message to the White House about his preference with respect to a pending presidential appointment. The purposes of the FCC chairman as well as those of the administration were thus served by the encounter between Hyde and Califano.

As an intelligence system, the White House staff also helped Johnson in his relationship with the FCC by gathering information about people who might be considered for appointment to that agency.

Partly, this was a matter of merely throwing additional names into the hopper. Sometimes, however, it also involved a contact with an outside party whose reaction to a pending appointment could be sounded out, and who might be flattered by the appearance of being consulted in advance about such a decision.

In 1966, for example, shortly before Johnson made his decision on the FCC chairmanship, Robert Kintner, a presidential aide who had been brought to the White House to serve in a liaison role with the broadcast industry, met with Sol Taishoff, publisher of *Broadcasting* magazine, the most influential journal in its field. In a memo to the president on this meeting, Kintner wrote:

> Taishoff said the most able Commissioner was Rosel Hyde, who could be Chairman with the least repercussions. Sol said that you might name Hyde to the unexpired term of Chairman Henry and select a new Commissioner for the full six-year term.[18]

Interestingly enough, the course of action recommended by Taishoff was precisely the path that Johnson ultimately followed.

Although they operated largely behind the scenes, White House staff members were quite sensitive to the public image of the actions the president took with respect to the bureaucracy in the communications field. In 1966 Robert Kintner made an assiduous effort to persuade Jack Gould, a *New York Times* reporter who specialized in communications topics, to look more kindly upon the president's selection of Hyde as FCC chairman. In an editorial the *Times* had taken a jaundiced view of the Hyde appointment, as had Gould in a subsequent article. The *Times* editorial said that Hyde "has been more noted for amiability than vigor in his many years" with the FCC,[19] while Gould's newspaper column described the new chairman as "miscast as the people's champion." [20]

To persuade Gould to take a more favorable view of Johnson's decision, Kintner arranged a meeting between the columnist and the president in June of 1966. Prior to that meeting, he also sent Johnson a number of memoranda that advised the president not only on the topics that Gould would probably question him about but also on the strategy Johnson should follow in answering the reporter's questions. For example, he told Johnson to "offset Gould's appraisal of Hyde with a positive statement of your belief in his ability and your impartiality in appointing him." [21]

Whatever he thought of Kintner's advice in areas in which he was himself very well-informed, the president could not have been disappointed with the results of the Gould interview. Shortly after meeting with Johnson, Gould wrote a glowing column in the *Times* about the Johnson administration's communications policy.[22] So faithfully did it reflect the president's views that it might well have been drafted by the White House itself. It was clear that whatever he may have thought of Johnson from a distance, Gould was very much impressed by him in the flesh. In this case at least, a White House staff member's effort to manipulate the press proved highly successful.

One of the most unpleasant assignments White House staff members can get in their go-between role in relationships with the bureaucracy is to transmit what they anticipate will be received as unpleasant information—engaging in a "trouble-shooting" operation. In May of 1966 Robert Kintner was asked to sound out Nicholas Johnson about the possibility of Johnson's leaving his post of maritime administrator and becoming an FCC commissioner. As noted earlier, Johnson had become anathema to all the groups directly concerned with the work of the maritime agency.

For Kintner such a meeting had awkward possibilities, as his description to the president of his visit with Nicholas Johnson reveals:

> While he says he wants nothing in Washington, Johnson was cold as to being a member of the FCC, reasoning that it would look as though he was moved from a more important job as Maritime Administrator with 2500 employees and a $350 million budget to membership in a 7-man Commission. However, he expressed some interest in the chairmanship of the FCC, but I mentioned that, while you had not made a decision, I thought you were thinking in another direction—I was not sure.[23]

After receiving this memorandum from Kintner, the president scribbled a note on the bottom: "Bob—Talk to Warren Woodward [a mutual friend] to see if Nick Johnson could be talked into a 6 yr. commissionership with possibility of becoming chairman—L."[24] Eventually, either reason, ambition, or political pressure prevailed, and Nicholas Johnson agreed to accept the FCC post that was offered to him.

Another White House aide, Ernest Goldstein, was involved in an equally ticklish situation in 1968. The two most activist FCC commissioners, Nicholas Johnson and Kenneth Cox, had sent letters to Oklahoma radio and television stations that were designed to discover how much time these stations were allotting to news and public affairs programming. This inquiry reflected their fear that many stations in that state neglected these areas in their broadcast schedules. The letters also inquired into the employment records of the stations with respect to minority groups, and the attention paid to the problems of these groups in news broadcasts. Similar letters were sent to networks that had outlets in Oklahoma.[25]

These letters aroused strong protests in Oklahoma and in broadcasting circles generally. Strictly speaking, the letters were unofficial. They were sent by the two commissioners on their own initiative, without support of the commission. But the broadcasters were vehement in expressing the fear that they were being intimidated—that two commissioners with the power to vote against the renewal of their licenses were introducing standards of performance that previously had not been used in FCC license renewal decisions.

These protests quickly came to White House attention. Sen. Mike Monroney of Oklahoma, a Democrat who was coming up for reelection in 1968, complained to the White House about the damage "this harassment" could do to his political prospects.[26] FCC Chairman Hyde also was displeased by the entire controversy and privately advised the White House that if an applicant refused to answer the Johnson-Cox letter, its license still would be renewed if everything else was in order.[27]

Goldstein called Nicholas Johnson and invited him to the White House. At their meeting he emphasized to Johnson the "need for team work in a Commission" and "the obligation of Federal agencies to use regular procedures which do not harass the citizen." According to Goldstein, "Nick got the message," and about a week later the White House aide reported to the president that the two commissioners had "modified and clarified" their positions. "However, the broadcasters still feel threatened, and nothing further can be done in this case. As for the future, one would hope for a little more teamwork." [28]

Occasionally, members of the White House staff became involved in communications problems on behalf of the president that only can be described as less than presidential. Television reception at the Johnson ranch in Texas was subject to a good deal of interference at certain times during the year, particularly when there were temperature inversions in the atmosphere. Eventually this problem reached the desk of Special Assistant to the President Marvin Watson and was the subject of technical inquiries by both the FCC and the White House Communications Agency.

One proposed solution to this problem would have involved a nationwide change in broadcast frequencies. The political implications of such a step were, however, obvious to all. Col. Jack Albright was then in charge of the White House Communications Agency, the organization responsible for ensuring that the White House itself had an adequate communications system. He put the situation this way in a memo to Watson:

> . . .changing frequencies nation-wide, is, in my opinion, an impractical proposal and might engender nation-wide publicity and animosity if it became known that the reason for the change was to accommodate television to the LBJ ranch. In addition, it most likely would cost homeowners some small amount of money to modify their television sets.[29]

In the end, Watson and the president agreed that discretion was the better part of political valor and that it would be necessary for Lyndon Johnson to accept the price of poor television reception in order to enjoy the blessings of life on the banks of the Pedernales.

As a technique to control bureaucracy, White House monitoring has the obvious advantage of being carried out by officials who are not, like agency appointees, likely to be seduced by either their agency or its clientele. To be sure, a White House staff member's support of the president sometimes may be diluted by devotion to his or her own career. But in their dealings with other administrative agencies, presidential aides still have the presidency as their chief focus of institutional loyalty within the executive branch.

However, for some presidents this may not be enough. A major limitation of White House monitoring is that it is reactive. "Trouble-shooting" of the kind that presidential aides were engaged in with respect to the FCC, for example, leaves the initiative very largely in the hands of the executive agency, which means that the pace of policy development will be set, for the most part, by the agency. If the White House has policy priorities of its own, it has no institutional mechanism for forcing these concerns to the top of the agency's agenda.

Recognizing this, some presidents will prefer to place their faith in the first strategy of White House control—using their power of appointment to presidentialize the bureaucracy. Since it is the agencies that ultimately control the action, it may be more important to influence decisions at their source inside the corridors of bureaucracy than to try to affect them by an ex-post-facto system of remote control monitoring by White House aides. Of course, these are not mutually exclusive alternatives. Every modern president has made substantial efforts both to presidentialize the bureaucracy through the judicious selection of agency executives and to strengthen or refine White House mechanisms for monitoring the actions and decisions of executive agencies.

Sometimes, however, a third option may be even more attractive for a president—establishing a White House agency that can pull the bureaucracy in policy directions that it is unlikely to take on its own.

White House Staff Organizations

When Lyndon Johnson left the White House in 1969, he was succeeded by a president, Richard M. Nixon, who was very dissatisfied with his limited ability to influence the work of the executive organizations that deal with communications problems. Neither his power to make appointments to communications agencies such as the FCC nor the capacity of his staff to monitor bureaucratic activity in this field was sufficient for Nixon.

What Nixon sorely wanted was some mechanism through which the White House itself could initiate action in the development of communications policy. Accordingly, he sent to Congress in 1970 a reorganization plan that set up an Office of Telecommunications Policy (OTP) in the White House. Besides advising the president on communications issues, the OTP's ostensible purpose was to carry out certain telecommunications functions that had long been part of the president's responsibility, including the management of the portion of the radio spectrum that is allocated to governmental use.[30]

Under President Johnson these functions had been performed by an obscure unit in the Office of Emergency Planning called the Office of Telecommunications Management (OTM). After a single meeting with Johnson when he first arrived at the White House, the OTM director never met or discussed communications issues with the president again. His subordinate status was nettling to this official, and the widespread knowledge that he never got to see the president virtually nullified his standing and influence in the Washington community. He was subject to ridicule at Senate hearings, where he appeared to testify on behalf of OTM. The chairman of a subcommittee handling OTM appropriations, Sen. John Pastore of Rhode Island, described him as "the presidential advisor who never gets to see the President."[31] Nixon's OTP, on the other hand, was designed from the start to be an agency with clout in the telecommunications field. The president named as director Clay Whitehead, an ambitious and aggressive young administrator with strong professional credentials and very good access to the White House. Shortly after taking office, Whitehead held a press conference at which he proclaimed that the new agency would be a vigorous protagonist of the administration's point of view on a number of critical communications policy issues. It was especially important in Whitehead's view to speed the development of cable television as a new entry in the nation's communications system. He also was convinced that the public interest was best protected by encouraging competition in the communications industry rather than by closely regulating its activities.

One of the first things Whitehead did when he took over the OTP was to send a shot across the bow of the FCC, the flagship communications agency in the executive branch. If the FCC did not address the issues the president considered important, Whitehead said, then the OTP would take the lead in doing so. In a speech before the communications bar association in Washington, Whitehead made it clear that he would be happy to entertain complaints from those who were dissatisfied with the work of the FCC. In a question period afterwards, one listener asked whether he should in the future take his complaints to the FCC or the OTP. "You go," Whitehead answered, "where you think you can get the best deal." [32]

This brash challenge to the FCC's preeminent position among Washington's communications agencies was a far cry from the public caution that White House officials in the Johnson administration always displayed in their relations with the agency. These officials constantly emphasized that the FCC was an independent agency not under the president's control. As a Johnson aide, Myer Feldman, put in a letter responding to one citizen aggrieved by an FCC decision: "As you know, the Federal Communications Commission is an independent agency, and it would be inappropriate for the Administration to interfere with its decisional activities." [33] Or as another presidential assistant, Jack Valenti, responded in a letter to a complaint that the FCC had failed to renew a radio license: "As you know, White House staff assistants cannot intervene with any government agency or department about matters such as this. I'm sure that your renewal application will be given careful consideration by the Federal Communications Commission." [34]

Over the course of the OTP's brief history, Whitehead did succeed in making the agency a significant player in the bureaucratic give-and-take that was at the center of communications policy making in the executive branch. The principal role of the OTP in this process was as an action-forcing mechanism—stimulating decisions on issues that had long been stalemated by disagreement within the communications community about what steps the government should take.

This was certainly a useful contribution. Communications organizations such as the FCC tended to move very slowly in tackling tough issues. They nibbled away at them in tried and true incremental style.[35] This slow pace often irritated those who were affected by FCC decisions. Members of Congress were under constant pressure from constituents who wanted to know when the FCC was going to hand down a particular decision.

Perhaps the greatest success the OTP achieved in performing this action-forcing role was the temporary settlement of the cable television issue that had plagued the FCC for many years. In 1970 the OTP was able to get the various parties involved to agree on a set of rules that would protect the interests of established networks and stations while permitting the new cable systems to develop. The OTP's role in this case drew high praise from a number of independent observers:

> It was successful in forging a compromise because of the vacuum created by prior FCC indecisiveness in developing an overall cable policy, and the OTP's willingness to exert pressure in private sessions on groups representing broadcasters, cable system owners, and copyright holders.[36]

The OTP also was instrumental in inducing the FCC to recognize that the sky would not fall in if there were some degree of deregulation in the radio industry. This innovation in policy eventually won broad support from both liberals and conservatives in the communications community.

But in spite of this success at forcing action, the OTP obviously could not serve as a model for the president's relationship with bureaucracy in all areas of policy. If its example were followed elsewhere, there would be a proliferation of presidential agencies all over the White House landscape. An extraordinarily top-heavy presidential establishment would result, with the overloaded circuits and delayed decisions that an overly centralized administrative system inevitably brings. Of course, from the Nixon administration's point of view, the OTP's value did not lie entirely in its role in revamping communications policy. It also was seen as playing an important part in the administration's unrelenting campaign against the news media—an involvement that eventually contributed to the OTP's demise.[37] When the Nixon White House fell from grace during the Watergate affair, OTP became one of the chief targets of the president's critics.

Of course, other alternatives are open to presidents who are dissatisfied with their ability to control the bureaucracy through use of their appointing power or the monitoring activity of White House staff members. They can, for example, create an ad hoc body that will generate proposals that the bureaucratic apparatus is believed to be suppressing or neglecting. President Johnson did this when he appointed a Task Force on Communications Policy during the twilight of his administration.

The report of this task force put a heavy emphasis on market competition rather than government regulation as the chief means through which consumer interests could be protected in the communications field. Released during the last months of Johnson's term as president, the report had little effect on his presidency. But it greatly affected the design and development of communications policy during the Nixon years. Its strong stance in favor of deregulation was thoroughly in tune with the view of the Nixon White House, and the creation of the OTP itself can be traced to one of the main task force recommendations.

During the Carter administration another alternative to the OTP model of White House control emerged. The development of communications policy was one of the Domestic Policy Staff's concerns, at least insofar as it generated issues of sufficient importance to warrant presidential attention. For most presidents, this Carter strategy may be a more desirable arrangement than the OTP model, since it confines White House intervention in bureaucratic decision making to those few "big-ticket" items that require presidential attention. From the president's point of view, one of the major disadvantages of an organization like the OTP is that it develops an institutional interest of its own in intervening in many issues that are not really important enough to merit White House attention.

As noted earlier, the alternative ways of relating to bureaucracy that have been examined here reflect differing degrees of White House distrust of the permanent government. Presidents who are most at ease with the bureaucracy will center their efforts at control on the appointing power to make sure that agencies are run by administration loyalists. Presidents who are somewhat more suspicious of bureaucracy will increase the amount of White House monitoring of agency decision making. Chief executives with the greatest distrust of bureaucracy will turn to White House organizations such as the OTP to ensure that the executive apparatus does not sabotage their efforts to achieve their goals.

Presidential assessments of the strategies necessary to improve their control over bureaucracy may not always be accurate. It already has been pointed out that the Nixon administration underestimated the value of using agency appointees to impose presidential priorities on bureaucracy. It sought instead to shift control over decision making from the bureaucracy to the White House and only saw the error of its ways as the president's second term was beginning. Hence, the strategy the White House chooses to increase its control over bureaucracy actually may have the opposite effect.

Coping with Bureaucracy: Perils for Presidents

The strategies of control that are discussed in the previous sections reflect the need presidents feel to use coping mechanisms to deal with the bureaucratic establishment they inherit when they take office. These mechanisms certainly play an essential role in the governing process in the United States. However, there is also a common tendency among presidents to exaggerate the amount of trouble the bureaucracy actually will give them. Studies have shown a very strong predisposition among career civil servants to go along with a newly elected chief executive.[38] Contrary to what many White House staff members are prone to believe, true cases of bureaucratic sabotage of presidential directives are not easy to find in the executive branch.[39]

Moreover, distrust of bureaucracy sometimes blinds presidents to the fact that the strategies they use in dealing with executive agencies may be damaging to the White House. Lewis Thomas has written fluently and extensively about the aberrant tendencies of the human body's immunological system, which, although designed to protect against infection and other threats to physical well-being, can also overreact in ways that are themselves perilous to human health.[40] Similarly, presidential appointees in the executive branch, who are supposed to immunize the president from the ill effects of bureaucratic machinations, can do more to impair the success of an administration than any of the bureaucratic obstructions that they are appointed to protect the president against.

President Johnson, for example, had a great deal of trouble getting his cabinet members to do the things he wanted them to do. Even worse, on more than one occasion he regarded their activities as seriously injuring his administration. The Justice Department under Ramsey Clark moved much more aggressively on the anti-trust front than the president wanted, and White House efforts to restrain Clark in cases involving IBM and a railroad merger were quite unsuccessful. As one irritated White House aide described the attorney general: "If he thought he was right, no one could persuade him to change his position, up to and including the President. Clark merely overlooked White House objection to some of his decisions and went on his merry way." [41]

An even more acrimonious relationship developed between Johnson and his secretary of the interior, Stewart Udall. Not many months before they were scheduled to leave office, Udall reminded Johnson that it was customary for presidents at the end of their tenure in office to set aside some acreage of public lands as parks. The president liked the idea and told Udall to draw up a plan to this effect. Such a plan eventually was prepared, setting aside more than six million acres as parklands.

As time went by, however, Johnson's enthusiasm for the project seemed to wane. The legality of so large an addition to the parklands came into question, opposition developed in Congress, and an additional irritant entered the picture when Udall proposed that DC Stadium be named after Robert F. Kennedy, a long-time Johnson nemesis. Undaunted, Udall prepared press kits announcing the parklands decision, which was expected to come two days before Johnson left office. Some of these kits were handed out to reporters from weekly newspapers even before Johnson had made his decision. When word reached him that the wire services were carrying this announcement, the president was furious and berated Udall: "The President was very unhappy and bawled me out good that he hadn't made a decision and we turned it loose. I lamely tried to explain." [42]

Thus it was that on the very last day of Johnson's term in office, he was standing in his bedroom still discussing what to do about these parkland additions with an aide, W. DeVier Pierson. At this pivotal moment in history, with American troops locked in combat in Vietnam and the peace negotiations stalled in Paris, the president finally made his decision. "These are just too big," Johnson said to Pierson. "A President shouldn't take this much land without the approval of Congress." [43] So he signed proclamations putting only the four smallest additions into effect—fewer than 400,000 acres.

Easily the worst experience that Johnson had with a cabinet member was his fight with his secretary of labor, Willard Wirtz. In 1968 Wirtz drew up a reorganization plan for the department that was designed to coordinate all its manpower training activities through one simplified organizational structure. Relying on assurances provided by presidential aide Joseph Califano, the department believed that this plan had the approval of the president.

But in late October of 1968, the president let it be known that he was, in fact, opposed to the plan. After consulting with his senior aides, the secretary of labor decided to issue his reorganization order in spite of the president's opposition. This was a step he was legally entitled to take under the reorganization authority granted him by Congress. Enraged by this act of defiance, Johnson summoned Wirtz to a meeting in the White House and ordered him to rescind his reorganization order.[44] Wirtz refused to do so, reminding the president that the action he had taken was within the law.

Thereafter, the fur began to fly. Johnson asked for Wirtz's resignation. Wirtz replied that the president still had a resignation letter from him on file—a letter that had been tendered following President Kennedy's assassination. He refused to supply another letter, and said that the president would have to fire him. Later that same evening, however, Wirtz drafted a letter of resignation and sent it to the president. But Johnson refused to accept this letter until Wirtz rescinded his reorganization plan. Since Wirtz refused to do so until his letter of resignation was accepted, an impasse developed. The efforts of various presidential emissaries to change Wirtz's mind were unsuccessful, including a visit from Assistant Attorney General Warren Christopher, who outlined to the secretary of labor the procedures available to the president for removing a refractory cabinet member from office.[45]

Ultimately, the reorganization plan was neither rescinded nor put into effect, but remained in limbo throughout the remaining months of the Johnson administration. After Richard Nixon took office in 1969, the new secretary of labor, George Shultz, quickly reorganized manpower activities very much along the lines of the Wirtz proposal.[46]

What these various episodes of conflict between Johnson and his cabinet members clearly reveal is that a president's sorest trials may come not from the bureaucracy but from the people he appoints to control it. The family of political appointees a president brings with him when he takes office is a quarrelsome one. Because its members come from the uneasy coalition of groups that supported the president's election, it is riven by ideological and other differences. Once they have taken office, the members of the family also acquire and play varying institutional roles that bring them into competition and conflict.[47]

Much the same set of problems tends to arise whether the president is making cabinet appointments or using either of the other control strategies we have discussed—having White House aides monitor bureaucratic activities or setting up White House staff organizations to goad administrative agencies into taking action. White House aides, as the events of Watergate so clearly demonstrated, can help get a president into as well as out of trouble, and our review of OTP's brief life during the Nixon administration points up the pitfalls of using staff organizations to control the bureaucracy. None of these strategies protect the president against the risk of being hoist with his own petard.

Presidential difficulties in governing the executive branch do not necessarily spring, as is so often suggested, from the lethargy or obstinacy of the career bureaucracy. They may come just as easily from the rivalries and ambitions of the members of his own official family, whether located in the executive departments or on his White House staff. The public image of an administration's performance in office can be more severely damaged by disputes within this family than by the bureaucratic maneuvering and foot-dragging that White House officials so often complain about. The stronger a president builds his defenses against bureaucracy, the more likely these defenses are to be a source of trouble for him.

NOTES

1. The research on which this article is based has been supported by a grant from the Russell Sage Foundation, for which the author would like to express his gratitude. Byron Shafer at Russell Sage was of particular help on this project. Roger Brown and Kenneth Kato provided valuable assistance in conducting the research.
2. Henry Jones Ford, *The Rise and Growth of American Politics* (New York: The Macmillan Co., 1898), 283.
3. The antecedents and consequences of Nixon's strategic choices are traced in Richard P. Nathan, *The Plot That Failed: Nixon and the Administrative Presidency* (New York: John Wiley & Sons, 1975).
4. For general discussions of the president's use of his appointing power, see Dean C. Mann with Jameson W. Doig, *The Assistant Secretaries: Problems and Processes of Appointment* (Washington, D.C.: The Brookings Institution, 1965); G. Calvin Mackenzie, *The Politics of Presidential Appointments* (New York: The Free Press, 1981); and Nelson W. Polsby, *Consequences of Party Reform* (New York: Oxford University Press, 1983), 90-105. For a detailed analysis of recent regulatory appointments, see U.S. Senate, Committee on Commerce, *Appointments to the Regulatory Agencies: The Federal Communications Commission and the Federal Trade Commission (1949-1974)*, 94th Cong., 2d sess. (1976).
5. Newton Minow, oral history interview, March 19, 1971, 21-22, LBJ Library.
6. Interview, Max Paglin, Washington, D.C., August 17, 1979.
7. The story is told in Erwin G. Krasnow, Lawrence D. Longley, and Herbert A. Terry, *The Politics of Broadcast Regulation*, 3d ed. (New York: St. Martin's Press, 1982), 192-205.
8. Interview, E. William Henry, Washington, D.C., October 19, 1979.
9. Ibid.
10. Interview, Rosel Hyde, Washington, D.C., October 23, 1979.
11. "Now it's the Hyde era at the FCC," *Broadcasting*, June 27, 1966, 29-30.

12. For a detailed analysis of the Johnson family's holdings in the communications industry, see the *Wall Street Journal,* March 23, 1964, A1 and March 24, 1964, A1. When Johnson became president, his Texas Broadcasting Company was a multimillion dollar enterprise.
13. Interview, General James D. O'Connell, Falls Church, Virginia, September 11, 1979.
14. Memo, Joe Califano to the President, September 20, 1967, Ex FG 11-8-1, WHCF, LBJ Library.
15. Memo, DeVier Pierson to the President, February 17, 1968, Ex UT 1, WHCF, LBJ Library.
16. Ibid.
17. Memo, Jim Jones to the President, June 30, 1967, Ex FG 228, WHCF, LBJ Library.
18. Memo, Robert E. Kintner to the President, May 2, 1966, C.F. Pe 2, WHCF, LBJ Library.
19. *New York Times,* June 20, 1966.
20. *New York Times,* June 26, 1966.
21. Memo, Robert E. Kintner to the President, June 27, 1966, filed with Kintner memo to Marvin Watson, June 27, 1966, C.F. FG 228, WHCF, LBJ Library.
22. *New York Times,* July 3, 1966.
23. Memo, Robert E. Kintner to the President, May 7, 1966, filed with Marvin Watson memo to the President, June 14, 1966, "June 14, 1966" folder, Appointment File (Diary Backup), LBJ Library.
24. Ibid.
25. "Cox, Johnson polling 59 Oklahoma stations," *Broadcasting,* April 15, 1968, 9; "FCC Checks Oklahoma Radio-TV Stations," *Washington Post,* April 13, 1968, C11; and letter, Kenneth A. Cox and Nicholas Johnson to Leonard H. Goldenson, April 11, 1968, and letters, Kenneth A. Cox and Nicholas Johnson to Oklahoma Broadcasters, April 12, 1968, C. F. FG 228, WHCF, LBJ Library.
26. Memo, Ernest Goldstein to the President, April 17, 1968, CF. FG 228, WHCF, LBJ Library.
27. Ibid.
28. Memo, Ernest Goldstein to the President, April 22, 1968, C.F. FG 228; and memo, Ernest Goldstein to the President, May 2, 1968, C.F. FG 228, WHCF, LBJ Library.
29. Memo, Jack A. Albright to Marvin Watson, December 14, 1966, Ex PP 13-2/Texas, WHCF, LBJ Library.
30. For a description of these functions, see U.S. House of Representatives, Hearings before a Subcommittee of the Committee on Government Operations, *Reorganization Plan No. 1 of 1970,* 91st Cong., 2d sess. (1970), 4.
31. See U.S. Senate, *Independent Offices and Department of HUD Appropriation, 1970,* Part 1, 91st Cong., 1st sess., 1969, 87-88.
32. See "Whitehead offers to listen to losers," *Broadcasting,* February 1, 1971, 35-36.
33. Letter, Myer Feldman to Milton Rygh, April 21, 1964, Gen FG 228, WHCF, LBJ Library.
34. Letter, Jack Valenti to R. S. Bell, Jr., December 14, 1964, Gen. FG 228, WHCF, LBJ Library.
35. For an excellent description of FCC decision-making processes, see Krasnow et al., esp. 133-142, 271-285.

36. Ibid., 71.
37. The Nixon administration's war on the news organizations is described in William E. Porter, *Assault on the Media: The Nixon Years* (Ann Arbor, Mich.: The University of Michigan Press, 1976).
38. For a further discussion of this point, see Francis E. Rourke, "Grappling with the Bureaucracy," in *Politics and the Oval Office*, ed. Arnold J. Meltsner (San Francisco, Calif.: Institute for Contemporary Studies, 1981), 135-138.
39. Even the Nixon administration, which had an inordinate suspicion of bureaucracy, secured a great deal of cooperation from it. See, in this connection, Richard L. Cole and David A. Caputo, "Presidential Control of the Senior Civil Service: Assessing the Strategies of the Nixon Years," *American Political Science Review* 73 (June 1979): 399-413.
40. See, for example, Lewis Thomas, *The Medusa and the Snail* (New York: Bantam Books, 1980), 75-82.
41. George Christian, *The President Steps Down: A Personal Memoir of the Transfer of Power* (New York: The Macmillan Co., 1970), 239.
42. Stewart L. Udall, oral history interview: tape 4, October 31, 1969, 13, LBJ Library.
43. Lyndon B. Johnson, *The Vantage Point: Perspectives of the Presidency, 1963-1969* (New York: Holt, Rinehart & Winston, 1971), 562-563; and W. DeVier Pierson, oral history interview: tape 1, March 19, 1969, 20-21, LBJ Library.
44. The meeting was held in the Cabinet Room. Larry Temple notes that Johnson commonly used the Cabinet Room for small meetings when he wanted to set a stiff, formal tone. See Larry Temple, oral history interview: tape 2, June 12, 1970, 26, LBJ Library.
45. For an account of the meeting between Christopher and Wirtz, see note, Larry Temple to President, Oct. 23, 1968, "Dept. of Labor Reorganization Plans" folder, Box 2 (1852), Files of Larry Temple, LBJ Library.
46. As chairman of an outside task force, Shultz had recommended reorganization of the manpower training area as early as 1967. See James Gaither, oral history interview: tape 5, March 24, 1970, 33, LBJ Library.
47. The character of this family is aptly described by Hugh Heclo, *A Government of Strangers* (Washington, D.C.: The Brookings Institution, 1977).

14. THE PRESIDENCY AND CONGRESS

Roger H. Davidson

In the dog days of August 1982, Speaker Thomas P. O'Neill, Jr., the highest Democratic officeholder in the land, found himself playing an unaccustomed role. He was in the well of the House of Representatives, pleading for passage of a tax increase drafted by Senate Republicans and endorsed by a Republican president. It was too bad, he said, that new taxes had to be imposed less than a year after the president's vaunted tax cuts and that the vote came just a few months before midterm elections. Pointing his finger to the Republican side of the aisle and singling out freshmen who (as he put it) had ridden into office on Ronald Reagan's coattails, he urged them to remember they were citizens first and politicians second. He concluded:

> I ask you today as the leader of the opposition party, as a leader opposed to the President of the United States in most of his philosophies. The President is right. We need this tax bill. I ask for your vote.[1]

A standing, cheering ovation followed the Speaker's words; the bill passed by a 226-207 margin.

Not that Speaker O'Neill was signing up for the president's team. During most of the 97th Congress, he chafed under White House initiatives and pressures from the Republican-controlled Senate to cut social programs he supported and divert funds into military spending. It was O'Neill who first voiced the complaint that Reagan's agenda was "unfair" to those on the lower rungs of the economic ladder—a theme that proved effective in the 1982 elections.

Speaker O'Neill's roller-coaster fortunes during the 97th Congress speak volumes about relations between the White House and Capitol Hill. The Constitution offers no simple or direct formula for working out this relationship, even though its success is undoubtedly the leading institutional question posed by the document. Throughout history the relationship has proven delicate, multifaceted, and constantly changing.

Like a pair of wrestlers in a ring, presidents and Congresses are locked in a contest for advantage. Some of their moves lead to real body contact; others are evasive or for dramatic effect. Both must seize their political opportunities; yet each finds it convenient to cede ground to the other. Confrontation is built into the relationship. Legislators are suspicious of White House occupants (not only presidents but their advisers as well) and the attention they get; they fear that presidents would rather operate without so much as a nod in their direction. All the so-called strong presidents in fact have been accused of "usurpation" at one time or another. Presidents and their advisers, by the same token, sometimes regard Congress as a nuisance or an anachronism. Some of them come to believe that a little usurpation is required to make the system work.

Sources of Conflict

The designer of the nation's capital, Major Pierre L'Enfant, followed logic and advice when he placed the president and Congress on opposite sides of the city. Congress would occupy a single large building on Jenkins Hill, the highest promontory. On a plain a mile or so to the northwest would be the executive mansion. A broad avenue was to link them for ceremonial exchanges of communications; but a bridge spanning Tiber Creek was not built until the third decade of the nineteenth century. Characteristically, the Capitol faced eastward and the executive mansion northward, their backs turned on each other.[2]

Constitutional Conflicts

"An invitation to struggle" is the way one constitutional scholar describes the Constitution's delineation of powers between the two elected branches.[3] Article I invests Congress with "all legislative powers," which embrace nearly all the governmental functions known to eighteenth-century thinkers. Reflecting the founders' Whig heritage, the powers include the historic parliamentary power of the purse, in addition to broad economic powers and even a hand in foreign and defense policies—traditionally royal prerogatives. Finally, Congress was granted in section 8 an elastic power to make all laws "necessary and proper" to carry out its enumerated powers.

In working out these policies, however, the Constitution spreads authority across the two branches. Although Congress possesses "all legislative powers," the president can veto legislation passed by the two houses. The president concludes treaties with foreign nations, but these must be ratified with the "advice and consent" of the Senate. The Constitution does not say how the Senate is to render its advice and consent. At first George Washington tried to consult the Senate personally regarding a treaty with the southern Indians; but the encounter was so uncomfortable that Washington left in a huff, and neither he nor any of his successors ever again attempted to seek direct advice.[4] Senate opposition killed ratification of the Treaty of Versailles in 1919 and 1920. Senate interest in the 1978 Panama Canal treaties was so keen that nearly half the senators visited Panama to talk personally with its government leaders, and several senators rewrote the treaties by authoring crucial amendments.

In short, the Constitution blends executive and legislative authority and assigns each branch special duties. The resulting arrangement is usually called "separation of powers," but it is actually something quite different: separate institutions sharing the same powers. The arrangement was designed, as James Madison put it, so that "these departments be so far connected and blended as to give to each a constitutional control over the others." [5]

Different Constituencies

Presidents and their running mates are, as some of them are fond of pointing out, the only nationally elected public officials. To gain election they must construct electoral coalitions that are national in scope. Practically speaking, this means crisscrossing the nation in search of votes and support—in the process brushing against a host of local concerns. Although local commitments may be made, presidential candidates must shape successful appeals that transcend local politics. Members of Congress, acting singly, represent these same local concerns and thus have a somewhat different perspective on them.

As transplanted locals, senators and representatives tend to see the nation's problems through their constituents' eyes. Even if they concede that a certain local benefit is bad public policy, they may not oppose it. Especially on economic issues—for example, public works, farm programs, import restrictions—members usually give unqualified support to their district's needs because, as they see it, no one else is likely to do so.[6] A president or cabinet member who is pursuing, for example, macro-economic policy mandates or more efficient distribution of military installations will find the welfare of auto workers or a given area's Camp Swampy standing in the way.

From the president's point of view, the key to winning victories on Capitol Hill is to build coalitions of members whose constituencies benefit or at least are indifferent to the consequences of given policies. In an institution in which stopping policies is easier than enacting them, the objective often is to avoid singling out sizable numbers of constituencies for adverse policy effects. This is not an easy assignment, especially if economic output and productivity fail to provide a cushion of growth to sweeten the pot. Distributing hardships, in other words, is more hazardous politically than distributing benefits.

Disparities in constituencies are underscored by a disparity in the way that voters judge presidents and members of Congress. Studies of presidential popularity ratings since Franklin D. Roosevelt's administration show that presidents tend to be judged on the basis of general criteria—economic boom or bust, the presence or absence of wars or other types of crises, the effects of policies on given groups.[7] Legislators, by contrast, tend to be assessed on the basis of their personalities, their communication with the district, and their service to the district in material ways. Relatively few voters, it seems, mention policy issues in rating their representatives.[8] Not only do presidents and legislators serve different constituencies; they labor under divergent incentives.

Different Time Perspectives

The president and members of Congress also operate under different timetables. It is commonly claimed that while legislators look only to the next election—every two years, in the case of House members—presidents can take a longer perspective. The opposite is more nearly the truth. Presidents work in a four-year time frame. Once they have been reelected, presidents are lame ducks who have nothing to run for except the historical record books: "running for the Nobel Peace Prize," as Thomas E. Cronin puts it. In reality, no president since Dwight D. Eisenhower has enjoyed that luxury. Even at that, a one-term president is an old-timer compared with other political appointees in the executive branch, whose average tenure has been only 18 months.[9]

A president's political timetable in practice is briefer than the four-year term. Presidents and their advisers face the harsh fact that their honeymoon with Congress usually is short-lived. They are aware of the need to strike quickly and preempt the nation's agenda. Formerly, presidents accomplished this by submitting packages of legislative proposals, sometimes with catchy labels like "New Deal," "Fair Deal," or "New Frontier." President Reagan, whose goals lay less in enacting new laws than in curtailing old ones, relied instead upon the budget process to carry out his proposals for drastically shifting national priorities.

While the two-year electoral cycle affects the pace of Capitol Hill business, it does not dominate the policy-making timetable of members or their committees. After all, the average senator's or representative's tenure exceeds that of presidents and their appointed executives. Today's typical House member has been in Congress for about five terms (10 years); the typical senator for nearly two terms (11 years). Committee and subcommittee leaders boast even greater longevity. Most of them have witnessed the evolution of issues over a number of years, perhaps even a generation. They have watched administrations, and their policies, come and go. Most legislators, then, will be in office longer than the presidents they deal with, and many of them have more stable policy perspectives.

Sources of Cooperation

Despite the built-in tensions between the two branches of government, cooperation is at least as common as conflict. Day in and day out, Congress and the president work together. Bills get passed and signed into law: the 94 volumes of *United States Statutes at Large,* in which all enactments are compiled, testify to the cooperative impulses of the two branches. Presidential appointments are confirmed by the Senate; budgets are approved and the government is kept afloat—although sometimes just barely. Cooperation is evident even when the White House and the Capitol are in the hands of opposing parties.

Constitutional Blending of Powers

As we have seen, the Constitution separated the instruments of governmental powers rather than the powers themselves. Quite obviously, accommodation between the branches is essential to make the intricate mechanism work. As Justice Joseph Story once wrote, the framers sought to "prove that rigid adherence to [separation of powers] in all cases would be subversive of the efficiency of government and result in the destruction of the public liberties." [10] And Justice Robert Jackson wrote in 1952, "While the Constitution diffuses power the better to secure liberty, it also contemplates that practice will integrate the dispersed powers into a workable government." [11]

Cooperation—or at least civilized give and take—is more the rule than the exception. White House personnel screening and selection, when it functions effectively, takes congressional preferences into account. Within the president's party, various Capitol Hill factions sponsor and lobby for sympathetic candidates; floor and committee leaders must be informed, if not always catered to, during the selection process. Most cabinets include a sprinkling of former members of Congress, chosen not only to appeal to Capitol Hill but to bring political savvy to the administration's councils. Unusually sensitive appointments—for example, in the wake of forced resignations, scandals, or acute policy conflicts—will be made with an eye to pacifying congressional factions.

Once sent to Capitol Hill, the president's appointments are traditionally accorded great respect. Not since the Eisenhower administration has a cabinet designee been turned down: Lewis L. Strauss was rejected as secretary of commerce by a 46-49 vote on the Senate floor in 1959. A combination of policy differences and questions of integrity led to the defeat. Subcabinet nominees are almost always approved.

Certain types of appointees demand special congressional scrutiny. Regulatory commissioners are, after all, located in the nether world between the legislative and executive branches. While nominated by the president, these appointees are not strictly members of the president's administration. Supreme Court appointees also lie outside the executive branch and are subject to serious Senate review. During the Nixon administration, two nominees to the supreme bench—Clement Haynsworth and G. Harrold Carswell—were rejected by the Senate after questions were raised about their competence and dedication to civil rights. Only a couple of years earlier, President Lyndon B. Johnson failed in two Supreme Court nominations—one of them withdrawn, the other not acted upon.

In general, though, few nominees are turned down outright. Of the 106,616 nominations submitted in 1981 by Ronald Reagan (the great bulk of them military officers), 105,284 were confirmed. None were rejected. But 33 were withdrawn (the most notable being Ernest Lefever, nominated as assistant secretary of state for human rights). Going unconfirmed were 1,299. Some of these were eventually approved; others were later withdrawn, and still others were simply left vacant—a White House tactic for holding firm while avoiding a direct clash with Congress.

In exercising other constitutionally blended powers, deference is paid at both ends of Pennsylvania Avenue. Presidents are expected to take strong initiatives; if they do not, Congress will voice equally strong complaints. When presidential initiatives are presented and pushed, Congress can be expected to follow suit in a majority of instances. Yet congressional committees and subcommittees remain jealous of their prerogatives and jurisdictions: their viewpoints must be checked out before new executive initiatives are launched and their wishes accommodated in negotiations.

Coinciding Interests

Partisan or ideological ties often bind the two branches. Presidents and congressional leaders have consulted informally on issues ever since the first Congress, when George Washington sought the advice of Rep. James Madison. Regular meetings between the chief executive and House and Senate leaders have occurred since Theodore Roosevelt's time. Today, congressional leaders of the president's party are two-way conduits, communicating legislative views to the president and, conversely, informing lawmakers of executive preferences and intentions. As Senate Majority Leader Howard H. Baker, Jr., described the relationship during the Reagan administration:

> [T]he majority leadership of this body has a special obligation to see to it that the President's initiatives are accorded full and fair hearing on Capitol Hill. By the same token, we have a special duty to advise the President and his counselors concerning parliamentary strategy and tactics.[12]

Ideological or factional affinities sometimes enable presidents to forge Capitol Hill coalitions outside their own party lines. Reagan was by no means the first conservative president to capitalize on the presence of "Boll Weevil" Democrats in Congress. Eisenhower and Nixon also bargained with southern Democrats to pass compromise White House measures and thwart more liberal alternatives. (Senate Majority Leader Lyndon B. Johnson used to carry a laminated scorecard showing how much legislation he had helped pass for President Eisenhower.)

These same Dixie conservatives were the bane of liberal presidents such as Franklin D. Roosevelt, Harry S Truman, and John F. Kennedy. Yet these chief executives could enlist help from moderate or liberal Republicans. Passage of Truman's internationalist foreign policy initiatives would have been far more difficult without the bipartisan imprint of Republican Sen. Arthur Vandenberg. Senate passage of the 1964 Civil Rights Act hinged on support from Republican Minority Leader Everett McKinley Dirksen who, though no liberal, became convinced that civil rights was "an idea whose time had come."

Thus the White House must seek out votes from a wide range of lawmakers on both sides of the aisle. There is plainly no other way to get legislative results. As FDR declared in his second State of the Union address, the "impulse of common purpose" remains a potent cause of cooperation between the legislative and executive branches.[13]

Public Expectations

Regardless of the policy commitments of the two branches, the basic need to sustain the federal government stimulates cooperation. Legislators and presidents have several common interests: winning elections, maximizing policy objectives, and keeping the government running. Sometimes there is little more to compel cooperation than the need to keep the government solvent. In 1981, Republican senators faced, many of them for the first time, the question of supporting their president's call for a hike in the national debt ceiling in order to fund government operations. Most of them opposed debt hikes on philosophical grounds; many had never voted for them. During a heated meeting on the issue, Strom Thurmond, the senior Republican and the Senate's president pro tempore, rose and addressed his colleagues:

> Gentlemen, I understand you are concerned that you always opposed an increase in the debt limit. Some of you served in the House, and you never voted to increase it. Well, neither have I. But I never had Ronald Reagan for President before, so I'm going to vote for it, and I believe you should too.[14]

Thurmond's appeal helped sway his wavering colleagues. The debt limit hike passed by a 64-34 margin, with Democrats holding back until a majority of Republicans went on record to support their chief executive.

The President as Legislator

Political scientists have long called the president "the chief legislator" because of his crucial role in the legislative process. This is a metaphor. Presidents do not directly introduce legislation nor do they appear as witnesses or participate in floor debate. (President Carter, however, met at the White House in 1977 to "testify" before congressional committee members on his energy proposals.) But the president can propose legislation, deputize allies and agents in Congress, and use or threaten to use the veto power.

The President's Legislative Powers

The president's legislative role springs from Article II, Section 3, of the Constitution: "He shall from time to time give to the Congress information on the state of the Union, and recommend to their consideration such measures as he shall judge necessary and expedient." Since Woodrow Wilson, these addresses have been delivered in person, recently during prime television time. Presidents focus attention, publicize priorities, and mobilize public opinion. By so doing they supply Congress with something that its scattered and decentralized structure prevents it from providing itself—an agenda.

Setting the Agenda. Framing agendas is what the presidency is all about. Within the White House, priorities are established for using the president's precious commodities of time, energy, and influence. Setting the national agenda poses the same problem written large: how to control other political actors rather than be dominated by their initiatives. That has been the essence of leadership for all presidents with extensive program goals—Wilson, the two Roosevelts, Jackson, and others at certain moments. Ronald Reagan's early days in the White House dramatically exemplified leadership through agenda control. It was easy enough for some to say after the fact that "Reaganomics" was an unworkable mixture of incompatible and wrong-headed decisions. (White House advisers such as David A. Stockman, director of the Office of Management and Budget, apparently understood the inconsistencies from the start.[15]) The Reagan program swept through the nation's capital not because it was a "better idea," but because it was the only game in town. Acting swiftly and communicating skillfully, the new president had imposed his agenda at both ends of Pennsylvania Avenue.

Agenda setting assumes that other actors welcome presidential leadership. For Congress, such leadership meets a need it has rarely been able to fulfill on its own. The First Congress lost no time turning to Treasury Secretary Alexander Hamilton for guidance on weighty economic matters. As time passed, Congress more and more equipped itself to respond to presidential initiatives, through the standing committee system and later through expert staffs. But central leadership from within is Congress's notoriously weak suit, especially in the contemporary "reformed" Congress with its panoply of committees, subcommittees, informal caucuses, and party bodies. Thus Congress is vulnerable to manipulation by presidents who understand its traits.

Presidents communicate their agenda in a variety of ways—not only in State of the Union addresses, but in special messages, reports, and required documents such as annual budgets. Through them presidents highlight priorities, provoke public debate, stimulate congressional deliberation, and exhort for attention and support. Modern Congresses also expect the president to translate executive proposals into draft bills or to give explicit guidance on legislation that does not originate in the White House. When such guidance is not forthcoming, complaints are heard. Thus in 1982 a Reagan employment and training bill to replace the tainted CETA program was slow to appear. Sen. Dan Quayle and other Labor and Human Resources Committee Republicans threatened to launch their own bill and proceed with hearings whether the administration produced a bill or not. At the last moment the threat worked and the White House sent up its own proposal.

How do presidents arrive at their legislative priorities? Many arise from long-held beliefs or convictions like those held by Wilson or Reagan. Others are byproducts of a style or frame of mind; the New Deal emerged from Franklin D. Roosevelt's pragmatic optimism. Other elements may stem from campaign promises, platform planks, or demands of influential backers or powerful lobbies. Needless to say, there are far more claimants for White House support than can ever be satisfied.

From the perspective of presidents and their supporters, some priorities are decidedly more pressing than others. Charles Bingman, a federal career executive, describes three agenda levels for incoming administrations: a priority agenda, an uncertainty agenda, and an unformed agenda.[16] The *priority agenda* is what an administration knows it wants to do in given areas and what its campaign supporters expect it to accomplish. For better or worse, this agenda is part of the baggage a new president brings to the White House. It consumes the energies of presidents and their advisers during their early months in office and often forms the trademark for the entire administration. In its *uncertainty* agenda, the new crowd knows it wants to move in a certain direction but is uncertain exactly what steps to take. The administration therefore looks around for formulas that fit its ideological and programmatic goals. Finally, the *unformed agenda* consists of a host of problems that the incoming political leaders did not anticipate or did not understand. It is a special challenge for presidents and their advisers to move into these second and third agenda levels, adapting their known goals to unfamiliar or emerging problems. Outsiders, including the permanent bureaucracy, can help the White House identify and clarify its stance at these agenda levels.

The formal mechanisms for sifting and choosing the "president's program" from the thousands of possible proposals are budgeting and central clearance. These functions are performed by White House staff aides and by OMB, the president's management arm. The annual budget season, during which the president reaches final decisions on the budget submitted for the following fiscal year, is a high point of agenda setting. Options are outlined, major decisions are posed, and at some point the president must say yes or no. A great part of federal spending (about three-quarters) is relatively "uncontrollable" because it has been mandated by prior actions of president and Congress and cannot be changed without revising the legislation. But within the budget's discretionary portion, presidents can indicate clearly the directions they wish to take. Indeed, the budget is such a powerful instrument of priority setting and agenda control that President Reagan chose it, rather than a list of new proposals, as the vehicle for his initial program. In addition to budget requests, federal departments and agencies submit to the White House their reactions to proposals in the pipeline. Along with White House staffers, OMB selects the approaches that fit best with the president's objectives. The final say, of course, rests with the president, although not all decisions reach his desk.

The Veto Power. The president's other direct window on the legislative process is the veto power. The Constitution (Article I, Section 7) requires the president to approve or disapprove bills passed by Congress. If the president disapproves, a two-thirds vote in both houses is needed to override the veto. Because presidents usually can muster one-third plus one of their own supporters, their vetoes are overturned rarely. Of the 2,391 vetoes from Presidents Washington through Carter, fewer than 4 percent were overridden by Congress.

If agenda setting is the carrot, vetoing is the stick in the president's array of powers. However, the veto is not merely a negative power; the most potent vetoes are those that are never used but are merely posed as threats. At each stage of the legislative process, lawmakers, lobbyists, and staff members ask, in one way or another, "What is the White House willing to live with?" Supporters of the bill normally would rather have it passed than not, even if they must yield points to the president to gain his signature. During times of conflict, however, lawmakers who oppose the president are not above passing a bill they know will be vetoed. Then they can take the issue to the country, portraying the president as heartless or unresponsive. Of course, presidents can play the same game, portraying their detractors as irresponsible spendthrifts.

The veto decision is a collective White House judgment. Presidents receive advice from their aides, OMB staff members, agency officials, legislators, and interest group representatives. Veto decisions usually are rationalized by one or more of the following considerations: 1) The bill may be regarded as unconstitutional by the president, the most common rationale prior to Jackson and a reason that still occasionally is given. 2) The measure encroaches upon the president's independence. Sometimes legislators load so many limitations onto a bill that presidents conclude their role will be compromised. 3) The bill is unwise public policy. 4) The bill as written is impossible to administer. 5) The bill will cost too much—a favorite theme of modern presidents.

Coalition Building

"Merely placing a program before Congress is not enough," President Johnson once declared. "Without constant attention from the administration, most legislation moves through the congressional process at the speed of a glacier." [17] The president's most important power over Congress is an ability to construct coalitions to push and support presidential initiatives. No task is more central to presidential leadership, and no task is more difficult or misunderstood. As Cronin puts it:

> The office does not guarantee political leadership; it merely offers incumbents an invitation to lead politically. It is in this sense that those best suited to the job are those who can creatively shape their political environment and savor the rough-and-tumble give-and-take of political life. [18]

Perhaps the rarest of all executive talents is the ability to build support among legislators. Franklin Roosevelt and Johnson had this talent in abundance; they truly enjoyed lobbying members of Congress and were uncommonly successful in recruiting allies. Wilson and Reagan had their periods of success, though both faced increased resistance as their administrations matured. Other presidents have had tougher sledding on Capitol Hill. Some, such as Nixon or Carter, displayed real distaste or lack of talent in dealing with Congress. Indeed, their inability to build coalitions was in a very real sense the measure of the shortcomings of their administrations.

In applying persuasive and bargaining powers, presidents must approach Congress, as a complex and decentralized institution, on at least four fronts: the congressional leaders, especially those of the president's own party; the scattered committee and subcommittee work groups of Capitol Hill; the individual members of Congress; and

Congress as a whole, as the object of media attention and grass-roots pressure.

Congressional Leaders. Presidents meet periodically with formal House and Senate leaders from their own party and occasionally from the opposing party as well. From these meetings party leaders gain valuable information on the president's plans and programs that can be turned into the coin of influence in dealing with their colleagues. Needless to say, face-to-face meetings with the president are only the tip of the iceberg. Leaders who are responsible for shepherding the administration's program through the Capitol Hill labyrinth may confer with White House staff as well.

Two Reagan administration examples illustrate how White House actions can help or hinder legislative leaders in advancing the president's cause. During the June 1981 struggle to approve the Gramm-Latta budget package backed by President Reagan, House Republican leaders were conspicuously aided by the president. A steady stream of legislators was called off the floor to take personal calls from Reagan. "I just wanted to tell you the president's on the phone," John H. Rousselot announced gleefully to his House colleagues.[19] Needless to say, leaders are buoyed by the knowledge that "the president's on the phone" backing up their actions. On the other hand, Senate Majority Leader Baker's effort late in 1982 to take up a controversial arms control nomination opposed by North Carolina Sen. Jesse Helms was undercut by the president. Baker had assured the White House that he had the votes to confirm the nomination, but when he moved to take it up, Helms rose to announce that the president would soon withdraw the name. Although Baker hastily dropped the matter, he was not amused by the White House reversal.[20] Failing to inform leaders on the Hill of current strategy is an unforgivable sin: legislative leaders would rather go down to defeat on a clearly defined issue than have the rug pulled out from under them by quixotic White House maneuvering.

What do presidents get out of their contacts with congressional leaders? At best they gain loyalty and support. Accurate information about Congress's mood as well as advice about where to look in seeking votes are other benefits. Sometimes the message is not what the president wants to hear. Early in 1983, Senate Republican leaders, apparently encouraged by White House aides, assumed the task of informing the president that cuts in military spending had to be proposed. Thus, congressional allies not only sustain and support but also inform or even warn.

Capitol Hill Work Groups. Bargaining with a few influential leaders no longer ensures passage of the president's program. Today Congress embraces numerous work groups—committees, subcommittees, task forces, and informal caucuses. Indeed, the proliferation of these groups is perhaps the distinguishing characteristic of the modern Congress. In the 98th Congress there were 107 *standing* work groups (committees and subcommittees) in the Senate and nearly 150 in the House. The average senator held nearly 10 seats on standing work groups, while the average representative held between five and six assignments. Leadership posts are nearly as numerous: every senator, regardless of party, is eligible to serve as chairman or ranking minority member on at least one standing committee or subcommittee. Even in the much larger House of Representatives, well over half the members hold such leadership posts.[21]

Informal voting-bloc groups outside the standing committee system also allow members to involve themselves in policies of interest to them. Before 1970 there were only a handful of informal caucuses; today there are about 80 of them. The Northeast-Midwest Coalition, known as the "Frost Belt Caucus," looks after regional interests; so do the Rural Caucus and the High Altitude Coalition. Industry concerns are voiced by such groups as the Textile Caucus, the Senate Steel Caucus, or the Mushroom Caucus. Other groups include the Black Caucus, Hispanic Caucus, Arts Caucus, and the Environmental Study Group. Informal groups have grown and prospered because they perform useful functions for individual members, in particular assistance with legislative, political, and electoral goals. For many members, such groups offer alternative channels of information and voting cues that are tailored to the legislators' own values as members of regional, ethnic, issue, or ideological blocs.

On any given subject, therefore, not one but many work groups may be involved. This confronts executive agencies with a bewildering array of access points in Congress. Formerly, a White House aide or agency lobbyist could forge alliances with the handful of legislators who served on the relevant committee. Those members could be counted on to carry the word to their colleagues. Today, liaison officers from executive agencies work with voting-bloc groups and frequently canvass large numbers of members, not excluding the most junior ones. As one State Department liaison officer observed, "It used to be that all one had to do was to contact the chairman and a few ranking members of a committee; now all 435 members and 100 senators have to be contacted." [22]

Individual Lawmakers. Much has been made of the autonomy of today's senators and representatives. Yet they are not free of outside influences; quite the contrary. Indeed, given the multiplicity of interested citizens and groups, and their unprecedented invasion of electoral politics, "special interests" are as powerful and pervasive today as they have ever been. One effect is that it is hard to pigeonhole legislators according to their party labels; rather, today's elected politicians are encouraged by circumstances to construct their own political parties out of bits and pieces of appeals tailored to attract their constituencies. Members march not only to different drummers but to *many* different drummers—first one, then the other. A different but equally evocative metaphor was used by John B. Breaux, who with colleagues from Louisiana and Florida went along with Reagan's 1981 budget package in exchange for White House reconsideration of sugar price supports, which it had opposed as inflationary. Asked if his vote could be bought, Breaux replied, "No, but it can be rented." [23] Sooner or later, presidents and their aides must "retail" their appeals, going individually to members of Congress to sell the White House position, ask for votes, and provide incentives for support.

Presidents always have had to make these personal, informal overtures. Washington dispatched Treasury Secretary Hamilton to consult with members; Jefferson socialized in the White House with congressional allies. The modern presidency, with its stress on legislative programs, led to the assignment of White House staffers to conduct day-to-day relations with Capitol Hill. Roosevelt and Truman dispatched close aides to contact members and help build support for legislation. Eisenhower set up the first separate congressional liaison office, under Wilton B. "Jerry" Persons and then Bryce Harlow.[24] Eisenhower's legislative goals were modest, and the style of his liaison staff was low-key and mainly bipartisan.

In 1961 President Kennedy expanded legislative liaison to advance his New Frontier legislation, appointing Lawrence F. O'Brien to head the renamed Office of Congressional Relations. O'Brien, the father of modern legislative liaison, dispatched staff aides to Congress to familiarize themselves with members from each geographical area, learn their interests, and plan how to win their votes for the president's program. Departmental and agency liaison activities were coordinated to complement White House efforts.

Presidents since Kennedy have added their individual touches, but all have continued the liaison apparatus. Nixon elevated his first liaison head, Bryce Harlow, to cabinet status; Ford enlarged the staff; Carter added computers to analyze congressional votes and target members for persuasion. In other respects, Carter's liaison operation drew less than rave reviews. Speaker O'Neill reportedly was miffed when he was denied extra tickets to Carter's inaugural; and he claimed to have met with top Carter aide Hamilton Jordan (whom he dubbed "Hannibal Jerkin") only three times in four years. While the inexperience of Carter's liaison people may have contributed to this appearance of ineptitude, Carter's own indifference to Congress was probably more to blame. When a president gives only sporadic attention to a function, staff productivity is bound to suffer.

Effective congressional liaison embraces a wide variety of services that aid legislators in their careers and induce them to go along with the president's initiatives. Being able to announce government contracts or projects in one's state or district is a valuable privilege, and liaison officers make an effort to relay this information so members can make such announcements. Special White House tours are a popular item. So are invitations to White House dinners and social events. President Reagan became famous for dispensing gift cuff links and theater tickets along with brief homilies on the legislation at hand, aided by index cards. Campaign appearances with the president, including opportunities for press photos, are valued for the favorable impression they convey that the lawmaker "has the ear" of the chief executive. By the same token, astute presidents avoid personal campaign appearances that might harm incumbents' reelection chances. Reagan's 1982 campaign schedule was a deft combination of appearances in areas where the president was popular and avoidance of areas where his programs were a liability.

Conversely, lawmakers who defy the White House can be made to pay a price for their independence. Legislators who belittle the president may expect a cool reception or tough phone calls from the president's advisers or even from the president himself. After he began attacking the Vietnam War, Sen. J. William Fulbright was banished from White House state dinners, even though his position as chairman of the Senate Foreign Relations Committee normally would have ensured invitations. More recently, Sen. Robert Packwood's criticisms of Reagan led the White House to remove his name from a party fund-raising letter and, later, to aid efforts to oust him as chairman of the Republican Senatorial Campaign Committee. After Republican Rep. Marc L. Marks delivered a speech on the House floor that was critical of Reagan, he reported receiving an "intimidating" phone call from a cabinet member implying that White House officials might hinder his job-seeking efforts after he retired from Congress.[25] There were even reports that the White House had compiled a "bad-boy list" of Republicans slated for disciplining. Withholding favors, it seems, is as important as conferring them. However, vendettas or "hit lists" may be counterproductive, because they place the president in the unseemly posture of appearing to squash honest disagreement.

Presidents and their staffs, then, devote large amounts of time to granting or withholding resources in order to cultivate support on Capitol Hill. This includes not only patronage—executive and judicial posts—but also construction projects, government installations, offers of campaign support, access to strategic information, plane rides on Air Force One, White House meetings, signed photographs, and countless other favors both large and small that can be traded for needed votes. Some of these services may seem petty or even tawdry, but it is out of a patchwork of such appeals that legislative majorities are often constructed.

The Public Fever Chart. Washington decision makers are endlessly fascinated by what "the people" are thinking; and, as Richard Neustadt has pointed out, their response to the president depends on their assessment of public sentiment.[26] Put another way, to lead Congress, a president must first convince the public. With public support, Congress can be coaxed, goaded, or intimidated into following the president's initiatives; without that support, members have added incentives to act independently.[27]

Presidents and their advisers realize they must act quickly to win support for their programs. Every modern president, no matter how popular, faces the fading of the "honeymoon period" when public hopes and approval run high. Popularity invariably slips as the administration remains in office. For some presidents, such as Eisenhower, the decline is minimal. For others, such as Truman, Johnson, Nixon, and Carter, the decline is precipitous. For all presidents, it means a brief-lived "window of opportunity" early in the term when bold initiatives are expected and most apt to receive favorable reaction.

The brevity of the honeymoon period led Reagan and his advisers to move fast to imprint the president's priorities upon public policy. Rather than choose the lengthy, laborious path of pushing proposals through the authorizing committees of Congress, the administration shrewdly concentrated its efforts on the budget process as a short-cut way of shifting spending patterns. The honeymoon would be brief, they reasoned, and committees would be unwilling to curtail programs they

379

had developed and nurtured. By passing budget targets, committees were given spending ceilings and told to conform. When the painful process yielded results somewhat short of the administration's goals, a second budget resolution was prepared and pushed through. The administration's gamble paid off: Reagan's popularity, and his plans for solving the nation's economic ills, persuaded the public to give unstinting support to "Reaganomics" during the early months of 1981. Members of Congress faced an unprecedented volume of mail, much of it voicing the same simple message: support the president. Enough lawmakers followed these instructions that Reagan enjoyed stunning legislative victories early in his administration.

The downfall of presidents, as measured by survey results, can constrict presidential leadership just as surely as honeymoon support can enhance it. Thus, as Nixon's popularity slipped in the wake of the Watergate scandal, the Democratically controlled Congress grew bolder in defying the White House and insisting on its own programs. The same thing has happened in other administrations. During Reagan's second year, Republican leaders on Capitol Hill forced him to accept new taxes that he had pledged to avoid; by the third year, Congress openly revolted against the Reagan program—a revolt that extended to both chambers and many shades of the political spectrum.

Events or trends can boost or depress a president's popularity. Some think the downward pull on presidential popularity is caused by a "coalition of minorities" phenomenon: every time a president decides or acts on an issue, he alienates those people who feel intensely on the opposite side. As the president makes more and more decisions over time, the number of alienated people grows.[28] Others hold that downturns are caused by the "fickle" segment of the public, those who are least knowledgeable, involved, or committed. They uncritically accept a new president's proposals, but when things go wrong, they quickly turn against him.[29] Neither of these views is totally persuasive. Public opinion fluctuations indicate that shifts flow not just from the coalition of minorities and the quirks of the least-informed people, but from wars, economic cycles, scandals, and other events.

As the most visible and understandable part of the government, the president tends to be praised or blamed for whatever happens in the public arena.[30] In today's competitive and hostile environment, it seems easier for presidents to fall short than to live up to expectations. If presidents are the unwitting recipients of windfall support, they are also the undeserved objects of criticism when things go wrong.

To neutralize or reverse erosions of public support, presidents are often tempted to "take their case to the people." The assumption is that Congress, the press, and other Washington power centers are excessively negative and cynical and that a vast reservoir of support exists "out there" in the nation if only the president can unleash and exploit it. Thus, a "fireside chat," a nationally televised address, a carefully staged symbolic event, or a nationwide tour may be able to reverse the president's fortunes. In an all-out White House campaign on an issue, the support of state and local officials will be mobilized. Members of interest groups will be brought to Washington and briefed by the White House public liaison office. Media exposure will be orchestrated to highlight White House policy objectives.

"Going public" on an issue is not without its risks. The president may raise expectations that cannot be fulfilled, make inept presentations, lose control over the issue, anger legislators whose support is needed, or put forward hastily conceived proposals. "Going to the country" is a potent weapon, but if the president already has overall support on Capitol Hill, such concerted efforts are not necessary.

Patterns of Interbranch Control

Shifts in power between Congress and the president are a recurring feature of American politics. The power balance is influenced by partisan control of the two chambers and by issues, circumstances, and personalities. Legislative-executive relationships are not zero-sum games, however. If one branch is up, the other is not necessarily down. Internal power fluctuations—within the executive branch or within the two legislative chambers—complicate the ebb and flow of power.

Of all the factors that affect interbranch relationships, partisan control is the most obvious. Three patterns have occurred historically. Both the executive and legislative branches may be controlled by the same party—a situation we might term, albeit euphemistically, *party government.* Or the president's party may control one but not both houses of Congress, a *truncated majority* situation. Finally, there may be *divided government,* with Congress and the White House in the hands of opposing partisans.

Party Government

In nearly 70 percent of the Congresses in this century, the same party has controlled the White House and both houses of Congress. But this orderly state of affairs is less common than it once was, as Table 14-1 indicates. One-party control has marked less than half the

Table 14-1 Partisan Control of Presidency and Congress, 1901-1985

	Congresses Since 1901	*Congresses Since 1947*
Party Government	29	9
Truncated Majority	4	2
Divided Government	9	8
Total Congresses	42	19

Congresses that have convened since 1947. During much of this period, tensions between the White House and Capitol Hill were high. The Carter administration, with its awkward and fitful efforts at legislative leadership, is only the most recent demonstration that one-party dominance does not necessarily produce interbranch harmony.

The rarity of party government in the modern era results from the overall decline in party identification and the rise of ticket-splitting by voters. Party labels are worn lightly these days, and voters split their loyalties as freely as they do their ballots. Thus, politicians at all levels are tempted to fashion their own candidacies, bypassing partisan appeals and relying on personal qualities or campaign technology. The Democrats remain the choice of a plurality of voters, and their candidates usually capture a majority of the votes cast in federal elections. In the House of Representatives this has translated into something approaching permanent control, inasmuch as House members have methods of constituency outreach that allow them to build personal reelection coalitions and insulate themselves from nationwide swings in attitudes.[31] At the presidential and senatorial levels, however, party disaggregation has produced more competitive contests: national tides matter, and candidates can win by minimizing partisan appeals.[32] This accounts in large part for the ability of the Republicans to capture the White House and even the Senate by stressing nonparty voter appeals. But whichever party benefits or loses, the decline of party support per se betokens continued division of control of the branches of government.

Eras of true legislative harmony—party government in the parliamentary sense of the term—are in this country few and far between: Wilson's first administration (1913-1917); Roosevelt's celebrated "New Deal" (1933-36); and the palmiest days of Johnson's "Great Society" (1963-1965). For good or ill, these were periods of frantic lawmaking, which produced landmark legislation and innovative governmental programs.

Wilson's "New Freedom." Wilson's first administration must have seemed a textbook fulfillment for a man who idolized the British Constitution and saw himself as a kind of prime minister shepherding his party's program into law. The president's leadership was timely because in 1910 insurgents had stripped the House Speaker of important prerogatives, leaving a power vacuum that was temporarily filled by the party caucuses. "Ever mindful of the unique powers of the British prime minister," notes one historian, "Wilson sought to establish as never before the position of the President as leader of both his party and the nation." [33] Wilson conferred repeatedly with the Democratic majority leaders—Sen. John Worth Kern of Indiana and Rep. Oscar Underwood of Alabama—not only at the White House but also in the little-used president's room at the Capitol. He had a special telephone line installed to reach party leaders quickly and directly. He stressed the importance of party loyalty: Democrats could freely differ and debate an issue in their caucus, but they should close ranks once the majority had decided the party's course.

Calling upon Democratic majorities in the two chambers, Wilson won approval for such monumental acts as the Underwood-Simmons Tariff Act, which reduced duties on 958 articles and provided for an income tax and tax levies; the Federal Reserve Act, which gave the federal government control over the nation's credit system; the Federal Trade Commission Act, giving the federal government authority to crack down on unfair competition in business; and the Clayton Antitrust Act, which reinforced and strengthened the Sherman Antitrust Act. The Smith-Lever Act formalized the agricultural extension system as a joint undertaking of the Agriculture Department and the nation's land-grant colleges.

With the backing of Democratic majorities in the House and Senate, Wilson in two years had wrought fundamental changes in the nation's tariffs, business laws, banking system, and agricultural education and research. Further legislation flowed from the ensuing 64th Congress (1915-1917). But the advent of World War I clouded Wilson's party government; in the last two years of his administration Congress was in Republican hands and his postwar peace plan in ruins.

"The Roosevelt Revolution." Franklin Roosevelt's first term, especially the celebrated first "hundred days," was another era of party government. A few days after taking office, Roosevelt called a special session of Congress to consider emergency banking legislation. By unanimous consent Democratic leaders introduced the act to conform to Roosevelt's wishes and grant him new powers over banking and currency. The bill was completed by the president and his advisers at two o'clock one morning. When it went to Capitol Hill, it was still in rough form, but before the 40 minutes allocated for House debate had expired, shouts of "Vote! Vote!" were heard on the House floor. As there were no copies of the bill in the House, the Speaker recited the text from a penciled draft bearing last-minute corrections. After only 38 minutes, the House passed the bill, sight unseen, with a unanimous shout.[34]

The Roosevelt "hundred days" was perhaps the most remarkable period of legislative innovation in the nation's history. After the Emergency Banking Act, Congress passed laws pertaining to the budget, taxation, unemployment relief, federal grants to the states, agricultural subsidies, federal supervision of investment securities, public ownership of public utilities, refinancing of home mortgages, federal bank deposit insurance, financial reorganization of the railroads, industrial self-regulation, public works, and an industrial recovery program. More acts followed in the 74th Congress (1935-1937).

Momentous as Roosevelt's initial achievements were, they did not ensure a smooth course with Congress after 1937. The second Roosevelt administration confronted such explosive issues as antilynching, tax reform, farm policies, and the president's disastrous Court-packing scheme. "Deadlock on the Potomac" was the way one historian described relations between the White House and Congress in the late 1930s.[35]

Johnson's "Great Society." The Great Society legislative out-pouring of the mid-1960s, like Wilson's New Freedom a half-century before, grew from a germinating process that had extended over a decade or more. During the Eisenhower administration of the 1950s, Capitol Hill Democrats developed and refined in hearings and reports a lengthy agenda of proposed programs—most notably Medicare, aid to education, employment and training, civil rights, and environmental preservation. When Democrat John F. Kennedy came to office in 1961, this agenda was ready for action. Although initially stalled in Congress, Kennedy's program had begun to gain momentum when he was assassinated in November 1963.[36] Seizing upon the wave of feeling that followed the tragedy, Lyndon B. Johnson, a master legislative tactician, pushed through the remainder of the Kennedy agenda and added other programs including the war on poverty and the food stamp program.

The unpopularity of the Republican party's 1964 presidential candidate, Sen. Barry Goldwater, brought a tide of new Democrats to Washington—more than two-to-one majorities in both chambers—to help build Johnson's Great Society. "The obstacles to that [Democratic] program had simply been washed away by the Goldwater debacle," James L. Sundquist writes.[37]

The legislative record of the 89th Congress (1965-1967) reads like a roll call of contemporary government programs: Medicare/Medicaid, Voting Rights Act of 1965, Older Americans Act, Freedom of Information Act, National Foundation on the Arts and the Humanities, highway beautification, urban mass transit, clean water, and the Departments of Transportation and Housing and Urban Development, among others. The legislative output rivalled Roosevelt's "hundred days" and might justifiably be called a second New Deal. Yet, as before, the honeymoon with Congress was short-lived. Johnson's consensus began to fall apart even before the 89th Congress adjourned, a casualty of escalating involvement in the Vietnam conflict.

Periods of "party government" as productive as these three are not problem free. The pace of lawmaking is sometimes so rapid that political institutions require years to absorb the new programs. Succeeding generations may retrench or even reverse ill-considered or ineffective programs. Some New Deal enactments, like the first Agricultural Adjustment Act and the National Industrial Recovery Act, were of this type. Important portions of Johnson's Great Society proved expensive or ineffectual and were dismantled (like the War on Poverty) or cut back (like food stamps) in the 1980s. One generation's achievements can prove another's stumbling blocks.

Few eras of party control produce so much legislation. More than control of the two branches is needed for legislative productivity. High turnover on Capitol Hill, a landslide presidential election, a sense of national urgency—these are among the forces that turn party control into party government.

Truncated Majorities

Truncated majorities are relative rarities in modern national politics. In only four Congresses in the twentieth century has the president's party controlled just one of the two chambers: the 62nd (1911-1913), the 72nd (1931-1933), the 97th (1981-1982) and the 98th

(1983-1985). In every case, a Republican president—William Howard Taft, Herbert Hoover, and Ronald Reagan—faced a Republican Senate and a Democratic House. In the first two instances, the president's party had controlled both houses at the start of his term, but swings toward the Democratic party captured the House in midterm elections. In both those cases, Democrats went on to capture both branches of government two years later. Thus, the truncated majorities were byproducts of momentous social or economic events or a political realignment.

The truncated Republican majorities of the 1980s flowed from sources less dramatic than social upheaval or political realignment. First, the Republicans captured nearly all the closely contested Senate seats, including those of several vulnerable Democratic incumbents. A second reason was the Republicans' strength in the sparsely populated states of the Upper Plains and the Mountain West which are "overrepresented" in the Senate. In raw votes, Democratic senatorial candidates outpolled their opponents by a margin of about 51 to 48 percent in 1980 and 55 to 45 percent in 1982.

Whether it was luck, skillful Republican campaigning, the electorate's desire for change, or some other combination of circumstances, there was no denying that split-chamber control dramatically shaped the record of the 97th Congress. The media spotlighted President Reagan's successes in winning votes in the Democratic-controlled House, but it was Republican control of the Senate that provided the motor power for the administration's economic program. The fate of Reagan's 1981 budget and tax proposals probably hinged on Senate control by his party. In 1982, when the president's budget and tax leadership was challenged, it was Republican Senate leaders who grasped the initiative and moved in to fill the void.

Truncated majorities, then, do not always produce legislative stalemate. Before he left office in 1913, President Taft signed bills to create the territory of Alaska, establish the Department of Labor and regulate interstate traffic in liquor. Under Hoover, the 72nd Congress passed the Glass-Steagall Banking Act, the Federal Home Loan Bank Act, the Reconstruction Finance Corporation Act, and the Twentieth and Twenty-first Amendments. President Reagan's first year yielded a legislative outburst of a magnitude that recalled the early days of the New Deal nearly 50 years before.

President Reagan's initial success with Congress illustrates how a truncated majority can push its goals into policies. Even before his election, Reagan met with congressional Republicans on the Capitol steps to pledge a united front in reducing the size of the federal government. Once in power, White House and Senate leaders worked in tandem to set forth the agenda and keep pressure on the House of Representatives for action. Senate Republican leaders conceived the strategy of using the so-called budget reconciliation procedure to effect their goals. By lumping spending cuts into a single measure, they were able to bypass the authorizing committees, which take a proprietary interest in programs they have conceived and nurtured over the years. This approach also gave legislators some protection for supporting cuts that hurt their states or districts. The budgetary strategy was implemented with uncommon speed as the Senate reported and passed reconciliation resolutions substantially before the House did. This put the pressure on Democratic leaders and gave Republican leaders the leverage to forge alliances with conservative Democrats to provide a Reagan majority in the House. The president's own lobbying—with members one-on-one, and with the public through appeals for grass-roots support—persuaded legislators to go along with the package, even when they had reservations about specific program shifts. When a reconciliation measure devised by House committee leaders proved unsatisfactory to the White House, a bipartisan substitute package was hastily put together. It was filled with penciled-in additions, crossed out items, misnumbered pages, and even the phone number of a budget staff aide. Majority Leader Jim Wright complained:

> There never has been an administration that has demanded to dictate so completely to the Congress, certainly not Lyndon Johnson in his heyday or Franklin Roosevelt in his. I don't know what it will take to satisfy them. I guess for the Congress to resign and give them our voting proxy cards.[38]

With the Republican-Southern Democratic coalition holding firm, the House went along with Reagan's demands.

Like legislative outbursts in the past, the Reagan juggernaut soon ran out of steam. As constituents felt the effects of budget cuts, grass-roots support for "Reaganomics" sagged. Members, too, harbored misgivings about the way the budget process had roughed up the authorizing committees. In 1982 the president's budget and tax leadership was challenged. The Republican Senate grasped the initiative, drafting a corrective tax measure that eventually passed in modified form. When the 1982 midterm elections boosted Democratic ranks in the House, Reagan's extraordinary legislative leadership was undermined even further.

Divided Government

Government divided between the two parties has become common-place in modern times: eight of the 19 Congresses between 1947 and 1985 have been in the hands of the party opposed to the president. This includes two years of the Truman presidency, all but two years of Eisenhower's, and all of Nixon's and Ford's.

Under divided government, interbranch relationships range from lukewarm to hostile. During the Eisenhower administration, Democratic Congresses refrained from attacking the popular president, developing instead modest legislative alternatives and pushing them in election years. Hostility marked the relations between President Truman and the Republican Congress of 1947-1948, which he called the "awful 80th Congress" during his 1948 reelection campaign. The same hostility marked relations between Nixon and Democratic Congresses (1969-1974).

Today, as a result of shifting and indistinct party lines, politicians at both ends of Pennsylvania Avenue are in business for themselves. Like others in the "Me Generation," they are putting their career interests first. For legislators, this usually means picking their way carefully among issues, keeping some daylight between themselves and the president. For White House occupants, it means constructing coalitions for each new issue and reaching beyond party leaders to shape public opinion and bargain with individual lawmakers.

The psychology of divided government wears upon presidents and their advisers. No doubt it has something to do with the swift cycles of presidential popularity, not to mention the string of one-term presidencies. It also explains why some ex-White House aides are beguiled by the parliamentary system as a way to ensure working majorities for the chief executive's plans and programs.[39]

Assessing the President's Success

Shifts of influence between the White House and Capitol Hill are a recurrent feature of American politics. Scholars are tempted to designate certain eras as times of "congressional government" or "presidential government." Certainly there is an ebb and flow of power between the two branches, but one must be cautious in making such generalizations.

For one thing, influence in the legislative process is difficult to measure with certainty. Who really initiates legislation? A president may draw publicity by articulating a proposal and giving it currency, but the real origins may be embedded in years of political agitation, congressional hearings, or academic discussion. What exactly is "the president's program?" Major proposals are publicized by the president, but what of minor proposals? Lyndon Johnson used to announce support for measures already assured of passage to boost his record of success. Thus, not all measures endorsed by a president ought to be given equal weight. And who actually wields the decisive influence in passing a piece of legislation? Presidential lobbying may be persuasive, but no major legislation passes Congress without help from many quarters. For these and other reasons, measuring White House influence over legislation is hazardous.

The ups and downs of Congress and the presidency should be interpreted with care. The structure of either branch can be influenced by rapid changes in issues, circumstances, or personalities. Even during periods when one branch is in eclipse, it may exert potent influence. Nor are legislative-executive struggles zero-sum games. If one branch gains power, it does not mean that the other branch necessarily loses it. Generally speaking, expanding governmental authority since World War II has augmented the authority of both branches. Their growth rates may differ and their temporary fortunes diverge, but the lesson thus far has been that there is enough work for both branches. Finally, power shifts may affect some issues but not others. In foreign relations, cycles of isolationism and internationalism, nonintervention- ism and interventionism, have followed each other at fairly regular intervals.

Our constitutional system demands mutual accommodation on the part of the two political branches. Neither the presidency nor Congress is monolithic and neither dominates all facets of policy. Nonetheless, the two branches are fated to confront each other; they can be adversaries even when controlled by the same political party. The relationship between president and Congress, then, yields temporary winners and losers but is unlikely to produce a long-term victor or vanquished.

NOTES

* The views expressed in this chapter are those of the author alone and do not represent the views or positions of the Congressional Research Service.

1. U.S., Congress, House, *Congressional Record,* daily ed. 97th Cong., 2d sess., August 19, 1982, H6634. See also Ward Sinclair, "High Theater, Starring Tip and Cast of 434," *Washington Post,* August 20, 1982, A-1.

2. James S. Young, *The Washington Community, 1800-1828* (New York: Columbia University Press, 1966), 75-76.
3. Edward S. Corwin, *The President: Office and Powers, 1787-1957,* 4th rev. ed. (New York: New York University Press, 1957), 171.
4. William Maclay, *Journal of William Maclay,* ed. Edgar S. Maclay (New York: D. Appleton & Co., 1890), 128-133.
5. James Madison, Alexander Hamilton, and John Jay, *The Federalist Papers,* introduction by Clinton Rossiter (New York: New American Library, 1961), no. 48, 308.
6. Thomas E. Cavanagh, "Role Orientations of House Members: The Process of Representation." (Paper delivered at the annual meeting of the American Political Science Association, Washington, D.C., August 31-September 3, 1979), 20.
7. See, for example, Stephen J. Wayne, "Great Expectations: What People Want from Presidents," in *Rethinking the Presidency,* ed. Thomas E. Cronin (Boston: Little, Brown & Co., 1982), 185-199.
8. Glenn R. Parker and Roger H. Davidson, "Why Do Americans Love Their Congressmen So Much More Than Their Congress?" *Legislative Studies Quarterly* 7 (February 1979): 53-61.
9. Hugh Heclo, *A Government of Strangers: Executive Politics in Washington* (Washington, D.C.: The Brookings Institution, 1977), 103-105.
10. Joseph Story, *Commentaries on the Constitution of the United States,* 5th ed. (Boston: Little, Brown & Co., 1905), pt. I, 396.
11. *Youngstown Sheet & Tube Co. v. Sawyer,* 343 US 579, 635 (1952).
12. U.S., Congress, Senate, *Congressional Record,* daily ed., 97th Cong., 2d sess., December 23, 1982, S16115.
13. U.S., Congress, *Congressional Record,* 43d Cong., 2d sess., January 3, 1934, 7.
14. John H. Averill, "Thurmond Joins Insiders at Last," *Los Angeles Times,* April 25, 1982, pt. I, 12.
15. William Grieder, "The Education of David Stockman," *Atlantic Monthly* (December 1981): 38, 44-47.
16. *Management* 3 (1982): 6.
17. Lyndon B. Johnson, *The Vantage Point* (New York: Holt, Rinehart & Winston, 1971), 448.
18. Thomas E. Cronin, *The State of the Presidency,* 2d ed. (Boston: Little, Brown & Co., 1980), 168.
19. U.S., Congress, House, *Congressional Record,* daily ed., 97th Cong., 1st sess., June 25, 1981, H3365.
20. Mary McGrory, "Sen. Baker, Ever Decorous, Yanks at His Middleman's Strings," *Washington Post,* January 13, 1983, A-3.
21. Roger H. Davidson, "Subcommittee Government: New Channels of Policy Making," in *The New Congress,* ed. Thomas E. Mann and Norman J. Ornstein (Washington, D.C.: American Enterprise Institute for Public Policy Research, 1981), 109-111.
22. Daniel P. Mulhollan and Arthur G. Stevens, "Congressional Liaison and the Rise of Informal Groups in Congress" (Paper delivered at the annual meeting of the Western Political Science Association, Chicago, Illinois, 1979), 5.
23. *Congressional Quarterly Weekly Report,* July 4, 1981, 1169.
24. Stephen J. Wayne, *The Legislative Presidency* (New York: Harper & Row, 1978), 142.

25. Jack Nelson, "President's 'Bad-Boy' List Aims for Republican Unity," *Los Angeles Times,* May 23, 1982, pt. I, 1.
26. Richard E. Neustadt, *Presidential Power: The Politics of Leadership from FDR to Carter* (New York: John Wiley & Sons, 1980), 64.
27. George C. Edwards III, *Presidential Influence in Congress* (San Francisco: W. H. Freeman & Co., 1980), 86-115.
28. John E. Mueller, *War, Presidents, and Public Opinion* (New York: John Wiley & Sons, 1973), 205-208.
29. James A. Stimson, "Public Support for American Presidents: A Cyclical Model," *Public Opinion Quarterly* 40 (Spring 1976): 1-21.
30. James David Barber, *Presidential Character,* 2d ed. (Englewood Cliffs, N.J.: Prentice-Hall, 1977), 5.
31. Robert S. Erikson, "Malapportionment, Gerrymandering, and Party Fortunes in Congressional Elections," *American Political Science Review* 66 (December 1972): 1295-1300; Thomas E. Mann and Raymond E. Wolfinger, "Candidates and Parties in Congressional Elections," *American Political Science Review* 74 (September 1980): 617-632.
32. Barbara Hinckley, "Incumbency and Presidential Vote in Senate Elections," *American Political Science Review* 64 (September 1970): 836-842.
33. E. David Cronon, ed., *The Political Thought of Woodrow Wilson* (Indianapolis: The Bobbs-Merrill Co., 1965), lii.
34. William Leuchtenburg, *Franklin D. Roosevelt and the New Deal, 1932-1940* (New York: Harper & Row, 1963), 43-44.
35. James Macgregor Burns, *Roosevelt: The Lion and the Fox* (New York: Harcourt, Brace, 1956), 337-342.
36. James L. Sundquist, *Politics and Policy: The Eisenhower, Kennedy, and Johnson Years* (Washington, D.C.: The Brookings Institution, 1968), 481.
37. Ibid.
38. *New York Times,* June 17, 1981, A25.
39. Lloyd C. Cutler, "To Form A Government," *Foreign Affairs* 59 (Fall 1980): 126-143.

15. THE PRESIDENCY AND THE JUDICIARY

Robert Scigliano

The presidency and the judiciary share a common power under different names and perform similar tasks although in different ways. The framers of the Constitution arranged matters so that the two branches might act from a common interest in restraining Congress, but some of their sharpest differences have been with each other.

The Common Power

The executive and judicial branches are part of a system of separated powers that has its origin more in a theory of government than in its practice, especially in the works of the English philosopher John Locke and the French philosopher Baron de Montesquieu. Writing in the late seventeenth century, Locke seems to have been the first person to speak of executive power as something distinct from legislative power. The person who holds this power, he says, executes laws made by the legislative authority or, put another way, employs the common force as directed by the legislature. Before civil society or government existed, each man was in a state of nature, executing the laws of nature for himself. The state of nature continues to exist internationally in the absence of a world government, for each nation, like each person in the original state of nature, executes the law of nations for itself. Locke says that executive power in foreign relations, which he calls "federative power," almost always is given to the person who wields "domestic" executive power. There is no separate judicial power in Locke's scheme; judging is considered to be part of executive power. For example, Locke refers to "the administration of justice" as an element of the execution of the laws. However, he does consider judging to be a distinct activity, if not a distinct power, and insists on the need for "indifferent [impartial] and upright" judges.[1]

Montesquieu is the bridge between Locke and the American framers. Writing in the first part of the eighteenth century, about a half century after Locke, he was "the oracle who is always consulted and cited" on the subject of separation of powers, according to *The Federalist*. Adopting Locke's view that the power of judging is executive in nature, Montesquieu called this power at first, executive power relating to domestic matters, and then simply, executive power. We don't know why he did this, but perhaps he wanted to emphasize that, in his opinion, the courts typically executed the laws. Montesquieu renamed Locke's federative power "executive power in relation to external matters." [2]

Apparently influenced by Locke and Montesquieu, many Americans at the time of the founding thought of judges as engaged in the execution of the laws. According to John Adams, only the legislative and executive powers were "naturally distinct," and Thomas Paine wrote, "so far as regards the execution of the laws, that which is called the judicial power is strictly and properly the executive power of every country." In the Constitutional Convention, Gouverneur Morris observed that "the judiciary was part of the executive." Madison saw "an analogy between the executive and judicial departments [branches] in several respects" and mentioned that both the executive and the judges executed, interpreted and applied the laws. [3]

Madison was right. Executive officials necessarily interpret and apply laws when enforcing them, and judges enforce laws when they interpret and apply them. Consider the industrial foremen during World War II who wanted to invoke the National Labor Relations Act to protect their efforts to organize a labor union. The executive agency charged with enforcing the act had to decide that foremen were "employees" before it could extend the act's protections to them; and the courts agreed with the designation, thereby supporting enforcement of the act. (Unfortunately for the unionizing foremen, Congress then legislated foremen out of the labor law.) [4]

Many framers thought that judges could be associated rather closely with the president. A presidential cabinet containing the chief justice and the heads of the executive departments was proposed at the Constitutional Convention. In one version, called a Council of State, the president could "submit any matter to the discussion" of his cabinet and could "require the written opinions" of its members. The chief justice, who would preside over the Council in the president's absence, had the specific duty to "recommend such alterations of and additions to the laws of the U.S. as may in his opinion be necessary to the due administration of Justice, and such as may promote useful learning and inculcate sound morality throughout the nation." [5] These proposals failed because most of the framers were opposed to saddling the president with a council, not because they were opposed to a Supreme Court justice's membership on it. Indeed, in the final version of the

Constitution they did not prohibit judges from also serving in the executive branch, even though they did not allow members of Congress or the executive to serve in each other's ranks, or members of Congress to be judges. Thus a Supreme Court justice could be an ambassador and a secretary of state could be a member of the Supreme Court although neither official could be a senator or representative.[6]

President George Washington, who was fastidious in observing constitutional proprieties, saw nothing amiss in sending Chief Justice John Jay his circulars to department secretaries asking for legislation to be recommended to Congress. On numerous occasions Washington and Secretary of the Treasury Alexander Hamilton consulted the chief justice on matters of foreign policy and national security, including the constitutionality of Washington's Neutrality and Whiskey Rebellion proclamations. The president asked the Supreme Court as a whole for its written opinion on questions related to American neutrality in a war that had broken out in Europe at the end of 1792; he also asked Chief Justice Oliver Ellsworth, Jay's successor, for his written opinion concerning the House of Representatives' demand for papers connected with the Jay Treaty.

When Jay, as Washington's special ambassador to Great Britain, negotiated that treaty, he was a member of the Supreme Court; a few years later, Ellsworth, in a similar appointment by John Adams, negotiated a settlement of differences between the United States and France while serving on the Court. Jay served for about six months in 1789 as chief justice and Washington's secretary of foreign affairs until Thomas Jefferson was able to assume the latter office; and when John Marshall was appointed to succeed Ellsworth as chief justice in 1801, he continued as secretary of state for several weeks until replaced by James Madison.[7]

Congress saw nothing wrong with using judges to assist the executive. When it enacted Hamilton's plan for funding the public debt in 1790, it accepted the Treasury secretary's recommendation that the chief justice be a member of the commission to manage the fund for paying off the debt. A pension law that was passed in 1791 to handle the claims of Revolutionary War veterans made federal judges, in effect, aides to the secretary of war, for they were to examine pension claims and submit their reports to the secretary, who would approve or correct the reports and forward them to Congress. Supreme Court justices were included in the task, for in those days they "rode circuit," that is, periodically conducted court with district judges in the territorial circuits to which they were assigned.[8]

Thus in the earliest years of the Republic, presidents and Congress alike engaged judges in the business of the executive branch with hardly a thought that they might be violating the principle of separation of powers. We can assume that Washington, most members of Congress, and the justices of the Supreme Court, including Jay, Ellsworth, and Marshall, acted with some notion of what the Constitution allowed because they had been delegates to the national or state ratifying conventions.

Yet a stricter notion of separation of powers, one that placed the judiciary at a greater distance from the presidency, was emerging in the 1790s. No serious objections were made to the departmental "caretaker" duties performed by Chief Justices Jay and Marshall, but the appointments of Jay and Ellsworth as ambassadors did draw criticism, especially within the Senate when those nominations were approved. Senator Charles Pinckney, who had also been a delegate at the Constitutional Convention, urged a constitutional amendment in 1800 to prohibit federal judges from holding any other office. "If the President can hold out to the judges the temptation of being envoys, or giving them other offices," said Pinckney, "it might have a tendency to influence them in opinion." The Supreme Court itself decided that formal advice-giving to the President was improper, and in 1793 replied to Washington's request for answers to questions with a polite no. "Your judgment will discern what is right," the president was told. By this time, the chief justice's name had been dropped from circulars that Washington sent to his department secretaries and, not long after, the practice of informal advice-giving by individual members of the Court seemed to decline.

All members of the Supreme Court balked when Congress assigned them the task of deciding the pension claims of veterans in their circuit courts. "Neither the legislative nor the executive branch can constitutionally assign to the judicial any duties but such as are properly judicial, and to be performed in a judicial manner," said two justices in the New York circuit court; "the business is not of a judicial nature," decided two others in the Pennsylvania circuit; and, argued one justice in the North Carolina circuit, "the legislative, executive, and judicial departments are each formed in a separate and independent manner." The justices (together with the district judge) in the New York court said they were willing to "execute the act in the capacity of commissioners," that is, to consider themselves to be acting not as judges but, apparently, as executive officers; the others refused any cooperation. The Supreme Court acting in its own right never decided the question because Congress amended the law to relieve the judiciary of any responsibility for enforcing it.[9]

The president and the judiciary further adjusted their relations after the 1790s, moving toward sharper institutional separation and a clearer differentiation of the common power they exercised. Jefferson's eight years in the presidency hastened the separation. Little common ground existed between the judiciary and a president who regarded it as "the stronghold" of his defeated Federalist enemy: "There the remains of federalism are to be preserved and fed from the treasury, and from that battery all the works of republicanism are to be beaten down and erased." Nor could Jefferson possibly have enjoyed easy relations with John Marshall, whom he held to be a "crafty chief judge" and who in turn considered Jefferson's character "totally to unfit him for the chief magistracy."[10]

In the view of separation of powers that has prevailed since the 1790s, Supreme Court justices are supposed to have little to do with the executive branch (or the legislative branch, for that matter). For a justice to enter into executive service, as Jay, Ellsworth, and, in a small way, Marshall did, would be considered improper; in fact, only Justice Robert H. Jackson has done it since then, acting as the chief American prosecutor at the trials of the defeated Nazi leadership in Nuremberg, Germany. Many persons today would probably disapprove of a justice serving even in a quasi-judicial capacity off the Court, as Chief Justice Earl Warren did in chairing the commission that investigated the assassination of President John F. Kennedy, and as a number of justices had done previously, usually without a murmur of criticism. It still seems acceptable for justices to speak out, in a nonpartisan way, on matters that directly affect the court system; Chief Justice Burger has made a practice of giving the president and Congress his views on judicial workloads, the need for more judges, and reforms in the Court's jurisdiction. Perhaps most Americans would not object to the long-standing though intermittent practice of justices giving the president their views on appointments to the Supreme Court or lower federal courts, although it is interesting that this kind of advice-giving has always taken place privately.

Public sentiment is strongly opposed to judges acting as informal presidential advisers or helpers (as speech writers, for example). Such activities have not been an issue until recently, partly because they were not generally known until long after they had occurred, when correspondence or biographies of justices were published, but mostly because they seem not to have taken place very often. Apart from Chief

Justice Jay's assistance to the Washington administration, which was conducted before the protocol between justices and the executive had been established, not many justices have been involved in significant ways with the executive branch. Such involvement appears to be a phenomenon of this century (or perhaps judicial secrets have been harder to keep in modern America) and seems to have taken place mainly between justices and the presidents who appointed them. In each instance, the parties were continuing a previous political relationship.

This issue came to a head in 1968 when President Lyndon Johnson nominated Justice Abe Fortas, an old friend whom he had appointed to the Court three years earlier, to succeed Earl Warren as chief justice. Fortas's activities as a presidential adviser already had been widely reported in the press, and his nomination as chief justice led to further investigation of his ties to the White House. One account called him "a close and confidential adviser on everything from race riots to Vietnam." These reports were offered in the Senate as a major reason why Fortas should not be approved for the chief justiceship (he was not), and the justice's supporters as well as his critics expressed concern about judicial politicking at the White House.[11]

No executive position has been held by a Supreme Court justice since Justice Jackson in 1946; no justice has performed judicial functions outside the Court since Earl Warren in 1964; and none has overtly lent his services as a White House adviser since Fortas. Chief Justice Burger, who attained his position after Fortas resigned in May 1969 in response to disclosures of questionable financial dealings, apparently invoked President Richard Nixon's aid in 1970 to dampen a Republican-led campaign in the House of Representatives to impeach Justice William O. Douglas. The charges against Douglas were so weak that there was no chance that the campaign would succeed, and Burger's argument that the affair could harm the Court might be considered to fall within his proper concerns. The White House claimed that Burger's visit to discuss the Douglas matter was for the purpose of reassuring the president on his decision, just taken, to send American forces into Cambodia, but the chief justice quickly issued a denial.

Since the Fortas affair, presidents have refrained from nominating their friends or political associates to the Court in order to avoid charges of "cronyism," a term that Nixon used in the 1968 election in indirect criticism of the Fortas nomination. The closest any nominee since 1968 has come to being a "crony" of the president has been

William H. Rehnquist, who was an assistant attorney general at the time Nixon appointed him in 1971; but it is hard to describe as a presidential intimate a man whose name Nixon could hardly remember and whom he once called a "clown" because of his taste in clothes.[12]

In short, precedent more than constitutional requirements has tended to separate judges and executive officials. Today we hardly ever think of them as sharing a common power—the execution of laws—but they do.

The Two Executives

In their execution of the laws, the president and the judiciary play complementary parts. As a federal court described the relationship in an 1837 decision: "the judicial and executive powers are closely allied; they are necessary to each other in the discharge of the duties of both departments." [13] The differences between the two branches are important, to be sure. The president is an active agent in law enforcement with an energy—sometimes referred to as "force" by the framers—that pervades the entire government. He is an Argus with hundreds of thousands of eyes; his subordinates in the executive branch ceaselessly watch over the laws and those to whom they apply. He can do many things, do them with dispatch and, as the framers wished, do them secretly when necessary. Those who are slow to yield to him are prodded, and those who might be thinking of violating his orders are admonished. When prods and threats fail, the president's minions take the recalcitrant and disobedient to court to be coerced into compliance, punished for their disobedience, or, if they are fortunate, informed that they have not offended the laws after all.

Judges, on the other hand, are (or were intended to be) passive in their enforcement of the laws. They "can take no active resolution whatever," according to *The Federalist*. Theirs is the power of judgment, really not a power at all. To overcome their "natural feebleness," the Constitution gave them their offices during good behavior (practically speaking, for life) and prohibited legislative reductions in their salaries.[14] Yet, although judges act only upon the specific parties in cases brought to them, they, too, serve law enforcement generally, for many persons take note of what happens in court and govern themselves accordingly.

Like the president, the Supreme Court primarily supervises the work of others. Several hundred judges in the federal district (trial) courts and, above them, in the federal courts of appeals handle nearly all judicial business before it gets to the Supreme Court, which few cases do. The thousands of state court judges also act under the Court's supervision when their business involves "federal questions." Under today's expanded notion of federal authority, this covers a great deal of their litigation. The Supreme Court alone decides about 250 to 300 cases a year on their merits nowadays, less than a handful of which come into the Court without first having passed through other tribunals.

The executive assists the judiciary in several ways. It assigns marshalls to the judges to serve their writs and other orders, to make arrests, to guard their prisoners, and to transport those convicted by them to prisons it maintains. Moreover, it brings the judges much of their business. The executive arm of government institutes all criminal cases and a large portion of the civil cases that are tried in courts as well; and the government is often the defendant in other civil suits. In the 12 months ending on June 30, 1981, the government was a party, one way or another, in more than two-fifths of the 211,863 cases that were filed in federal district courts, and in nearly all of the minor criminal and civil matters tried before United States magistrates, who are appointed by district judges to hear such cases. The government was a party in about one-half of the appeals filed in the federal courts of appeals, which, incidentally, come to the appellate courts laterally from decisions of federal agencies as well as vertically from the district courts. In the 1980 term of the Supreme Court, which extended from October of that year to the summer of 1981, the executive was a party in nearly half the 277 cases that were decided on their merits.[15]

These figures only partly tell the story of the relationship between the executive and the judiciary. Consider the Supreme Court's caseload of 4,203 appeals in its 1980 term. The Court itself decides in nearly all appeals whether to accept cases, but it needs help in managing its agenda. The executive, through the solicitor general and his staff, who are located in the Justice Department but exercise considerable autonomy, provide a good measure of this help. The solicitor general almost always decides whether the government will appeal its defeats in lower courts to the Supreme Court, and the Court relies on him to approve only the most deserving cases. (In the 1980 term, the government appealed only 60 of its 664 lower court defeats, compared with 1,543 defeats that were appealed by its adversaries.)

The solicitor general helps out in other ways. He sometimes tells the Court which appeals by the government's adversaries are worth hearing and, increasingly over the past few decades, he has entered into other people's litigation in his capacity as *amicus curiae,* or friend of the court. In the 1980 term, the solicitor general suggested cases for review to the justices 44 times and threw the government's support to other parties in at least 33 cases that were being considered on their merits. Quite often, the Court will invite him to enter other people's fights, as it did in *Brown* v. *Board of Education* (1954), the case that ruled segregation in public education to be unconstitutional, and in *Baker* v. *Carr* (1962), which set the stage for the Court's "one person, one vote" doctrine in legislative reapportionment decisions. What seems still more remarkable, the solicitor general will on rare occasion come into Court to say that the government did not deserve to win a case in district court or the court of appeals.[16]

What does the executive ask of the Supreme Court justices in return? Only that they do their jobs in administering justice. Of course, the executive has its own idea of what justice requires: it would not have gone to trial, appealed its defeats, defended its victories in appellate court, or offered its friendly advice to the Court if it did not believe it was in the right. So in wishing that the Supreme Court—and the judiciary, in general—do what is just, the executive wants the courts to decide its way. And the courts usually do. In the 1980 term, the Supreme Court accepted for decision about 66 percent of the government's appeals, and 80 percent of the appeals supported by the government as *amicus curiae*. In comparison, the Court accepted only 3 percent of the appeals of the executive's defeated opponents. The executive branch does very well, too, in cases decided by the Court on their merits; it was on the winning side as party and *amicus* in 75 percent of the decisions in which victory could be declared.[17] Clearly, the executive branch is very active and persuasive in the Supreme Court, whether in getting into Court and keeping its adversaries out or in winning cases for itself and its friends.

What we have been describing is "tough" and "soft" law enforcement. The president is a tough executive and judges are soft executives. Unlike the president, whose hand grasps a sword in his capacity as commander of the armed forces, or Congress, whose collective hand clutches a purse, the judiciary, exercising judgment, holds the scales of justice. And judgment, *The Federalist* observes, is "easily overpowered, awed, or influenced" by the strength of the executive or the willfulness of the legislature.[18]

The tough executive, keeping his sword in scabbard and out of view, sometimes presents himself as softer than he is. What he executes, he or his defenders sometimes say, are laws passed by Congress— neglecting to mention that these laws in all likelihood were approved or even recommended by him. The Constitution, a president might add, imposes law enforcement as a duty, yet he and his subordinates seem to enjoy their work. He certainly resents interference with it, for he not only threatens and arrests but also calls out the military power of the nation to overcome resistance. Moreover, he cites his duty to execute the laws to justify some unusual actions: Washington's issuance of a Neutrality Proclamation in time of foreign war, Lincoln's proclamation of a blockade of southern ports during the Civil War, and Truman's seizure of the steel industry during the Korean War, for example. And when the tough executive really has his spirits aroused, he speaks of the duty imposed by his constitutional oath "to execute the Office of President," not simply the laws of Congress, and "to preserve, protect, and defend the Constitution of the United States," not simply support it. Whatever the tough executive may say about his power, ordinary citizens recognize it in the vast array of law enforcers, administrators, investigators, prosecutors, and jailers—all of them backed by the military might of the commander in chief.[19]

The exercise of judicial power looks quite different from the exercise of executive power. Wearing robes, sitting singly or collegially, judges seem to be onlookers above the fray, usually saying little and almost never in harsh tones. Tocqueville put the matter well:

> The judicial power is by its nature devoid of action; it must be put in motion in order to produce a result. When it is called upon to repress a crime, it punishes the criminal; when a wrong is to be redressed, it is ready to redress it; when an act requires interpretation, it is prepared to interpret it; but it does not pursue criminals, hunt out wrongs, or examine evidence of its own accord.[20]

Thus it is not the judges who are to be blamed for a defendant's presence in court, but the tough executive's prosecutor or the civil plaintiff's attorney. If it is a trial court, the judge will carefully explain to the criminal defendant his rights against the government or assure the plaintiff and the defendant in a civil trial of his neutrality in their contest. Occasionally, he will dismiss a case or find a statute unconstitutional. It is true that most persons accused of crime are convicted and nearly all civil suits end in a victory for one side or the other, but it is, as the trial judge may inform the parties, not his hand that has come down harshly but that of the law or the Constitution itself. Don't blame me, his tone implies, if things have gone badly with you or, if you must find fault with somebody, blame the jury—for they rendered the verdict. With this, the soft executive moves to the next case, turning over the criminally convicted to agents of the tough executive, and usually leaving one—or both—of the parties in a civil proceeding the poorer for having pursued their rights in court. The loser may appeal his case to a higher court, where again he will be treated with courtesy and perhaps sympathy—but probably no better result.

In this view of things, it is hard to think of judges as being in law enforcement, or even as being part of government; indeed they sometimes speak as though they were not. This is the secret of their power, for the work of judges is best done when they are thought to be different from busy administrators and busybody legislators. Perhaps this is what Montesquieu had in mind when he said that "the power of judging is, in a certain respect, nothing"—that it is also, in another respect, quite something. It is most effective when kept out of sight, when its actions are supported by judgment and the source of judgment is seen to be the will of the lawmaker. Judges forget the advantage that comes from being regarded as "the living oracles" of the law when they exercise "raw judicial power," that is, when they move into the domains of lawmaking and rough, exposed execution of the laws.[21]

The Limited Alliance

The framers believed that the powers of government had to be separated to secure the liberty of citizens and that the legislative power had to be restrained to preserve separation of powers. In the words of *The Federalist,* "the legislative department is everywhere extending the sphere of its activity and drawing all power into its impetuous vortex." The framers sought to restrain Congress by dividing it and by strengthening its rivals, the presidency and the judiciary, through an array of checks and balances directed against it. To be precise, they considered the House of Representatives, with its numerous members elected directly by the people for brief two-year terms, to be the main embodiment of the legislative power.[22]

The Constitution established two limited "alliances" against the "enterprising ambition" of the legislative power. One, between the president and the Senate against the House of Representatives, was to lead the Senate "to support the constitutional rights of the [executive], without being too much detached" from its own branch of government, in return for which the Senate received a share in presidential appointments and treatymaking. The other alliance, which is of present interest, was between the president and the judiciary against Congress as a whole, but, above all, against the House. The hope was that these two "weaker branches" of government would support each other against congressional encroachments on themselves and against legislative oppressions originating in the people. The "alliance" would be based on a shared interest in self-defense and, secondarily, in a common concern with protecting rights, especially those of property, against popular majorities. Only the self-interested basis for alliance will be examined.

As we have pointed out, many of the framers wanted there to be a link between judges and the executive branch in some of its activities. Their method for choosing judges and the president not only brought these officials somewhat close to each other but placed them some distance from both Congress and the people. Special electors, selected either by popular vote or by the state legislatures, would elect the president, and the president would appoint judges with the Senate's consent. Second, the terms of the president and judges were lengthened beyond those of the House of Representatives: the presidential term to four years and indefinite reeligibility and judicial terms to life—if the judges behaved themselves. The executive's major share in appointing judges meant that the judiciary would tend to reflect the constitutional and general political views of the presidency, although generally not the views of any single president.[23]

The president and the judges were granted powers to resist congressional encroachments (or perhaps, the judges had simply assumed theirs since the earliest days). The president's power, the veto, was considered a legislative power. The courts' power came to be called judicial review. Although it extended to review of actions by the president as well as by Congress, judicial review almost always was referred to as the power to review the constitutionality of legislative actions.

Some framers would have gone further in drawing the executive and judicial branches together. They made several attempts in the convention to establish a "council of revision" within which the president and members of the Supreme Court would exercise veto power over national and state legislation. The council would strengthen the president's confidence when dealing with the legislative branch, Madison and other leading members of the Convention argued. But its opponents said that such a body would form an "*improper* coalition" between the president and the Supreme Court. It might cause the justices to "embark *too far* in the political views" of the executive branch. Each time the proposal came up, it was rejected.[24]

How has this intended "alliance" worked·out? Have presidents and judges protected each other against the encroachments of Congress?

This is a difficult question to answer. In some but by no means all of their conflicts with Congress, the president and the judiciary have supported each other. Several times in American history, Congress has contested the president's right to freely remove executive officials whom he appointed with the consent of the Senate.[25] But the president's authority to remove executive officers did not reach the courts until the 1920s when an Oregon postmaster challenged his removal by Woodrow Wilson in violation of an 1876 law that required Senate consent. The outcome was the famous case of *Myers* v. *United States* (1926), in which the Supreme Court sided with the president by ruling that all attempts by Congress to limit his removal power were unconstitutional. In a later case, *United States* v. *Lovett* (1946), the Court again protected the president against an attempt by Congress to exercise a legislative power of removal, declaring void an appropriation rider that forbade the payment of salaries to three named executive officers unless the president renewed, and the Senate confirmed, their appointments. In other, fairly recent conflicts with Congress, however, the courts have not supported the president. Only nine years after it ruled in the *Myers* case that Congress could not limit the president's right to remove executive officials, the Supreme Court, in the case of *Rathbun* v. *United States* (1935), decided that congressional limits were permissible if the officials were members of agencies (in this instance, the Federal Trade Commission) engaged in "quasi-legislative" or "quasi-judicial" activities. And in 1958, the Court said in *Wiener* v. *United States* that the president's power to remove such officials was limited whether Congress wrote limits into law or not.[26]

A second area in which judges recently have refused to support the president is in his right to withhold information. This became an issue in the aftermath of Watergate, when President Nixon was suspected of having authorized or (as happened) having covered up an attempted forced entry at the Democratic Party's national headquarters at the Watergate Hotel in June 1972. Critical to the case of presidential complicity were tape recordings of conversations held at the White House before and after the incident. Presidents since Washington had claimed a right to withhold information that was sought by Congress or by others, usually for reasons related to the national interest. Never before had their claims been seriously challenged. Congress and its committees, it generally was said, had avoided a court test for fear of losing to the executive. When the Senate committee investigating the Watergate affair went to court in 1974 to obtain the White House tapes and related documents, it failed in its effort, which ended in the court of appeals. The committee did not pursue the appeal to the Supreme Court because the Court was then considering a case brought by the Watergate special prosecutor, who was seeking the release of the same information. The Court ruled that the materials had to be produced; and, when transcripts of damaging presidential conversations were introduced in the criminal proceeding, the Senate committee obtained indirectly what it could not get on its own authority. The Supreme Court knew that its decision in *United States* v. *Nixon* would gravely undermine Nixon's position with Congress. Indeed, the Court expedited its review of the case, over objections presented in the president's brief, by taking the appeal directly from the federal district court without an intervening hearing in the court of appeals, and then rushing its own deliberations to judgment. The Court's haste did not seem necessary to the criminal proceeding, but it did help those legislators who needed conclusive evidence for the impeachment of the president.[27]

Another dispute between the presidency and Congress was settled judicially in 1983. Since 1932, and increasingly since the 1970s, Congress has been making its delegations of authority to the executive conditional, reserving the right to repeal legislation unilaterally or to cancel executive actions taken pursuant to authority delegated by it. Presidents since Roosevelt have criticized the "legislative veto" for bypassing their own power to veto repeal measures and for interfering with their execution of the laws. For its part, Congress has argued that it may delegate authority to the executive conditionally, or not, and that the legislative veto is necessary for congressional control over a bureaucracy grown vast. Then, in June 1983, the Supreme Court sided with the executive in the case of *Immigration and Naturalization Service* v. *Chadha*, which involved a Kenyan citizen who sought to avoid deportation to his country. The attorney general had ruled that Chadha could remain in the United States and the House of Representatives, exercising the "one-house veto" permitted by law in such cases, had overruled him. All exercises of legislative power, the Court declared, henceforth must pass both houses of Congress and be submitted to the president.[28]

On their part, presidents have not always come to the aid of the judiciary when Congress has attacked its authority or members. Some presidents have applied gentle dissuasion to Congress. Nixon, for example, acted on Chief Justice Burger's request to discourage House Republicans from pressing their efforts to impeach Justice Douglas. Few situations have called for more vigorous action, because Congress has been irritated with the judiciary more often than it has been resolved to act against it. Even when presidents have kept silent, congressional squalls usually have spent their force unaided from the outside. Since the 1950s, however, attempts in Congress to deprive the federal courts (especially the Supreme Court) of jurisdiction over certain matters or to overrule the Court by amending the Constitution, have assumed more threatening proportions.

During this recent period, the judiciary could have used the president's help but did not get it. President Dwight D. Eisenhower was silent while Congress fought over legislation to deprive the Supreme Court of appellate jurisdiction in cases concerning internal security and related matters, and one bill came fairly close to being enacted. Presidents Gerald R. Ford and Richard M. Nixon also were quiet during congressional fights over laws or amendments affecting school busing, school prayers, and abortions. Nixon has revealed in his *Memoirs* that he once contemplated recommending a constitutional amendment "against forced integration and housing," but was glad that he had not.[29]

In most of Congress's serious threats to the judiciary, the president, far from being helpful or even neutral, has sided with the attackers. Andrew Johnson did veto a bill to deprive the Supreme Court of its appellate jurisdiction in habeas corpus cases, which contributed to his own troubles with Congress, but this was an exception. (The law was enacted over Johnson's veto.) Thomas Jefferson actually instigated impeachment action against John Pickering, a federal district judge, in 1803, and against Samuel Chase, a justice of the Supreme Court, in 1804. (The Senate convicted Pickering, removing him from office, but Chase escaped that fate and, by his good fortune, probably saved other members of the Supreme Court from impeachment.) Indeed, Jefferson and many in his party wished to use the impeachment power as a political weapon to purge the judiciary of its more obnoxious Federalists. Jefferson also was behind the repeal in 1802 of a law, enacted in the waning days of John Adams's presidency, that had established a circuit court system staffed by 16 judges. The repeal required Supreme Court justices to return to holding circuit court themselves. More important, by abolishing their positions, it removed the Federalist circuit judges from office without impeachment.

In 1937 Franklin Roosevelt urged Congress to pass a measure that would have enabled him to appoint six more justices to the Supreme Court. The purpose of adding to the Court, he claimed, was to assist the aging members on the bench, but his real motive was to lessen

Court opposition to his New Deal legislation. Only once before—and then to tie the president's hands, not to affect decisions of the Court—had Congress changed the Supreme Court's size for a clearly political reason: in 1866 it ruled that no appointments were to be made to the Court until its membership fell from nine justices to six. Congress protected the Supreme Court in 1937 by refusing to enact Roosevelt's Court-reform bill.[30]

President Ronald Reagan endorsed proposals to amend the Constitution to allow the states to prohibit abortions and to allow prayers in public schools. But as of August 1983, he had not lent the strength of his office to his endorsements, and congressional support for the measures had not been strong enough to secure their passage.

Presidency versus Judiciary

Presidents and judges occasionally have regarded each other, rather than Congress, as the encroacher upon their constitutional rights. Usually presidents have considered judges the transgressor, probably because the courts have many more opportunities to affect the actions of presidents than presidents have to affect those of judges. On a few occasions presidents have pressed attacks on the courts through Congress, notably Jefferson in the repeal of the circuit court act and Roosevelt in the attempt to increase the size of the Supreme Court. But only twice have presidents unilaterally breached what the Supreme Court has considered to be the boundary between the executive and judiciary. In each instance (both in times of war), they substituted for the regular courts of law special courts staffed by military officers. President James K. Polk authorized such courts during the Mexican War to condemn ships seized for trade with the enemy in American-occupied territory; President Lincoln authorized them in the Civil War for trials of civilians who were suspected of disloyal activities in states where the regular courts were functioning. War, and with it the reasons for which the special courts had been established, had ended before either decision was handed down, and neither president was still in office at the time. As a result, there was little reaction from the executive branch to what the Supreme Court had done. Presidents Franklin D. Roosevelt and Harry S. Truman made use of special military courts for the trial of enemy Germans and Japanese, but their actions, although challenged at the time, were later sanctioned by the Supreme Court.[31]

Much more often than judges, presidents have regarded the other "executive" as having encroached upon their constitutional powers.

Sometimes judges have earned this disfavor by telling presidents that the Constitution required them to perform acts that presidents thought they had a constitutional right not to perform. For example, the court trying Burr for treason summoned Jefferson to appear in Richmond as a witness and to bring along certain documents, unless he could satisfy the court that he should be excused. The president's objections to the subpoena were only intensified because his enemy of old, John Marshall, was presiding at the Burr trial in his capacity as a circuit court judge. (Congress, at Jefferson's urging, had sent Supreme Court justices back on circuit duty in 1802.) The court that tried some of the Watergate defendants similarly instructed Richard Nixon to turn over documents that were in his possession.

Sometimes the unwelcome news from judges is that presidents must stop doing something they thought they had a right to do. Several federal and state judges during the Civil War told Lincoln that he had no right to suspend the writ of habeas corpus and keep under military arrest persons suspected of disloyalty or draft evasion. In a rash of judicial decisions, culminating in *Train* v. *City of New York* (1975), the judiciary told Nixon that he could not impound (refuse to spend) money appropriated by Congress for social programs.[32]

Taking American history as a whole, however, the courts have not been unduly hard on the office of president. According to the foremost study on the subject, Glendon Schubert's *The Presidency in the Courts,* the Supreme Court has declared unconstitutional only a small number of presidential orders— perhaps 16 between 1789 and 1956. Eight more have been voided between then and 1975. The Court has approved many more of the president's actions. It upheld Lincoln's engaging the country in civil war, including the blockading of southern ports, without congressional authorization. It declared the president's right to remove most executive officials, as already seen. It said that the president—in this case Franklin Roosevelt, who was settling differences with the new Communist government in Russia—could use executive agreements for a purpose similar to treaties without the need of Senate consent; and later that the president—now Jimmy Carter, settling differences with the Communist government in China—could terminate the United States' defense treaty with Taiwan, also without Senate consent. Finally, the Court steadfastly refused to entertain suits that challenged the constitutionality of the Vietnam War.[33]

To be sure, some Supreme Court decisions have been adverse to presidential claims of constitutional authority. Three such decisions already have been mentioned: *Rathbun* v. *United States,* and *Wiener* v.

United States, which limited the president's power of removal; and *Nixon* v. *United States,* limiting his power to withhold information. In *Youngstown Sheet and Tube Company* v. *Sawyer* (1952), the Court told President Truman that he lacked constitutional authority to seize most of the nation's steel mills when a strike threatened that industry during the Korean War. In *New York Times* v. *United States* (1971), it rejected the argument made on behalf of the Nixon administration that the executive had a constitutional right "to protect the nation against publication of information whose disclosure would endanger the national security." This decision led to the release of a purloined documentary history of the Vietnam War, the Pentagon Papers, which had been prepared within the Defense Department. And in *United States* v. *District Court* (1972), it ruled that the executive needed search warrants to eavesdrop by electronic means on domestic organizations that were bent on subversion and violence, though not necessarily to spy on foreigners involved in such activities.[34]

Encroachments on the president's authority also include those judicial decisions that have held his actions to be unsupported by legislation. An early case of this type, *Gilchrist* v. *Collector of Charleston* (1808), decided by Justice William Johnson on circuit, hampered Jefferson's ability to enforce the Embargo Act by declaring that the act did not authorize certain of his Treasury secretary's instructions to customs collectors. In a more recent decision, *Cole* v. *Young* (1956), the Warren Court struck at President Eisenhower's executive branch Loyalty-Security Program by ruling that Congress had not intended to allow the summary dismissal of government officials in nonsecurity sensitive positions. This and other cases of the period indicate the Court's willingness to restrain the president without challenging his constitutional authority directly.[35]

The number of judicial encroachments on the president are greater still if we count invalidations by the courts of congressional statutes that he endorsed or initiated. The courts can strike at the president through the legislative branch, just as he can work through that branch to strike at them, and it is often the case that the president is more affronted than Congress when courts declare that Congress has, without authority, enacted legislation. When the Supreme Court declared unconstitutional a law to tax income, Grover Cleveland did not seem to mind, for he had let it be enacted without his signature. The same cannot be said about Franklin D. Roosevelt and his New Deal measures. The Court's decision in *Schecter Poultry Corporation* v. *United States* (1935) that Congress had no constitutional power to regulate wages, hours, and prices in trade and industry, or to delegate broad powers of regulation to the president, must have seemed to him to be as much an encroachment on his conduct as its earlier decision that he had no authority to remove a member of the Federal Trade Commission, in *Rathbun* v. *United States.*[36] The courts have on numerous occasions declared laws void that give the president authority to act. Thus, in one way or another, American presidents frequently have had reason to feel poorly treated by the courts.

The weapon of judicial defense against executive intrusions is judicial review. But what weapon can the president wield when he thinks the courts have invaded his domain? Must he obey the commands of judges when he thinks they infringe upon his rights under the Constitution? Must he obey commands that he thinks invade Congress's authority? Most Americans probably think "yes" is the only possible reply. They might say that the essence of the judicial administration of justice is in deciding cases and controversies, and that this function is undermined when anyone, including the president, stands "above the law" by refusing to accept the outcome of judicial cases. But *The Federalist* seems to indicate that the president may decide whether to enforce court judgments against others and that both he and Congress may decide whether to obey judgments they think are unwarranted. "The judiciary must ultimately depend upon the aid of the executive arm even for the efficacy of its judgments," it says in one place; elsewhere it refers to the judiciary's "total incapacity to support its usurpations [of authority] by force." [37]

A more recent opinion is that of an eminent member of the District of Columbia Court of Appeals, a judge of populist inclinations, who stated in a 1968 law journal essay that "if the [Supreme] Court is too far out of touch with the people, the Congress and the executive can annul its directives simply by refusing to execute them, or the people can do so by constitutional amendment." [38]

In a few circumstances, presidents have refused to do as the courts have ordered. Jefferson refused to show up at Burr's trial, furnish the requested documents to the court, or even answer the court's subpoena. (He did send some papers to the government's attorney with permission to make them available as he saw fit.) Similarly, Jefferson had his attorney general tell customs collectors to ignore Justice William Johnson's decision that executive instructions to them violated the Embargo Act (but then asked Congress to give him the authority he claimed he already had to issue them). Lincoln refused to acknowledge several judicial decisions ordering him or his commanders to release persons from military custody, the most famous of which concerned the case of *Ex parte Merryman* (1861).

Presidents also have threatened that they would disregard judicial commands, anticipating confrontations that never happened. Jefferson would not have had delivered William Marbury's commission for a judicial office if the Supreme Court had ordered it in the case of *Marbury* v. *Madison*—or so he said privately several years later. Lincoln informed Congress in 1863 that he would not "return to slavery any person who is free by the terms of [the Emancipation] Proclamation or by any of the acts of Congress." In a rather enigmatic note to himself he added, "[if] such return shall be held to be a legal duty by the proper court of final resort. . . I will promptly act as may then appear to be my personal duty." Franklin D. Roosevelt twice threatened—also privately—to disobey the Supreme Court. The first time was when it was considering cases that challenged Roosevelt's authority to take the country off the gold standard. (As it happened, the Court's decision in *Norman* v. *Baltimore Railroad Company* (1935) left his action intact.) The second instance occurred when the Court, to Roosevelt's annoyance, agreed to decide whether he could appoint a special military tribunal to try Nazi saboteurs landed from submarines on the American coast. The Court affirmed his authority in *Ex parte Quirin* (1942).[39]

Most recently, in the Watergate tapes case, President Richard Nixon hinted that he might not give over the tapes, whatever the Supreme Court ordered. As his counsel said in oral argument before the justices, "This matter is being submitted to this Court for its guidance and judgment with respect to the law. The president, on the other hand, has his obligations under the Constitution." Because Nixon realized, as he has stated in his *Memoirs,* that defiance of a clear ruling against him would have brought about his impeachment, he considered "abiding" by an unfavorable ruling without actually "complying" with it, that is, provide only excerpts of the tapes in his possession. Nixon required at least a month to carry off his plan, and, to stall that long, he needed a division of opinion on the Court—perhaps, he thought, only a single dissent. But the Court ruled against him unanimously.[40]

No president, so far as we know, has continued to enforce a law after the courts have definitively ruled it to be unconstitutional, nor has any president argued that he had such a right. However, Jefferson implied that he did in commenting on his duty toward the Sedition Act. So did Martin Van Buren, whose views were influenced by Jefferson's. In Jefferson's case, federal judges, including justices of the Supreme

Court on circuit duty, had upheld the validity of the Sedition Act in prosecutions by the Adams administration of newspaper editors and others. When he came into office, Jefferson, in his own words, "discharged every person under punishment under the Sedition law because I considered, and now consider [in 1804], that law to be a nullity." Van Buren's stand was even stronger. A president, he declared, would violate his oath of office and open himself to impeachment if he executed an unconstitutional law. If a president has a right—or duty—to refuse to support laws he thinks are void, even when the courts have said otherwise, is he not free—or required—to continue enforcing them when he disagrees with judicial decisions that have ruled them void? [41]

Jefferson and Lincoln sought to justify noncompliance with judicial decisions that were aimed directly at them, in contrast to those that affected them through invalidations of congressional laws. Neither addressed his remarks to the courts, however. When he was informed that Chief Justice Marshall wanted papers for the Burr trial, Jefferson wrote to the government attorney in the case that it was "the necessary right of the president of the United States to decide, independently of all other authority, what papers coming to him as president the public interest permits to be communicated." As to Marshall's power to require his appearance in court as a witness: "Would the executive be independent of the judiciary, if he were subject to the *commands* of the latter, and to imprisonment for disobedience; if the several courts could bandy him from pillar to post, keep him constantly trudging from north to south and east to west, and withdraw him entirely from his constitutional duties?" [42]

Lincoln explained to Congress, with Chief Justice Roger B. Taney's *Merryman* decision obviously in mind, that if he had exercised legislative power in suspending the writ of habeas corpus (which he thought he had not), his action was justified by public necessity and supported by his oath of office, to "preserve, protect, and defend the Constitution." Lincoln left it to his attorney general to answer Taney, which he did by asserting executive independence of judicial commands. "No court or judge," the attorney general declared, "can take cognizance of the political acts of the president or undertake to revise and reverse his political decisions." The president, he added, was "eminently and exclusively political in all his principal decisions." [43]

Aside from the plea of public necessity, how can presidential assertions of independence from judicial control be justified? The justification, it seems, derives from the principle of separation of powers. The Constitution makes the three branches of government equal and independent of each other; checks and balances serve to keep them that way. Judges need not accept actions by Congress or the president that they consider to be unconstitutional. Why should the president not have a similar right when he believes that judicial actions regarding his authority, or Congress's for that matter, lack constitutional support? Do not equality and independence imply reciprocity among the branches of government? At the very least, should not the president be able to require the courts to reaffirm their opinions of his powers one or more times before he accepts their decisions as conclusive? [44]

The president has a case against judicial determination of his powers and control of his actions. But to accept it is to raise other questions. Would not it tend to make him superior to law or to the judges whom the Constitution makes guardians of the law? Is there not a danger in this, as Harry S. Truman expressed when asked if he would accept what the Supreme Court might decide in the steel seizure case? "Certainly," Truman replied, he had "no ambition to be a dictator." [45] But again, the judicial case against the president tends to make judges superior to him in violation of the principle of separation of powers upon which a government of laws rests.

The claims of the two branches cannot be resolved on the level of principle because they are incompatible. Nor can one of the claims be chosen as preferable in principle to the other because both are essential to the constitutional system. What statesmen must try to do is to compromise when conflicts arise from these claims and, when it is necessary to act on a choice, to say as little publicly as possible.

Conclusion

As we have seen, the powers of the presidency and the judiciary have a common origin in the doctrines of Locke and Montesquieu. These powers interact in law enforcement. The framers assumed that presidents and judges would be the weaker parts of American government. To enhance their shared interest in supporting each other against the excesses of Congress, they drew these officials toward each other. We then examined the presidency and judiciary in their relations with Congress and each other.

The reader will have noticed that executive-judicial relationships have experienced conflict as well as harmony and that conflict has occupied a larger place in recent years. The framers did not expect the presidency and the courts to stand by each other in all their disputes, but only those in which Congress was the aggressor. If they thought that separation of powers usually would be imperiled by the legislature, they did not believe this would always be the case. Indeed, it is hard to say whether Congress was constitutionally at fault in some of its conflicts with the presidency or judiciary. Moreover, those framers who foresaw connections between the two branches did not calculate on the connections weakening as they have. Nor, it seems, did anyone foresee the impressive growth of presidential and judicial power that has taken place over the years, especially in this century.

It is interesting to compare relations between the presidency and the judiciary a generation ago and today. Schubert's study of those relations assesses them in the following terms: "In every major constitutional crisis between the executive and the judiciary, the president emerged the victor." The courts "normally do not attempt to second-guess the president on fundamental issues of public policy." The judiciary "can neither force him [the president] to do anything, nor prevent him from doing anything he may decide to do." [46] Prior to the 1950s, the courts probably were not quite so weak; since then they certainly have been much stronger. Indeed, they have in fact told the president what to do and kept him from doing things he wanted to do, willingly second-guessing him on matters of major importance. He has been informed that he cannot pocket-veto legislation during short congressional recesses, that he cannot refuse to spend appropriated funds, that he cannot conduct electronic surveillance of subversives without search warrants, that he cannot prevent the printing by newspapers of classified documents, and that he must turn over documents for use in criminal trials. The courts also have ordered his subordinates about more frequently in cases in which presidential authority has been less obviously at stake. And federal officials, including cabinet secretaries—but not prosecutors, members of Congress, or judges—recently have lost their absolute immunity from private suits when engaged in their official responsibilities; in a case decided in 1982, the president came within one vote on the Supreme Court of losing some of his immunity as well. Finally, although the judiciary formerly excluded many executive actions from their scrutiny by stating that they raised political and not judicial questions, the Supreme Court has discarded large parts of the doctrine of "political questions" since the 1950s. [47]

This surge of judicial power, which has been directed not just at the presidency, seems to originate in more than the willfulness of judges or in any strength given them by the Constitution. Once the foot-draggers in our governmental system, the courts have become an advance guard urging on the president, Congress, and the state governments. It is as if the Supreme Court, the leader in this movement, had decided after its showdown with the New Deal in 1937 that never again would it be exposed to serious attack on its weaker, left flank. In any event, the judiciary, the least democratic and, in constitutional intent, the weakest of the branches of the national government, has become the instrument of powerful democratic forces in our society.

NOTES

* The author wishes to acknowledge the research opportunity provided him by the White Burkett Miller Center of Public Affairs of the University of Virginia.

1. John Locke, *Two Treatises of Government,* ed. Peter Laslett (New York: New American Library, 1965), *Second Treatise,* paragraphs 87-88, 125, 131, 145-148, 219.
2. Alexander Hamilton, James Madison, and John Jay, *The Federalist,* ed. Jacob E. Cooke (Middletown, Conn.: Wesleyan University Press, 1961), no. 47, 324. Baron de Montesquieu, *The Spirit of Laws,* trans. Thomas Nugent (New York: Hafner Publishing Co., 1949), book 11, chap. 6, 151-156.
3. Robert Scigliano, *The Supreme Court and the Presidency* (New York: Free Press, 1971), 4.
4. Robert Scigliano, "Trade-Unionism and the Industrial Foreman," *Journal of Business,* 57 (October 1954): 293-300.
5. *The Records of the Federal Convention of 1787,* ed. Max Farrand (New Haven: Yale University Press, 1937), vol. 2, proposal of G. Morris and C. Pinckney, 342; see also Ellsworth's proposal, 328.
6. Constitution of the United States, Art. I, sec. 6(2).
7. *Diaries of George Washington, 1748-1799,* ed. John C. Fitzpatrick (Boston: Houghton Mifflin & Co., 1925), vol. 4, 139, 143; Frank Monaghan, *John Jay: Defender of Liberty* (Indianapolis: Bobbs-Merrill Co., 1935); and Samuel B. Crandall, *Treaties: Their Making and Enforcement;* Studies in History, Economics and Public Law (New York: Columbia University Press, 1904), vol. 21, 115-116, 120. See also *Supreme Court and the Presidency,* passim; and Russell Wheeler, "Extrajudicial Activities of the Early Supreme Court," in *Supreme Court Review, 1973,* ed. Philip B. Kurland (Chicago: University of Chicago Press, 1974), 123-158.
8. See Alexander Hamilton, Report Relative to a Provision for the Support of Public Credit, Jan. 9, 1790, in Hamilton, *Papers,* ed. Harold C. Syrett and Jacob E. Cooke (New York: Columbia University Press, 1962), vol. 6, 107. Act of March 23, 1791, in Hayburn's Case, 1 Law. Ed. 436 (1792), 437-438n.
9. Scigliano, *Supreme Court and Presidency,* 83. Charles Warren, *The Supreme Court in United States History,* rev. ed. (Boston: Little, Brown & Co., 1926), vol. 1, 111; Hayburn's Case, 407, 436-438.

10. Letter to John Dickinson, Dec. 19, 1801, in Thomas Jefferson, *Writings,* ed. Andrew A. Lipscomb and Albert E. Bergh (Washington: Thomas Jefferson Memorial Association, 1903), vol. 10, 302. Letter to Thomas Ritchie, Dec. 25, 1820, ibid., vol. 15, 298. Albert J. Beveridge, *Life of John Marshall* (Boston: Houghton Mifflin & Co., 1919), vol. 2, 537.

11. See the discussion of extrajudicial activity in *Supreme Court and Presidency,* chap. 3, "Out-of-Court Relations," 61-84. For additional information on Justice Fortas, see Bob Woodward and Scott Armstrong, *The Brethren: Inside the Supreme Court* (New York: Simon & Schuster, 1979), 127. For Chief Justice Burger's views on such activity, see "Why Courts Are in Trouble: Interview with Chief Justice Warren E. Burger," *U.S. News & World Report,* March 31, 1975, 138-139.

12. Woodward and Armstrong, *The Brethren,* 87-88, 189. Joseph Califano, Jr., *A Presidential Nation* (New York: W. W. Norton & Co., 1975), 254, accepts the White House's version of Burger's 1970 visit.

13. U.S. v. Kendall, 26 Fed. Cas. 702(1837), 749-50, Circ. Ct., Dist. of Col., No. 15, 517.

14. *The Federalist,* no. 70, 472; no. 78, 522-523.

15. Computed from data provided in *Annual Report of the Director of the Administrative Office of the United States Courts, 1981* (Washington, D.C.: U.S. Government Printing Office, 1981), Tables 4, 5, and 6, 126-127 (district courts); ibid., Table 13, 138 (magistrates); ibid., Tables 1 and 2, 124 (courts of appeals). "Office of the Solicitor General," in *Annual Report of the Attorney General of the United States,* 1981 (Washington, D.C.: U.S. Government Printing Office, 1983), Table 3, 5 (Supreme Court).

16. Computed from data provided in "Office of Solicitor General," 1, and Tables II-A and II-B, 3, 4. Brown v. Board of Education, 347 U.S. 483 (1954); Baker v. Carr, 369 U.S. 186 (1962). See Wade H. McCree, Jr., "The Solicitor General and His Client," *Washington University Law Quarterly,* 59 (1981), 337-47.

17. "Office of the Solicitor General," Table II, 5.

18. *The Federalist,* no. 78, 522-523.

19. Constitution, Art. II, sec. 1(9). See Abraham Lincoln, Message to Congress in Special Session, July 4, 1861, in Lincoln, *Collected Works,* ed. Roy P. Basler et al. (New Brunswick, N.J.: Rutgers University Press, 1953), vol. 4, 430.

20. Alexis de Tocqueville, *Democracy in America,* ed. Phillips Bradley (New York: Vintage Books, 1954), vol. 1, 103-104.

21. *The Federalist,* no. 78, 523n., has Montesquieu say that the judicial power "is next to nothing," but Montesquieu's words are "en quelque façon nulle." Blackstone, *Commentaries on the Laws of England,* Facsimile of 1st ed. (Chicago: University of Chicago Press, 1979), vol. 1, 69; Doe v. Bolton, 410 U.S. 179 (1973), White dissenting, 222.

22. *The Federalist,* no. 48, 333; see ibid., 334, no. 51, 350.

23. Ibid., no. 51, 350; ibid., no. 49, 339.

24. See, e.g., ibid., no. 78, 524. *Records of Federal Convention,* vol. 1, 21, 97-98, 138; vol. 2, 73-80 (the first quotation is on page 75); also, an attempt was made to allow the president and Supreme Court separately to disapprove legislation, ibid., vol. 2, 298-302. *The Federalist,* no. 73, 499.

25. See President Andrew Jackson, "Protest," April 15, 1834, in *A Compilation of the Messages and Papers of the Presidents, 1789-1897,* ed. James D. Richardson (Washington, D.C.: Bureau of National Literature and Art, 1901), vol. 3, 72-73.

John W. Burgess, *Reconstruction and the Constitution, 1866-1876* (New York: Charles Scribner's Sons, 1902), 157-194; James F. Rhodes, *History of the United States, 1850-1877* (New York: Macmillan, 1906), vol. 6, 105, 112, 139.

26. Myers v. U.S., 272 U.S. 52 (1926); U.S. v. Lovett, 328 U.S. 303 (1946); Rathbun v. U.S., 295 U.S. 602 (1935); Wiener v. U.S., 357 U.S. 349 (1958).

27. Joseph E. Kallenbach, *The American Chief Executive* (New York: Harper & Row, 1966, 423. Senate Select Committee on Presidential Campaign Activities v. Nixon, 498 F. 2d 725 (1974), Circ. Ct., Dist. of Col.; U.S. v. Nixon, 418 U.S. 683 (1974), Woodward and Armstrong, *The Brethren,* 342-346.

28. *Immigration and Naturalization Service v. Chadha, New York Times,* June 24, 1983, B5.

29. See generally Walter F. Murphy, *Congress and the Court* (Chicago: University of Chicago Press, 1962). Richard Nixon, *Memoirs* (New York: Grosset & Dunlap, 1978), 444.

30. Scigliano, *Supreme Court and Presidency,* 26-29, 44-51.

31. Jecker v. Montgomery, 13 How. 498 (1851); Ex parte Milligan, 4 Wall. 2 (1866); Ex parte Quirin, 317 U.S. 1 (1942); In re Yamashita, 327 U.S. 1 (1946).

32. Train v. City of New York, 420 U.S. 35 (1975).

33. Glendon A. Schubert, Jr., *The Presidency in the Courts* (Minneapolis: University of Minnesota Press, 1957), states on page 355 that there were 14 cases and lists 16 cases in the Appendix on pages 303 to 320; an updating of Schubert's list can be found in Michael A. Genovese, *The Supreme Court, the Constitution, and Presidential Power* (Lanham, Md.: University Press of America, 1980), Appendix, 303-320. The Prize Cases, 2 Black 635 (1863); U.S. v. Belmont, 30 U.S. 324 (1937) and U.S. v. Pink, 315 U.S. 203 (1942); Goldwater v. Carter, 444 U.S. 996 (1979); Mora v. McNamara, 389 U.S. 934 (1967) and Mass. v. Laird, 400 U.S. 886 (1970).

34. Youngstown Sheet and Tube Co. v. Sawyer, 343 U.S. 579 (1952); New York Times v. U.S., 403 U.S. 713 (1971); U.S. v. District Court, 407 U.S. 297 (1972).

35. Gilchrist v. Collector of Charleston, 10 Fed. Cas. 355 (1808), Circ. Ct., S. Car., No. 5420; Cole v. Young, 351 U.S. 536 (1956). See also Peters v. Hobby, 349 U.S. 331 (1955).

36. Schecter Poultry Corp. v. U.S., 295 U.S. 495 (1935).

37. The Federalist, nos. 78 and 81, 523, 545. The framers mainly thought of judicial review in terms of legislation, as these two numbers testify, because Congress was considered to be the main source of constitutional encroachments.

38. J. Skelly Wright, "The Role of the Supreme Court in a Democratic Society—Judicial Activism or Restraint," *Cornell Law Review,* 54 (November 1968): 11.

39. Ex parte Merryman, 17 Fed. Cas. 144 (1861), Circ. Ct., Md., No. 9487. Jefferson, Letter to George Hay, *Writings,* vol. 11, 215; Lincoln, Fragment [c. Aug., 26 1863?], *Collected Works,* vol. 6, 41, and Annual Message to Congress, Dec. 8, 1863, ibid., vol. 7, 51; Norman v. Baltimore & Ohio Railroad, 294 U.S. 240 (1935); Ex parte Quirin, 317 U.S. 1 (1942).

40. James D. St. Clair, *U.S. Law Week,* July 16, 1974, vol. 43, 3012; Nixon, *Memoirs,* 1043, 1052.

41. Jefferson, Letter to Mrs. John Adams, July 22, 1804, in *Writings,* vol. 2, 43; Martin Van Buren, *Inquiry into the Origin and Course of Political Parties in the United States* (New York: Hurd & Houghton, 1867), 342-343.

42. Jefferson, Letter to Hay, June 12, 1807, in *Writings*, vol. 2, 228; ibid., June 20, 1807, 241 (emphasis in original).
43. Scigliano, *Supreme Court and Presidency*, 41, 43.
44. See Tocqueville, *Democracy in America*, vol. 1, 106.
45. Truman, quoted in *New York Times*, May 2, 1952, 1.
46. Schubert, *Presidency in the Courts*, 4, 347-348, 354.
47. Butz v. Economou, 438 U.S. 478 (1978); Fitzgerald v. Nixon, 102 S. Ct. 2690 (1982).

Part VI

PRESIDENTS AND POLICY

Earlier parts of this book have been explicit in relating the presidency to other components of the political system. Here the accent is on policy making within the White House—domestic, economic, and foreign. In Chapter 16, Paul Light describes the policy-making process as "The Presidential Policy Stream"—"a stream of people and ideas that flows through the White House." In Light's analogy, the policy stream consists of four "currents"—problems, solutions, assumptions, and players—that are narrowed into final decisions by two "filters": resources ("to make and market the president's agenda") and opportunities ("to present the national agenda to Congress and the public"). Light concludes that presidential success is a matter of combining "the 'right' problems with the 'right' solutions, assumptions, and players."

Underlying Light's orderly taxonomy of the elements of presidential policy making, however, is that image of the stream—rapid, fluid, uncertain, and ever changing beneath the surface clarity. And bounding the presidential stream, shaping and being shaped by its course, are its banks—the rest of the political system. Both of these themes—fluid complexity and, even with the focus on the White House, the presidency's connections with the rest of the system—come through strongly in Chapter 17, "The Presidency and Domestic Policy: Organizing the Department of Education," a case study by Willis D. Hawley and Beryl A. Radin.

The idea for a federal education department is about a hundred years old, but its political birthdate is October 1975, when presidential candidate Jimmy Carter endorsed it in a successful appeal for the support of the National Education Association. Soon after Carter's election, however, a complex array of goals was attached to the department proposal, which Hawley and Radin classify as "symbolic status, political advantage, efficiency, effectiveness, and educational change." These goals were of varying importance and differing meaning to an equally varied and different constellation of political actors in Congress, the bureaucracy, the interest groups, and the Executive Office of the President. Carter's initial proposal had been for a department that would "consolidate the grant programs, job training, early childhood education, literacy training, and many other functions scattered throughout the government." The department that eventually was created in late 1979, after running the gamut (or swirling down the policy stream) of goals and actors, was a pale fulfillment of this promise.

The story of Carter's Department of Education illustrates the constraints on presidential policy making that are imposed by the political system. W. Bowman Cutter's case study in Chapter 18, "The Presidency and Economic Policy: A Tale of Two Budgets," suggests that even when the political problems are solved, other difficulties may await. Both Carter, in constructing the federal budget for fiscal year 1980, and Ronald Reagan, doing the same for fiscal year 1982, managed to overcome extraordinary political obstacles en route to securing Congress's assent to a policy of fiscal austerity. Having navigated these straits, however, each was blindsided by sudden changes in the economy that sent their budget deficits skyrocketing.

With the world outside the White House gates so threatening, presidents naturally are tempted to gather as much control over policy into the Oval Office as possible. Historically, presidents have been most able to do this in foreign policy. When Richard Nixon and his national security adviser, Henry Kissinger, assumed power in 1969, they did everything they could to seal out the public, the press, Congress, and the bureaucracy from participation in—or even knowledge of—foreign policy making. Yet according to Chapter 19, "The Presidency, the Bureaucracy, and Foreign Policy: Lessons from Cambodia," the results were not only disastrous, but the sources of the disaster were directly traceable to the White House-centered style: excessive secrecy, isolation from dissenting views, and an infiltration of personal psychology into public policy. The difficult lesson for presidents seems to be that the only thing worse than presidential dependence on the rest of the political system is presidential independence.

16. THE PRESIDENTIAL POLICY STREAM

Paul Light

Presidential policy is the product of a stream of people and ideas that flows through the White House. At the start of the term, the stream is often swollen with campaign promises and competing issues. The president's major task is to narrow the stream into a manageable policy agenda. By the end of the term, the stream is reduced to a trickle, and the president's major task is to pass the initial programs and get re-elected.

The stream itself is composed of four currents that come together in the White House. The first current carries the *problems* that confront an administration during its term: budget deficits, energy shortages, international crises. The second current carries the different *solutions* that emerge as answers to the problems: tax and spending cuts, solar energy research, summit diplomacy. The third current carries the *assumptions* that define the problems and solutions: economic forecasts, missile tests, guesses about Soviet intentions. The fourth current carries the *players* who participate in the presidential policy debate: presidents, their staffs, cabinet members, commissions.

Although these four currents carry the essential ingredients of presidential policy, they are narrowed into final decisions by two filters: *resources* and *opportunities*. Resources are needed to make and market the president's agenda; they include time and energy to make decisions, information and expertise to evaluate choices, public approval and party seats in Congress to win passage, and money and bureaucrats to implement final legislation. Opportunities are needed to present the national agenda to Congress and the public; these depend upon the ebb and flow of the major policy calendars and upon presidential cycles of increasing effectiveness and decreasing influence.

The four currents—problems, solutions, assumptions, and players—often flow together before they reach the presidency: problems find players; solutions find assumptions; problems find solutions, and so on. In theory, all potential problems, solutions, players, and assumptions exist somewhere in the presidential policy stream. In reality, presidents see only a fraction of the problems and solutions that merit attention. Most presidents deliberately structure the policy stream to limit the flow of problems and solutions to a manageable level, leaving the filtering decisions to the White House staff. Presidents who will not delegate (Jimmy Carter) or do not watch the evolving process (Ronald Reagan) are sometimes overwhelmed. The key to narrowing the policy stream to a final agenda of presidential priorities—and to winning reelection or a place in history—is to combine the "right" problems with the "right" solutions, assumptions, and players. Presidents differ, of course, in their ability to make these matches.

Before looking at each policy current separately, it is important to recognize that, like a stream, the policy process is extremely fluid. A change of problems—from economics to defense, from foreign affairs to domestic programs—has a rippling effect on the rest of the stream. A change of players—from Alexander Haig to George Shultz, from Edwin Meese to James Baker—significantly affects the kinds of problems and solutions that emerge from the filtering process. A change of assumptions—from optimistic to pessimistic, from best-case to worst-case—has a major influence on players who control the winnowing decisions. And a change of solutions—from supply-side to tax-side, from MX race-track to MX dense-pack—affects assumptions and problems.

Moreover, because the process is so fluid, few fixed rules apply. There is no required sequence for channeling the four currents into a policy agenda; no rule on where to start. Although the filtering process generally begins with the selection of a problem and continues with a search for a solution, some decisions start with a solution and only then move to the problem. Still other decisions start with a pessimistic forecast or an ambitious staff player. The presidential policy stream often transcends constitutional and legal boundaries, taking on a life of its own. The very notion that there is a presidential policy stream suggests a dynamic, often unpredictable process that is much less mechanical and orderly than our civics books have led us to believe.

Currents of Presidential Policy

Problems

Over time, the current of problems changes, and different issues merit presidential attention. The current includes old problems that have been discussed for decades and new problems that have just been noticed, large problems that appear to be virtually unsolvable and small problems that border on the routine. Although some problems seem to demand presidential action because of their seriousness, presidents retain considerable discretion over the choice of issues for their policy agendas. In 1969, Richard Nixon concentrated on foreign problems—détente with the Soviet Union, the Vietnam War, a new China policy—while largely ignoring domestic policy. In 1977, Jimmy Carter concentrated on domestic problems—energy, hospital cost containment, electoral reform, welfare reform—at the expense of foreign policy. In 1981, Ronald Reagan concentrated on economic problems—inflation, budget deficits, tax rates—while largely avoiding foreign and domestic policy.

Although presidents have wide leeway, some problems move through the presidential policy stream with more visibility than others. Medical care for the aged was a prominent problem long before President John F. Kennedy selected it for his domestic agenda in 1961; welfare reform was a problem on at least two presidential agendas before Carter tackled it in 1977. The rise and fall of problems within the presidential policy stream involves the combined interests of Congress, lobbyists, bureaucrats, and presidents, all looking for problems that match their political and policy goals.

Once a problem is "discovered," it may produce intense activity for several years. But hot issues usually cool off quickly. During the past decade, civil rights and education virtually disappeared from the domestic problem list, only to return as campaign issues for 1984. They were replaced by energy, welfare reform, social security deficits, and deregulation—issues that were not in the current 20 years ago.

The movement of problems within the presidential policy stream involves two simple patterns.[1] First, some problems surface so quickly and involve such controversy that all other issues are submerged. In 1981, Reagan's tax and spending cuts dominated the presidential agenda; little room was left for competing issues, including school prayer and abortion, until 1982. Other issues may dominate the problem current, not because of their controversial nature, but because of their appeal as easy targets for presidential success. In the late 1970s and early 1980s, economic deregulation greatly interested presidents: first railroad, then airline and trucking, now telecommunications. Second, some problems exhaust themselves over time, dropping from the policy currents. Often a problem proves so difficult that presidents and other policy makers finally let it drop. Richard Nixon, Gerald Ford, and Jimmy Carter all tried to tackle welfare reform and all eventually gave up.

On the other hand, some problems disappear from the presidential agenda because they appear to be resolved. One reason education dropped from the problem current is that Kennedy and Lyndon B. Johnson were remarkably successful in winning passage of their legislative agenda. Between 1961 and 1968, Congress passed a long string of education programs: aid to primary and secondary education, aid to higher education, Headstart, the Teacher Corps, library and school construction, school lunches, teacher education. For a decade after Johnson, many policy makers believed that the problems were solved. When education returned to the agenda in 1977, the problem was to build an executive department to house the programs as well as to find the money in a tight budget to pay for them. When education returned once more in 1983, however, the problem was defined as a decline in school quality, an implicit criticism of the Kennedy and Johnson programs. Perhaps some problems can never be completely resolved, returning at uncertain intervals in the policy stream.

Although individual problems come and go within the current, presidents generally think in terms of problem clusters: domestic, economic, defense and foreign affairs. Domestic and economic issues concern what happens *inside* the nation—even if the causes are international—while defense and foreign problems are about what happens *outside* the nation—even if the results are felt within the United States. These problem clusters are treated differently in the institutional presidency. Domestic problems usually move through the Office of Policy Development (known as the Domestic Council under Nixon and Ford, then as the Domestic Policy Staff under Carter); economic problems through the Council of Economic Advisers and the Office of Management and Budget; and foreign and defense problems through the National Security Council. The players in each cluster are generally separate (domestic policy aides rarely interact with national security staff), and the lines of communication radiate to different corners of the executive branch. Yet even if presidents think in terms of these "subpresidencies," [2] the distinctions frequently are blurred in reality. Foreign crises may cause severe economic problems at home; defense problems outside the United States may cause domestic problems, particularly if the solutions call for deep domestic spending cuts (Reagan) or draft registration (Carter).

Once the problem current enters the White House policy stream, the critical question is why some problems are selected and others ignored. Why did Carter pick energy shortages and welfare reform but neglect national health insurance? Why did Kennedy choose education and medical care for the aged but delay civil rights? Why did Reagan mention school prayer and tuition tax credits in his 1983 State of the Union address but not abortion? All problems carry some level of benefits that make them attractive to presidents. Although the levels vary from problem to problem, president to president, and year to year, they exist nonetheless. Theoretically, presidents could assign specific values to every problem in the policy stream, then choose the problems with the highest returns. Realistically, they can estimate only the rough rewards of one problem over another, either through public opinion or their own political instincts.

Ultimately, then, benefits are in the eye of the beholder. School prayer was an inviting problem for Ronald Reagan but of no interest to liberal Democrats; equal rights for women was an attractive problem for Gerald Ford but not for more conservative Republicans. The reason why one president will see value in a problem when another does not is goals. Presidents want to be reelected, because they care about their place in history, or because they truly believe the problems are important.

Consider these goals that shape the problem current. First, most first-term presidents want to be reelected to a second term. Although the Twenty-second Amendment limits presidents to two terms, reelection remains a powerful first-term goal. Reelection keeps presidents somewhat faithful to their campaign pledges in the first two years of the term: too many broken promises fracture the electoral coalition. Reelection leads presidents to search for new problems to rekindle campaign fervor in the third and fourth years. Reelection certainly guides presidents' decisions about when and where to change their course. Although there is considerable talk among former presidential aides of a single six-year term, reelection is the critical goal that makes presidents accountable to public opinion.

Second, presidents are interested in the judgment of history. As Thomas Cronin notes, "Both Kennedy and Nixon . . . wanted history to record that they had laid the foundation for peace not only in their own time but also for generations to come." [3] Herbert Stein, Nixon's chief economic adviser, also commented on the glory of foreign policy: "Presidents like to associate themselves personally with dramatic events, for reasons of vanity as well as of politics. There is hardly anything in economic action that can compete with the televised picture of the president alighting from Air Force One on the Peking airfield." [4] In recent polls of American historians, activist presidents who serve during periods of international crisis, lead the nation to war, veto more bills, and win greater legislative success rank higher in "greatness" than their more passive peers.[5] These lessons are not lost on new presidents.

Third, all presidents are interested in shaping the government in their own image. Presidents enter office with very strong beliefs about what should and should not be done. Each has a view of what constitutes good public policy. Reagan's attraction to budget and tax cuts was not just a play for electoral or historical support. It reflected his ideological beliefs about the size and role of government. Carter's concern for human rights in foreign policy was not simply a gesture to his religious followers or a pose for the history books. It sprang from his personal faith and moral convictions. Johnson's war on poverty was not a campaign ploy. It centered on his own experience in the depression and his recruitment into the New Deal tradition. Clearly, presidents select certain problems because they believe they are right.

The emphasis presidents place on each of these three goals varies. Preoccupied with history, Nixon installed the White House taping system to keep accurate transcripts for his own memoirs. Johnson seemed to be unusually involved in the reelection process, relishing the drive for the presidency more than the office itself. Carter may have been most concerned about his belief in humane foreign policies. Goals also change during the term. If Carter made most decisions on the basis of his beliefs at the start of his term, staff members report that he made most decisions on the basis of politics at the end.

Individual presidents may differ in their goals, yet changes in the electoral process over the past two decades have elevated the importance of reelection. With the ever-lengthening campaigns, presidents may become lame ducks if they do not announce their own reelection intentions as early as possible. For instance, with Alan Cranston, Walter Mondale, John Glenn, and several other Democrats already running hard by January 1983, Reagan was under considerable pressure to enter the contest, too. The critical question for students of politics is whether the start of the campaigns so early in the term limits the president's more "noble" goals of historical greatness and good policy.

Solutions

Solutions to problems take the form of legislation, executive orders, regulations, symbolic maneuvers, vetoes, or commissions. Even doing nothing is a possible solution in the presidential policy stream.

Sometimes presidents truly want to solve a problem; other times they only want to appear as if they want to solve it. Whatever the motive, presidents have a number of solutions at their disposal.

Once Reagan decided that budget deficits were a problem, he could adopt a standard "revenue-side" solution, raising taxes and cutting spending, or an unorthodox "supply-side" solution, cutting taxes as well as spending. Reagan chose the untested supply-side program, then added a massive $1.6 trillion defense buildup alongside his domestic spending cuts and three-year tax reduction. The program clearly did not reduce deficits. Reagan's 1983 budget forecast annual deficits of more than $100 billion into the late 1980s. Yet the success or failure of the program must be viewed in terms of the president's objectives. If Reagan's primary concerns were cutting the size of the federal government and easing the tax burden on corporations and the upper income class, his solution was a success.

The solution current has two basic features. First, each problem can have a number of potential solutions. As one Carter domestic policy aide told me: "There's never any shortage of people telling you what to do. They come out from under every rock with their own answer to the problems. Energy is a great example. We got ideas ranging from solar to geothermal to coal gasification to offshore drilling to conservation. It was more an exercise in picking the right ones."

Second, and more important, most solutions are designed to answer more than one problem. Indeed, when solutions are designed to solve multiple problems, the chances for legislative passage increase. Carter's hospital cost containment plan was advertised as a solution to four different problems: inflation, by holding down medical costs; deficits, by holding down Medicare and Medicaid spending; social security bankruptcy, by freeing up room for higher payroll taxes; and urban health shortages, by providing more doctors for inner cities. That the program did not pass is a tribute to the combined efforts of the American Medical Association and the hospital lobbies, who did not agree that hospital cost containment was the proper solution to the various problems.

The B-1 bomber is another example of a solution with more than one problem. Originally advertised as the new class of long-range bombers, the B-1 was cancelled by Carter. It reappeared in 1981 as a short-term solution to Reagan's "window of vulnerability." No longer new, the B-1 was promoted as a stopgap until a new "Stealth" bomber was ready.

Whatever the problem, presidents rarely develop solutions from scratch. As one author notes of defense planning:

> Programs have a life of their own and individual Secretaries of Defense can only nourish or slow them. In 1962, Robert McNamara introduced the idea of STRICOM, a rapidly moving strike command that could fight anywhere from the Arctic to the tropical jungle. By 1982, 20 years later, the same idea had been lifted to the concept of Rapid Deployment Joint Task Force. Then, finally, by [Secretary Caspar] Weinberger, to a new Central Command that can deploy strike forces over the troubled third world, and the blistering Middle East. But it is still based at the old STRICOM headquarters. . . .[6]

Thus, what may seem like a new program in a new administration often may be an old solution in a different package.

Obviously, presidential programs are often different.[7] Some solutions are large-scale and controversial, while others are small-scale and routine. Some programs demand federal funding to succeed, others rely on regulation. Some programs expand the federal role, while others contract it. These differences affect the likelihood of congressional passage.

Large-scale programs are more "expensive" politically than small-scale. They are more complex and thereby require more time to draft and explain. They are more controversial and thereby demand more time to move through Congress. They involve more conflict, both inside and outside the White House, and thereby absorb more political resources for bargaining. Moreover, because the presidential policy process does not end with the announcement of an idea, large-scale solutions usually exact more long-term resource costs. As Reagan discovered in 1981, winning a legislative war requires more than one victory. Not only did Reagan have to win initial passage of his tax cuts, but he had to defend them from counterattacks when the economy worsened in 1982. Presidential programs are more often the result of a sequence of minor battles instead of one major confrontation.

Solutions are actually the product of a string of decisions. First, presidents must decide whether to act. A president may understand the importance of a problem but still be unable or unwilling to propose a solution. A president may want the acclaim that comes from finding the problem but not the costs of winning a solution. Second, presidents then must decide just what to put into the solution. The choices are many. Should it involve legislation or executive action; include a specific proposal to Congress or an effort to veto a bill already passed; be new and innovative or a simple modification of past legislation; center on a large, complicated package or a small, modest bill; rely on spending or regulation to accomplish its ends; be short-term or leave more time for full implementation; be sent to Congress as a "take-it-or-leave-it" omnibus package or as a series of smaller, self-contained proposals? Although the list of questions is rarely so straightforward, each choice must be made at some point in the current of solutions.

Once the president decides to act, costs determine why some solutions are adopted and others ignored. Just as presidents weigh benefits in selecting problems, they measure costs in adopting solutions. First, presidents are very aware of *budget costs*. In an era of tight budgets and high deficits, new programs must pass the budget test before presidents will adopt them. Second, presidents assess *political costs*. Although presidents are interested in public reactions, they are concerned most directly with the question "Will it fly on Capitol Hill?" Presidents try to reduce their political costs in Congress by bargaining over pet projects, trading votes on other bills, assigning credit or blame, timing their requests to avoid overloading in important committees, lobbying to direct congressional attention to their priorities, and using the power of the presidency to stimulate public pressure. Certainly, trips to Camp David and invitations to White House dinners do not sway votes on major bills, but they do make it easier for members of Congress to stay in the habit of supporting the president longer.

Third, presidents are aware—sometimes only dimly—of *technical costs*. Unfortunately, the question "Will it work?" is asked only occasionally. Presidents appear much less concerned with workability than with budget and political costs. According to Martin Anderson, a domestic policy aide under Nixon and director of the Office of Policy Development under Reagan, Nixon's 1969 welfare reform plan never passed the technical hurdle: "No one seemed to clearly comprehend that there was, in fact, no way out of the dilemma presented by the conflicting goals of reasonably high welfare payments, low tax rates, and low cost. To some it seemed that the plan was 'such a good thing' that the possibility of it not being possible was never seriously considered." [8]

Presidents view costs, like benefits, differently. Among recent presidents, Reagan may be the most preoccupied with budget costs, while Johnson may have been overconcerned with politics. Since 1970, however, budget costs have become the dominant influence in the search for solutions. This major change in presidential policy making was evident in the Ford, Carter, and Reagan administrations: if a solution could not pass the budget hurdle, it was dropped. Concern with budgetary effects is, of course, a product of staggering deficits since the early 1970s. Yet, as the budget has grown in importance, the attention to technical issues has declined. Reagan's supply-side economic program and defense expansion surmounted both the budget and political hurdles, but as Office of Management and Budget Director David Stockman acknowledged in an interview in *The Atlantic,* they never passed the test of workability.[9] The critical issue is whether the three costs can ever be compatible. Do budget questions rule out potentially workable solutions? Do political costs conflict with budget considerations? And, if they are incompatible, which cost should come first?

Assumptions

Assumptions tell presidents what the world is like. They help presidents to understand the causes of problems and the effects of solutions. Some assumptions are based on complicated models of how the economy behaves; others are simple guesses about what the Soviets believe. Because there is always some uncertainty about how the world works, presidents often must make choices among competing assumptions. The president must decide, for example, whether the Soviets are basically evil (Reagan's assumption in a 1983 speech to evangelical Christians) or somewhat more humane (Carter's assumption until the invasion of Afghanistan).

As presidents make choices among competing problems and solutions, they must rely on the best available assumptions, which are themselves the results of subjective and sometimes conflicting estimates: How bad is the problem? Can it be solved? What are the benefits? How much will it cost? Will it work? What will the public think? When will the economy improve? Most of these questions cannot be answered in any objective sense. Presidents are no more gifted at fortunetelling than other human beings; they must rely on the best assumptions available. In early 1983, for example, Reagan was forced to choose between an optimistic economic forecast backed by supply-siders and a pessimistic forecast supported by more traditional advisers.

Assumptions may be the most important but least understood current in the presidential policy stream. Assumptions help presidents to predict the future, understand the present, and analyze the past. They help players recognize problems and work out solutions. Because assumptions are not always based on a complete knowledge of objective reality, conflict in the White House over which assumptions should be made can be intense. Indeed, assumptions are sometimes designed after the fact to build support or undermine opposition. Presidents may select a problem and adopt a solution for political, philosophical, or personal reasons, and only then prepare the evidence of need. Moreover, because presidents often see the world as they want it to be, not as it actually is, assumptions can become the critical flaw in a presidential program. For example, Reagan's overly optimistic assumption of economic recovery early in his term made change more difficult later on.

The role of assumptions in the presidential policy stream has become increasingly important during the last decade. In the 1970s, spending on federal programs, including Social Security, was increased automatically with rises in the Consumer Price Index (CPI). Thus, assumptions about future inflation became crucial for forecasting budget deficits. Much of what government now does is "uncontrollable" in the normal legislative process; thus assumptions have become the central element in telling policy makers when and where to act.

In all areas of presidential policy making, mistaken assumptions can have a dramatic effect. For example, although there was widespread concern in 1982 and 1983 about a short-term and long-term Social Security financing problem, even the experts disagreed about how much money was involved. The Social Security Administration based its 1981 estimates on five different sets of assumptions. Assumption I was geared to optimistic economic and demographic figures: lower inflation, lower unemployment, higher economic growth. Assumption II(A) based on Reagan's economic assumptions, was also optimistic. After Reagan's overly optimistic budget forecast in 1981, Social Security actuaries devised a more realistic II(B), or intermediate, assumption. Assumption III, initially the most pessimistic, projected higher inflation, higher unemployment, and lower growth. However, under pressure from the new Social Security Commissioner, the actuaries came up with a fifth estimate called "Worst-Case."

With five different assumptions, says one Social Security administrator, "Congress tends to buy off on the most optimistic estimates, when even the pessimistic ones aren't pessimistic enough. Congress sees the optimistic figures and concludes there isn't much of a problem, while we're fighting to make them see how bad it is." Indeed, one of the reasons why Social Security faced deficits in the early 1980s is that Carter based his 1977 reforms on intermediate assumptions instead of pessimistic ones, leaving a very narrow margin of safety that did not prove large enough in the 1980-1983 recession.

Presidents also must make choices on foreign and defense policy assumptions, which have their own sources of error. As Richard Betts, an expert on why surprise attacks succeed, argues, "estimates can never be perfect . . . because the facts—even 'hard' facts about the number and quality of Soviet military forces—cannot speak for themselves." [10] Questions about Soviet weapons and intentions dominate defense and foreign policy, particularly as presidents try to guess what the next problem will be. Do the Soviets think they can win a limited nuclear war? How accurate are the new SS-20 intermediate missiles? How strong is the Soviet economy? What are the Soviets' intentions in Afghanistan, Poland, and Africa? Because American intelligence gathering is limited, the answers to these and other questions are often speculative. Reagan was far more likely to perceive Soviet threats and a "window of vulnerability" than Carter.

Assumptions also shape foreign policy solutions. Will the Trident submarine pose a deterrent to the Soviets? How accurate are the U.S. cruise missiles? Will the MX deter Soviet aggression in the Third World? Can the United States fight and win a limited nuclear war? Assumptions about what the Soviets will do in response to U.S. actions are crucial both to theories of deterrence and to the legislative debate. During the 1978 congressional debate over MX, for example, Pentagon officials presented this scenario of what a Soviet planner would think with and without MX:

> *Without MX.* If I attack his forces . . . and his only response is counter value . . . then my residual ICBM forces may be enough to deter him from responding . . . and he may be subject to blackmail."
> *With MX.* If I attack his forces . . . then I must either use my residual forces or lose them. This would escalate the conflict and invite further retaliation. And he still has the capability to promptly attack my residual ICBM forces and counter value targets. Therefore, in this case, an attack is probably not worth it.

This "We know that they know that we know" assumption forms a large part of defense and foreign policy planning.

The choice of assumptions is also critical to the federal budget. The budget is extremely sensitive to changes in economic assumptions. In 1983, for instance, most of the increases in projected deficits came from changed assumptions. Of the $1.4 trillion in newly estimated deficits in the 1983-1986 period, $822 billion came from a more pessimistic economic outlook, not from any deliberate government action. Moreover, if the new forecast proved too optimistic, automatic increases in spending would force the deficits even higher. If the gross national product grew by only one percentage point less per year than the Reagan forecast, the five-year deficit would increase by another

$152 billion; if unemployment fell at just one percentage point less per year, the deficit would increase by $121 billion. How can the president and Congress pass a budget when mistakes cost so much? The usual answer is to make the assumptions fit the budget, not vice versa. As Allen Schick, a budget specialist formerly with the Congressional Research Service, explains:

> It is politically difficult for a president to publish best-guess projections about the future course of the economy. To project rising prices or higher unemployment is to pronounce one's budget policy a failure. Economic forecasts are congenitally optimistic; they project the next year to be more favorable than the one preceding it. Unemployment and inflation will abate, economic growth will be vigorous, interest rates will decline. With these projections, it is easy to promise a balanced budget, not right away, but within a few years.[11]

Most problems are selected on the basis of worst-case assumptions. Why solve the problem if it is not bad? The emphasis shifts to best-case assumptions for selling solutions. Why pass the program if it will not work? Once a solution is enacted and implemented, presidents shift back to worst-case. What would happen if the solution was dismantled? In 1981, Stockman used dire projections of huge budget deficits to define the federal spending problem (worst-case) and hopeful projections of increased productivity to sell the president's program (best-case). By 1983, the Reagan administration was relying on very negative economic projections. For the first time in the administration, White House forecasts were more, not less, pessimistic than the Congressional Budget Office projections. Indeed, in 1983 Stockman publicly admitted the administration's "inability to predict the economy for one year," adding, "that should be evident after the experience that we've gone through."[12] The administration's new argument was that 1983 was not the year to cancel tax cuts or increase domestic spending. Unlike in 1981, congressional Democrats countered with optimism, accusing the White House of "low-balling" the economic forecast.

The result of such debate over assumptions is that the worst-case rhetoric about *problems* leads to greater public panic: Is Social Security going bankrupt? Is nuclear war inevitable? In contrast, best-case assumptions about *solutions* lead toward higher public expectations about the future. In 1977, Jimmy Carter proclaimed that Social Security would be solvent into the next century. It is unsurprising that public confidence in the system was undermined when the problem reappeared scarcely three years later.

Players

Several thousand people actively engage in presidential policy making: White House staffers, cabinet secretaries, OMB analysts, bureaucrats, old friends, pollsters, the first lady, the vice president, and a host of lesser lights. Certainly the most important player is the president. As Abraham Lincoln once said to his cabinet after a heated debate: "One Aye, Seven Nays. The Ayes have it." Yet the mix of players can have an important bearing on the president's final decisions. When Shultz replaced Haig as Reagan's secretary of state, the constellation of advice changed immediately. As a former director of OMB and secretary of the Treasury, Shultz brought a much stronger economic background to his foreign policy views. Suddenly international trade was elevated as a problem in the Reagan White House. Shultz also began to participate in White House debates on the economy. He was widely seen as a powerful force in persuading Reagan of the need for a pessimistic budget forecast in 1983, as well as deeper defense cuts. There is no question that Shultz changed the direction of the Reagan agenda. Nor is there any doubt that Shultz had to compete with and against other players for the president's support.

At least four major offices fight to influence the president's policy agenda. The largest is the *Office of Management and Budget,* which has primary control over the president's annual budget and the legislative clearance process. Each year federal departments are required to submit detailed budgets and legislative priorities to OMB, which reviews all of the requests, makes "final" budget decisions, and assigns priorities to each piece of legislation. Budget and clearance responsibilities give OMB considerable leverage in dealing with the president and the executive branch, and in Stockman's first months as Reagan's budget director they were skillfully manipulated.

The second major policy office is the *Council of Economic Advisers,* which is responsible for preparing the president's annual economic report and thereby has an important role in developing the most important set of forecasts and projections. However, unlike OMB, CEA has no formal power over the budget or legislation. The OMB director is guaranteed access to the White House, but the CEA chairman must battle for a chance to speak. Reagan's first CEA chairman, Murray Weidenbaum, was unable to crack Stockman's control of economic advice; his replacement, Martin Feldstein, was initially more successful.

The third major policy agency is the *Office of Policy Development,* which originally was named the Domestic Council in 1970. OPD is primarily responsible for the review of domestic policy issues for possible elevation to the president's agenda. Unlike OMB, which reviews all executive branch requests, OPD can be more selective, performing an important role in bringing major problems and solutions to the president's attention. OPD is the domestic counterpart of the fourth major policy office, the *National Security Council.* The NSC staff acts as a much smaller version of the departments of State and Defense and has evolved into a powerful alternative source of advice.[13]

Perhaps the most important feature of these four offices is their competition *against* the executive branch for White House influence. CEA competes with the Treasury Department; OPD competes with Health and Human Service, Housing and Urban Development, and Transportation, among others; NSC competes with State and Defense; OMB competes with almost all of the departments. Although departments sometimes gain a measure of influence through a skillful secretary, the White House policy offices have an important advantage in their proximity to the president. In the "us-versus-them" mentality that often dominates the White House, presidents frequently conclude that the executive branch simply cannot be trusted to follow the presidential point of view faithfully.

Within the White House, however, the four policy offices are not the only competitors. The Congressional Relations Office, Public Liaison Office, Vice President's Office, Office of the Trade Representative, Counsel's Office, and Press Office participate in the policy debate, usually through the device of a "paper loop" that circulates proposals within the White House. At the very top, the president's chief of staff exercises the ultimate control over the movement of ideas in and out of the Oval Office. H. R. Haldeman (Nixon), Donald Rumsfeld (Ford), Hamilton Jordan (Carter), and Edwin Meese, James Baker, and Michael Deaver (Reagan) all became powerful "gate keepers" in the presidential policy stream.

If players influence presidential decisions, the question is why some are included and others ignored. The first step in answering the question is to separate *advice* from *influence.* Presidents receive a great deal of advice from members of their staffs, but they do not always agree with it. Advice is the expression of a player's view of what should or should not be done. In 1983, supply-siders advised Reagan not to adopt a pessimistic economic forecast, lest Congress turn to tax increases. Their advice did not equal influence. Influence occurs only when presidents accept advice.

Unlike more traditional definitions of influence—player A causes player B to do something B otherwise would not have done—this view allows for a wide range of compromise and bargaining inside the White House. Influence varies by problem areas, by stages of the policy process, and by degree. One adviser might be influential only in economic policy, only in the agenda-setting stage of the process, and only 50 percent of the time; another might be influential only in defense policy, only in the implementation stage, but 90 percent of the time. This definition of influence also allows for change over time. For example the supply-siders lost in 1983, but they won in 1981. Thus, when looking at the players, two questions arise: Who has the opportunity to give advice? Who wins the final arguments?

In the competition to advise the president, two elements are important: physical proximity to the Oval Office and the president's own system of management. The closer an adviser is located to the president, the greater the opportunity to give advice. Although the Old Executive Office Building is scarcely 100 yards from the West Wing of the White House, former Vice President Walter F. Mondale once said that it was "like being in Baltimore." Mondale attributed much of his success in the Carter administration to finally winning a West Wing office. Proximity gives a player a "window" on what other players are doing and what the president wants.

Second, presidents vary in how they structure the movement of players in and out of the Oval Office. Some prefer to meet players face to face, while others rely primarily on written recommendations. More importantly, some presidents structure the White House organization to limit access, while others permit greater give-and-take. In a *hierarchical* system, advice usually flows up to the president through a small number of gate keepers. Under Nixon, H. R. Haldeman used this kind of system to limit access. If Haldeman did not want the president to consider an argument, it was never presented to him. In a *competitive* system, presidents seek advice from a wider range of players, often assigning responsibility for the same problems to different advisers simultaneously. Under Franklin D. Roosevelt, this approach increased the amount and quality of the advice that moved into the White House but also increased the conflict among staff members. In a *collegial* system, presidents organize their staffs like the "spokes of a wheel." President Kennedy was advised in an informal setting by a number of close aides—a collegial approach that worked with considerable success in the Cuban missile crisis. Although most presidents use a blend of all three management styles, they must eventually choose between more or less staff access. Under a hierarchical system, fewer players will be allowed to participate; under a competitive and collegial system, more players will be given access.

Once players give their advice, what then determines the fight for influence? First, players vary in their persuasive skills. Some advisers are more effective in presenting an argument than others. In the Nixon White House, for example, Daniel Moynihan, who became a senator from New York, was able to persuade the president on the merits of a costly welfare reform package. As one of Moynihan's chief opponents described him:

> . . . [H]e had great persuasive resources. In the sea of dark gray and blue that surrounded Nixon, Moynihan, in his cream-colored suit and red bow tie, gleamed like a playful porpoise. He was a charming Irish rogue, a delightful dinner companion, a fascinating teller of tales. His presence lighted the gloom of national policy deliberations, and even his opponents liked to have him around. The President liked to read his memoranda, sometimes even searching through the pile on his desk to find them.[14]

Second, and more importantly, presidents vary in the degree to which they can be persuaded. Consider James Fallows's portrait of President Carter:

> During the first year came . . . indications that Carter did not really know *what* he wanted to do in such crucial areas as taxes, welfare, energy, and the reorganization of government. In each of these areas, Carter's passionate campaign commitments turned out to be commitments to generalities, not to specific programs or policies. After taking office, he commissioned panels of experts to tell him what to do, usually giving them instructions no more detailed than his repeated exhortation to "Be Bold!"[15]

Carter's openness to persuasion gave his advisers more room for influence. Other presidents have been less flexible on major policy questions. Reagan, for example, steadfastly refused to drop the third year of his tax cut but showed considerable willingness to be persuaded on what his staff euphemistically called "revenue enhancers." Because presidents cannot take positions on all the problems and solutions presented to them, they are always open to persuasion on some part of their policy agenda. Because Nixon concentrated on foreign policy, he was persuadable on domestic and economic policy; because Reagan concentrated on economic policy, he was persuadable on foreign and defense policy.

The Filtering Process

As the policy stream flows through the White House, presidents must choose among the competing problems, solutions, assumptions, and players that make up the policy agenda. Because presidents cannot do everything, they must narrow the stream to a rather short list of priorities.

This presidential filtering process must serve two often competing demands in the policy stream. First, the filtering process must *merge* problems, solutions, assumptions, and players into final decisions. When the process fails, presidential proposals may face immediate defeat. Reagan's 1981 Social Security package, rejected by the Senate 96 to 0, is an example of a decision that moved through the filtering process without being matched with the political players. Second, the filtering process must *regulate* the flow of problems and solutions into the Oval Office. If too few items reach the president, important problems, solutions, assumptions, and players may be neglected. If too many items come to his attention, serious overloading may result. According to Schick, Reagan's economic program was the product of too many players working to solve too many problems. Supply-siders who cared about taxes, monetarists who cared about the money supply, and old-fashioned conservatives who cared about deficits all had some say about the Reagan program:

> The supply-siders got tax cuts; the deficitists got spending reductions; the monetarists got low money growth.... The price of these internal fissures was contradictory economic policy. Monetary restraint clashed with fiscal expansionism, producing soaring interest rates and a sharp downturn in the economy. The monetary targets could not support the economic targets.[16]

In the search for the best match of problems, solutions, assumptions, and players, the policy stream expands to include a wider current of ideas. In regulating the flow into the president, however, the stream must narrow. Here the important question is "How much is enough?" How many problems should a president tackle? How many solutions should be reviewed? How many players should be involved? While Carter spread himself over too many problems, perhaps Reagan limited himself to too few. While Kennedy opened the stream to too many players, perhaps Nixon did not listen to enough.

In answering "How much?" presidents often must choose between waiting for a comprehensive review of problems and solutions or taking action.[17] If the president delays in setting the legislative agenda, others may do it for him. Congress, interest groups, and the executive branch are eager to rush in where presidents fear to tread. Although presidential scholar Richard Neustadt maintains that the first year of a term is a "learning time for the new President who has to learn—or unlearn—many things about his job," most White House staff members see the first year as the greatest opportunity for successful action. As Lyndon B. Johnson told his staff at the start of 1965:

> I keep hitting hard because I know this honeymoon won't last. Every day I lose a little more political capital. That's why we have to keep at it, never letting up. One day soon, I don't know when, the critics and the snipers will move in and we will be at stalemate. We have to get all we can, now, before the roof comes down." [18]

Stockman also understood the need to "move it or lose it." During the transition he warned President-elect Reagan: "If bold policies are not swiftly, deftly and courageously implemented in the first six months, Washington will quickly become engulfed in political disorder commensurate with the surrounding economic disarray." [19]

The risk of moving quickly is that presidents can make mistakes. Stockman soon recognized the danger. As he acknowledged in his *Atlantic Monthly* interviews, the budget was put together so fast "that it probably should have been put together differently." [20]

As presidents try to both merge and regulate the policy stream, they rely on two filters: resources and opportunities. As problems, solutions, assumptions, and players pass through these two filters, final decisions are set.

Resources

Resources "pay" for the final decisions presidents make. Some resources pay the costs of arriving at the decisions; others pay the costs of winning congressional passage; still others pay the costs of implementing the policies. Three basic kinds of resources are used for decision making, political marketing, and program implementation. These resources finance the presidential agenda.

Decision-making Resources. The most basic decision-making resource is *time*. Players need time to digest new ideas, form coalitions to influence the president, and review solutions. Similarly, problems need time to find sponsors, build public support, and locate solutions.

In theory, each presidential term starts with 1,461 days. In reality, the start of the reelection campaign early in the third year limits the available policy time to approximately 700 days. For particular policies, time can be much shorter. According to Stockman, there were only 20 to 25 days to build the Reagan economic program at the start of 1981.

Energy is a second decision-making resource. One only has to look at the "before" and "after" pictures of presidents to notice the wearing effect of the office on the individual. Similarly, some problems, solutions, and assumptions consume more energy than others. Few Carter staff members would equate the stress of the Iranian hostage crisis with the lesser demands of routine domestic policy.

A third decision-making resource is *information*. Knowledge about problems, solutions, and assumptions often varies significantly. Presidents can predict the accuracy of an MX missile within 200 yards on a normal East-to-West flight range but do not know the accuracy on the North-South arctic path to the Soviet Union. What would the magnetic fields at the North Pole do to the complex MX-guidance system? Presidents still have few proven theories on how the Social Security program affects the economy. As one economist warned the National Commission on Social Security Reform, "relatively little good evidence" is available to policy makers on the subject. Using the "best that economic theory and statistical techniques have to offer," economists "have produced a series of studies that can be selectively cited by the true believers of conflicting hunches or by people with political agendas that they seek to advance."[21]

A final decision-making resource is *expertise*. This resource applies specifically to the players, who must know how to bring problems, solutions, and assumptions together into final decisions. Policy expertise is more than the sum of an individual's experience in government. It is the skill that comes from learning.

Political Resources. The policy stream also absorbs political resources. As Vice President Mondale noted on leaving office, "a president . . . starts out with a bank full of good will and slowly checks are drawn on that, and it's very rare that it's replenished. It's a one-time deposit." [22] This political capital is composed of public approval and seats in Congress. For several reasons, among them the simple decay of support and presidential mistakes, capital is depleted during the term. At least since 1960, all presidents have experienced a loss in public support over time; since 1934, all presidents have lost party seats in Congress in every midterm election. Like Mondale, many White House players see political capital as a finite resource that is spent with each choice of a problem, solution, or assumption. Clearly, some problems, solutions, and assumptions are more "expensive" politically than others.

Program Resources. Just as presidents need resources to make and sell final decisions, they need them for implementation, that is, for converting legislation into actual government activity. The most basic program resources are federal dollars and employees. However, program resources also can include supplies, land, computer time, and new equipment. Carter's MX missile "race-track" plan had a staggering list of resource needs. Designed as an elaborate shell game in the Nevada-Utah desert, the program required 200 MX missiles, numerous decoy missiles, 4,600 hardened concrete shelters, 8,500 miles of heavy-duty roadbed, huge new trucks to carry the missiles, new launchers, new computers, and 40,000 square miles of land. Each of the 200 missiles cost $50 million in the Carter budget, but construction and maintenance expenses of the entire program would have boosted the final price tag to $500 million per missile. Moreover, construction required 50,000 workers, 190 billion gallons of water, and 100 million tons of concrete—all to be transported somehow to the desert. Critics argued that construction alone would have caused a decade-long concrete shortage.

In the early and mid-1980s, program resources are in short supply. There is virtually no money in the federal budget for new programs and very little room for growth in old programs. With indexation of the federal tax code scheduled to begin in 1985, the federal government will face even greater shortages in funding for spending programs. With the hiring freeze and reductions-in-force (RIFs) in the first year of the Reagan administration, fewer federal employees are available to administer and enforce presidential policies. The same is true at the state level. Although the RIFs in domestic agencies did not concern the Republican president, shortages of military personnel threatened the Reagan defense program. New tanks and ships need new drivers and crews. New computer systems and communication networks need new programmers and specialists.

Opportunities

Once the filtering process has merged a problem with a solution, a set of assumptions, and a collection of players, and has found the decision-making, political, and program resources to pay for the combination, the White House must decide when to present the idea to Congress and the public. With the steady increase in its workload, in particular more committee and subcommittee meetings and greater constituency demands, Congress offers fewer opportunities for presidential influence. Indeed, one of Carter's critical mistakes in filtering his legislative agenda was to flood the congressional tax-writing committees with proposals. Most of Carter's program had to move through the Senate Finance Committee and House Ways and Means Committee. His economic stimulus package (January 1977), hospital cost containment plan (April 1977), Social Security financing proposal (May 1977), welfare reform bill (August 1977), urban assistance plan (January 1978), and tax reform measure (January 1978) all moved through Congress with little thought of the opportunities for legislative review.

Policy Calendar. The timing of the president's requests to Congress is critical to their success. According to John Kessel, there is a presidential policy cycle that begins sometime "after Labor Day when programs to be proposed to Congress are readied. Fall is probably the time of the heaviest work load for the policy-staffer in the White House, because work is still progressing on Capitol Hill on the present year's program at the same time preparations for the next year are being made." [23] The calendar continues with basic choices on the budget in December, major messages to Congress in January and February (including the State of the Union address, the budget message, and the economic report), congressional decision making in the spring and summer, vacations in August, and a return to planning in September and October.

In the Johnson administration, for example, the policy sequence began in the spring and followed a clear order: visits to universities and contacts with outside experts and "idea men" in government in April, May and June; internal discussions of ideas in July; appointment of outside task forces in August; receipt and review of task-force reports and agency proposals in September, October, and November; White House meetings and final presidential decisions on the program in December; and preparation of messages to Congress and introduction of bills in January, February, and March.[24]

The policy calendars of recent administrations have emphasized two periods as offering the greatest opportunity to set the national agenda: January-February and August-September. The winter opportunity arises with the presentation of the formal messages and the start of a new congressional session; the summer opportunity comes with the end of Congress's August recess and a brief chance to introduce replacements for proposals that already have failed. Like resources, opportunities are finite. Even though every year in the term offers some opportunity for presidential agenda setting, the first year remains critical. Because White House priorities absorb so much time, energy, and other resources and involve such high stakes, they often remain on the legislative calendar for several years before Congress reaches a final decision. Thus, the first winter and summer offer the best opportunities for presidential policy. Problems and solutions presented later in the term may simply have to wait, regardless of how important or innovative they are.

Cycles of Influence. Although presidents are guaranteed a certain number of opportunities to introduce policy when they enter office—four State of the Unions, four budgets, etc.—they can create additional opportunities through the *cycle of increasing effectiveness.* Whatever the initial level of information and expertise, presidents and their staffs learn over time, becoming more effective in managing their scarce opportunities. Carter, for example, became more adept at handling Congress as his term wore on and he learned how to use his limited policy opportunities. Presidents can create opportunities for new ideas through carefully staged public events or through skillful manipulation of the press. A president's effectiveness in using these informal opportunities always grows over time, as a simple byproduct of learning the ropes.

Just as presidents can create opportunities through the cycle of increasing effectiveness, they can lose opportunities through the *cycle of decreasing influence.* As public approval and party seats drop during the term—one month-to-month, the other at the midterm election—presidents lose opportunities for influence. Even though they become more effective at finding opportunities for ideas, Congress and the public become less interested. Moreover, even the formal opportunities lose effectiveness later in the term. Major messages, televised addresses, and press conferences carry less weight.

Filtering and Policy

Why are resources and opportunities so important as policy filters? The reason is that presidents enter office with different amounts of each. Ford had only two years in his brief term, Johnson had five.

Ford had fewer than 150 party faithful in the House, Johnson once had more than 290. Carter and Reagan had little expertise in national policy making, Nixon had little in domestic affairs. Carter's Georgia staff had little background in national policy, too, which left considerable room for learning, while Reagan's legislative staff had considerable expertise in legislative lobbying. These kinds of differences tell a great deal about the policy stream as it flows through an administration. The resources and opportunities at the start of a term determine both the quantity and quality of the president's policy agenda.

Conclusion

If presidential policy is the product of a highly dynamic stream, the final issue is whether the stream has changed its course during the past decades. The problems have changed, but have they become more difficult? Is cutting government spending more difficult than increasing it? Kennedy and Johnson selected problems that seemed to demand expanded government, while Carter and Reagan picked problems that seemed to require contracted government. Nor did Kennedy and Johnson have to tackle any of the new "single issues" such as abortion and school prayer. Perhaps the most important change in the past 20 years has been the rise of a new class of "constituentless" issues— problems, such as energy conservation, which have few supporters but many potential enemies.

The solutions also have changed. Spending and regulation are no longer the popular response to national problems, but it is not yet clear what kinds of solutions will replace them. The players have changed, too. The rise of the National Security Council staff and the Office of Policy Development has shaped a new pool of players who compete for the president's attention and support. Moreover, most White House aides argue that interest groups are penetrating further into the policy process in recent years. As presidents reach out to interest groups to help pass their programs, interest groups reach further in to draft legislation and influence decisions.

Perhaps the most important area of change—or lack of change—is in assumptions. Despite new methods of forecasting and computer analysis, presidents do not seem much closer to being able to predict problems or solutions accurately. Much of the policy process still rests on best guesses about what will or will not happen. Even in the very short-term, players have difficulty predicting what will happen. Stockman was willing to admit in early 1983 that we cannot predict even the next year, let alone five years out. That may be the most serious obstacle to presidents as they continue to search for problems and solutions. If problems are more controversial in this era of single-issue politics, if solutions are more constrained by tight budgets and personnel shortages, if players are more competitive for presidential influence, there is even greater need for accurate assumptions. Unfortunately, presidents still look into their crystal balls and see pretty much what they want to see.

NOTES

1. See Jack L. Walker, "Setting the Agenda in the U.S. Senate: A Theory of Problem Selection," *British Journal of Political Science* (1977): 438.
2. Thomas E. Cronin, *The State of the Presidency* (Boston: Little, Brown & Co., 1980), 143-186.
3. Ibid., 146.
4. Herbert Stein, "The Chief Executive as Chief Economist," in *Contemporary Economic Problems: 1981-1982,* ed. William Fellner (Washington, D.C.: American Enterprise Institute for Public Policy Research, 1982), 61-62.
5. Paul C. Light, "Correlates of Greatness," unpublished paper, 1979.
6. Theodore H. White, "Weinberger at the Ramparts," *New York Times Magazine,* February 6, 1983, 20.
7. Paul C. Light, "Passing Nonincremental Policy: Presidential Influence in Congress," *Congress and the Presidency* (Winter 1982).
8. Martin Anderson, *Welfare: The Political Economy of Welfare Reform in the United States* (Stanford, Cal.: Hoover Institution Press, 1978), 143-144.
9. William Greider, "The Education of David Stockman," *The Atlantic,* 248 (December 1981): 38, 44-47.
10. Richard K. Betts, "Strategic Intelligence Estimates: Let's Make them Useful," *Parameters* (December 1980): 21.
11. Allen Schick, "How the Budget Was Won and Lost," in *President and Congress: Assessing Reagan's First Year,* ed. Norman J. Ornstein (Washington, D.C.: American Enterprise Institute for Public Policy Research, 1982), 36.
12. David Stockman, "Face the Nation," February 6, 1983.
13. I. M. Destler, "National Security II: The Rise of the Assistant (1961-1981)," in *The Illusion of Presidential Government,* ed. Hugh Heclo and Lester M. Salamon (Boulder, Colo.: Westview Press, 1982).
14. Anderson, *Welfare,* 6.
15. James Fallows, "The Passionless Presidency," *The Atlantic,* (May 1979): 40.
16. Schick, "How the Budget Was Won and Lost," in *President and Congress,* ed. Ornstein, 40.
17. Paul C. Light, *The President's Agenda: Domestic Policy Choice from Kennedy to Carter* (Baltimore: Johns Hopkins University Press, 1982), 41.
18. Quoted in Jack Valenti, *A Very Human President* (New York: W. W Norton & Co., 1975), 144.
19. "The Stockman Manifesto," *Washington Post,* December 14, 1980, D-1.
20. Greider, "The Education of David Stockman," 27-54.
21. Henry Aaron, *Economic Effects of Social Security* (Washington: The Brookings Institution, 1983), 51, 82.

22. *Washington Post,* January 21, 1981, A-24.
23. John Kessel, *The Domestic Presidency* (Boston: Duxbury Press, 1975), 9.
24. Norman C. Thomas and H. C. Wolman, "Policy Formulation in the Institutionalized Presidency: The Johnson Task Forces," in *The Presidential Advisory System,* ed. Thomas E. Cronin and S. D. Greenberg (New York: Harper & Row, 1969), 132.

17. THE PRESIDENCY AND DOMESTIC POLICY: ORGANIZING THE DEPARTMENT OF EDUCATION

Willis D. Hawley and Beryl A. Radin

On October 17, 1979, President Jimmy Carter signed the act that established a cabinet-level Department of Education. With this action, Carter delivered on a campaign promise made in October 1975 to the National Education Association (NEA) to establish a department that would "consolidate the grant programs, job training, early childhood education, literacy training, and many other functions scattered throughout the government. The result would be a stronger voice for education at the federal level."[1] This campaign promise, often repeated, won for Carter the NEA's first endorsement of a presidential candidate in its 119-year history. With politically active members in every part of the country, the NEA was an important force both within the Democratic party and among the electorate.

However, the department that emerged from the decision process was, with few exceptions, simply a reincarnation in cabinet form of education programs within the Education Division of the old Department of Health, Education and Welfare (HEW). While Carter was able to claim success because a new department opened in May 1980, it fell far short of what he had envisioned. The few programs that were not drawn from HEW were transferred from the departments of Justice, Labor, Housing and Urban Development, Defense, and Agriculture. (See Table 17-1).

The decision processes that explain the establishment of the new department provide a fascinating case study in domestic policy making in the executive branch.[2] We hope to shed some light on two aspects of the federal policy process. First, we offer a glimpse of presidential involvement in policy making, including the influence of presidential style, techniques of leadership, dependence on staff, and sensitivity to the institutionalized processes of decision making. Jimmy Carter's personal predilection for concrete, technical questions has been detailed elsewhere.[3] But his personal involvement in this particular issue also is extremely important.

Table 17-1 Budget, Personnel, and Programs of the U.S. Department of Education

Budget authority:	$14.2 billion
Personnel:	17,000
Programs:	152 programs from six agencies:

— *Education Division* including elementary, secondary, and postsecondary education programs and research activities (Department of Health, Education and Welfare).

— *Office for Civil Rights* education and vocational rehabilitation-related activities (Department of Health, Education and Welfare).

— *Overseas Dependents' Schools* (Department of Defense).

— *Vocational Rehabilitation Program* (Rehabilitation Services Administration, Department of Health, Education and Welfare).

— *Law enforcement student loan programs* (Department of Justice).

— *The College Housing Loan Program* (Department of Housing and Urban Development).

— *Migrant education programs* (Department of Labor).

— *Special Institutions* for which the Department of Health, Education and Welfare exercises budgetary oversight, including Howard University, Gallaudet College, the American Printing House for the Blind, and the National Technical Institute for the Deaf.

— *Telecommunications Nonbroadcast Demonstration Program* (Department of Health, Education and Welfare).

— *Department of Agriculture Graduate School.*

— Certain *science education programs* (National Science Foundation).

SOURCE: President's Reorganization Project, Office of Management and Budget, September 1979.

Second, the creation of the Department of Education (ED) exemplifies the complex decision processes within the executive branch. This complexity is illustrated by the actions of individuals within the president's immediate staff, the vice president's office, the Office of Management and Budget (OMB), and the Domestic Policy staff, as well as top officials of executive departments and agencies.

This chapter examines these general topics in the context of the political processes that narrowed a comprehensive presidential proposal to almost trivial dimensions. It attempts to answer the question: Why did the Department of Education emerge as it did, given that other possibilities existed?

Goals and Actors

Our analysis centers on the goals that were at issue during the formulation, adoption, and early implementation of the proposal to establish a Department of Education. Among other things, examining the goals held by actors such as the Executive Office of the President (EOP), Congress, interest groups, and the federal bureaucracy allows us to see why a presidential issue plays out the way it does. Goals structure the debate, help to determine the processes through which issues are decided, and influence the criteria by which conflict is resolved. In the politics of reorganization, goals also have implications for organizational structure.[4]

These goals are woven into a multistage policy process that is at once discontinuous, truncated, nonlinear, fragmented, and often circular. There are many types of decisions that involve different actors at particular stages of the process. At each new stage—and through new actors—the question of goals is raised again. At each subsequent stage, some goals are avoided, newly articulated, or reopened for debate.

Goals for Establishing the Department of Education

Because issues often evolve from more than one source, most deliberations about policies engage several goals at one time or another. The process of coalition building avoids specific detail to accommodate a broad range of interests. The ED proposal was no exception.

Proposals for the creation of a separate department of education have hovered around the American political landscape for more than 100 years and have been debated seriously for two decades. By mid-1977, after Carter's election, five general concerns or goals were associated with the proposal for a new department. These goals, which shaped the organizational alternatives that were considered, were: symbolic status, political advantage, efficiency, effectiveness, and change.

Symbolic Status. The problem that advocates of symbolic status addressed was simple: the United States is the only nation in the world that does not have an education ministry or department. Perhaps more important to them was the sense that the failure to have a cabinet-level agency for education issues indicated that education did not have a status equal to other service sectors in the society such as agriculture, labor, and business. Thus the goal was clear-cut: to get a cabinet-level department. Many advocates believed that higher status and visibility, and a place at the cabinet table, would translate into increased federal funding for education.

Political Advantage. Advocates of reorganization of the federal education enterprise—the White House, members of Congress, interest groups, and career bureaucrats, among them—frequently acted in terms of partisan and personal political advantage. The decision to create a department, the programs it would encompass, and its internal structure affected members of Congress whose support was needed for this issue, and even more important, for other issues on the president's agenda. Congressional ED advocates tried to curry favor with the interest groups in return for support on election day. At the same time these groups were calculating the advantages and disadvantages of various proposals with which they were identified. Finally, some bureaucrats mobilized opposition to reorganization as a way of protecting their own programs and constituents.

Efficiency. Arguments based on efficiency are the most common reasons given for administrative reorganization of any type. In the case of the federal education bureaucracy, the classic public administration diagnosis of problems was made: overlap and duplication pervaded the federal education enterprise. Administrative operations inside the Office of Education and the larger HEW "holding company" were characterized by redundancy and multiple layers of decision. For example, a proposed education regulation had as many as 14 levels to clear and took an average of 519 days to publish, more than twice the 240-day deadline set by Congress in section 431 of the General Education Provision Act.[5]

The product of a more efficient system presumably would be either savings to the taxpayer or the delivery of more service for the same cost. It was argued that efficiency also would result in less delay in the preparation of regulations and other decisions. Advocates of this argument were not concerned about the outcomes of bureaucratic processes; they were concerned only about the process itself.

Effectiveness. Others argued that a separate department of education would improve existing educational services and address problems that federal programs had failed to solve, such as inequities in educational opportunity. Advocates of greater effectiveness sought to take programs that already were in place and make them work better.

Ostensibly, programmatic reforms would be made possible by better and more integrated organizational structures. One proposal called for an Office for Civil Rights (OCR) in the new department because a large percentage of complaints that were handled by HEW's OCR were related to education. Effectiveness advocates also hoped to remedy problems of intergovernmental relations by making federal programs more responsive to state and local needs.

Change in American Education. The effectiveness and change goals overlap. But while the effectiveness proponents saw the problem in terms of incremental improvements in the existing program, advocates of the change goal argued for fundamental reforms in the way educational issues were perceived and in the federal government's role in inducing change. Problems were identified in terms of both programmatic deficiencies and a professional monopoly of school administrators and teachers who, it was argued, dominated education policies at all levels and resisted attempts to change the system. As a result, they claimed, coherent federal policies could not develop.

Actors

Literally hundreds of individuals and groups played a role in the identification and pursuit of different policy alternatives related to the establishment of the Department of Education. However, on any given decision about either the general structure or the inclusion of an activity or program within the department, relatively few actors were influential. Because numerous specialized issues were debated during the policy process, the cast of characters shifted over time and by issue. These characters were drawn from four clusters of actors that played significant roles throughout the process: the Executive Office of the President, Congress, interest groups, and the bureaucracy. Other actors, of course, were involved at various stages. The media were always a concern because of their ability to shape public opinion. And in an era of public skepticism about bureaucracy in general, how a proposal for a new bureaucracy would "play in Peoria" was especially important.

Each cluster of actors contained diverse views, so none could be regarded as expressing a single opinion. But they did share common types of goals, as shown in Table 17-2.

The Executive Office of the President. Although the public perceived that the EOP supported a single position (the president's), a number of separate views actually were expressed within this group.

Actors included the president himself, the vice president, the White House staff, the President's Reorganization Project (PRP), and OMB. While several of the president's important advisers based their recommendations largely on the political advantage goal, the PRP analyzed reorganization programs more on principles of effectiveness and change.

Congress. Because it was a reorganization issue, jurisdiction over the education department was given to the Senate Governmental Affairs Committee and the House Government Operations Committee, rather than to the Senate Human Resources and the House Education and Labor authorizing committees. In addition to the members and staff of those committees, the debate involved individual legislators who were concerned with either particular programs or ideological arguments. The mixture of congressionally expressed goals included symbolic status, political advantage, and efficiency.

Interest Groups. A coalition representing most of the large education organizations (more than 100) was organized in support of the department; the NEA was dominant within that coalition. Strong opposition to the department came from the American Federation of Teachers (AFT), an AFL-CIO affiliate and an arch rival of the NEA. The AFT argued the importance of maintaining the coalition of education and labor and was concerned about an education-only department dominated by NEA. Other groups became involved when specific programs were debated. For example, the Children's Defense Fund actively opposed the transfer of the Head Start program into the new department. Whatever their particular position, however, interest groups were concerned with the symbolic, political, and efficiency goals.

The Bureaucracy. This cluster included the HEW bureaucracy, other federal agencies that were affected by the proposals, and the

Table 17-2 Predominant Goals of Actors

	Executive Office of President	Congress	Interest Groups	Bureaucracy
Symbolic Status		X	X	X
Political Advantage	X	X	X	X
Efficiency	X	X	X	
Effectiveness	X			X
Change	X			

department itself once it was created. While HEW Secretary Joseph A. Califano, Jr., personally opposed the department, he did not involve his department in the reorganization controversy. Relationships between interest groups and career bureaucrats, however, influenced certain decisions. Some bureaus that would be affected by the proposals—for example, the feeding programs in Agriculture and Indian education programs in the Bureau of Indian Affairs—became involved as their constituencies worked to narrow the scope of the department.

The Policy Process

The Department of Education was developed through three stages of the policy process: initial policy formulation, enactment, and early implementation. These stages are not as neatly differentiated in practice as they are in textbooks; policy formulation occurred throughout the process, and the enactment stage overlapped with the other two. The stages, however, can be treated as sequential.

Policy Formulation

Carter's campaign promise for a separate department rested primarily on the political advantage and symbolic status arguments. Immediately following the election, the proposal made its way onto the presidential agenda, and policy development on ED's structure began in earnest in Congress and the White House.

Congress and Interest Groups. As chairman of the Senate Governmental Affairs Committee, Abraham Ribicoff introduced a bill shortly after the 1976 election to establish an education department. Ribicoff's push for a department had begun in the 89th Congress (1965-1967), and he had introduced similar legislation in almost every session of Congress since then. Ribicoff's experience as former secretary of HEW was the basis for his belief that education issues received short shrift in HEW's massive bureaucracy. He also wanted to support fellow Democrat Carter's plans to reorganize the government.

Ribicoff's plan attracted more than 50 cosponsors by mid-1977, but as most observers pointed out, their support was "a mile wide and an inch deep." Senate support for the concept of a department was strong, but there was little discussion of its structure. To minimize conflict over specifics, Senator Ribicoff waited for President Carter to define his proposal. As a result, the Senate avoided discussing the particular structure that the bill outlined until midway through the process of considering the legislation.

Interest group advocates for a department also directed their attention to the symbolic importance of the department. The NEA clearly took the lead in support, and the endorsement of most of the large education organizations (such as the PTA, the Council of Chief State School Officers, and the National Association of School Boards) followed. Arguments about efficiency were expressed but with little passion. Rather, these groups argued—often abstractly—that a separate department would foster more effective, capable, and visible leadership:

> If excellence is what we seek for our children ... education must have a voice that is sustained and concentrated.... We need a secretary of education who can concentrate solely on the problems of education and not be bogged down with the crushing problems of health and welfare too.[6]

Moreover, the interest groups argued that political demands would be more directly and clearly expressed because a department would foster a better national appreciation of the importance of public support for education.

Those who supported the department for symbolic reasons cared little about the details of organizational structure. As long as there was a cabinet-level agency devoted to education, it really did not matter to them what form it took. While advocates of this position were not opposed to any special organizational configuration, neither were they willing to fight for the inclusion of particular programs. As a result, they laid little groundwork with members of Congress on the substantive issues about programs.

In contrast to the interest groups, Ribicoff and the staff of the Governmental Affairs Committee were interested in promoting a relatively broad department in keeping with the goals of efficiency, good management, and coordination of federal programs. The long list of cosponsors in the Senate developed without apparent conflict on these issues. Few anticipated strong opposition to the bill.

In the policy development phase, the House was largely uninvolved. It was not until passage of the bill was approaching in the Senate that a House sponsor was decided upon. Texas Democrat Jack Brooks, chairman of the House Government Operations Committee, was finally convinced by President Carter to introduce a companion bill to S. 991. Brooks had expressed deep reservations about Carter's reorganization plans. "In fact," Carter has commented, "because of Jack Brooks's opposition, as the new Congress prepared to convene, I could not get any Democratic member to introduce my proposed reorganization legislation!" [7] Brooks finally agreed to sponsor the education reorganization bill out of a sense of partisan loyalty.

Clearly the lead for the Department of Education initiative was in the Senate. It was important to the character of the issues raised and to the outcome of congressional action that the Senate Governmental Affairs Committee had jurisdiction over reorganization matters. The members of that committee, unlike those on Human Resources, were not experts on education matters, and Ribicoff and the staff were given considerable latitude. Because the issue was debated in organizational terms rather than as a question of substantive education policy, arguments based on effectiveness were not salient to most members.

The Executive Office of the President. While support was building in the Senate, congressional leaders waited for the president to act. Given his campaign promise and his commitment to reorganization, Carter was expected to move quickly to establish the department.

Early in the life of the administration, Carter asked some of his advisers—HEW Secretary Califano, Vice President Walter Mondale, OMB Director Bert Lance, and domestic adviser Stuart Eizenstat—to evaluate how to proceed with a study of options for the organization of federal education activities. Rather than introducing a bill immediately, Carter established a special study team within the President's Reorganization Project to examine the alternatives for structuring federal education programs. His concerns as president were for effectiveness and change as well as the political advantage of his candidate days.

Carter's initiatives, in education and other policy areas, to reorganize the federal government in order to provide better delivery of government services followed from his experiences in Georgia. As governor, Carter enacted a massive reorganization of state government and frequently emphasized the reorganization approach as a method to attain change. Because reorganization was an integral part of Carter's program, the PRP was established within OMB. Previous reorganization studies, such as Lyndon Johnson's 1964 Task Force on Government Organization and the 1971 Ash Council Study under President Richard Nixon, were one-time, "blue ribbon" task forces. The PRP, by contrast, was to be "tucked" into OMB and depend mainly on Washington careerists, education specialists, and junior-level analysts.

The Education Study Team was established within the PRP in April 1977, given a six-month life, and charged to examine all the alternatives. It began its work with assurances from Carter aide

Hamilton Jordan that its task was general and that concerns for political feasibility, while important, should not dominate its analysis. The study team itself had a decidedly academic character. Politics would be the White House's responsibility; the PRP's job was to conduct a careful, but general, study.

PRP attempts to involve interest groups early in substantive decisions about structure were extensive but fruitless. Apparently wary of being coopted, most waited for PRP to unveil its own proposals. There were opponents of the department, such as the AFT, but they did not work together as an effective coalition. The relative quiescence of other interest groups that might be affected by re-organization (with the exception of the adamant, steadfast Head Start advocates and the commodity and nutrition interest groups that were fighting the transfer of child nutrition from the Agriculture Department) fooled the department's advocates. Thus, within the administration and the Senate Governmental Affairs Committee staff, there was little sense of how intense the opposition to the department would be.

To the PRP analysts, the symbolic goal that was so important to the interest groups did not seem worth pursuing for three reasons. First, the goal had no demonstrable payoff for students (it begged questions of program effectiveness); second, PRP's analysis showed no relationship between attainment of cabinet status and the subsequent funding of programs; and third, PRP concluded that the problems of American education could not be solved by the federal government doing more of the same thing—an assumption that was implicit in the symbolic goal.

The PRP did not treat political advantage (Congress's main concern) as a goal to be served by reorganization either. And few people in PRP believed that there were great savings and other improvements in efficiency to be gained from reorganization.[8] That left the goals of effectiveness and change by which to judge the consequences of restructuring the administration of federal education programs.

The effectiveness goal, symbolized by the motto "if it's not broke, don't fix it," was a cornerstone of the entire PRP study. While many programs seemed "broke," this preoccupation forced analysts to examine proposals from the "bottom up" and to show how reorganization would make programs more effective. In addition, the education study took place in an atmosphere of substantial national concern about shrinking student enrollments, declining test scores, school violence, and high levels of teen-age unemployment. These concerns led to an emphasis on the federal government's responsibility to facilitate change in American education.

The PRP was not the only group involved in policy development that saw significant change as an important goal of reorganization. Civil rights groups that favored the department believed that increasing the federal role in education was the most effective way to rectify racial and ethnic inequities within the society. Other groups argued for less federal intervention on the assumption that once local school administrators were unfettered from central control, they would be far more creative in dealing with their own districts' problems. While these groups advocated a separate education department, they subscribed to very different theories of social change.

The PRP staff believed that the key to achieving effectiveness and change was to link school-based education more effectively with other social services and with so-called "nontraditional sources of learning," such as job training, television, adult education, libraries, and child care. The structural considerations that flowed from this approach moved PRP in the direction of a broad department that would enhance the potential for coordinating all such services at the local level. Thus, the PRP concluded that the president should endorse a department of education and human development that incorporated education and social service activities. To create a narrow department was seen as less desirable than simply upgrading the status of education programs within HEW. The diffuse support for change from several sources appeared to PRP to justify its approach. It had taken its own analyses seriously and had reason to believe that the president was interested in using reorganization as a tool for strengthening not just federal programs, but American education as a whole.

The PRP's proposal for a broad department was submitted to the president in late November 1977 with the initial endorsement of OMB Director James McIntyre. McIntyre had been the deputy director of OMB under Lance and replaced him as director after his resignation in September. Although McIntyre did not enjoy the close personal relationship with the president that his predecessor had, he was very familiar with Carter's reorganization program and style from his service to Carter in Georgia.

The PRP, however, was not the only source of presidential advice on this issue within the EOP. The budget side of OMB contained critics of a broad department of education and human development. The White House staff and legislative liaison team opposed the PRP proposal because it would require extensive political bargaining at a time when other domestic initiatives by the administration, such as welfare reform, were in trouble, and when international issues (SALT negotiations, the Panama Canal treaties, and the energy crisis) were preempting the White House's attention. These developments were seen—especially by the president's staff—as more important. At the time, the PRP's education reorganization plan seemed more than anyone wanted.

Outside of the PRP, then, the political advantage goal of reorganization was what counted to the EOP. The president's personal staff believed that a department should be created because it met the administration's campaign commitments. Such a department, however, should be narrow in scope. The interest groups advocating a department let the White House know, in no uncertain terms, that cabinet status for education was essential. A broad proposal like the PRP's would lead to controversy and perhaps failure.

At this stage of the process, the president did not appear to be personally comfortable with arguments based only on political advantage. In late November 1977, he decided that, given the advice of most of his top staff, the PRP plan for a broad department was not politically possible. At the same time, he made it known that he wanted a proposal outlining a department of education that "was as broad as possible," a desire that was open to definitional dispute.

For almost three months, the PRP and the White House staff debated what was politically possible and desirable. PRP's proposals generally prevailed. In April 1978 the president sent to the Hill a proposal that looked very much like the one endorsed by Senator Ribicoff. It was consistent with—although narrower than—the "structure" Carter had proposed during the campaign. Both the president's bill and Ribicoff's called for a new department that would include the Education Division of HEW, much of the HEW Office for Civil Rights, all Indian and migrant education programs, school feeding programs, the Department of Defense's Overseas Dependent Schools, the Head Start program, most of the Education Directorate from NSF, and numerous small programs.

Enactment

Congress had before it two very similar proposals in spring 1978. Both rested more on abstract theories of political science than on concrete evidence about the effects of reorganization. The Department of Energy—the most recent of federal departments—was viewed more as a negative than a positive model.

Effectiveness and Change Goals

Some members of Congress viewed the PRP proposal as change for its own sake. In truth, some in the PRP believed that a broad department would shift the balance of power in education policy making from the narrow, professional interest groups such as NEA and the Council of Chief State School Officers to a wider array of actors. This belief could not be propounded publicly since those were the groups whose support made the department a possibility. Indeed, most of the decision-making arenas that surrounded the department were not congenial to change arguments. Many existing bureaucracies opposed drastic changes of any sort. There was some risk that if educational change became the issue, both government operations committees in Congress would defer to tradition and allow the authorizing committees to consider the proposals, blocking the momentum of Carter's campaign promise. OMB and the PRP were forced, reluctantly, to defer to Carter's personal aides and the Domestic Policy Staff regarding political calculations.

The change goal, then, if it was to have any chance of steering reorganization toward a more comprehensive and radical approach, would have required that careful and active presidential attention be given to the proposal. Although comprehensive reorganization that would encompass more than education was appealing in theory to many groups, in practice, it meant substantial, diligent homework on the part of the president to realign and rebuild coalitions and to calculate all the potential costs to the affected constituencies. These large-scale, complex negotiations were not high on the administration's priority list. Furthermore, political destabilization and political realignment—even if potentially valuable—posed too many risks. As Native American leaders put it after years of decrying the treatment of Indian education by the Department of the Interior, "They may be bastards, but they're our bastards."

The effectiveness goal also had serious limitations as a base upon which to build a department. Most members of the Senate Governmental Affairs Committee and House Government Operations Committee knew little about education and other human resource programs. For effectiveness arguments to carry weight, they had to be weighty themselves; most members had little time for such matters. Thus, even when there was agreement among the analysts, the PRP tended to back away from assertions about effectiveness and offer simpler and more appealing efficiency arguments when the decision shifted from the analytical to the political. For example, in its effort to transfer the child nutrition programs from Agriculture to the new department, the PRP began by using the effectiveness argument that as long as these programs were housed in USDA, they would necessarily be geared more to farm income maintenance than to school feeding priorities. Because this argument was not convincing, the PRP switched to the efficiency argument that the programs were almost always administered by the local boards of education.

In addition, arguments about the ineffectiveness of programs were not politically attractive to an administration that basically supported the goals of the programs it wanted to change. At the same time reorganization was being advocated, so were budget increases for Title I compensatory education programs, higher education, and Head Start. It was difficult for the administration to push for more funding for certain programs and then argue that not until reorganization would these same programs really be effective.

Efficiency, Symbolic, and Political Goals

Not surprisingly, as the enactment process progressed, presidential attention turned increasingly to the goal of efficiency and at the same time returned to the basic Carter campaign theme—the symbolic importance of a separate department. Issues of political advantage also became more salient.

In response to interest group pressure, the Senate debates had narrowed the department significantly by removing both Head Start and feeding programs from the proposal. At the same time, successful lobbying by vocational rehabilitation groups, such as the Council for Exceptional Children and the American Coalition for Citizens with Disabilities, prompted Democratic Sen. Muriel Humphrey to sponsor an amendment to move certain programs out of HEW and into the new department. There was no significant interest group opposition to the transfer, and the amendment passed in committee by a voice vote. After further narrowing, the bill passed the Senate by a vote of 72 to 11 at the end of September 1978.

In the House, the department confronted its first real legislative opposition. Government Operations Committee Chairman Jack Brooks was less concerned with education issues than his Senate counterpart, Abraham Ribicoff. After months of negotiations, Carter had managed to persuade Brooks to sponsor the Department of Education bill. But Brooks saw his job as simply getting a bill passed and devoted little attention to the programmatic scope of the department. The bill was reported out of his committee in August 1978 only after the Indian education, child nutrition, and National Science Foundation (NSF) science education transfers had been deleted, and even then it never reached a vote in the House. House opposition to the act was led by conservative Republicans John Erlenborn from Illinois and Robert Walker from Pennsylvania. Dilatory amendments stalled activity long enough so that Congress adjourned without a vote.

As late as the spring of 1979 opposition to the department remained sporadic and ill defined. Some objections had been overcome as the scope of the proposal narrowed and programs were eliminated. Republican Senators William Roth, and John Danforth had their fear of a federal monolith alleviated when language that emphasized the importance of state and local control over education was strengthened. But after the Senate passed the bill easily for the second time in April 1979, and the House Government Operations Committee seemed to be moving forward, opposition to the department mobilized in full force.

Some argued that the department was unnecessary, others focused on its probable effects. Some liberals claimed that the department would fragment the HEW coalition in Congress, thus diminishing federal support for education; others feared that domination of the department by professional educators and state and local officials would reduce the aggressiveness of federal action with respect to civil rights enforcement. (This was the position taken by several Black members of Congress.) Conservatives such as Representative Erlenborn pictured the proposed department as a bureaucratic tool for further extending federal influence over education much the same way as education ministries in other nations controlled local education.

As political opposition mounted, the symbolic arguments for the department gained strength, and advocates formed an effective 125-organization coalition called the Ad Hoc Committee for a Cabinet Department of Education, led by Allan Cohen, a former state official from Illinois. The White House met weekly with representatives from these groups to plan strategy and coordinate lobbying of members of Congress. Despite these joint efforts, the House head counts by the administration's congressional liaison staff dropped from two-thirds in favor to a near dead heat, 10-vote margin just a few days before the vote.

As uncertainty grew, so did the threat of political disaster for the administration and its willingness to barter on programs and structure. Even a little lobbying by specialized interest groups paid off. More personnel cuts were promised in the name of efficiency, and trades were made for administration support on other issues. An assistant secretary-ship for nonpublic schools was promised to attract support from Catholics and conservatives. Indian schools were sent back to Interior in an effort to smooth over rising controversy between the Indians and the government over federal treaty issues. Hispanics won the promise of a separate office for bilingual education. Civil rights advocates were successful in achieving passage of the "Rosenthal amendment," which requires that the Office for Civil Rights report directly to Congress. Most science curriculum development was "given back" to NSF. Even the museum interests were assured that their $13 million program would have a reporting line directly to the new secretary.

In the end, then, the issue was reduced to its simplest terms: the department itself. Structure became irrelevant, and with it the change and effectiveness goals. The symbolic issue and rhetorical assertions of efficiency, although politically persuasive, were largely unrelated to specific characteristics of the department. The bill that passed the House by a handful of votes in July 1979 was a pale shadow of the structure imagined by the president and the bill introduced by Senator Ribicoff two and a half years earlier.

Early Implementation

The complexity and fragmentation of political power and policy making at the federal level creates a situation in which presidential issues that seemingly are resolved at one stage of the policy process are resurrected in the next stage. The implementation of the bill to establish the department was no exception: it provided new opportunities to pursue old goals, albeit in different ways. The Department of Education bill had passed largely because of its symbolic appeal. In this new phase of policy development, however, the goals of change and program effectiveness, which had been slighted during the adoption process in the face of political expediency, resurfaced. President Carter and Vice President Mondale hailed passage of the ED bill as a new dawn for American education. At the East Room signing ceremony attended by 200 education officials, congressional advocates, and a class of fourth-graders from Washington's Brent Elementary School, Carter declared, "I don't know what history will show, but my guess is that the best move for the quality of life in America in the future might very well be the establishment of this new Department of Education." [9] Having lost most of what he had hoped to gain through organizational restructuring, the president returned to the theory of politics that had brought him to Washington in the first place. He believed that change could be brought about by people who were not wedded to the status quo. Leadership, not organizational structure, was the answer.

In his selection of Shirley Hufstedler as secretary of the new department, the president articulated. this theory clearly. Hufstedler was a distinguished jurist who knew about education, although not about education programs. She did not have much administrative experience. Her advocacy of specific education policies had been confined to her actions as a pro-civil-rights judge who had authored a significant opinion that guaranteed rights to children with limited English-speaking ability. Since she was virtually unknown to the traditional education interests, Hufstedler's nomination stirred little opposition.

Upon taking office, Secretary Hufstedler asserted the change goal. She expressed optimism that the answers to vexing educational problems could be found and facilitated, and she sounded the call for educational excellence. To help her get the transition effort off the ground, Hufstedler brought a staff of trusted advisers from California. These close personal advisers did not want permanent positions in the department; their loyalty was to the new secretary. Important appointments to the department were made with White House involvement, continuing the same approach that had led to Hufstedler's own nomination. Interest groups scurried about to identify the new staff, many of whom had not been directly involved in federal education policy and had no experience in education except as students or parents.

Not surprisingly, the task of designing the department's organizational structure was not given high priority. During the period between congressional passage in late 1979 and the opening of the department in May 1980, task forces were organized to study possible structures, but the secretary gave little attention to the work of the transition team at Buzzard's Point, located in Washington's southwest corner far from the department offices. Since the secretary believed that people make a difference, she was not ready to engage in fights about structure. When particular task force proposals for restructuring were opposed by major interest groups, Hufstedler yielded to political advantage goals.

A case in point was the debate over placement of the "gifted and talented" program within the new department. The program task force had examined three possible organizational settings: in research and development (R&D), in elementary and secondary programs, or in the Office of Special Education. The task force recommended the first option, arguing that more innovative programs would be achieved in an

R&D office. However, several influential lobbying groups wanted the program to remain in the Office of Special Education for two principal reasons: first, to minimize disruption, and second, because the majority of programs already were being administered by the state special education offices. Those advocates got their wish.

Other matters also distracted the attention of the secretary and her advisers from organizational issues. The president's reelection strategists wanted to present the department in a way that capitalized on political support from groups such as NEA. Campaign-related demands on the secretary were predictable but not anticipated, and they diverted attention away from the reorganization agenda.

In the original strategy for reorganization, the president had intended that OMB would maintain an active role in implementation. But OMB virtually abandoned that effort. By late 1979, after the bill's passage, the education study team had been disbanded, and the leaders within the PRP who were committed to organizational strategies for bringing about change and improved programs had left or were leaving, most to return to their permanent positions. Efficiency issues had not stirred the White House, and the symbolic goal was achieved by enactment itself. The White House believed that the matter had been resolved when good people were appointed to be in charge of the new department. Understandably, the budget and the presidential election dominated the presidential agenda.

Conclusion

Most decisions about the structure of the Department of Education essentially were made in the adoption stage of the policy process as a result of arguments for efficiency, symbolic status, and political advantage. Rhetorically, at least, efficiency goals pushed out other goals. Although the PRP never argued that substantial savings would result from reorganization, efficiency dominated the debate because it was easier to defend and more difficult to oppose. The only goal that continued in a "pure" form from start to finish was the goal of symbolic status. In organizational terms, at the end of the Carter presidency the structure of the Department of Education represented a triumph of symbolic concerns with the attendant loss of a major opportunity to change the role of the federal government in education or make widely criticized programs more effective. Finally, during the policy process, political goals shifted from maximizing benefits to minimizing costs. As the outcome became less certain (which it usually does in legislative struggles), each one of the other goals was evaluated and redefined for

Table 17-3 Predominant Goals Analyzed by Stages in the Policy Process

	Agenda Setting	Formulation	Adoption Enactment	Transition/ Implementation
Symbolic Status	X	X	X	X
Political Advantage	X		X	X
Efficiency			X	
Effectiveness		X		X
Change		X		

its effect on political support. The political analysis of costs and benefits superseded logical analyses from the other perspectives. Table 17-3 summarizes the emphasis that was placed on different goals at different stages of the policy process.

What, then, does this case tell us about the complexity of the decision processes within the executive branch and about presidential involvement in decision making?

Decision Processes within the Executive Branch

The story of the creation of the Department of Education provides a graphic illustration of the type of conflict that can be found in executive branch decision making. The conflict over establishing the department had many sources—political, personal, and institutional. Even before its official term in the White House began, the Carter executive office was plagued by political infighting that continued throughout the administration. Part of the conflict may be attributed to the clash of political styles between Carter's "old guard" advisers from Georgia and the Washington experts he quickly realized had to be incorporated into his administration. Often, the concerns of the actors within the White House, the executive office (particularly OMB), and executive branch agencies reflected very different perceptions.

Because its function was temporary, the PRP—the institutional mechanism the president established to carry out his reorganization—lacked political muscle within the White House. Even when congressional action was completed and the president, through the PRP, might have influenced change, he handed the ball to the new secretary instead. Her theory of change had little to do with reorganization. Moreover, because she was a newcomer in Washington, she was not in a position to mediate the conflicts that were involved.

Most students of American politics note that the federal bureaucracy has a mind of its own—or at least of its constituents—and that presidents accordingly find it hard to give coherence and direction to domestic policy. But the ED case also points to the difficulty presidents may have in controlling their own staffs. Carter was not able to bring cohesion to the executive office on this issue. Indeed, the PRP and the White House staff were able to pursue their differing interpretations of what the president wanted. The PRP staff believed that Carter was clear about the type of department he wanted. The White House staff, on the other hand, had a different interpretation of Carter's priorities: they argued that to push for a broad department would undermine the president's ability to attain other aspects of his program.

Presidential Involvement

For reorganization to be substantive (that is, to enhance effectiveness and change), it requires forceful and continuing leadership. The more sweeping the change that is desired, the more presidential attention is required. Thus, if President Carter wanted reorganization, why did he not provide the leadership for it?

Carter was, of course, involved with more pressing matters, and there was no independent constituency for "good government" to push him to raise the issue higher on his agenda. This case suggests that the lower the priority of an issue to the president, the more likely it is that staff will determine the outcome. In this particular instance, the staff was divided between the PRP on the one side and the president's personal and political staff on the other.

Although Carter believed that reorganization had important implications for change, in many ways his approach to this issue was closer to that of an academician than of a politician. He failed to understand the political consequences of the effort, either in terms of the issues that were being confronted or the relationships among components of the Executive Office staff. Carter may not have wavered on the substantive issues that were involved in the Department of Education reorganization, but he did demonstrate sporadic and often unpredictable levels of intensity in pursuing his goal.

Carter's involvement in the Department of Education issue is similar in some ways to his involvement in welfare reform. In their study of Carter's welfare reform proposal, Laurence Lynn and David Whitman note that presidents commonly want to "establish new directions for government and to leave a legacy of programmatic achievement and administrative reform." [10] Their analysis of the Roosevelt, Eisenhower, and Johnson administrations indicates that despite the very different historical circumstances in which these presidents governed, each had to make the most of the opportunities that confronted him during his tenure. The experiences of these three presidents

> suggest that, despite wide variations in intellectual and personal style, presidents are successful at policymaking when they demonstrate a tenacity of purpose, a vision that transcends the details of programs and legislation, a sense of personal involvement in the issue, as shown by the visible willingness to spend time mobilizing support and overcoming opposition, and, perhaps, some emotion. Some combination of personal interest, talented subordinates, political acumen, a strategic sense, and general knowledge of the issues is necessary if the president is to move the government in new directions of his choosing.[11]

But on the welfare reform issue (as on education reorganization), Lynn and Whitman found that Carter was attracted to discrete technical matters, not inspired to a "noble calling." He did not confront conflict among his advisers. Finally, he did not demonstrate a sustained awareness of the political significance of his actions.[12]

In the final analysis, of course, Carter delivered on his campaign promise. A Department of Education was created. But the department, as it emerged through the various stages of the policy process, was not the broad structural embodiment of change that Carter had envisioned. Clearly, the task of bringing about significant reorganization demanded political leadership. Jimmy Carter did not provide it.

NOTES

1. Carter's first public statement specifically endorsing the creation of an education department occurred during a meeting with Iowa teachers on November 21, 1975.
2. This analysis of how the Department of Education was established and how it came to be structured is one installment of an extensive study being conducted by the authors. An earlier version of this essay was presented at the annual meeting of the American Political Science Association, New York, September 3-6, 1981. We want to thank Marilyn Zlotnik for her able assistance to us on this chapter as well as the larger study.
3. Laurence Lynn, Jr., and David Whitman, *The President as Policymaker: Jimmy Carter and Welfare Reform* (Philadelphia: Temple University Press, 1981).
4. See Lester M. Salamon, "The Goals of Reorganization: A Framework for Analysis," *Administration and Society* (February 1981): 471-500; Frederick C.

Mosher, *Governmental Reorganizations: Cases and Commentary* (New York: Bobbs Merrill Co., 1967); and Harold Seidman, *Politics, Position and Power: The Dynamics of Federal Organization,* 2d ed. (New York: Oxford University Press, 1977).

5. James T. McIntyre, Jr., "For Creation of a Department of Education," *New York Times,* June 6, 1979, A27.
6. John Ryor, "The Case for a Federal Department of Education," *Phi Delta Kappa* (April 1977): 9.
7. Jimmy Carter, *Keeping Faith: Memoirs of a President* (New York: Bantam Books, 1982), 71.
8. Salamon, "The Goals of Reorganization."
9. Steven R. Weisman, "Carter Signs Measure Creating a Department of Education," *New York Times,* October 18, 1979, A1.
10. Lynn and Whitman, *The President as Policymaker,* 3.
11. Ibid., 15.
12. Ibid., 272-280.

18. THE PRESIDENCY AND ECONOMIC POLICY: A TALE OF TWO BUDGETS

W. Bowman Cutter

Since 1980, the federal budget has monopolized Washington's attention. During the Reagan administration's first months, public debate centered upon the enormous budget changes the president envisioned, and the press heralded the triumphal procession of his policies through Congress. Soon afterwards, however, the debate began to shift to the effects of those policies as they produced, within a year, the largest deficits in American history.

Long before Ronald Reagan, however, federal budget making was in trouble. Between 1950 and 1980, the budget developed an unsustainable dynamic. It grew rapidly. Its underlying structure became progressively more difficult for public policy to control. Moreover, the tax system—a progressive rate structure that allowed revenues to rise steeply in times of high inflation—permitted spending to increase almost automatically. For much of this period, there was enough slack in the economy to enable this dynamic to proceed without causing noticeable damage. During the mid-1960s, strong economic growth provided the necessary safety margin. In the early 1970s, reductions in defense spending paid for expanding social programs. But by the late 1970s, the slack had run out. The economy had been performing below expectations for a decade. Major categories of federal spending were all rising steadily in relation to the gross national product (GNP). Federal taxes were a high and rapidly increasing percentage of GNP. By 1980, there was a broad consensus among economists that the economy was faltering under the combination of spending, deficits, tax rates, and tax burdens.

Presidents Jimmy Carter and Ronald Reagan both tackled these problems. But a successful policy of change requires more than policy analysis or the exercise of will. In the fiscal year 1980 budget, Carter made, what was for the time, an unprecedented effort to alter the course of federal spending, but the structure of the budget and its linkages to the performance of the economy ultimately defeated him.

Similarly, a lack of understanding of the federal budget structure led the Reagan administration to commit itself very early to far more than it could ever sustain.

This chapter examines the general characteristics of the federal budget process, Carter's and Reagan's individual efforts to cope with the problems of budget making, and finally the skills future presidents will need to meet the challenge of budget management.

The Budget Process

The budget process, a central Washington ritual, is one of the principal institutions in our political-economic structure. A task of immense complexity, it is the forum in which the fundamental question of government and politics—Who gets what?—is answered. As such, the budget process handles the basic stuff of modern government—not the instance of crisis when a president's visibility allows him to dominate easily, but the hard, gritty, unrelenting questions of resource allocation. How much does the Department of Defense get? What water project or federal building will be built? Should funds go for Social Security increases, for nuclear fusion research, or for foreign aid? How much does the federal government owe the states and why?

These are the questions that are asked by local congressional districts, single-issue political groups, and major blocs in our society. Because the answers matter to almost everyone in America, the principal institutions and actors in our political system inevitably play roles in the budget process. The all-inclusive nature of the process adds enormously to its complexity. No decision in Washington that has important financial stakes for someone or some group is made quickly, simply, or even only once. Issues are decided, reinterpreted, restated, and brought back for discussion. The budget process is so complex, so extensive, so long that there is always the opportunity to raise an issue again.

The Formal Process

The formal budget process for any given fiscal year begins almost 19 months before the start of that fiscal year. For example, the process for fiscal year 1980, which ran from October 1, 1979, to September 30, 1980, began in March 1978. In the spring of each year, the Office of Management and Budget (OMB) begins its planning for the impending budget season. Macroeconomic projections are considered; major spending, tax, and deficit alternatives are defined; and, in most years, meetings are held with the president to discuss the major budget issues. This planning period usually concludes when OMB gives budget guidance to the executive agencies—spending ceilings and direction regarding particular budget categories.. Then, throughout the late spring and summer, the departments and agencies of the executive branch prepare their detailed budgets. These budgets are submitted to OMB in early September.

The fall budget-decision process is divided into three periods. First, throughout September, the OMB staff carefully analyzes the agency budgets. Second, during October and the first half of November, the OMB staff presents its analysis of these budgets to OMB's director and other senior political officials in a series of budget review meetings. The resulting decisions are then "passed back" to the agencies as OMB decisions. Throughout this period, the president also is kept informed of events and emerging problems. Finally, OMB and the agencies negotiate those OMB decisions with which the agencies disagree; the most important unfinished issues are taken to the president in appeal meetings.

Usually at the end of the appeals process, a final economic and budgetary overview meeting is held with the president, who then attempts to finish making all of his decisions by Christmas. In late January, after the budget documents are completed, the president proposes his budget to Congress. This concludes the first half of the formal budget process.

When the president's budget reaches Congress, it is first considered in a series of general testimonies by the House and Senate Budget Committees. After these testimonies, the budget committees begin to develop the First Budget Resolution, a statement by the Congress of the general shape it intends for the budget. If Congress and the president rely on similar economic assumptions, the overall outline of the budget that is defined by the First Budget Resolution differs little from the budget proposed by the president. But when the economic assumptions are divergent—as they were in President Reagan's 1982 and 1983 budgets—the differences become substantial and extremely difficult to resolve.

With this general outline completed, the appropriations committees fill in the details during the summer by making specific funding decisions for individual programs. These "details" often include major questions of policy. Even after accepting a budget that resembles the president's, Congress often fashions specific programs that are completely different. Finally, the formal budget process is finished when these detailed decisions are brought together in a Second Budget Resolution, which gives the nation a budget by the beginning of the fiscal year on the first of October.

The formal budget process seems to take forever: 19 months pass from the start of spring planning in March to the beginning of the fiscal year; 31 months pass to the end of the fiscal year. During that period, economic crises, world events, changes in programs, and shifts in political mood can greatly affect the budget. The budget is linked closely to the economy, and it can change form completely as the economy changes. The 1979 oil crisis and the 1981-1982 economic recession altered the respective budgets of Presidents Carter and Reagan in precisely this way. Finally, a president's term is 50 percent completed by the beginning of his first budget year, and 75 percent completed when it ends. Usually a president does not receive useful information on the results of his first budget until the last year of his first term.

The Informal Process

The informal budget process is even more extensive than the formal process. While there is a main, procedural path, there is no single budget process. Issues arise through every means that ingenious spending advocates can invent. A suggestion to the president that he speak at a particular forum so that he will find it hard to avoid making a desired spending commitment, an almost unnoticed change in a regulation, a statement of general policy goals placed at the last moment in testimony to Congress—all can be part of the budget process. The most difficult budget issues are frequently presented to a president or a Congress as being cost-free policy concerns that are unrelated to such grubby issues as money. Such issues blindside presidents and budget officials from all directions every day. The consequent need for a permanently skeptical outlook gives budget officials a bad name.

The budget process is not a green eye shade, accounting task. It is, instead, the point at which wishes and dreams confront reality. And bridging the gap between dreams and reality in the public sector is more difficult today than at any other time. Today there is much less room to maneuver on the margins. Consequently, those who feel that OMB has been arbitrary on any particular issue are, to a degree, correct. From 1977 to 1981, I served as the Executive Associate Director for Budget—the direct manager of the federal budget—in

President Carter's OMB. Other budget advisers and I often acknowledged to the president that a cabinet secretary's argument was correct on the merits and his particular program reasonably effective, but that it was not affordable and should not be given the priority of some other program—a difficult position to maintain to a secretary who quite naturally felt those other programs were wastes of the taxpayers' dollars.

As a result, disputes often are not resolved amicably. The failure to fund the favorite idea of a secretary, senator, or a representative is viewed, at best, as a mindless inability to see truth and political advantage, at worst as personal animosity. OMB staff are routinely accused of being against housing, education, medical care, old people, farmers, conservation, veterans, the U.S. economy, world economic stability, and national security. In my first week in office, OMB came within a vote of being subpoenaed by the House Armed Services Committee because the budget examining staff had recommended that no funds be provided for the Edward Hebert Medical College of the Armed Forces. Midway through the president's term, a senior member of Congress threatened to have me fired because I had written a letter to the Hill suggesting that a choice would have to be made between one of two solvent refined coal plants. He also said that I must be a Republican because no Democrat would do a thing like that. Years after the end of the Carter presidency, there were cabinet and subcabinet officers still angry with OMB. None of this is unique to the Carter administration. The budget that amicably encompasses the combined wishes of the executive branch agencies, Congress, and outside interests does not exist.

The Process Today

The budget process has become far more visible in the last decade than ever before. It used to be that an understanding of the importance of the budget process, and of OMB in particular, was valuable inside knowledge of Washington. No more. OMB is now a stopping point on every special interest group's list. The economic difficulties of the 1970s and the declining discretionary margin of the government brought the federal budget into the center of the political process. Then, with the advent of the Reagan administration, the budget process became the central obsession of government. President Reagan's commitments to tax cuts and major budget reductions forced two years of nonstop budget debate upon the executive branch and the Congress.

Yet, despite its importance and visibility, the budget process today is a facade, a mock ritual. No one in the process has enough power to forge a long-term resolution. The process does not permit purposeful, long-term decisions about public spending. It defines some of the spending out of existence by treating it as "off-budget." It is not broad enough to include some of the most important resources that the federal government spends or allocates. The process involves the interaction of so many institutions and actors, at so many points along the way, that consistency or clarity of direction, or results of any kind, are difficult to achieve.

These problems with the process lead to significant problems of budgetary results. Many times the process arrives at no definitive conclusions at all. For the 1982 budget year, a Second Budget Resolution was never passed because Congress could not bring itself to acknowledge the enormous emerging deficits. Parts of the appropriations process have not been completed for years. State Department and foreign aid programs have functioned without appropriations, on what are called continuing resolutions, for several years.[1] In 1982, both the executive and the congressional budget processes were built upon exceedingly improbable economic assumptions because no one would face the implications of the real assumptions. The entire process, therefore, proceeded on the basis of economic projections that every single individual actor disavowed. So long as tough budget choices can be avoided or obscured, the process will continue to produce budgets that are based upon unlikely assumptions. Sound economic policy making will replace misleading illusory nonbudgets only when the most difficult budgetary choices are confronted.

President Carter's Fiscal Year 1980 Budget

In early 1978, barely one year into his presidency, President Jimmy Carter and his principal advisers—Charles Shultze, the chairman of the Council of Economic Advisers (CEA); Michael Blumenthal, secretary of the Treasury; and James McIntyre, director of OMB—were deeply concerned about the rising level of inflation and the force of its momentum. What to do about it was debated throughout the early months of 1978—well before inflation developed into the all-purpose whipping boy of the 1980 election.

At the same time, OMB had become equally worried about an apparent surge in spending and an impending deficit that was much too large. In March 1978, my staff predicted that the fiscal year 1980 deficit would be at least $55 billion if no action was taken—$15 billion higher than the $40-billion deficit it forecast for 1979. To allow the deficit to rise by almost 40 percent in a time of accelerating inflation seemed profoundly wrong—wrong in strictly economic terms, wrong politically, and wrong in light of the president's public commitments to budget control. This was the conclusion at OMB, and we determined to act.

In a long set of discussions in May and June 1978, the president was told in detail—and understood in detail—what a substantial reduction in the deficit would entail. The tax cut the administration already had proposed would have to be reduced, which would require immediate consultations with congressional leaders. No new programs of any significant size could be introduced. Existing programs for the cities, for transportation, for the environment—which already provided benefits and had clients and constituents, most of them Democrats— had to be held down or cut back. Legal changes would have to be proposed to Congress to permit reductions in such untouchables as Social Security and Medicare—the flagships of Democratic party rhetoric. Agency operational costs would have to be reduced, federal salary increases limited, and federal hiring restricted.

No one involved had any illusions about the difficulty of this effort for this president. In June 1978, Jimmy Carter was not particularly popular. The "incompetence" and "inconsistency" issues had emerged already. His White House was not widely admired. The Democratic party's traditional constituencies questioned his caution, conservatism, and apparent skepticism about their programs. He was already working with a relatively low reserve of personal authority.

But any president confronting such controversial issues would have found himself in a terribly difficult position. Conservatives would be pleased with the direction the president was taking but displeased with its moderate scope. The president would get no credit from them. On the other hand, much of the Democratic party would despise the entire effort. A widely prevailing view held that there was no problem with public spending that a little more spending would not cure, and that the deficit had relatively little to do with inflation.

The president had an extremely difficult program to sell. He had to convince one set of skeptics that a policy of restraint was appropriate, while he persuaded another that too much restraint would be unfair to those who depended upon federal programs. He needed the backing of his cabinet and of the senior civil service that operates the government. He needed governors, mayors, and members of Congress to support, or at least accept, the changes.

On May 25, 1978, the president discussed the economy, the budget, and his intentions with the cabinet. He spoke for about 10 to 15 minutes—quietly, as always, with more emotion than was normal, and very much on point. The economic situation worried him deeply, he said, and he was concerned that inflation not get out of control. His economic advisers would provide the specifics, but he wanted the cabinet to hear from him, at the earliest possible moment, that he had decided to propose an extremely austere 1980 budget. He knew his decision would cause difficulties for some of them, but he needed their cooperation and support. Then, the president left the cabinet room and Vice President Walter Mondale spoke briefly.

The vice president said that he traveled more than anyone else in the room, and he believed inflation was the greatest single issue on the minds of the American people. There was, he said, too great an acceptance in Washington of the view that the country had only two economic options, unacceptable inflation or unacceptable unemployment. The administration was fighting to preserve a third option: bringing the economy around and into balance. "But the American people do not believe us yet, and unless we can convince them we will get wiped out in the fall midterm elections, and in later elections."

Up to this point, the cabinet had listened attentively—as a captive audience they had little choice—but as members began to speak, a wide range of views became immediately apparent. Some were highly supportive. Others simply did not believe the projected deficit figures. Others felt the president should withdraw or reduce the proposed tax cut: "Going up with as restrained a budget as OMB proposes will be viewed as ludicrously inconsistent with a tax cut." A few disliked particular aspects of the planned cuts: "Personnel cuts are one of the most asinine policies we have. They are insanity. The President could gain more by cutting fraud and abuse through adding people." And some disagreed with the politics of the proposed strategy:

> Let's look at reality. How will this be perceived by the American people. We are destroying our political base in the name of fiscal responsibility. You do this, and no one will go in and pull the Democratic levers in 1980. You are creating a Republican President with a Democratic Congress; this is a Nixon-Ford presentation.

The unambiguous support the president needed was very difficult for the cabinet to give. Department heads are tested daily for virtue and constancy by the constituencies of their departments. Groups that depend on housing programs do not applaud secretaries of the Department of Housing and Urban Development who subordinate those programs to an abstraction—even one called inflation. And—

which made it harder—this was a Democratic president asking a Democratic cabinet to support budget restraint. The request ran against the grain of almost 50 years of accepted party practice, tried and true rhetoric, and hardened ideology. Jimmy Carter had the enormous misfortune to be a Democratic president who was required to acknowledge the existence of budgetary limits and to try to alter strong-running budgetary currents.

Restraint alone might not have been too difficult. But Carter also had to choose among federal programs, and the choice he felt compelled to make ran against the grain of his party. Jimmy Carter had concluded that defense spending should be increased. The president's evolving attitude toward the defense budget had been a source of muted displeasure among many Democrats for more than a year. In his 1976 campaign, he had argued that the defense budget could be reduced by more efficient management. But in June 1977, he directed Secretary of Defense Harold Brown to announce the administration's decision to increase spending by 3 percent in real terms, that is, 3 percent above the rate of inflation—a measure taken in part to convince the other members of NATO to raise their own defense budgets. By the summer of 1978, it was obvious that President Carter was considering extending that defense commitment through a second budget year.

For two years the president had been moving toward the view that Soviet defense increases had to be countered by sustained increases in the U.S. defense establishment. He was already hearing from the White House staff that one of the costs of defense increases would be his own political hide. At the same time, the Department of Defense irritated him as an institution. He found it impossible to believe that a $150 billion a year department could not save a billion or two by being more efficient. The Pentagon's appetite seemed insatiable. He was willing to grant its claims a high priority, but that concession never seemed to get him anything. For instance, public acknowledgment by the military services that Carter seemed to understand their needs would have been enormously helpful to a president as exposed on the high wire as this one was. Acknowledgment of the difficulties the defense increases posed for domestic programs also would have been valuable. But he never got such generous responses. The Pentagon's attitude was more, "Thanks a lot but what's for dessert?" A year and a half later, a few months after the president had committed himself to the largest sustained rate of increase in peacetime defense budgets in American history, the chief of staff of the Army would testify that he had a "hollow army": no acknowledgment of the presidential effort, no analysis of trends, just a "hollow army."

Despite the political risks, President Carter believed in the importance of his defense initiatives. Moreover, they probably appealed to his sense of himself as commander-in-chief—one of the few presidential roles actually specified by the Constitution. On defense issues a president could feel as if he were making strategic decisions that other world leaders watched, that swayed blocs of senators, that were presidential. Domestic issues, on the other hand, must sometimes make a president feel like the chairman of the local zoning commission. He is inundated with highly specific requests for programs he has never heard of, or wishes he had never heard of.

President Carter recognized that defense increases would not come free; they could only be paid for by cutting domestic programs that had enormous emotional appeal for Democrats. Black voters had been crucial to the president's 1976 primary campaign and to his election. The possibility that their programs might be cut in favor of defense was profoundly disturbing to many members of the administration and more than disturbing to Democrats outside the government. The budgets of these programs—regardless of their merits—were regarded as Democratic litmus tests.

The president knew he owed a great deal to black voters; he was genuinely distressed about black unemployment rates, teen-age unemployment, and urban poverty. He was also a Democrat who accepted the view that good Democrats funded these programs. But at the same time, he had grown increasingly skeptical of their true value. Spending more on public service employment might give everyone involved a warm feeling, but did it really do any good? In any case, he had to make choices, and these programs were beginning to slip in priority.

In sum, Carter had to bring the total growth of spending down, but he felt he had no choice but to raise defense spending. The only way he could accomplish both objectives was to cut the programs of the one constituency that really supported him. Reports on the economy were making clear that there were limits to the ambitions or conceits of government. These limits required budget choices that raised conflicts impossible to resolve. The consensus necessary to enforce these choices seemed unobtainable.

By the fall of 1978, the 1980 budget had become a prominent public issue. Its general direction was widely known. The standard Washington game of leaking OMB's budget "marks" prior to budget publication flourished with more than normal intensity. The president had met or was scheduled to meet leaders of the groups his staff had briefed earlier in the year.

In December the Democratic party's difficulty with the politics of budget restraint became apparent. As luck would have it, the party's second midterm convention was held that month in Memphis, Tennessee. Midterm conventions, whatever their broader procedural merits, are bound to be tough on incumbent Democratic presidents. The party believes deeply in positive government—one that searches out social problems and defines programmatic solutions. Its grass-roots constituencies are absolutist: each problem is important, each should be solved immediately. But a president must balance problems, solutions, resources, and opportunities. He always will appear to be waffling, temporizing, insufficiently responsive—particularly to a convention whose stated midterm role is to give him guidance on his policies and programs.

In this case the convention not only had these normal, built-in dissatisfactions; it also had the issue of President Carter's budget to chew on. And chew it did. In his speech to the convention on December 9, 1978, Sen. Edward Kennedy tore into President Carter's budget policies:

> I support the fight against inflation. But no such fight can be effective or successful unless the fight is fair. The party that tore itself apart over Vietnam in the 1960's cannot afford to tear itself apart today over budget cuts in basic social programs.
>
> There could be few more divisive issues for America and for our party than a Democratic policy for drastic slashes in the federal budget at the expense of the elderly, the poor, the black, the sick, the cities and the unemployed.

The convention's response to Senator Kennedy's speech was enthusiastic and positive. As the *New York Times* reported, "The audience voiced strong support of his position with applause, cheers and two standing ovations, a more visibly supportive response than President Carter received when he addressed the full conference last night." One person on the podium, who had the assigned task of defending the president's position, said later that he was physically afraid of an audience for the first time in his life. Certainly the convention made clear that if President Carter continued to pursue his stated budget policies, he would risk major problems with an important part of the Democratic party. It also marked a clear point at which the gulf between President Carter and Senator Kennedy really began to open.

This gulf profoundly affected the second half of President Carter's term in office. The presence of Senator Kennedy—who owned the left wing of the Democratic party—first as an undeclared and then a declared opponent, made President Carter's effort to forge a moderate policy alternative to the developing Republican critiques even more difficult—and ultimately impossible—than the task would have been in any case.

In January 1979, President Carter announced a budget for fiscal year 1980 of $532 billion in spending and $503 in receipts. The projected $29-billion deficit hit the mark he had set publicly the previous November. The domestic budget fell in real terms; grants to state and local governments fell in real terms. Reductions of $600 million in Medicare and Social Security were recommended. Defense spending was projected to grow 3 percent in real terms. For all the political obstacles, Congress was persuaded to accept the new policy of budgetary austerity.

The president had made his choice—and sold it. But had he really? And what did it get him?

Because federal spending is intricately related to economic conditions, when a president proposes a budget, he is also providing, explicitly, an economic forecast upon which that budget depends. Forecasts are chancy things, particularly in a volatile economy. But as Jimmy Carter was about to discover, a president is held responsible for his budget proposals no matter what happens to the economy.

President Carter's 1980 budget predicted economic growth of 3.2 percent, inflation of 6.3 percent, and unemployment of 6.2 percent. A year later, in January 1980, the new forecast for 1980 was dramatically bleaker: economic growth of −1.0 percent, inflation of 10.4 percent, unemployment of 7.5 percent. Jimmy Carter was hit simultaneously with three of the four factors that automatically force spending up: low economic growth, high inflation, high unemployment. (The fourth factor is high interest rates; in two months Carter was faced with those as well.) His revised 1980 budget, which reflected the later forecasts, was for $564 billion in spending—an increase of $32 billion. The new predicted deficit had grown to $40 billion.

The financial community went crazy. Financial leaders, market newsletters, and various market soothsayers predicted economic collapse as the best of the fates awaiting the nation. In the year that had passed since Carter's initial 1980 budget proposal, times and needs had changed. The fall of the shah of Iran had precipitated another oil shortage; oil prices had more than doubled. Inflation had risen to a markedly high level and, more importantly, had become a matter of national concern and anxiety. It was a fact—but clearly a politically trivial one—that virtually all of the $32-billion spending increase that was forecast in January 1980 was caused by either drastically changed economic circumstances or defense increases that generally were approved of by the financial world. But the 1980 budget no longer seemed to represent a policy of restraint; rather it appeared symptomatic of the uncontrolled appetite of the federal monster.

After a period of intense turmoil in the markets—the long-term bond market practically disappeared after the prime interest rate hit 21 percent—the president announced in February 1980 that administration officials would meet immediately with the Democratic congressional leadership to consider reactions to the budget he had proposed only six weeks earlier. In effect, events had forced the president to withdraw and reconsider his budget. After a widely published 11-day series of all-day meetings with members of Congress, President Carter presented at the end of March 1980 reductions of $3 billion in his 1980 budget and $17 billion in the 1981 budget, whose 19-month cycle had just begun.

In late October 1980, shortly after the end of fiscal year 1980 and approximately one week before the presidential elections, final budget figures were announced. Federal spending had reached $579 billion, the deficit $59 billion. Spending had grown by $48 billion from the time the budget was proposed to the end of the fiscal year; the deficit had doubled from the $29-billion mark that President Carter had first established. These figures did not go unnoticed in the press. Candidate Reagan attacked them as indicative of Carter's mismanagement of the economy. The restrained budget of 1980 upon which Jimmy Carter had spent so much political capital ended up as a symbol of his profligacy and loss of control. He lost his bid for reelection by a landslide.

President Reagan's First Year:
Three Seasons

Euphoria

Ronald Reagan arrived in Washington with a mandate and blueprint for change. Within 45 days of his inauguration on January 20, 1981, he proposed the broadest, most radical, and most explicit agenda for economic and budgetary change that any president had ever presented to the American people. Head on, he directly and simultaneously tackled all of the problems that had been converging upon the economy and the government. Because the budget is at the heart of American government he would confront it immediately and reduce it sharply regardless of who complained. Because high taxes had become a serious drag on the economy, he would put into effect the largest—by several multiples—corporate and personal tax cuts in American history. Because America's defenses were, in Reagan's view, dangerously weak, military spending would be increased sharply and quickly.

Reagan's theory was that the budget reductions would reverse Wall Street's dismal expectations regarding inflation and future economic growth. The tax cuts would jolt the "supply side" of the economy—workers, savers, and investors—into responding far more favorably than standard economic theory allowed for. The new, improved economy would provide lower inflation, lower interest rates, lower unemployment, higher economic growth, and increased tax revenues. (The revenues were needed because Reagan's budget cuts were far smaller than his tax cuts.) The budget deficit would be slightly higher in 1982 than Carter's proposed $27 billion but would decline rapidly after that. By 1984, the books would balance. Surpluses thereafter would be so great that tax rates would be indexed, that is, automatically reduced annually.

Nothing so typified the early period of the Reagan transition and presidency as David Stockman and his "Dunkirk" memorandum. Stockman, a young, two-term representative from Michigan who was considered able, highly ideological, and enormously sure of himself, had not been a visible part of the Reagan campaign, nor was he widely known in Washington. But within weeks after the election, his economic position paper—and, many believed, declaration of candidacy for OMB director—entitled "Avoiding a GOP Economic Dunkirk" spread through the city. It warned that "an initial [Reagan] economic policy package that includes the tax cuts but does not contain *decisive, credible elements* on matters of outlay control, future budget authority reduction, and a believable plan for curtailing the federal government's massive direct and indirect credit absorption will generate pervasive expectations of a continuing 'Reagan inflation.' " Stockman concluded his memorandum by urging that "to prevent early dissolution of the incipient Republican majority only one remedy is available: an initial Administration economic program so bold, sweeping and sustained that it totally dominates the Washington agenda during 1981," and "holds promise of propelling the economy into vigorous expansion and the financial markets into a bullish psychology."

The Dunkirk memorandum was not drafted by someone lacking self-confidence. In fact, the memorandum and the man who wrote it—confirmed on January 27, 1981, as OMB director—almost perfectly symbolized the incoming Reagan administration. The administration in its early days was marked by a very special philosophical cohesion. To one accustomed to the raging policy debates within Jimmy Carter's administration—on oil price decontrol, health insurance, the budget generally—the apparent fact that Ronald Reagan's appointees seemed to share a common purpose, to agree with each other about major goals and tasks, was striking by itself. So was their arrogance. Several months after the inauguration a young and junior Reagan White House staff member said to me: "We all have wondered why you had the OMB career staff prepare such enormous budget review books. Dave [Stockman] doesn't need them; he knows what to do." I wondered, at the time, if they would "know" with as much certainty a year from then.

By the end of the November-January transition period, the broad viewpoint of Stockman's "Dunkirk memorandum" dominated the advice being given to Ronald Reagan. The pace quickened immediately after President Reagan's inauguration. Within days, Stockman was on the Hill with his "black book," an OMB loose-leaf binder that contained a long list of suggested budget cuts. With a lag of about 12 hours, the black book itself began to circulate through Washington. The book was general, its list was long, and it revealed no specific policy. But there was not much in the domestic budget it left untouched. Public service jobs? Out. The Economic Development Agency? Out. The Urban Development Action Grant Program? The Legal Services Corporation? Alcohol Loan Guarantees? Out, out, out.

Then, in late January, the Reagan administration followed up on the black book by announcing that the president would reveal the major pieces of his economic budget policy on February 18 and would present a specific revised budget in early March. Reagan's speech and the budget that followed were blockbusters. The speech, delivered with Reagan's genius for conveying his message in simple, untortured terms, underlined all of the general points upon which he had campaigned, in the hard, specific terms Stockman had advocated. The Reagan tax and budget changes represented a view of the government radically different from that of any of his post-World War II predecessors. They embodied almost total change—the cancellation of programs, reversals of course, the termination of departments. Above all, the strategy was a presidential one. It was a "big" view of the world. At one level, at least, it was a consistent view. It treated real problems, and it involved real choices. It was a strategy the president could convey clearly to the American people, and one he could use to guide his administration.

For 1985, the Reagan program projected $250 billion of tax cuts; $50 billion of defense increases; and about $80 billion of reductions. Almost half of the budget cuts were unspecified. Those tough battles were deferred to a time when the president, inevitably, would be weaker politically. But several years of defense increases were sold as necessary to American security. And a three-year tax reduction program was proposed that would begin in 1981.

Certain imbalances within the Reagan program were disturbing. It was based upon untested and widely disbelieved economic assumptions. It required an acceptance of deficits much larger than those that congressional Republicans regularly had tantrums about only a few years ago. It constituted a high-return, high-risk strategy that would lead either to dramatic improvements in economic performance, as the president's economists believed, or, as many others feared, to an equally dramatic worsening of the budget and economic situation.

Legislative Victory

Whatever the long-term implications of Reagan's budget, the combination of a popular president, a confident, united Republican congressional party, and worried, divided Democrats allowed little latitude for quibbling in 1981. Pursuing budget reductions his way, Ronald Reagan won more legislative victories in his first few months in office than President Carter won in four years. And the Democrats on the Hill voted by large majorities for budget cuts they would have laughed at had Jimmy Carter proposed them. The Democratic party was not prepared to take on Ronald Reagan. The loss of the presidency, the Senate, and the then widely projected possibility of losing the House in 1982 unnerved most of the Democratic party and prevented it for almost a year from recasting itself as an effective opposition party.

At the end of Ronald Reagan's triumphant first six months, Congress endorsed his 1982 budget. With David Stockman's adept management of Congress during most of the session, Reagan's tax policy passed virtually without change. In the press, "Reagan-triumphant-Democratic-humiliation" stories were routine. Even when presenting their own alternatives, Democrats voted in droves for changes they would have bitterly opposed a year earlier. Moreover, their alternatives lost to the far more extreme Reagan versions.

By midsummer 1981, the Reagan "revolution" seemed to have completely changed long-held assumptions about politics and public issues. During the first six months of the 97th Congress, in one of the nation's periodic policy spasms, tax and budget changes of enormous importance had been rushed through with little thought or reflection. The joint topics of tax and budget reductions had completely dominated the legislative and political agenda. There was no debate about new federal program initiatives in 1981. It was almost impossible to find a member of Congress who did not begin every speech with a body-and-soul commitment to cutting the budget. The fiercest advocates of domestic spending between 1976 and 1980 turned meekly to the task of trimming their favorite programs. Within one year of his inauguration, Ronald Reagan had put into place the basics of his entire presidential campaign program.

Apostasy and Reality

At the zenith of President Reagan's first year, nothing seemed likely or even able to counter the Reagan revolution. A seemingly endless series of legislative victories, coupled with several remarkable personal television performances by the president, gave the overwhelming impression that the Reagan blueprint not only had been quickly written into law, but had, in fact, already succeeded. When Ronald Reagan left Washington for his vacation in August 1981, he left behind a six-month record of political, legislative, and public achievement that few presidents have equaled.

But, a month and a half later, it began to become apparent that the most essential element for success had never been tied down. Depending upon one's level of objectivity, either the economy never performed as it "should" have or the Reagan program never recognized hard economic realities. In any case, from August on, the Reagan program steadily unraveled. The projected capital investment surge never took place. The federal funds rate never approached the low levels projected in President Reagan's budget. The prime rate hovered above 16 percent. The long-term money markets virtually disappeared. And the budget deficit—and the economic worries stemming from the deficit—were not going away.

In a major television speech in September, President Reagan was forced to propose a new round of budget cuts—which the Congress, reverting to a more normal executive-congressional relationship during the next weeks, completely ignored—and to defer, indefinitely, his earlier commitment to a balanced budget by 1984. For the next few months one administration spokesman after another confessed that he had always believed in the salutory effects of large deficits. In November 1981, the respected economic forecasting firm Data Resources Inc. (DRI), noting that "the budget really is in its worst condition since World War II," reported:

> The financial community lives with the day-to-day necessity of underwriting the securities to finance the federal deficits. Investors have kept real interest rates on long-term securities at high levels even after four months of easier monetary policies. So long as the administration does not face up to the budget problem, the bond market can have little more than temporary cyclical rallies, and the rates which govern housing and business fixed investment activity will remain in a range which seriously retards otherwise healthy recoveries for these sectors.

However, the real bombshell in the fall of 1981 was the Stockman revelations. William Greider's *Atlantic* article, published in December but circulated throughout Washington in early November, made very clear that David Stockman, the creator of the Reagan program and its most important public advocate, had had enormous doubts about the program almost from its inception.[2] While he was publicly excoriating critics of the Reagan program, Stockman in private was experiencing many of the same doubts. For example,

- When Henry Kaufman of Soloman Brothers expressed concern about the economics of a budget policy that cut taxes and raised defense spending at the same time, Stockman conceded to Greider that this argument might be right.
- While the public was debating Reagan's tax program, which rationalized major tax cuts with the argument that increased national income would bring in more revenue, Stockman was saying in private: "I never believed that just cutting taxes alone will cause output and employment to expand. . . ."
- At a time when Secretary of Defense Caspar Weinberger was testifying that every penny in the enormously increased defense budget was critical to American survival, and President Reagan was backing him up, Stockman sounded a note much closer to administration critics:

> As soon as we get past this first phase in the process, I'm really going after the Pentagon. The whole question is blatant inefficiency, poor deployment of manpower, contracting idiocy. . . . Hell, I think there's a kind of swamp of $10 to $30 billion worth of waste that can be ferreted out if you really push hard.

They got a blank check. We didn't have time during the February-March period to do anything with defense. Where are we going to cut? Domestic? Or struggle all day and night with defense? So I let it go. But it worked perfectly, because they got so goddamned greedy that they got themselves strung way out there on a limb.

● Finally, as the year wore on, Stockman's private mood changed:

There was a certain dimension of our theory that was unrealistic. . . . Whenever there are great strains or changes in the economic system, it tends to generate crackpot theories, which then find their way into the legislative channels.[3]

There were many who were beginning to believe that this last prediction of David Stockman's had already come true in 1981.

It is very easy for someone who has been involved in the budget process to sympathize with Director Stockman. The numbers are confusing. Program and budget views often seem to be based on conflicting analytical mythologies. Change is very, very hard. Nevertheless, David Stockman's admissions seriously damaged the Reagan budget program. The winter of 1981, as the economy was entering a highly inconvenient and unexpected recession, was a bad time for the high priest of the Reagan policy to recant in public.

The first completely Reagan budget—the 1983 fiscal year budget—was published in February 1982. It had been preceded by weeks of leaks and counterleaks from within the administration concerning the enormous deficits that were beginning to be projected and what to do about them. But publication of the final budget made clear that the president had not been swayed from his tax and spending policies. The budget continued unchanged the administration's multiyear personal and business tax reduction proposals. It proposed a 19 percent increase in spending for defense. At the same time, it proposed that all other spending be held constant. The budget projected deficits of $90 billion for 1983; $80 billion for 1984; and $70 billion for 1985.

Within days, two problems became apparent. First, on its own terms, the projected deficit was unacceptable. The country was not prepared to accept a $90-billion deficit from a president who had campaigned against Jimmy Carter's $60-billion deficit. Moreover, Congress was not going to accept the president's budget priorities. Congress had gone along in 1981, but in 1983 it would not raise defense by almost 20 percent and cut every domestic program on the books. Second, the budget lacked credibility. Within weeks, the Congressional Budget Office and others provided starkly different deficit projections, ones which ran from $150 billion in 1983, to well over $200 billion by 1986. The administration's highly optimistic economic assumptions were doubted, and CBO's projections, which spelled enormous problems for the economy, were believed.

The Reagan budget did not survive the spring. Like Carter before him, but for different reasons, Reagan had to renegotiate his published budget. In the end, faced with an economy far worse than anyone had contemplated, continuing high interest rates, and a bleak outlook for Republicans in November, Reagan agreed to go along with a set of tax increases inspired by Republican Sen. Robert Dole.

The spring negotiations averted an immediate crisis, but the Reagan budget policies emerged in shambles. The former widespread consensus for increased defense spending diminished as its implications for the domestic economy became better understood. Congress made clear that there was very little room for more domestic budget cuts. President Reagan's standing in the polls during his first 15 months had fallen faster than any previous president, although it began to rise again with the economic recovery in 1983. Like presidents before him, Ronald Reagan had a much narrower operating margin by midterm. The opportunities for dramatic policy breakthrough now seemed behind the president. Almost inevitably, Reagan faced, for the balance of his first term, two and one-half years of tough slogging — defending and backing away from a policy that had been conceived in haste, proposed in the midst of euphoria, and shredded to pieces by mid-1982.

Conclusion

The budget is the fundamental issue that presidents of the 1980s will encounter. Structural deficits approaching $200 billion, which have developed as a consequence of Reagan administration policies, pose central obstacles to sustained economic improvement. Reducing these deficits will require wrenching changes in both taxing and spending, changes that can be accomplished only through a budget process that in itself needs substantial renovation.

The presidency is the only institution in the political process that affords an overall view of these issues. The president is the only figure who can consider the most general choices and provide the necessary sustained direction. To be successful, a president must develop both a strategic perspective on the substance of these problems and a fundamental understanding of their procedural and constitutional context. A strategic perspective must encompass a clear-eyed view of the country's economic and budgetary problems: of their complex, intertwined relationship with other problems of public policy and of the simultaneous actions that must occur if the problems are to be solved.

However, for such a perspective to mean anything, a president must also have a realistic perception of his own office. Modern presidents are treated as mythic beings. We regard our presidents as the Shilluk of the Upper Nile did their kings, as symbols of nature at rest or the world gone awry. We praise or castigate them for their possession or lack of heroic qualities. We regard them as larger than life, figures who determine the fate of nations and men. In every White House mess conversation, there is much talk of "the boss said" or "the old man wants." The "who talked with the president last" syndrome is standard in every White House.

But on many issues it does not matter what "the old man" thinks. No matter what priorities or objectives a president assigns himself, events will intervene. A president cannot choose all issues that will affect his presidency. President Carter did not choose the 1979 oil crisis, nor President Reagan the war in Lebanon. An increasingly complex, interdependent, resource-hungry world randomly hurls problems at a president; with luck he can influence some of the outcomes. Further, a president does not have one, clear, homogeneous public interest to which to appeal. The American people hold many contradictory views. Our political system, certainly the budget process, invariably favors the short run over the long run. On any issue the abstract, analytically "right" position—if there ever is one—invariably is the wrong position politically. And there are at least as many public opinions as there are issues.

No president can act alone. He must function through the work of others in the executive branch. A president's closest advisers in the White House sometimes know little about the real government. The politics of governance are different from and tougher than the politics of campaigns. A president must pay inordinate attention to the nurturing of his own position within the executive branch lest he lose the ability to act at all.

A president will never be allowed to forget that he has competition. Sen. Russell Long abruptly reminded President Carter of this in early 1977. After the president made a brief statement to a gathering of senators about his plans to eliminate 18 water projects, Senator Long, whose state was to lose two of these projects, stood up. "I," he said, "am Russell Long, chairman of the Senate Finance Committee." His message was not difficult to understand.

In sum, the issues that confront presidents do not appear as clear generalities. The president cannot just decide to show restraint, or emphasize investment, or cut waste, and have anything happen. He must show what he means through his decisions on countless specific issues. Each of these specifics brings with it a range of arguments, personalities, analyses, and political effects. Each raises questions of need that cannot be evaluated, of different perspectives, of appropriate roles. These specifics do not resolve themselves naturally into a clear general course of action. Even a president's own advisers are often more of an obstacle than a help; they have their own, often conflicting, views as to what is good for him. A president will find that the most difficult part of being president—apart from the fact that his powers do not match up well with his responsibilities—is the enormous exercise of will required to chart a clear course against the claims of all the specifics.

This is a difficult context in which to lead, but it is not an impossible one. A president's efforts to mobilize the executive branch and contend with Congress, the interest groups, and the press can do much to shift the odds in his favor. A president must operate without illusions. He must understand the true nature of the budget problem. He must appreciate the political environment in which he operates. He must define a genuinely achievable course of action and be able to explain it—not as another six-point program but in relation to issues that are important in the lives of the voters. He must struggle to avoid being captive to his own mythologies.

Every incoming president believes in cabinet government and wastes several months until he discovers it will not work. Every president believes that the discovery of vast amounts of waste will ease his budget problems. Few presidents like the awful trade-offs among taxes, budgets, programs, and the economy, so they pretend they do not exist. President Carter continued to propose national health insurance long after it became clear that it was unaffordable. President Reagan stayed with supply-side economic theology because it denied the existence of or need for trade-offs. The Democrats of the early 1980s became noticeably vague when the topic turned to budget control and entitlement programs. Presidents badly underestimate the importance of a plausible link between their policy views and reality.

Although few do, presidents should worry at length about building and maintaining loyalty, discipline, morale, and esprit within the executive branch. A president should appoint a senior, retired civil servant as an assistant and adviser on the management of the permanent government. He should fire political appointees who will not support his programs. On the other hand, he should reward excellence, effectiveness and loyal support. Presidents have signing ceremonies, trips on Air Force One, bill-signing pens, pictures, White House movies, telephone calls, promotions and many other ways to convey approval. But they rarely do so thoughtfully and systematically. As a result, the deputy assistant secretaries who are slogging away in the agencies get nothing for being loyal to the president.

A president must insist upon consistency. He need not enter every fight, nor force a complete meshing of all the decisions he makes, but he should state where he is going and be perceived as going there. This requires strategic decisions. Whatever one thinks of Ronald Reagan's policies, his presidential strategy was brilliant. He defined a strategy and followed it consistently. Jimmy Carter wounded his presidency, perhaps fatally, by not doing so. He allowed the various factions within the administration to fight out every issue, but he never decided—or told anyone—where he wanted to go. The result was a series of policies that were too compromised to have any bite to them.

A president must use carefully the few unmatched advantages the presidency possesses: the power to define a problem clearly and with a single voice, the power to appeal to a presidential constituency, and above all the power to set the nation's agenda. When a president asks for something of a general nature, ordinary Americans try to deliver. They make sacrifices, they accept restraint. However, they cannot deliver several things at once. They cease to listen to multiple, contradictory messages. Here, too, a president must function without illusions. There is a limit to how much the American people will hear, even from him. To set an agenda implies having made strategic choices.

To master the problems of the budget, a president must define an agenda and a strategy; he must make his own branch of government acknowledge that he has a strategy; he must allocate scarce resources to infinite needs and he must contend with competition. These are not easy tasks, but upon them may rest the success of modern government.

NOTES

1. When a fiscal year begins and Congress has not yet enacted all the regular appropriation bills for that year, it passes a joint resolution "continuing appropriations" for government agencies at rates generally based on their previous year's appropriations.
2. William Greider, "The Education of David Stockman," *The Atlantic*, 248 (December 1981): 38, 44-47.
3. Ibid.

19. THE PRESIDENCY, THE BUREAUCRACY, AND FOREIGN POLICY: LESSONS FROM CAMBODIA

Michael Nelson and Thomas Tillman

The making of American foreign policy, unlike domestic and economic policy making, is predominantly an executive branch activity. Although the language of those provisions of the Constitution that bear explicitly on foreign affairs is ambiguous on the issue of whether Congress or the executive, if either, is in charge, their implications are not and seldom have been. Presidential ascendancy over Congress flowed from the Constitutional Convention's decisions to make the executive, in striking contrast to the legislature, a single-person office chosen independently by a national constituency. These decisions endowed the executive alone with qualities of energy, unity, secrecy, and legitimacy that are structurally advantageous to the conduct of foreign policy.

Executive Primacy

The first century-and-a-half of American history under the Constitution bore out executive primacy. Although presidents had to struggle to invigorate the enumerated powers of their office in domestic policy, they usually were able to get their way when deciding how the United States should deal with other countries. Sometimes this came about through explicit congressional assent— Senate ratification of treaties submitted by the president, for example. More often, however, presidents succeeded by *faits accomplis*: George Washington's proclamation of American neutrality in the Anglo-French War, James Monroe's doctrine against European intervention in the Western Hemisphere, and Woodrow Wilson's 14-point proposal for postwar settlement were all unilaterally proclaimed. James Polk secretly negotiated for the annexation of Texas and by sending troops into disputed territory provoked the war with Mexico. Without congressional consultation, Presidents William McKinley, William Howard Taft, Woodrow Wilson, and Calvin Coolidge dispatched American forces into foreign countries. Since Washington's administration, presidential decisions about which foreign governments to recognize have gone uncontested. Indeed, treaties themselves gave way to executive agreements based on presidential authority alone as the main form of contract between American and foreign governments.

When criticized for their assertiveness, presidents invariably invoked the number and selection-based strengths of their constitutional office. James Sundquist summarizes the standard (and politically persuasive) presidential response: "quick decision was imperative; ... the move had to be made, or negotiations conducted, in secret, and only the executive could maintain confidentiality; ... only the president has the essential information, ... effective intercourse with other nations requires the United States to speak with a single voice, which can only be the president's." [1]

Arguments such as those Sundquist cites became especially compelling in the post-World War II period. As in the other wars, vast temporary powers had been granted the executive. What made World War II different was the aftermath. Instead of lapsing into relative isolation from world political affairs, the United States entered into a "Cold War" with the Soviet Union. New technologies of nuclear weapons and intercontinental delivery systems raised the spectre of instant destruction.

These developments made the executive's constitutional strengths appear more important in peacetime than in past wars. Increased reliance not only on executive agreements but on secrecy in all diplomacy made the conduct of foreign policy a shared power with Congress in only the most nominal sense. The Republican 80th Congress (1947-1949), angrily partisan on domestic political issues, readily assented to such far-reaching Truman adminstration initiatives as the Marshall Plan, the North American Alliance, and Point Four. Congress supported the American role in the Korean War, which it never had been asked to declare, with annual military appropriations, as it did the war in Vietnam in the 1960s and early 1970s. In the intervening years between Korea and Vietnam, it wrote virtual blank checks in advance support of whatever actions the administrations of Dwight D. Eisenhower and John F. Kennedy might decide to take in the Middle East, Berlin, Cuba, and elsewhere.

Much has been made in the post-Vietnam era of Congress's recent resurgence in national security policy making. Although the last decade or so has been an exceptional period of congressional assertiveness, the exception has been of a kind that demonstrates the rule of executive dominance. When Congress has tried to seize the reins, it generally has done so in ways that are negative, such as limitations on discretionary war making by presidents and short-term prohibitions on trade or military assistance to the Soviet Union, Vietnam, and Turkey.

Congress's weaknesses in foreign policy making can be partially explained by its institutional character: large, diverse, unwieldy, and slow. As Sundquist observes, Congress can "disrupt the policy the president pursues, but it cannot act affirmatively to carry out a comprehensive substitute policy of its own." [2] Congress also is constrained by public expectations of the institution: voters want their own representatives and senators to concern themselves more with local than national interests, which leaves out most foreign policies.[3] Not surprisingly, Congress has been consistently more vigorous on the minority of national security issues with a clear domestic politics coloration, such as support of Israel and Greece, nations that have vocal and well-organized ethnic lobbies in this country.

Rise of the Bureaucracy

Far more important than Congress's occasional assertiveness in foreign policy making has been the steady post-World War II rise in the power and influence of the bureaucracy within the executive branch. This seems curious in at least one regard. With the exception of secrecy, bureaucracy lacks all of the constitutional qualities that historically have caused and sustained executive primacy over Congress: energy, unity, and legitimacy. But the foreign affairs bureaucracy, with its distinctive brand of organizational complexity, offered or developed other useful qualities—geographical reach, internal hierarchy, professional expertise and continuity—that Congress lacked and that presidents increasingly needed to conduct day-to-day policy in an ever more threatening and complicated world. Also, like other executive departments, the foreign affairs bureaucracy exists in a state of formal subordination to the president: its rise in power posed no overt threat to presidential power or constitutional legitimacy. Finally, to some extent, the bureaucracy came to rule by filling a vacuum. Presidents, like representatives and senators, tend to be creatures of domestic politics; their confidence is lowest in the very policy area in which the permanent government's is greatest. As Roger Morris explains, on most policies the bureaucracy "simply ruled by default, just by being there, in the vacuum left by executive, congressional, and public inattention." [4]

One index of the shift in power to the bureaucracy was sheer size: the growth of the State Department from about 1,700 foreign service officers spending $15 million in 1930 to levels five and twenty times larger, respectively, by the 1960s;[5] the proliferation of civilian agencies such as the United States Information Agency and the Central Intelligence Agency; and the unprecedented maintenance of an enormous and expensive "garrison state" in peacetime.

Even more important than sheer expansion was the new conventional wisdom that it reflected. As Dean Acheson said in his farewell address to the State Department in 1953, national security in the atomic age is "a problem which must be dealt with wisely and justly and quietly by people who are expert at it." [6] Such men, Acheson did not need to add, were to be found in the bureaucracy. They came in two varieties: career civil servants at the middle levels of their departments and agencies, and "wise men," the few hundred eastern lawyers, bankers, foundation executives, and other leaders of the foreign policy "establishment" who occupied the ranks from which presidents of both parties were expected to choose their high-ranking appointees.

Whatever the formal trappings of power, then, executive primacy in national security policy making came to mean not presidential but bureaucratic primacy in the post-World War II period. Even when presidents chose to assert themselves, they usually found that "the bureaucracy commanded the flow of information to senior officials, variously pressured and lobbied the nominal decisionmakers to protect bureaucratic interests, and then controlled the daily execution of policy." [7]

The presidency of John F. Kennedy was not distinctive in this regard, but it was in two others: it had, first, a remarkable number of embarrassing foreign policy failures and, second, an unusually skillful corps of administration apologists to pass the blame for them on to the bureaucracy. These efforts by Kennedy administration alumni, however self-serving they may have been, produced a vigorous debate over who the proper arbiters of foreign policy within the executive apparatus should be: the elected chief executive and his staff or the permanent bureaucracy?

The debate is worth describing in its own right—we do so in the section that follows and, in the conclusion, we enter it. More important, it was a debate that had consequences. These, too, we describe and, using the case of American foreign policy in Cambodia, illustrate.

The Debate:
White House vs. Bureaucracy

Historian and former Kennedy adviser Arthur M. Schlesinger, Jr., begins the foreign policy-making chapter of his administration memoirs by describing "one muddle after another—the Department's acquiescence in the Bay of Pigs, the fecklessness of its recommendations after the disaster, the ordeal of trying to change its attitude in Laos," and several others. The department Schlesinger was referring to in this passage was the "tradition-ridden ... formless and impenetrable" Department of State. "But resistance was no less great at Defense," he adds, and elsewhere he singles out the CIA for particular abuse.[8] Schlesinger was hardly alone in such assessments: John Kenneth Galbraith, a Harvard economist and Kennedy's ambassador to India, insisted that it was the bureaucracy's outdated, deeply ingrained view of communism as a monolith that brought about America's ill-fated intervention in the Vietnam War.[9]

Clearly, New Frontier scholar-politicians such as Schlesinger and Galbraith had a stake in shifting blame for Vietnam and other administration failures from the political echelons in which they had served to the career bureaucracy. Their hope, as Kennedy himself half-facetiously put it, of "establishing a secret office of 30 people or so to run foreign policy, while maintaining the State Department as a facade in which people might contentedly carry papers from bureau to bureau" was hardly disinterested.[10] But whatever their motives, the indictment they made of the executive foreign policy establishment was extremely perceptive and influential.

The wellspring of most pathologies of foreign policy making, as these critics saw it, was the bureaucracy's preoccupation with its own organizational interests at the expense of all others. Francis Rourke notes their argument that "bureaucracies push for policies designed to serve not so much the national interest as their own hegemonial ambitions as organizations—competing more for primacy in the governmental structure of the United States than with any foreign adversary."[11] Such selfishness, the argument went, poisons agencies' behavior in their two major areas of responsibility and power: first, as givers of information and policy advice to the president so that he can make intelligent foreign policy decisions and, second, as faithful agents of policy implementation once those decisions have been made.

Policy Advice

After World War II, presidential decisions in foreign policy increasingly became based on information and advice supplied by executive departments and agencies. The problem with this, critics argued, was that these bureaucracies seemed less interested in informing presidential decisions than in predetermining them through selected information and biased advice. Henry Kissinger observes in his memoirs that such behavior has been pervasive:

> The strong inclination of all departments is to narrow the scope for presidential decision, not to expand it. They are organized to develop a preferred policy, not a range of choices. If forced to present options, the typical department will present two absurd alternatives as straw men bracketing its preferred option—which usually appears in the middle position. A totally ignorant decisionmaker could easily satisfy his departments by blindly choosing Option 2 of any three choices which they submit to him.[12]

Morton Halperin facetiously characterized these three options as "You can blow up the world, do as we say, or surrender to the Kremlin." But according to James C. Thomson, Jr., it was exactly those choices that the foreign policy agencies offered President Lyndon B. Johnson in the summer of 1964 when he asked them to work up as wide a range of Vietnam courses as possible and was advised almost unanimously to bomb the North ("or blow up the world, or scuttle-and-run.")[13]

Ironically, two characteristics of the foreign affairs bureaucracy that were intended to enhance its accountability to the president—internal hierarchy and the postwar consolidation of the military services into a single Department of Defense—were said to have made it all the more difficult for him to overcome these information distortions. Hierarchy, observes Rourke, makes "it impolitic for subordinates to disagree openly with superior officials who control job assignments and other avenues of career advancement."[14] (Franklin Roosevelt liked to quote a veteran foreign service officer's advice to his colleagues: "You can get to be a Minister if a) you are loyal to the service; b) you do nothing to offend people; c) if you are not intoxicated at public functions.") As for military consolidation, it meant that the Army, Navy, and Air Force would speak with one voice instead of three. Disagreements that formerly reached the president's ears, taking up his time but also offering him several realistic choices, now tended to be smoothed out within the Pentagon.

Policy Implementation

Liberal critics also found pathological self-interest at work in the bureaucracy's exercise of its second major function: policy implementation. Departments and agencies, they noted, tend to resist any change in policy that disrupts their standard operating procedures (SOPs), the routines that organizations develop to handle problems or situations they expect to face. SOPs are indispensable for regimenting the workload of government agencies. In addition, one of their purported virtues is to keep low- and middle-level subordinates accountable to their elected and appointed superiors by making them "go by the book." Ironically, however, SOPs often become sources of leverage over the president and his staff, who are unfamiliar with day-to-day operating procedures and must defer to the agencies on such matters. One oft-noted consequence is that agencies can be very slow in implementing new policy decisions and equally slow in halting or altering existing policies. To corrupt a phrase from physics, "bureaucracies at rest tend to stay at rest, and bureaucracies in motion tend to stay in motion," or even accelerate.[15]

Postwar history abounds in stories of bureaucratic inertia and bureaucratic momentum. One of the most frequently cited examples of inertia is President Kennedy's inability to effect the removal of American Jupiter missiles from Turkey. Kennedy raised the removal issue in early 1961; an administration study supported his position a year later. Throughout 1962 Kennedy told State Department officials that the missiles had to go. But, much to the president's anger, they still were in place at the time of the Cuban missile crisis in October and were used by the Soviet Union to justify its installation of missiles in Cuba.[16] State's explanation was that it had been doing what it always did in such cases: consulting with all the nations that would be affected by an order prior to acting on it.

Bureaucratic momentum has been equally troublesome to the White House. The Cuban missile crisis offers another example: in accordance with the Strategic Air Command's standard operating procedure, bombers were moved to civilian airports, even though the intent of Defense Secretary Robert McNamara's "no cities doctrine" was to "encourage the Soviet Union to attack only American military centers."[17] But nowhere was the power of bureaucratic momentum more evident than during the course of American involvement in Vietnam, where the decision to use the Air Force led "inescapably to the assignment of ground combat forces to protect the air bases . . . and the activities of such ground forces inevitably escalated from a simply protective role to 'search and destroy' activities against the enemy to forestall enemy attacks upon these bases." [18]

Standard operating procedures and other organizational routines were not the only sources of inertia and momentum cited by bureaucracy's critics. They also argued that agencies' discretion in implementing executive orders limits a president's ability to make policy. Presidential decisions seldom can be so specific that they eliminate all leeway in implementation. But in the service of personal or organizational self-interests, departmental officials frequently abused the proper discretion that is allowed them. As Graham Allison writes, departmental "players who supported the decision will maneuver to see it implemented and may go beyond the spirit if not the letter of the decision," while "those who opposed the decision . . . will maneuver to delay implementation, to limit implementation to the letter but not the spirit, and even to have the decision disobeyed." [19] Alexander George offers a less cynical but equally consequential explanation of the same phenomenon. He argues that while "subversive" behavior by middle-level department personnel rarely reflects "conscious 'sabotage' of the president's will," it nonetheless occurs because of their tendency to adjust policy decisions to the "perceptions, objectives, and constraints" inherent in their roles. [20]

A final aspect of both bureaucratic advice and implementation, it was argued, is the absence of central coordination and direction of agencies' activities. As foreign policy issues became more complex, they inevitably cut across jurisdictional lines, involving two or more of the approximately 30 departments, agencies, and bureaus that take part in the development of American foreign policy. The issue of American troop deployment in Europe, for example, is "critical to our defense posture (Defense), our balance of payments (Treasury), and our relations with several important countries, including the Soviet Union (State)." [21] Yet few argued the desirability of having each component of foreign policy handled by only one organization, with the "eggs in one basket" dependence that would imply.

The Consequences: White House Ascendancy

Liberal critics in the late 1960s saw the weaknesses of the civilian and military foreign policy-making bureaucracies quite clearly. Their foresight into the consequences of their criticisms, however, was less keen. The State Department's power, tenuous even in the best of times because of long-standing conservative dislike and the department's lack of a domestic constituency, was shattered by this assault from its traditional liberal friends. A similar consensus kept Congress and the public as impotent in foreign policy as ever. In addition to their general uninterest, they still were considered too dovish for conservative tastes, yet not "reliable" enough to overcome liberal suspicions, born of pre-World War II isolationism, that voters and their elected representatives are, in Walter Lippman's phrase, "too pacifist in peace and too bellicose in war." [22]

The power of the military bureaucracy, although also attacked by liberals, was in contrast more secure. The Pentagon enjoyed continuing conservative ideological support from the outside and high morale within, as well as a large domestic constituency of veterans and other beneficiaries of the defense pork barrel that overflows into virtually every congressional district. Thus, the inevitable effect of the liberals' evenhanded campaign against the foreign policy bureaucracy was to reduce the power of its already vulnerable civilian agencies and increase, relatively speaking, military power. Still, ex-New Frontiersmen argued, all this was an acceptable price because they were placing their confidence in the White House to take charge, bring boldness and good sense to foreign policy, and keep the Pentagon in line.

Although liberals paved the way for presidents to expand their foreign policy-making power, it was a conservative Republican administration that took advantage of the opportunity. The liberals' critique of the foreign affairs bureaucracy corresponded perfectly with the attitudes of President Richard M. Nixon, who took office in 1969, and his special assistant for national security affairs, Henry Kissinger. Kissinger's disdain "for the institutions and men who had governed American policy since World War II" was apparent in his scholarly writings, which criticized the "rigid" and "fatuous" diplomacy of the period.[23] Inadvertently echoing Kennedy's "secret office" daydream, he told a reporter: "There are 20,000 people in the State Department and 50,000 in Defense . . . and they all want to do what I'm doing. So the problem becomes: how do you get them to push papers around, spin their wheels, so that you can get your work done?"[24] Nixon's dislike of the foreign affairs establishment was even more intense than Kissinger's; it had despised him ever since he had exposed one of its members, Alger Hiss, as a subversive in 1947.

Policy Advice

Central to the Nixon administration's concentration of foreign policy-making power in the White House was the expansion, reorganization, and invigoration of the office of the White House national security adviser, which Nixon set in motion immediately after his inauguration. Kissinger, who headed the National Security Council staff, and Morton Halperin, his aide and former Harvard associate, engineered the office's new structure and increased its professional staff from 18 under predecessor Walt Rostow to more than 50.[25]

An important element in the reorganization was the creation of the National Security Study Memorandum, or "Nisim" as it came to be known. A Nisim was supposed to begin when Nixon or Kissinger decided he wanted to find out all he could about a particular foreign policy problem. Kissinger then would circulate among all concerned agencies a short memo asking them to send up whatever advice and information they had that was pertinent. The bureaucracy's varied responses would be collated and passed on to the National Security Council Review Group, which Kissinger also chaired. Kissinger's role in all this, as Halperin described it, was merely that of a "traffic cop," who decided whether a study was of sufficient quality to pass on to Nixon or needed to be sent back to the agencies for further work, but who did not shape it to accord with his own views.

In theory, the Nisim was a marvelous device for informing presidential decisions—a sure cure for the narrow bureaucratic information-giving the Kennedy alumni had been criticizing. As President Nixon assured Americans in 1970:

> The new NSC system is designed to make certain that clear policy choices reach the top, so that the various positions can be fully debated in the meeting of the council.... I refuse to be confronted with a bureaucratic consensus that leaves me no options but acceptance or rejection.[26]

Liberals applauded the new system, especially since the highly respected Kissinger was to head it. "Excellent ... very encouraging," was Schlesinger's response. "I'll sleep better with Henry Kissinger in Washington," remarked former Kennedy adviser Adam Yarmolinsky.[27]

In practice, however, Nisims served a different purpose, at least on issues of central concern to the Nixon White House. They were devices the administration used "to keep the departments occupied and under the illusion that they were participating in the policy-making process while decisions were actually made in the White House." [28] Former Kissinger aide Roger Morris explains that Kissinger essentially controlled the entire Nisim process. "As Review Group chairman ... he could veto, order redraftings, insert amendments, and generally shape the content and tone of the paper"; as national security adviser, it was his cover memo on each Nisim that first caught the president's eye.[29] Thus could the "traffic cop" snarl the traffic and then drive off himself on a clear road.

Decision

To be sure, the reorganization of the NSC staff meant that the White House now was freed from the pathologies of advice inherent in bureaucracy-centered foreign policy making. But Kissinger and Nixon proceeded to transplant many of them to the White House itself. If executive agencies had been guilty of giving presidents only the information they wanted to give, so were Nixon and Kissinger often guilty of receiving only what they wanted to receive. In February 1969, for example, Kissinger deleted the discussion of unilateral withdrawal from an options paper on Vietnam that he had commissioned for the NSC from the Rand Corporation. Later, when the American ambassador to Cambodia, Emory Swank, began expressing mild reservations about U.S. policy there, Kissinger had him reassigned to Norfolk. Secretary of the Interior Walter Hickel, who brought Nixon the bad news that college students were rebelling, was fired almost immediately.

Nixon and Kissinger also created pathologies of decision distinctive to the White House. As Irving Janis has argued, any time decision making becomes concentrated in the hands of a few, the potential arises for "groupthink"—"a mode of thinking that people engage in when they are deeply involved in a cohesive in-group, when the members' strivings for unanimity override their motivation to realistically approve alternative courses of action." [30] He notes that "some chief executives ... probably become more dependent than others on an inner circle of advisers and establish group norms that encourage unanimity." Although writing in general terms, Janis could not have described more accurately what actually took place in the Nixon White House, where the president surrounded himself with a handful of close personal advisers and worked in the area of foreign affairs almost entirely with Kissinger alone.

Such isolation suggests another defect in the foreign policy making of the White House-centered style: the excessive influence of personality on policy. As cultural and impersonal bureaucratic influences on decision making decline, the importance of presidential character grows. Kissinger and Nixon shared an unusual propensity for working alone. "I've always acted alone," Kissinger once commented, and

"Americans admire that enormously. Americans admire the cowboy leading the caravan alone astride his horse." [31] Similarly, "to prevent the face-to-face confrontations he so disliked and dreaded," Nixon "insisted on isolating himself" and "making decisions in private, like a judge." [32] Nixon also was especially prone to project his ego onto the world stage. Other presidents have done this (Kennedy's first reaction to the missiles in Cuba was "He can't do this to me!"), but none converted political crises into personal crises as readily as Nixon.

Implementation

The pervasiveness of White House influence on the foreign policy making of the Nixon administration makes it easy to forget just how powerful the bureaucracy remained in the second traditional area of bureaucratic power: policy implementation. Allison stated it succinctly in a report to the Commission on the Organization of the Government for the Conduct of Foreign Policy: "Implementation is at least half the problem in most important government decisions and actions," and "bureaucracies dominate implementation." [33]

This condition is, of course, inherent in modern government. A few people may be able to decide what should be done, but they usually must depend on large organizations to actually do it. What was different by the time Nixon came into office was the power of the Pentagon, more ascendant over State than ever in the wake of the ex-New Frontiersmen's critical assault. The course of American involvement in Cambodia vividly illustrates the consequences of this pathology and others present in the strategy of foreign policy making practiced by the Nixon White House.

Cambodia

For centuries Cambodia occupied a precarious position in Southeast Asia, with hostile neighbors periodically ravaging its countryside and annexing parts of its territory. By the time the French imposed a protectorate over the Kingdom of Cambodia in 1864, the country had nearly been consumed by Siam (Thailand) and Vietnam. Although France saved Cambodia from complete eradication, it did so only to create a buffer between Vietnam, its primary colonial concern in the region, and Siam, where the British had strong trade interests. France did little to develop Cambodia, treating it somewhat like "a granary for Cochin China." [34]

Like most of Asia, Cambodia experienced a significant increase in nationalist fervor after World War II. The catalyst of Cambodian nationalism was Prince Norodom Sihanouk, who was crowned king in 1941. An eccentric, Sihanouk nonetheless commanded enormous popularity and led a brilliant campaign to rid his country of French domination in the early 1950s. France, bogged down by the costly war in Vietnam, had little choice but to concede Cambodia its independence, which was officially recognized at the Geneva Conference on Indochina in 1954. The next year Sihanouk abdicated the throne so that he could head up the newly established, popularly elected government.

Fighting continued throughout most of Indochina after 1954, but the neutral status granted Cambodia at Geneva and Sihanouk's success at "playing his neighbors off against one another, exploiting both their ambitions and their weaknesses" kept Cambodia virtually unscathed by war.[35] The United States, which gradually assumed France's role in the region, was disappointed with Cambodia's strict neutralist position. Sihanouk, mindful of the French experience, was in turn suspicious of American intentions in his country. Relations between the United States and Cambodia during the early 1960s grew increasingly tense. In 1963 Sihanouk renounced American aid and two years later broke off diplomatic relations because he felt Cambodia was becoming too dependent on the United States and, more importantly, because he believed Hanoi was going to win the Vietnam War and he feared being closely allied with the losing side. A pragmatic leader, Sihanouk "made a point of controlling the violent racial antipathies" his subjects felt for the Vietnamese.[36] He also appeased Hanoi as much as possible without fully committing Cambodia either to communism or the war. In 1963, for example, he shifted Cambodia's economic policies leftward by nationalizing banks and foreign trade.

The series of events that provoked America's military involvement in Cambodia began several years later, when Sihanouk tolerated Vietnamese Communist use of the border areas adjoining South Vietnam as base camps and allowed them to land supplies at the port of Sihanoukville. These Communist base camps in Cambodia's eastern provinces considerably frustrated the American strategy in Indochina because Cambodia's neutrality legally deterred the United States from taking decisive action against them. In January 1968, however, Sihanouk himself began to express concern about the expanding Vietnamese presence in his country. At a meeting with the American ambassador to India, Chester Bowles, he hinted that he would not oppose small-scale operations along the border.[37]

Small-scale operations, however, were not what eventually were carried out. In February 1969, a few weeks after President Nixon's inauguration, General Creighton Abrams, the commander of American forces in Vietnam, renewed a longstanding Pentagon request for a short-duration B-52 bombing attack on the North Vietnamese camp that he believed to be the headquarters from which Hanoi and the Viet Cong were directing their war efforts in South Vietnam. A little more than a month later, Nixon approved the bombing mission, code-named "Breakfast." Subsequently, other missions were requested and approved. Over a 14-month period, 3,630 B-52 raids were flown in "Breakfast" and related missions, leaving 108,000 tons of bombs inside the Cambodian border.[38] By the time of the last U.S. raid in August 1973, 539,129 tons of bombs had been dropped, more than three times the tonnage used against Japan during World War II.[39]

American bombing missions did not destroy the Vietnamese Communist forces in eastern Cambodia; they merely dislodged them, driving them deeper into Cambodia and "into increasing conflict with the Cambodian authorities," according to General Abrams.[40] The presence of Vietnamese forces deep within Cambodian territory destabilized the Sihanouk regime, resulting in Sihanouk's overthrow in March 1970 by his premier, Gen. Lon Nol, and his cousin, Prince Sirik Matak. Government instability allowed Cambodia's own Communists, the Khmer Rouge, to grow from a rag-tag bunch of a few thousand in 1970 to an impressive fighting force of 60,000 three years later that would terrorize the Cambodian people.

Whether the United States bombed Cambodia with Sihanouk's consent still has not been determined conclusively.[41] Other questions, however, are more critical for understanding foreign policy making during the Nixon years: How were the decisions to bomb and later to invade Cambodia reached and how were they eventually implemented?

Policy Advice and Decision

The most arresting characteristic of the 1969 decision to bomb Cambodia and its implementation was the administration's reliance on secrecy. In the Lippmann tradition, Kissinger and Nixon believed the nation was better off excluding the public and its elected representatives in Congress from participation or even knowledge of security matters of such import. According to Marvin and Bernard Kalb, Kissinger "felt that if it became known that the United States was . . . extending the bombing into Cambodia, this would prompt a wave of angry denunciations from an increasingly disillusioned Congress and antiwar critics across the country" that "would only complicate the Administration's plans for peace in Vietnam." [42] Similarly, Nixon argues in his memoirs that "the problem of domestic antiwar protest" made secrecy necessary. "My administration was only two months old," he adds, "and I wanted to provoke as little public outcry as possible at the outset." [43]

The White House's obsession with keeping the B-52 bombing missions secret even led to the falsification of official bombing records. Before every mission,

> the pilots and navigators of the planes ... were told privately to expect the ground controllers to direct them to drop their bombs on a set of coordinates [over Cambodia] that were different from those they had just received [for targets in South Vietnam] .... After the bombs were released, the plane's radio operator—who was not supposed to know of the diversion—called his base by high-frequency radio to say that the mission had been accomplished. At base, the intelligence division which also knew nothing of the change entered the original South Vietnamese coordinates on the poststrike report. ... The night's mission over Cambodia entered the records as having taken place in Vietnam. The bombing was not merely concealed; the official, *secret* records showed that it had never happened.[44]

The administration took severe and sometimes illegal measures to prevent the press from uncovering the full extent of operations in Cambodia. On May 9, 1969, a few hours after a story by William Beecher appeared in the *New York Times* that revealed the first B-52 bombings of Cambodia, White House officials initiated a wiretap on the home telephone of NSC aide Morton Halperin, whom they suspected (wrongly, as it turned out) of having leaked the information to Beecher. During the next two weeks, other NSC staff members— Daniel Davidson, Helmut Sonnenfeldt, Richard Sneider, and Richard Moose—also were wiretapped. By September 1969, such prominent newsmen as Henry Brandon of the London *Sunday Times,* Marvin Kalb of CBS News, and Hedrick Smith of the *New York Times* were under surveillance.

This extraordinary zeal for secrecy was a product of the style of decision making described earlier as groupthink. Only Nixon, Kissinger, Secretary of Defense Melvin Laird, Secretary of State William Rogers, members of Kissinger's NSC staff, and a handful of top military officials participated in the bombing debate. Potential dissenters, including the secretary and the chief of staff of the Air Force, were excluded; Ellsworth Bunker, the American ambassador to South Vietnam, actually was told that there would be no bombings. Another condition of groupthink that characterized the White House's decision to bomb Cambodia was the practice of "bolstering." As Alexander George explains it, bolstering occurs when

> the expected gains from the preferred alternative are magnified and its expected costs/risks are minimized. Similarly, the expected gains from rejected alternatives are downgraded, their expected costs/risks are magnified.[45]

Kissinger and Nixon both played up the hoped-for gains of the bombing, while neglecting the potentially disastrous consequences of failure. Kissinger recalls that "to bomb base areas from which North Vietnamese soldiers had expelled all Cambodians so that they could more effectively kill Americans—at the rate of four hundred a week—was a minimum defensive reaction fully compatible with international law." [46]

But aerial bombing of the Vietnamese sanctuaries in Cambodia proved inadequate to destroy them. Nothing illustrates this better than the code name chosen for the supposedly one-shot bombing raid in early 1969: "Breakfast." It is a bounded image, one that can stand alone as intended or, at most, with a subsequent "Lunch" and "Supper." In Cambodia, though, each futile set of bombings led to another— "Lunch," "Snack," "Dinner," "Dessert," and "Supper"—before the image was exhausted and a new terminology had to be invented— "Patio," "Freedom Raid," and so on.

In early 1970 the White House decided to launch a large-scale ground attack on the enemy's Cambodian sanctuaries, a decision made with the same obsessive secrecy as the 1969 bombing of Cambodia. In addition to top military officials, only Kissinger and Nixon knew the details of the invasion. When Secretary of State Rogers voiced opposition to escalation, his department was all but excluded from the decision-making process. Defense Secretary Laird was kept largely uninformed because he opposed the use of American troops in the invasion force. Congress was not consulted in any serious way. (Kissinger and Nixon did discuss the ground attack informally with John Stennis, the chairman of the Senate Armed Services Committee and a long-time Vietnam hawk, who they knew would support it.) Even the head of the Cambodian government, Lon Nol, was not advised. Yet when American and South Vietnamese troops drove the North Vietnamese and Viet Cong forces deeper into his country, Lon Nol's government was destabilized and forced to fight a tremendously costly war against Vietnamese Communists and eventually Cambodian Communists.

The strategy taken by Kissinger and Nixon, then, was one of tolerating, much less accepting, only advice that supported their preconceived beliefs. The decision to invade Cambodia was reached in isolation from the rest of the government. Nixon's recollection of the night and morning before the invasion illustrates just how private the final decision was:

> That night I sat alone going over the decision one last time. It was still not too late to call the operation off.... I took a pad and began to make a list of the pluses and minuses.... Early the next morning, I showed Kissinger my notes.... "Now that we have made the decision there must be no recriminations among us," I said. "Not even if the whole thing goes wrong. In fact, *especially* if the whole thing goes wrong." [47]

I. M. Destler regards Nixon's Cambodia decision as "a frightening confirmation" of the "built-in isolation" of the presidency and the problem of "maintaining contact with reality." [48] But in addition to these pathologies of the office, the president's personal character colored his decision to invade Cambodia. The decision was prompted by what Nixon perceived as serious challenges to his personal authority. First, there were "the bums blowing up campuses." In his speech to the American people in April on the night following the invasion, Nixon made clear that it was to this threat "that the United States and he, the President, must respond":

> If when the chips are down, the world's most powerful nation, the United States of America, acts like a pitiful, helpless giant, the forces of totalitarianism and anarchy will threaten free nations and free institutions throughout the world. [49]

Second, there were the Senate's recent rejections of two of his Supreme Court nominees, Clement Haynsworth and G. Harrold Carswell, the latter on April 8. To Kissinger, he said: "Those senators think they can push Nixon around on Haynsworth and Carswell. Well, I'll show them who's tough." [50]

Enraged by these challenges and motivated by repeated screenings of the film *Patton*, Nixon resolved to launch the sudden invasion, then shocked even the military leaders who had supported the plan with his vitriol. The morning after Americans crossed the border into Cambodia, Nixon curtly interrupted a progress briefing by the Joint Chiefs of Staff to harangue them in locker-room language on the need to "electrify people with bold decisions." " 'Let's go blow the hell out of them,' he shouted, while the Chiefs, Laird and Kissinger sat mute with embarrassment and concern." [51] George Smiley, the central character in John Le Carre's *Tinker, Tailor, Soldier, Spy,* tells his superior that there is a lot to be learned from the cover an enemy agent chooses. If he constructs a false identity that is five years younger than he, for example, that says something about his vanity. Nixon's cover, H. R. Haldeman records in *The Ends of Power,* was instability: " 'I call it the Madman Theory, Bob. I want the North Vietnamese to believe I've reached the point where I might do *anything* to stop the war.' " [52]

Implementation

It is possible if inadvisable, for foreign policy decisions to be made by a small group on the basis of advice and information supplied by an only slightly larger one. Implementation of those decisions, however, necessarily involves large-scale bureaucracies. With that involvement goes a certain delegation of power. Nothing illustrates this better than the way in which the bombing of Cambodia was carried out by the Air Force.

The Air Force's posture within the postwar military has been that of the textbook bully: powerful but insecure. Its power comes from the primacy in modern warfare of air-delivered nuclear weapons. Its insecurity is born of air power's essentially trivial role in the limited wars that, ironically, are characteristic of the nuclear age. In Korea, the Air Force felt it had been slighted; in Vietnam, it decided, it was not about to be. By swinging its considerable political weight and by playing to Johnson's and Nixon's desire to battle the North while keeping American casualties low, the Air Force got its foot in the door.

Air Force SOPs then came into play. Once bombers were assigned to Southeast Asia, they had to be kept busy. In a classified study, a senior Pentagon analyst likened the result to a fire hose "running under full pressure most of the time and pointed with the same intensity at whichever area is allowed, regardless of its relative importance in the scheme of things." [53] In late 1968, the power of the fire hose was such that President Johnson was able to stop bombing the North without raising military ire only because he allowed the Air Force to bomb Laos instead. When the Paris Peace Agreement of early 1973 ended the bombing in Laos and Vietnam, the full force of the fire hose was turned on Cambodia. During the next half-year, as many bombs were dropped on Cambodia in an average month as had been dropped on it in all of 1972: a total of 257,465 tons. As former Director of the CIA William Colby explained, "Cambodia was then the only game in town." [54]

The fire hose is only representative of the importance of the military bureaucracy's standard operating procedures in the implementation of American policy in Indochina. All through the Vietnam War, the Air Force dropped its bombs, despite a host of strategic studies that demonstrated the ineffectiveness of strategic bombing. (One survey of the bombing of Germany during World War II "proved conclusively that the strategic bombing had not worked; on the contrary, it had intensified the will of the German population to resist." [55]) The Army massed large troop formations for battle as in World War II and Korea, even though such tactics were inappropriate for guerrilla fighting; and the Navy, after decades spent perfecting the procedures of sea battle, shelled the shores of Indochina's rivers as if there were enemy ships in the jungle.

Sometimes the results were blackly humorous. From the start, American military advisers insisted on remaking the primitive Cambodian army in the American brigade and division command model, even though its own more diffuse structure was better suited to fighting guerrillas. In one instance an American general demanded that Cambodian authorization forms be written in English, which few natives knew. The Cambodians drew up a form in both English and Khmer, but it was turned down by the general, who said it "had no ability to interface carbon papers between the copies." Instead, he imported trained English-speaking Filipinos to take over from the Cambodian quartermasters.[56]

Consequences

The White House policy of air and ground attacks against Vietnamese Communist sanctuaries in eastern Cambodia drove the battle deeper into the neutral nation's interior. A third of the Cambodian people became refugees; Phnom Penh's population swelled from 600,000 to 2,000,000; starvation became commonplace in what had been a rice-exporting nation.

The chaos and destruction of the war were perfect breeding grounds for Cambodia's previously tiny guerrilla force, the Khmer Rouge, which seized control of the country in April 1975. The Khmer Rouge, under the leadership of Pol Pot, were ruthless in their exercise of power. Their first official action was to move approximately three and a half million people—including the lame, the sick, and the dying—from Phnom Penh and other towns to the countryside to work in the fields. The human costs of this action, as one might expect, were devastating. Disease and starvation enveloped the country, already ravaged by five years of war. Thousands who either opposed the new regime or were suspected of doing so were tortured or killed. Cambodia was decimated; perhaps as much as half the population died.

Almost immediately after the Khmer Rouge and the North Vietnamese secured their respective victories in Cambodia and South Vietnam, border disputes between the two sides escalated into armed conflict. The Khmer Rouge had never forgiven Hanoi for what they regarded as its outright betrayal of Cambodian communism at the 1954 Geneva Peace Conference and later at the 1973 Paris Peace Agreement. They also feared that Hanoi now would try to fulfill "the Vietnamese Communists' old ambition of imposing a federation dominated by Hanoi on all Indochina." [57] Hanoi, on the other hand, had its own fears of encirclement by China and Cambodia. Relations between the Socialist Republic of Vietnam and the Republic of Democratic Kampuchea (as Cambodia was renamed) deteriorated rapidly as fighting escalated in 1978. In December, Vietnam launched a large-scale invasion of Cambodia. Vietnamese troops swept quickly through the country, seizing the capital, Phnom Penh, in early 1979.

Kissinger vehemently defends the Nixon administration's Cambodian policies in both volumes of his memoirs. It is not that what the United States did in Cambodia was wrong, he argues, but that it was not enough. In the second volume, *The Years of Upheaval*, Kissinger insists that if our Cambodian bombing campaign in 1973 had not been "torpedoed" by "domestic turmoil," the Khmer Rouge would have agreed to a cease-fire. This, he says, "would have bought a transitional period to ease the fate of the Cambodian people and perhaps spare them the genocidal suffering that the abdication of their friends and the ferocity of their conquerors eventually inflicted on them." [58]

Yet whatever the United States could have accomplished by its 1973 bombing could not have undone what it already had done. Until the American bombing of 1969 and the invasion of 1970, Cambodia had managed to escape the destruction of the war by playing the Americans and North Vietnamese against each other; afterward, this was impossible. The ultimate irony was that in trying to keep Vietnamese Communists from using Cambodia, the White House set events in motion that, by war's end, had made Cambodia a part of Vietnam.

Conclusion

Foreign policy should be forged not by "professionals" in the bureaucracy but by the White House, argued mid-sixties liberals.

Whatever their motives, their case was strong: organizational pathologies inherent in large-scale bureaucracy simply preclude vigorous
initiatives in foreign affairs. The Nixon years showed the limits of this
position—White House power does not automatically generate the
national good and cannot eliminate bureaucratic influence entirely—
but they do not necessarily invalidate it.

The best defense of presidential ascendancy in foreign policy rests
not on ostensibly pragmatic considerations of who-does-what-best, as
Nixon, Kissinger, and the Kennedy alumni had it, but rather on
constitutional democratic theory. The president is the only elected
member of the executive establishment. Unlike members of Congress,
he is in the branch of government whose constitutional duties and
inherent institutional advantages (unified leadership and the ability to
act flexibly and with dispatch) mandate its primacy in foreign policy
making. Unlike the career bureaucrats in the executive branch, he is
elected by the people and can be held accountable by them for his
conduct. The presidency is a political office, and in a democratic system
governmental legitimacy is rooted in public support.

The Cambodia debacle of Kissinger and Nixon does not refute
this defense of presidential leadership in foreign affairs because
Kissinger and Nixon did not abide by the principle of democratic
accountability. Indeed, so secret was their conduct that the people *could*
not hold them accountable for it. Nor are Kissinger's and Nixon's
failures evidence of bureaucracy's virtues or, for that matter, of
Congress's, which some chastened liberal scholars hastened to celebrate
after the consequences of their earlier wish for White House ascendancy became clear. Arthur M. Schlesinger, Jr., accurately pointed out
the flaws in the congressional primacy argument when he noted that
even an avowedly antipresidential congressional initiative, such as the
1973 War Powers Resolution, is futile. It flatly gives presidents a
power to begin war (which the Constitution does not) and asks
Congress to review his decision within 60 days—the very time when
war fever is likely to be at its highest.[59] Congress's power in foreign affairs is, at best, a restraint on the executive.

The ideal arrangement for making American foreign policy is
through elected presidents who accept the vital role of bureaucracy as
supplier of information prior to decision and vehicle for implementation
afterward, but also strive to weed out or mitigate its pathologies. "An
ideal system," writes Erwin Hargrove, "would give the president
analytic help [and] provide for administrative follow-through and intergovernmental coordination for presidential purposes."[60]

So far, however, presidents have been reluctant to break away from the White House-centered system and rejuvenate the bureaucracy. Presidents find the national security adviser and his staff more attuned to their immediate political needs than the State Department. As Leslie Gelb points out, the foreign service careerists who shape State Department advice to the president are more interested in "bilateral and long-term relationships with other nations and regions" than in "thinking about potential political costs to the president." Because they can count on more empathetic advice from the NSC staff, "presidents usually do not have much patience with [State] ... and soon stop listening." [61]

A good example of this can be found in the Carter administration's decision to rescue the American hostages taken captive in Iran in November 1979. As Gelb explains, "the State Department tried to define the issue from a long-term perspective, arguing that if we did not alienate the new regime, there would be a reasonable chance that the hostages would be released eventually and that Iran would gravitate back toward the United States." The White House and NSC staff, on the other hand, "began to define the problem in terms of America's impotence before a third-rate state and argued that unless the president took firm action ... American credibility in the world would suffer—as would the president's electoral chances." [62] President Carter eventually stopped listening to State and ordered the ill-fated rescue mission, prompting Secretary Cyrus Vance to resign in protest.

In truth, the present system of "ad hoc, personal, 'political' staff instrumentalities serving the president" in foreign policy making poorly serves not only the nation's needs, but also the president's, according to I. M. Destler. By emphasizing "the president's role as a decider of specific issues," it pushes the public's expectations of what the president can do well beyond what he can conceivably deliver. [63] Americans have come to expect superhuman feats from their presidents in national security matters, but presidents, as humans, rarely can satisfy them. To arrive at a more practicable and continuous approach to foreign policymaking, Destler concludes, a president must entrust the State Department with the power and responsibility to inform presidential foreign policy decisions and coordinate their implementation. By transferring the analytic expertise of the White House national security staff to State, the president would give the department the wherewithal and, one would hope, the confidence to develop policy options from a broad political perspective. If the secretary then linked this policy staff to operational and budgetary decisions, the cautious resistance of the department's many subunits might be overcome.

These reforms will not work unless the president backs up his people and policies, making clear to all in government that the chain of command runs from him to the secretary, from the secretary to the department, and from the department to the rest of the government's foreign affairs apparatus. The president must be especially supportive of his secretary of state. To avoid any confusion as to who his principal adviser is in foreign policy matters, Destler recommends that the president "eliminate the assistant for national security affairs and place in . . . a position a notch lower" a foreign policy facilitator with primarily managerial and supervisory tasks.[64]

Early in his administration Ronald Reagan showed promising signs of revamping the office of his national security adviser along these lines: his first adviser, Richard Allen, was assigned to play a scaled-down, managerial role. But Allen's replacement with William Clark restored the advisory status of the post to a level matched only by Kissinger and Carter's national security adviser, Zbigniew Brzezinski.

Changes in the foreign policy-making process will not come easily. As Hargrove points out, "Presidents achieve fame for policy, not administration." [65] But after years of foreign policy disasters such as Cambodia, during which presidents have achieved not fame but infamy for their and the bureaucracy's actions abroad, new presidents may realize that the time and energy that reconstructing and leading State will require will be time and energy wisely spent by any standard, including a political one.

NOTES

* The authors would like to thank Bernard Cohen, Ernest May, and Francis Rourke for their comments and suggestions.

1. James L. Sundquist, *The Decline and Resurgence of Congress* (Washington: The Brookings Institution, 1981), 92.
2. Ibid., 306.
3. Ibid., chap. 7.
4. Roger Morris, *Uncertain Greatness: Henry Kissinger and American Foreign Policy* (New York: Harper & Row, 1977), 32-33.
5. Arthur M. Schlesinger, Jr., *A Thousand Days* (Boston: Houghton Mifflin Co., 1965), 409.
6. Morris, *Uncertain Greatness*, 8.
7. Ibid., 32.
8. Schlesinger, *Thousand Days*, 293.

9. John Kenneth Galbraith, *How to Control the Military* (New York: Signet Books, 1969), 16-17.

10. Schlesinger, *Thousand Days*, 406.

11. Francis E. Rourke, *Bureaucracy and Foreign Policy* (Baltimore: Johns Hopkins University Press, 1972), 4.

12. Henry Kissinger, *The White House Years* (Boston: Little, Brown & Co., 1979), 43.

13. James C. Thomson, Jr., "How Could Vietnam Happen? An Autopsy," *The Atlantic* (April 1968): 52.

14. Rourke, *Bureaucracy*, 25.

15. Ibid., 50.

16. Graham T. Allison, *Essence of Decision* (Boston: Little, Brown & Co., 1971), 142.

17. Ibid., 139.

18. Rourke, *Bureaucracy*, 53.

19. Allison, *Essence*, 173.

20. Alexander L. George, *Presidential Decisionmaking in Foreign Policy* (Boulder, Colo.: Westview Press, 1980), 117.

21. I. M. Destler, *Presidents, Bureaucrats, and Foreign Policy* (Princeton, N.J.: Princeton University Press, 1972), 13.

22. Walter Lippman, *Essays in the Public Philosophy* (Boston: Little, Brown & Co., 1955), 20.

23. Quoted in Morris, *Uncertain Greatness*, 53.

24. Quoted in William Shawcross, *Sideshow: Nixon, Kissinger, and the Destruction of Cambodia* (New York: Washington Square Press, 1979), 84.

25. I. M. Destler, "National Security: The Rise of the Assistant (1961-1981)," in *The Illusion of Presidential Government*, ed. Hugh Heclo and Lester M. Salamon (Boulder, Colo.: Westview Press, 1981), 264.

26. Quoted in Destler, *Presidents*, 119.

27. Quoted in Shawcross, *Sideshow*, 79.

28. Ibid., 84. As Richard Allen, Nixon's chief foreign policy adviser during the 1968 campaign and heir to Kissinger's job in the Reagan administration, put it, Kissinger "knew at the time that the best of these studies wouldn't see the light for a year. He kept them busy. He wanted to demoralize the bureaucracy by keeping them overwhelmed." Quoted in Seymour M. Hersh, *The Price of Power: Kissinger in the Nixon White House* (New York: Summit Books, 1983), 35.

29. Morris, *Uncertain Greatness*, 81.

30. Irving L. Janis, *Victims of GroupThink* (Boston: Houghton Mifflin Co., 1972), 9.

31. Quoted in Morris, *Uncertain Greatness*, 2.

32. Quoted in Kissinger, *White House*, 48; Destler, *Presidents*, 125.

33. Graham T. Allison, ed., *Adequacy of Current Organization: Defense and Arms Control*, vol. 4 (Washington, D.C.: U.S. Government Printing Office, 1976), 45.

34. Shawcross, *Sideshow*, 43.

35. Ibid., 51.

36. Ibid., 132.

37. Ibid., 70.

38. Ibid., 26-28.

39. Ibid., 297.

40. Ibid., 113.

41. *Henry Kissinger: An Interview with David Frost*, transcript of NBC News Special Report, October 11, 1979, 10. Frost quotes remarks made by Sihanouk at a special press conference on March 28, 1969.

> No chief of state in the world, placed in the same situation as I am, would agree to let foreign aircraft bomb his own country. They've never dared to say I would authorize such bombings but they have said I wouldn't oppose them. Well, I will oppose it for the simple reason they've never been able to kill a single communist. They've only killed ordinary peasants, male and female. I don't want to run the risk, because of their bombing of the communists, of seeing the escalation of the war extend to Cambodia. That is, I will, in all cases, oppose all bombings on Cambodian territory under whatever pretext.

42. Marvin and Bernard Kalb, *Kissinger* (Boston: Little, Brown & Co., 1974), 132.
43. Richard Nixon, *RN: The Memoirs of Richard Nixon* (New York: Grosset & Dunlap, 1978), 382.
44. Shawcross, *Sideshow*, 30-31. Kissinger's original hope had been that the pilots somehow could be kept from knowing that they were bombing Cambodia. Hersh, *Price of Power*, 60.
45. George, *Presidential Decisionmaking*, 38.
46. Kissinger, *The White House Years*, 252.
47. Nixon, *RN*, 450-451.
48. George Reedy, quoted in Destler, *Presidents*, 86-87.
49. Quoted in Shawcross, *Sideshow*, 147.
50. Quoted in Hersh, *Price of Power*, 187-188.
51. Quoted in Shawcross, *Sideshow*, 152.
52. Quoted in H. R. Haldeman, *The Ends of Power* (New York: Times Books, 1978), 83. Hersh argues that Nixon derived the "madman theory" from President Dwight D. Eisenhower's 1953 threat to drop an atomic bomb on North Korea if it refused to negotiate an end to the Korean War, and that it underlay Nixon's entire Vietnam policy. *Price of Power*, 52-53.
53. Shawcross, *Sideshow*, 92.
54. Quoted in ibid., 265.
55. David Halberstam, *The Best and the Brightest* (New York: Fawcett Crest, 1969), 200.
56. Shawcross, *Sideshow*, 191.
57. Ibid., 387.
58. Henry Kissinger, *The Years of Upheaval* (Boston: Little, Brown & Co., 1982), 368-369.
59. Arthur M. Schlesinger, Jr., *The Imperial Presidency* (New York: Popular Library, 1974), 456-457.
60. Erwin C. Hargrove, *The Power of the Modern Presidency* (New York: Alfred A. Knopf, 1974), 248.
61. Leslie H. Gelb, "Muskie and Brzezinski: The Struggle over Foreign Policy," *New York Times Magazine*, July 20, 1980, 34.
62. Ibid.
63. I. M. Destler, "National Security Management: What Presidents Have Wrought," *Political Science Quarterly*, Volume 95, Number 4, Winter 1980-81, 583, 586.
64. Ibid., 587.
65. Hargrove, *Modern Presidency*, 249.

CONTRIBUTORS

Roger G. Brown teaches political science at Iowa State University. His articles on the presidency and the political parties have appeared in the *Political Science Quarterly* and *Presidential Studies Quarterly*. He currently is completing a book on presidential party leadership since 1960.

W. Bowman Cutter is a partner in the Washington, D.C., firm of Coopers & Lybrand, where he heads their business planning group. A former executive associate director for budget in the Office of Management and Budget, he has written articles for *The Atlantic* and *The New Republic*. He currently is writing a book about the federal budget.

Roger H. Davidson is Senior Specialist in American Government and Public Administration at the Congressional Research Service of the U.S. Library of Congress. He teaches government and politics at the University of Maryland and is the author of *The Role of the Congressman* (1969) and coauthor of *Congress in Crisis* (1966), *On Capitol Hill* (1972), *Congress Against Itself* (1977), and *Congress and Its Members* (1981).

George C. Edwards III teaches political science at Texas A&M University. He is the author of *Presidential Influence in Congress* (1980), *Implementing Public Policy* (1980), and *The Public Presidency* (1983), coauthor of *The Policy Predicament* (1978), and coeditor of *Studying the Presidency* (1983) and *Public Policy-Making* (1976). His forthcoming books include edited volumes on policy implementation and presidential policy making and a text on the presidency.

James Fallows, the former chief speech writer for President Jimmy Carter, is Washington editor of *The Atlantic*. He is coauthor of *Who Runs Congress?* (1972), *The System* (1976), and *Inside the*

System (1976), and is author of *The Water Lords* (1971) and *National Defense* (1981), which won the American Book Award. He has written numerous articles for magazines including *The Washington Monthly,* of which he once was editor.

Morris P. Fiorina teaches government at Harvard University. He is the author of *Representatives, Roll Calls, and Constituencies* (1974), *Congress: Keystone of the Washington Establishment* (1977), and *Retrospective Voting in American National Elections* (1981). He has written numerous articles for the *American Political Science Review, Daedalus,* and *The Washington Monthly,* among others.

Michael Baruch Grossman teaches political science at Towson State University. He is the author of *The City and the Council: Views from the Inside and the Outside* (1974) and of articles in the *Political Science Quarterly* and the *Washington Journalism Review,* among others. He is the coauthor with Martha Kumar of *Portraying the President: The White House and the News Media* (1981) and of two forthcoming works, *Washington Politics and the News Media* and a book on the White House and interest groups.

Willis D. Hawley is dean of George Peabody College for Teachers of Vanderbilt University, where he teaches education and political science. He is the author of *Nonpartisan Elections and the Case for Party Politics* (1973) and coauthor of *Theoretical Perspectives on Urban Politics* (1974), *Improving the Quality of Urban Management* (1974), and *Strategies for Effective Desegregation* (1983). He served as Director of the Education Study, President's Reorganization Project, in 1977 and 1978, and is completing a study, with Beryl Radin, of the development and implementation of the plans to establish the U.S. Department of Education.

Samuel Kernell teaches political science at the University of California, San Diego. He has written several articles for the *American Political Science Review* and other journals and is coauthor of *Strategy and Choice in Congressional Elections* (1981). He currently is writing books on the rise of the public presidency and on voting in advanced democracies.

Martha Joynt Kumar teaches political science at Towson State University and is Secretary-Treasurer of the Presidency Research Group. She is a contributor to *The Judiciary Committees* (1975) and to *Studying the Presidency* (1983). She is the coauthor with Michael Grossman of *Portraying the President: The White House and the News Media* (1981) and of two forthcoming works, *Washington Politics and the News Media* and a book on the White House and interest groups.

Paul Light teaches political science at Georgetown University and George Washington University and is a guest scholar at the Brookings Institution. He served as an APSA Congressional Fellow with Rep. Barber Conable and the National Commission on Social Security Reform, and with Sen. John Glenn and the Glenn presidential campaign committee. He is the author of *The President's Agenda: Domestic Policy Choice from Kennedy to Carter* (1982) and *Vice-Presidential Power: Advice and Influence in the White House* (1983) and is at work on a book about the social security compromise.

Michael Nelson teaches political science at Vanderbilt University and is a former editor of *The Washington Monthly*. His articles have appeared in the *Journal of Politics, The Public Interest, Saturday Review, Harvard Business Review, The Virginia Quarterly Review, Newsweek,* and *Congress and the Presidency,* among others, and he has won writing awards for his essays on classical music and baseball. He is coauthor of *The Culture of Bureaucracy* (1979) and *Presidents, Politics, and Policy* (1984).

Paul J. Quirk teaches political science at Ohio State University. He is the author of *Industry Influence in Federal Regulatory Agencies* (1981) and the coauthor of a forthcoming book about the politics of deregulation.

Beryl A. Radin is the Director of the Washington Public Affairs Center of the School of Public Administration of the University of Southern California. She is the author of *Implementation, Change and the Federal Bureaucracy* (1977), as well as a number of other works that deal with federal policy and organization.

Francis E. Rourke teaches political science at Johns Hopkins University and is President of the Presidency Research Group. He is the author of several books about executive branch politics, including *Secrecy and Publicity: Dilemmas of Democracy* (1961), *Bureaucracy and Foreign Policy* (1972), and *Bureaucracy, Politics, and Public Policy* (1978). He currently is engaged in a Russell Sage Foundation supported study of the presidency and the bureaucracy.

Robert Scigliano teaches political science at Boston College. He is the author of *South Vietnam: Nation Under Stress* (1963), *The Courts* (1962), and *The Supreme Court and the Presidency* (1971) and coauthor of two American Political Science Association monographs, *Representation* (1978) and *Citizenship* (1983). He is engaged in a study, parts of which have been published, of war and foreign relations under the Constitution.

Stephen Skowronek teaches political science at the University of California at Los Angeles. He is the author of *Building a New American State: The Expansion of National Administrative Capacities, 1877-1920* (1982). He currently is engaged in a historical study of the presidency and policy change.

Thomas Tillman is a doctoral candidate in political science at Johns Hopkins University.

Jeffrey Tulis teaches politics at Princeton University and serves as Associate Director of its Presidency Study Program. He is coauthor of *The President in the Constitutional Order* (1981) and currently is writing *The Rhetorical Presidency*.

Jack L. Walker teaches political science at the University of Michigan and is the former director of its Institute for Public Policy Studies. He is the author of *Race and the City* (1973) and numerous articles in the *American Political Science Review*. He is coauthor of *Dynamics of the American Presidency* (1964) and currently is at work on a study of the origins and maintenance of interest groups in America.